Exploring Macroeconomics

ROBERT L. SEXTON

Pepperdine University

Exploring Macroeconomics **6e**

ROBERT L. SEXTON

Pepperdine University

SOUTH-WESTERN
CENGAGE Learning®

Australia • Brazil • Japan • Korea • Mexico • Singapore • Spain • United Kingdom • United States

SOUTH-WESTERN
CENGAGE Learning®

Exploring Macroeconomics, 6e

Robert L. Sexton

Vice President of Editorial, Business:
Jack W. Calhoun

Editor-in-Chief: Joe Sabatino

Sr. Acquisitions Editor: Steve Scoble

Developmental Editor: Daniel Noguera

Editorial Assistant: Allyn Bissmeyer

Associate Marketing Manager: Betty Jung

Sr. Content Project Manager: Colleen A. Farmer

Media Editor: Sharon Morgan

Manufacturing Planner: Kevin Kluck

Sr. Marketing Communications Manager:
Sarah Greber

Production Service: Cenveo® Publisher Services

Sr. Art Director: Michelle Kunkler

Internal and Cover Designer: Beckmeyer Design

Cover Image: ©Simon McCombs/Getty Images, Inc.

Rights Acquisitions Specialist (Text): Sam Marshall

Rights Acquisitions Specialist (Photo):
Deanna Ettinger

For product information and technology assistance, contact us at
Cengage Learning Customer & Sales Support, 1-800-354-9706

For permission to use material from this text or product,
submit all requests online at www.cengage.com/permissions
Further permissions questions can be emailed to
permissionrequest@cengage.com

ExamView® is a registered trademark of eInstruction Corp. Windows is a registered trademark of the Microsoft Corporation used herein under license. Macintosh and Power Macintosh are registered trademarks of Apple Computer, Inc. used herein under license. © 2008 Cengage Learning. All Rights Reserved.

Cengage Learning WebTutor™ is a trademark of Cengage Learning.

Library of Congress Control Number: 2011944040

ISBN-13: 978-1-111-97031-4
ISBN-10: 1-111-97031-9

South-Western
5191 Natorp Boulevard
Mason, OH 45040
USA

Cengage Learning products are represented in Canada by Nelson Education, Ltd.

For your course and learning solutions, visit www.cengage.com
Purchase any of our products at your local college store or at our preferred online store www.cengagebrain.com

Printed in the United States of America
1 2 3 4 5 6 7 16 15 14 13 12

To Leo Rosenberg

Thanks for Inspiring and Mentoring Me

Brief Contents

Table of Contents

part **4**
Macroeconomic Foundations

5 The Macroeconomic Models

CHAPTER 14
Aggregate Demand and Aggregate Supply 376

CHAPTER 15
The Aggregate Expenditure Model 418

6 Macroeconomic Policy

part

7 The Global Economy

Preface

Exploring Macroeconomics, **6th Edition,** was written to not only be a student-friendly textbook, but one that was relevant, one that focused on those few principles and applications that demonstrate the enormous breadth of economics to everyday life. This text is lively, motivating, and exciting, and it helps students relate economics to their world.

The Section-by-Section Approach

Many students are not lacking in ability but, rather, are lacking a strategy. Information needs to be moved from short-term memory to long-term memory and then retrieved. Learning theory provides several methods for helping students do this.

Exploring Macroeconomics uses a section-by-section approach in its presentation of economic ideas. Information is presented in small, self-contained sections rather than in large blocks of text. Learning theorists call this *chunking.* That is, more information can be stored in the working memory as a result of learning in smaller blocks of information. Also, by using shorter bite-sized pieces, students are not only more likely to read the material but also more likely to reread it, leading to better comprehension and test results. Learning theorists call this *rehearsal.*

Unlike standard textbook construction, this approach is distinctly more compatible with the modern communication style with which most students are familiar and comfortable: short, intense, and exciting bursts of information. Rather than being distracted and discouraged by the seeming enormity of the task before them, students are more likely to work through a short, self-contained section before getting up from their desks. More importantly, instructors benefit from having a student population that has actually read the textbook and prepared for class!

In executing the section-by-section approach in *Exploring Macroeconomics,* every effort has been made to take the intimidation out of economics. The idea of sticking to the basics and reinforcing student mastery, concept by concept, has been done with the student in mind. But students aren't the only ones to benefit from this approach. The section-by-section presentation allows instructors greater flexibility in planning their courses.

Exploring Macroeconomics was created with flexibility in mind in order to accommodate a variety of teaching styles. Many of the chapters are self-contained, allowing instructors to customize their course. For example, in Part 3, the theory of the firm chapters can be presented in any order. The theory of the firm chapters are introduced in the textbook from the most competitive market structure (perfect competition) to the least competitive market structure (monopoly). After all, almost all firms face a downward-sloping demand curve, not just monopolists. However, instructors who prefer can teach monopoly immediately following perfect competition because each chapter is self-contained. And for those who do not have sufficient time to cover the Aggregate expenditure model, the Fiscal Policy chapter has an extensive section on the multiplier.

Each chapter is comprised of approximately 6–10 short sections. These sections are self-contained learning units, typically presented in 3–6 pages that include these helpful learning features:

- **Key Questions.** Each section begins with a list of questions that highlight the primary ideas that students should learn from the material. These questions are intended to serve as a preview and to pique interest in the material to come. They also serve as landmarks: if students can answer these questions after reading the material, they have prepared well.

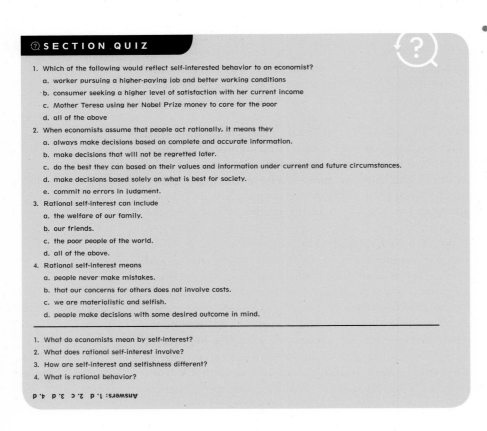

Economics: A Brief Introduction   1.1

What is economics?   What is the economic problem?

What is scarcity?

⊘ SECTION QUIZ

1. Which of the following would reflect self-interested behavior to an economist?
   a. worker pursuing a higher-paying job and better working conditions
   b. consumer seeking a higher level of satisfaction with her current income
   c. Mother Teresa using her Nobel Prize money to care for the poor
   d. all of the above
2. When economists assume that people act rationally, it means they
   a. always make decisions based on complete and accurate information.
   b. make decisions that will not be regretted later.
   c. do the best they can based on their values and information under current and future circumstances.
   d. make decisions based solely on what is best for society.
   e. commit no errors in judgment.
3. Rational self-interest can include
   a. the welfare of our family.
   b. our friends.
   c. the poor people of the world.
   d. all of the above.
4. Rational self-interest means
   a. people never make mistakes.
   b. that our concerns for others does not involve costs.
   c. we are materialistic and selfish.
   d. people make decisions with some desired outcome in mind.

1. What do economists mean by self-interest?
2. What does rational self-interest involve?
3. How are self-interest and selfishness different?
4. What is rational behavior?

Answers: 1. d 2. c 3. d 4. d

- **Section Quizzes.** It is also important that students learn to self-manage. They should ask themselves: How well am I doing? How does this relate to what I already know? The section-by-section approach provides continual self-testing along every step of the way. Each section ends with 4–10 multiple-choice questions emphasizing the important points in each section. It also includes 4–6 open-ended questions designed to test comprehension of the basic points of the section just covered. Answers for multiple choice questions are provided in the Section Quiz box, and answers for the open-ended questions are provided at the end of each chapter so students can check their responses. If students can answer these Section Quiz questions correctly, they can feel confident about proceeding to the next topic.

- **NEW! Student Questions** Over the years, student questions have been tracked. These FAQs (Frequently Asked Questions) are highlighted in the margins and offset by an icon with students raising their hands in class.

Does elasticity affect the size of the deadweight loss?

● **NEW! Economic Content Standards (ECS)** from the National Council of Economic Education are set in the margin where the content is introduced. This addition helps to establish clear learning objectives and ties the text to these objectives.

ECS
economic content standards

Public goods provide benefits to more than one person at a time, and their use cannot be restricted to only those people who have paid to use them. If a good or service cannot be withheld from those who do not pay for it, providers expect to be unable to sell it profitably and, therefore, will not produce it.

Other End-of-Chapter Materials Include:

● **Interactive Summary.** Each chapter ends with an interactive summary of the main ideas in the chapter. Students can fill in the blanks and check their answers against those provided at the end of the summary. It is a useful refresher before class or tests and a good starting point for studying.

● **Key Terms and Concepts.** A list of key terms concludes each chapter. If students can define all these terms, they have a good head start on studying.

● **Problems.** Each chapter provides a list of exercises to test students' comprehension and mastery of the material. Organized in chronological order to follow the chapter, students can easily refer back to the chapter content for review and support as they proceed through the exercises.

---

90 PART 1 Introduction

Interactive Summary

Fill in the blanks:

1. Because of scarcity, certain economic questions must be answered regardless of the level of affluence of the society or its political structure. Three fundamental questions that inevitably must be faced in a world of scarcity are (1) _____ will be produced? (2) _____ the goods and services be produced? (3) _____ the goods and services produced?

2. Market economies largely rely on a(n) _____ decision-making process, where literally millions of individual producers and consumers of goods and services determine what will be produced.

3. Most countries, including the United States, have _____ economies, in which the government and private sector determine the allocation of resources.

4. The _____ -cost method is the most appropriate method for producing a given product.

13. If an economy is operating _____ its production possibilities curve, it is not at full capacity and is operating _____. Such an economy's actual output is less than _____ output.

14. By putting _____ resources to work or by putting already employed resources to _____ uses, we could expand output.

15. _____ requires society to use its resources to the fullest extent—getting the _____ we can out of our scarce resources.

16. If the production possibilities curve is concave from below (that is, bowed outward from the origin), it reflects _____ opportunity costs of producing additional amounts of a good.

17. On a bowed production possibilities curve (concave to the origin), the opportunity costs of producing additional units of a good rises as society produces more of that good. This relationship is called the law of _____.

Key Terms and Concepts

externality 212	public good 224	adverse selection 229
positive externality 212	private good 224	moral hazard 231
negative externality 212	free rider 225	winner's curse 231
transferable pollution rights 220	common resource 226	
Coase theorem 222	asymmetric information 228	

Problems

1. Indicate which of the following activities create a positive externality, a negative externality, or no externality at all.
   a. During a live theater performance, an audience member's cell phone loudly rings.
   b. You are given a flu shot.
   c. You purchase and drink a soda during a break from class.
   d. A college fraternity and sorority clean up trash along a two-mile stretch on the highway.
   e. A firm dumps chemical waste into a local water reservoir.
   f. The person down the hall in your dorm plays loud music while you are trying to sleep.

2. Draw a standard supply-and-demand diagram for televisions, and indicate the equilibrium price and output.
   a. Assuming that the production of televisions generates external costs, illustrate the effect of the producers being forced to pay a tax equal to the external costs generated, and indicate the equilibrium output.
   b. If instead of generating external costs, television production generates external benefits, illustrate the effect of the producers being given a subsidy equal to the external benefits generated, and indicate the equilibrium output.

Visual Learning Features

Imagery is also important for learning. Visual stimulus helps the learning process. This text uses pictures and visual aids to reinforce valuable concepts and ideas. Information is often stored in visual form; thus, pictures are important in helping students retain important ideas and retrieve them from their long-term memory. Students want a welcoming, magazine-looking text; a brain-friendly environment. The most consistent remark we have received from *Exploring Macroeconomics* adopters is that their students are reading their book, and reading the text leads to better test performance.

At every turn this text has been designed with interesting graphics so that visual cues help students learn and remember:

How many workers could be added to this jackhammer and still be productive (not to mention safe)? If more workers were added, how much output would be derived from each additional worker? Slightly more total output might be realized from the second worker, because the second worker would be using the jackhammer while the first worker was taking a break from "the shakes." However, the fifth or sixth worker would clearly not create any additional output, as workers would just be standing around for their turn. That is, the marginal product (additional output) would eventually fall because of diminishing marginal product.

BRUCE BURKHARDT/CORBIS

- **Photos.** The text contains a number of colorful pictures. They are not, however, mere decoration; rather, these photos are an integral part of the book, for both learning and motivation purposes. The photos are carefully placed where they reinforce important concepts, and they are accompanied by captions designed to encourage students to extend their understanding of particular ideas.

- **Exhibits.** Graphs, tables, and charts are important economic tools. These tools are used throughout *Exploring Macroeconomics* to illustrate, clarify, and reinforce economic principles. Text exhibits are designed to be as clear and simple as possible, and they are carefully coordinated with the text material.

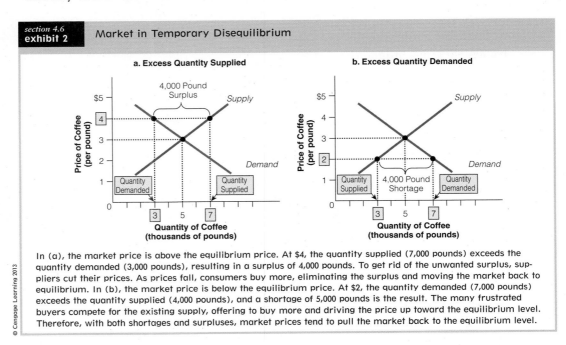

section 4.6 exhibit 2 — Market in Temporary Disequilibrium

In (a), the market price is above the equilibrium price. At $4, the quantity supplied (7,000 pounds) exceeds the quantity demanded (3,000 pounds), resulting in a surplus of 4,000 pounds. To get rid of the unwanted surplus, suppliers cut their prices. As prices fall, consumers buy more, eliminating the surplus and moving the market back to equilibrium. In (b), the market price is below the equilibrium price. At $2, the quantity demanded (7,000 pounds) exceeds the quantity supplied (4,000 pounds), and a shortage of 5,000 pounds is the result. The many frustrated buyers compete for the existing supply, offering to buy more and driving the price up toward the equilibrium level. Therefore, with both shortages and surpluses, market prices tend to pull the market back to the equilibrium level.

© Cengage Learning 2013

Applications

There are numerous applications to everyday life situations scattered throughout the text. These applications were chosen specifically with students in mind, and they are designed to help them find the connection between economics and their life. With that, economic principles are applied to everyday problems and issues, such as teen smoking, property rights and song swapping, crime, gift giving, and many others. There are also five special types of boxed applications scattered throughout each chapter:

- **In the News.** These applications focus primarily on current news stories that are relevant and thought-provoking. These articles are placed strategically throughout the text to solidify particular concepts. In an effort to emphasize the breadth and diversity of the situations to which economic principles can be applied, these articles have been chosen from a wide range of sources.

in the news Is a Diamond Monopoly Forever?

At one time, the De Beers diamond company had control of roughly 80 percent of the world's output of diamonds. However, today De Beers accounts for less than 40 percent of diamond production. Increased competition and the discovery of new diamond deposits has finally broken the monopoly in the diamond industry. A number of producers from countries such as Russia, Canada, and Australia chose to start distributing diamonds outside of the De Beers channel, thus effectively ending the monopoly. De Beers realized it was no longer profitable to buy diamonds to keep them off the market. Also, the demand for diamond jewelry had fallen. To keep its share of the market from falling further, De Beers has differentiated its diamonds by branding with a mark visible only with a microscope. Other diamond firms have followed suit to assure customers that these diamonds are mined under ethical and environmentally friendly conditions. By branding diamonds, sellers are assuring their customers that they are not buying "blood" diamonds that have been exported from war-ravaged areas of Africa where the revenues are used to bolster military efforts. De Beers's new strategy has been effective; it is now more profitable today with a 40 percent market share than when it maintained an 80 percent market share.

© PETER HORREE/ALAMY

- **Global Watch.** Whether we are concerned with understanding yesterday, today, or tomorrow, and whether we are looking at a small, far-away country or a large next door neighbor, economic principles can strengthen our grasp of many global issues. "Global Watch" articles were chosen to help students understand the magnitude and character of the changes occurring around the world today and to introduce them to some of the economic causes and implications of these changes. To gain a greater perspective on a particular economy or the planet as a whole, it is helpful to compare important economic indicators around the world. For this reason, "Global Watch" applications are sometimes also used to present relevant comparative statistics.

global watch Why are Some Countries Rich?

In the beginning of this chapter we asked why is the average citizen of the United States is 40 times richer than those of Ethiopa, Mali and Sierra Leone? But perhaps the question we should have been asking is how did particular countries prosper while others did not? Nations are not inherently rich or poor. Government policies can make the difference.

According to Professor Daron Acemoglu of MIT, the reason why some nations succeed and others don't comes down to the soundness and transparency of their government institutions—the ability of a nation's citizen to own property, freely elect representatives and live without fear of crime and corruption.

COURTESY OF KATHERINE SEXTON

- **Using What You've Learned.** Economic principles aren't just definitions to memorize; they are valuable tools that can help students analyze a whole host of issues and problems in the world around them. Part of learning economics is learning when and how to use new tools. These special boxes are scattered throughout the text as a way of reinforcing and checking students' true comprehension of important or more difficult concepts by assessing their ability to apply what they have learned to a real-world situation. Students can check their work against the answer given in the self-contained box, providing them with immediate feedback and encouragement in the learning process.

use
what you've learned   ## Is That Really a Free Lunch, a Freeway, or a Free Beach?

The expression, "There's no such thing as a free lunch," clarifies the relationship between scarcity and opportunity cost. Suppose the school cafeteria is offering "free" lunches today. Although the lunch is free to you, is it really free from society's perspective? The answer is no, because some of society's scarce resources will have been used in the preparation of the lunch. The issue is whether the resources that went into creating that lunch could have been used to produce something else of value. Clearly, the scarce resources that went into the production of the lunch—the labor and materials (food-service workers, lettuce, meat, plows, tractors,

fertilizer, and so forth)—could have been used in other ways. They had an opportunity cost and thus were not free.

Do not confuse free with a zero monetary price. A number of goods—freeways, free beaches, and free libraries, for instance—do not cost consumers money, but they are still scarce. Few things are free in the sense that they use none of society's scarce resources. So what does a free lunch really mean? It is, technically speaking, a "subsidized" lunch—a lunch using society's scarce resources, but one that the person receiving it does not have to pay for personally.

- **Policy Application.** These features focus primarily on news stories that involve a government policy decision based upon economic concepts. These applications are scattered throughout the text as a way of reinforcing important or more difficult concepts.

policy
application   ## The Fed's Exit Strategy

The depth and breadth of the global recession has required a highly accommodative monetary policy. Since the onset of the financial crisis nearly two years ago, the Federal Reserve has reduced the interest-rate target for overnight lending between banks (the federal-funds rate) nearly to zero. We have also greatly expanded the size of the Fed's balance sheet through purchases of longer-term securities and through targeted lending programs aimed at restarting the flow of credit.

These actions have softened the economic impact of the financial crisis. They have also improved the functioning of key credit markets, including the markets for interbank lending, commercial paper, consumer and small-business credit, and residential mortgages.

My colleagues and I believe that accommodative policies will likely be warranted for an extended period. At some point, however, as economic recovery takes hold, we will need to tighten monetary policy

The exit strategy is closely tied to the management of the Federal Reserve balance sheet. When the Fed makes loans or acquires securities, the funds enter the banking system and ultimately appear in the reserve accounts held at the Fed by banks and other depository institutions. These reserve balances now total about $800 billion, much more than normal. And given the current economic conditions, banks have generally held their reserves as balances at the Fed.

But as the economy recovers, banks should find more opportunities to lend out their reserves. That would produce faster growth in broad money (for example, M1 or M2) and easier credit conditions, which could ultimately result in inflationary pressures—unless we adopt countervailing policy measures. When the time comes to tighten monetary policy, we must either eliminate these large reserve balances or, if they remain, neutralize any potential undesired effects on the economy.

Instructor Resources

The 6th Edition offers an array of instructor resources designed to enhance teaching.

Instructor's Resource CD-ROM

The Instructor's Resource CD-ROM will include electronic versions of the Instructor's Manual, Test Bank, and PowerPoint® slides, as well as ExamView® testing software.

Instructor's Manual

Prepared by Gary Galles (Pepperdine University), the Instructor's Manual, available online and on the Instructor's Resource CD-ROM, follows the textbook's concept-by-concept approach in two parts: chapter outlines and teaching tips. The Teaching Tips section provides analogies, illustrations, and examples to help instructors reinforce each section of the text. Answers to all of the end-of-chapter text questions can also be found in the Instructor's Manual.

Test Bank

Test bank questions, available online and on the Instructor's CD-ROM, have been thoroughly updated. The test bank includes approximately 150 test questions per chapter, consisting of multiple-choice, true-false, and short-answer questions.

ExamView® Testing Software

ExamView®—Is an easy-to-use test creation software compatible with Microsoft Windows and Apple computers. Instructors can add or edit questions, instructions, and answers, and select questions by previewing them on the screen, selecting them randomly, or selecting them by number.

Microsoft PowerPoint® Presentation Slides

- **Lecture Presentation in PowerPoint.** This PowerPoint presentation covers all the essential sections presented in each chapter of the book. Graphs, tables, lists, and concepts are animated sequentially to visually engage students. Additional examples and applications are used to reinforce major lessons. The slides are crisp, clear, and colorful. Instructors may adapt or add slides to customize their lectures.
- **Exhibits from the Text in PowerPoint.** Every graph and table within the text has been recreated in PowerPoint. These exhibits are available within the lecture presentation, but we have also made them available as a separate batch of slides for those instructors who don't want the lecture slides.

Both the Lecture and Exhibit PowerPoint presentations are available for downloading at the Sexton Companion Web site: **www.cengagebrain.com**

Student Resources

The 6th Edition offers an array of resources to help students test their understanding of chapter concepts and enhance their overall learning. Found at the student Companion Web site, these interactive resources provide exam preparation and help students get the most from their Principles of Economics course.

Interactive Quizzes

Students can test their understanding of the chapter's concepts with the interactive quiz. Each quiz contains multiple-choice questions, like those found on a typical exam. Questions include detailed feedback for each answer, so that students may know instantly whether they have answered correctly or incorrectly. In addition, they may email the results of the quiz to themselves or their instructor, with a listing of correct and incorrect answers. An Internet connection is required to take the quizzes.

Key Term Glossary, Flashcards, and Crossword Puzzles

As a study aid, students may use the glossary terms as flashcards to test their knowledge. Students can state the definition of a term, then click on the term to check the correctness of their statement. Students can also test their knowledge in a fun way with the Crossword Puzzles.

Economics with Steven Tomlinson Videos

Cengage South-Western is excited to announce its continuous agreement with *Tomlinson Economics Videos*, featuring award-winning teacher and professional communicator, Steven Tomlinson (PhD, Stanford). These Web-based lecture videos—*Economics with Steven Tomlinson, Economic JumpStart®*, and *Economic LearningPath®*—are sure to engage your students, while reinforcing the economic concepts they need to know.

Complete Online Economics Course

Whether using these videos to deliver online lectures for a distance learning class or as the required text for your Principles course, *Economics with Steven Tomlinson* presents and develops the fundamentals of economics. While this video text offers comprehensive coverage of economic principles, with more than 40 hours of video lecture, you can offer your students an exceptional value package and a richer learning experience by pairing the video text with Sexton's 6th Edition.

Economic LearningPath® Videos

These segments provide a full resource for students to review what you have covered, reinforce what they have learned, or expand their knowledge of topics that you may not have time to cover in your course.

Visit **http://www.cengage.com/economics/tomlinson/learningpath.html**

Global Economic Watch

The global economic downturn, the most important economic event in generations, unfolds day to day and hour to hour. Cengage Learning's Global Economic Watch is a powerful online portal for bringing current events into the classroom.

The Watch includes:

- A content-rich blog of breaking news, expert analysis, and commentary
- A real-time database of hundreds of relevant and vetted journal, newspaper, and periodical articles, videos, and podcasts—updated four times daily
- A thorough overview and timeline of events leading up to the global economic crisis

CengageNOW

New to this edition! Now every homework and test assignment provides both assessment and learning. CengageNOW robust course management system provides the power of learning by offering targeted help for students completing homework, quizzes, and tests. Students can perform their own errors analysis and learn from every assignment. The timing and availability of solutions are, of course, controlled by instructors.

CengageNOW Offers:

- **Auto-graded homework**, test bank, and eBook are all in one resource.
- **Easy-to-use course management option** offers flexibility and continuity from one semester to another.
- **Different levels of feedback and engaging students resources** guide students through material and solidify learning.
- **The most robust and flexible** assignment options in the industry.
- **The ability to analyze student work** from the gradebook and generate reports on learning outcomes.

APLIA™

Created by Paul Romer, one of the nation's leading economists, Aplia enhances teaching and learning by providing online interactive tools and experiments that help economics students become "active learners." This application allows a tight content correlation between Sexton's 6th Edition and Aplia's online tools.

Students Come to Class Prepared

It is a proven fact that students do better in their course work if they come to class prepared. Aplia's activities are engaging and based on discovery learning, requiring students to take an active role in the learning process. When assigned online homework, students are more apt to read the text, come to class better prepared to participate in discussions, and are more able to relate to the economic concepts and theories presented. Learning by doing helps students feel involved, gain confidence in the materials, and see important concepts come to life.

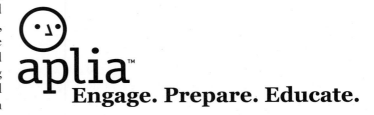

Assign Homework in an Effective and Efficient Way

Now you can assign homework without increasing your workload! Together, Sexton and Aplia provide the best text and technology resources to give you multiple teaching and learning solutions. Through Aplia, you can assign problem sets and online activities that automatically give feedback and are tracked and graded, all without requiring additional effort. Since Aplia's assignments are closely integrated with Sexton's 6th Edition, your students are applying what they have learned from the text to their homework.

Contact your local Cengage South-Western representative to find out how you can incorporate this exciting technology into your course. For more information, please visit: **www.aplia.com**.

CourseMate

New to this edition! *Economics CourseMate: Engaging, Trackable, Affordable.* Economics CourseMate brings course concepts to life with interactive learning, study, and exam preparation tools that support the printed textbook. Watch student comprehension soar as your class works with the printed textbook and the text-specific website. Economics CourseMate goes beyond the book to deliver what you need!

Engagement Tracker

How do you know your students have read the material or viewed the resources you've assigned? How can you tell if your students are struggling with a concept? Engagement Tracker assesses student preparation and engagement. Use the tracking tools to see progress for the class as a whole or for individual students.

Identify students at risk early in the course. Uncover which concepts are most difficult for your class. Monitor time on task. Keep your students engaged.

Interactive Teaching and Learning Tools

Economics CourseMate includes interactive teaching and learning tools:
• Quizzes
• Flashcards
• Videos
• Graphing Tutorials
• News, Debates, and Data

Interactive eBook

In addition to interactive teaching and learning tools, Economics CourseMate includes an interactive eBook. Students can take notes, highlight, search, and interact with embedded media specific to their book. Use it as a supplement to the printed text, or as a substitute—the choice is up to your students with CourseMate.

Go to **login.cengage.com** to access these resources within CourseMate.

About the Author

Robert L. Sexton is Distinguished Professor of Economics at Pepperdine University. Professor Sexton has also been a Visiting Professor at the University of California at Los Angeles in the Anderson Graduate School of Management and the Department of Economics.

Professor Sexton's research ranges across many fields of economics: economics education, labor economics, environmental economics, law and economics, and economic history. He has written several books and has published numerous reference articles, many in top economic journals such as *The American Economic Review, Southern Economic Journal, Economics Letters, Journal of Urban Economics*, and *The Journal of Economic Education*. Professor Sexton has also written more than 100 other articles that have appeared in books, magazines, and newspapers.

Professor Sexton received the Pepperdine Professor of the Year Award in 1991, a Harriet and Charles Luckman Teaching Fellow in 1994, Tyler Professor of the Year in 1997, and received the Howard A. White Award for Teaching Excellence in 2011.

Professor Sexton resides in Agoura Hills, California, with his wife, Julie, their three children, Elizabeth, Katherine, and Tommy and their dog Mally.

Acknowledgments

I would like to extend special thanks to the following colleagues for their valuable insight during the manuscript phase of this project. I owe a debt of gratitude to Edward Merkel, Troy University; Doug McNiel and Salvador Contreras, McNeese State University; David McClough, Ohio Northern University; Tim Bettner, University of La Verne; Inge O'Connor, Syracuse University; William Coomber, University of Maryland; Michael Marlow, Cal Poly; Nand Arora, Cleary University; Carlos F. Liard, Central Connecticut State University; Howard Cochran, Belmont University; Abdulhamid Sukar, Cameron University; Harry Karim, Los Angeles Community College; Maria DaCosta, University of Wisconsin-Eau Claire; Kelli Mayes-Denker, Carl Sandburg College; Elnora Farmer, Griffin Technical College; Robert Shoffner, Central Piedmont Community College; Mark Strazicich, Appalachian State University; Tanja Carter, El Camino College; and Jeffrey Phillips, SUNY Morrisville.

I also wish to thank Gary Galles of Pepperdine University for his help preparing the ancillaries that accompany the 6th Edition, and Mike Ryan of Gainesville State College for providing an invaluable verification of the text and updating the Test Bank.

I am truly indebted to the excellent team of professionals at Cengage Learning. My appreciation goes to Steve Scoble, Senior Acquisitions Editor; Daniel Noguera, Developmental Editor; Colleen Farmer, Senior Content Project Manager; and Michelle Kunkler, Senior Art Director. Also thanks to Joe Sabbatino, Editor-in-Chief; Betty Jung, Associate Marketing Manager, Jack Calhoun, VP/Editorial Director, and the Cengage Sales Representatives. I sincerely appreciate your hard work and effort.

In addition, my family deserves special gratitude—my wife, Julie; my daughters, Elizabeth and Katherine; and my son, Tommy. They are an inspiration to my work. Also, special thanks to my brother Bill for all of his work that directly and indirectly helped this project come to fruition.

Thanks to all of my colleagues who reviewed this material for the 6th Edition. From very early on in the revision all the way up to publication, your comments were very important to me.

Robert L. Sexton

© SIMON McCOMB/STONE/GETTY IMAGES, INC.

part

Introduction

The Role and Method of Economics

FUSE/JUPITERIMAGES

As you begin your first course in economics, you may be asking yourself why you're here. What does economics have to do with your life? Although we can list many good reasons to study economics, perhaps the best reason is that many issues in our lives are at least partly economic in character.

A good understanding of economics would allow you to answer such questions as, Why do 10 A.M. classes fill up more quickly than 8 A.M. classes during registration? Why is it so hard to find an apartment in cities such as San Francisco, Berkeley, and New York? Why is teenage

unemployment higher than adult unemployment? Why is the price of your prescription drugs so high? How does inflation impact you and your family? Will higher taxes on cigarettes reduce the number of teenagers smoking? If so, by how much? Why do female models make more than male models? Why is it easier for college graduates to find jobs in some years rather than others? Do houses with views necessarily sell faster than houses without views? Why do people buy houses near noisy airports? Why do U.S. auto producers like tariffs (taxes) on imported cars? Is outsourcing jobs to India a good idea? Is globalization good for the economy? The study of economics improves your understanding of these and many other concerns.

Economics is a unique way of analyzing many areas of human behavior. Indeed, the range of topics to which economic analysis can be applied is broad. Many researchers discover that the economic approach to human behavior sheds light on social problems that have been with us for a long time: discrimination, education, crime, divorce, political favoritism, and more. In fact, your daily newspaper is filled with economics. You can find economics on the domestic page, the international page, the business page, the sports page, the entertainment page, and even the weather page—economics is all around us.

However, before we delve into the details and models of economics, it is important that we present an overview of how economists approach problems—their methodology. How does an economist apply the logic of science to approach a problem? And what are the pitfalls that economists should avoid in economic thinking? We also discuss why economists disagree.

NATALIAYEROMINA/SHUTTERSTOCK.COM

Why do female models make more money than male models?

Economics: A Brief Introduction   1.1

🗀 What is economics?

🗀 What is scarcity?

🗀 What is the economic problem?

Economics—A Word with Many Different Meanings

Some people think economics involves the study of the stock market and corporate finance, and it does—in part. Others think that economics is concerned with the wise use of money and other matters of personal finance, and it is—in part. Still others think that economics involves forecasting or predicting what business conditions will be in the future, and again, it does—in part. The word *economics* is, after all, derived from the Greek *Oeconomicus*, which referred to the management of household affairs.

Precisely defined, **economics** is the study of the choices we make among our many wants and desires given our limited resources. What are resources? **Resources** are inputs—land, human effort, and skills, and machines and factories, for instance—used to produce goods and services. The problem is that our unlimited wants exceed our limited resources, a fact that we call **scarcity**. That is, scarcity exists because human wants for goods and services exceed the amount of goods and services that can be produced using all of our available resources. So scarcity forces us to decide how best to use our limited resources. This is **the economic problem**: Scarcity forces us to choose, and choices are costly because

economics the study of choices we make among our many wants and desires given our limited resources

resources inputs used to produce goods and services

scarcity exists because our unlimited wants exceed our limited resources

the economic problem scarcity forces us to choose, and choices are costly because we must give up other opportunities that we value

ROBERT L. SEXTON

Newspapers and websites are filled with articles related to economics—either directly or indirectly. News headlines may cover topics such as unemployment, deficits, financial markets, health care, Social Security, energy issues, war, global warming, and so on.

ECS

economic
content
standards

Productive resources are limited. Therefore, people cannot have all the goods and services they want. As a result, they must choose some things and give up others.

we must give up other opportunities that we value. Consumers must make choices on what to buy, how much to save, and how much to invest of their limited incomes. Workers must decide what types of jobs they want, when to enter the workforce, where they will work, and number of hours they wish to work. Firms must decide what kinds of goods and services to produce, how much to produce, and how to produce those goods and services at the lowest cost. That is, consumers, workers, and firms all face choices because of scarcity, which is why economics is sometimes called the study of choice.

The economic problem is evident in every aspect of our lives. You may find that the choice between shopping for groceries and browsing at the mall, or between finishing a research paper and going to a movie, is easier to understand when you have a good handle on the "economic way of thinking."

Economics Is All Around Us

The tools of economics are far reaching. In fact, other social scientists have accused economists of being imperialistic because their tools have been used in so many fields outside the formal area of economics, like crime, education, marriage, divorce, addiction, finance, health, law, politics, and religion. Every individual, business, social, religious, and governmental organization faces the economic problem. Every society, whether it is capitalistic, socialistic, or totalitarian, must also face the economic problem of scarcity, choices, and costs.

Even time has an economic dimension. In fact, in modern culture, time has become perhaps the single most precious resource we have. Everyone has the same limited amount of time per day, and how we divide our time between work and leisure (including study,

---

in the ~~news~~   **Who Studies Economics?**

© PICTORIAL PRESS LTD/ALAMY

The study of economics is useful in many career paths. Here is a short list of some relatively well-known people who studied economics in college.

Politicians, Policy Makers, and Supreme Court Justices
George H. W. Bush, former U.S. President (Yale)
Ronald Reagan, former U.S. President (Eureka College)
Gerald Ford, former U.S. President (University of Michigan)
Arnold Schwarzenegger, body builder/actor/ governor (University of Wisconsin)
Sandra Day-O'Connor, retired U.S. Supreme Court Justice (Stanford)
Stephen Breyer, U.S. Supreme Court Justice (Stanford)

(continued)

in the **news**   Who Studies Economics? (Cont.)

Anthony Kennedy, U.S. Supreme Court Justice (Stanford and London School of Economics)

Kofi Annan, former Secretary General of the United Nations (Macalester College)

Billionaires

Sam Walton, founder of Walmart (University of Missouri)

Warren Buffett, financier (Columbia School of Business, Masters in Economics)

Meg Whitman, former President and CEO of eBay, Inc. (Princeton)

Ted Turner, media tycoon (Brown)

Steve Ballmer, CEO of Microsoft (Harvard)

Donald Trump, real-estate/television mogul (University of Pennsylvania—Wharton)

Paul Otellini, President and CEO of Intel (University of San Francisco)

Celebrities

John Elway, former NFL quarterback (Stanford University)

Mick Jagger, lead singer of the Rolling Stones (London School of Economics)

Cate Blanchett, actress (Melbourne University)

Scott Adams, cartoonist, creator of Dilbert (Hartwick College)

Tiger Woods, golfer (Stanford)

Bill Belichick, NFL head coach, New England Patriots (Wesleyan University)

According to Bob McTeer, former President and CEO of the Federal Reserve Bank of Dallas, "My take on training in economics is that it becomes increasingly valuable as you move up the career ladder. I can't think of a better major for corporate CEOs, congressmen (and women), or presidents of the United States. You've learned a systematic, disciplined way of thinking that will serve you well."

sleep, exercise, and so on) is a distinctly economic matter. If we choose more work, we must sacrifice leisure. If we choose to study, we must sacrifice time with friends or time spent sleeping or watching television. Virtually everything we decide to do, then, has an economic dimension.

Living in a world of scarcity involves trade-offs. As you are reading this text, you are giving up other things you value: shopping, spending time on Facebook, text messaging with friends, going to the movies, sleeping, or working out. When we know what the trade-offs are, we can make better choices from the options all around us, every day. George Bernard Shaw stated, "Economy is the art of making the most of life."

Why can't we ever eliminate scarcity?

② SECTION QUIZ

1. If a good is scarce,

   a. it only needs to be limited.

   b. it is not possible to produce any more of the good.

   c. our unlimited wants exceed our limited resources.

   d. our limited wants exceed our unlimited resources.

2. Which of the following is true of resources?

   a. Their availability is unlimited.

   b. They are the inputs used to produce goods and services.

   c. Increasing the amount of resources available could eliminate scarcity.

   d. Both b and c.

(*continued*)

3. If scarcity were not a fact,

   a. people could have all the goods and services they wanted for free.

   b. it would no longer be necessary to make choices.

   c. poverty, defined as the lack of a minimum level of consumption, would also be eliminated.

   d. all of the above would be true.

4. Economics is concerned with

   a. the choices people must make because resources are scarce.

   b. human decision makers and the factors that influence their choices.

   c. the allocation of limited resources to satisfy unlimited wants.

   d. all of the above.

---

1. What is the definition of economics?

2. Why does scarcity force us to make choices?

3. Why are choices costly?

4. What is the economic problem?

5. Why do even "non-economic" issues have an economic dimension?

Answers: 1. c 2. b 3. d 4. d

1.2

Economic Behavior

🗁 What is self-interest?   🗁 What is rational behavior?

🗁 Why is self-interest not the same as
   selfishness?

Do people really pursue their self-interest? Do people really think that way?

Self-Interest

Economists assume that most individuals act *as if* they are motivated by self-interest and respond in predictable ways to changing circumstances. In other words, self-interest is a good predictor of human behavior in most situations. For example, to a worker, self-interest means pursuing a higher-paying job and/or better working conditions. To a consumer, it means gaining a higher level of satisfaction from limited income and time.

We seldom observe employees asking employers to cut their wages and increase their workload to increase a company's profits. And how often do you think customers walk into a supermarket demanding to pay more for their groceries? In short, a great deal of human behavior can be explained and predicted by assuming that most people act *as if* they are motivated by their own self-interest in an effort to increase their *expected* personal satisfaction. When people make choices, they often do not know with certainty which choice is best. But they *expect* the best outcome from that decision—the one that will yield the greatest satisfaction.

Critics will say people don't think that way, and the critics might be right. But economists are arguing that people *act* that way. Economists are observing and studying what people do—their actions. We largely leave what people think to psychologists and sociologists.

There is no question that self-interest is a powerful force that motivates people to produce goods and services. But self-interest can include benevolence. Think of the late Mother Teresa, who spent her life caring for others. One could say that her work was in her self-interest, but who would consider her actions selfish? Similarly, workers may be pursuing self-interest when they choose to work harder and longer to increase their charitable giving or saving for their children's education. That is, self-interest to an economist is not a narrow monetary self-interest. The enormous amount of money and time donated to victims of Hurricane Katrina is an example of self-interest too—the self-interest was to help others in need. However, our charitable actions for others are influenced by cost. We would predict that most people would be more charitable when the tax deductions are greater or that you may be more likely to offer a friend a ride to the airport when the freeway was less congested. In short, the lower the cost of helping others, the more help we would expect to be offered.

In the United States, people typically give more than $250 billion annually to charities. They also pay more money for environmentally friendly goods, "giving" a cleaner world to the future. Consumers can derive utility or satisfaction from these choices. It is clearly not selfish—it is in their best interest to care about the environment and those who are less fortunate than themselves.

REUTERS/DAVID J. PHILLIP/POOL/LANDOV

Enormous amounts of resources (time and money) were donated to the Hurricane Katrina victims. If individuals are acting to promote the things that interest them, are these self-interested acts necessarily selfish? Acting in one's own self-interest is only selfish if one's interests are selfish.

What Is Rational Behavior?

Economists assume that people, for the most part, engage in rational, or purposeful, behavior. And you might think that could not possibly apply to your brother, sister, or roommates. But the key is in the definition. To an economist, **rational behavior** merely means that people do the best they can, based on their values and information, under current and anticipated future circumstances. That is, people may not know with complete certainty which decisions will yield the most satisfaction and happiness, but they select the one that they *expect* to give them the best results among the alternatives. It is important to note that it is only the person making the choice that determines its rationality. You might like red sports cars while your friend might like black sports cars. So it would be rational for you to choose a red sports car and your friend to choose a black sports car.

Economists assume that people do not intentionally make decisions that will make them worse off. Most people act purposefully. They make decisions with some *expected* outcome in mind. Their actions are rational and purposeful, not random and chaotic. Individuals all take purposeful actions when they decide what to buy and produce. They make mistakes and are impacted by emotion, but the point is that they make their decisions with some expected results in mind. In short, rational self-interest means that individuals try to weigh the expected benefits and costs of their decisions, a topic we will return to in Chapter 2.

What do economists mean when they say people are rational?

rational behavior
people do the best they can, based on their values and information, under current and anticipated future circumstances

Does being rational mean you don't make mistakes?

Adam Smith (1723–1790)

Adam Smith was born in a small fishing village just outside of Edinburgh, Scotland, in 1723. At age 4, gypsies (called *tinkers* in Scotland) kidnapped Smith, but he was rescued through the efforts of his uncle. He began studying at Glasgow College when he was just 14 and later continued his studies at Oxford University. He returned to Glasgow at age 28 as a professor of philosophy and logic. (Until the nineteenth century, economics was considered a branch of philosophy, thus Smith neither took nor taught a class in economics.) He later resigned that position to become the private tutor to the stepson of Charles Townshend.

Although known for his intelligence, warm hospitality, and charitable spirit, Smith was not without his eccentricities. Notorious for his absent-mindedness, there is a story about Smith taking a trip to a tanning factory and, while engaged in conversation with a friend, walking straight into a large tanning vat. Another tale features Smith walking 15 miles in his sleep, awakening from his sleepwalk to the ringing of church bells, and scurrying back home in his nightgown. Most astonishing and unfortunate, Smith, without explanation, had the majority of his unpublished writings destroyed before his death in 1790.

Adam Smith is considered the founder of economics. He addressed problems of both economic theory and policy in his famous book, *An Inquiry into the Nature and Causes of the Wealth of Nations,* published in 1776. The book was a success from the beginning, with its first edition selling out in just six months, and people have continued to read it for well over two centuries.

Smith believed that the wealth of a nation did not come from the accumulation of gold and silver—the prevailing thought of the day. Smith observed that people tend to pursue their own personal interests and that an "invisible hand" (the market) guides their self-interest, increasing social welfare and general economic well-being. Smith's most power-

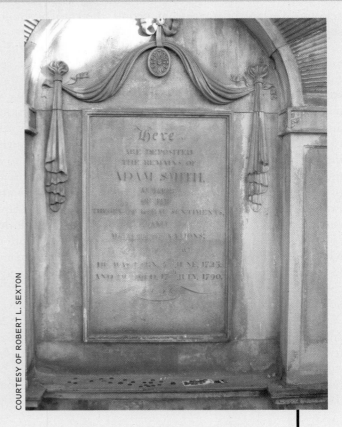

COURTESY OF ROBERT L. SEXTON

Smith is buried in a small cemetery in Edinburgh, Scotland. The money left on the grave site is usually gone by morning; the homeless prey on the donations to use for food and spirits. Adam Smith is probably smiling somewhere. He had a reputation as a charitable man—"a scale much beyond what might have been expected from his fortunes."

ful and enduring contribution was this idea of an invisible hand of market incentives channeling individuals' efforts and promoting social welfare.

Smith also showed that through division of labor and specialization of tasks, producers could increase their output markedly. While Smith did not invent the market, he demonstrated that free markets, unfettered by monopoly and government regulation, and free trade were at the very foundation of the wealth of a nation. Many of Smith's insights are still central to economics today.

1. Which of the following would reflect self-interested behavior to an economist?

    a. worker pursuing a higher-paying job and better working conditions

    b. consumer seeking a higher level of satisfaction with her current income

    c. Mother Teresa using her Nobel Prize money to care for the poor

    d. all of the above

2. When economists assume that people act rationally, it means they

    a. always make decisions based on complete and accurate information.

    b. make decisions that will not be regretted later.

    c. do the best they can based on their values and information under current and future circumstances.

    d. make decisions based solely on what is best for society.

    e. commit no errors in judgment.

3. Rational self-interest can include

    a. the welfare of our family.

    b. our friends.

    c. the poor people of the world.

    d. all of the above.

4. Rational self-interest means

    a. people never make mistakes.

    b. that our concerns for others does not involve costs.

    c. we are materialistic and selfish.

    d. people make decisions with some desired outcome in mind.

---

1. What do economists mean by self-interest?

2. What does rational self-interest involve?

3. How are self-interest and selfishness different?

4. What is rational behavior?

Answers: 1. d 2. c 3. d 4. d

Economic Theory   1.3

▷ What are economic theories?

▷ What can we expect from theories?

▷ Why do we need to abstract?

▷ What is a hypothesis?

▷ What is empirical analysis?

▷ What is the *ceteris paribus* assumption?

▷ What are microeconomics and macroeconomics?

Economic Theories

A **theory** is an established explanation that accounts for known facts or phenomena. Specifically, economic theories are statements or propositions about patterns of human behavior that occur expectedly under certain circumstances. These theories help us sort out

theory statement or proposition used to explain and predict behavior in the real world

and understand the complexities of economic behavior and guide our analysis. We expect a good theory to explain and predict well. A good economic theory, then, should help us better understand and, ideally, predict human economic behavior.

Abstraction Is Important

Economic theories cannot realistically include every event that has ever occurred. A theory weeds out the irrelevant facts from the relevant ones. We must abstract. A road map of the United States may not include every creek, ridge, and gully between Los Angeles and Chicago; indeed, such an all-inclusive map would be too large and too detailed to be of value. A road map designating major interstate highways will provide enough information to travel by car from Los Angeles to Chicago. Likewise, an economic theory is more useful when it ignores the details that are not relevant to the questions being investigated.

Without abstraction or simplification, the world is too complex to analyze. For the same reason, economists make a number of simplifying *assumptions* in their models. Sometimes economists make very strong assumptions, such as that all people are rational decision makers or that all firms attempt to maximize profits. Of course, this may not hold for every single person or firm. Only when we test our models using these assumptions do we find out if they were too simplified or too limiting.

COURTESY OF ROBERT L. SEXTON

How is economic theory like a map? Much like a road map, economic theory is more useful when it ignores details that are not relevant to the questions that are being investigated.

Developing a Testable Proposition

hypothesis a testable proposition

The beginning of any theory is a **hypothesis**, a testable proposition that makes some type of prediction about behavior in response to certain changes in conditions based on our assumptions. In economic theory, a hypothesis is a testable prediction about how people will behave or react to a change in economic circumstances. For example, if we notice an increase in the price of coffee beans (per pound), we might hypothesize that sales of coffee beans will drop, or if the price of coffee beans (per pound) decreases, our hypothesis might be that coffee bean sales will rise. Once we state our hypothesis, we test it by comparing what it predicts will happen to what actually happens.

Using Empirical Analysis

empirical analysis the use of data to test a hypothesis

To determine whether our hypothesis is valid, we must engage in **empirical analysis**. That is, we must examine the data to see whether our hypothesis fits well with the facts. If the hypothesis is consistent with real-world observations, we can accept it; if it does not fit well with the facts, we must "go back to the drawing board."

Determining whether a hypothesis is acceptable is more difficult in economics than it is in the natural or physical sciences. Chemists, for example, can observe chemical reactions under laboratory conditions. They can alter the environment to meet the assumptions of the hypothesis and can readily manipulate the variables (chemicals, temperatures, and so on) crucial to the proposed relationship. Such controlled experimentation is seldom possible in economics. The laboratory of economists is usually the real world. Unlike chemists in their labs, economists cannot easily control all the variables that might influence human behavior.

From Hypothesis to Theory

After gathering their data, economic researchers must evaluate the results to determine whether their hypothesis is supported or refuted. If supported, the hypothesis can be tentatively accepted as an economic theory.

Every economic theory is on life-long probation; the hypothesis underlying an economic theory is constantly being tested against empirical findings. Do the observed findings support the prediction? When a hypothesis survives a number of tests, it is accepted until it no longer predicts well.

Science and Stories

Much of scientific discovery is expressed in terms of stories, not unlike the stories told by novelists. This similarity is not accidental. The novelist tries to persuade us that a story could almost be true; the scientist tries to persuade us that certain events fall into a certain meaningful pattern. The scientist does not (or is not supposed to) invent the underlying "facts" of the story, whereas the novelist is not so constrained. However, a scientist does select *certain* facts from among many facts that could have been chosen, just as the novelist chooses from an infinite number of possible characters and situations to make the story most persuasive. In both cases, the author "invents" the story. Therefore, we should not be surprised to find order in economic theory any more than we are surprised to find order in a good novel. Scientists would not bother to write about "life" if they were not convinced that they had stories worth telling.

How is scientific discovery like the stories presented by novelists?

What makes a story "worth telling?" When we look for order in nature, we cannot suppose that the "facts" are a sufficient basis for understanding observed events. The basic problem is that the facts of a complex world simply do not organize themselves. Understanding requires that a *conceptual order* be imposed on these "facts" to counteract the confusion that would otherwise result. For example, objects of different weights falling freely in the air do **not** travel at *precisely* the same rate (largely because of the different effects of air resistance). Yet this piece of information is generally much less significant than the fact that falling bodies do travel at *almost* the same rate (which presumably would be identical in a vacuum). By focusing on the most significant fact—the similarity, not the difference—Galileo was able to impose order on the story of gravity.

In the same way, to interpret the impact of rising housing prices on the amount of housing desired, economists must separate out the impact of increasing wealth, population, and other contributing factors. Failing to do so would obscure the central insight that people tend to buy less housing at higher prices. Without a story—a theory of causation—scientists could not sort out and understand the complex reality that surrounds us.

The *Ceteris Paribus* Assumption

Virtually all economic theories share a condition usually expressed by the Latin phrase *ceteris paribus*. A rough translation of the phrase is "letting everything else be equal" or "holding everything else constant." When economists try to assess the effect of one variable on another, they must keep the relationship between the two variables isolated from other events that might also influence the situation that the theory tries to explain or predict. In other words, everything else freezes so we can see how one thing affects another. For example, if the price of tomatoes falls, we would expect to see more people buy tomatoes. But if the government recently recommended not buying tomatoes because they have been infected by a bug that causes intestinal problems, people would buy fewer, not more, at lower prices. Does that mean you throw out your theory that people buy more at lower prices? No, we just did not freeze the effects of news from the government, which had a greater impact on purchases than lower prices did.

ceteris paribus holding all other things constant

Why is the ceteris paribus so important?

Let's return to the gravity example. Suppose you drop a feather and a brick off the Eiffel Tower on a windy day. We would expect the brick to win the race. But if we could hold everything constant in a vacuum, then we would expect them to hit the ground at the same time. The law of gravity needs the *ceteris paribus* assumption, too.

If I study harder, I will perform better on the test. That sounds logical, right? Holding other things constant (*ceteris paribus*), your theory is likely to be true. However, what if you studied harder but inadvertently overslept the day of the exam? What if you were so sleepy during the test that you could not think clearly? Or what if you studied the wrong material? Although it might look like additional studying did not improve your performance, the real problem could be the impact of other variables, such as sleep deficiency or how you studied.

Why Are Observation and Prediction Harder in the Social Sciences?

Working from observations, scientists try to make generalizations that will enable them to predict certain events. However, observation and prediction are more difficult in the social sciences than in physical sciences such as physics, chemistry, and astronomy. Why? The major reason for the difference is that the social scientists, including economists, are concerned with *human* behavior. And human behavior is more variable and often less readily predictable than the behavior of experiments observed in a laboratory. However, by looking at the actions and the incentives faced by large groups of people, economists can still make many reliable predictions about human behavior.

Why Do Economists Predict on a Group Level?

Economists' predictions usually refer to the collective behavior of large groups rather than to that of specific individuals. Why is this? Looking at the behaviors of a large group allows economists to discern general patterns of actions. For example, consider what would happen if the price of air travel from the United States to Europe was reduced drastically, say from $1,000 to $400, because of the invention of a more fuel-efficient jet. What type of predictions could we make about the effect of this price reduction on the buying habits of typical consumers?

What Does Individual Behavior Tell Us?

Let's look first at the responses of individuals. As a result of the price drop, some people will greatly increase their intercontinental travel, taking theater weekends in London or week-long trips to France to indulge in French food. Some people, however, are terribly afraid to fly, and the price reduction will not influence their behavior in the slightest. Others might detest Europe and, despite the lowered airfares, prefer to spend a few days in Aspen, Colorado, instead. A few people might respond to the airfare reduction in precisely the opposite way from ours: At the lower fare, they might make fewer trips to Europe, because they might believe (rightly or wrongly) that the price drop would be accompanied by a reduction in the quality of service, greater crowding, or reduced safety. In short, we cannot predict with any level of certainty how a given individual will respond to this airfare reduction.

What Does Group Behavior Tell Us?

Why is group behavior more predictable than individual behavior?

Group behavior is often more predictable than individual behavior. When the weather gets colder, more firewood will be sold. Some individuals may not buy firewood, but we can predict with great accuracy that a group of individuals will establish a pattern of buying more firewood. Similarly, while we cannot say what each individual will do, within a group of persons, we can predict with great accuracy that more flights to Europe from Los Angeles will be sold at lower prices than at higher prices, holding other things such as income and preferences constant. We cannot predict exactly how many more airline tickets will be sold at $400 than at $1,000, but we can predict the direction of the impact and approximate the extent of the impact. By observing the relationship between the price of goods and services and the quantities people purchase in different places and during different time periods, it is possible to make some reliable generalizations about how much people will react to changes in the prices of goods and services. Economists use this larger picture of the group for most of their theoretical analysis.

Economists and Survey Data

Economists do not typically use survey data. Economists prefer to look at revealed preferences (how people actually behave) rather than declared preferences (how they say they behave). Participants in surveys may consciously or subconsciously fib, especially when it costs almost nothing to fib. Measuring revealed preferences will generally give us more accurate results.

REUTERS/ARKO DATTA

Professors Oster and Jensen, by measuring revealed preferences, found that rural Indian families who had cable TV had lower birth rates than those with no television.

The Two Branches of Economics: Microeconomics and Macroeconomics

Conventionally, we distinguish between two main branches of economics: microeconomics and macroeconomics. **Microeconomics** deals with the smaller units within the economy, attempting to understand the decision-making behavior of firms and households and their interaction in markets for particular goods or services. Microeconomic topics include discussions of health care, agricultural subsidies, the price of everyday items such as running shoes, the distribution of income, and the impact of labor unions on wages. **Macroeconomics**, in contrast, deals with the **aggregate**, or total economy; it looks at economic problems as they influence the whole of society. Topics covered in macroeconomics include discussions of inflation, unemployment, business cycles, and economic growth. To put it simply, microeconomics looks at the trees while macroeconomics looks at the forest.

microeconomics
the study of household and firm behavior and how they interact in the marketplace

macroeconomics
the study of the whole economy, including the topics of inflation, unemployment, and economic growth

aggregate the total amount—such as the *aggregate level of output*

---

② SECTION QUIZ

1. Economists use theories to

    a. abstract from the complexities of the world.

    b. understand economic behavior.

    c. explain and help predict human behavior.

    d. do all of the above.

    e. do none of the above.

2. The importance of the *ceteris paribus* assumption is that it

    a. allows one to separate normative economic issues from positive economic ones.

    b. allows one to generalize from the whole to the individual.

    c. allows one to analyze the relationship between two variables apart from the influence of other variables.

    d. allows one to hold all variables constant so the economy can be carefully observed in a suspended state.

(*continued*)

3. When we look at a particular segment of the economy, such as a given industry, we are studying

    a. macroeconomics.

    b. microeconomics.

    c. normative economics.

    d. positive economics.

4. Which of the following is most likely a topic of discussion in macroeconomics?

    a. an increase in the price of a pizza

    b. a decrease in the production of stereos by a consumer electronics company

    c. an increase in the wage rate paid to automobile workers

    d. a decrease in the unemployment rate

    e. the entry of new firms into the software industry

---

1. What are economic theories?

2. What is the purpose of a theory?

3. Why must economic theories be abstract?

4. What is a hypothesis? How do we determine whether it is tentatively accepted?

5. Why do economists hold other things constant *(ceteris paribus)*?

6. Why are observation and prediction more difficult in the social sciences?

7. Why do economic predictions refer to the behavior of groups of people rather than individuals?

8. Why is revealed preference preferred to declared preference?

9. Why is the market for running shoes considered a microeconomic topic?

10. Why is inflation considered a macroeconomic topic?

Answers: 1. d 2. c 3. b 4. d

1.4

Pitfalls to Avoid in Scientific Thinking

📂 If two events usually occur together, does it mean one event caused the other to happen?

📂 What is the fallacy of composition?

In our discussion of economic theory we have not yet mentioned that there are certain pitfalls to avoid that may hinder scientific and logical thinking: confusing correlation and causation, and the fallacy of composition.

Confusing Correlation and Causation

correlation when two events occur together

causation when one event brings about another event

Without a theory of causation, no scientist could sort out and understand the enormous complexity of the real world. But one must always be careful not to confuse correlation with causation. In other words, the fact that two events usually occur together (**correlation**) does not necessarily mean that one caused the other to occur (**causation**). For example, say a groundhog awakes after a long winter of hibernation, climbs out of his hole, and sees his shadow—then six weeks of bad weather ensue. Did the groundhog cause the bad weather?

Perhaps the causality runs in the opposite direction. A rooster may always crow before the sun rises, but it does not cause the sunrise; rather, the early light from the sunrise causes the rooster to crow.

Why Is the Correlation between Ice Cream Sales and Property Crime Positive?

Did you know that when ice cream sales rise, so do property crime rates? What do you think causes the two events to occur together? The explanation is that property crime

ERIC ISSELEE/SHUTTERSTOCK.COM

In Europe, the stork population has fallen and so have birth rates. Does this mean that one event caused the other to occur?

---

in the **news**   **Sex on Television and Teenage Pregnancy**

When it comes to television programming, sex sells—maybe too well. According to a Rand Corporation study authored by Anita Chandra, there is a link between teenagers' exposure to sexual content on TV and teen pregnancies. Specifically, the study found that teens exposed to high levels of sexual content on television were twice as likely to be involved in a pregnancy in the following three years compared to teens with limited exposure. The results were published in the November 2008 edition of the journal *Pediatrics*.

The study's author is quick to point out that the factors leading to teen pregnancies are varied and complex—but warns it is important for parents, teachers, and pediatricians to understand that television can be one of them.

© ALLSTAR PICTURE LIBRARY/ALAMY

consider this:

While sex on television may lead to increases in teen pregnancy, isn't it possible the causality runs in the opposite direction—teenagers who are more susceptible to teen pregnancy watch shows with more sexual content? In addition, there are a host of other variables that could be much more statistically significant, such as low self-esteem, single-parent households, household income, years of schooling, heavy drug and alcohol use, GPA, child abuse, peer pressure, and so on.

In fact, more women of all ages, not just teenagers, are having children out of wedlock. Actually, the teen birth rate was much higher in 1957 than it is today. The growing concern is over the rise in unwed teenage mothers. However, births to single teens actually account for a smaller percentage of all non-marital births than 20 years ago—so is television to blame? Heed the author's warning: "The reasons for the rise in teen pregnancies are varied and complex."

If there is a correlation between more sex on television and increased teenage pregnancy, does that necessarily mean that television is responsible for the rise in teenage pregnancy?

fallacy of composition
the incorrect view that what is true for the individual is always true for the group

peaks in the summer because of warmer weather, more people on vacations (leaving their homes vacant), teenagers out of school, and so on. It just happens that ice cream sales also peak in those months because of the weather. It is the case of a third variable causing both to occur. Or what if there were a positive correlation between sales of cigarette lighters and the incidence of cancer? The suspect might well turn out to be the omitted variable (the so-called "smoking gun"): the cigarette. Or what if research revealed that parents who bought parenting books were "better" parents. Does that prove the books work? Or is it possible that people who would buy books on parenting tend to be "better" parents? That is, it might be about the parents, not the book. Causality is tricky stuff. Be careful.

The Fallacy of Composition

Economic thinking requires us to be aware of the problems associated with aggregation (adding up all the parts). One of the biggest problems is the **fallacy of composition**. This fallacy states that even if something is true for an individual, it is not necessarily true for many individuals as a group. For example, say you are at a football game and you decide to stand up to get a better view of the playing field. This works as long as the people seated around you don't stand up. But what happens if everyone stands up at the same time? Then your standing up does nothing to improve your view. Thus, what is true for an individual does not always hold true in the aggregate. The same can be said of getting to school early to get a better parking place—what if everyone arrived early? Or studying harder to get a better grade in a class that is graded on a curve—what if everyone studied harder? Or what if you are a wheat farmer and you decide to clear some additional land to plant even more wheat to get more income from the additional wheat that is sold. Sounds good if you were the only one. But what if all wheat farmers do the same thing? There would be so much additional wheat produced that the price would come down and you might be worse off. These are all examples of the fallacy of composition.

---

⑦ SECTION QUIZ

1. Which of the following statements can explain why correlation between Event A and Event B may not imply causality from A to B?

    a. The observed correlation may be coincidental.

    b. A third variable may be responsible for causing both events.

    c. Causality may run from Event B to Event A instead of in the opposite direction.

    d. All of the above can explain why the correlation may not imply causality.

2. Ten-year-old Tommy observes that people who play football are larger than average and tells his mom that he's going to play football because it will make him big and strong. Tommy is

    a. committing the fallacy of composition.

    b. violating the *ceteris paribus* assumption.

    c. mistaking correlation for causation.

    d. committing the fallacy of decomposition.

3. The fallacy of composition

    a. is a problem associated with aggregation.

    b. assumes that if something is true for an individual, then it is necessarily true for a group of individuals.

    c. is illustrated in the following statement: If I stand up at a football game, I will be able to see better; therefore, if we all stood up, we would all see better.

    d. all of the above are true.

(continued)

1.5

Positive Statements and Normative Statements

▭ What is a positive statement?   ▭ Why do economists disagree?

▭ What is a normative statement?

Positive Statement

Most economists view themselves as scientists seeking the truth about the way people behave. They make speculations about economic behavior, and then, ideally, they assess the validity of those predictions based on human experience. Their work emphasizes how people *do* behave, rather than how people *should* behave. In the role of scientist, an economist tries to observe patterns of behavior objectively, without reference to the appropriateness or inappropriateness of that behavior. This objective, value-free approach, based on the scientific method, is called positive analysis. In positive analysis, we want to know the impact of variable *A* on variable *B*. We want to be able to test a hypothesis. For example, the following is a **positive statement**: If rent controls are imposed, vacancy rates will fall. This statement is testable. A positive statement does not have to be a true statement, but it does have to be a testable statement.

positive statement an objective, testable statement that describes what happens and why it happen

Keep in mind, however, that it is doubtful that even the most objective scientist can be totally value free in his or her analysis. An economist may well emphasize data or evidence that supports a hypothesis, putting less weight on other evidence that might be contradictory. This tendency, alas, is human nature. But a good economist/scientist strives to be as fair and objective as possible in evaluating evidence and in stating conclusions based on the evidence. In some sense, economists are like engineers; they try to figure out how things work and then describe what would happen if you changed something.

What is the difference between positive statements and normative statements?

Normative Statement

Economists, like anyone else, have opinions and make value judgments. And when economists, or anyone else for that matter, express opinions about an economic policy or statement, they are indicating in part how they believe things should be, not stating facts about the way things are. In other words, they are performing normative analysis. **Normative statements** involve judgments about what should be or what ought to happen. For example, normative questions might include: Should the government raise the minimum wage? Should the government increase spending in the space program? Should the government give "free" prescription drugs to senior citizens?

normative statement a subjective, contestable statement that attempts to describe what should be done

Positive versus Normative Analysis

The distinction between positive and normative analysis is important. It is one thing to say that everyone should have universal health care, an untestable normative statement, and quite another to say that universal health care would lead to greater worker productivity, a testable positive statement. It is important to distinguish between positive and normative analysis because many controversies in economics revolve around policy considerations that contain both. For example, what impact would a 3 percent reduction in income taxes across the board have on the economy? This question requires positive analysis. Whether we should have a 3 percent reduction in income taxes requires normative analysis as well. When economists are trying to explain the way the world works, they are scientists. When economists start talking about how the economy should work rather than how it does work, they have entered the normative world of the policy maker. In short, positive statements are attempts to *describe* what happens and why it happens, while normative statements are attempts to *prescribe* what should be done. Positive analysis can demonstrate the consequences of a particular policy but cannot prove that a particular policy is good or bad. However, it is also important to remember that a good understanding of positive analysis is crucial to making effective policy prescriptions—normative analysis.

Does positive analysis prove a policy is good?

Disagreement Is Common in Most Disciplines

Although economists do frequently have opposing views on economic policy questions, they probably disagree less than the media would have you believe. Disagreement is common in most disciplines: Seismologists differ over predictions of earthquakes or volcanic eruption; historians can be at odds over the interpretation of historical events; psychologists disagree on proper ways to raise children; and nutritionists debate the efficacy of particular vitamins and the quantities that should be taken.

The majority of disagreements in economics stem from normative issues; differences in values or policy beliefs result in conflict. For example, a policy might increase efficiency at the expense of a sense of fairness or equity, or it might help a current generation at the expense of a future generation. Because policy decisions involve trade-offs, they will always involve the potential for conflict.

Freedom versus Fairness

Some economists are concerned about individual freedom and liberty, thinking that any encroachment on individual decision making is bad, other things being equal. People with this philosophic bent are inclined to be skeptical of any increased government involvement in the economy.

On the other hand, some economists are concerned with what they consider an unequal, "unfair," or unfortunate distribution of income, wealth, or power, and view governmental intervention as desirable in righting injustices that they believe exist in a market economy. To these persons, the threat to individual liberty alone is not sufficient to reject governmental intervention in the face of perceived economic injustice.

The Validity of an Economic Theory

Aside from philosophic differences, a second reason helps explain why economists may differ on any given policy question. Specifically, they may disagree about the validity of a given economic theory for the policy in question—that is, they disagree over the positive analysis. Why would they disagree over positive analysis? For at least two reasons. One, a particular model may yield mixed results: some empirical evidence supporting it and some not. Two, the information available may be insufficient to make a compelling theory.

Often Economists Do Agree

Although you may not believe it after reading the previous discussion, economists don't always disagree. In fact, according to a survey among members of the American Economic

Association, most economists agree on a wide range of issues, including the effects of rent control, import tariffs, export restrictions, the use of wage and price controls to curb inflation, and the minimum wage.

It seems like economists always disagree on important issues. Is that true?

According to studies, most economists agree that these statements are correct:

1. A ceiling on rents (rent control) reduces the quantity and quality of rental housing available (93 percent agree).
2. Tariffs and import quotas usually reduce general economic welfare (93 percent agree).
3. The United States should not restrict employers from outsourcing work to foreign countries (90 percent agree).
4. Fiscal policy (e.g., tax cuts and/or increases in government expenditure) has significant stimulative impact on an economy that is less than fully employed (90 percent agree).
5. Flexible and floating exchange rates offer an effective international monetary arrangement (90 percent agree).
6. The gap between Social Security funds and expenditures will become unsustainably large within the next 50 years if the current policies remain unchanged (85 percent agree).
7. The United States should eliminate agricultural subsidies (85 percent agree).
8. Local and state governments in the United States should eliminate subsidies to professional sport franchises (85 percent agree).
9. A large budget deficit has an adverse effect on the economy (83 percent agree).
10. A minimum wage increases unemployment among young and unskilled (79 percent agree).
11. Effluent taxes and marketable pollution permits represent a better approach to pollution control than imposition of pollution ceilings (78 percent agree).
12. Economists favor expanding competition and market forces in education (67 percent agree).[1]

Steps on How to Do Well in This (or any other) Course

1. Are you motivated to learn? Link your motivation to goals. I want an A in this class. I want to graduate. I want to go to medical school or law school. I want a college degree. Setting goals demonstrates an intention to achieve and activates learning. School is really about learning to learn and hopefully, learning to enjoy learning. Students must find satisfaction in learning based on the understanding that the goals are useful to them. Put yourself in the right mind set. In short, learning is most effective when an individual is ready to learn. If you are not ready for Step 1, the other nine steps are less useful.

2. Do you attend class and take good notes? Listen actively—think before you write but be careful not to fall behind. Try to capture the main points of the lecture. You cannot take down everything. Leave space in your notebook so you can fill in with greater clarity when reading or re-reading text. This is also a good time to edit your notes. Review your notes within 24 hours of lecture. This way you will be reviewing rather than relearning!

3. Do you read before class? Stay current. If you are studying Chapter 3 when the lecture is on Chapter 6, it will harm your performance. While perfection is not necessary, do the best you can to read the material before it is covered in lecture.

4. Do you just highlight when you read? Don't. It is too passive. Finish a section and summarize it in your own words. Afterward, compare it with the section checks and summary at the end of the chapter to see if you caught all the main points. Do NOT read something without learning anything. That's a waste of time. Train your mind to learn—questioning, reciting, reviewing while you read will make you an active reader and a better student.

---

[1]Richard M. Alston, J. R. Kearl, and Michael B. Vaughn, "Is there Consensus among Economists in the 1990s?" *American Economic Review* (May 1992): 203-09; Robert Whaples, "Do Economists Agree on Anything? Yes!" *Economists' Voice* (November 2006): 1–6.

5. When do you study? Break up your study time, to keep it fresh. Don't study when you are tired. Know when you function best. To many people, an hour of studying in the day is worth two at night! That is, reading in the morning after a good night's sleep may be much more productive than when you are tired late at night. Study in 20- to 50-minute chunks with 5- to 10-minute breaks. This has proven to be the most effective way to study.

6. How do you study? Study actively. Study by doing. Work problems, like in physics, chemistry, or engineering. Go back and forth between problems, examples, and text. That is, practice, practice, and practice. There are many problems throughout the text and on the website. Do them. The late John Wooden (famous basketball coach at UCLA) would often quote Ben Franklin, "Failing to prepare is preparing to fail." Have you worked on your self-confidence? Before you look up the answer to a question, assign a "confidence factor" to your work. On a scale of 1-10, how confident are you that you are right? Be honest with yourself. The more often you prove yourself right, the less test anxiety you will have.

7. Do you work for understanding? Can you explain the concepts to others? If you can explain it to others, perhaps in a study group, you will really know it. There is no better way to learn something than by teaching it to others.

8. Do you find a quiet place to study with few distractions? Music and TV are not conducive to quality study time. This will only impair concentration. If you find your mind wandering, get up and walk around for a couple of minutes. Try to relax before you start studying, and associate reading with relaxation, not anxiety. Set a goal of how much you want to accomplish in each session and try to increase it gradually.

9. Do you apply your reading and lectures to your daily life? Retention is always greater when you can make the connection between the course and your life. Read the *In the News* features and the real world examples throughout the text and see how the economic principles apply to your everyday life. Economics should also help you better understand the events you read about in the newspaper and on the internet.

10. Do you cram for tests? Don't. It will not work well in economics and perhaps not in any analytical field. Study regularly, with greater review being the only difference in your study habits prior to a test. Try to have all your material read two days prior to exam so the remaining time can be devoted to review. Cramming for tests leads to fatigue, test anxiety, and careless mistakes. Get plenty of sleep. Treat being in school as having a full-time job— put in your time regularly and you won't need or want to cram. In short, don't procrastinate!

ⓧ SECTION QUIZ

1. Which of the following is a positive statement?

   a. New tax laws are needed to help the poor.

   b. Teenage unemployment should be reduced.

   c. We should increase Social Security payments to the elderly.

   d. An increase in tax rates will reduce unemployment.

   e. It is only fair that firms protected from competition by government-granted monopolies pay higher corporate taxes.

2. Positive statements

   a. are testable.

   b. are attempts to describe what happens and why it happens.

   c. do not have to be a true statement.

   d. All of the above are true.

(*continued*)

⑦ S E C T I O N   Q U I Z (Cont.)

3. Normative statements

    a. attempt to describe what happens and why it happens.

    b. are objective and testable.

    c. attempt to describe the way the world works.

    d. are subjective and attempt to prescribe what should be done.

4. The statement "the government should increase spending for the space program" is

    a. objective and testable.

    b. a positive statement.

    c. subjective, prescriptive, and normative.

    d. a fact and very important for the defense of our country.

5. Which of the following statements is (are) true?

    a. Economists disagree but most often over normative issues.

    b. Economists do agree over a wide range of issues.

    c. Disagreement is also common in other disciplines.

    d. All of the above statements are true.

---

1. What is a positive statement? Must positive statements be testable?

2. What is a normative statement? Is a normative statement testable?

3. Why is the positive/normative distinction important?

4. Why do policy disagreements arise among economists?

Answers: 1. d 2. d 3. d 4. c 5. d

Interactive Summary

Fill in the blanks:

1. Economics is the study of the choices we make among our many wants and desires given our _____ resources.

2. _____ occurs because our unlimited wants exceed our limited resources.

3. Resources are _____ used to produce goods and services.

4. The economic problem is that _____ forces us to choose, and choices are costly because we must give up other opportunities that we _____.

5. Living in a world of scarcity means _____.

6. _____ deals with the aggregate (the forest), or total economy, while _____ deals with the smaller units (the trees) within the economy.

7. Economists assume that individuals act as if they are motivated by _____ and respond in _____ ways to changing circumstances.

8. Economists believe that it is _____ for people to anticipate the likely future consequences of their behavior.

9. Actions have _____.

10. Rational self-interest implies that people do not make _____ mistakes.

11. Economic _____ are statements or propositions used to _____ and _____ patterns of human economic behavior.

12. Because of the complexity of human behavior, economists must _____ to focus on the most important components of a particular problem.

13. A(n) _____ in economic theory is a testable prediction about how people will behave or react to a change in economic circumstances.

14. _____ analysis is the use of data to test a hypothesis.

15. In order to isolate the effects of one variable on another, we use the _____ assumption.

16. When two events usually occur together, it is called _____.

17. When one event brings on another event, it is called _____.

18. The _____ is the incorrect view that what is true for an individual is always true for the group.

19. The objective, value-free approach to economics, based on the scientific method, is called _____ analysis.

20. _____ analysis involves judgments about what should be or what ought to happen.

21. _____ analysis is descriptive; normative analysis is _____.

22. "A tax increase will lead to a lower rate of inflation" is a(n) _____ economic statement.

Answers: 1. limited; unlimited 2. Scarcity 3. inputs 4. scarcity; value 5. trade-offs 6. Macroeconomics; microeconomics 7. self-interest; predictable 8. rational 9. consequences 10. systematic 11. theories; explain; predict 12. abstract 13. hypothesis 14. Empirical 15. *ceteris paribus* 16. correlation 17. causation 18. fallacy of composition 19. positive 20. Normative 21. Positive; prescriptive 22. positive

Key Terms and Concepts

economics 3
resources 3
scarcity 3
the economic problem 3
rational behavior 7
theory 9

hypothesis 10
empirical analysis 10
ceteris paribus 11
microeconomics 13
macroeconomics 13
aggregate 13

correlation 14
causation 14
fallacy of composition 16
positive statement 17
normative statement 17

Section Quiz Answers

1.1   Economics: A Brief Introduction

1. **What is the definition of economics?**
Economics is the study of the choices we make among our many wants and desires given our limited resources.

2. **Why does scarcity force us to make choices?**
Scarcity—the fact that our wants exceed what our resources can produce—means that we are forced to make choices on how best to use these limited resources.

3. **Why are choices costly?**
In a world of scarcity, whenever we choose one option, we also choose to do without something else that we also desire. The want that we choose not to satisfy is the opportunity cost of that choice.

4. **What is the economic problem?**
Scarcity forces us to choose, and choices are costly because we must give up other opportunities that

we value. This is the economic problem. Every individual, business, social, religious, and governmental organization faces the economic problem. Every society, whether it is capitalistic, socialistic, or totalitarian, must also face the economic problem of scarcity, choices, and costs.

5. **Why do even "non-economic" issues have an economic dimension?**
Even apparently non-economic issues have an economic dimension because economics concerns anything worthwhile to some human being (including love, friendship, charity, etc.) and the choices we make among those things we value.

1.2   Economic Behavior

1. **What do economists mean by self-interest?**
By self-interest, economists simply mean that people try to improve their own situation (as they see it, not necessarily as others see it). Self-interest can also include benevolence.

2. What does rational self-interest involve?

Economists consider individuals to be acting in their rational self-interest if they are striving to do their best to achieve their goals with their limited income, time, and knowledge, and given their expectations of the likely future consequences (both benefits and costs) of their behavior.

3. How are self-interest and selfishness different?

Self-interest means people are striving to do their best to achieve their goals, which may or may not be selfish. Parents working more hours to give more to their children or a favorite charity can be self-interested but are not selfish.

4. What is rational behavior?

Rational behavior is when people do the best they can based on their values and information, under current and anticipated future consequences. Rational individuals weigh the benefits and costs of their actions and they only pursue actions if they perceive their benefits to be greater than the costs.

1.3 Economic Theory

1. What are economic theories?

A theory is an established explanation that accounts for known facts or phenomena. Economic theories are statements or propositions about patterns of human behavior that are expected to take place under certain circumstances.

2. What is the purpose of a theory?

The purpose of a theory is primarily to explain and predict well. Theories are necessary because the facts of a complex world do not organize themselves.

3. Why must economic theories be abstract?

Economic theories must be abstract because they could not possibly include every possible event, circumstance, or factor that might affect behavior. Like a road map, an economic theory abstracts from some issues to focus more clearly and precisely on the central questions it is designed to understand.

4. What is a hypothesis? How do we determine whether it is tentatively accepted?

A hypothesis is a testable proposal that makes some type of prediction about behavior in response to certain changed conditions. An economic hypothesis is a testable proposal about how people will behave or react to a change in economic circumstances. It is tentatively accepted if its predictions are consistent with what actually happens. In economics, testing involves empirical analysis to see whether the hypothesis is supported by the facts.

5. Why do economists hold other things constant (*ceteris paribus*)?

The hold other things constant, or *ceteris paribus*, assumption is used in economics because in trying to assess the effect of one variable on another, we must isolate their relationship from other important events or variables that might also influence the situation the theory tries to explain or predict.

6. Why are observation and prediction more difficult in the social sciences?

Observation and prediction are more difficult in the social sciences than in physical sciences because social sciences are concerned with human behavior, which is more variable and often less readily predictable than the behavior of experiments observed in a laboratory. Social scientists can seldom run truly "controlled" experiments like those of the biological scientists.

7. Why do economic predictions refer to the behavior of groups of people rather than individuals?

Economists' predictions usually refer to the collective behavior of large groups rather than individuals because looking at the behaviors of a large group of individuals allows economists to discern general patterns of actions and therefore make more reliable generalizations.

8. Why is revealed preference preferred to declared preference?

Researchers find that their results are more accurate when they observe what people do (revealed preferences) rather that what they say they do (declared preferences).

9. Why is the market for running shoes considered a microeconomic topic?

Because a single industry is "small" relative to the economy as a whole, the market for running shoes (or the running-shoe industry) is a microeconomic topic.

10. Why is inflation considered a macroeconomic topic?

Inflation—a change in the overall price level—has effects throughout the entire economy, rather than just in certain small areas of the economy, which makes it a macroeconomic topic.

1.4 Pitfalls to Avoid in Scientific Thinking

1. What is the relationship between correlation and causation?

Correlation means that two things are related; causation means that one thing caused the other to occur. Even though causation implies correlation, correlation does not necessarily imply causation.

2. **What types of misinterpretation result from confusing correlation and causation?**

Confusing correlation between variables with causation can lead to misinterpretation where a person "sees" causation between two variables or events where none exists or where a third variable or event is responsible for causing both of them.

3. **What is the fallacy of composition?**

The fallacy of composition is the incorrect idea that if something is true for an individual, it must also be true for many individuals as a group.

4. **If you can sometimes get a high grade on an exam without studying, does it mean that additional studying does not lead to higher grades? Explain your answer.**

In some instances a student can get a high grade on an exam without studying. However, because additional studying increases mastery of the material, additional studying would typically increase test performance and grades. That is, even though added studying would not raise grades in some unusual situations, as a generalization, additional studying does lead to higher grades.

1.5   Positive Statements and Normative Statements

1. **What is a positive statements? Must positive statements be testable?**

Positive statements focus on how people actually behave, rather than on how people should behave.

They deal with how variable *A* impacts variable *B*. Positive statements must be testable to determine whether their predictions are borne out by the evidence.

2. **What is a normative statement? Is a normative statement testable?**

Normative statements focus on what should be or what ought to happen; they involve opinions about the desirability of various actions or results. Normative statements are not testable, because it is not scientifically possible to establish whether one value judgment is better than another value judgment.

3. **Why is the positive/normative distinction important?**

It is important to distinguish between positive and normative statements because many controversies in economics revolve around policy considerations that contain both. Deciding whether a policy is good requires both positive analysis (what will happen) and normative analysis (is what happens good or bad).

4. **Why do policy disagreements arise among economists?**

As with most disciplines, economists do disagree. However, the majority of those disagreements stem from differences in normative analysis, because the evidence cannot establish whether one set of value judgments is better or more appropriate than other sets of value judgments.

Problems

1. In most countries the birth rate has fallen as incomes and the economic opportunities for women have increased. Use economics to explain this pattern.

2. Write your own definition of economics. What are the main elements of the definition?

3. Are the following topics ones that would be covered in microeconomics or macroeconomics?
   a. the effects of an increase in the supply of lumber on the home-building industry
   b. changes in the national unemployment rate
   c. changes in the inflation rate
   d. changes in the country's economic growth rate
   e. the price of concert tickets

4. Identify which of the following headlines represents a microeconomic topic and which represents a macroeconomic topic.
   a. "U.S. Unemployment Rate Reaches Historic Lows"
   b. "General Motors Closes Auto Plant in St. Louis"
   c. "OPEC Action Results in a General Increase in Prices"
   d. "Companies Increase the Cost of Health Care for Employees"
   e. "Lawmakers Worry about the Possibility of a U.S. Recession"
   f. "Colorado Rockies Make Outfielder Highest Paid Ballplayer"

5. The Environmental Protection Agency asks you to help it understand the causes of urban pollution. Air pollution problems are worse the higher the Air Quality Index. You develop the following two hypotheses. Hypothesis I: Air pollution will be a greater problem as the average temperature increases in the urban area. Hypothesis II: Air pollution will be a greater problem as the population increases in the urban area.

   Test each hypothesis with the facts given in the following table. Which hypothesis fits the facts better? Have you developed a theory?

Metropolitan Statistical Area	Days with Polluted Air*	Average Maximum Temperature	Population (thousands)
Cincinnati, OH	30	64.0	1,979
El Paso, TX	13	77.1	680
Milwaukee, WI	12	55.9	1,690
Atlanta, GA	24	72.0	4,112
Philadelphia, PA	33	63.2	5,101
Albany, NY	8	57.6	876
San Diego, CA	20	70.8	2,814
Los Angeles, CA	80	70.6	9,519

*Air Quality Index greater than 100 (2002) **Source:** U.S. Dept. of Commerce, Bureau of Census, 2002 Statistical Abstract of the United States, Tables Nos. 30 and 363; U.S. EPA, Air Trends Report, 2002, EPA.Gov/airtrends/factbook.

6. Do any of the following statements involve fallacies? If so, which ones do they involve?
   a. Because sitting in the back of classrooms is correlated with getting lower grades in the class, students should always sit closer to the front of the classroom.
   b. Historically, the stock market rises in years the NFC team wins the Super Bowl and falls when the AFC wins the Super Bowl; I am rooting for the NFC team to win for the sake of my investment portfolio.
   c. When a basketball team spends more to get better players, it is more successful, which proves that all the teams should spend more to get better players.
   d. Gasoline prices were higher last year than in 1970, yet people purchased more gas, which contradicts the law of demand.
   e. An increase in the amount of money I have will make me better off, but an increase in the supply of money in the economy will not make Americans as a group better off.

7. In the 1940s, Dr. Melvin Page conducted a national campaign to stop people other than infants from drinking milk. According to Page, milk was a dangerous food and a leading cause of cancer. He pointed to the fact that more people died of cancer in Wisconsin, the nation's leading milk producer, than any other state as proof of his claim. How would you evaluate Dr. Page's claim?

8. Are the following statements normative or positive, or do they contain elements of both normative and positive statements?
   a. A higher income-tax rate would generate increased tax revenues. Those extra revenues should be used to give more government aid to the poor.
   b. The study of physics is more valuable than the study of sociology, but both should be studied by all college students.
   c. An increase in the price of corn will decrease the amount of corn purchased. However, it will increase the amount of wheat purchased.
   d. A decrease in the price of butter will increase the amount of butter purchased, but that would be bad because it would increase Americans' cholesterol levels.
   e. The birth rate is reduced as economies urbanize, but it also leads to a decreased average age of developing countries' populations.

9. In the debate about clean air standards we have often heard the statement, "A nation as rich as the United States should have no pollution." Why is this a normative statement? Would it help you make a decision on national air quality standards? Describe two positive statements that might be useful in determining the air *quality standards.*

10. Answer the following questions:
    a. What is the difference between self-interest and selfishness?
    b. Why does inaction have consequences?
    c. Why are observation and prediction more difficult in economics than in chemistry?
    d. Why do economists look at group behavior rather than individual behavior?

11. Using the map analogy from the chapter, talk about the importance of abstraction. How do you abstract when taking notes in class?

Appendix

Working with Graphs

Graphs Are an Important Economic Tool

Sometimes the use of visual aids, such as graphs, greatly enhances our understanding of a theory. It is much the same as finding your way to a friend's house with the aid of a map rather than with detailed verbal or written instructions. Graphs are important tools for economists. They allow us to understand better the workings of the economy. To economists, a graph can be worth a thousand words. This textbook will use graphs throughout to enhance the understanding of important economic relationships. This appendix provides a guide on how to read and create your own graphs.

The most useful graph for our purposes is one that merely connects a vertical line (the *y*-axis) with a horizontal line (the *x*-axis), as seen in Exhibit 1. The intersection of the two lines occurs at the *origin,* which is where the value of both variables is equal to zero. In Exhibit 1, the graph has

y-axis
the vertical axis on a graph

x-axis
the horizontal axis on a graph

four quadrants, or boxes. In this textbook, we will be primarily concerned with the shaded box in the upper-right corner. This portion of the graph deals exclusively with positive numbers. Always keep in mind that moving to the right on the horizontal axis and moving up along the vertical axis both lead to higher values.

Using Graphs and Charts

Exhibit 2 presents three common types of graphs. The pie chart in Exhibit 2(a) shows the revenues received from various taxes levied on households and corporations. Each slice in the pie chart represents the percentage of finances that are derived from different sources—for example, personal income taxes account for 43 percent of the federal government's tax revenues. Therefore, pie charts are used to show the relative size of various quantities that add up to 100 percent.

Exhibit 2(b) is a bar graph that shows the unemployment rate by age and sex in the United States. The height of the line represents the unemployment rate. Bar graphs are used to show a comparison of quantities.

Exhibit 2(c) is a time-series graph. This type of graph shows changes in the value of a variable over time. This visual tool allows us to observe important trends over a certain time period. In Exhibit 2(c) we see a graph that shows trends in the inflation rate over time. The horizontal axis shows us the passage of time, and the vertical axis shows us the inflation rate (annual percent change). From the graph, we can see the trends in the inflation rate from 1961 to 2005.

pie chart
visual display showing the relative size of various quantities that add up to 100 percent

bar graph
visual display showing the comparison of quantities

time-series graph
visual tool to show changes in a variable's value over time

variable
something that is measured by a number, such as your height

Using Graphs to Show the Relationship between Two Variables

Even though the graphs and chart in Exhibit 2 are important, they do not allow us to show the relationship between two variables (a variable is something that is

---

appendix **exhibit 1** Plotting a Graph

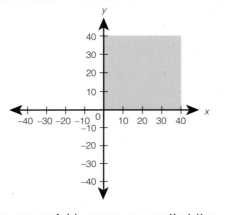

In the upper-right corner, we see that the graph includes a positive figure for the *y*-axis and the *x*-axis. As we move to the right along the horizontal axis, the numerical values increase. As we move up along the vertical axis, the numerical values increase.

© Cengage Learning 2013

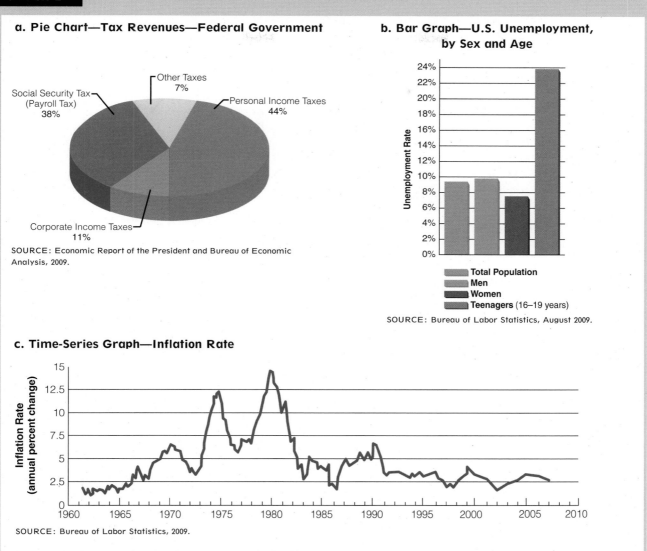

appendix
exhibit 2   Pie Chart, Bar Graph, and Time-Series Graph

a. Pie Chart—Tax Revenues—Federal Government

Other Taxes
7%

Social Security Tax
(Payroll Tax)
38%

Personal Income Taxes
44%

Corporate Income Taxes
11%

SOURCE: Economic Report of the President and Bureau of Economic Analysis, 2009.

b. Bar Graph—U.S. Unemployment, by Sex and Age

Unemployment Rate

- Total Population
- Men
- Women
- Teenagers (16–19 years)

SOURCE: Bureau of Labor Statistics, August 2009.

c. Time-Series Graph—Inflation Rate

Inflation Rate (annual percent change)

SOURCE: Bureau of Labor Statistics, 2009.

measured by a number, such as your height). To more closely examine the structures and functions of graphs, let's consider the story of Josh, an avid skateboarder who has aspirations of winning the Z Games next year. He knows that to get there, he'll need to put in many hours of practice. But how many hours? In search of information about the practice habits of other skateboarders, he searches the Internet, where he finds the results of a study that looked at the score of each Z Games competitor in relation to the amount of practice time per week spent by each skateboarder. As Exhibit 3 shows, the results of the study indicate that skateboarders had to practice 10 hours per week to receive a score of 4, 20 hours per week to receive a

score of 6, 30 hours per week to get a score of 8, and 40 hours per week to get a perfect score of 10. How does this information help Josh? By using a graph, he can more clearly understand the relationship between practice time and overall score.

A Positive Relationship

The study on scores and practice times reveals what is called a direct relationship, also called a positive relationship. A **positive relationship** means that the variables change in the same direction. That is, an increase

positive relationship
when two variables change in the same direction

appendix
exhibit 3   A Positive Relationship

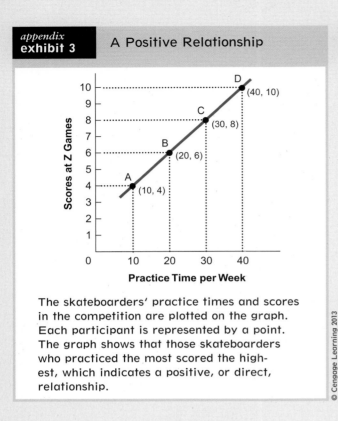

appendix
exhibit 3   A Positive Relationship

The skateboarders' practice times and scores in the competition are plotted on the graph. Each participant is represented by a point. The graph shows that those skateboarders who practiced the most scored the highest, which indicates a positive, or direct, relationship.

© Cengage Learning 2013

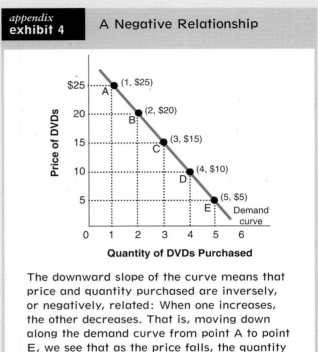

appendix
exhibit 4   A Negative Relationship

The downward slope of the curve means that price and quantity purchased are inversely, or negatively, related: When one increases, the other decreases. That is, moving down along the demand curve from point A to point E, we see that as the price falls, the quantity purchased increases. Moving up along the demand curve from point E to point A, we see that as the price increases, the quantity purchased falls.

© Cengage Learning 2013

in one variable (practice time) is accompanied by an increase in the other variable (overall score), or a decrease in one variable (practice time) is accompanied by a decrease in the other variable (overall score). In short, the variables change in the same direction.

A Negative Relationship

When two variables change in opposite directions, they have an inverse relationship, also called a **negative relationship**. That is, when one variable rises, the other

negative relationship
when two variables change in opposite directions

variable falls, or when one variable decreases, the other variable increases.

The Graph of a Demand Curve

Let's now examine one of the most important graphs in economics—the demand curve. In Exhibit 4, we see Emily's individual demand curve for DVDs. It shows the price of DVDs on the vertical axis and the quantity of DVDs purchased per month on the horizontal axis. Every point in the space shown

represents a price and quantity combination. The downward-sloping line, labeled "Demand curve," shows the different combinations of price and quantity purchased. Note that the higher the price of the DVDs, as shown on the vertical axis, the smaller the quantity purchased, as shown on the horizontal axis, and the lower the price shown on the vertical axis, the greater the quantity purchased shown on the horizontal axis.

In Exhibit 4, we see that moving up the vertical price axis from the origin, the price of DVDs increases from $5 to $25 in increments of $5. Moving out along the horizontal quantity axis, the quantity purchased increases from zero to five DVDs per month. Point A represents a price of $25 and a quantity of one DVD, point B represents a price of $20 and a quantity of two DVDs, point C a price of $15 and a quantity of three DVDs, and so on. When we connect all the points, we have what economists call a curve. As you can see, curves are sometimes drawn as straight lines for ease of illustration. Moving down along the curve, we see that as the price falls, a greater quantity is demanded; moving up the curve to higher prices, a smaller quantity is demanded. That is, when DVDs become less expensive, Emily buys more DVDs. When

DVDs become more expensive, Emily buys fewer DVDs, perhaps choosing to go to the movies or buy a pizza instead.

Using Graphs to Show the Relationship among Three Variables

Although only two variables are shown on the axes, graphs can be used to show the relationship among three variables. For example, say we add a third variable—income—to our earlier example. Our three variables are now income, price, and quantity purchased. If Emily's income rises—say she gets a raise at work—she is now able and willing to buy more DVDs than before at each possible price. As a result, the whole demand curve shifts outward (to the right) compared with the old curve. That is, the new income gives her more money to use buying more DVDs. This

shift is seen in the graph in Exhibit 5(a). On the other hand, if her income falls—say she quits her job to go back to school—she would have less income to buy DVDs. A decrease in this variable causes the whole demand curve to shift inward (to the left) compared with the old curve. This shift is seen in the graph in Exhibit 5(b).

The Difference between a Movement along and a Shift in the Curve

It is important to remember the difference between a movement between one point and another along a curve and a shift in the whole curve. A change in one of the variables on the graph, like price or quantity purchased, will cause a movement along the curve, say from point A to point B, as shown in Exhibit 6. A change in one of the variables not shown (held constant in order to show only the relationship between price and quantity), such as income in our example, will cause the whole curve to shift. The change from D_1 to D_2 in Exhibit 6 shows such a shift.

Slope

In economics, we sometimes refer to the steepness of a line or curve on a graph as the slope. A slope can be either positive (upward sloping) or negative (downward sloping). A curve that is downward sloping represents an inverse, or negative, relationship between the two variables and slants downward from left to right, as seen in Exhibit 7(a). A curve that is upward sloping represents a direct, or positive, relationship between the two variables and

slope
the ratio of rise (change in the *y* variable) over run (change in the *x* variable)

---

appendix exhibit 5   Shifting a Curve

a. Demand Curve with Higher Income

Price of DVDs / Quantity of DVDs Purchased

D
D (with higher income)

b. Demand Curve with Lower Income

Price of DVDs / Quantity of DVDs Purchased

D (with lower income)
D

© Cengage Learning 2013

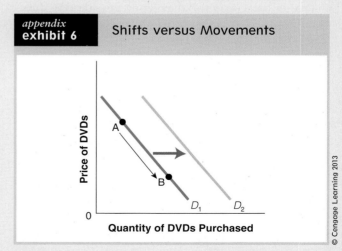

appendix exhibit 6   Shifts versus Movements

Price of DVDs / Quantity of DVDs Purchased

A
B
D_1 D_2

© Cengage Learning 2013

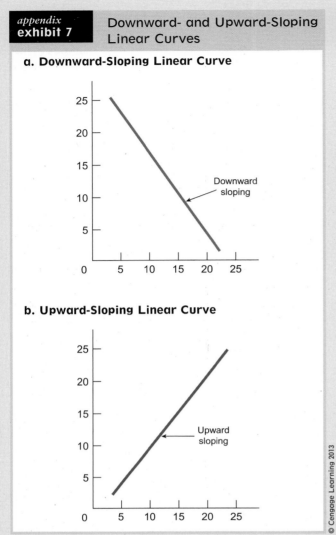

appendix exhibit 7   Downward- and Upward-Sloping Linear Curves

a. Downward-Sloping Linear Curve

Downward sloping

b. Upward-Sloping Linear Curve

Upward sloping

© Cengage Learning 2013

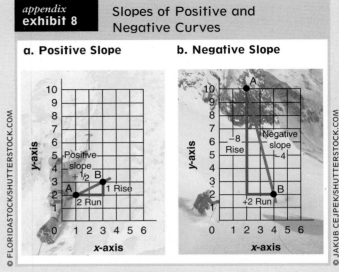

appendix exhibit 8   Slopes of Positive and Negative Curves

a. Positive Slope

Positive slope +½

A   B   1 Rise

2 Run

© FLORIDASTOCK/SHUTTERSTOCK.COM

b. Negative Slope

A

−8 Rise   Negative slope −4

B

+2 Run

© JAKUB CEJPEK/SHUTTERSTOCK.COM

Exhibit 8(a), the slope of the positively sloped linear curve from point A to B is 1/2, because the rise is 1 (from 2 to 3) and the run is 2 (from 1 to 3). In Exhibit 8(b), the negatively sloped linear curve has a slope of −4: a rise of −8 (a fall of 8, from 10 to 2) and a run of 2 (from 2 to 4) gives us a slope of −8/2, or −4. Notice the appropriate signs on the slopes: the negatively sloped line carries a minus sign and the positively sloped line, a plus sign.

Finding the Slope of a Nonlinear Curve

In Exhibit 9, we show the slope of a nonlinear curve. A nonlinear curve is a line that actually curves. Here the slope varies from point to point along the curve. However, we can find the slope of this curve at any given point by drawing a straight line tangent to that point on the curve. A tangency is when a straight line just touches the curve without actually crossing it. At

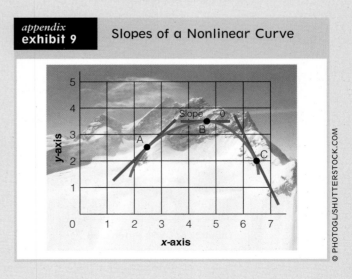

appendix exhibit 9   Slopes of a Nonlinear Curve

Slope = 0

A   B

C

© PHOTOGL/SHUTTERSTOCK.COM

slants upward from left to right, as seen in Exhibit 7(b). The numeric value of the slope shows the number of units of change of the *y*-axis variable for each unit of change in the *x*-axis variable. Slope provides the direction (positive or negative) as well as the magnitude of the relationship between the two variables.

Measuring the Slope of a Linear Curve

A straight-line curve is called a linear curve. The slope of a linear curve between two points measures the relative rates of change of two variables. Specifically, the slope of a linear curve can be defined as the ratio of the change in the *Y* value to the change in the *X* value. The slope can also be expressed as the ratio of the rise over the run, where the rise is the vertical change and the run is the horizontal change.

Exhibit 8 shows two linear curves, one with a positive slope and one with a negative slope. In point A, we see that the positively sloped line that is tangent to the curve has a slope of 1: the line rises 1 and runs 1. At point B, the line is horizontal, so it has zero slope. At point C, we see a slope of –2, because the negatively sloped line has a rise of –2 (a fall of 2) for every run of 1.

Remember, many students have problems with economics simply because they fail to understand graphs, so make sure that you understand this material before going on to Chapter 2.

Key Terms and Concepts

y-axis 26
x-axis 26
pie chart 26

bar graph 26
time-series graph 26
variable 26

positive relationship 27
negative relationship 28
slope 29

Problems

1. The following table gives the prices and quantity demanded of oranges (pounds) for the week of December 10–16.

Price ($/lb.)	Quantity Demanded (lbs.)
$0.80	0
0.70	3
0.60	4
0.50	5
0.40	7

   a. Plot the data from the table into a graph.
   b. Is it a positive or negative relationship? Explain.

Answer

We have created a negatively sloped demand curve. That is, the price and quantity demanded of oranges are inversely related:

$$\uparrow P \Rightarrow \downarrow Q_D \quad \text{and} \quad \downarrow P \Rightarrow \uparrow Q_D$$

Individual demand curve of a customer for oranges of a certain grade, Week of December 10–16.

The demand curve records the pounds of oranges a consumer desires at various prices in a given week, holding all other factors fixed. Because the individual desires more oranges at lower prices, the demand curve slopes downward.

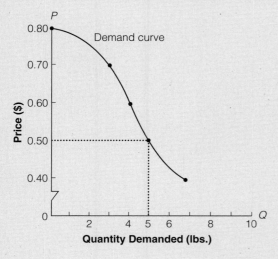

2. Which of the following will lead to a positive relationship? A negative relationship?
    a. hours studied and grade in a course
    b. the price of ice cream and the amount of ice cream purchased
    c. the amount of seasonal snowfall and the sale of snow shovels

    Answer
    a. positive
    b. negative
    c. positive

3. Below is Emily's demand curve for pizza. How do we add income, a third variable, to price and quantity purchased on our graph? Using a graph, explain what would happen if Emily had an increase in income. What would happen if Emily has a decrease in income?

    Answer

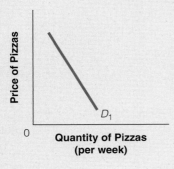
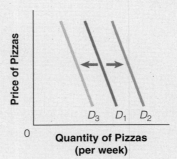

    When income increases, Emily can purchase more pizzas at each and every price—a rightward shift from D_1 to D_2. If Emily's income falls, her demand will shift leftward from D_1 to D_3.

4. Use the information in the following table to plot a graph. Is it a positive or negative relationship? What is the slope?

x	y
1	2
2	4
3	6
4	8
5	10

    Answer

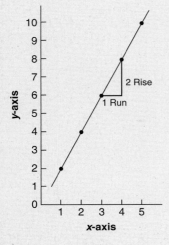

    $$\text{Positive Slope} = \frac{\text{Rise}}{\text{Run}} = \frac{2}{1} = +2$$

5. What is a pie chart? Bar graph? Time-series graph?

Answer

Pie charts are used to show the relative size of various quantities that add up to 100 percent. Bar graphs are used to show a comparison of quantities of similar items. Time-series graphs allow us to see important trends over a period of time.

Economics: Eight Powerful Ideas

COURTESY OF ROBERT SEXTON

You're thinking about cutting class and going to the beach? Is the expected marginal benefit greater than the expected marginal cost? What if it is expected to be windy and rainy? What if you have a final next class period, and today is the review? Do these scenarios affect your decision?

Studying economics may teach you how to "think better," because economics helps develop a disciplined method of

thinking about problems. A student of economics becomes aware that, at a basic level, much of economic life involves choosing one course of action rather than another—making choices among our conflicting wants and desires in a world of scarcity. Economics provides insights about how to intelligently evaluate these options and determine the most appropriate choices in given situations.

This chapter presents eight powerful ideas that will help you understand the economic way of thinking. The economic way of thinking provides a logical framework for organizing and analyzing your understanding of a broad set of issues, many of which do not even seem directly related to economics as you now know it.

The basic ideas that you learn in this chapter will occur repeatedly throughout the text. If you develop a good understanding of these principles and master the problem-solving skills inherent in them, they will serve you well for the rest of your life. Learning to think like an economist takes time. Like most disciplines, economics has its own specialized vocabulary, including such terms as *elasticity, comparative advantage, supply and demand, deadweight loss,* and *consumer surplus.* Learning economics requires more than picking up this new terminology; however, it also involves using its powerful tools to improve your understanding of a whole host of issues in the world around you.

IDEA 1: People Face Scarcity and Costly Trade-offs

📂 What are goods and services?

📂 What are tangible and intangible goods?

📂 What are economic goods?

📂 Why do we have to make choices?

📂 What do we give up when we have to choose?

Introduction

This chapter presents eight powerful ideas that serve as the foundation of economics. Most of economics is really knowing certain principles well and knowing how and when to apply them. These few basic ideas will occur repeatedly throughout the text and are presented in this chapter as a preview of what is to come. if you develop a good understanding of these principles and master the problem-solving skills inherent in them, they will serve you well for the rest of your life.

The first three ideas focus on individual behavior: people face scarcity and costly trade-offs; people are rational decision makers and engage in marginal thinking; and people respond predictably to incentives. The next three ideas emphasize the interaction of people: specialization and trade makes people better off; markets can improve economic efficiency; and appropriate government policies can improve economic outcomes. The final two ideas are about how the economy as a whole interacts: government policies may help stabilize the economy, and increased productivity leads to economic growth.

scarcity
exists when human wants (material and nonmaterial) exceed available resources

COURTESY OF ROBERT L. SEXTON

All the things you see here—grass, trees, rocks, animals—are considered land to economists.

Human Wants Exceed Available Resources

Eonomics is concerned primarily with scarcity—how we satisfy our unlimited wants in a world of limited resources. We may want "essential" items such as food, clothing, schooling, and health care.

We may want many other items, such as vacations, cars, computers, and concert tickets. We may want more friendship, love, knowledge, and so on. We also may have many goals—perhaps an A in this class, a college education, and a great job. Unfortunately, people are not able to fulfill all their wants and desires, material and nonmaterial. Or, in the words of Mick Jagger, "You can't always get what you want." And as long as human wants exceed available resources, scarcity will exist.

Scarcity and Resources

Our desires and wants could all be met if we had unlimited resources. Unfortunately, resources are scarce: they are desirable and limited. Consequently, people have to make choices.

As we learned in the last chapter, a resource is anything that can be used to produce something else. Resources are costly because they have alternative uses. When we use land for a new football stadium that same land cannot be used for something else that is valuable like an office building or a hotel.

The scarce resources used in the production of goods and services can be grouped into four categories: labor, land, capital, and entrepreneurship.

labor
the physical and human effort used in the production of goods and services

Labor is the total of both physical and mental effort expended by people in the production of goods and services. The services of a teacher, nurse, cosmetic surgeon, professional golfer, and an electrician all fall under the general category of labor.

land
the natural resources used in the production of goods and services

Land includes the "gifts of nature" or the natural resources used in the production of goods and services. Economists consider land to include trees, animals, water, minerals, and so on, along with the physical space we normally think of as land.

capital
the equipment and structures used to produce goods and services

Capital is the equipment and structures used to produce goods and services. Office buildings, tools, machines, and factories are all considered capital goods. When we invest in factories, machines, research and development, or education, we increase the potential to create more goods and services in the future. Capital also includes **human capital**—the productive knowledge and skill people receive from education and on-the-job training.

human capital
the productive knowledge and skill people receive from education, on-the-job training, health, and other factors that increase productivity

entrepreneurship
the process of combining labor, land, and capital to produce goods and services

Entrepreneurship is the process of combining labor, land, and capital to produce goods and services. Entrepreneurs make the tough and risky decisions about what and how to produce goods and services. Entrepreneurs are always looking for new ways to improve production techniques or to create new products. They are lured by the chance of making a profit. It is this opportunity to make a profit that leads entrepreneurs to take risks.

Profits provide the financial incentive and income for entrepreneurs for their effort and risk if they are successful. Losses provide the financial incentive to let entrepreneurs know that resources are not being used efficiently.

Entrepreneurship is not just about new technology. It's also about the introduction of new goods, new production methods, new markets, new sources of raw materials, and new organizational structures.

However, not every entrepreneur is a Bill Gates or a Henry Ford. In some sense, we are all entrepreneurs when we try new products or when we find better ways to manage our households or our study time. Rather than money, then, our profits might take the form of greater enjoyment, additional time for recreation, or better grades.

What Are Goods and Services?

goods
items we value or desire

Goods are the items that we value or desire to satisfy our wants. Goods tend to be **tangible**—objects that can be seen, held, tasted, or smelled, such as shirts, pizzas, and perfume.

tangible goods
items we value or desire that we can reach out and touch

intangible goods
goods that we cannot reach out and touch, such as friendship and knowledge

Goods that we cannot reach out and touch are called **intangible goods**, which includes fairness for all, friendship, leisure, knowledge, security, prestige, respect, and health.

services
intangible items of value provided to consumers, such as education

Services are intangible acts for which people are willing to pay, such as legal counsel, medical care, and education. Services are intangible because they are less overtly visible, but they are certainly no less valuable than goods.

All goods and services, whether tangible or intangible, are produced from scarce resources and can be subjected to economic analysis. Scarce goods created from scarce resources are called **economic goods**. These goods are *desirable but limited* in amount.

Oxygen to breathe is *not* scarce because it is desirable and abundant. Garbage is *not* scarce because it is abundant but not desirable. However, freedom, books, vacations, computers, cell phones, cars, houses, drinkable water, clean air, health, and sunlight in December in Anchorage, Alaska, are all scarce. That is, for most people, all of these things are desirable but limited in amount—that is, scarce.

Without enough economic goods for all of us, we are forced to compete. That is, scarcity ultimately leads to competition for the available goods and services, a subject we will return to often in the text.

economic goods
scarce goods created from scarce resources—goods that are desirable but limited in supply

What Are Bads?

In contrast to goods, **bads** are those items that we do not desire or want. For most people, garbage, pollution, weeds, and crime are bads. People tend to eliminate or minimize bads, so they will often pay to have bads, like garbage, removed. The elimination of the bad—garbage removal, for example—is a good.

bads
items that we do not desire or want, where less is preferred to more, like terrorism, smog, or poison oak

Does Everyone Face Scarcity?

We all face scarcity because we cannot have all the goods and services we desire. However, because we all have different wants and desires, scarcity affects everyone differently. For example, a child in a developing country may face a scarcity of food and clean drinking water, while a rich man may face a scarcity of garage space for his growing antique car collection. Likewise, a harried middle-class working mother may find time for exercise particularly scarce, while a pharmaceutical company may be concerned with the scarcity of the natural resources it uses in its production process. Its effects may vary, but no one can escape scarcity.

We often hear it said of rich people that "He has everything," or "She can buy anything she wants." Actually, even the richest person must live with scarcity and must, at some point, choose one want or desire over another. That is, even rich people have finite income. And of course, we all have only 24 hours in a day! The problem is that as we get more affluent, we learn of new luxuries to provide us with satisfaction. Wealth, then, creates a new set of wants to be satisfied. No evidence indicates that people would not find a valuable use for additional income, no matter how rich they became. Even the wealthy individual who decides to donate all her money to charity faces the constraints of scarcity. If she had greater resources, she could do still more for others.

Not even millionaire lottery winners can escape scarcity. They may become less content as the excitement wears off and they begin looking for new satisfactions. After winning his second $1 million scratch-off lottery, a 78-year-old man from Michigan said, "I am now going for three."

Scarcity even exists for billionaires Bill and Melinda Gates.

Will Scarcity Ever Be Eradicated?

It is probably clear by now that scarcity never has and never will be eradicated. The same creativity that develops new methods to produce goods and services in greater quantities also reveals new wants. Fashions are always changing. Clothes and shoes that are

What is the difference between a want and a need?

"in" one year will likely be "out" the next. New wants quickly replace old ones. It is also quite possible that over a period of time, a rising quantity of goods and services will not increase human happiness. Why? Because our wants may grow as fast—if not faster—than our ability to meet those wants.

Wants versus Needs

To an economist, the terms *wants* and *needs* are very different. In fact, it is difficult to objectively define a need. To most, a need is something you must have and don't currently possess. But it can be used to describe a trivial wish, a want, or something that is essential for survival. A need can be more or less urgent, depending on the circumstances. Whenever you hear somebody say, "I need a new car," "I need a vacation," or "I need new clothes," always be sure to ask: What does the person really mean?

During rush hour, freeways can get very congested. Perhaps we should have an express lane for people who have urgent needs. What do you think of this idea? Imagine the number of people who would develop what they felt were urgent needs if the "urgent need" lane was much shorter than the other lanes. It would be inevitable that the system would fall apart. In fact, it would be fun to guess what might be defined as an urgent need when you are stopped by the urgent need police. It might include: "I am really in a hurry because I have to get home to clean my apartment," or "I need to get back to the dorm to type a term paper that is overdue." "Oh, shoot, I left the dog in the house." Many people would perceive their needs as more urgent than other people's urgent needs. This is a reason that the concept of need falls apart as a means of explaining behavior. It is impossible to make the concept of need useful when it is so hard to define or compare those "needs" among people.

Need as a concept ignores scarcity and the fact that choices may change with circumstances and trade-offs. In a world of scarcity, we have unlimited wants in the face of limited resources. That is, we all must make choices because we have competing wants and limited resources. Whenever we choose, we can satisfy one want but we leave other wants not satisfied. We might satisfy our want for a new car but it may leave other wants, like a trip to Hawaii, tuition, or paying rent, unfilled. That is, every want that is satisfied leaves other wants that are unsatisfied.

Scarcity Forces Us to Choose

Doesn't the fact that we face scarcity mean we have to compete for the limited resources?

Each of us might want a nice home, two luxury cars, wholesome and good-tasting food, a personal trainer, and a therapist, all enjoyed in a pristine environment with zero pollution. If we had unlimited resources, and thus an ability to produce all the goods and services everyone wants, we would not have to choose among those desires. However, we all face scarcity, and as a consequence, we must make choices. If we did not have to make meaningful economic choices, the study of economics would not be necessary. The essence of economics is to understand fully the implications that scarcity has for wise decision making.

Trade-Offs

In a world of scarcity, we all face trade-offs. If you spend more time at work you might give up an opportunity to go shopping at the mall or watch your favorite television show. Time spent exercising means giving up something else that is valuable—perhaps relaxing with friends or studying for an upcoming exam. Or when you decide how to spend your income, buying a new car may mean you have to forgo a summer vacation. Businesses have trade-offs, too. If a farmer chooses to plant his land in cotton this year, he gives up the opportunity to plant his land in wheat. If a firm decides to produce only cars, it gives up the opportunity to use those resources to produce refrigerators or something else that people value. Society, too, must make trade-offs. For example, the federal government faces trade-offs when it comes to spending tax revenues; additional resources used to enhance the environment may come at the expense of additional resources to provide health, education, or national defense.

To Choose Is to Lose

Every choice involves a cost. Anytime you are doing something, you could be doing something else. The highest or best forgone opportunity resulting from a decision is called the **opportunity cost**. Another way to put it is that "to choose is to lose," or, "An opportunity cost is the highest valued opportunity lost." It is important to remember that the opportunity cost involves the next highest valued alternative, not all alternatives not chosen. For example, what would you have been doing with your time if you were not reading this book? That alternative is what you give up, not all the things you could have been doing. To get more of anything that is desirable, you must accept less of something else that you also value.

opportunity cost
the value of the best forgone alternative that was not chosen

Every choice you make has a cost, an opportunity cost. All productive resources have alternative uses regardless of who owns them—individuals, firms, or government. For example, if a city uses land for a new school, the cost is the next-best alternative use of that land—perhaps, a park. To have a meaningful understanding of cost, you must be able to compare the alternative opportunities that are sacrificed in that choice.

Bill Gates, Tiger Woods, and Oprah Winfrey all quit college to pursue their dreams. Tiger Woods dropped out of Stanford (an economics major) to join the PGA golf tour. Bill Gates dropped out of Harvard to start a software company. Oprah Winfrey dropped out of Tennessee State to pursue a career in broadcasting. At the early age of 19, she became the co-anchor of the evening news. LeBron James (Miami Heat), Kobe Bryant (LA Lakers), and Alex Rodriguez (New York Yankees) understood opportunity cost; they didn't even start college, and it worked out well for them. Staying in, or starting, college would have cost each of them millions of dollars. We cannot say it would have been the wrong decision to stay in or never start college, but it would have been costly. Their opportunity cost of staying in or going to or starting college was high.

Is an opportunity cost all the things you give up when you make a choice?

Money Costs and Nonmoney Costs

If you go to the store to buy groceries, you have to pay for the items you bought. This money cost is an opportunity cost, because you could have used that money to purchase other goods or services. However, additional opportunity costs include the nonprice costs incurred to acquire the groceries—time spent getting to the grocery store, finding a parking place, actual shopping, and waiting in the checkout line. The nonprice costs are measured by assessing the sacrifice involved—the value you place on what you would have done with that time if you had not gone shopping. So the cost of grocery shopping is the price paid for the goods, plus the nonprice costs incurred. Or your concert ticket may have only been $50. But what if you had to wait in line for six hours in the freezing cold? Waiting and enduring the cold are costs, too. Seldom are costs just dollars and cents. Shopping at a large discount store may save you on the money price, but cost you time waiting in long checkout lines. Also, buying food in bulk quantities may be less expensive per ounce, but cost inventory space in your pantry, or the food may spoil before it is eaten.

Remember that many costs do not involve money but are still costs. Do I major in economics or engineering? Do I go to Billy Madison University or Tech State University? Should I get an MBA now or work and wait a few years to go back to school?

Choices have present and future consequences. What if I decide *not* to study for my final exams? What future consequences will I bear? Flunk out of school? Not get into graduate school?

The famous poet, Robert Frost, understood that choices have costs. In his poem, "The Road Not Taken," he writes, "two roads diverged in a yellow wood, and sorry I could not travel both."

TIMOTHY EPP/SHUTTERSTOCK.COM

UPI/JOHN ANGELILLO/LANDOV

Economic questions are all around you. Take for instance the people who lined up to buy the latest Apple iPhone. Not only did it cost them money to purchase the item, but it also cost them time waiting in line—time that they might have spent doing other things. Choices like this one are all around us. By studying economics, we can better understand these choices and hopefully make better ones.

Policy makers are unavoidably faced with opportunity costs, too. Consider airline safety. Both money costs and time costs affect airline safety. New airline safety devices cost money (luggage inspection devices, smoke detectors, fuel tank safeguards, new radar equipment, and so on), and time costs are quite evident with the new security checks. Time waiting in line costs time doing something else that is valuable. New airline safety requirements could also actually cost lives. If the new safety equipment costs are passed on in the form of higher airline ticket prices, people may choose to travel by car, which is far more dangerous per mile traveled than by air. Opportunity costs are everywhere! And the real cost of anything is what you have to give up to get it.

The Opportunity Cost of Going to College or Having a Child

The average person often does not correctly calculate opportunity costs. For example, the (opportunity) cost of going to college includes not just the direct expenses of tuition and books. Of course, those expenses do involve an opportunity cost because the money used for books and tuition could be used to buy other things that you value. But what about the nonmoney costs? That is, going to college also includes the opportunity cost of your time. Specifically, the time spent going to school is time that could have been spent on a job earning, say, $30,000 over the course of an academic year. What about room and board? That aspect is a little tricky because you would presumably have to pay room and board whether you went to college or not. The relevant question may be how much more it costs you to live at school rather than at home (and living at home may have substantial nonmoney costs). Even if you stayed at home, your parents would sacrifice something; they could rent your room out or use the room for some other purpose such as storage, guest room, home office, a sibling's room, and so on.

How often do people consider the full opportunity of raising a child to age 18? The obvious money costs include food, visits to the doctor, clothes, piano lessons, time spent at

Is That Really a Free Lunch, a Freeway, or a Free Beach?

The expression, "There's no such thing as a free lunch," clarifies the relationship between scarcity and opportunity cost. Suppose the school cafeteria is offering "free" lunches today. Although the lunch is free to you, is it really free from society's perspective? The answer is no, because some of society's scarce resources will have been used in the preparation of the lunch. The issue is whether the resources that went into creating that lunch could have been used to produce something else of value. Clearly, the scarce resources that went into the production of the lunch—the labor and materials (food-service workers, lettuce, meat, plows, tractors,

fertilizer, and so forth)—could have been used in other ways. They had an opportunity cost and thus were not free.

Do not confuse free with a zero monetary price. A number of goods—freeways, free beaches, and free libraries, for instance—do not cost consumers money, but they are still scarce. Few things are free in the sense that they use none of society's scarce resources. So what does a free lunch really mean? It is, technically speaking, a "subsidized" lunch—a lunch using society's scarce resources, but one that the person receiving it does not have to pay for personally.

soccer practices, and so on. According to the Department of Agriculture, a middle-income family with a child born in 2011 can expect to spend about $300,000 for food, shelter, and other necessities to raise that child through age 17. And that does not include college. Other substantial opportunity costs are incurred in raising a child as well. Consider the opportunity cost of one parent choosing to give up his or her job to stay at home. For a parent who makes that choice, the time spent in child raising is time that could have been used earning money and pursuing a career.

⑦ SECTION QUIZ

1. Scarcity occurs because our _____ wants exceed our _____ resources.

   a. limited; unlimited

   b. unlimited; limited

   c. limited; unlimited

   d unlimited; unlimited

2. Scarcity and rarity are

   a. the same because both words means the good is limited in supply.

   b. different because something might be rare, but if it is not desirable, it is not scarce.

   c. different because scarcity only affects poor people and rarity only affects rich people.

   d. All of the above are true.

3. Scarce resources include

   a. labor—the human effort used in producing goods and services.

   b. land—the natural resources used in the production of goods and services.

   c. capital—the equipment and structures used to produce goods and services.

   d. entrepreneurship—the process of combining labor, land, and capital to produce goods and services.

   e. all of the above.

4. To economists, needs

   a. are difficult to define.

   b. can be more or less urgent, depending on the circumstances.

   c. are hard to compare among people.

   d. ignore scarcity and the fact that choices may change with circumstances and trade-offs.

   e. all of the above.

5. Which of the following statements is true?

   a. The opportunity cost of a decision is always expressed in monetary terms.

   b. The opportunity cost of a decision is the value of the best forgone alternative.

   c. Some economic decisions have zero opportunity cost.

   d. The opportunity cost of attending college is the same for all students at the same university but may differ among students at different universities.

   e. None of the above statements is true.

6. Money costs

   a. are not opportunity costs, since they involve money.

   b. are opportunity costs, because you could have used that money to buy other goods and services.

   c. are always the only relevant opportunity costs.

   d. both (a) and (c).

(*continued*)

⓺ SECTION QUIZ (Cont.)

7. Which of the following involve an opportunity cost?

   a. choosing to go to law school rather than business school

   b. the money I used to pay for my new laptop

   c. new airline safety regulations

   d. all of the above

8. Which of the following are the opportunity costs of going to college?

   a. tuition

   b. books needed for classes

   c. the job I was going to take if I did not go to school

   d. all of the above

---

1. What must be true for something to be an economic good?

2. Why does scarcity affect everyone?

3. How and why does scarcity affect each of us differently?

4. Why might daylight be scarce in Anchorage, Alaska, in the winter but not in the summer?

5 Would we have to make choices if we had unlimited resources?

6 What do we mean by opportunity cost?

7 Why was the opportunity cost of going to college higher for LeBron James (Miami Heat star) than for most undergraduates?

8. Why is the opportunity cost of time spent getting an MBA typically lower for a 22-year-old straight out of college than for a 45-year-old experienced manager?

Answers: 1. b **2.** b **3.** e **4.** e **5.** b **6.** b **7.** d **8.** d

---

2.2

IDEA 2: People Engage in Rational Decision Making and Marginal Thinking

📁 What is rational decision making?

📁 What do we mean by marginal thinking?

📁 What is the rule of rational choice?

📁 Why do we use the word *expected* with marginal benefits and costs?

Do People Engage in Rational Decision Making?

Recall from Chapter 1 that economists assume that people, for the most part, engage in rational, or purposeful, behavior. That is, people systematically and purposefully do the best they can, based on their values and information, under current and anticipated future circumstances. In short, as rational individuals, we are influenced by an array of incentives, social norms, and past experiences. We act the way we do because we do not want to make ourselves worse off. Even if everyone does not behave rationally all the time, the assumption of **rational decision making** is still very useful in explaining most of the choices that individuals make.

Many Choices We Face Involve Marginal Thinking

Some decisions are "all or nothing," like whether to start a new business or go to work for someone else, or whether to attend graduate school or take a job. But rational people know that many decisions are not black and white. Many choices we face involve how *much* of something to do rather than whether to do something. It is not *whether* you eat but *how much* will you eat? Or how many caffe lattes will I buy this week? Or how often do I change the oil in my car? Or how much of my check do I spend, and how much do I save? Your instructors hope that the question is not *whether* you study this semester but *how much* you study. You might think to yourself, "If I studied a little more, I might be able to improve my grade," or, "If I had a little better concentration when I was studying, I could improve my grade." That is, spending more time has an additional expected benefit (a higher grade) and an additional expected cost (giving up time to do something else that is valuable, such as watching TV or sleeping). These examples reflect what economists call **marginal thinking** because the focus is on the additional, or marginal, choices available to you. Or think of marginal as the edge—marginal decisions are made around the edge of what you are currently doing. Marginal choices involve the effects of adding or subtracting from the current situation. In short, they are the small (or large) incremental changes to a plan of action.

Businesses are constantly engaged in marginal thinking. For example, firms have to decide whether the additional (marginal) revenue received from increasing production is greater than the marginal cost of that production.

Always watch out for the difference between average and marginal costs. Suppose an airline had 10 unoccupied seats on a flight from Los Angeles to New York, and the average cost was $400 per seat (the total cost divided by the number of seats—$100,000/250). If 10 people are waiting on standby, each willing to pay $300, should the airline sell them the tickets? Yes! The unoccupied seats earn nothing for the airline. What are the additional (marginal) costs of a few more passengers? The marginal costs are minimal—slight wear and tear on the airplane, handling some extra baggage, and 10 extra in-flight meals. In this case, thinking at the margin can increase total profits, even if it means selling at less than the average cost of production.

Another good example of marginal thinking is an auction. Prices are bid up marginally as the auctioneer calls out one price after another. When bidders view the new price (the marginal cost) to be greater than the value they place on the good (the marginal benefit), they withdraw from further bidding.

In trying to make themselves better off, people alter their behavior if the expected marginal benefits from doing so outweigh the expected marginal costs, which is the **rule of rational choice**. Economic theory is often called marginal analysis because it assumes that people are always weighing the expected marginal benefits against the expected marginal costs. The term *expected* is used with *marginal benefits* and *marginal costs* because the world is uncertain in many important respects, so the actual result of changing behavior may not always make people better off. However, as a matter of rationality, people are assumed to engage only in behavior that they think ahead of time will make them better off. That is, individuals will only pursue an activity if their expected

rational decision making
people do the best they can, based on their values and information, under current and anticipated future circumstances.

ECS
economic content standards

Effective decision making requires comparing the additional costs of alternatives with the additional benefits. Most choices involve doing a little more or a little less of something: few choices are "all or nothing" decisions.

marginal thinking
focusing on the additional, or marginal, choices; marginal choices involve the effects of adding or subtracting, from the current situation, the small (or large) incremental changes to a plan of action

rule of rational choice
individuals will pursue an activity if the expected marginal benefits are greater than the expected marginal costs

TARAS VYSHNYA/SHUTTERSTOCK.COM

During rush hour some drivers will switch into and out of lanes if they perceive one lane is moving faster that another. This is a marginal adjustment. The same is true of lines in a supermarket. People are constantly weighing the marginal benefits and marginal costs of changing lanes and/or lines.

marginal benefits are greater than their expected marginal costs of pursuing that activity one step further, $E(MB) > E(MC)$.

This fairly unrestrictive and realistic view of individuals seeking self-betterment can be used to analyze a variety of social phenomena.

Suppose that you have to get up for an 8 A.M. class but have been up very late. When the alarm goes off at 7 A.M. you are weighing the marginal benefits and marginal costs of an extra 15 minutes of sleep. If you perceive the marginal benefits of 15 additional minutes of sleep to be greater than the marginal costs of those extra minutes, you may choose to hit the snooze button. Or perhaps you may decide to blow off class completely. But it's unlikely that you will choose that action if it's the day of the final exam—because it is now likely that the **net benefits** (the difference between the expected marginal benefits and the expected marginal costs) of skipping class have changed. When people have opportunities to make themselves better off they usually take them. And they will continue to seek those opportunities as long as they expect a net benefit from doing so.

To determine the optimal or best public policy program, voters and government officials must compare the expected marginal benefits against the expected marginal costs of providing a little more or a little less of the program's services.

Rational decision makers will follow the rule of rational choice. This is simply the rule of being sensible, and most economists believe that individuals act *as if* they are sensible and apply the rule of rational choice to their daily lives. It is a rule that can help us understand our decisions to study, walk, shop, exercise, clean house, cook, and perform just about every other action.

It is also a rule that we will continue to use throughout the text. Because whether it is consumers, producers, or policy makers, they all must compare the expected marginal benefits and the expected marginal cost to determine the best level to consume, produce, or provide public programs.

net benefit
the difference between the expected marginal benefits and the expected marginal costs

Do government policy makers have to weigh their expected marginal benefits against their expected marginal costs?

Zero Pollution Would Be Too Costly

Let's use the concept of marginal thinking to evaluate pollution levels. We all know the benefits of a cleaner environment, but what would we have to give up—that is, what marginal costs would we have to incur—to achieve zero pollution? A lot! You could not drive a car, fly in a plane, or even ride a bicycle, especially if everybody else were riding bikes, too (because congestion is a form of pollution). How would you get to school or work, or go to the movies or the grocery store? Everyone would have to grow their own food because transporting, storing, and producing food uses machinery and equipment that pollute. And even growing your own food would be a problem because many plants emit natural pollutants. We could go on and on. The point is *not* that we shouldn't be concerned about the environment; rather, we have to weigh the expected marginal benefits of a cleaner environment against the expected marginal costs of a cleaner environment. This discussion is not meant to say the environment should not be cleaner, only that zero pollution levels would be far too costly in terms of what we would have to give up.

Optimal (Best) Levels of Safety

Like pollution, crime and safety can have optimal (or best) levels that are greater than zero. Take crime. What would it cost society to have zero crime? It would be prohibitively costly to divert a tremendous amount of our valuable resources toward the complete elimination of crime. In fact, it would be impossible to eliminate crime totally. Even reducing crime significantly would be costly. Because lower crime rates are costly, society must decide how much it is willing to give up. The additional resources for crime prevention can only come from limited resources, which could be used to produce something else that people may value even more.

If you decide to buy a more expensive diamond ring for your fiancee, what are the expected marginal benefits? What are the expected marginal costs? What did you give up— part of a down payment for a house, a nicer honeymoon?

The same is true for safer products. Nobody wants defective tires on their cars, or cars that are unsafe and roll over at low speeds. The optimal amount of risk may not be zero. The issue is not safe versus unsafe products but rather, *how much* safety we want. It is not risk versus no-risk but rather, *how much* risk we are willing to take. Additional safety can only come at higher costs. To make all products perfectly safe would be impossible, so we must weigh the benefits and costs of safer products. In fact, according to one study by Sam Peltzman, a University of Chicago economist, additional safety regulations in cars (mandatory safety belts and padded dashboards) in the late 1960s may have had little impact on highway fatalities. Peltzman found that making cars safer led to more reckless driving and more accidents. The safety regulations did result in fewer deaths per automobile accident, but the total number of deaths remained unchanged because more accidents occurred.

Shouldn't all products be perfectly safe?

Reckless driving has a benefit in the form of getting somewhere more quickly, but it can also have a cost—an accident or even a fatality. Most people will compare the marginal benefits and marginal costs of safer driving and make the choices that they believe will get them to their destination safely.

⑦ SECTION QUIZ

1. Which of the following demonstrates marginal thinking?

   a. deciding to never eat meat

   b. deciding to spend one more hour studying economics tonight because you think the improvement on your next test will be large enough to make it worthwhile to you

   c. working out an extra hour per week

   d. both (b) and (c)

2. Which of the following best reflects rational decision-making behavior?

   a. analyzing the total costs of a decision

   b. analyzing the total benefits of a decision

   c. undertaking an activity as long as the total benefits exceed the total costs

   d. undertaking an activity whenever the marginal benefit exceeds the marginal cost

   e. undertaking activities as long as the marginal benefit exceeds zero

3. Individual gallons of milk at a local grocery story are priced at $4, but two gallons purchased at the same time are priced at $6 for two. The marginal cost of buying a second gallon of milk on a shopping trip is

   a. $6.

   b. $4.

   c. $3.

   d. $2.

   e. none of the above.

4. The results of which of the following activities would marginal thinking help improve?

   a. studying

   b. driving

   c. shopping

   d. looking for a place to park your car

   e. all of the above

---

1. What are marginal choices? Why does economics focus on them?

2. What is the rule of rational choice?

(*continued*)

⑦ SECTION QUIZ (Cont.)

3. How could the rule of rational choice be expressed in terms of net benefits?

4. Why does rational choice involve expectations?

5. What is rational decision making?

6. Why do students often stop taking lecture notes when a professor announces that the next few minutes of material will not be on any future test or assignment?

7. If you decide to speed to get to a doctor's appointment and then get in an accident due to speeding, does your decision to speed invalidate the rule of rational choice? Why or why not?

8. If pedestrians felt far safer using crosswalks to cross the street, how could adding crosswalks increase the number of pedestrian accidents?

9. Imagine driving a car with daggers sticking out of the steering wheel—pointing directly at your chest. Would you drive more safely? Why?

Answers: 1. d 2. d 3. d 4. e

2.3

IDEA 3: People Respond Predictably to Changes in Incentives

📂 Can we predict how people will respond to changes in incentives?

📂 What are positive incentives?

📂 What are negative incentives?

A subsidy on hybrid electric vehicles would be a positive incentive that would encourage greater production and consumption of these vehicles. A wide variety of incentives are offered at the federal, state, and local levels to encourage the expanded use of alternative-fuel vehicles.

Changes in Incentives Change Individual Behavior

Because most people are seeking opportunities to make themselves better off, they respond to changes in incentives. If you can figure out what people's incentives are, there is a good chance you can predict their behavior. That is, they are reacting to changes in expected marginal benefits and expected marginal costs. In fact, much of human behavior can be explained and predicted as a response to changing incentives. That is, changes in incentives cause people to change their behavior in predictable ways.

Positive and Negative Incentives

Almost all of economics can be reduced to incentive stories, where consumers and producers are driven by incentives that affect expected costs or benefits. An incentive induces people to respond to a reward or a punishment. We just discussed that most rational people predictably respond to changes in incentives by weighing the expected marginal benefits against the expected marginal cost. Prices, wages, profits, taxes, and subsidies are all examples of economic incentives. Incentives can be classified into two types: positive and negative. **Positive incentives** are those that either

positive incentive
an incentive that either reduces costs or increases benefits, resulting in an increase in an activity or behavior

increase benefits or reduce costs and thus result in an increased level of the related activity or behavior. **Negative incentives**, on the other hand, either reduce benefits or increase costs, resulting in a decreased level of the related activity or behavior. For example, a tax on cars that emit lots of pollution (an increase in costs) would be a negative incentive that would lead to a reduction in emitted pollution. On the other hand, a subsidy (the opposite of a tax) on hybrid cars—part electric, part internal combustion—would be a positive incentive that would encourage greater production and consumption of hybrid cars. Human behavior is influenced in predictable ways by such changes in economic incentives, and economists use this information to predict what will happen when the benefits and costs of any choice are changed. In short, economists study the incentives and consequences of particular actions.

Because most people seek opportunities that make them better off, we can predict what will happen when incentives are changed. If salaries increase for engineers and decrease for MBAs, we would predict fewer people would go to graduate school in business and more would go into engineering. A permanent change to a much higher price of gasoline would lead us to expect fewer gas guzzlers on the highway. People who work on commission tend to work harder. If the price of downtown parking increased, we would predict that commuters would look for alternative methods to get to work that would save money. If households were taxed to conserve water, economists would expect people to use less water—and substantially less water than if they were simply asked to conserve water. Some people are charitable and some people are stingy, but if you change the tax code to give even greater deductions for charitable contributions, we can predict *more* people will be charitable, even some of those who are stingy. Incentives matter.

negative incentive
an incentive that either increases costs or reduces benefits, resulting in a decrease in the activity or behavior

economic content standards

People respond predictably to positive and negative incentives.

? SECTION QUIZ

1. Positive incentives make actions _____ likely; negative incentives make actions _____ likely.

   a. more; more

   b. more; less

   c. less; more

   d. less; less

2. A higher price is a _____ incentive to buyers and a _____ incentive to sellers.

   a. positive; positive

   b. positive; negative

   c. negative; positive

   d. negative; negative

3. Because most people seek opportunities that make people better off,

   a. it makes it more difficult to predict behavior.

   b. we can predict what will happen when incentives are changed.

   c. we cannot predict as well as we could if their behavior was random and chaotic.

   d. None of the above is true.

4. If households, water usage was taxed, economists would expect

   a. people to use less water.

   b. people to use less water, but they would not reduce their consumption by as much as they would if they were asked to conserve water.

   c. they would not reduce their water consumption because people need water.

   d. none of the above.

(continued)

5. Who would be most likely to drop out of college before graduation?

    a. an economics major who wishes to go to graduate school

    b. a math major with a B+ average

    c. a chemistry major who has been reading about the great jobs available for people with chemistry degrees

    d. a star baseball player who has just received a multi-million dollar contract offer after his junior year

---

1. What is the difference between positive incentives and negative incentives?

2. According to the rule of rational choice, would you do more or less of something if its expected marginal benefits increased? Why?

3. According to the rule of rational choice, would you do more or less of something if its expected marginal costs increased? Why?

4. How does the rule of rational choice imply that young children are typically more likely to misbehave at a supermarket checkout counter than at home?

5. Why do many parents refuse to let their children have dessert before they eat the rest of their dinner?

Answers: 1. b   2. c   3. b   4. a   5. d

2.4

IDEA 4: Specialization and Trade Can Make Everyone Better Off

specializing
concentrating in the production of one, or a few, goods

comparative advantage
occurs when a person or country can produce a good or service at a lower opportunity cost than others

📂 What is the relationship between opportunity cost and specialization?

📂 What are the advantages of specialization in production?

Without specialization and division of labor, this car and crew would not be as competitive. Imagine how much time would be lost if one person was changing four tires.

WALTER G ARCE/SHUTTERSTOCK.COM

Why Do People Specialize?

As you look around, you can see that people specialize in what they produce. They tend to dedicate their resources to one primary activity, whether it be performing brain surgery, driving a cab, or making bagels. Why? The answer, short and simple, is opportunity costs. By concentrating their energies on only one, or a few, activities, individuals are **specializing**. This focus allows them to make the best use of (and thus gain the most benefit from) their limited resources. A person, a region, or a country can gain by specializing in the production of the good in which they have a comparative advantage. That is, if they can produce a good or service at a lower opportunity cost than others, we say that they have a **comparative advantage** in the production of that good or service. Comparative advantage changes over time for many reasons, including changes in resources, prices, and events that occur in other countries. For example, the United States once had a comparative advantage in producing shoes, but now imports most of its shoes from foreign countries.

We All Specialize

We all specialize to some extent and rely on others to produce most of the goods and services we want. The work that we choose to do reflects our specialization. For example, we may specialize in selling or fixing automobiles. The wages from that work can then be used to buy goods from a farmer who has chosen to specialize in the production of food. Likewise, the farmer can use the money earned from selling his produce to get his tractor fixed by someone who specializes in that activity.

Specialization is evident not only among individuals but among regions and countries as well. In fact, the story of the economic development of the United States and the rest of the world involves specialization. Within the United States, the Midwest with its wheat, the coastal waters of the Northeast with its fishing fleets, and the Northwest with its timber are each examples of regional specialization.

Bangladesh exports low-cost garments to mass-market retailers like Walmart. U.S. workers are a lot more productive in building airplanes and a little more productive in producing clothes than Bangladeshi workers. If the two countries divide the work according to comparative advantage, then the U.S. workers would specialize in the tasks at which they are most productive, airplanes. And the the Bangladeshi workers would concentrate on the tasks where their productivity is only slightly less, clothing.

REUTERS/ANDREW BIRAJ/LANDOV

The Advantages of Specialization

In a small business, every employee usually performs a wide variety of tasks—from hiring to word processing to marketing. As the size of the company increases, each employee can perform a more specialized job, with a consequent increase in output per worker. The primary advantages of specialization are that employees acquire greater skill from repetition, they avoid wasted time in shifting from one task to another, and they do the types of work for which they are best suited—and specialization promotes the use of specialized equipment for specialized tasks.

The advantages of specialization are seen throughout the workplace. For example, in larger firms, specialists conduct personnel relations, and accounting is in the hands of full-time accountants instead of someone with half a dozen other tasks. Owners of small retail stores select the locations for their stores primarily through guesswork, placing them where they believe sales will be high or where empty low-rent buildings are available. In contrast, larger chains have store sites selected by experts who have experience in analyzing the factors that make different locations relatively more desirable, such as traffic patterns, income levels, demographics, and so on. In short, workers will earn more by specializing in doing the things that they do relatively well because that entails the least sacrifice in opportunities forgone. It also important to remember that even if everyone had similar skills and resources, specialization could still lead to greater production because the concentration of production of some goods and services in one location can sometimes reduce the costs of production.

Specialization and Trade Lead to Greater Wealth and Prosperity

Trade, or voluntary exchange, directly increases wealth by making both parties better off (or they wouldn't trade). It is the prospect of wealth-increasing exchange that leads to productive specialization. That is, trade increases wealth by allowing a person, a region, or a nation to specialize in those products that it produces at a lower opportunity cost and to trade them

AP PHOTO/PRNEWSFOTO/APPLE

The entrepreneurs at Apple have learned how to combine almost 500 generic parts to make something of much greater value. The whole is greater than the sum of the parts. There is not one person at Apple or in the world who could put together an iPhone all alone. It takes many people, making many parts, living all over the world. In other words, specialization and exchange has given us the ability to do things we do not even understand.

use what you've learned   Comparative Advantage

Q Should an attorney who types 100 words per minute hire an administrative assistant to type her legal documents, even though he can only type 50 words per minute? If the attorney does the job, she can do it in five hours; if the administrative assistant does the job, it takes him 10 hours. The attorney makes $100 an hour, and the administrative assistant earns $10 an hour. Which one has the comparative advantage (the lowest opportunity cost) in typing documents?

A If the attorney types her own documents, it will cost $500 ($100 per hour × 5 hours). If she has the administrative assistant type her documents, it will cost $100 ($10 per hour × 10 hours). Clearly, then, the lawyer should hire the administrative assistant to type her documents, because the administrative assistant has the comparative advantage (lowest opportunity cost) in this case, despite being half as good in absolute terms.

ECS

economic content standards

When individuals, regions, and nations specialize in what they can produce at lower costs and then trade with others, both production and consumption increase.

for products that others produce at a lower opportunity cost. That is, we trade with others because it frees up time and resources to do other things that we do better.

In short, if we divide tasks and produce what we do *relatively* best and trade for the rest, we will be better off than if we were self-sufficient—that is, without trade. Imagine life without trade, where you were completely self-sufficient—growing your own food, making your own clothes, working on your own car, building your own house—do you think you would be better off? For example, say the United States is better at producing wheat than is Brazil, and Brazil is better at producing coffee than is the United States. The United States and Brazil would each benefit if the United States produces wheat and trades some of it to Brazil for coffee. Coffee growers in the United States could grow coffee in expensive greenhouses, but it would result in higher coffee costs and prices, while leaving fewer resources available for employment in more beneficial jobs, such as wheat production.

In the words of growth theorist, Paul Romer, "There are huge potential gains from trade. Poor countries can supply their natural and human resources. Rich countries can supply their know-how. When these are combined, everyone can be better off. The challenge is for a country to arrange its laws and institutions so that both sides can profitably engage in trade." Standards of living can be increased through trade and exchange. In fact, the economy as a whole can create more wealth when each person specializes in a task that he or she does relatively best. And through specialization and trade, a country can gain a greater variety of goods and services at a lower cost. So while counties may be competitors in the global market, they are also partners.

② SECTION QUIZ

1. The person, region, or country that can produce a good or service at a _____ opportunity cost than other producers has a _____ advantage in the production of that good or service.

   a. higher; comparative

   b. lower; absolute

   c. lower; comparative

   d. higher; absolute

(*continued*)

② S E C T I O N   Q U I Z (Cont.)

2. Specialization is important for
   a. individuals.
   b. businesses.
   c. regions.
   d. nations.
   e. all of the above.

3. People can gain by specializing in the production of a good in which
   a. they have a comparative advantage.
   b. they have an absolute advantage.
   c. they have a lower opportunity cost.
   d. they have a higher opportunity cost.
   e. both (a) and (c).

4. If a country wants to maximize the value of its output, each job should be carried out by the person who
   a. has the highest opportunity cost.
   b. has a comparative advantage in that activity.
   c. can complete the particular job most rapidly.
   d. enjoys that job the least.

5. If resources and goods are free to move across states, and if Florida producers choose to specialize in growing grapefruit and Georgia producers choose to specialize in growing peaches, then we could reasonably conclude that
   a. Georgia has a comparative advantage in producing peaches.
   b. Florida has a comparative advantage in producing peaches.
   c. the opportunity cost of growing peaches is lower in Georgia than in Florida.
   d. the opportunity cost of growing grapefruit is lower in Florida than in Georgia.
   e. all of the above except (b) are true.

6. Kelly is an attorney and also an excellent typist. She can type 120 words per minute, but she is pressed for time because she has all the legal work she can handle at $75.00 per hour. Kelly's friend Todd works as a waiter and would like some typing work (provided that he can make at least his wage as a waiter, which is $25.00 per hour). Todd can type only 60 words per minute.
   a. Kelly should do all the typing because she is faster.
   b. Todd should do the typing as long as his earnings are more than $25.00 and less than $37.50 per hour.
   c. Unless Todd can match Kelly's typing speed, he should remain a waiter.
   d. Todd should do the typing, and Kelly should pay him $20.00 per hour.
   e. Both a and c are correct.

---

1. Why do people specialize?
2. What do we mean by comparative advantage?
3. Why does the combination of specialization and trade make us better off?
4. If you can mow your lawn in half the time it takes your spouse or housemate to do it, do you have a comparative advantage in mowing the lawn?
5. If you have a current comparative advantage in doing the dishes, and you then become far more productive than before in completing yard chores, could that eliminate your comparative advantage? Why or why not?
6. Could a student who gets a C in one class but a D or worse in everything else have a comparative advantage over someone who gets a B in that class but an A in everything else? Explain this concept using opportunity cost.

Answers: 1. c   2. e   3. e   4. b   5. e   6. b

IDEA 5: Markets Can Improve Economic Efficiency

📁 How does a market economy allocate scarce resources?

📁 What are the important signals that market prices communicate?

📁 What are the effects of price controls?

How Does the Market Work to Allocate Resources?

In a world of scarcity, competition is inescapable, and one method of allocating resources among competing uses is the market economy. The market economy provides a way for millions of producers and consumers to allocate scarce resources. For the most part, markets are efficient. To an economist, **efficiency** is achieved when the economy gets the most out of its scarce resources. In short, efficiency makes the economic pie as large as possible.

Competitive markets are powerful—they can make existing products better and/or less expensive, they can improve production processes, and they can create new products, from video games to life-saving drugs. Buyers and sellers indicate their wants through their action and inaction in the marketplace, and it is this collective "voice" that determines how resources are allocated. But how is this information communicated? Market prices serve as the language of the market system. By understanding what these market prices mean, you can get a better understanding of the vital function that the market economy performs.

Markets may not always lead to your desired tastes and preferences. You may think that markets produce too many pet rocks, chia pets, breast enhancements, and face lifts. Some markets are illegal—the market for cocaine, the market for stolen body parts, the market for child pornography, and the market for indecent radio announcers. Markets do not come with a moral compass; they simply provide what buyers are willing and able to pay for and what sellers are willing and able to produce.

Market Prices Provide Important Information

Market prices send signals and provide incentives to both buyers and sellers. These prices communicate information about the relative availability of products to buyers, and they provide sellers with critical information about the relative value that consumers place on those products. In short, buyers look at the price and decide how much they are willing and able to demand and sellers look at the price and decide how much they are able and willing to supply. The market price reflects the value a buyer places on a good and the cost to society of producing that good. Thus, market prices provide a way for both buyers and sellers to communicate about the relative value of resources. To paraphrase Adam Smith, prices adjust like an "invisible hand" to direct buyers and sellers to an outcome that is socially desirable. We will see how this works beginning in Chapter 4.

The basis of a market economy is voluntary exchange and the price system that guides people's choices and produces solutions to the questions of what goods to produce and how to produce and distribute them.

Take something as simple as the production of a pencil. Where did the wood come from? Perhaps the Northwest or Georgia. The graphite may have come from the mines in Michigan and the rubber may be from Malaysia. The paint, the glue, the metal piece that holds the eraser—who knows? The point is that market forces coordinated this production activity among literally thousands of people, some of whom live in different countries and speak different languages. The market brought these people together to make a pencil that sells for 25 cents at your bookstore. It all happened because the market economy provided the incentive

---

efficiency
when an economy gets the most out of its scarce resources

economic content standards

Markets exist when and where buyers and sellers interact. This interaction determines market prices and thereby allocates goods and services.

Prices provide incentives for buyers and sellers. Higher prices for a good or service provide incentives for buyers to purchase less of that good or service and for producers to make or sell more of it. Lower prices for a good or service provide incentives for buyers to purchase more of that good or service and for producers to make or sell less of it.

What is the invisible hand?

for people to pursue activities that benefit others. This same process produces millions of goods and services around the world, from automobiles and computers to pencils and paper clips.

What Effect Do Price Controls Have on the Market System?

Government policies called **price controls** sometimes force prices above or below what they would be in a market economy. Unfortunately, these controls often impose harm on the same people they are trying to help, in large part by short-circuiting the market's information-transmission function. That is, price controls effectively strip the market price of its meaning for both buyers and sellers (as we will see in Chapter 5). A sales tax also distorts price signals, leading to a misallocation of resources (as we will see in Chapter 6).

price controls
government-mandated minimum or maximum prices

---

⑦ SECTION QUIZ

1. Markets
   a. for the most part are efficient.
   b. provides a way for millions of of producers and consumers to allocate scarce resources.
   c. may not always lead to your desired tastes and preferences.
   d. All of the above statements are true.

2. Efficiency
   a. makes the size of the economic pie as large as possible.
   b. is achieved when the economy gets the most of of its resources.
   c. Both (a) and (b) are true.
   d. None of the above is true.

3. Which of the following is (are) true statement(s)?
   a. Prices provide *incentives* for buyers and sellers.
   b. Higher prices for a good or service provide incentives for buyers to purchase less of that good or service and for producers to make or sell more of it.
   c. Lower prices for a good or service provide incentives for buyers to purchase more of that good or service and for producers to make or sell less of it.
   d. All of the above statements are correct.

4. Price controls
   a. assure that society distributes its resources fairly.
   b. distort price signals.
   c. prevent the natural system of supply and demand from working.
   d. Both (b) and (c) are true.

---

1. Why must every society choose some manner in which to allocate its scarce resources?

2. How does a market system allocate resources?

3. What do market prices communicate to others in society?

4. How do price controls undermine the market as a communication device?

Answers: 1. d   2. c   3. d   4. d

IDEA 6: Appropriate Government Policies Can Improve Market Outcomes

📂 Why is it so important that the government protect our property rights?

📂 Why can't we rely exclusively on the "invisible hand" of the market to determine economic decisions?

📂 What are market failures?

📂 Does the market distribute income fairly?

Property Rights and the Legal System

ECS

economic content standards

An important role for government in the economy is to define, establish, and enforce property rights. A property right to a good or service includes the right to exclude others from using the good or service and the right to transfer the ownership or use of the resource to others.

In a market economy, private individuals and firms own most of the resources. For example, when consumers buy houses, cars, or pizzas, they have purchased the right to use these goods in ways they, not someone else, see fit. These rights are called property rights. Property rights are the rules of our economic game. If well-defined, property rights give individuals the incentive to use their property efficiently. That is, owners with property rights have a greater incentive to maintain, improve, and conserve their property to preserve or increase its value.

The market system can only work if the government enforces the rules. That is, one of the key functions of government is to provide a legal framework that protects and enforces property rights and contracts. Markets, like baseball games, need umpires. It is the government that plays this role when it defines and protects the rights of people and their property through the legal system and police protection. That is, by providing rules and regulations, government can make markets work more efficiently. Private enforcement is possible, but as economic life becomes more complex, political institutions have become the major instrument for defining and enforcing property rights.

The government defines and protects property rights through the legal system and public policy. The legal system ensures the rights of private ownership, the enforcement of contracts and the legal status for businesses. The legal system serves as the referee, imposing penalties on violators of our legal rules. Property rights also include intellectual property—the property rights that an owner receives through patents, copyrights and trademarks. These rights give the owner long-term protection that encourages individuals to write books, music and software programs and invent new products. In short, well-defined property rights encourage investment, innovation, exchange, conservation, and economic growth.

Market Failure

market failure
when the economy fails to allocate resources efficiently on its own

The market mechanism is a simple but effective and efficient general means of allocating resources among alternative uses. When the economy fails to allocate resources efficiently on its own, however, it is known as **market failure**. For example, a steel mill might put soot and other forms of "crud" into the air as a byproduct of making steel. When it does, it imposes costs on others not connected with using or producing steel from the steel mill. The soot may require homeowners to paint their homes more often, entailing a cost. And studies show that respiratory diseases are greater in areas with more severe air pollution, imposing costs that may even include life itself. In addition, the steel mill might discharge chemicals into a stream, thus killing wildlife and spoiling recreational activities for the local

in the news   Song Swapping on the Net

If you were a rock star, would you want to put a stop to bootlegged music on the Internet?

- Yes, it violates copyright laws and cheats the artist.
- Yes, but unlicensed music sharing is inevitable.
- No, it will only increase the size of my audience.
- No, it hurts only record companies, which charge too much anyway.

Song swapping on the Net allows you to search for almost any song you can think of, find the song on a fellow enthusiast's hard drive, and then download it for yourself, right now—for the unbeatable cost of zero, free, nada, gratis.

MARC PAGANI PHOTOGRAPHY/SHUTTERSTOCK.COM

consider this:

Song swapping on the Net has set the stage for an interesting battle over copyright laws and intellectual property rights. Is sharing songs with others on the Internet underground piracy, or is it sharing someone's purchased possession? Is it a "personal use" right to share music online—like sharing a CD with a friend?

Napster and Grokster may be gone, but "free" music and videos are alive and well. The network is still wide open. It is a tough war to win, and the people trading music illegally online have little chance of being caught. Also, many young music lovers do not see downloading music without paying the copyright as a crime. The industry must innovate its way out. One reason that illegal downloading took off was because the industry did not keep up with the technology. The music industry continued to sell CDs and tapes when buyers had the technology to download songs.

A recent survey by the Institute for Policy Innovation concludes that the "piracy" of recorded music costs the U.S. recording industries billions of dollars annually in lost revenue and profits. In addition, the study states that recorded music piracy costs American workers significant losses in jobs and earnings, and lost tax revenues to the government.

Incentives play an important part in this story, too. If the price is zero, the probability of being caught is close to zero, and people do not view it as illegal, then you would expect many to download music illegally rather than purchase. However, the flipside of the story is that when talented producers and artists do not get royalties for their artistic work, you will see a lot less of it—especially quality music. Incentives matter.

population. In this case, the steel factory does not bear the costs of its polluting actions, and it continues to emit too much pollution. In other words, by transferring the pollution costs onto society, the firm lowers its costs of production and so produces more than the ideal output—which is inefficient because it is an overallocation of resources.

Markets sometimes produce too little of a good—research, for example. Therefore, the government might decide to subsidize promising scientific research that could benefit many people—such as cancer research. When one party prevents other parties from participating in

Am I sharing or stealing if I download a song from a site like Limewire or The Pirate Bay?

Can markets fail to allocate resources efficiently?

mutually beneficial exchange, it also causes a market failure. This situation occurs in a monopoly, with its single seller of goods. Because the monopolist can raise its end price above the competitive price, some potential consumers are kept from buying the goods they would have bought at the lower price, and inefficiency occurs. Whether the market economy has produced too little (underallocation) or too much (overallocation), the government can improve society's well-being by intervening. The case of market failure will be taken up in more detail in Chapter 8.

We cannot depend on the market economy to always communicate accurately. Some firms may have market power to distort prices in their favor. For example, the only regional cement company in the area has the ability to charge a higher price and provide lower-quality services than if the company were in a highly competitive market. In this case, the lack of competition can lead to higher prices and reduced product quality. And without adequate information, unscrupulous producers may be able to misrepresent their products to the disadvantage of unwary consumers.

When such conditions of restricted competition arise, the communication system of the marketplace is disrupted, causing the market to function inefficiently, to the detriment of consumers. For this reason, since 1890, the federal government has engaged in antitrust activities designed to encourage competition and discourage monopoly conditions. Specifically, the Antitrust Division of the Department of Justice and the Federal Trade Commission attempt to increase competition by attacking monopolistic practices.

In sum, government *can* help promote efficiency when there is a market failure—making the economic pie larger.

Does the Market Distribute Income Fairly?

Sometimes a painful trade-off exists between how much an economy can produce efficiently and how that output is distributed—the degree of equality. An efficient market rewards those that produce goods and services that others are willing and able to buy. But this does not guarantee a "fair" or equal distribution of income. That is, how the economic pie is divided up. A market economy cannot guarantee everyone adequate amounts of food, shelter, and health care. That is, not only does the market determine what goods are going to be produced and in what quantities, but it also determines the distribution of output among members of society.

As with other aspects of government intervention, the degree-of-equity argument can generate some sharp disagreements. What is "fair" for one person may seem highly "unfair" to someone else. One person may find it terribly unfair for some individuals to earn many times the amount earned by other individuals who work equally hard, and another person may find it highly unfair to ask one group, the relatively rich, to pay a much higher proportion of their income in taxes than another group pays.

Government Is Not Always the Solution

However, just because the government could improve the situation does not mean it will. After all, the political process has its own set of problems, such as special interests, shortsightedness, and imperfect information. For example, government may reduce competition through tariffs and quotas, or it may impose inefficient regulations that restrict entry. Consequently, government, like markets, has shortcomings and imperfections; the cost of government policies can exceed the benefits. Citizens failing to understand the difference between actual and ideal government performance will find it difficult to to decide the appropriate role for government.

ROBERT L. SEXTON

Even though designating these parking spaces for disabled drivers may not be an efficient use of scarce parking spaces (because they are often not used), many believe it is fair to give these drivers a convenient spot. The debate between efficiency and equity is often heated.

1. The government defines and protects property rights through
   a. the legal system.
   b. police protection.
   c. the military.
   d. all of the above.

2. Well-defined property rights encourage
   a. investment.
   b. innovation.
   c. conservation.
   d. exchange.
   e. economic growth.
   f. all of the above.

3. A market failure is said to occur
   a. when costs are imposed on some people without their consent.
   b. when the market economy fails to allocate resources efficiently.
   c. when one party prevents others from participating in mutually beneficial exchange.
   d. All of the above are examples of market failure.

4. The government redistributes income through
   a. taxes.
   b. subsidies.
   c. transfer payments.
   d. all of the above.

---

1. Why do owners with clear property rights have incentives to use their property efficiently?
2. How does the government use taxes, subsidies, and transfer payments to redistribute income toward lower-income groups?
3. Why would the government want to prevent market conditions of insufficient competition?
4. Why can markets sometimes fail to allocate resources efficiently?

Answers: 1. d 2. f 3. d 4. d

IDEA 7: Government Policies May Help Stabilize the Economy

2.7

▱ What can happen when total spending is insufficient?

▱ What can happen when total spending is excessive?

▱ What is inflation, and what causes it?

▱ Why is a stable monetary environment important?

▱ How can the government policies help stabilize the economy?

▱ Can government policies used to stabilize the economy be counterproductive?

The market mechanism does not always assure fulfillment of macroeconomic goals, most notably full employment and stable prices. Sometimes total spending is insufficient, and unemployment occurs; sometimes total spending is excessive, and inflation occurs. Both inflation and unemployment affect economic growth and standards of living. Almost everyone is affected directly or indirectly by high rates of unemployment or inflation.

Inflation

What is inflation, and what causes it? Inflation is an increase in the overall price level in the economy. Sustained inflation is usually caused by government printing too much money. When the government prints too much money, money loses its value. In its extreme form, inflation can lead to complete erosion in faith in the value of money. In Germany after both World Wars, prices increased so rapidly that people in some cases finally refused to take paper money, insisting instead on payment in goods or metals with some intrinsic worth.

A stable monetary environment can lead to price stability and enable producers and consumers to better coordinate their plans and decisions through the market. An increase in the overall price level increases burdens on people with fixed incomes when the inflation is not anticipated. It hurts savers, but helps those who have borrowed at a fixed rate. Moreover, inflation can raise one nation's prices relative to prices in other countries, which will either lead to difficulties in financing purchases of foreign goods or to a decline in the value of the national currency relative to that of other countries. Also, inflation imposes costs on people who devote resources to protecting themselves from expected inflation. The redistributional impact of inflation need not be the result of conscious public policy; it just happens.

Both inflation and unemployment affect economic growth and standards of the living. Almost everyone is affected directly or indirectly by high rates of unemployment and inflation.

Unemployment

When the economy is producing at less than its capacity, there will be some unemployment. Unemployment will vary by age, sex, and race. It will also vary by work experience, years of schooling, and skill level.

Unemployment statistics do not always give us an accurate picture of the economy. There are discouraged workers who are so disillusioned by the economy they stop looking for work and are no longer counted as unemployed. There are also workers who take part-time jobs when they are looking for full-time jobs.

What causes unemployment? Some of it results from a downswing in a business cycle, the unpredictable fluctuations in the economy. Other unemployment occurs because people are changing jobs, different skills needed by employers, or there are seasonal fluctuations in demand.

During the 1930s, the unemployment rate rose to more than 20 percent of the labor force, and among some groups, such as women and minority workers, unemployment rates were even higher. The concern over unemployment manifested itself in the passage of the Employment Act of 1946, committing the government to "promote maximum employment, production, and purchasing power." The act also implied that the government should respond to fluctuations in the economy through the use of stabilization policies.

More recently, as a result of a severe global recession, unemployment in many countries has remained high with many workers remaining unemployed for long periods of time. In 2009, 45 percent of unemployed workers had been without a job for at least 27 weeks. This is the longest downturn since World War II. The financial and psychological damage to the unemployed will last for years.

Government policies called fiscal policy, use taxes, and government spending to try to help stabilize the economy. If there is an unemployment problem, policy makers may lower taxes and/or increase government spending to stimulate demand. Alternatively, if there is a problem with persistent inflation, policy makers may raise taxes and/or reduce government spending.

Also, the Federal Reserve can use monetary policy to change the money supply and interest rates in an effort to achieve price stability, high employment, and economic growth. Many economists believe that these government policies play an important role in stabilizing the economy.

However, other economists believe the government policies are not effective and can be counterproductive. Because some government spending occurs for reasons other than macroeconomic stabilization—like money spent on defense and health care—government programs may have counterproductive effects on employment and inflation. And there are problems of time lags and the higher interest rate effect of expansionary fiscal policy, which can crowd out private investment and spending. This debate is important and will be discussed in the macroeconomic portion of the text.

ⓠ SECTION QUIZ

1. When total spending is insufficient, it can lead to
   a. economic growth.
   b. inflation.
   c. unemployment.
   d. none of the above.

2. When total spending is excessive it can lead to
   a. budget surpluses.
   b. inflation.
   c. unemployment.
   d. all of the above.

3. Inflation
   a. is when there is an increase in the overall price level in the economy.
   b. can be caused by the government printing too much money.
   c. can cause people to lose faith in the value of money.
   d. All of the above are true.

4. A stable monetary environment
   a. can lead to price stability.
   b. enables producers and consumers to better coordinate their plans and decisions.
   c. Both (a) and (b) are true.
   d. None of the above is true.

5. Unanticipated inflation
   a. redistributes income.
   b. increases burdens on people with fixed incomes when the inflation is not anticipated.
   c. hurts savers, but helps those who have borrowed at a fixed rate.
   d. can raise one nation's prices relative to prices in other countries.
   e. can cause all of the above.

6. The government may help stabilize the economy
   a. by providing a stable monetary environment.
   b. by using changes in government spending.
   c. by using changes in taxes.
   d. using any of the above.

1. What is inflation?
2. What causes inflation?
3. Why is a stable monetary environment so important?
4. What was the Employment Act of 1946?

Answers: 1. c   2. b   3. d   4. c   5. e   6. d

IDEA 8: Higher Productivity Growth Leads to Greater Long-Run Economic Growth

📂 What is economic growth? 📂 What is productivity?
📂 Do differences in growth rates matter?

Defining Economic Growth

Economic growth
the economy's abilities to produce more goods and services

Economic growth is usually measured by the annual percentage change in real (indexed for inflation) output of goods and services per capita (real GDP per capita), reflecting the expansion of the economy over time. We focus on per capita measures because we want to adjust for the effect of increased population on economic well-being. An increase in population, *ceteris paribus,* will lower the standard of living because more people will be sharing a fixed real GDP. Long-run economic growth is a *sustained* increase in real output per capita. However, economic growth rates do not reveal anything about the distribution of output and income. For example, a country could have extraordinary growth in per capita output, and yet the poor might achieve little or no improvement in their standard of living.

In Exhibit 1, we see that most of the increase in world GDP per capita has occurred in the last 200 years. Over the past millennium, world population rose twenty-two fold. Per capita income increased thirteen fold, world GDP nearly three-hundred fold. This contrasts sharply with the preceding millennium, when world population grew by only a sixth, and there was no advance in per capita income. From the year 1000 to 1820, the advance in per capita income was a slow crawl—the world average rose about 50 percent. Most of the growth went to accommodate a fourfold increase in population—stagnant economic growth rates mean little changes in the standard of living. The average Englishman was probably no better off in 1800 than he was in 1500. Life expectancy in England was less than 40 years in 1800. The effects of the Industrial Revolution had a huge impact beginning in the mid-1800s. Since then, world development has been much more dynamic. Per capita income rose more than eightfold, population more than fivefold.

Was the standard of living higher two hundred years ago, when we had fewer people?

Because of increased economic growth, the people of the world are better fed, better sheltered, and better protected against diseases. Global life expectancies have risen despite increases in population. This is not to say that millions of people do not still live in poverty. Admittedly, averages conceal a lot, but even the poorest countries of the world are better off than they were 60 years ago.

According to Stanford economist Paul Romer, "Economic growth springs from better recipes, not just from more cooking." Better recipes lead to permanent and continuing change. It is these better recipes that lead us down the path of innovation, the path of breakthroughs—organizational, intellectual, and technological. These are the ideas that can transform societies.

Small Differences in Growth Rates Matter

If Nation A and Nation B start off with the same population and the same level of real GDP, will a slight difference in their growth rates over a long period of time make much of a difference? Yes. In the first year or two, the difference will be small. However, after a decade the difference will be large, and after 50 or 100 years, it will be huge. In the words of Nobel laureate Robert Lucas, "Once one starts to think about differences in growth rates among countries, it is hard to think about anything else."

in the news Rockefeller and Carnegie

Are you richer than they were? John D. Rockefeller (left) and Andrew Carnegie (right) were the wealthiest Americans who ever lived. John D. Rockefeller had wealth valued at $200 billion in today's dollars (Bill Gates' estimated worth is about $50 billion), and Andrew Carnegie had wealth valued at $100 billion in today's dollars. But were they richer than you? Look what long-run economic growth has done for you. Rockefeller and Carnegie could not travel by air, ride in a car, turn on an air conditioner on a hot and humid day, watch HDTV, text message their friends, download music, or use Facebook, Skype, or Twitter. And medicine was far less advanced. Improvements in

Rockefeller: (1839–1937)

© PICTORIAL PRESS LTD/ALAMY

Carnegie: (1835–1919)

© ARCHIVE PICS/ALAMY

medical technology and sanitation have increased life expectancies about 50 percent since their day.

Because of differences in growth rates, some countries will become richer than others over time. If they achieve relatively slower rates of economic growth, today's richest countries will not remain the richest over time. And with even slight improvements in economic growth, today's poorest countries will not remain poor for long. China and India have both experienced spectacular economic growth over the past 20 years. Because of this economic growth, much of the world is now poorer than these two heavily populated countries. Other countries, such as Ireland, once one of the poorest countries in Western Europe, is now one of the richest. Because of past economic growth, the "richest" or "most-developed" countries today have many times the market output of the "poorest" or "least-developed" countries.

Economic Growth, Productivity, and the Standard of Living

The only way an economy can increase its rate of consumption in the long run is by increasing the amount it produces. Whether a country's standard of living rises, levels off, or declines over time depends for the most part on productivity growth. **Productivity** is the amount of goods and services a worker can produce per hour. Sustained economic growth occurs when workers' productivity rises. For example, slow growth of capital investment can lead to slower growth in labor productivity and, consequently, slower growth rates in real wages. On the other hand, increases in productivity and the associated higher real wages can be the result of carefully crafted economic policies, such as tax policies that stimulate investment or programs that encourage research and development. The only way an economy can increase its rate of consumption in the long run is by increasing the amount it produces.

Saving and investment are critical components of long-run economic growth and living standards. Families save for many things, including housing, medical expenses, taxes, retirement, children's education, vacations, automobiles, and so on. When money is saved in a bank or other financial institution, this money will earn interest because those savings are loaned to firms. An interest rate is the price of money that is borrowed or saved and is determined by the interaction of supply and demand. Higher real (that is, adjusted for inflation) interest rates provide an incentive for people to save more and borrow less. Lower real interest rates provide an incentive for people to borrow more and save less. Thus, higher (real) interest rates reduce investment spending by firms and household spending on housing cars and other major purchases.

Productivity
output per worker

When firms invest in new production techniques, new capital (machines and factories), and new technology, it makes labor more productive, which in turn leads to increases in incomes and living standards. Of course, investing in new physical or human capital involves a trade-off—giving up consumption today in anticipation of greater future production and consumption. For example, college is expensive but you hope the future payoff from this investment in human capital will lead to greater consumption and production in the future.

What Factors Contribute to Increases in Productivity?

There are a number of major factors that contribute to productivity growth. These include physical capital, human capital, natural resources, technological change as well as improvements in economic institutions and incentives. Today's workers generally produce more output than workers in the past. And workers in some countries, like the United States, generally produce more output than workers in most other countries. Workers with higher productivity usually have more physical capital to work with, like buildings and computers, are more educated, and have benefited from tremendous technological advancements.

Rate of productivity growth will be higher in countries that provide incentives for innovation, investment in research and development, and physical and human capital. These incentives can be in the form of copyrights or patents.

in the news   Results of Long-Run Economic Growth

The American economy is in a rough patch. But the long-term trends are good—and there is a price to economic pessimism. When a presidential election year collides with iffy economic times, the public's view of the U.S. economy turns gloomy. Perspective shrinks in favor of short-term assessments that focus on such unpleasant realities as falling job counts, sluggish GDP growth, uncertain incomes, subprime mortgage woes, and wobbly financial markets.

Taken together, it's enough to shake our faith in American progress. The best path to reviving that faith lies in gaining some perspective—getting out of the short-term rut—casting off the blinders that focus us on what will turn out to be mere footnotes in a longer-term march of progress. . . . In the exhibit you can see what many goods Americans can now afford because of long-run economic growth.

SOURCE: W. Michael Cox and Richard Alm, "How Are We Doing?" *The American*, July/August 2008.

The Results of Long-Run Economic Growth

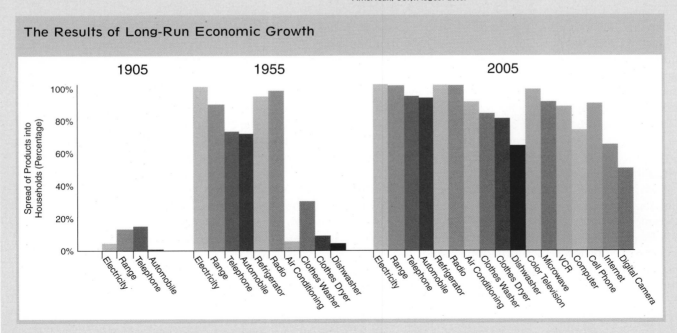

② SECTION QUIZ

1. Economic growth is measured by
   a. the percentage change in nominal GDP.
   b. the percentage change in nominal GDP per capita.
   c. the percentage change in real GDP.
   d. the percentage change in real GDP per capita.

2. Growth in real per capita output
   a. says nothing about the distribution of output.
   b. has been far more common in the last 200 years than before.
   c. can make poorer countries richer over time.
   d. All of the above are true.

3. Productivity growth
   a. is a primary determinant of a country's standard of living.
   b. is a primary cause of growth in real wages.
   c. is the only way in the long run for an economy to increase its potential real consumption per capita over time.
   d. is crucially affected by saving and investment over time.
   e. All of the above are true.

4. Which of the following can add to productivity growth?
   a. physical capital
   b. human capital
   c. discovery of new natural resources
   d. technological advances
   e. All of the above can add to productivity growth.

---

1. What is long-run economic growth, and why do we use a per capita measure?
2. Why is economic growth important?
3. Do small differences in growth rates matter?
4. What is labor productivity?
5. What role do saving and investment have in economic growth?
6. What factors lead to increases in labor productivity?

Answers: 1. d 2. d 3. e 4. e

Interactive Summary

Fill in the blanks:

1. As long as human _____ exceed available _____, scarcity will exist.

2. Something may be rare, but if it is not _____ it is not scarce.

3. The scarce resources that are used in the production of goods and services can be grouped into four categories: _____, _____, _____, and _____.

4. Capital includes human capital, the _____ people receive from _____.

5. Entrepreneurs are always looking for new ways to improve _____ or _____. They are lured by the chance of making a(n) _____.

6. _____ goods include fairness, friendship, knowledge, security, and health.

7. _____ are intangible items of value, such as education, provided to consumers.

8. Scarce goods created from scarce resources are called _____ goods.

9. Scarcity ultimately leads to _____ for the available goods and services.

10. Because we all have different _____, scarcity affects everyone differently.

11. Economics is the study of the choices we make among our many _____ and _____.

12. In a world of scarcity, we all face _____.

13. The highest or best forgone alternative resulting from a decision is called the _____.

14. The cost of grocery shopping is the _____ paid for the goods plus the _____ costs incurred.

15. Many choices involve _____ of something to do rather than whether to do something.

16. Economists emphasize _____ thinking because the focus is on additional, or _____, choices, which involve the effects of _____ or _____ the current situation.

17. The rule of rational choice is that in trying to make themselves better off, people alter their behavior if the _____ to them from doing so outweigh the _____ they will bear.

18. In acting rationally, people respond to _____.

19. If the benefits of some activity _____ and/or if the costs _____, economists expect the amount of that activity to rise. Economists call these _____ incentives. Likewise, if the benefits of some activity _____ and/or if the costs _____, economists expect the amount of that activity to fall. Economists call these _____ incentives.

20. Because most people seek opportunities that make them better off, we can _____ what will happen when incentives are _____.

21. People _____ by concentrating their energies on the activity to which they are best suited because individuals incur _____ opportunity costs as a result.

22. If a person, a region, or a country can produce a good or service at a lower opportunity cost than others can, we say that they have a(n) _____ in the production of that good or service.

23. The primary advantages of specialization are that employees acquire greater _____ from repetition, they avoid _____ time in shifting from one task to another, and they do the types of work for which they are _____ suited.

24. We trade with others because it frees up time and resources to do other things we do _____.

25. Produce what we do _____ best and _____ for the _____.

26. Market prices serve as the _____ of the market system. They communicate information about the _____ to buyers, and they provide sellers with critical information about the _____ that buyers place on those products. This communication results in a shifting of resources from those uses that are _____ valued to those that are _____ valued.

27. The basis of a market economy is _____ exchange and the _____ system that guides people's choices regarding what goods to produce and how to produce those goods and distribute them.

28. _____ can lead the economy to fail to allocate resources efficiently, as in the cases of pollution and scientific research.

29. Sometimes a painful trade-off exists between how much an economy can produce _____ and how that output is _____.

30. In the case of market _____, appropriate government policies could improve on market outcomes.

31. Sometimes total spending is insufficient, and _____ occurs.

32. Sometimes total spending is excessive, and _____ occurs.

33. A stable _____ environment can lead to price stability

34. Government policies called _____ policy use taxes and government spending to try to help stabilize the economy.

35. The Federal Reserve can use _____ policy to change the money supply and interest rates in an effort to achieve price stability, high employment, and economic growth.

36. The only way an economy can increase its rate of consumption in the long run is by increasing the amount it _____.

37. Whether a country's living standard of living rises, levels off, or declines over time depends for the most part on _____ growth.

38. _____ is the amount of goods and services a worker can produce per hour and _____ economic growth occurs when workers' productivity rises.

Answers: 1. wants; resources 2. desirable 3. land; labor; capital; entrepreneurship 4. knowledge and skill; education and on-the-job training 5. production techniques; products; profit 6. Intangible 7. Services 8. economic 9. competition 10. wants and desires 11. wants; desires 12. trade-offs 13. opportunity cost 14. price; nonprice 15. how much 16. marginal; marginal; adding to; subtracting from 17. expected marginal benefits; expected marginal costs 18. incentives 19. rise; fall; positive; fall; rise; negative 20. predict; changed 21. specialize; lower 22. comparative advantage 23. skill; wasted; best 24. better 25. relatively; trade; rest 26. language; relative availability of products; relative value; less; more 27. voluntary; price 28. Market failure 29. efficiency; distributed 30. failure 31. unemployment 32. inflation 33. monetary 34. fiscal 35. monetary 36. produces 37. productivity 38. productivity; sustained

Key Terms and Concepts

scarcity 35
labor 36
land 36
capital 36
human capital 36
entrepreneurship 36
goods 36
tangible goods 36
intangible goods 36

services 36
economic goods 37
bads 37
opportunity cost 39
rational decision making 43
marginal thinking 43
rule of rational choice 43
net benefit 44
positive incentive 46

negative incentive 47
specializing 48
comparative advantage 48
efficiency 52
price controls 53
market failure 54
economic growth 60
productivity 61

Section Quiz Answers

2.1   IDEA 1: People Face Scarcity and Costly Trade-offs

1. What must be true for something to be an economic good?

An economic good, tangible or intangible, is any good or service that we value or desire. This definition includes the reduction of things we don't want—bads—as a good.

2. Why does scarcity affect everyone?

Because no one can have all the goods and services that he or she desires, we all face scarcity as a fact of life.

3. How and why does scarcity affect each of us differently?

Because our desires and the extent of the resources we have available to meet those desires vary, scarcity affects each of us differently.

4. Why might daylight be scarce in Anchorage, Alaska, in the winter but not in the summer?

For a good to be scarce means we want more of it than we are able to have. Residents of Anchorage typically have all the daylight they wish in the summer, when the sun sets just before midnight, but they have only a few hours of daylight during the winter months. If daylight is desirable, it is limited in the winter.

5. **Would we have to make choices if we had unlimited resources?**

We would not have to make choices if we had unlimited resources, because we would then be able to produce all the goods and services anyone wanted, and having more of one thing would not require having less of other goods or services.

6. **What do we mean by opportunity cost?**

The opportunity cost of a choice is the highest valued forgone opportunity resulting from a decision. It can usefully be thought of as the value of the opportunity a person would have chosen if his most preferred option was taken away from him.

7. **Why was the opportunity cost of going to college higher for LeBron James (Miami Heat star) than for most undergraduates?**

The forgone alternative to LeBron James of going to college—starting a highly paid professional basketball career sooner than he could otherwise—was far more lucrative than the alternatives facing most undergraduates. Because his forgone alternative was more valuable for LeBron James, his opportunity cost of going to college was higher than for most.

8. **Why is the opportunity cost of time spent getting an MBA typically lower for a 22-year-old straight out of college than for a 45-year-old experienced manager?**

The opportunity cost of time for a 45-year-old experienced manager—the earnings he would have to give up to spend a given period getting an MBA—is higher than that of a 22-year-old straight out of college, whose income earning alternatives are far less.

2.2   IDEA 2: People Engage in Rational Decision Making and Marginal Thinking

1. **What are marginal choices? Why does economics focus on them?**

Marginal choices are choices of how much of something to do, rather than whether to do something. Economics focuses on marginal choices because those are the sorts of choices we usually face: Should I do a little more of this or a little less of that?

2. **What is the rule of rational choice?**

The rule of rational choice is that in trying to make themselves better off, people alter their behavior if the expected marginal benefits from doing so outweigh the expected marginal costs they will bear. If the expected marginal benefits of an action exceed the expected marginal costs, a person will do more of that action; if the expected marginal benefits of an action are less than the expected marginal costs, a person will do less of that action.

3. **How could the rule of rational choice be expressed in terms of net benefits?**

Because net benefits are expected to be positive when expected marginal benefits exceed expected marginal cost to the decision maker, the rule of rational choice could be restated as: People will make choices for which net benefits are expected to be positive.

4. **Why does rational choice involve expectations?**

Because the world is uncertain in many important respects, we can seldom know for certain whether the marginal benefits of an action will in fact exceed the marginal costs. Therefore, the rule of rational choice deals with expectations decision makers hold at the time they make their decisions, recognizing that mistakes can be made.

5. **What is rational decision making?**

Rational decision making is when people do the best they can based on their values and information, under current and anticipated future consequences. Rational individuals weigh the marginal benefits and marginal costs of their actions and they only pursue actions if they perceive the marginal benefits to be greater than the marginal costs.

6. **Why do students often stop taking lecture notes when a professor announces that the next few minutes of material will not be on any future test or assignment?**

The benefit, in terms of grades, from taking notes in class falls when the material discussed will not be tested or "rewarded," and when the benefits of lecture note taking are smaller in this situation, students do less of it.

7. **If you decide to speed to get to a doctor's appointment and then get in an accident due to speeding, does your decision to speed invalidate the rule of rational choice? Why or why not?**

No. Remember, the rule of rational choice deals with expectations at the time decisions were made. If you thought you would get in an accident due to speeding in this situation, you would not have decided to speed. The fact that you got in an accident doesn't invalidate the rule of rational choice; it only means your expectations at the time you decided to speed were incorrect.

8. If pedestrians felt far safer using crosswalks to cross the street, how could adding crosswalks increase the number of pedestrian accidents?

Just like safer cars can lead people to drive less safely, if pedestrians felt safer in crosswalks, they might cross less safely, such as taking less care to look both ways. The result of pedestrians taking less care may well be an increase in the number of pedestrian accidents.

9. Imagine driving a car with daggers sticking out of the steering wheel—pointing directly at your chest. Would you drive more safely? Why?

Because the cost to you of an accident would be so much higher in this case, you would drive far more safely as a result.

2.3   IDEA 3: People Respond Predictably to Changes in Incentives

1. What is the difference between positive incentives and negative incentives?

Positive incentives are those that either increase benefits or decrease costs of an action, encouraging the action; negative incentives are those that either decrease benefits or increase costs of an action, discouraging the action.

2. According to the rule of rational choice, would you do more or less of something if its expected marginal benefits increased? Why?

You would do more of something if its expected marginal benefits increased, because then the marginal expected benefits would exceed the marginal expected costs for more "units" of the relevant action.

3. According to the rule of rational choice, would you do more or less of something if its expected marginal costs increased? Why?

You would do less of something if its expected marginal costs increased, because then the marginal expected benefits would exceed the marginal expected costs for fewer "units" of the relevant action.

4. How does the rule of rational choice imply that young children are typically more likely to misbehave at a supermarket checkout counter than at home?

When a young child is at a supermarket checkout counter, the benefit of misbehaving—the potential payoff to pestering Mom or Dad for candy—is greater. Also, because his parents are less likely to punish him, or to punish him as severely, in public as in private when he pesters them, the costs are lower as well. The benefits of misbehavior are higher and the costs are lower at a supermarket checkout counter, so more child misbehavior is to be expected there.

5. Why do many parents refuse to let their children have dessert before they eat the rest of their dinner?

Children often find that the costs of eating many foods at dinner exceed the benefits (e.g., "If it's green, it must be disgusting."), but that is seldom so of dessert. If parents let their children eat dessert first, children would often not eat the food that was "good for them." But by adding the benefit of getting dessert to the choice of eating their other food, parents can often get their children to eat the rest of their dinner, too.

2.4   IDEA 4: Specialization and Trade Can Make Everyone Better Off

1. Why do people specialize?

People specialize because by concentrating their energies on the activities to which they are best suited, individuals incur lower opportunity costs. That is, they specialize in doing those things they can do at lower opportunity costs than others, and let others who can do other things at lower opportunity costs than they can specialize in doing them.

2. What do we mean by comparative advantage?

A person, region, or country has a comparative advantage in producing a good or service when it can produce it at a lower opportunity cost than other persons, regions, or countries.

3. Why does the combination of specialization and trade make us better off?

Trade increases wealth by allowing a person, region, or a nation to specialize in those products that it produces relatively better than others and to trade for those products that others produce relatively better than they do. Exploiting our comparative advantages, and then trading, allows us to produce, and therefore consume, more than we could otherwise from our scarce resources.

4. If you can mow your lawn in half the time it takes your spouse or housemate to do it, do you have a comparative advantage in mowing the lawn?

Your faster speed at mowing the lawn does not establish that you have a comparative advantage in mowing. That can only be established relative to other tasks. The person with a comparative advantage in mowing lawns is the one with the lowest opportunity cost, and that could be your spouse or housemate in this case. For instance, if you could earn $12 an hour, mowing the lawn in half an hour implies an opportunity cost of $6 of forgone output elsewhere. If your spouse or housemate could only earn $5 per hour (because he or she was less than half as productive doing other things compared to you), the opportunity cost of that person mowing the lawn in an hour is $5. In this case, your spouse or housemate has a comparative advantage in mowing the lawn.

5. If you have a current comparative advantage in doing the dishes, and you then become far more productive than before in completing yard chores, could that eliminate your comparative advantage? Why or why not?

The opportunity cost of you doing the dishes is the value of other chores you must give up to do the dishes. Therefore, an increase in your productivity doing yard chores would increase the opportunity cost of doing the dishes, and could well eliminate your current comparative advantage in doing the dishes compared to other members of your family.

6. Could a student who gets a C in one class but a D or worse in everything else have a comparative advantage over someone who gets a B in that class but an A in everything else? Explain this concept using opportunity cost.

A student who gets a C in a class is less good, in an absolute sense, at that class than a student who gets a B in it. But if the C student gets Ds in other classes, he is relatively, or comparatively, better at the C class, while if the B student gets As in other classes, she is relatively, or comparatively, worse at that class.

2.5   IDEA 5: Markets Can Improve Economic Efficiency

1. Why must every society choose some manner in which to allocate its scarce resources?

Every society must choose some manner in which to allocate its scarce resources because the collective wants of its members always far outweigh what the scarce resources nature has provided can produce.

2. How does a market system allocate resources?

A market system allows individuals, both as producers and consumers, to indicate their wants and desires through their actions—how much they are willing to buy or sell at various prices. The market then acts to bring about that level of prices that allows buyers and sellers to coordinate their plans.

3. What do market prices communicate to others in society?

The prices charged by suppliers communicate the relative availability of products to consumers; the prices consumers are willing to pay communicate the relative value consumers place on products to producers. That is, market prices provide a way for both consumers and suppliers to communicate about the relative value of resources.

4. How do price controls undermine the market as a communication device?

Price controls—both price floors and price ceilings—prevent the market from communicating relevant information between consumers and suppliers. A price floor set above the market price prevents suppliers from communicating their willingness to sell for less to consumers. A price ceiling set below the market price prevents consumers from indicating their willingness to pay more to suppliers.

5. Why can markets sometimes fail to allocate resources efficiently?

Markets can sometimes fail to allocate resources efficiently. Such situations, called market failures, represent situations such as externalities, where costs can be imposed on some individuals without their consent (e.g., from dumping "crud" in their air or water), where information in the market may not be communicated honestly and accurately, and where firms may have market power to distort prices in their favor (against consumers' interests).

2.6   IDEA 6: Appropriate Government Policies Can Improve Market Outcomes

1. Why must every society choose some manner in which to allocate its scarce resources?

Every society must choose some manner in which to allocate its scarce resources because the collective wants of its members always far outweigh what the scarce resources that nature has provided can produce.

2. How does a market system allocate resources?

A market system allows individuals, both as producers and consumers, to indicate their wants and desires through their actions—how much they are willing to buy or sell at various prices. The market then acts to bring about that level of prices that allows buyers and sellers to coordinate their plans.

3. What do market prices communicate to others in society?

The prices charged by suppliers communicate the relative availability of products to consumers; the prices consumers are willing to pay communicate the relative value consumers place on products to producers. That is, market prices provide a way for both consumers and suppliers to communicate about the relative value of resources.

2.7   IDEA 7: Government Policies May Help Stabilize the Economy

1. What is inflation?

Inflation is an increase in the overall price level in the economy.

2. What causes inflation?

Sustained inflation is usually caused by government printing too much money. When the government prints too much money; money loses its value. The high inflation of the 1970s was associated with rapid growth in the quantity of money and the recent low inflation rates have been associated with slow growth in the quantity of money.

3. Why is a stable monetary environment so important?

A stable monetary environment can lead to price stability and enable producers and consumers to better coordinate their plans and decisions through the market. Inflation can redistribute income randomly. An increase in the overall price level increases burdens on people with fixed incomes when the inflation is not anticipated. Unanticipated inflation hurts savers, but helps those who have borrowed at a fixed rate. Also, inflation can raise one nation's prices relative to prices in other countries, which will either lead to difficulties in financing purchase of foreign goods or to a decline in the value of the national currency relative to that of other countries.

4. What was the Employment Act of 1946?

Answer: The passage of the Employment Act of 1946 committed the government to "promote maximum employment, production, and purchasing power." The act also implied that the government should respond to fluctuations in the economy through the use of stabilization policies.

5. What government policy changes might be effective in increasing employment in recessions?

Government policies to stimulate the economy, such as decreasing taxes or increasing government purchases, could potentially increase employment in recessions.

6. What government policy changes might be effective in controlling inflation?

Government policies to control inflation can include increasing taxes, decreasing government purchases, and reducing the growth in the money supply through the banking system.

2.8   IDEA 8: Higher Productivity Growth Leads to Greater Long-Run Economic Growth

1. What is long-run economic growth and why do we use a per capita measure?

Economic growth is usually measured by the annual percentage change in real output of goods and services per capita (real GDP per capita), reflecting the expansion of the economy over time. We focus on per capita because we want to isolate the effect of increased population on economic growth.

2. Why is economic growth important?

Because of increases in economic growth, the people of the world are better fed, better sheltered, and better protected against disease. Global life expectancies have risen despite increases in population.

3. Do small differences in growth rates matter?

Because of differences in growth rates, over time some countries will become richer than others. With relatively slower economic growth, today's richest countries will not be the richest for very long. On the other hand, with even slight improvements in economic growth, today's poorest countries will not remain poor for long.

4. What is labor productivity?

Whether a country's living standard rises, levels off, or declines over time depends for the most part on productivity growth. For example, slow growth of capital investment can lead to lower labor productivity and, consequently, lower wages. On the other hand, increases in productivity and higher wages can occur as a result of carefully crafted economic policies, such as tax policies that stimulate investment or programs that encourage research and development. The only way an economy can increase its rate of consumption in the long run is by increasing the amount it produces.

5. What role do saving and investment have in economic growth?

Saving and investment are critical components of long-run economic growth and living standards. When money is put in a savings account in a bank or other financial institution, that money will earn interest because those savings are loaned to firms. An interest rate is the price of money that is borrowed or saved and I determined by the interaction of supply and demand. Higher real (that is, adjusted for inflation) rates provide an incentive for people to save more and borrow less. Lower real interest rates provide an incentive for people to borrow more and save less. Thus, higher (real) interest rates reduce investment spending by firms and household spending on housing cars and other major purchases.

6. What factors lead to increases in labor productivity?

Labor productivity increases as firms invest in new production techniques, acquire new capital (machines and factories), and incorporate new technology. This makes labor more productive leading to increases in incomes and living standards. Of course, investing in new physical or human capital involves a trade-off—giving up consumption today in anticipation of greater future production and consumption. There are five major factors that contribute to growth in productivity. These include physical capital, human capital, natural resources, technological change, and improvements in economic institutions and incentives.

Problems

1. Which of the following goods are scarce?
   a. garbage
   b. salt water in the ocean
   c. clothes
   d. clean air in a big city
   e. dirty air in a big city
   f. a public library

2. Explain the difference between poverty and scarcity.

3. The automotive revolution after World War II reduced the time involved for travel and shipping goods. This innovation allowed the U.S. economy to produce more goods and services since it freed resources involved in transportation for other uses. The transportation revolution also increased wants. Identify two ways the car and truck revealed new wants.

4. The price of a one-way bus trip from Los Angeles to New York City is $150.00. Sarah, a school teacher, pays the same price in February (during the school year) as in July (during her vacation), so the cost is the same in February as in July. Do you agree?

5. McDonald's once ran a promotion that whenever St. Louis Cardinal's slugger Mark McGwire hit a home run into the upper deck at Busch Stadium, McDonald's gave anyone with a ticket to that day's game a free Big Mac. If holders of ticket stubs have to stand in line for 10 minutes, is the Big Mac really "free"?

6. List some things that you need. Then ask yourself if you would still want some of those things if the price were five times higher. Would you still want them if the price were 10 times higher?

7. List the opportunity costs of the following:
   a. going to college
   b. missing a lecture
   c. withdrawing and spending $100 from your savings account, which earns 5 percent interest annually
   d. going snowboarding on the weekend before final examinations

8. Which of the following activities require marginal thinking, and why?
   a. studying
   b. eating
   c. driving
   d. shopping
   e. getting ready for a night out

9. Should you go to the movies this Friday? List the factors that affect the possible benefits and costs of this decision. Explain where uncertainty affects the benefits and costs.

10. Explain why following the rule of rational choice makes a person better off.

11. Which of the following are positive incentives? Negative incentives? Why?
    a. a fine for not cleaning up after your dog defecates in the park
    b. a trip to Hawaii paid for by your parents or significant other for earning an A in your economics course
    c. a higher tax on cigarettes and alcohol
    d. a subsidy for installing solar panels on your house

12. Modern medicine has made organ transplants a common occurrence, yet the number of organs that people want far exceeds the available supply. According to CNN, 10 people die each day because of a lack of transplantable organs like kidneys and livers. Some economists have recommended that an organ market be established through which doctors and others could pay people for the right to use their organs when they die. The law currently forbids the sale of organs. What do you think of such a proposal? What kind of incentives would an organ market provide for people to allow others to use their organs? What would happen to the supply of organs if, instead of relying on donated kidneys, livers, and retinas, doctors and hospitals could bid for them? What drawbacks would a free market in organs have? Have you made arrangements to leave your organs to your local organ bank? Would you do so if you could receive $50,000 for them?

13. Throughout history, many countries have chosen the path of autarky, choosing to not trade with other countries. Explain why this path would make a country poorer.

14. Farmer Fran can grow soybeans and corn. She can grow 50 bushels of soybeans or 100 bushels of corn on an acre of her land for the same cost. The price of soybeans is $1.50 per bushel and the price of corn is $0.60 per bushel. Show the benefits to Fran of specialization. What should she specialize in?

15. Which region has a comparative advantage in the following goods:
    a. wheat: Colombia or the United States?
    b. coffee: Colombia or the United States?
    d. timber: Iowa or Washington?
    e. corn: Iowa or Washington?

16. Why is it important that the country or region with the lower opportunity cost produce the good? How would you use the concept of comparative advantage to argue for reducing restrictions on trade between countries?

17. People communicate with each other in the market through the effect their decisions to buy or sell have on prices. Indicate how each of the following would affect prices by putting a check in the appropriate space.
    a. People who see an energetic and lovable Jack Russell Terrier in a popular TV series want Jack Russell Terriers as pets. The price of Jack Russell Terriers _____ Rises _____ Falls
    b. Aging retirees flock to Tampa, Florida, to live. The price of housing in Tampa _____ Rises _____ Falls
    c. Weather-related crop failures in Colombia and Costa Rica reduce coffee supplies. The price of coffee _____ Rises _____ Falls
    d. Sugarcane fields in Hawaii and Louisiana are replaced with housing. The price of sugar _____ Rises _____ Falls
    e. More and more students graduate from U.S. medical schools. The wages of U.S. doctors _____ Rise _____ Fall
    f. Americans are driving more, and they are driving bigger, gas-guzzling cars like sport utility vehicles. The price of gasoline _____ Rises _____ Falls

18. Prices communicate information about the relative value of resources. Which of the following would cause the relative value and, hence, the price of potatoes to rise?
    a. Fungus infestation wipes out half the Idaho potato crop.
    b. The price of potato chips rises.
    c. Scientists find that eating potato chips makes you better looking.
    d. The prices of wheat, rice, and other potato substitutes fall dramatically.

19. Imagine that you are trying to decide whether to cross a street without using the designated crosswalk at the traffic signal. What are the expected marginal benefits of crossing? The expected marginal costs? How would the following conditions change your benefit–cost equation?
    a. The street was busy.
    b. The street was empty, and it was 3 A.M.
    c. You were in a huge hurry.
    d. A police officer was standing 100 feet away.
    e. The closest crosswalk was a mile away.
    f. The closest crosswalk was 10 feet away.

chapter three

Scarcity, Trade-Offs, and Production Possibilities

Goods and services can be distributed many different ways: prices, first come/first served, random selection (like a lottery), majority rule, according to need, equal shares, and so on. Each method has advantages and disadvantages. What are the benefits and costs of different allocative systems?

Some methods of resource allocation might seem bad and counterproductive; physical violence has been used since the beginning of time, as people, regions, and countries attacked one another to gain control over resources.

We could argue that government should allocate scarce resources on the basis of equal shares or according to need. However, this approach

poses problems because of diverse individual preferences, the difficulty of ascertaining needs, and the negative work and investment incentives involved. In command economies, resource allocation is determined by central planners rather than in the market. Consequently, the planners do not get markets signals regarding consumers' preferences and producers' costs, and shortages and surpluses ensue. When prices are used to allocate resources, the seller produces something a consumer wants and takes the money from the sale and buys what she wants. If something other than price is used, say force, what incentive does a producer have to produce the good, if she knows it can be taken from her? People will not produce as much in this kind of world. Incentives matter. For many goods and services, consumers wait in line—called queuing. This is another way to distribute goods and services. People routinely queue at concerts or sporting events, to purchase groceries, to mail a parcel at the post office, to use a public toilet at a ball game, or to enter a congested highway. What are the costs of waiting in line?

Most queuing problems can be resolved by the market if people are willing to pay a higher price. For example, what if your grocery store charged you 5 percent to use the express lane, donating the express fee to charity? Or what if a store had a "discount line" that gave you coupons for waiting longer in line? However, the question remains, how do you create a system that simultaneously satisfies concerns about efficiency, time, money, and fairness?

This chapter builds on the foundations of the preceding chapters. We have learned that we have unlimited wants and limited resources—that is, we all face scarcity. And scarcity forces us to choose. To get one thing we like, we usually have to give up something else we want—that is, people face trade-offs. Recognizing these trade-offs will allow us to make better decisions.

Every economy must transform the resources that nature provides into goods and services. Economics is the study of that process. This chapter begins with a discussion of how every economy must respond to three fundamental questions: What goods and services will be produced? How will the goods and services be produced? Who will get the goods and services?

In this chapter, we introduce our first economic models: the circular flow model and the production possibilities curve. In the circular flow model, we show how decisions made by households and firms interact with each other. Our second model, the production possibilities curve, illustrates many of the most important concepts in economics: scarcity, trade-offs, increasing opportunity costs, efficiency, investment in capital goods, and economic growth.

3.1 The Three Economic Questions Every Society Faces

- ▱ What goods and services will be produced?
- ▱ How will the goods and services be produced?
- ▱ Who will get the goods and services?

The Three Economic Questions

Because of scarcity, certain economic questions must be answered, regardless of a society's level of affluence or its political structure. We will consider three fundamental questions that every society inevitably faces: (1) What goods and services will be produced? (2) How will the goods and services be produced? (3) Who will get the goods and services produced? These questions are unavoidable in a world of scarcity.

If producers decide what to produce in a market economy, why do we describe it as consumer sovereignty?

What Goods and Services Will Be Produced?

How do individuals control production decisions in market-oriented economies? Questions arise such as whether society should produce more baseball stadiums or more schools. Should Apple produce more iPhones or laptops? The government has a limited budget, too, and must make choices on how much to spend on defense, health care, highways, and education. In short, consumers, firms, and governments must all make choices about what goods and services will be produced and each one of those decisions has an opportunity cost—the highest valued alternative forgone. In the marketplace, the answer to these and other similar questions is that people "vote" in economic affairs with their dollars (or pounds or yen). This concept is called **consumer sovereignty**. Consumer sovereignty explains how individual consumers in market economies determine what continues to be produced.

How do we decide which colors and options to include with these cars?

High-definition televisions, DVD players, cell phones, iPods, camcorders, and computers, for example, became part of our lives because consumers "voted" hundreds of dollars apiece on these goods. Consumers "voted" fewer dollars on regular color televisions and more on high definition televisions. Similarly, vinyl record albums gave way to tapes, CDs to downloadable music, as consumers voted for these items with their dollars. If consumers vote for more fuel efficient cars and healthier foods, then firms that wish to remain profitable must listen and respond.

How Different Types of Economic Systems Answer the Question "What Goods and Services Will Be Produced?"

Economies are organized in different ways to answer the question of what is to be produced. The dispute over the best way to answer this question has inflamed passions for centuries. Should a central planning board make the decisions, as in North Korea and Cuba? Sometimes this highly centralized economic system is referred to as a **command economy**. Under this type of regime, decisions about how many tractors or automobiles to produce are largely determined by a government official or committee associated with the central planning organization. That same group decides on the number and size of school buildings, refrigerators, shoes, and so on. Other countries, including the United States, much of Europe, and increasingly, Asia and elsewhere have largely adopted a decentralized decision-making process where literally millions of individual producers and consumers of goods and services determine what goods, and how many of them, will be produced. A country that uses such a decentralized decision-making process is often said to have a **market economy**. Actually, no nation has a pure market economy. The United States, along with most countries, is said to have a **mixed economy**. In such an economy, the government and the private sector together determine the allocation of resources.

consumer sovereignty
consumers vote with their dollars in a market economy; this accounts for what is produced

command economy
an economy in which the government uses central planning to coordinate most economic activities

market economy
an economy that allocates goods and services through the private decisions of consumers, input suppliers, and firms

mixed economy
an economy where government and the private sector determine the allocation of resources

How Will the Goods and Services Be Produced?

All economies, regardless of their political structure, must decide how to produce the goods and services that they want—because of scarcity. Goods and services can

Consumers say no to some new products. If consumers do not like a product, like the Ford Edsel above, it becomes unprofitable and will eventually disappear. Sometimes they become collector's items years later.

BRASILIAO/SHUTTERSTOCK.COM

Which transplant patient should receive the available kidney? What are benefits and costs of different allocative systems?

labor intensive
production that uses a large amount of labor

capital intensive
production that uses a large amount of capital

generally be produced in several ways. Firms may face a trade-off between using more machines or more workers. For example, a company might decide to move its production to a plant in another country that uses more workers and fewer machines.

A ditch can be dug by many workers using their hands, by a few workers with shovels, or by one person with a backhoe. Someone must decide which method is most appropriate. From this example, you might be tempted to conclude that it is desirable to use the biggest, most elaborate form of capital. But would you really want to plant your spring flowers with huge earthmoving machinery? That is, the most capital-intensive method of production may not always be the best. The best method is the least-cost method.

What Is the Best Form of Production?

The best or "optimal" form of production will usually vary from one economy to the next. For example, earthmoving machinery is used in digging large ditches in the United States and Europe, while in developing countries, shovels are often used. Why do these optimal forms of production vary? Compared with capital, labor is relatively inexpensive and plentiful in developing countries but relatively scarce and expensive in the United States. In contrast, capital (machines and tools, mainly) is comparatively plentiful and relatively inexpensive in the United States but scarcer and more costly in developing countries. That is, in developing countries, production tends to be more labor intensive, or labor driven. In the United States, production tends to be more capital intensive, or capital driven. Each nation tends to use the production processes that conserve its relatively scarce (and thus relatively more expensive) resources and use more of its relatively abundant resources.

Who Will Get the Goods and Services Produced?

In every society, some mechanism must exist to determine how goods and services are to be distributed among the population. Who gets what? Why do some people get to consume or use far more goods and services than others? This question of distribution is so important

use what you've learned   Market Signals

Q Adam was a college graduate with a major in art. A few years ago, Adam decided that he wanted to pursue a vocation that utilized his talent. In response, he shut himself up in his studio and created a watercolor collection. With high hopes, Adam put his collection on display for buyers. After several years of displaying his art, however, the only one interested in the collection was his 18-year-old sister, who wanted the picture frames for her room. Recognizing that Adam was having trouble pursuing his chosen occupation, Adam's friend Karl told him that the market had failed. In the meantime, Adam turned to house painting (interior and exterior) and business was booming. Adam hired five workers and would often be painting all day and into the evenings and weekends. Do you think the market has failed?

A No. Markets provide important signals, and the signal being sent in this situation is that Adam should look for some other means of support—something that society values. Remember the function of consumer sovereignty in the marketplace. Clearly, consumers were not voting for Adam's art. The market seems to be telling Adam: less painting on canvas and more painting on walls, doors, and trim.

that wars and revolutions have been fought over it. Both the French and Russian revolutions were concerned fundamentally with the distribution of goods and services. Even in societies where political questions are usually settled peacefully, the question of the distribution of income is an issue that always arouses strong emotional responses. As we will see, in a market economy with private ownership and control of the means of production, the amounts of goods and services an individual can obtain depend on her or his income. Income, in turn, will depend on the quantity and quality of the scarce resources the individual controls. Income is also determined by the price others are willing and able to pay for what you have to sell. If you are a medical doctor and make $300,000 a year, that is income you will have available to buy goods and services. If you also own a condominium you rent out in Aspen, Colorado, you will have an even greater amount of income to spend on goods and services. Markets reward education, hard work, and training. Education (years of schooling) and earnings are highly (positively) correlated. Oprah Winfrey made a lot of money because she had unique and marketable skills as a talk show host. This basis for distribution may or may not be viewed as "fair," an issue we will look at in detail later in this book.

In a market economy, who decides what and how much to produce?

Castaway and Resource Allocation

In the movie *Cast Away*, a plane crash leaves Chuck Noland (Tom Hanks) stranded on a deserted island, as in the classic 18th century novel *Robinson Crusoe*. In this simple island economy, Noland had to find a way to survive. His behavior was restricted by the resources that he salvaged from the crash and what he could find on the island. He was by himself, so property rights were not an issue. However, he still had to answer the *what, how,* and *for whom* questions. In this chapter, you will discover these are the three questions that every society must face—even the simplest island economy. To Noland, the *for whom* question, who get the goods and services produced, was pretty easy: He was the only one on the island; he got what was produced. The *what* question, what goods and services would be produced, was pretty easy, too: He was trying to survive, so he was looking to produce food, shelter, and clothing. The *how* question, how will the goods and services be produced, was where this scene becomes interesting. How to best use his scarce resources? Noland salvaged several boxes from the plane crash. After a failed attempt to leave the island, he decided to open the boxes to see whether they contain anything useful. He first found a pair of ice skates. He uses the blade of the skate as a knife to open coconuts, to cut a dress to convert into a fishing net, and to sharpen a stick to use as a spear for catching fish. He uses the laces from the skate and the bubble wrap in the package to dress an injury. He uses the raft as a lean-to for his shelter. He builds a fire and even "makes" a friend out of a volleyball— Wilson. In short, Noland uses his entrepreneurial talents to try to make the best use of the scarce resources in order to survive on the island.

Singer Beyonce gets paid a lot of money because she controls scarce resources: her talent and her name recognition. As we will see in Chapter 5, people's talents and other goods and services in limited supply relative to demand will command high prices.

Chuck Noland (Tom Hanks) had to make the best use of his scarce resources to survive on the island.

ⓘ SECTION QUIZ

1. Which of the following is not a question that all societies must answer?

   a. How can scarcity be eliminated?

   b. What goods and services will be produced?

   c. Who will get the goods and services?

   d. How will the goods and services be produced?

   e. All of the above are questions that all societies must answer.

2. Economic disputes over the distribution of income are generally associated with which economic question?

   a. Who should produce the goods?

   b. What goods and services will be produced?

   c. Who will get the goods and services?

   d. How will the goods and services be produced?

3. The private ownership of property and the use of the market system to direct and coordinate economic activity are most characteristic of

   a. a command economy.

   b. a mixed economy.

   c. a market economy.

   d. a traditional economy.

4. The degree of government involvement in the economy is greatest in

   a. a command economy.

   b. a mixed economy.

   c. a market economy.

   d. a traditional economy.

5. The best method of production is

   a. the capital-intensive method.

   b. the labor-intensive method.

   c. the same under all circumstances.

   d. the lowest cost method.

6. When _____ is relatively scarce, _____ methods of production will be relatively less expensive.

   a. capital; capital-intensive

   b. capital; labor-intensive

   c. labor; capital-intensive

   d. labor; labor-intensive

   e. Both (b) and (c) are true.

---

1. Why does scarcity force us to decide what to produce?

2. How is a command economy different from a market economy?

3. How does consumer sovereignty determine production decisions in a market economy?

4. Do you think that what and how much an economy produces depends on who will get the goods and services produced in that economy? Why or why not?

5. Why do consumers have to "vote" for a product with their dollars for it to be a success?

6. Why must we choose among multiple ways of producing the goods and services we want?

7. Why might production be labor intensive in one economy but be capital intensive in another?

8. If a tourist from the United States on an overseas trip notices that other countries don't produce crops "like they do back home," would he be right to conclude that farmers in the other countries produce crops less efficiently than U.S. farmers?

9. In what way does scarcity determine income?

10. What are the most important functions of the market system?

Answers: 1. a 2. c 3. c 4. a 5. d 6. e

The Circular Flow Model

📁 What are product markets?

📁 What is the circular flow model?

📁 What are factor markets?

How do we explain how the millions of people in an economy interact when it comes to buying, selling, producing, working, hiring, and so on? A continuous flow of goods and services is bought and sold between the producers of goods and services (which we call firms) and the buyers of goods and services (which we call households). A continuous flow of income also moves from firms to households as firms buy inputs to produce the goods and services they sell. In our simple economy, these exchanges take place in product markets and factor markets.

product markets
markets where households are buyers and firms are sellers of goods and services

factor (or input) markets
markets where households sell the use of their inputs (capital, land, labor, and entrepreneurship) to firms

simple circular flow model
an illustration of the continuous flow of goods, services, inputs, and payments between firms and households

Product Markets

Product markets are the markets for consumer goods and services. In the product market, households are buyers and firms are sellers. Households buy the goods and services that firms produce and sell. The payments from the households to the firms, for the purchases of goods and services, flow to the firms at the same time as goods and services flow to the households.

Factor Markets

Factor or input markets are where households sell the use of their inputs (capital, land, labor, and entrepreneurship) to firms. In the factor market, households are the sellers and firms are the buyers. Households receive money payments from firms as compensation for the labor, land, capital, and entrepreneurship needed to produce goods and services. These payments take the form of wages (salaries), rent, interest payments, and profit.

The Simple Circular Flow Model

The simple circular flow model is illustrated in Exhibit 1. In the top half of the exhibit, the product markets, households purchase goods and services that firms have produced. In the lower half of the exhibit, the factor (or input) markets, households sell the inputs that firms use to produce goods and services. Households receive income (wages, rent, interest, and profit) from firms for the inputs used in production (capital, land, labor, and entrepreneurship).

So we see that in the simple circular flow model, income flows from firms to households (factor markets), and spending flows from households to firms (product markets). The simple circular flow model shows how households and firms interact in product markets and factor markets and how the two markets are interrelated.

LAYLAND MASUDA/SHUTTERSTOCK.COM

A teacher's supply of labor generates personal income in the form of wages in the factor market, which she can use to buy automobiles, vacations, food, and other goods in the product market. Suppose she buys an automobile in the product market; the automobile dealer now has revenue to pay for his inputs in the factor market—wages to workers, payment for new cars to replenish his inventory, rent for his building, and so on.

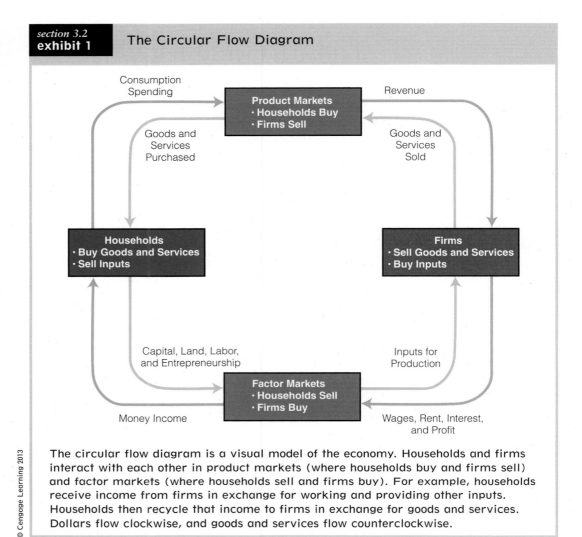

section 3.2
exhibit 1   The Circular Flow Diagram

The circular flow diagram is a visual model of the economy. Households and firms interact with each other in product markets (where households buy and firms sell) and factor markets (where households sell and firms buy). For example, households receive income from firms in exchange for working and providing other inputs. Households then recycle that income to firms in exchange for goods and services. Dollars flow clockwise, and goods and services flow counterclockwise.

Are households always buyers and firms always sellers?

⑦ SECTION QUIZ

1. In a circular flow diagram,

   a. goods and services flow in a clockwise direction.

   b. goods and services flow in a counterclockwise direction.

   c. product markets appear at the top of the diagram.

   d. factor markets appear at the left of the diagram.

   e. both (b) and (c) are true.

2. Which of the following is true?

   a. In the product markets, firms are buyers and households are sellers.

   b. In the factor markets, firms are sellers and households are buyers.

   c. Firms receive money payments from households for capital, land, labor, and entrepreneurship.

   d. All of the above are true.

   e. None of the above is true.

(*continued*)

ⓘ SECTION QUIZ (Cont.)

3. In the circular flow model,

   a. firms supply both products and resources.

   b. firms demand both products and resources.

   c. firms demand resources and supply products.

   d. firms supply resources and demand products.

4. The circular flow model

   a. traces the flow of goods and services among firms and households.

   b. traces the flow of payments among firms and households.

   c. includes both product markets and factor markets.

   d. All of the above are true.

1. Why does the circular flow of money move in the opposite direction from the flow of goods and services?

2. What is bought and sold in factor markets?

3. What is bought and sold in product markets?

Answers: 1. b 2. e 3. c 4. d

The Production Possibilities Curve

3.3

📂 What is a production possibilities curve?

📂 What are unemployed resources?

📂 What are underemployed resources?

📂 What is efficiency?

📂 What is the law of increasing opportunity costs?

production possibilities curve
the potential total output combinations of any two goods for an economy given the available factors of production and the available production technology that firms use to turn their inputs into outputs.

The Production Possibilities Curve

The economic concepts of scarcity, choice, and trade-offs can be illustrated visually by means of a simple graph called a production possibilities curve. The production possibilities curve represents the potential total output combinations of any two goods for an economy, given the available factors of production and the available production technology that firms use to turn their inputs into outputs. That is, it illustrates an economy's potential for allocating its limited resources in producing various combinations of goods, in a given time period.

The Production Possibilities Curve for Grades in Economics and History

What would the production possibilities curve look like if you were "producing" grades in two of your classes—say, economics and history? Exhibit 1 shows a hypothetical production possibilities curve for your expected grade in economics (on the vertical axis), and your expected grade in

Because Tia and Tamera only have so many hours a week to study, studying more for economics and less for history might hurt their grade in history, *ceteris paribus.* Life is full of trade-offs.

COURTESY OF ROBERT L. SEXTON

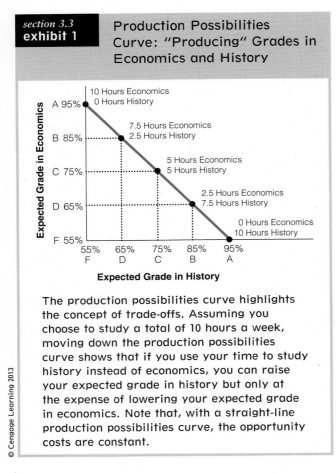

section 3.3
exhibit 1
Production Possibilities Curve: "Producing" Grades in Economics and History

The production possibilities curve highlights the concept of trade-offs. Assuming you choose to study a total of 10 hours a week, moving down the production possibilities curve shows that if you use your time to study history instead of economics, you can raise your expected grade in history but only at the expense of lowering your expected grade in economics. Note that, with a straight-line production possibilities curve, the opportunity costs are constant.

history (on the horizontal axis). Suppose you have a part-time restaurant job, so you choose to study 10 hours a week. You like both courses and are equally adept at studying for both.

We see in Exhibit 1 that the production possibilities curve is a straight line. For example, if you spend the full 10 hours studying economics, your expected grade in economics is 95 percent (an A), and your expected grade in history is 55 percent (an F). Of course, this outcome assumes you can study zero hours a week and still get a 55 percent average or study the full 10 hours a week and get a 95 percent average. Moving down the production possibilities curve, we see that as you spend more of your time studying history and less on economics, you can raise your expected grade in history but only at the expense of lowering your expected grade in economics. Specifically, moving down along the straight-line production possibilities curve, the trade-off is one lower percentage point in economics for one higher percentage point in history. That is, with a straight-line production possibilities curve, the opportunity costs are constant.

Of course, if you were to increase your overall study time, you would expect higher grades in both courses. But that would be on a different production possibilities curve. Along the production possibilities curve shown in Exhibit 1, we assume that technology and the number of study hours are given.

The Production Possibilities Curve for Food and Shelter

To illustrate the production possibilities curve more clearly, imagine living in an economy that produces just two goods, food and shelter. The fact that we have many goods in the real world makes actual decision making more complicated, but it does not alter the basic principles being illustrated. Each point on the production possibilities curve shown in Exhibit 2 represents the potential amounts of food and shelter that we can produce in a given period, with a given quantity and quality of resources in the economy available for production.

section 3.3
exhibit 2   Production Possibilities Curve: The Trade-Off between Food and Shelter

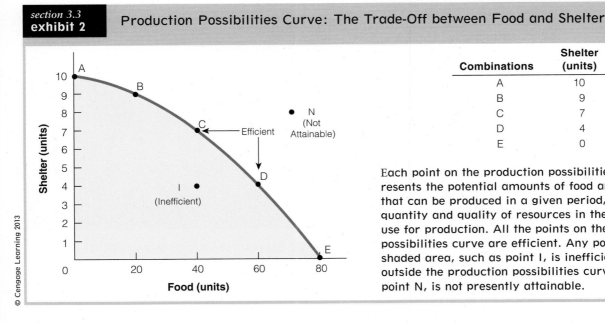

Combinations	Shelter (units)	Food (units)
A	10	0
B	9	20
C	7	40
D	4	60
E	0	80

Each point on the production possibilities curve represents the potential amounts of food and shelter that can be produced in a given period, with a given quantity and quality of resources in the economy to use for production. All the points on the production possibilities curve are efficient. Any point in the shaded area, such as point I, is inefficient. Any point outside the production possibilities curve, such as point N, is not presently attainable.

Notice in Exhibit 2 that if we devote all our resources to making shelters, we can produce 10 units of shelter but no food (point A). If, on the other hand, we choose to devote all our resources to producing food, we end up with 80 units of food but no shelters (point E).

In reality, nations rarely opt for production possibility A or E, preferring instead to produce a mixture of goods. For example, our fictional economy might produce 9 units of shelter and 20 units of food (point B) or perhaps 7 units of shelter and 40 units of food (point C). Still other combinations along the curve, such as point D, are possible.

Off the Production Possibilities Curve

The economy cannot operate at point N (not attainable) during the given period because not enough resources are currently available to produce that level of output. However, it is possible the economy can operate inside the production possibilities curve, at point I (inefficient). If the economy is operating at point I, or any other point inside the production possibilities curve, it is not at full capacity and is operating inefficiently; perhaps because of widespread unemployment. In short, the economy is not using all its scarce resources efficiently; as a result, actual output is less than potential output.

When you are inside the production possibilities curve, is it just because there are unemployed labor resources?

---

use **what you've learned**   # The Production Possibilities Curve

Q Imagine that you are the overseer on a small island that only produces two goods, cattle and wheat. About a quarter of the land is not fertile enough for growing wheat, so cattle graze on it. What would happen if you tried to produce more and more wheat, extending your planting even to the less fertile soil?

A Under the law of increasing opportunity cost, as you plant more and more of your acreage in wheat, you would move into some of the rocky, less fertile land, and, consequently, wheat yields on the additional acreage would fall. If you try to plant the entire island with wheat, you would find that some of the rocky, less fertile acreage would yield virtually no extra wheat. It would, however, have been great for cattle grazing—a large loss. Thus, the opportunity cost of using that marginal land for wheat rather than cattle grazing would be high. The law of increasing

opportunity cost occurs because resources are not homogeneous (identical) and are not equally adaptable for producing cattle and wheat; some acres are more suitable for cattle grazing, while others are more suitable for wheat growing. This relationship is shown in Exhibit 3, where the vertical lines represent the opportunity cost of growing 10 more bushels of wheat in terms of cattle production sacrificed. You can see that as wheat production increases, the opportunity cost in terms of lost cattle production rises.

section 3.3 exhibit 3   **Opportunity Costs for Cattle and Wheat**

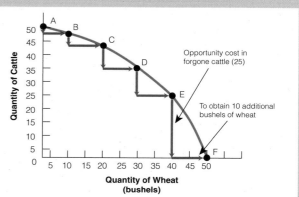

Opportunity cost in forgone cattle (25)

To obtain 10 additional bushels of wheat

Quantity of Wheat (bushels)

The opportunity cost of each 10 bushels of wheat in terms of forgone cattle is measured by the vertical distances. Moving from point A to point F, the opportunity cost of wheat in terms of forgone cattle rises.

Why can't a point inside the production possibilities curve be best?

When is an economy efficient?

Inefficiency and Efficiency

Suppose for some reason employment is widespread or resources are not being put to their best uses. The economy would then be operating at a point inside the production possibilities curve, such as I in Exhibit 2, where the economy is operating inefficiently. At point I, 4 units of shelter and 40 units of food are being produced. By putting unemployed resources to work or by putting already employed resources to better uses, we could expand the output of shelter by 3 units (moving to point C) without giving up any units of food. Alternatively, we could boost food output by 20 units (moving to point D) without reducing shelter output. We could even get more of both food and shelter by moving to a point on the curve between C and D. Increasing or improving the utilization of resources, then, can lead to greater output of all goods. You may recall from Chapter 2, an efficient use of our resources means that more of everything we want can be available for our use. Thus, *efficiency* requires society to use its resources to the fullest extent—getting the most from our scarce resources and wasting none. If resources are being used efficiently—that is, at some point along a production possibilities curve—then more of one good or service requires the sacrifice of another good or service.

Economists say that the economy is efficient when there are no opportunities for improvement left. This is the case when the economy is on the production possibilities curve. Notice that once the efficient points on the production possibilities curve are reached, there is no way to produce more of one good without producing less of the other. This is exactly the point we made in the last chapter: people face scarcity and costly trade-offs. Efficiency does not tell us which point along the production possibilities curve is *best,* but it does tell us that points inside the curve cannot be best, because some resources are wasted.

The Law of Increasing Opportunity Cost

As in Exhibit 2, the production possibilities curve in Exhibit 4 is not a straight line like that in Exhibit 1. It is concave from below (that is, bowed outward from the origin). Looking at Exhibit 4, you can see that at low food output, an increase in the amount of food produced will lead to only a small reduction in the number of units of shelter produced. For example, increasing food output from 0 to 20 (moving from point A to point B on the curve) requires the use of resources capable of producing 1 unit of shelter. In other words, for the first 20 units of food, 1 unit of shelter must be given up. When food output is higher, however, more units of shelter must be given up when switching additional resources from the production of shelter to food. Moving from point D to point E, for example, an increase in food output of 20 (from 60 to 80) reduces the production of shelters from 4 to 0. At this point, then, the cost of those 20 additional units of food is 4 units of shelter, considerably more than the 1 unit of shelter required in the earlier scenario. This difference shows us that opportunity costs do not remain constant but rise because more units of food and fewer units of shelter are produced. It is this **increasing opportunity cost**, then, that is represented by the bowed production possibilities curve.

increasing opportunity cost
the opportunity cost of producing additional units of a good rises as society produces more of that good

What Is the Reason for the Law of Increasing Opportunity Cost?

The basic reason for the increasing opportunity cost is that some resources and skills cannot be easily adapted from their current uses to alternative uses. And, the more you produce of one good, the more you are forced to employ inputs that are relatively more suitable for producing other goods. For example, at low levels of food output, additional increases in food output can be obtained easily by switching relatively low skilled carpenters from making shelters to producing food. However, to get even more food output, workers who are less well suited or appropriate for producing food (i.e., they are better adapted to making shelters) must be released from shelter making to increase food output. For example, a skilled carpenter may be an expert at making shelters but a very bad farmer because he lacks

section 3.3 exhibit 4	Increasing Opportunity Cost and the Production Possibilities Curve

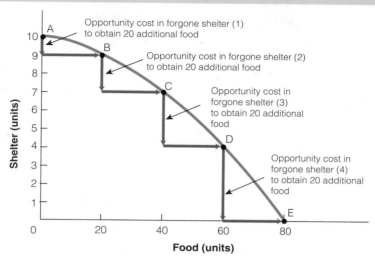

The production possibilities curve also illustrates the opportunity cost of producing more of a given product. For example, if we are to increase food output from 40 units to 60 units (moving from point C to point D), we must produce 3 fewer units of shelter. The opportunity cost of those 20 additional units of food is the 3 units of shelter we must forgo. We can see that, moving down the curve from A to E, each additional 20 units of food costs society more and more shelter—the law of increasing opportunity cost.

the training and skills necessary in that occupation. So using the skilled carpenter to farm results in a relatively greater opportunity cost than using the unskilled carpenter to farm. The production of additional units of food becomes increasingly costly as progressively lower-skilled farmers (but good carpenters) convert to farming.

In short, resources tend to be specialized. As a result, we lose some of their productivity when we transfer those resources from producing what they are relatively good at to producing something they are relatively bad at.

ⓘ SECTION QUIZ

1. A point beyond the boundary of an economy's production possibilities curve is
   a. efficient.
   b. inefficient.
   c. attainable.
   d. unattainable.
   e. both attainable and efficient.

2. Which of the following is consistent with the implications of the production possibilities curve?
   a. If the resources in an economy are being used efficiently, scarcity will not be a problem.
   b. If the resources in an economy are being used efficiently, more of one good can be produced only if less of another good is produced.
   c. Producing more of any one good will require smaller and smaller sacrifices of other goods as more of that good is being produced in an economy.
   d. An economy will automatically attain that level of output at which all of its resources are fully employed.
   e. Both (b) and (c) are consistent with the implications of the production possibilities curve.

(*continued*)

⊘ SECTION QUIZ (Cont.)

3. Consider a production possibilities curve for an economy producing bicycles and video game players. It is possible to increase the production of bicycles without sacrificing video game players if

   a. the production possibilities curve shifts outward due to technological progress.

   b. the production possibilities curve shifts outward due to increased immigration (which enlarges the labor force).

   c. the economy moves from a point inside the production possibilities curve to a point on the curve.

   d. any of the above occurs.

   e. either (a) or (b), but not (c), occurs.

4. What determines the position and shape of a society's production possibilities curve?

   a. the physical resources of that society

   b. the skills of the workforce

   c. the level of technology of the society

   d. the number of factories available to the society

   e. all of the above

5. Which of the following is the most accurate statement about a production possibilities curve?

   a. An economy can produce at any point inside or outside its production possibilities curve.

   b. An economy can produce only on its production possibilities curve.

   c. An economy can produce at any point on or inside its production possibilities curve, but not outside the curve.

   d. An economy can produce at any point inside its production possibilities curve, but not on or outside the curve.

6. A _____ production possibilities curve illustrates _____ costs of production.

   a. straight-line; constant

   b. straight-line; increasing

   c. bowed-outward; constant

   d. bowed-outward; increasing

   e. Both (a) and (d) are true.

7. Which statement(s) is/are true about the law of increasing opportunity cost?

   a. Some resources and skills cannot be easily adapted from their current uses to alternative uses.

   b. The more you produce of one good, the more you are forced to employ inputs that are relatively more suitable for producing other goods.

   c. Resources tend to be specialized so we lose some of their productivity when we transfer those resources from producing what they are relatively good at to producing something at which they are relatively bad.

   d. All of the above are true.

---

1. What does a production possibilities curve illustrate?

2. How are opportunity costs shown by the production possibilities curve?

3. Why do the opportunity costs of added production increase with output?

4. How does the production possibilities curve illustrate increasing opportunity costs?

5. Why are we concerned with widespread amounts of unemployed or underemployed resources in a society?

6. What do we mean by efficiency, and how is it related to underemployment of resources?

7. How are efficiency and inefficiency illustrated by a production possibilities curve?

8. Will a country that makes being unemployed illegal be more productive than one that does not? Why or why not?

9. If a 68-year-old worker in the United States chooses not to work at all, does that mean that the United States is functioning inside its production possibilities curve? Why or why not?

Answers: 1. d 2. b 3. d 4. e 5. c 6. e 7. d

Economic Growth and the Production Possibilities Curve

3.4

📁 How much should we sacrifice today to get more in the future?

📁 How do we show economic growth on the production possibilities curve?

Generating Economic Growth

How have some nations been able to rapidly expand their outputs of goods and services over time, while others have been unable to increase their standards of living at all?

The economy can only grow with qualitative or quantitative changes in the factors of production—land, labor, capital, and entrepreneurship. Advancement in technology, improvements in labor productivity, or new sources of natural resources (such as previously undiscovered oil) could lead to outward shifts of the production possibilities curve.

In terms of the production possibilities curve, an outward shift in the possible combinations of goods and services produced leads to economic growth, as seen in Exhibit 1. With growth comes the possibility of having more of both goods than was previously available. Suppose we were producing at point C (7 units of shelter, 40 units of food) on our original production possibilities curve. Additional resources and/or new methods of using them (technological progress) can lead to new production possibilities, creating the potential for more of all goods (or more of some with no less of others). These increases will push the production possibilities curve outward. For example, if we invest in human capital by training the workers making the shelters, it will increase the productivity of those workers. As a result, they will produce more units of shelter. Ultimately, then, we will use fewer resources to make shelters, freeing them to be used for farming, which will result in more units of food. Notice that at point F (future) on the new curve, we can produce 9 units of shelter and 70 units of food, more of both goods than we previously could produce, at point C.

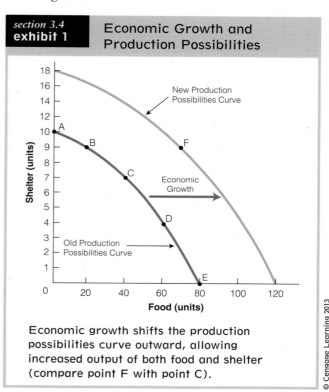

section 3.4 exhibit 1 Economic Growth and Production Possibilities

Economic growth shifts the production possibilities curve outward, allowing increased output of both food and shelter (compare point F with point C).

© Cengage Learning 2013

Growth Does Not Eliminate Scarcity

With all of this discussion of growth, it is important to remember that growth, or increases in a society's output, does not make scarcity disappear. When output grows more rapidly than population, people are better off. But they still face trade-offs; at any point along the production possibilities curve, to get more of one thing, you must give up something else. There are no free lunches on the production possibilities curve.

Can economic growth eliminate the problem of scarcity?

Capital Goods versus Consumption Goods

Economies that choose to invest more of their resources for the future will grow faster than those that don't. To generate economic growth, a society must produce fewer consumer goods—video games, DVD players, cell phones, cars, vacations, and so on—in the present and produce more capital goods—machines, factories, tools, education, and the like. The society that devotes a larger share of its productive capacity to capital goods than to

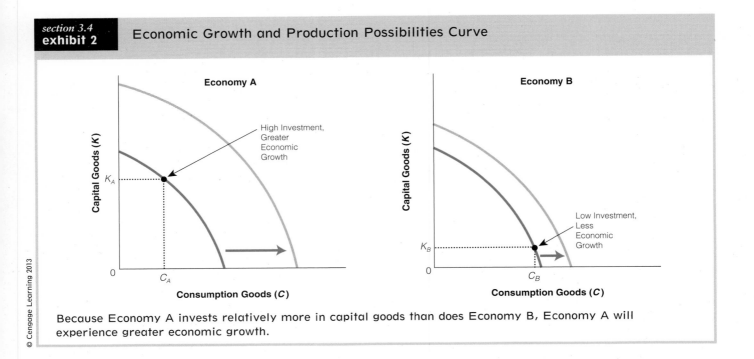

section 3.4 exhibit 2   Economic Growth and Production Possibilities Curve

Because Economy A invests relatively more in capital goods than does Economy B, Economy A will experience greater economic growth.

consumer goods will experience greater economic growth. It must sacrifice some present consumption of consumer goods and services to experience growth in the future. Why? Investing in capital goods, such as computers and other new technological equipment, as well as upgrading skills and knowledge, expands the ability to produce in the future. It shifts the economy's production possibilities curve outward, increasing the future production capacity of the economy. That is, the economy that invests more now (consumes less now) will be able to produce, and therefore consume, more in the future. In Exhibit 2, we see that Economy A invests more in capital goods than Economy B. Consequently, Economy A's production possibilities curve shifts outward further than does Economy B's over time.

section 3.4 exhibit 3   The Effects of a Technological Change on the Production Possibilities Curve

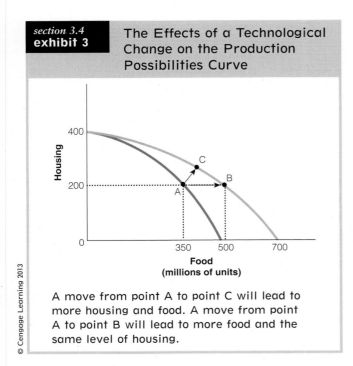

A move from point A to point C will lead to more housing and food. A move from point A to point B will lead to more food and the same level of housing.

The Effects of a Technological Change on the Production Possibilities Curve

In Exhibit 3, we see that a technological advance does not have to impact all sectors of the economy equally. There is a technological advance in food production but not in housing production. The technological advance in agriculture causes the production possibilities curve to extend out further on the horizontal axis, which measures food production. We can move to any point on the new production possibilities curve. For example, we could move from point A on the original production possibilities curve to point B on the new production possibilities curve. This would lead to 150 more units of food and the same amount of housing—200 units. Or, we could move from point A to point C, which would allow us to produce more units of both food and housing. How do we produce more housing, when the technological advance occurred in agriculture? The answer is that the technological advance in agriculture allows us to produce more from a given quantity of resources. That is, it allows us to shift some of our resources out of agriculture into housing. This is actually an ongoing story in U.S. economic history. In colonial days, about 90 percent of the population made a living in agriculture. Today it is less than 3 percent.

How can we produce more of two goods when there is a technology advance in only one of the goods?

⑦ SECTION QUIZ

1. Which of the following is most likely to shift the production possibilities curve outward?

   a. an increase in unemployment

   b. a decrease in the stock of physical or human capital

   c. a decrease in the labor force

   d. a technological advance

2. Suppose Country A produces few consumption goods and many investment goods while Country B produces few investment goods and many consumption goods. Other things being equal, you would expect

   a. per capita income to grow more rapidly in Country B.

   b. population to grow faster in Country B.

   c. the production possibilities curve for Country A to shift out more rapidly than that of Country B.

   d. that if both countries started with identical production possibilities curves, in 20 years, people in Country B will be able to produce more consumer goods than people in Country A can.

   e. that both (c) and (d) are true.

3. A virulent disease spreads throughout the population of an economy, causing death and disability. This event can be portrayed as

   a. a movement from a point on the production possibilities curve to a point inside the curve.

   b. a movement from a point on the production possibilities curve to the northeast.

   c. a movement along the production possibilities curve to the southeast.

   d. an outward shift of the production possibilities curve.

   e. an inward shift of the production possibilities curve.

1. What is the essential question behind issues of economic growth?

2. What is the connection between sacrifices and economic growth?

3. How is economic growth shown in terms of production possibilities curves?

4. Why doesn't economic growth eliminate scarcity?

5. If people reduced their saving (thus reducing the funds available for investment), what would that change do to society's production possibilities curve over time?

Answers: 1. d 2. c 3. e

Interactive Summary

Fill in the blanks:

1. Because of scarcity, certain economic questions must be answered regardless of the level of affluence of the society or its political structure. Three fundamental questions that inevitably must be faced in a world of scarcity are (1) _____ will be produced? (2) _____ the goods and services be produced? (3) _____ the goods and services produced?

2. Market economies largely rely on a(n) _____ decision-making process, where literally millions of individual producers and consumers of goods and services determine what will be produced.

3. Most countries, including the United States, have _____ economies, in which the government and private sector determine the allocation of resources.

4. The _____ -cost method is the most appropriate method for producing a given product.

5. Methods of production used where capital is relatively scarce will be _____, and methods of production used where labor is relatively scarce will be _____.

6. In a market economy, the amount of goods and services one is able to obtain depends on one's _____, which depends on the quality and quantity of the scarce _____ he or she controls.

7. The markets where households are buyers and firms are sellers of goods and services are called _____ markets.

8. The markets where households sell the use of their _____ (capital, land, labor, and entrepreneurship) to _____ are called _____ or _____ markets.

9. The simple _____ model shows the continuous flow of goods, services, inputs, and payments through the _____ and _____ markets among households and _____.

10. A(n) _____ curve represents the potential total output combinations of any two goods for an economy.

11. On a production possibilities curve, we assume that the economy has a given quantity and quality of _____ and _____ available to use for production.

12. On a straight-line production possibilities curve, the _____ are constant.

13. If an economy is operating _____ its production possibilities curve, it is not at full capacity and is operating _____. Such an economy's actual output is less than _____ output.

14. By putting _____ resources to work or by putting already employed resources to _____ uses, we could expand output.

15. _____ requires society to use its resources to the fullest extent—getting the _____ we can out of our scarce resources.

16. If the production possibilities curve is concave from below (that is, bowed outward from the origin), it reflects _____ opportunity costs of producing additional amounts of a good.

17. On a bowed production possibilities curve (concave to the origin), the opportunity costs of producing additional units of a good rises as society produces more of that good. This relationship is called the law of _____.

18. Resources tend to be specialized, so we lose some of their productivity when we transfer those resources from what they are relatively _____ at producing to something they are relatively _____ at producing.

19. To generate economic growth, a society must produce _____ consumer goods and _____ capital goods in the present.

20. Advancements in _____, improvements in _____, or new _____ could all lead to outward shifts of the production possibilities curve.

21. Increases in a society's output do not make _____ disappear. Even when output has grown more rapidly than population so that people are made better off, they still face _____.

22. The production possibilities curve can be used to illustrate the economic concepts of _____ (resource combinations outside the production possibilities curve are unattainable), _____ (selecting among the alternative bundles available along the production possibilities curve), _____ (how much of one good you give up to get another unit of the second good as you move along the production possibilities curve), _____ (being on the production possibilities curve rather than inside it), and _____ (shifting the production possibilities curve outward).

Key Terms and Concepts

consumer sovereignty 75
command economy 75
market economy 75
mixed economy 75

labor intensive 76
capital intensive 76
product markets 79
factor (or input) markets 79

simple circular flow model 79
production possibilities curve 81
increasing opportunity cost 84

Section Quiz Answers

3.1 The Three Economic Questions Every Society Faces

1. Why does scarcity force us to decide what to produce?

Because our wants exceed the amount of goods and services that can be produced from our limited resources, it must be decided which wants should have priority over others.

2. How is a command economy different from a market economy?

A command economy makes decisions about what and how much to produce centrally by members of a planning board or organization. A market economy makes those decisions as the result of decentralized decision making by individual producers and consumers, coordinated by their offers to buy and sell on markets.

3. How does consumer sovereignty determine production decisions in a market economy?

Consumer sovereignty determines production decisions in a market economy because producers make what they believe consumers will "vote" for by being willing to pay for them.

4. Do you think that what and how much an economy produces depends on who will get the goods and services produced in that economy? Why or why not?

Who will get the goods produced in an economy affects the incentives of the producers. The less a producer will benefit from increased production, the smaller are incentives to increase production, and the smaller will be total output in an economy.

5. Why do consumers have to "vote" for a product with their dollars for it to be a success?

In the market sector, products can be profitable only if they attract dollar votes from consumers.

6. Why must we choose among multiple ways of producing the goods and services we want?

We must choose among multiple ways of producing the goods and services we want because goods can generally be produced in several ways, using different combinations of resources.

7. Why might production be labor intensive in one economy but be capital intensive in another?

Production will tend to be labor intensive where labor is relatively plentiful, and therefore relatively less expensive; it will tend to be capital intensive where capital is relatively plentiful, and therefore relatively less expensive. When the manner of production is different in different situations because factors of production have different relative prices, each of those methods will be more efficient where they are used.

8. If a tourist from the United States on an overseas trip notices that other countries don't produce crops "like they do back home," would he be right to conclude that farmers in the other countries produce crops less efficiently than U.S. farmers?

No. The different ways of farming in different areas reflect the different relative scarcities of land, labor, and capital they face. Factors of production that are relatively scarce in an economy are also relatively costly there as a result. Producers there economize on the use of those more costly resources by using more of relatively less scarce, and less costly, resources instead. For example, where land is scarce, it is intensively cultivated with relatively cheaper (less scarce) labor and capital, but where capital is scarce, relatively cheaper (less scarce) land and labor are substituted for capital.

9. In what way does scarcity determine income?

Relative scarcity determines the market values of the scarce resources people offer to others in exchange for income.

10. What are the most important functions of the market system?

They transmit information through price signals, they provide incentives, and they distribute income.

3.2   The Circular Flow Model

1. Why does the circular flow of money move in the opposite direction from the flow of goods and services?

The circular flow of money moves in the opposite direction from the flow of goods and services because the money flows are the payments made in exchange for the goods and services.

2. What is bought and sold in factor markets?

The factors of production—capital, land, labor, and entrepreneurship—are sold in factor, or input, markets.

3. What is bought and sold in product markets?

Consumer and investment goods and services are sold in product markets.

3.3   The Production Possibilities Curve

1. What does a production possibilities curve illustrate?

The production possibilities curve illustrates the potential output combinations of two goods in an economy operating at full capacity, given the inputs and technology available to the economy.

2. How are opportunity costs shown by the production possibilities curve?

Opportunity cost—the forgone output of one good necessary to increase output of another good—is illustrated by the slope, or trade-off, between the two goods at a given point on the production possibilities curve.

3. Why do the opportunity costs of added production increase with output?

Opportunity costs of added production increase with output because some resources cannot be easily adapted from their current uses to alternative uses. At first, easily adaptable resources can be switched to producing more of a good. But once those easily adapted resources have been switched, producing further output requires the use of resources less well adapted to expanding that output, raising the opportunity cost of output.

4. How does the production possibilities curve illustrate increasing opportunity costs?

Increasing opportunity costs are illustrated by a bowed (concave from below) production possibilities curve. It shows that initial units of one good can be produced by giving up little of another good, but progressive increases in output will require greater and greater sacrifices of the other good.

5. Why are we concerned with widespread amounts of unemployed or underemployed resources in a society?

We are concerned with widespread amounts of unemployed or underemployed resources in a society because, if we could reduce the extent of unemployed or underemployed resources, people could have more scarce goods and services available for their use.

6. What do we mean by *efficiency,* and how is it related to underemployment of resources?

Efficiency means getting the most we can out of our scarce resources. Underemployment of resources means a society is not getting the most it can out of these resources, either because they are not fully employed or because they are not matched to the uses best suited to them.

7. How are efficiency and inefficiency illustrated by a production possibilities curve?

Efficient combinations of outputs are illustrated by points on the production possibilities curve, along which more of one good can be produced only if less of some other good is also produced. Inefficient combinations of outputs are illustrated by points inside the production possibilities curve, because more of both goods could then be produced with the resources available to the economy.

8. Will a country that makes being unemployed illegal be more productive than one that does not? Why or why not?

A more productive economy is one that makes the best use of those who wish to work. Making unemployment illegal (as was true in the old USSR) does not eliminate underemployment, nor does it guarantee that people and other resources are employed where they are most productive (especially because it is more difficult to search for a better job when you are working than when you are not working).

9. **If a 68-year-old worker in the United States chooses not to work at all, does that mean that the United States is functioning inside its production possibilities curve? Why or why not?**

Individuals who choose retirement rather than work must consider themselves better off not working, when all the relevant considerations are taken into account. They are therefore as fully employed, given their circumstances, as they would like to be, and so the choice does not imply that the United States would be inside its production possibilities curve as a result. However, if such workers became more willing to work, that would shift the U.S. production possibilities curve outward.

3.4   Economic Growth and the Production Possibilities Curve

1. **What is the essential question behind issues of economic growth?**

The essential question behind issues of economic growth is: How much are we willing to give up today to get more in the future?

2. **What is the connection between sacrifices and economic growth?**

The more current consumption is sacrificed in an economy, the larger the fraction of its current resources it can devote to producing investment goods, which will increase its rate of economic growth.

3. **How is economic growth shown in terms of production possibilities curves?**

Economic growth—the expansion of what an economy can produce—is shown as an outward shift in the production possibilities curve, with formerly unattainable output combinations now made possible.

4. **Why doesn't economic growth eliminate scarcity?**

Economic growth doesn't eliminate scarcity because people's wants still exceed what they are capable of producing, so that trade-offs among scarce goods must still be made.

5. **If people reduced their saving (thus reducing the funds available for investment), what would that change do to society's production possibilities curve over time?**

The less people save, the slower the capital stock of the economy will grow through new investment (because saving is the source of the funds for investment), and so the slower the production possibilities curve would shift out over time.

Problems

1. What are the three basic economic questions? How are decisions made differently in a market economy than in planned economies?

2. Recently the American Film Institute selected *Citizen Kane* as the best movie of all time. *Citizen Kane* is a fictional psychological biography of one of the most powerful newspaper publishers in history, William Randolph Hearst. *Avatar* has made the most money of any film in history. Unlike *Avatar*, *Citizen Kane* was not a box office success. Do you think Hollywood will make more movies like *Avatar* or like *Citizen Kane?* Why?

3. As women's wages and employment opportunities have expanded over the past 50 years, Americans have purchased more and more labor-saving home appliances like automatic washers and dryers, dishwashers, and microwave ovens. Do you think these phenomena are related? Could higher wages and better job opportunities lead to a more capital-intensive way of performing household chores? Explain.

4. Identify where the appropriate entries go in the circular flow diagram.

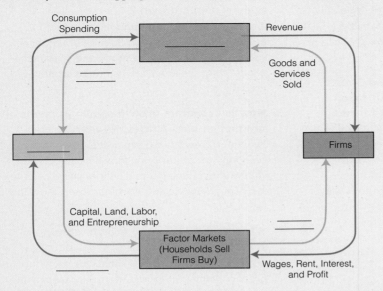

5. Identify whether each of the following transactions takes place in the factor market or the product market.
   a. Billy buys a sofa from Home Time Furniture for his new home.
   b. Home Time Furniture pays its manager her weekly salary.
   c. The manager buys dinner at Billy's Café.
   e. After he pays all of his employees their wages and pays his other bills, the owner of Billy's Café takes his profit.

6. Given the following production possibilities curve:

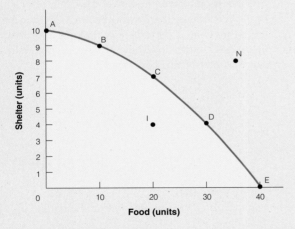

   a. Does this production possibilities curve show increasing opportunity costs? Explain.
   b. What is the opportunity cost of moving from point I to point D? Explain.
   c. What is the opportunity cost of moving from point C to point B?
   d. Which of points A–E is the most efficient? Explain.

7. During wartime, countries shift production from civilian goods, like automobiles and clothing, to military goods, like tanks and military uniforms. When the United States entered World War I in April 1917, for example, the federal government created the War Industries Board and charged it with determining production priorities and converting plants to meet war needs. In the following year, automobile production fell 43 percent as output of military vehicles soared. When the war ended, 19 months later, in November 1918, the government cancelled $2.5 billion in military contracts and the nation resumed normal production. Assuming that in 1917 the United States was at point A on the production possibilities curves shown, show what happened between April 1917 and November 1918. Show what happened once the war ended.

8. How would the following events be shown using a production possibilities curve for shelter and food?
   a. The economy is experiencing double-digit unemployment.
   b. Economic growth is increasing at more than 5 percent per year.
   c. Society decides it wants less shelter and more food.
   d. Society decides it wants more shelter and less food.

9. In *A Bend in the River,* Nobel Prize winner V. S. Naipaul describes an underdeveloped country in which the government's constantly changing tax policies and vague laws regarding property ownership cause entrepreneurs to become demoralized and unresponsive to economic opportunities. Could this be a case of idle or unemployed entrepreneurs? How can tax laws and rules governing property affect entrepreneurs' willingness to start new businesses or improve existing enterprises?

10. Using the following table, answer the questions:

	Combinations				
	A	**B**	**C**	**D**	**E**
Guns	1	2	3	4	5
Butter	20	18	14	8	0

   a. What are the assumptions for a given production possibilities curve?
   b. What is the opportunity cost of one gun when moving from point B to point C? When moving from point D to point E?
   c. Do these combinations demonstrate constant or increasing opportunity costs?

11. Economy A produces more capital goods and fewer consumer goods than Economy B. Which economy will grow more rapidly? Draw two production possibilities curves, one for Economy A and one for Economy B. Demonstrate graphically how one economy can grow more rapidly than the other.

12. Why one nation experiences economic growth and another doesn't is a question that has intrigued economists since Adam Smith wrote *An Inquiry into the Nature and Causes of the Wealth of Nations* in 1776. Explain why each of the following would limit economic growth.
   a. The politically connected elite secure a large share of a country's output and put the proceeds in Swiss banks.
   b. A country has a very low output per person.
   c. The national philosophy is to live for the moment and forget about tomorrow.
   d. The government closes all of the schools so more people will be available for work.
   e. The country fears military invasion and spends half of its income on military goods.

13. How does education add to a nation's capital stock?

14. A politician running for U.S. president promises to build new schools and new space stations during the next four years without sacrificing any other goods and services. Using a production possibilities curve between schools and space stations, explain under what conditions the politician would be able to keep his promise.

© SIMON McCOMB/STONE/GETTY IMAGES, INC.

part 2

Supply and Demand

Demand, Supply, and Market Equilibrium

The National Football League posted attendance of roughly 74,000 for Super Bowl XLIV in Miami. Just weeks before the game, however, tickets were selling on secondary ticket exchange sites such as StubHub and TicketMaster for anywhere from $1,200 to $3,500—well above face value. What does this tell us about the prices that fans are willing to pay and the number of tickets they are willing to buy? Why does the NFL set its ticket prices so low? Do scalpers "rip off" innocent buyers? A further look at supply and demand will help us answer these and many other questions.

According to Thomas Carlyle, a nineteenth-century philosopher, "Teach a parrot the term 'supply and demand' and you've got an economist." Unfortunately, economics is more complicated than that. However, if Carlyle was hinting at the importance of supply and demand, he was right on target. Supply and demand is without a doubt the most powerful tool in the economist's toolbox. It can help explain much of what goes on in the world and help predict what will happen tomorrow. In this chapter, we will learn about the law of demand and the law of supply and the factors that can change supply and demand.

We then bring market supply and market demand together to determine equilibrium price and quantity. We also learn how markets with many buyers and sellers adjust to temporary shortages and surpluses.

Do markets have to be physical places?

market
the process of buyers and sellers exchanging goods and services

Markets   4.1

📂 What is a market?   📂 Why is it so difficult to define a market?

Defining a Market

Although we usually think of a market as a place where some sort of exchange occurs, a market is not really a place at all. A **market** is the process of buyers and sellers exchanging goods and services. Supermarkets, the New York Stock Exchange, drug stores, roadside stands, garage sales, Internet stores, and restaurants are all markets.

Every market is different. That is, the conditions under which the exchange between buyers and sellers takes place can vary. These differences make it difficult to precisely define a market. After all, an incredible variety of exchange arrangements exist in the real world—organized securities markets, wholesale auction markets, foreign exchange markets, real estate markets, labor markets, and so forth.

Goods being priced and traded in various ways at various locations by various kinds of buyers and sellers further compound the problem of defining a market. For some goods, such as housing, markets are numerous but limited to a geographic area. Homes in Santa Barbara, California, for example (about 100 miles from downtown Los Angeles), do not compete directly with homes in Los Angeles. Why? Because people who work in Los Angeles will generally look for homes within commuting distance. Even within cities, separate markets for homes are differentiated by amenities such as more living space, newer construction, larger lots, and better schools.

In a similar manner, markets are numerous but geographically limited for a good such as cement. Because transportation costs are so high relative to the selling price, the good is not shipped any substantial distance, and buyers are usually in contact only with local producers. Price and output are thus determined in a number of small markets. In other markets, such as those for gold or automobiles, markets are global. The important point is not what a market looks like, but what it does—it facilitates trade.

The stock market involves many buyers and sellers; and profit statements and stock prices are readily available. New information is quickly understood by buyers and sellers and is incorporated into the price of the stock. When people expect a company to do better in the future, the price of the stock rises; when people expect the company to do poorly in the future, the price of the stock falls.

ECS
economic content standards
Prices send signals and provide incentives to buyers and sellers. When supply or demand changes, market prices adjust, affecting incentives. Understanding the role of prices as signals and incentives helps people anticipate market opportunities and make better choices as producers and consumers.

Buyers and Sellers

The roles of buyers and sellers in markets are important. Buyers, as a group, determine the demand side of the market. Buyers include the consumers who purchase the goods and

eBay is an Internet auction company that brings together millions of buyers and sellers from all over the world. The gains from these mutually beneficial exchanges are large. Craigslist also uses the power of the Internet to connect many buyers and sellers in local markets.

competitive market
a market where the many buyers and sellers have little market power—each buyer's or seller's effect on market price is negligible

services and the firms that buy inputs—labor, capital, and raw materials. Sellers, as a group, determine the supply side of the market. Sellers include the firms that produce and sell goods and services and the resource owners who sell their inputs to firms—workers who "sell" their labor and resource owners who sell raw materials and capital. The interaction of buyers and sellers determines market prices and outputs—through the forces of supply and demand.

In the next few chapters, we focus on how supply and demand work in a **competitive market**. A competitive market is one in which a number of buyers and sellers are offering similar products, and no single buyer or seller can influence the market price. That is, buyers and sellers have little market power. Because many markets contain a high degree of competitiveness, the lessons of supply and demand can be applied to many different types of problems.

The supply and demand model is particularly useful in markets like agriculture, finance, labor, construction, services, wholesale, and retail.

In short, a model is only as good as it explains and predicts. The model of supply and demand is very good at predicting changes in prices and quantities in many markets large and small.

? SECTION QUIZ

1. Which of the following is a market?

   a. a garage sale

   b. a restaurant

   c. the New York Stock Exchange

   d. an eBay auction

   e. all of the above

2. In a competitive market,

   a. there are a number of buyers and sellers.

   b. no single buyer or seller can appreciably affect the market price.

   c. sellers offer similar products.

   d. all of the above are true.

3. Which of the following is true?

   a. Differences in the conditions under which the exchange between buyers and sellers occurs make it difficult to precisely define a market.

   b. All markets are effectively global in scope.

   c. All markets are effectively local in scope.

   d. Both (a) and (b) are true.

4. Buyers determine the _____ side of the market; sellers determine the _____ side of the market.

   a. demand; demand

   b. demand; supply

   c. supply; demand

   d. supply; supply

(*continued*)

Demand 4.2

📂 What is the law of demand? 📂 What is a market demand curve?

📂 What is an individual demand curve?

The Law of Demand

Sometimes observed behavior is so pervasive it is called a law—the law of demand, for example. According to the **law of demand**, the quantity of a good or service demanded varies inversely (negatively) with its price, *ceteris paribus*. More directly, the law of demand says that, other things being equal, when the price (P) of a good or service falls, the quantity demanded (Q_D) increases. Conversely, if the price of a good or service rises, the quantity demanded decreases.

$$P \uparrow \Rightarrow Q_D \downarrow \text{ and } P \downarrow \Rightarrow Q_D \uparrow$$

Why Is There a Negative Relationship between Price and the Quantity Demanded?

The law of demand describes a negative (inverse) relationship between price and quantity demanded. When price goes up, the quantity demanded goes down, and vice versa. But why is this so? There are several reasons. Observed behavior tells us that consumers will buy more goods and services at lower prices than at higher prices. Businesses would not put items on sale if they did not think they could sell more at lower prices—that is, at a lower price, there is a greater quantity demanded.

Another reason for the negative relationship is what economists call **diminishing marginal utility**. In a given time period, a buyer will receive less satisfaction from each successive unit of a good consumed. For example, a second ice cream cone will yield less satisfaction than the first, a third will yield less satisfaction than the second, and so on.

ECS

economic content standards

Higher prices for a good or service provide the incentives for buyers to purchase less. Lower prices for goods or services provide incentives to purchase more of the good or service.

law of demand
the quantity of a good or service demanded varies inversely (negatively) with its price, *ceteris paribus*

diminishing marginal utility
the concept that in a given time period, an individual will receive less satisfaction from each successive unit of a good consumed

It follows from diminishing marginal utility that if people derive decreasing amounts of satisfaction from successive units, consumers will buy additional units only if the price is reduced.

Finally, there are the substitution and income effects of a price change. For example, if the price of pizza increases, the quantity of pizza demanded will fall because some consumers might switch from of pizza to hamburgers, tacos, burritos, submarine sandwiches or other foods that substitute for pizza. This is called the substitution effect of a price change. In addition, an increase in the price of pizza will reduce the quantity of pizza demanded because it reduces a buyer's purchasing power. Purchasing power is the quantity of goods a consumer can buy with a fixed income. So when the price of pizza rises, the decreased purchasing power of the consumer's income will usually lead the consumer to buy less pizza. Alternatively, when the price of a pizza falls, the increased purchasing power of the consumer's income will usually lead the consumer to buy a greater quantity of pizza. This is called the income effect of a price change.

Individual Demand

An Individual Demand Schedule

The individual demand schedule shows the relationship between the price of the good and the quantity demanded. For example, suppose Elizabeth enjoys drinking coffee. How many pounds of coffee would Elizabeth be willing and able to buy at various prices during the year? At a price of $3 a pound, Elizabeth buys 15 pounds of coffee over the course of a year. If the price is higher, at $4 per pound, she might buy only 10 pounds; if it is lower, say $1 per pound, she might buy 25 pounds of coffee during the year. Elizabeth's demand for coffee for the year is summarized in the demand schedule in Exhibit 1. Elizabeth might not be consciously aware of the amounts that she would purchase at prices other than the prevailing one, but that does not alter the fact that she has a schedule in the sense that she would have bought various other amounts had other prices prevailed. It must be emphasized that the schedule is a list of alternative possibilities. At any one time, only one of the prices will prevail, and thus a certain quantity will be purchased.

An Individual Demand Curve

By plotting the different prices and corresponding quantities demanded in Elizabeth's demand schedule in Exhibit 1 and then connecting them, we can create the individual demand curve for Elizabeth shown in Exhibit 2. From the curve, we can see that when the price is higher, the quantity demanded is lower, and when the price is lower, the quantity demanded is higher. The demand curve shows how the quantity of the good demanded changes as its price varies.

What Is a Market Demand Curve?

Although we introduced the concept of the demand curve in terms of the individual, economists usually speak of the demand curve in terms of large groups of people—a whole nation, a community, or a trading area. That is, to analyze how the market works, we will need to use market demand. As you know, every individual has his or her demand curve

Economists conducted an experiment with rats to see how they would respond to changing prices of different drinks (changing the number of times a rat had to press a bar). Rats responded by choosing more of the beverage with a lower price, showing they were willing to substitute when the price changed. That is, even rats seem to behave rationally—responding to incentives and opportunities to make themselves better off.

individual demand schedule
a schedule that shows the relationship between price and quantity demanded

individual demand curve
a graphical representation that shows the inverse relationship between price and quantity demanded

section 4.2 exhibit 1	Elizabeth's Demand Schedule for Coffee
Price of Coffee (per pound)	**Quantity of Coffee Demanded (pounds per year)**
$5	5
4	10
3	15
2	20
1	25

for every product. The horizontal summing of the demand curves of many individuals is called the **market demand curve**.

market demand curve
the horizontal summation of individual demand curves

Suppose the consumer group is composed of Peter, Lois, and the rest of their small community, Quahog, and that the product is still coffee. The effect of price on the quantity of coffee demanded by Lois, Peter, and the rest of Quahog is given in the demand schedule and demand curves shown in Exhibit 3. At $4 per pound, Peter would be willing and able to buy 20 pounds of coffee per year, Lois would be willing and able to buy 10 pounds, and the rest of Quahog would be willing and able to buy 2,970 pounds. At $3 per pound, Peter would be willing and able to buy 25 pounds of coffee per year, Lois would be willing and able to buy 15 pounds, and the rest of Quahog would be willing and able to buy 4,960 pounds. The market demand curve is simply the (horizontal) sum of the quantities Peter, Lois, and the rest of Quahog demand at each price. That is, at $4, the quantity demanded in the market would be 3,000 pounds of coffee (20 + 10 + 2,970 = 3,000), and at $3, the quantity demanded in the market would be 5,000 pounds of coffee (25 + 15 + 4,960 = 5,000).

In Exhibit 4, we offer a more complete set of prices and quantities from the market demand for coffee during the year. Remember, the market demand curve shows the amounts that all the buyers in the market would be willing and able to buy at various prices. For example, when the price of coffee is $2 per pound, consumers in the market collectively would be willing and able to buy 8,000 pounds per year. At $1 per pound, the amount collectively demanded would be 12,000 pounds per year. The market demand curve is the negative (inverse) relationship between price and the total quantity demanded, while holding all other factors that affect how much consumers are able and willing to pay constant, *ceteris paribus*. For the most part, we are interested in how the market works, so we will primarily use market demand curves.

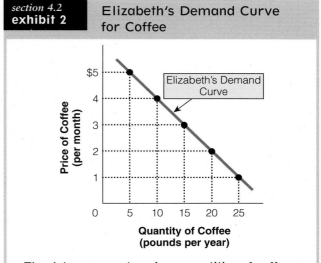

section 4.2
exhibit 2

Elizabeth's Demand Curve for Coffee

The dots represent various quantities of coffee that Elizabeth would be willing and able to buy at different prices in a given period. The demand curve shows how the quantity demanded varies inversely with the price of the good when we hold everything else constant— *ceteris paribus*. Because of this inverse relationship between price and quantity demanded, the demand curve is downward sloping.

© Cengage Learning 2013

---

section 4.2
exhibit 3

Creating a Market Demand Curve

a. Creating a Market Demand Schedule for Coffee

	Quantity of Coffee Demanded (pounds per year)							
Price (per pound)	Peter	+	Lois	+	Rest of Quahog	=	Market Demand
$4	20	+	10	+	2,970	=	3,000
$3	25	+	15	+	4,960	=	5,000

b. Creating a Market Demand Curve for Coffee

Peter	Lois	Rest of Quahog	Market Demand
D_{HOMER}	D_{MARGE}	D_S	D_M

© Cengage Learning 2013

section 4.2
exhibit 4   A Market Demand Curve

a. Market Demand Schedule for Coffee

Price (per pound)	Quantity Demanded (pounds per year)
$5	1,000
4	3,000
3	5,000
2	8,000
1	12,000

b. Market Demand Curve for Coffee

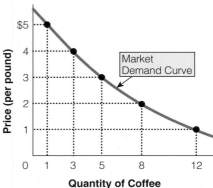

The market demand curve shows the amounts that all the buyers in the market would be willing and able to buy at various prices. We find the market demand curve by adding horizontally the individual demand curves. For example, when the price of coffee is $2 per pound, consumers in the market collectively would be willing and able to buy 8,000 pounds per year. At $1 per pound, the amount collectively demanded would be 12,000 pounds per year.

© Cengage Learning 2013

ⓘ SECTION QUIZ

1. If the demand for milk is downward sloping, then an increase in the price of milk will result in a(n)

   a. increase in the demand for milk.

   b. decrease in the demand for milk.

   c. increase in the quantity of milk demanded.

   d. decrease in the quantity of milk demanded.

   e. decrease in the supply of milk.

2. Which of the following is true?

   a. The law of demand states that when the price of a good falls (rises), the quantity demanded rises (falls), *ceteris paribus.*

   b. An individual demand curve is a graphical representation of the relationship between the price and the quantity demanded.

   c. The market demand curve shows the amount of a good that all buyers in the market would be willing and able to buy at various prices.

   d. All of the above are true.

3. Which of the following is true?

   a. The relationship between price and quantity demanded is inverse or negative.

   b. The market demand curve is the vertical summation of individual demand curves.

   c. A change in a good's price causes a movement along its demand curve.

   d. All of the above are true.

   e. Answers (a) and (c) are true.

(*continued*)

Shifts in the Demand Curve

4.3

📂 What is the difference between a change in demand and a change in quantity demanded?

📂 What are the determinants of demand?

📂 What are substitutes and complements?

📂 What are normal and inferior goods?

📂 How does the number of buyers affect the demand curve?

📂 How do changes in taste affect the demand curve?

📂 How do changing expectations affect the demand curve?

A Change in Demand versus a Change in Quantity Demanded

Understanding the relationship between price and quantity demanded is so important that economists make a clear distinction between it and the various other factors that can influence consumer behavior. A change in a good's own price is said to lead to a **change in quantity demanded**. That is, it "moves you along" a given demand curve. The demand curve is the answer to the question: "What happens to the quantity demanded when the price of the good changes?" The demand curve is drawn under the assumption that all other things are held constant, except the price of the good. However, economists know that price is not the only thing that affects the quantity of a good that people buy. The other variables that influence the demand curve are called *determinants of demand*, and a change in these other factors *shifts the entire demand curve*. These determinants of demand are called demand shifters and they lead to **shifts in the demand curve**.

change in quantity demanded
a change in a good's own price leads to a change in quantity demanded, a movement along a given demand curve

shifts in the demand curve
A change in one of the variables, other than the price of the good itself, that affects the willingness of consumers to buy.

Shifts in Demand ("PYNTE")

As illustrated in Exhibit 1, any event that increases the quantity demanded at every price shifts the demand curve to the right. Any event that decreases the quantity demanded at every price, shifts the demand curve to the left.

There are a number of variables that can shift the demand curve but here are some of the most important. It might be helpful to remember the old English spelling of the word pint—PYNTE. This acronym can help you remember the five principle factors that shift the demand curve for a good or service.

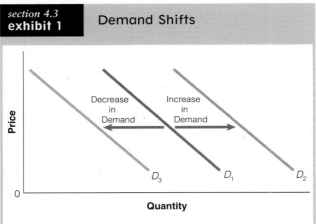

section 4.3 exhibit 1 Demand Shifts

Price

Decrease in Demand

Increase in Demand

D_3

D_1

D_2

0

Quantity

An increase in demand shifts the demand curve to the right, leading to an increase in quantity demanded at any given price. A decrease in demand shifts the demand curve to the left, leading to a decrease in quantity demanded at any given price.

Does a movement along the demand curve illustrate a change in demand or a change in quantity demanded?

substitutes
two good are substitutes if an increase (decrease) in the price of one good causes the demand curve for another good to shift to the right (left)

- Changes in the Prices of Related Goods and Services (P)
- Changes in Income (Y)
- Changes in the Number of Buyers (N)
- Changes in Tastes (T)
- Changes in Expectations (E)

Changes in the Prices of Related Goods and Services (P)

In deciding how much of a good or service to buy, consumers are influenced by the price of that good or service, a relationship summarized in the law of demand. However, sometimes consumers are also influenced by the prices of *related* goods and services—substitutes and complements.

Substitutes

Substitutes are generally goods for which one could be used in place of the other. To many, substitutes would include muffins and bagels, Crest and Colgate toothpaste, domestic and foreign cars, movie tickets and video rentals, jackets and sweaters, Exxon and Shell gasoline, and Nikes and Reeboks.

Two goods are **substitutes** if an increase (a decrease) in the price of one good makes consumers more (less) willing to buy another good. So two goods are substitutes if an increase (decrease) in the price of one good causes the demand curve for another good to shift to the right (left).

Complements

However, there are times when the price of a good may fall (rise), and it makes consumers more (less) willing to buy another good. If this relationship holds, the pair are complement goods. Complements are goods that "go together," often consumed and used simultaneously, such as skis and bindings, peanut butter and jelly, hot dogs and buns, digital music players and downloadable music, and printers and ink cartridges. For example, if the price of motorcycles falls, the quantity of motorcycles demanded will rise—a movement down along the demand curve for motorcycles. As more people buy motorcycles, they will demand more motorcycle helmets—the demand curve for motorcycle helmets shifts to the right. In short,

use what you've learned **Substitute Goods**

Q Can you describe the change we would expect to see in the demand curve for Pepsi if the relative price for Coca-Cola increased significantly?

A If the price of one good increases and, as a result, an individual buys more of another good, the two related goods are substitutes. That is, buying more of one reduces purchases of the other. In Exhibit 2(a), we see that as the price of Coca-Cola increases—a movement up along the demand curve for Coca-Cola, from point A to point B. The price increase for Coca-Cola causes a reduction in the quantity demanded of Coca-Cola. If the two goods are substitutes, the higher price for Coca-Cola will cause an increase in the demand for Pepsi (a rightward shift), as seen in Exhibit 2(b).

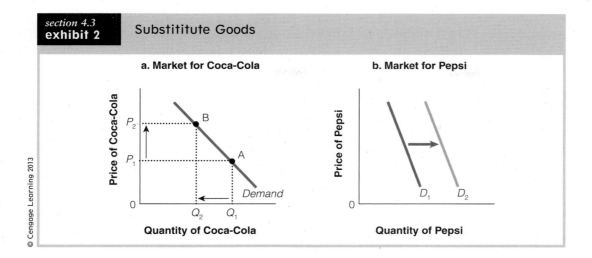

section 4.3
exhibit 2   Substititute Goods

a. Market for Coca-Cola

b. Market for Pepsi

© Cengage Learning 2013

two goods are **complements**, if an increase (decrease) in the price of one good shifts the demand curve for another good to the left (right).

complements
two goods are complements if an increase (decrease) in the price of one good shifts the demand curve for another good to the left (right)

Changes in Income (Y)

Why (Y)? The reason is because Macroeconomists use the letter (I) for investment, so Microeconomist often use the letter (Y) to denote income. Economists have observed that generally the consumption of goods and services is positively related to the income available to consumers. Empirical studies support the notion that as individuals receive more income,

USE
what you've learned   **Complementary Goods**

Q If the price of computers fell markedly, what do you think would happen to the demand for printers?

A If computers and printers are complements, the decrease in the price of computers will lead to

more computers purchased (a movement down along the demand curve from point A to point B) and an increase in the demand for printers (a rightward shift). Of course, the opposite is true, too—an increase in the price of computers will lead to fewer people purchasing computers (a movement up along the demand curve for computers from point B to point A) and a lower demand for printers (a leftward shift).

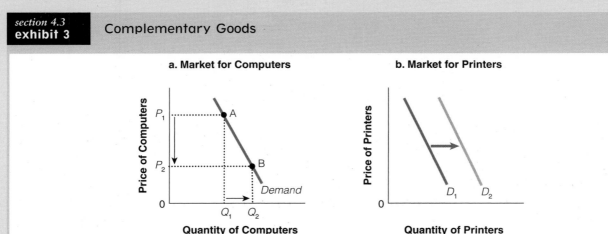

section 4.3
exhibit 3   Complementary Goods

a. Market for Computers

b. Market for Printers

© Cengage Learning 2013

they tend to increase their purchases of most goods and services. Other things held equal, rising income usually leads to an increase in the demand for goods (a rightward shift of the demand curve), and decreasing income usually leads to a decrease in the demand for goods (a leftward shift of the demand curve).

Normal and Inferior Goods

normal good
if income increases, the demand for a good increases; if income decreases, the demand for a good decreases

inferior good
if income increases, the demand for a good decreases; if income decreases, the demand for a good increases

If demand for a good increases when incomes rise and decreases when incomes fall, the good is called a **normal good**. Most goods are normal goods. Consumers will typically buy more CDs, clothes, pizzas, and trips to the movies as their incomes rise. However, if demand for a good decreases when incomes rise or if demand increases when incomes fall, the good is called an **inferior good**. These goods include inexpensive cuts of meat, second-hand clothing, or retread tires, which customers generally buy only because they cannot afford more expensive substitutes. As incomes rise, buyers shift to preferred substitutes and decrease their demand for the inferior goods. Suppose most individuals prefer hamburger to beans, but low-income families buy beans because they are less expensive. As incomes rise, many consumers may switch from buying beans to buying hamburgers. Hamburger may be inferior too; as incomes rise still further, consumers may substitute steak or chicken for hamburger. The term *inferior* in this sense does not refer to the quality of the good in question but shows that demand decreases when income increases and demand increases when income decreases. So beans are inferior not because they are low quality, but because you buy less of them as income increases.

Or if people's incomes rise and they increase their demand for movie tickets, we say that movie tickets are a normal good. But if people's incomes fall and they increase their demand for bus rides, we say bus rides are an inferior good. Whether goods are normal or inferior,

use what you've learned   Normal and Inferior Goods

Q Chester Field owns a high-quality furniture shop. If a boom in the economy occurs (higher average income per person and fewer people unemployed), can Chester expect to sell more high-quality furniture?

A Yes. Furniture is generally considered a normal good, so a rise in income will increase the demand for high-quality furniture, as shown in (a). However, if Chester sells unfinished, used, or low-quality furniture, the demand for his products might fall, as higher incomes allow customers to buy furniture that is finished, new, or of higher quality. Chester's furniture would then be an inferior good, as shown in Exhibit 4(b).

section 4.3
exhibit 4   Normal and Inferior Goods

a. Rising Income and a Normal Good

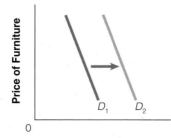

Quantity of High-Quality Furniture

b. Rising Income and an Inferior Good

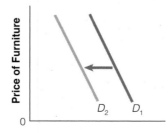

Quantity of Low-Quality Furniture

the point here is that income influences demand—usually positively, but sometimes negatively.

Changes in the Number of Buyers (N)

The demand for a good or service will vary with the size of the potential consumer population. The demand for wheat, for example, rises as population increases, because the added population wants to consume wheat products, such as bread or cereal. Marketing experts, who closely follow the patterns of consumer behavior regarding a particular good or service, are usually vitally concerned with the *demographics* of the product—the vital statistics of the potential consumer population, including size, race, income, and age characteristics. For example, market researchers for baby food companies keep a close watch on the birth rate.

In the midst of a recession, is it possible that many people will increase their demand for fast-food restaurants like McDonald's? It is not only possible, it actually happened! If declining income causes demand for a good to rise, is it a normal good or an inferior good?

Changes in Tastes (T)

The demand for a good or service may increase or decrease with changes in people's tastes or preferences. Changes in taste may be triggered by advertising or promotion, by a news story, by the behavior of some popular public figure, and so on. Changes in taste are particularly noticeable in apparel. Skirt lengths, coat lapels, shoe styles, and tie sizes change frequently.

Changes in preferences naturally lead to changes in demand. A person may grow tired of one type of recreation or food and try another type. People may decide they want more organic food; consequently, we will see more stores and restaurants catering to this change in taste. Changes in occupation, number of dependents, state of health, and age also tend to alter preferences. The birth of a baby might cause a family to spend less on recreation and more on food and clothing. Illness increases the demand for medicine and lessens purchases of other goods. A cold winter increases the demand for heating oil. Changes in customs and traditions also affect preferences, and the development of new products draws consumer preferences away from other goods. Compact discs replaced record albums, just as DVD players replaced VCRs. A change in information can also impact consumers' demand. For example, a breakout of *E. coli* or new information about a defective and/or dangerous product, such as a baby crib, can reduce demand.

Body piercing and tattoos have risen in popularity in recent years. The demand for these services has been pushed to the right. According to the Pew Research Center 36 percent of 18- to 25-year-olds have at least one tattoo.

Changes in Expectations (E)

Sometimes the demand for a good or service in a given period will increase or decrease because consumers expect the good to change in price or availability at some future date. If people expect the future price to be higher, they will purchase more of the good now before the price increase. If people expect the future price to be lower, they will purchase less of the good now and wait for the price decrease. For example, if you expect the price of computers to fall soon, you may be less willing to buy one today. Or, if you expect to earn additional income next month, you may be more willing to dip into your current savings to buy something this month.

Changes in Demand versus Changes in Quantity Demanded—Revisited

Economists put particular emphasis on the impact on consumer behavior of a change in the price of a good. We are interested in distinguishing between consumer behavior related to the price of a good itself (movements *along* a demand curve) and behavior related to changes in other factors (shifts of the demand curve).

As indicated earlier, if the price of a good changes, it causes a *change in quantity demanded*. If one of the other factors (determinants) influencing consumer behavior changes, it results in a *change in demand*. The effects of some of the determinants that cause changes in demand (shifters) are reviewed in Exhibit 5. For example, there are two different ways to curb teenage smoking: raise the price of cigarettes (a reduction in the quantity of cigarettes demanded) or decrease the demand for cigarettes (a leftward shift in the demand curve for cigarettes). Both would reduce the amount of smoking. Specifically, to increase the price of cigarettes, the government could impose a higher tax on manufacturers. Most of this would be passed on to consumers in the form of higher prices (more on this in Chapter 6). Or to shift the demand curve leftward, the government could adopt policies to discourage smoking, such as advertising bans and increasing consumer awareness of the harmful side effects of smoking—disease and death.

How is a change in demand different than a change in quantity demanded?

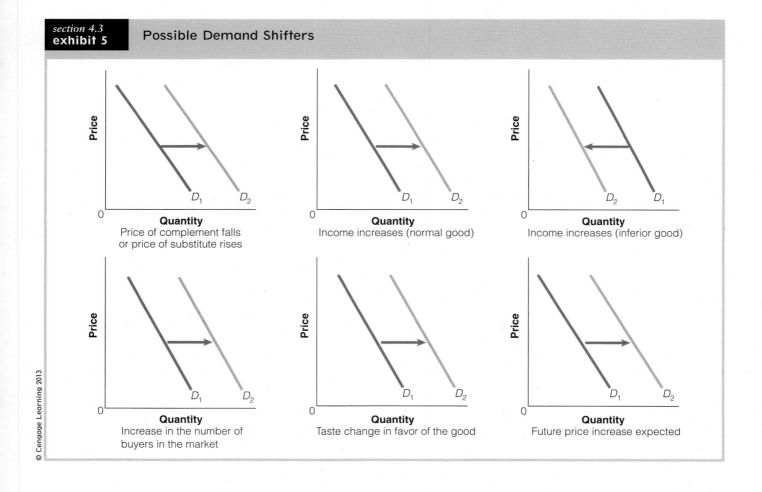

section 4.3 exhibit 5   **Possible Demand Shifters**

Price of complement falls or price of substitute rises

Income increases (normal good)

Income increases (inferior good)

Increase in the number of buyers in the market

Taste change in favor of the good

Future price increase expected

use what you've learned
Changes in Demand versus Changes in Quantity Demanded

Q How would you use a graph to demonstrate the two following scenarios? (1) Someone buys more pizzas because the price of pizzas has fallen; and (2) a student buys more pizzas because she just received a 20 percent raise at work, giving her additional income.

A In Exhibit 6, the movement from A to B is called an increase in quantity demanded; the movement from B to A is called a decrease in quantity demanded. Economists use the phrase "increase or decrease in quantity demanded" to describe movements along a given demand curve. However, the change from A to C is called an increase in demand, and the change from C to A is called a decrease in demand. The phrase "increase or decrease in demand" is reserved for a shift in the whole curve. So if an individual buys more pizzas because the price fell, we call it an increase in quantity demanded. However, if she buys more

pizzas even at the current price, say $15, we say it is an increase in demand. In this case, the increase in income was responsible for the increase in demand, because she chose to spend some of her new income on pizzas.

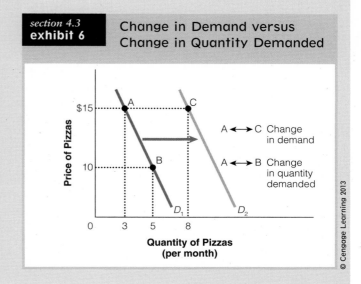

section 4.3
exhibit 6

Change in Demand versus Change in Quantity Demanded

© Cengage Learning 2013

---

② SECTION QUIZ

1. Which of the following would be most likely to increase the demand for jelly?

    a. an increase in the price of peanut butter, which is often used with jelly

    b. an increase in income; jelly is a normal good

    c. a decrease in the price of jelly

    d. medical research that finds that daily consumption of jelly makes people live 10 years *less,* on average

2. Which of the following would *not* cause a change in the demand for cheese?

    a. an increase in the price of crackers, which are consumed with cheese

    b. an increase in the income of cheese consumers

    c. an increase in the population of cheese lovers

    d. an increase in the price of cheese

3. Whenever the price of Good A decreases, the demand for Good B increases. Goods A and B appear to be

    a. complements.

    b. substitutes.

    c. inferior goods.

    d. normal goods.

    e. inverse goods.

(*continued*)

ⓘ SECTION QUIZ (Cont.)

4. Whenever the price of Good A increases, the demand for Good B increases as well. Goods A and B appear to be

   a. complements.

   b. substitutes.

   c. inferior goods.

   d. normal goods.

   e. inverse goods.

5. The difference between a change in quantity demanded and a change in demand is that a change in

   a. quantity demanded is caused by a change in a good's own price, while a change in demand is caused by a change in some other variable, such as income, tastes, or expectations.

   b. demand is caused by a change in a good's own price, while a change in quantity demanded is caused by a change in some other variable, such as income, tastes, or expectations.

   c. quantity demanded is a change in the amount people actually buy, while a change in demand is a change in the amount they want to buy.

   d. This is a trick question. A change in demand and a change in quantity demanded are the same thing.

6. Suppose CNN announces that bad weather in Central America has greatly reduced the number of cocoa bean plants and for this reason the price of chocolate is expected to rise soon. As a result,

   a. the current market demand for chocolate will decrease.

   b. the current market demand for chocolate will increase.

   c. the current quantity demanded for chocolate will decrease.

   d. no change will occur in the current market for chocolate.

7. If incomes are rising, in the market for an inferior good,

   a. demand will rise.

   b. demand will fall.

   c. supply will rise.

   d. supply will fall.

---

1. What is the difference between a change in demand and a change in quantity demanded?

2. If the price of zucchini increases, causing the demand for yellow squash to rise, what do we call the relationship between zucchini and yellow squash?

3. If incomes rise and, as a result, demand for jet skis increases, how do we describe that good?

4. How do expectations about the future influence the demand curve?

5. Would a change in the price of ice cream cause a change in the demand for ice cream? Why or why not?

6. Would a change in the price of ice cream likely cause a change in the demand for frozen yogurt, a substitute?

7. If plane travel is a normal good and bus travel is an inferior good, what will happen to the demand curves for plane and bus travel if people's incomes increase?

Answers: 1. b 2. d 3. a 4. b 5. a 6. b 7. b

Supply   4.4

📁 What is the law of supply?   📁 What is a market supply curve?
📁 What is an individual supply curve?

The Law of Supply

In a market, the answer to the fundamental question, "What do we produce, and in what quantities?" depends on the interaction of both buyers and sellers. Demand is only half the story. The willingness and ability of sellers to provide goods are equally important factors that must be weighed by decision makers in all societies. As with demand, the price of the good is an important factor. And just as with demand, factors other than the price of the good are also important to sellers, such as the cost of inputs or advances in technology. While behavior will vary among individual sellers, economists expect that, other things being equal, the quantity supplied will vary directly with the price of the good, a relationship called the **law of supply**. According to the law of supply, the higher the price of the good (P), the greater the quantity supplied (Q_S), and the lower the price of the good, the smaller the quantity supplied, *ceteris paribus*.

To get more oil, drillers must sometimes drill deeper or go into unexplored areas, and they still may come up dry. If it costs more to increase oil production, then oil prices would have to rise for producers to increase their output—the quantity supplied.

$$P \uparrow \Rightarrow Q_S \uparrow \text{ and } P \downarrow \Rightarrow Q_S \downarrow$$

The relationship described by the law of supply is a direct, or positive, relationship, because the variables move in the same direction.

law of supply
the higher (lower) the price of the good, the greater (smaller) the quantity supplied, *ceteris paribus*

A Positive Relationship between Price and Quantity Supplied

Firms supplying goods and services want to increase their profits, and the higher the price per unit, the greater the profitability generated by supplying more of that good. For example, if you were a coffee grower, wouldn't you much rather be paid $5 a pound than $1 a pound, *ceteris paribus*?

When the price of coffee is low, the coffee business is less profitable and less coffee will be produced. Some sellers may even shut down, reducing their quantity supplied to zero if the price is low enough.

There is another reason that supply curves are upward sloping. In Chapter 3, the law of increasing opportunity cost demonstrated that when we hold technology and input prices constant, producing additional units of a good will require increased opportunity costs. That is, when we produce something, we use the most efficient resources first (those with the lowest opportunity cost) and then draw on less efficient resources (those with a higher opportunity cost) as more of the good is produced. Because costs per unit are rising as they produce more, sellers must receive a higher price to increase the quantity supplied, *ceteris paribus*.

ECS
economic content standards

Higher prices for a good or service provide incentives for producers to make or sell more of it. Lower prices for a good or service provide incentives for producers to make or sell less of it.

An Individual Supply Curve

To illustrate the concept of an **individual supply curve**, consider the amount of coffee that an individual seller, Juan Valdés, is willing and able to supply in one year. The law of supply can be illustrated, like the law of demand, by a table or graph. Juan's supply schedule for

individual supply curve
a graphical representation that shows the positive relationship between the price and quantity supplied

section 4.4
exhibit 1   An Individual Supply Curve

a. Juan's Supply Schedule for Coffee

Price (per pound)	Quantity Supplied (pounds per year)
$5	80
4	70
3	50
2	30
1	10

Other things being equal, the quantity supplied will vary directly with the price of the good. As the price rises (falls), the quantity supplied increases (decreases).

b. Juan's Supply Curve for Coffee

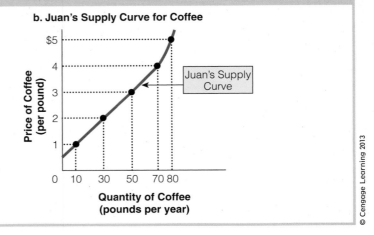

ECS

economic content standards

An increase in the price of a good or service enables producers to cover higher costs, ceteris paribus, causing the quantity supplied to increase, and vice versa.

market supply curve
a graphical representation of the amount of goods and services that sellers are willing and able to supply at various prices

coffee is shown in Exhibit 1(a). The combinations of price and quantity supplied were then plotted and joined to create the individual supply curve shown in Exhibit 1(b). Note that the individual supply curve is upward sloping as you move from left to right. At higher prices, it will be more attractive to increase production. Existing firms or growers will produce more at higher prices than at lower prices.

The Market Supply Curve

The **market supply curve** may be thought of as the horizontal summation of the supply curves for individual firms. The market supply curve shows how the total quantity supplied varies positively with the price of a good, while holding constant all other factors that affect how much producers are able and willing to supply. The market supply schedule, which reflects the total quantity supplied at each price by all of the coffee producers, is shown in Exhibit 2(a). Exhibit 2(b) illustrates the resulting market supply curve for this group of coffee producers.

section 4.4
exhibit 2   A Market Supply Curve

a. Market Supply Schedule for Coffee

Price (per pound)	Juan	+	Other Producers	=	Market Supply
$5	80	+	7,920	=	8,000
4	70	+	6,930	=	7,000
3	50	+	4,950	=	5,000
2	30	+	2,970	=	3,000
1	10	+	990	=	1,000

(Quantity Supplied (pounds per year))

b. Market Supply Curve for Coffee

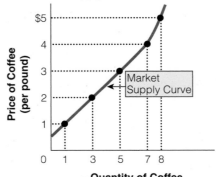

The dots on this graph indicate different quantities of coffee that sellers would be willing and able to supply at various prices. The line connecting those combinations is the market supply curve.

⑦ SECTION QUIZ

1. An upward-sloping supply curve shows that
   a. buyers are willing to pay more for particularly scarce products.
   b. sellers expand production as the product price falls.
   c. sellers are willing to increase production of their goods if they receive higher prices for them.
   d. buyers are willing to buy more as the product price falls.

2. Along a supply curve,
   a. supply changes as price changes.
   b. quantity supplied changes as price changes.
   c. supply changes as technology changes.
   d. quantity supplied changes as technology changes.

3. A supply curve illustrates a(n) _____ relationship between _____ and _____.
   a. direct; price; supply
   b. direct; price; quantity demanded
   c. direct; price; quantity supplied
   d. introverted; price; quantity demanded
   e. inverse; price; quantity supplied

4. Which of the following is true?
   a. The law of supply states that the higher (lower) the price of a good, the greater (smaller) the quantity supplied.
   b. The relationship between price and quantity supplied is positive because profit opportunities are greater at higher prices and because the higher production costs of increased output mean that suppliers will require higher prices.
   c. The market supply curve is a graphical representation of the amount of goods and services that suppliers are willing and able to supply at various prices.
   d. All of the above are true.

---

1. What are the two reasons why a supply curve is positively sloped?
2. What is the difference between an individual supply curve and a market supply curve?

Answers: 1. c 2. b 3. c 4. d

Shifts in the Supply Curve   4.5

📂 What is the difference between a change in supply and a change in quantity supplied?

📂 What are the determinants of supply?

📂 How does the number of suppliers affect the supply curve?

📂 How does technology affect the supply curve?

📂 How do taxes affect the supply curve?

A Change in Quantity Supplied versus a Change in Supply

Changes in the price of a good lead to changes in the quantity supplied by sellers, just as changes in the price of a good lead to changes in the quantity demanded by buyers. Similarly, a change in supply, whether an increase or a decrease, can occur for reasons other than changes in the price of the product itself, just as changes in demand may be due to factors (determinants) other than the price of the good. In other words, a change in the price of the good in question is shown as a movement along a given supply curve, leading to a change in quantity supplied. A change in any other factor that can affect seller behavior (seller's input prices, the prices of related products, expectations, number of sellers, and technology results in *a shift in the entire supply curve,* leading to a change in quantity supplied at every price.

Why is a change in supply different than a change in quantity supplied?

Shifts in Supply ("SPENT")

An increase in supply shifts the supply curve to the right; a decrease in supply shifts the supply curve to the left, as shown in Exhibit 1. Anything that affects the costs of production will influence supply and the position of the supply curve. We will now look at some of the possible determinants of supply—factors that determine the position of the supply curve—in greater depth.

There are a number of variables that can shift the supply curve but here are some of the most important. It might be helpful to remember the word "SPENT." This acronym can help you remember the five principle factors that shift the supply curve for a good or service.

- Changes in seller's input prices (S)
- Changes in the prices of related goods and services (P)
- Changes in expectations (E)
- Changes in the number of sellers (N)
- Changes in technology (T)

Changes in Seller's Input Prices (S)

Sellers are strongly influenced by the costs of inputs used in the production process, such as steel used for automobiles or microchips used in computers. For example, higher labor, materials, energy, or other input costs increase the costs of production, causing the supply curve to shift to the left at each and every price. If input prices fall, the costs of production decrease, causing the supply curve to shift to the right—more will be supplied at each and every price.

Changes in the Prices of Related Goods and Services (P)

The supply of a good increases if the price of one of its substitutes in production falls; and the supply of a good decreases if the price of one of its substitutes in production rises. Suppose you own your own farm, on which you plant cotton and wheat. One year, the price of wheat falls, and farmers reduce the quantity of wheat supplied, as shown in Exhibit 2(a). What effect does the lower price of wheat have on your cotton production? It increases the supply of cotton. You want to produce relatively less of the crop that has fallen in price (wheat) and relatively more of the now more attractive other crop (cotton). Cotton and wheat are *substitutes in production* because both goods can be produced using the same resources. Producers tend to substitute the production of more profitable products for that of less profitable products. So the decrease in the price in the wheat market has caused an increase in supply (a rightward shift) in the cotton market, as seen in Exhibit 2(b).

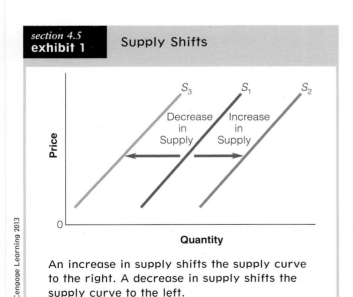

**section 4.5
exhibit 1**   **Supply Shifts**

An increase in supply shifts the supply curve to the right. A decrease in supply shifts the supply curve to the left.

If the price of wheat, a substitute in production, increases, then that crop becomes more profitable. This leads to an increase in the quantity supplied of wheat. Consequently, farmers will shift their resources out of the relatively lower-priced crop (cotton); the result is a decrease in supply of cotton.

Other examples of substitutes in production include automobile producers that have to decide between producing sedans and pick-ups or construction companies that have to choose between building single residential houses or commercial buildings.

Some goods are *complements in production*. Producing one good does not prevent the production of the other, but actually enables production of the other. For example, leather and beef are complements in production. Suppose the price of a beef rises and, as a result, cattle ranchers increase the quantity supplied of beef, moving up the supply curve for beef, as seen in Exhibit 2(c). When cattle ranchers produce more beef, they automatically produce more leather. Thus, when the price of beef increases, the supply of the related good, leather, shifts to the right, as seen in Exhibit 2(d). Suppose the price of beef falls, and as a result, the quantity supplied of beef falls; this leads to a decrease (a leftward shift) in the supply of leather.

Other examples of complements in production where goods are produced simultaneously from the same resource include: a lumber mill that produces lumber and sawdust or an oil refinery that can produce gasoline and heating oil from the same resource—crude oil.

section 4.5
exhibit 2   **Substitutes and Complements in Production**

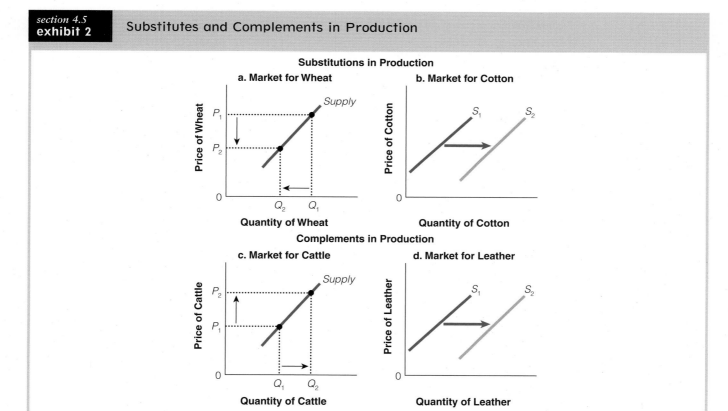

Substitutions in Production

a. Market for Wheat   **b. Market for Cotton**

Complements in Production

c. Market for Cattle   **d. Market for Leather**

If land can be used for either wheat or cotton, a decrease in the price of wheat causes a decease in the quantity supplied; a movement down along the supply curve in Exhibit 2(a). This may cause some farmers to shift out of the production of wheat and into the substitute in production—cotton—shifting the cotton supply curve to the right in Exhibit 2(b). If the price of the complement in production increases (cattle), it becomes more profitable and and as a result cattle ranchers increase the quantity supplied of beef, moving up the supply curve for beef, as seen in Exhibit 2(c). When cattle ranchers produce more beef, they also produce more leather. Thus, when the price of beef increases, the supply of the related good, leather, shifts to the right, as seen in Exhibit 2(d).

Changes in Expectations (E)

Another factor shifting supply is sellers' expectations. If producers expect a higher price in the future, they will supply less now than they otherwise would have, preferring to wait and sell when their goods will be more valuable. For example, if a cotton producer expected the future price of cotton to be higher next year, he might decide to store some of his current production of cotton for next year when the price will be higher. Similarly, if producers expect now that the price will be lower later, they will supply more now. Oil refiners will often store some of their spring supply of gasoline for summer because gasoline prices typically peak in summer. In addition, some of the heating oil for the fall is stored to supply it in the winter when heating oil prices peak.

Changes in the Number of Sellers (N)

We are normally interested in market demand and supply (because together they determine prices and quantities) rather than in the behavior of individual consumers and firms. As we discussed earlier in the chapter, the supply curves of individual suppliers can be summed horizontally to create a market supply curve. An increase in the number of sellers leads to an increase in supply, denoted by a rightward shift in the supply curve. For example, think of the number of gourmet coffee shops that have sprung up over the last 15 to 20 years, shifting the supply curve of gourmet coffee to the right. An exodus of sellers has the opposite impact, a decrease in supply, which is indicated by a leftward shift in the supply curve.

Changes in Technology (T)

Technological change can lower the firm's costs of production through productivity advances. These changes allow the firm to spend less on inputs and produce the same level of output. Human creativity works to find new ways to produce goods and services using

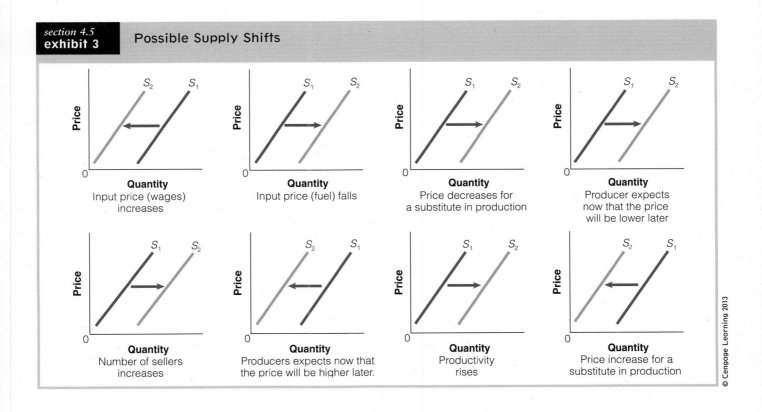

section 4.5
exhibit 3   **Possible Supply Shifts**

Input price (wages) increases

Input price (fuel) falls

Price decreases for a substitute in production

Producer expects now that the price will be lower later

Number of sellers increases

Producers expects now that the price will be higher later.

Productivity rises

Price increase for a substitute in production

© Cengage Learning 2013

fewer or less costly inputs of labor, natural resources, or capital. Because the firm can now produce the good at a lower cost it will supply more of the good at each and every price—the supply curve shifts to the right.

Change in Supply versus Change in Quantity Supplied—Revisited

If the price of a good changes, it leads to a change in the quantity supplied. If one of the other factors influences sellers' behavior, we say it results in a change in supply. For example, if production costs rise because of a wage increase or higher fuel costs, other things remaining constant, we would expect a decrease in supply—that is, a leftward shift in the supply curve. Alternatively, if some variable, such as lower input prices, causes the costs of production to fall, the supply curve will shift to the right. Exhibit 3 illustrates the effects of some of the determinants that cause shifts in the supply curve.

use what you've learned   Change in Supply versus Change in Quantity Supplied

Q How would you graph the following two scenarios: (1) the price of wheat per bushel rises; and (2) good weather causes an unusually abundant wheat harvest?

A In the first scenario, the price of wheat (per bushel) increases, so the quantity supplied changes (i.e., a movement along the supply curve). In the second scenario, the good weather causes the supply curve for wheat to shift to the right, which is called a change in supply (not quantity supplied). A shift in the whole supply curve is caused by one of the other variables, not by a change in the price of the good in question.

As shown in Exhibit 4, the movement from A to B is called an increase in quantity supplied, and the movement from B to A is called a decrease in quantity supplied. However, the change from B to C

is called an increase in supply, and the movement from C to B is called a decrease in supply.

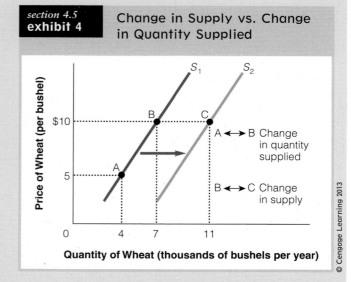

section 4.5 exhibit 4   Change in Supply vs. Change in Quantity Supplied

© Cengage Learning 2013

⊙ SECTION QUIZ

1. All of the following factors will affect the supply of shoes except one. Which will *not* affect the supply of shoes?

   a. higher wages for shoe factory workers

   b. higher prices for leather

   c. a technological improvement that reduces waste of leather and other raw materials in shoe production

   d. an increase in consumer income

2. The difference between a change in quantity supplied and a change in supply is that a change in

   a. quantity supplied is caused by a change in a good's own price, while a change in supply is caused by a change in some other variable, such as input prices, prices of related goods, expectations, or taxes.

   b. supply is caused by a change in a good's own price, while a change in the quantity supplied is caused by a change in some other variable, such as input prices, prices of related goods, expectations, or taxes.

   c. quantity supplied is a change in the amount people want to sell, while a change in supply is a change in the amount they actually sell.

   d. supply and a change in the quantity supplied are the same thing.

3. Antonio's makes the greatest pizza and delivers it hot to all the dorms around campus. Last week Antonio's supplier of pepperoni informed him of a 25 percent increase in price. Which variable determining the position of the supply curve has changed, and what effect does it have on supply?

   a. future expectations; supply decreases

   b. future expectations; supply increases

   c. input prices; supply decreases

   d. input prices; supply increases

   e. technology; supply increases

4. Which of the following is *not* a determinant of supply?

   a. input prices

   b. technology

   c. tastes

   d. expectations

   e. the prices of related goods

5. A leftward shift in supply could be caused by

   a. an improvement in productive technology.

   b. a decrease in income.

   c. some firms leaving the industry.

   d. a fall in the price of inputs to the industry.

---

1. What is the difference between a change in supply and a change in quantity supplied?

2. If a seller expects the price of a good to rise in the near future, how will that expectation affect the current supply curve?

3. Would a change in the price of wheat change the supply of wheat? Would it change the supply of corn, if wheat and corn can be grown on the same type of land?

4. If a guitar manufacturer increased its wages in order to keep its workers, what would happen to the supply of guitars as a result?

5. What happens to the supply of baby-sitting services in an area when many teenagers get their driver's licenses at about the same time?

Answers: 1. d 2. a 3. c 4. c 5. c

Market Equilibrium Price and Quantity

4.6

📁 What is the equilibrium price?

📁 What is a shortage?

📁 What is the equilibrium quantity?

📁 What is a surplus?

Equilibrium Price and Quantity

The **market equilibrium** is found at the point at which the market supply and market demand curves intersect. The price at the intersection of the market supply curve and the market demand curve is called the **equilibrium price**, and the quantity is called the **equilibrium quantity**. At the equilibrium price, the amount that buyers are willing and able to buy is exactly equal to the amount that sellers are willing and able to produce. The equilibrium market solution is best understood with the help of a simple graph. Let's return to the coffee example we used in our earlier discussions of supply and demand. Exhibit 1 combines the market demand curve for coffee with the market supply curve. At $3 per pound, buyers are willing to buy 5,000 pounds of coffee and sellers are willing to supply 5,000 pounds of coffee. Neither may be "happy" about the price; the buyers would probably like a lower price and the sellers would probably like a higher price. But both buyers and sellers are able to carry out their purchase and sales plans at the $3 price. At any other price, either suppliers or demanders would be unable to trade as much as they would like.

Shortages and Surpluses

What happens when the market price is not equal to the equilibrium price? Suppose the market price is above the equilibrium price, as seen in Exhibit 2(a). At $4 per pound, the quantity of coffee demanded would be 3,000 pounds, but the quantity supplied would be 7,000 pounds. At this price, a **surplus**, or excess quantity supplied, would exist. That is, at this price, growers would be willing to sell more coffee than demanders would be willing to buy. To get rid of the unwanted surplus, frustrated sellers would cut their price and cut back on production. And as price falls, consumers would buy more, ultimately eliminating the unsold surplus and returning the market to the equilibrium level.

What would happen if the market price of coffee were below the equilibrium price? As seen in Exhibit 2(b), at $2 per pound, the yearly quantity demanded of 7,000 pounds would be greater than the 3,000 pounds that producers would be willing to supply at that low price. So at $2 per pound, a **shortage** or excess quantity demanded of 4,000 pounds would exist. Some consumers are lucky enough to find coffee, but others are not able to find any sellers who are willing to sell them coffee at $2 per pound. Some frustrated consumers may offer to pay sellers more than $2. In addition, sellers noticing that there are disappointed consumers raise their prices. These actions by buyers and sellers cause the market price to rise. As the market price rises, the amount that sellers want to supply increases and the amount that

market equilibrium
the point at which the market supply and market demand curves intersect

equilibrium price
the price at the intersection of the market supply and demand curves; at this price, the quantity demanded equals the quantity supplied

equilibrium quantity
the quantity at the intersection of the market supply and demand curves; at the equilibrium quantity, the quantity demanded equals the quantity supplied

surplus
a situation where quantity supplied exceeds quantity demanded

shortage
a situation where quantity demanded exceeds quantity supplied

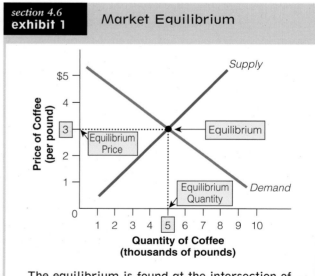

section 4.6
exhibit 1 Market Equilibrium

The equilibrium is found at the intersection of the market supply and demand curves. The equilibrium price is $3 per pound, and the equilibrium quantity is 5,000 pounds of coffee. At the equilibrium quantity, the quantity demanded equals the quantity supplied.

section 4.6
exhibit 2   Market in Temporary Disequilibrium

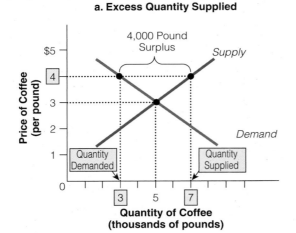

a. Excess Quantity Supplied

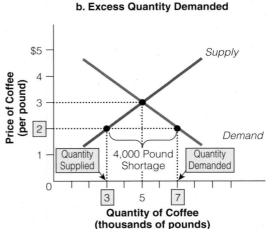

b. Excess Quantity Demanded

In (a), the market price is above the equilibrium price. At $4, the quantity supplied (7,000 pounds) exceeds the quantity demanded (3,000 pounds), resulting in a surplus of 4,000 pounds. To get rid of the unwanted surplus, suppliers cut their prices. As prices fall, consumers buy more, eliminating the surplus and moving the market back to equilibrium. In (b), the market price is below the equilibrium price. At $2, the quantity demanded (7,000 pounds) exceeds the quantity supplied (4,000 pounds), and a shortage of 5,000 pounds is the result. The many frustrated buyers compete for the existing supply, offering to buy more and driving the price up toward the equilibrium level. Therefore, with both shortages and surpluses, market prices tend to pull the market back to the equilibrium level.

use
what you've learned   Shortages

Q Imagine that you own a butcher shop. Recently, you have noticed that at about noon, you run out of your daily supply of chicken. Puzzling over your predicament, you hypothesize that you are charging less than the equilibrium price for your chicken. Should you raise the price of your chicken? Explain using a simple graph.

A If the price you are charging is below the equilibrium price (P_E), you can draw a horizontal line from that price straight across Exhibit 3 and see where it intersects the supply and demand curves. The point where this horizontal line intersects the demand curve indicates how much chicken consumers are willing to buy at the below-equilibrium price (P_1). Likewise, the intersection of this horizontal line with the supply curve indicates how much chicken producers are willing to supply at P_1. From this, it is clear that a shortage (or excess quantity demanded) exists, because consumers want more chicken (Q_D) than producers are willing to supply (Q_S) at this

relatively low price. This excess quantity demanded results in competition among buyers, which will push prices up and reduce or eliminate the shortage. That is, it would make sense to raise your price on chicken. As the price moves up toward the equilibrium price, consumers will be willing to purchase less (some will substitute fish, steak, or ground round), and producers will have an incentive to supply more chicken.

section 4.6
exhibit 3   Shortages

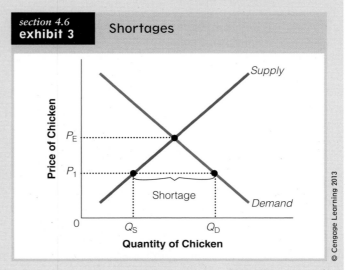

buyers want to buy decreases. The upward pressure on price continues until equilibrium is reached at $3.

Scarcity and Shortages

People often confuse scarcity with shortages. Remember most goods are scarce—desirable but limited. A shortage occurs when the quantity demanded is greater than the quantity supplied at the current price. We can eliminate shortages by increasing the price but we cannot eliminate scarcity.

ECS
economic content standards

A market exists when buyers and sellers interact. This interaction between supply and demand curves determines market prices and thereby allocates scarce goods and services.

in the news   Scalping and the Super Bowl

The Super Bowl is a high demand, limited supply sports event. The face value for general admission Super Bowl tickets, depending on what level, range from $600 to $800 and club seats go for $1,200. Many of the recipients of the tickets are corporate sponsors or are affiliated with the teams playing in the game. There are also some tickets that are allocated through a lottery. However, at the face value for the tickets at P_1, the quantity demanded far exceeds the quantity supplied as seen in Exhibit 4. In other words, the National Football League (NFL) has not priced their tickets equal to what the market will bear. Consequently, some fans are willing to pay much more, sometimes $6,000 to $7,000, for these tickets from scalpers, who buy the tickets at face value and try to sell them for a higher price. While ticket scalping is illegal in many states, scalpers will still descend on the host city to make a profit, even though the probability of arrest and conviction are substantial.

But is ticket scalping for athletic events and concerts really so objectionable? Could scalpers be transferring tickets into the hands of those who value them the most? The buyer must value attending the event more than the scalped price of the ticket or he would not buy the ticket. The seller would not sell her ticket unless she valued the money from the ticket more than attending the event. That is, the scalper has helped transfer tickets from those placing lower values on them to those placing higher values on them. The sponsors of the event are the losers, in the form of lost profits, for failing to charge the higher equilibrium market price. Why would the NFL not charge the higher price? Perhaps it sends a sign of goodwill to NFL fans, even if they have no appreciable chance of getting a ticket. That is, maybe the NFL is willing to take a hit on short-run profits to make sure they keep their base of fans (long-run profits).

section 4.6
exhibit 4   The Market for Super Bowl Tickets

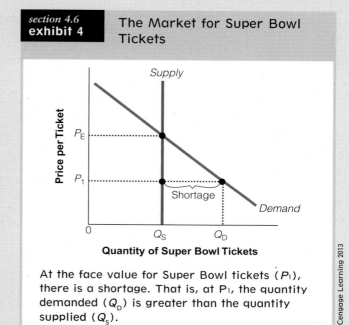

At the face value for Super Bowl tickets (P_1), there is a shortage. That is, at P_1, the quantity demanded (Q_D) is greater than the quantity supplied (Q_S).

© Cengage Learning 2013

AP PHOTO/KYLE ERICSON

ⓘ SECTION QUIZ

1. A market will experience a _____ in a situation where quantity supplied exceeds quantity demanded and a _____ in a situation where quantity demanded exceeds quantity supplied.

   a. shortage; shortage

   b. surplus; surplus

   c. shortage; surplus

   d. surplus; shortage

2. The price of a good will tend to rise when

   a. a temporary shortage at the current price occurs (assuming no price controls are imposed).

   b. a temporary surplus at the current price occurs (assuming no price controls are imposed).

   c. demand decreases.

   d. supply increases.

3. Which of the following is true?

   a. The intersection of the supply and demand curves shows the equilibrium price and equilibrium quantity in a market.

   b. A surplus is a situation where quantity supplied exceeds quantity demanded.

   c. A shortage is a situation where quantity demanded exceeds quantity supplied.

   d. Shortages and surpluses set in motion actions by many buyers and sellers that will move the market toward the equilibrium price and quantity unless otherwise prevented.

   e. All of the above are true.

---

1. How does the intersection of supply and demand indicate the equilibrium price and quantity in a market?

2. What can cause a change in the supply and demand equilibrium?

3. What must be true about the price charged for a shortage to occur?

4. What must be true about the price charged for a surplus to occur?

5. Why do market forces tend to eliminate both shortages and surpluses?

6. If tea prices were above their equilibrium level, what force would tend to push tea prices down? If tea prices were below their equilibrium level, what force would tend to push tea prices up?

Answers: 1. d 2. a 3. e

Interactive Summary

Fill in the blanks:

1. A(n) _____ is the process of buyers and sellers _____ goods and services.

2. The important point about a market is what it does—it facilitates _____.

3. _____, as a group, determine the demand side of the market. _____, as a group, determine the supply side of the market.

4. A(n) _____ market consists of many buyers and sellers, no single one of whom can influence the market price.

5. According to the law of demand, other things being equal, when the price of a good or service falls, the _____ increases.

6. An individual _____ curve reveals the different amounts of a particular good a person would be willing and able to buy at various possible prices in a particular time interval, other things being equal.

7. The _____ curve for a product is the horizontal summing of the demand curves of the individuals in the market.

8. A change in _____ leads to a change in quantity demanded, illustrated by a(n) _____ demand curve.

9. A change in demand is caused by changes in any of the other factors (besides the good's own price) that would affect how much of the good is purchased: the _____, _____, the _____ of buyers, _____, and _____.

10. An increase in demand is represented by a _____ shift in the demand curve; a decrease in demand is represented by a(n) _____ shift in the demand curve.

11. Two goods are called _____ if an increase in the price of one causes the demand curve for another good to shift to the _____.

12. For normal goods an increase in income leads to a(n) _____ in demand, and a decrease in income leads to a(n) _____ in demand, other things being equal.

13. An increase in the expected future price of a good or an increase in expected future income may _____ current demand.

14. According to the law of supply, the higher the price of the good, the greater the _____, and the lower the price of the good, the smaller the _____.

15. The quantity supplied is positively related to the price because firms supplying goods and services want to increase their _____ and because increasing _____ costs mean that the sellers will require _____ prices to induce them to increase their output.

16. An individual supply curve is a graphical representation that shows the _____ relationship between the price and the quantity supplied.

17. The market supply curve is a graphical representation of the amount of goods and services that sellers are _____ and _____ to supply at various prices.

18. Possible supply determinants (factors that determine the position of the supply curve) are _____ prices; _____; _____ of sellers and _____.

19. A fall in input prices will _____ the costs of production, causing the supply curve to shift to the _____.

20. The supply of a good _____ if the price of one of its substitutes in production falls.

21. The supply of a good _____ if the price of one of its substitutes in production rises.

22. The price at the intersection of the market demand curve and the market supply curve is called the _____ price, and the quantity is called the _____ quantity.

23. A situation where quantity supplied is greater than quantity demanded is called a(n) _____.

24. A situation where quantity demanded is greater than quantity supplied is called a(n) _____.

25. At a price greater than the equilibrium price, a(n) _____, or excess quantity supplied, would exist. Sellers would be willing to sell _____ than demanders would be willing to buy. Frustrated suppliers would _____ their price and _____ on production, and consumers would buy _____, returning the market to equilibrium.

Answers: 1. market; exchanging 2. trade 3. Buyers; Sellers 4. competitive 5. quantity demanded 6. demand 7. market demand 8. a good's price; movement along 9. prices of related goods; income; number; tastes; expectations 10. rightward; leftward 11. substitutes; right 12. increase; decrease 13. increase 14. quantity supplied; quantity supplied 15. profits; production; higher 16. positive; able 17. willing; able 18. seller's input; expectations; number of sellers; technology and the prices of related goods 19. lower; right 20. increases 21. decreases 22. equilibrium; equilibrium 23. surplus 24. shortage 25. surplus; more; lower; cut back; more

Section Quiz Answers

4.1 Markets

1. Why is it difficult to define a market precisely?

Every market is different. An incredible variety of exchange arrangements arise for different types of products, different degrees of organization, different geographical extents, and so on.

2. Why do you get your produce at a supermarket rather than directly from farmers?

Supermarkets act as middlepersons between growers of produce and consumers of produce. You hire them to do this task for you when you buy produce from them, rather than directly from growers, because they conduct those transactions at lower costs than you could. (If you could do it more cheaply than supermarkets, you would buy directly rather than from supermarkets.)

3. Why do the prices people pay for similar items at garage sales vary more than for similar items in a department store?

Items for sale at department stores are more standardized, easier to compare, and more heavily advertised, which makes consumers more aware of the prices at which they could get a particular good elsewhere, reducing the differences in price that can persist among department stores. Garage sale items are nonstandardized, costly to compare, and not advertised, which means people are often quite unaware of how much a given item could be purchased for elsewhere, so that price differences for similar items at different garage sales can be substantial.

4.2 Demand

1. What is an inverse relationship?

An inverse, or negative, relationship is one where one variable changes in the opposite direction from the other—if one increases, the other decreases.

2. How do lower prices change buyers' incentives?

A lower price for a good means that the opportunity cost to buyers of purchasing it is lower than before, and self-interest leads buyers to buy more of it as a result.

3. How do higher prices change buyers' incentives?

A higher price for a good means that the opportunity cost to buyers of purchasing it is higher than before, and self-interest leads buyers to buy less of it as a result.

4. What is an individual demand schedule?

An individual demand schedule reveals the different amounts of a good or service a person would be willing to buy at various possible prices in a particular time interval.

5. What is the difference between an individual demand curve and a market demand curve?

The market demand curve shows the total amounts of a good or service all the buyers as a group are willing to buy at various possible prices in a particular time interval. The market quantity demanded at a given price is just the sum of the quantities demanded by each individual buyer at that price.

6. Why does the amount of dating on campus tend to decline just before and during final exams?

The opportunity cost of dating—in this case, the value to students of the studying time forgone—is higher just before and during final exams than during most of the rest of an academic term. Because the cost is higher, students do less of it.

4.3 Shifts in the Demand Curve

1. What is the difference between a change in demand and a change in quantity demanded?

A change in demand shifts the entire demand curve, while a change in quantity demanded refers to a movement along a given demand curve, caused by a change in the good's price.

2. If the price of zucchini increases, causing the demand for yellow squash to rise, what do we call the relationship between zucchini and yellow squash?

Whenever an increased price of one good increases the demand for another, they are substitutes. The fact that some people consider zucchini an alternative to yellow squash explains in part why zucchini becomes more costly. Therefore, some people substitute into buying relatively cheaper yellow squash now instead.

3. If incomes rise and, as a result, demand for jet skis increases, how do we describe that good?

If income rises and, as a result, demand for jet skis increases, we call jet skis a normal good, because for most (or normal) goods, we would rather have more of them than less, so an increase in income would lead to an increase in demand for such goods.

4. **How do expectations about the future influence the demand curve?**

Expectations about the future influence the demand curve because buying a good in the future is an alternative to buying it now. Therefore, the higher future prices are expected to be compared to the present, the less attractive future purchases become, and the greater the current demand for that good, as people buy more now when it is expected to be cheaper, rather than later, when it is expected to be more costly.

5. **Would a change in the price of ice cream cause a change in the demand for ice cream? Why or why not?**

No. The demand for ice cream represents the different quantities of ice cream that would be purchased at different prices. In other words, it represents the relationship between the price of ice cream and the quantity of ice cream demanded. Changing the price of ice cream does not change this relationship, so it does not change demand.

6. **Would a change in the price of ice cream likely cause a change in the demand for frozen yogurt, a substitute?**

Yes. Changing the price of ice cream, a substitute for frozen yogurt, would change the quantity of frozen yogurt demanded at a given price. This change in price means that the whole relationship between the price and quantity of frozen yogurt demanded has changed, which means the demand for frozen yogurt has changed.

7. **If plane travel is a normal good and bus travel is an inferior good, what will happen to the demand curves for plane and bus travel if people's incomes increase?**

The demand for plane travel and all other normal goods will increase if incomes increase, while the demand for bus travel and all other inferior goods will decrease if incomes increase.

4.4 Supply

1. **What are the two reasons why a supply curve is positively sloped?**

A supply curve is positively sloped because (1) the benefits to sellers from selling increase as the price they receive increases, and (2) the opportunity costs of supplying additional output rise with output (the law of increasing opportunity costs), so it takes a higher price to make increasing output in the self-interest of sellers.

2. **What is the difference between an individual supply curve and a market supply curve?**

The market supply curve shows the total amounts of a good all the sellers as a group are willing to sell at

various prices in a particular time period. The market quantity supplied at a given price is just the sum of the quantities supplied by each individual seller at that price.

4.5 Shifts in the Supply Curve

1. **What is the difference between a change in supply and a change in quantity supplied?**

A change in supply shifts the entire supply curve, while a change in quantity supplied refers to a movement along a given supply curve.

2. **If a seller expects the price of a good to rise in the near future, how will that expectation affect the current supply curve?**

Selling a good in the future is an alternative to selling it now. Therefore, the higher the expected future price relative to the current price, the more attractive future sales become, and the less attractive current sales become. This will lead sellers to reduce (shift left) the current supply of that good, as they want to sell later, when the good is expected to be more valuable, rather than now.

3. **Would a change in the price of wheat change the supply of wheat? Would it change the supply of corn, if wheat and corn can be grown on the same type of land?**

The supply of wheat represents the different quantities of wheat that would be offered for sale at different prices. In other words, it represents the relationship between the price of wheat and the quantity of wheat supplied. Changing the price of wheat does not change this relationship, so it does not change the supply of wheat. However, a change in the price of wheat changes the relative attractiveness of raising wheat instead of corn, which changes the supply of corn.

4. **If a guitar manufacturer increased its wages in order to keep its workers, what would happen to the supply of guitars as a result?**

An increase in wages, or any other input price, would decrease (shift left) the supply of guitars, making fewer guitars available for sale at any given price, by raising the opportunity cost of producing guitars.

5. **What happens to the supply of baby-sitting services in an area when many teenagers get their driver's licenses at about the same time?**

When teenagers get their driver's licenses, their increased mobility expands their alternatives to baby-sitting substantially, raising the opportunity cost of baby-sitting. This change decreases (shifts left) the supply of baby-sitting services.

4.6   Market Equilibrium Price and Quantity

1. How does the intersection of supply and demand indicate the equilibrium price and quantity in a market?

The intersection of supply and demand indicates the equilibrium price and quantity in a market because at higher prices, sellers would be frustrated by their inability to sell all they would like, leading sellers to compete by lowering the price they charge; at lower prices, buyers would be frustrated by their inability to buy all they would like, leading buyers to compete by increasing the price they offer to pay.

2. What can cause a change in the supply and demand equilibrium?

Changes in any of the demand curve shifters or the supply curve shifters will change the supply and demand equilibrium.

3. What must be true about the price charged for a shortage to occur?

The price charged must be less than the equilibrium price, with the result that buyers would like to buy more at that price than sellers are willing to sell.

4. What must be true about the price charged for a surplus to occur?

The price charged must be greater than the equilibrium price, with the result that sellers would like to sell more at that price than buyers are willing to buy.

5. Why do market forces tend to eliminate both shortages and surpluses?

Market forces tend to eliminate both shortages and surpluses because of the self-interest of the market participants. A seller is better off successfully selling at a lower equilibrium price than not being able to sell at a higher price (the surplus situation) and a buyer is better off successfully buying at a higher equilibrium price than not being able to buy at a lower price (the shortage situation). Therefore, we expect market forces to eliminate both shortages and surpluses.

6. If tea prices were above their equilibrium level, what force would tend to push tea prices down? If tea prices were below their equilibrium level, what force would tend to push tea prices up?

If tea prices were above their equilibrium level, sellers frustrated by their inability to sell as much tea as they would like at those prices would compete the price of tea down, as they tried to make more attractive offers to tea buyers. If tea prices were below their equilibrium level, buyers frustrated by their inability to buy as much tea as they would like at those prices would compete the price of tea up, as they tried to make more attractive offers to tea sellers.

Problems

1. Is the market for laptop computers local, national, or global?

2. Sid moves from New York City, where he lived in a small condominium, to rural Minnesota, where he buys a big house on five acres of land. Using the law of demand, what do you think is true of land prices in New York City relative to those in rural Minnesota?

3. The following table shows Hillary's demand schedule for Cherry Blossom Makeup. Graph Hillary's demand curve.

Price (dollars per ounce)	Quantity Demanded (ounces per week)
$15	5 oz.
12	10
9	15
6	20
3	25

4. The following table shows Cherry Blossom Makeup demand schedules for Hillary's friends, Barbara and Nancy. If Hillary, Barbara, and Nancy constitute the whole market for Cherry Blossom Makeup, complete the market demand schedule and graph the market demand curve.

Price (dollars per ounce)	Quantity Demanded (ounces per week)			
	Hillary	Barbara	Nancy	Market
$15	5	0	15	
12	10	5	20	
9	15	10	25	
6	20	15	30	
3	25	20	35	

5. What would be the effects of each of the following on the demand for hamburger in Hilo, Hawaii? In each case, identify the responsible determinant of demand.
   a. The price of chicken falls.
   b. The price of hamburger buns doubles.
   c. Scientists find that eating hamburger prolongs life.
   d. The population of Hilo doubles.

6. What would be the effect of each of the following on the demand for Chevrolets in the United States? In each case, identify the responsible determinant of demand.
   a. The price of Fords plummets.
   b. Consumers believe that the price of Chevrolets will rise next year.
   c. The incomes of Americans rise.
   d. The price of gasoline falls dramatically.

7. The following graph shows three market demand curves for cantaloupe. Starting at point A,
   a. which point represents an increase in quantity demanded?
   b. which point represents an increase in demand?
   c. which point represents a decrease in demand?
   d. which point represents a decrease in quantity demanded?

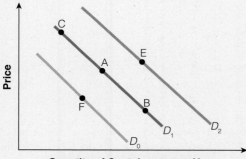

Quantity of Cantaloupes per Year

8. Using the demand curve, show the effect of the following events on the market for beef:
   a. Consumer income increases.
   b. The price of beef increases.
   c. An outbreak of "mad cow" disease occurs.
   d. The price of chicken (a substitute) increases.
   e. The price of barbecue grills (a complement) increases.

9. Draw the demand curves for the following goods. If the price of the first good listed rises, what will happen to the demand for the second good, and why?
   a. hamburger and ketchup
   b. Coca-Cola and Pepsi
   c. camera and film
   d. golf clubs and golf balls
   e. skateboard and razor scooter

10. If the price of ice cream increased,
    a. what would be the effect on the demand for ice cream?
    b. what would be the effect on the demand for frozen yogurt?

11. Using the graph below, answer the following questions.
    a. What is the shift from D_1 to D_2 called?
    b. What is the movement from B to A called?
    c. What is the movement from A to B called?
    d. What is the shift from D_2 to D_1 called?

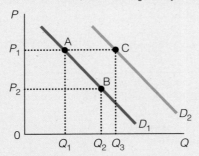

12. Felix is a wheat farmer who has two fields he can use to grow wheat. The first field is right next to his house and the topsoil is rich and thick. The second field is 10 miles away in the mountains and the soil is rocky. At current wheat prices, Felix just produces from the field next to his house because the market price for wheat is just high enough to cover his costs of production including a reasonable profit. What would have to happen to the market price of wheat for Felix to have the incentive to produce from the second field?

13. Show the impact of each of the following events on the oil market.
    a. OPEC becomes more effective in limiting the supply of oil.
    b. OPEC becomes less effective in limiting the supply of oil.
    c. The price for natural gas (a substitute for heating oil) rises.
    d. New oil discoveries occur in Alaska.
    e. Electric and hybrid cars become subsidized and their prices fall.

14. The following table shows the supply schedule for Rolling Rock Oil Co. Plot Rolling Rock's supply curve on a graph.

Price (dollars per barrel)	Quantity Supplied (barrels per month)
$ 5	10,000
10	15,000
15	20,000
20	25,000
25	30,000

15. The following table shows the supply schedules for Rolling Rock and two other petroleum companies. Armadillo Oil and Pecos Petroleum. Assuming these three companies make up the entire supply side of the oil market, complete the market supply schedule and draw the market supply curve on a graph.

Price (dollars per barrel)	Quantity Supplied (barrels per month)			
	Rolling Rock	Armadillo Oil	Pecos Petroleum	Market
$ 5	10,000	8,000	2,000	_____
10	15,000	10,000	5,000	_____
15	20,000	12,000	8,000	_____
20	25,000	14,000	11,000	_____
25	30,000	16,000	14,000	_____

16. If the price of corn rose,
    a. what would be the effect on the supply of corn?
    b. what would be the effect on the supply of wheat?

17. Using the graph below, answer the following questions:
    a. What is the shift from S_1 to S_2 called?
    b. What is the movement from A to B called?
    c. What is the movement from B to A called?
    d. What is the shift from S_2 to S_1 called?

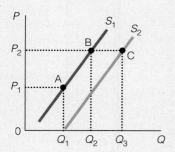

18. What would be the effect of each of the following on the supply of salsa in the United States? In each case, identify the responsible determinant of supply.
    a. Tomato prices skyrocket.
    b. Congress places a 26 percent tax on salsa.
    c. Ed Scissorhands introduces a new, faster vegetable chopper.
    d. J. Lo, Beyonce, and Adam Sandler each introduce a new brand of salsa.

19. What would be the effects of each of the following on the supply of coffee worldwide? In each case, identify the responsible determinant of supply.
    a. Freezing temperatures wipe out half of Brazil's coffee crop.
    b. Wages of coffee workers in Latin America rise as unionization efforts succeed.
    c. Indonesia offers big subsidies to its coffee producers.
    d. Genetic engineering produces a super coffee bean that grows faster and needs less care.
    e. Coffee suppliers expect prices to be higher in the future.

20. The following graph shows three market supply curves for cantaloupe. Compared to point A, which point represents
    a. an increase in quantity supplied?
    b. an increase in supply?
    c. a decrease in quantity supplied?
    d. a decrease in supply?

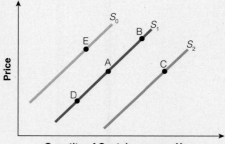

21. The following table shows the hypothetical monthly demand and supply schedules for cans of macadamia nuts in Hawaii.

Price	Quantity Demanded (cans)	Quantity Supplied (cans)
$ 6	700	100
7	600	200
8	500	300
9	400	400
10	300	500

a. What is the equilibrium price of macadamia nuts in Hawaii?

b. At a price of $7 per can, is there equilibrium, a surplus, or a shortage? If it is a surplus or shortage, how large is it?

c. At a price of $10, is there equilibrium, a surplus, or a shortage? If it is a surplus or shortage, how large is it?

22. When asked about the reason for a lifeguard shortage that threatened to keep one-third of the city's beaches closed for the summer, the Deputy Parks Commissioner of New York responded that "Kids seem to want to do work that's more in tune with a career. Maybe they prefer carpal tunnel syndrome to sunburn." What do you think is causing the shortage? What would you advise the Deputy Parks Commissioner to do in order to alleviate the shortage?

23. If a price is above the equilibrium price, explain the forces that bring the market back to the equilibrium price and quantity. If a price is below the equilibrium price, explain the forces that bring the market back to the equilibrium price and quantity.

24. The market for baseball tickets at your college stadium, which seats 2,000, is the following:

Price	Quantity Demanded	Quantity Supplied
$2	4,000	2,000
4	2,000	2,000
6	1,000	2,000
8	500	2,000

a. What is the equilibrium price?

b. What is unusual about the supply curve?

c. At what prices would a shortage occur?

d. At what prices would a surplus occur?

e. Suppose that the addition of new students (all big baseball fans) next year will add 1,000 to the quantity demanded at each price. What will this increase do to next year's demand curve? What is the new equilibrium price?

25. Assume the following information for the demand and supply curves for good Z.

Demand		Supply	
Price	Quantity Demanded	Price	Quantity Supplied
$10	10	$ 1	10
9	20	2	15
8	30	3	20
7	40	4	25
6	50	5	30
5	60	6	35
4	70	7	40
3	80	8	45
2	90	9	50
1	100	10	55

a. Draw the corresponding supply and demand curves.

b. What are the equilibrium price and quantity traded?

c. Would a price of $9 result in a shortage or a surplus? How large?

d. Would a price of $3 result in a shortage or a surplus? How large?

e. If the demand for Z increased by 15 units at every price, what would the new equilibrium price and quantity traded be?

f. Given the original demand for Z, if the supply of Z were increased by 15 units at every price, what would the new equilibrium price and quantity traded be?

chapter five

Markets in Motion and Price Controls

5.1 Changes in Market Equilibrium

5.2 Price Controls

When four floors of his building caved in, killing three of his neighbors, Uttamchand K. Sojatwala, owner of a successful textile business, refused to leave his two-bedroom, rent-controlled apartment in Mumbai, India. The city then cut off his electricity and water and threatened to arrest his wife, but he still wouldn't leave. In all, fifty-eight tenants refused to leave a rent-controlled apartment building that was considered too dangerous by city officials. Why did these residents take the risk? Cheap rent—$8.50 a month.

There is tremendous tension in "the market" for Mumbai rent-controlled properties between landlords who can't afford to keep up their properties and tenants who will go to extraordinary lengths to keep their units.

In the words of the great economist Alfred Marshall, "Like scissors that function by the interaction of two distinct blades, supply and demand interact to determine the price and quantity exchanged." In this chapter, we will study the impact of a change in one or more of the determinants of supply and demand and see how it impacts the market price and quantity exchanged. That is, if you want to know how an event or policy may affect the economy, you must know supply and demand. We will then explore the impact of price controls, which are government mandates to set a price above or below the equilibrium price. We will also see that policies can have unintended effects—adverse effects that the policy makers did not anticipate.

5.1 Changes in Market Equilibrium

- What happens to equilibrium price and quantity when the demand curve shifts?
- What happens to equilibrium price and quantity when the supply curve shifts?
- What happens when both supply and demand shift in the same time period?
- What is an indeterminate solution?

What causes the changes in the equilibrium price and equilibrium quantity?

When one of the many determinants of demand or supply (input prices, prices of related products, number of suppliers, expectations, technology, and so on) changes, the demand and/or supply curves will shift, leading to changes in the equilibrium price and equilibrium quantity. We first consider a change in demand.

A Change in Demand

A shift in the demand curve—caused by a change in the price of a related good (substitutes or complements), income, the number of buyers, tastes, or expectations—results in a change in both equilibrium price and equilibrium quantity, assuming the supply curve has not changed. But how and why does this relationship happen? The answer can be most clearly explained by means of an example. Suppose a new study claimed that two cups of coffee per day had significant health benefits. We would expect an increase in the demand for coffee. That is, at any given price, buyers want more coffee than before. At the original equilibrium, E_1, consumers want to buy Q_3 but sellers only want to sell Q_1, as seen in Exhibit 1. Market pressure drives the price up to a new equilibrium, E_2 at P_2. Both the equilibrium price and quantity rise because of the increase in demand. Notice that the rightward *shift in the demand curve causes a movement up along the supply curve*, causing an increase in quantity supplied.

If demand is greater than the current production schedule, then there will be shortages at the current price. Consequently some dealers were charging prices much higher than the sticker price for the 2010 Camaro when it first hit the showroom.

A Change in Supply

Like a shift in demand, a shift in the supply curve will also influence both equilibrium price and equilibrium quantity, assuming that demand for the product has not changed. For example, what impact would unfavorable weather conditions have in coffee-producing countries? Such conditions could cause a reduction in the supply of coffee. At any given price, sellers now want to sell less coffee. At the original equilibrium price of P_1, consumers still want to buy Q_1, but sellers are now only willing to supply Q_3. Thus, a shortage develops. Market pressure forces the price of coffee up until it reaches the new equilibrium at E_2, where the equilibrium price is P_2, and the equilibrium quantity is Q_2. A decrease in supply, *ceteris paribus*, will lead to a higher equilibrium price and a lower equilibrium quantity, as shown in Exhibit 2. Notice that the decrease in supply causes a *leftward shift in the supply curve, resulting in a movement up along the demand curve* causing a decrease in quantity demanded.

Changes in Both Supply and Demand

We have discussed that, as part of the continual process of adjustment that occurs in the marketplace, supply and demand can each shift in response to many different factors, with the market then adjusting toward the new equilibrium. We have, so far, only considered what happens when just one such change occurs at a time. In these cases, we learned that the results of the adjustments in supply and demand on the equilibrium price and quantity are predictable. However, both supply and demand will often shift in the same time period. Can we predict what will happen to equilibrium prices and equilibrium quantities in these situations?

As you will see, when supply and demand move at the same time, we can predict the change in one variable (price or quantity), but we are unable to predict the direction of the

In the summer of 2010, a severe drought and wildfires in Russia, the world's fourth largest wheat producer, destroyed roughly 20 percent of the country's wheat crop and sent prices soaring. From June of 2010 to August 2010, wheat prices more than doubled. The world wheat market was also impacted by unusually wet weather in Canada which prevented seeding and destroyed crops. The price of orange juice also rose probably thanks to bets placed on the likelihood of tropical storms. Coffee prices were also at a 13-year high, as a result of poor harvests. Taken together, the cost of breakfast rose over 20 percent in just two months.

ECS
economic content standards

Changes in supply or demand cause prices to change; in turn, buyers and sellers adjust their purchases and sales decisions.

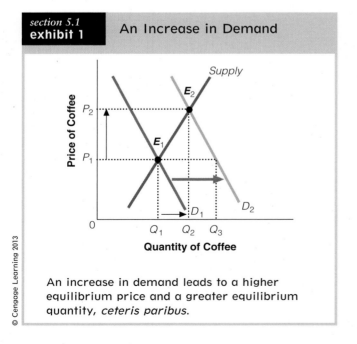

section 5.1 **exhibit 1**   An Increase in Demand

An increase in demand leads to a higher equilibrium price and a greater equilibrium quantity, *ceteris paribus.*

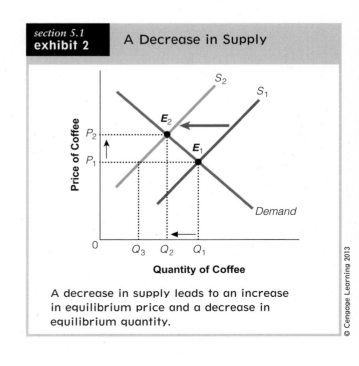

section 5.1 **exhibit 2**   A Decrease in Supply

A decrease in supply leads to an increase in equilibrium price and a decrease in equilibrium quantity.

use
what you've learned   Change in Demand

Q In ski resorts such as Aspen and Sun Valley, hotel prices are higher in February (in-season when more skiers want to ski) than in May (off-season when fewer skiers want to ski). If the May hotel prices were charged in February, what problem would arise? What if we charged February's price in May?

A In the (likely) event that supply is not altered significantly, demand is chiefly responsible for the higher prices in the prime skiing months. In Exhibit 3(a), if prices were maintained at the off-season rates (P_{MAY}) all year long, a shortage would exist—the difference between points A and B in Exhibit 3(a). This excess demand at the off-peak prices causes prime-season rates to be higher. After all, why would a self-interested resort owner rent you a room for less than its opportunity cost (what someone else would be willing to pay)? For example, at the Hotel Jerome in Aspen, the price per night of a Deluxe King room is almost six times higher

in late December (in-season) than it is in mid-May (off-season). In Exhibit 3(b), we see that if hotels were to charge the in-season price (P_{FEB}) during the off-season (May), a surplus would result—the difference between points C and D. Now, it would be this excess supply during the off-season (at in-season prices) that would cause the price to fall. Who needs all the empty rooms?

What would happen if the Hotel Jerome, pictured above, charged the lower out-of-season rate for resort rentals during peak ski season?

section 5.1
exhibit 3   The Market for Aspen Rentals

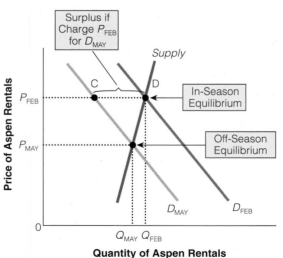

a. Charging May (Off-Season) Prices in February (In-Season)

b. Charging February (In-Season) Prices in May (Off-Season)

in the news   The Role of Prices in the Aftermath of Hurricane Katrina

The fallout from Hurricane Katrina has featured a lot of ignorance and demagoguery about prices. Let's look at some of it. One undeniable fact is that the hurricane disaster changed scarcity conditions. There are fewer stores, fewer units of housing, less gasoline, and a shortage of many other goods and services used on a daily basis. Rising prices are not only a manifestation of these changed scarcity conditions, they help us cope, adjust and get us on the road to recovery.

Here's a which-is-better question for you. Suppose a hotel room rented for $79 a night prior to Hurricane Katrina's devastation. Based on that price, an evacuating family of four might rent two adjoining rooms. When they arrive at the hotel, they find the rooms rent for $200; they decide to make do with one room. In my book, that's wonderful. The family voluntarily opted to make a room available for another family who had to evacuate or whose home was destroyed. Demagogues will call this price-gouging, but I ask you, which is preferable: a room available at $200 or a room unavailable at $79? Rising prices get people to voluntarily economize on goods and services rendered scarcer by the disaster.

After Hurricane Katrina struck, gasoline prices shot up almost a dollar nearly overnight. Some people have been quick to call this price-gouging, particularly since wholesalers and retailers were charging the higher price for gasoline already purchased and in their tanks prior to the hurricane. The fact of business is that what a seller paid for some-

thing doesn't necessarily determine its selling price. Put in a bit more sophisticated way: Historical costs have nothing to do with selling price. For example, suppose you maintained a 10-pound inventory of coffee in your cupboard. When I ran out, you'd occasionally sell me a pound for $2. Suppose there's a freeze in Brazil destroying much of the coffee crop, driving coffee prices to $5 a pound. Then I come around to purchase coffee. Are you going to charge me $2 a pound, what you paid for it, or $5, what it's going to cost you to restock your coffee inventory?

What about the house that you might have purchased for $50,000 in 1970 that you're selling today? If you charged me $250,000 for it, today's price for its replacement, as opposed to what you paid for it, are you guilty of price-gouging?

Recovering from Katrina means resources will have to be moved to the Gulf Coast. I ask you, how does one get electricians, plumbers and other artisans to give up their comfortable homes and livelihoods in Virginia and Pennsylvania and travel to Mobile and New Orleans to help in the recovery? If you said pay them higher prices, go to the head of the class. Higher prices, along with windfall profits, are economic signals of unmet human wants. As such, they encourage producers to meet those human wants. . . .

SOURCE: Walter Williams, "The Role of Prices in the Aftermath of Hurricane Katrina," September 14, 2005, © 2005, Creators Syndicate, Inc.

effect on the other variable with any certainty. The change in the second variable, then, is said to be *indeterminate,* because it cannot be determined without additional information about the size of the relative shifts in supply and demand. This concept will become clearer to you as we work through the following example.

An Increase in Supply and a Decrease in Demand

In Exhibits 4(a) and 4(b), we have an increase in supply and a decrease in demand. These changes will clearly result in a decrease in the equilibrium price, because both the increase in supply and the decrease in demand work to push this price down. This drop in equilibrium price (from P_1 to P_2) is shown in the movement from E_1 to E_2 in Exhibits 4(a) and 4(b).

What does it mean when it says that one of the variables is indeterminate?

section 5.1 exhibit 4 — Shifts in Supply and Demand

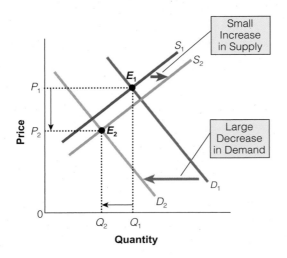

a. A Small Increase in Supply and a Large Decrease in Demand

If the decrease in demand (leftward shift) is greater than the increase in supply (rightward shift), the equilibrium price and equilibrium quantity will fall.

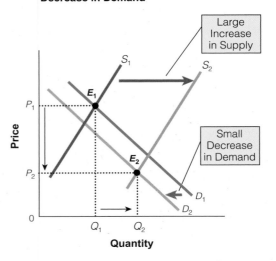

b. A Large Increase in Supply and a Small Decrease in Demand

If the increase in supply (rightward shift) is greater than the decrease in demand (leftward shift), the equilibrium price will fall and the equilibrium quantity will rise.

The effect of these changes on equilibrium price is clear, but how does the equilibrium quantity change? The impact on equilibrium quantity is indeterminate because the increase in supply increases the equilibrium quantity and the decrease in demand decreases it. In this scenario, the change in the equilibrium quantity will vary depending on the relative changes in supply and demand. If, as shown in Exhibit 4(a), the decrease in demand is greater than the increase in supply, the equilibrium quantity will decrease. If, however, as shown in Exhibit 4(b), the increase in supply is greater than the decrease in demand, the equilibrium quantity will increase.

section 5.1 exhibit 5 — An Increase in the Demand and Supply of HD Televisions

The increase in supply and demand caused an increase in the equilibrium quantity. Price is the indeterminate variable. Because the supply of HD televisions shifted more than the demand for HD televisions, the price of HD televisions has fallen.

An Increase in Demand and Supply

It is also possible that both supply and demand will increase (or decrease). This situation, for example, has happened with high-definition (HD) televisions (and with DVDs, laptops, cell phones, digital cameras, and other electronic equipment, too). As a result of technological breakthroughs and new factories manufacturing HD televisions, the supply curve for HD televisions shifted to the right. That is, at any given price, more HD televisions were offered than before. But with rising income and an increasing number of buyers in the market, the demand for HD televisions increased as well. As shown in Exhibit 5, both the increased demand and the increased supply caused an increase in the equilibrium quantity—more HD televisions were sold. The equilibrium price could have gone either up (because of increased demand) or down (because of increased supply), depending on the relative sizes of the demand and supply shifts. In this case, price is the indeterminate variable. However, in the case of HD televisions, we know that the supply curve shifted more than the demand curve, so that the effect of increased supply pushing prices down outweighed the effect of increased demand pushing prices up. As a result, the equilibrium price of HD televisions has fallen (from P_1 to P_2) over time.

section 5.1 **exhibit 6**	The Effect of Changing Demand and/or Supply		
	Supply Unchanged	**An Increase in Supply**	**A Decrease in Supply**
Demand unchanged	P unchanged Q unchanged	$P \downarrow$ $Q \uparrow$	$P \uparrow$ $Q \downarrow$
An increase in demand	$P \uparrow$ $Q \uparrow$	P indeterminate* $Q \uparrow$	$P \uparrow$ Q indeterminate*
A decrease in demand	$P \downarrow$ $Q \downarrow$	$P \downarrow$ Q indeterminate*	P indeterminate* $Q \downarrow$

*Indeterminate means it may increase, decrease, or remain the same, depending on the size of the change in demand relative to the change in supply.

© Cengage Learning 2013

The Combinations of Supply and Demand Shifts

The possible changes in demand and/or supply shifts are presented in Exhibit 6, along with the resulting changes in equilibrium quantity and equilibrium price in Exhibit 7. Even though you could memorize the impact of the various possible changes in demand and supply, it would be more profitable to draw a graph, as shown in Exhibit 7, whenever a situation of changing demand and/or supply arises. Remember that an increase in either demand or supply means a rightward shift in the curve, while a decrease in either means a leftward shift. Also, when both demand and supply change, one of the two equilibrium values, price or quantity, will change in an indeterminate manner (increase or decrease), depending on the relative magnitude of the changes in supply and demand.

Supply, Demand, and the Market Economy

Supply and demand are at the very foundation of the market system. They determine the prices of goods and services and determine how our scarce resources are allocated. What is truly amazing is how producers respond to the complex wants of the population without having tremendous shortages or surpluses, despite the fact that in a "free market," no single individual or agency makes decisions about what to produce. The market system provides a way for millions of producers and consumers to allocate scarce resources. Buyers and sellers indicate their wants through their actions and inactions in the marketplace, and this collective "voice" determines how resources are allocated. But how is this information communicated? Market prices serve as the language of the market system.

We often say the decision is made by "the market" or "market forces," but this is of little help in pinpointing the name and the place of the decision maker. In fact, no single person makes decisions about the quantity and quality of television, cars, beds, or any other goods or services consumed in the economy. Literally millions of people, both producers and consumers, participate in the decision-making process. To paraphrase a statement made popular by the first great modern economist, Adam Smith, it is as if an invisible hand works to coordinate the efforts of millions of diverse participants in the complex process of producing and distributing goods and services.

Market prices communicate important information to both buyers and sellers. They reveal information about the relative availability of products to buyers, and they provide sellers with critical information about the relative value that consumers place on those products. In effect, market prices provide a way for both buyers and sellers to communicate about the relative value of resources. This communication results in a shifting of resources from those uses that are less valued to those that are more valued.

section 5.1
exhibit 7   The Combination of Supply and Demand Shifts

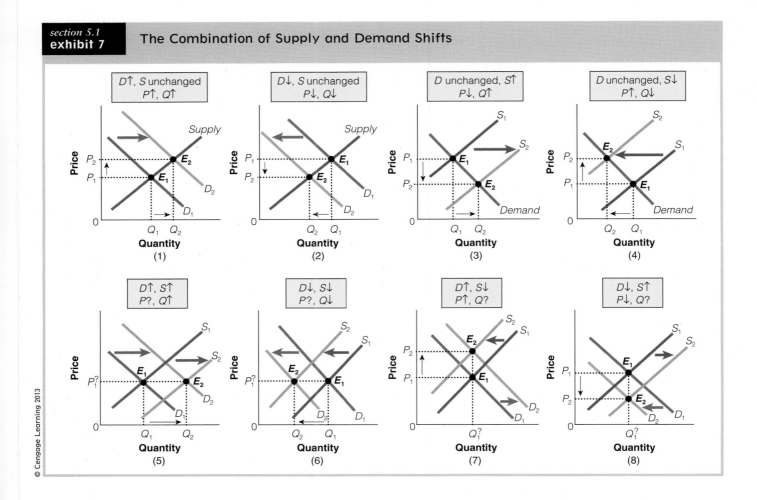

in the news College Enrollment and the Price of Going to College

Q How is it possible that the price of a college education has increased significantly over the past 37 years, yet many more students are attending college? Does this relationship defy the law of demand?

A If we know the price of a college education (adjusted for inflation) and the number of students enrolled in college for the two years 1970 and 2010, we can tell a plausible story using the analysis of supply and demand. In Exhibit 8(a), suppose that we have data for points A and B: the price of a

college education and the quantity (the number of college students enrolled in the respective years, 1970 and 2010). In Exhibit 8(b), we connect the two points with supply and demand curves and see a decrease in supply and an increase in demand. Demand increased between 1970 and 2010 for at least two reasons. First, on the demand side, as population grows, a greater number of buyers want a college education. Second, a college education is a normal good; as income increases, buyers increase their demand for a college education. Third, demand has increased because of the availability of student loans. Between 1999 and 2009, total federal aid to college students rose from $61.1 billion to $116.8 billion. If you include state aid, total

(*continued*)

section 5.1
exhibit 8   Market for College Education

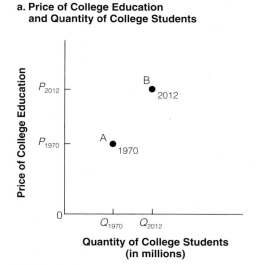

a. Price of College Education and Quantity of College Students

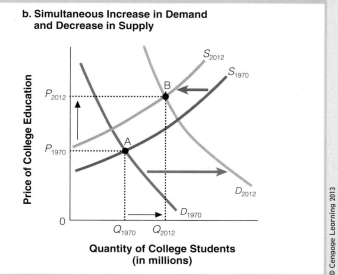

b. Simultaneous Increase in Demand and Decrease in Supply

© Cengage Learning 2013

government subsidies nearly doubled from $66.6 billion to $126.2 billion. The average amount of a federal student loan increased 180 percent from 1990 to 2008, after adjusting for inflation. On the supply side, several factors caused the supply curve for education to shift to the left: the cost of hiring new staff and faculty (and increases in their salaries), new equipment (computers, lab equipment, and library supplies), and buildings (additional classrooms, labs, cafeteria expansions, and dormitory space).

This situation does not defy the law of demand that states that there is an inverse relationship between price and quantity demanded, *ceteris paribus*. The truth is that supply and demand curves are shifting constantly. In this case, the demand (increasing) and supply (decreasing) caused price and quantity to rise.

use what you've learned   Supply and Demand Applications

Q During the second half of the twentieth century, demand for chicken increased because of rising income and the purported health benefits. However, as the demand for chicken increased, the price fell. Why? (*Hint:* Remember it is supply and demand.)

A Even though the demand for chicken did increase (a small rightward shift), the supply of chicken increased even more—technological advances in the poultry industry and many new suppliers caused the supply curve to shift rightward. In order for the price to fall, the supply must have shifted further to the right than the demand curve. The result is more chickens consumed at a lower price.

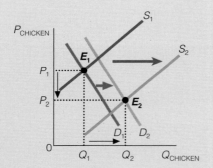

Q Suppose the demand for gasoline increases because of world economic growth and higher incomes. At the same time, supply decreases because of hostilities in the Middle East and refinery problems. What can we predict would happen to the price and quantity of gasoline?

A The increase in demand (rightward shift) and the decrease in supply (leftward shift) would lead to an increase in price. We are not sure about the quantity of gasoline consumed—it depends on the magnitude of the shifts in the demand and supply curves. That is, quantity is indeterminate.

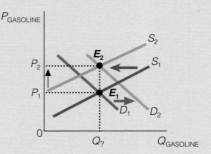

Q Suppose the demand for air travel decreases because of air safety concerns. At the same time, the price of jet fuel increases. What do you think will happen to the price and quantity of air travel?

A Safety concerns would result in a decrease in demand (leftward shift) for air travel and the higher input cost of jet fuel would lead to a decrease in supply (leftward shift). These factors reduce the quantity of air travel. The price change will depend on the magnitude of the shifts in the demand and supply curves. That is, price is indeterminate.

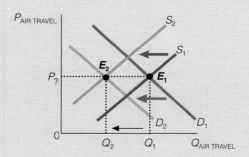

Q Hypothetically, suppose a new study reveals that sugar can have "huge" negative health consequences, causing a large decrease in demand. In addition, a slight reduction in the sugar yield occurs because of bad weather in sugar-producing areas. What do you think will happen to the price and quantity of sugar?

(*continued*)

use what you've learned   Supply and Demand Applications (Cont.)

A A large decrease in demand (leftward shift) for sugar and a small decrease in supply (leftward shift) because of bad weather lead to a reduction in price and a large reduction in quantity.

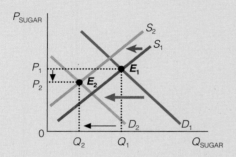

Q As the price of oil rises, many may switch to burning natural gas to save money. Can buyers of natural gas expect any surprises?

A If oil and natural gas are substitutes, then the higher price for oil will cause an increase in demand for natural gas (rightward shift). As a result, the price and quantity of natural gas will rise.

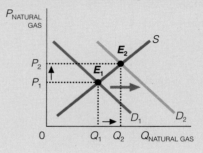

⊘ SECTION QUIZ

1. Other things equal, a decrease in consumer income would
   a. increase the price and increase the quantity of autos exchanged.
   b. increase the price and decrease the quantity of autos exchanged.
   c. decrease the price and increase the quantity of autos exchanged.
   d. decrease the price and decrease the quantity of autos exchanged.

2. An increase in the expected future price of a good by consumers would, other things equal,
   a. increase the current price and increase the current quantity exchanged.
   b. increase the current price and decrease the current quantity exchanged.
   c. decrease the current price and increase the current quantity exchanged.
   d. decrease the current price and decrease the current quantity exchanged.

3. Assume that airline travel is a normal good. Higher incomes would
   a. increase both the price and the quantity of airline travel.
   b. decrease both the price and quantity of airline travel.
   c. increase the price and decrease the quantity of airline travel
   d. decrease the price and increase the quantity of airline travel.

4. If you observed the price of a good increasing and the quantity exchanged decreasing, it would be most likely caused by a(n)
   a. increase in demand.
   b. decrease in demand.
   c. increase in supply.
   d. decrease in supply.

(*continued*)

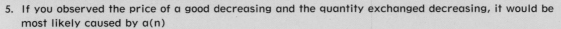

SECTION QUIZ (Cont.)

5. If you observed the price of a good decreasing and the quantity exchanged decreasing, it would be most likely caused by a(n)

   a. increase in demand.

   b. decrease in demand.

   c. increase in supply.

   d. decrease in supply.

6. If both supply and demand decreased, but supply decreased more than demand, the result would be

   a. a higher price and a lower equilibrium quantity.

   b. a lower price and a lower equilibrium quantity.

   c. no change in the price and a lower equilibrium quantity.

   d. a higher price and a greater equilibrium quantity.

   e. a lower price and a greater equilibrium quantity.

7. Which of the following are true statements?

   a. Changes in demand will cause a change in the equilibrium price and/or quantity, *ceteris paribus*.

   b. Changes in supply will cause a change in the equilibrium price and/or quantity, *ceteris paribus*.

   c. Supply and demand curves can shift simultaneously in response to changes in both supply and demand determinants.

   d. When simultaneous shifts occur in both supply and demand curves, we will be able to determine one, but not both, of the variables.

   e. All of the above are true.

---

1. Does an increase in demand create a shortage or surplus at the original price?

2. What happens to the equilibrium price and quantity as a result of a demand increase?

3. Does an increase in supply create a shortage or surplus at the original price?

4. Assuming the market is already at equilibrium, what happens to the equilibrium price and quantity as a result of a supply increase?

5. Why are evening and weekend long-distance calls cheaper than weekday long-distance calls?

6. What would have to be true for both supply and demand to shift in the same time period?

7. When both supply and demand shift, what added information do we need to know in order to determine in which direction the indeterminate variable changes?

8. If both buyers and sellers of grapes expect grape prices to rise in the near future, what will happen to grape prices and sales today?

9. If demand for peanut butter increases and supply decreases, what will happen to equilibrium price and quantity?

Answers: 1. d   2. a   3. a   4. d   5. b   6. a   7. e

Price Controls

☞ What are price controls?   ☞ What are price floors?

☞ What are price ceilings?   ☞ What is the law of unintended consequences?

Price Controls

Although nonequilibrium prices can occur naturally in the private sector, reflecting uncertainty, they seldom last for long. Governments, however, may impose nonequilibrium prices for significant periods. Price controls involve the use of the power of the state to establish prices different from the equilibrium prices that would otherwise prevail. The motivations for price controls vary with the market under consideration. For example, a **price ceiling**, a legal maximum price, is often set for goods deemed important to low-income households, such as housing. Or a **price floor**, a legal minimum price, may be set on wages because wages are the primary source of income for most people.

Price controls are not always implemented by the federal government. Local governments (and more rarely, private companies) can and do impose local price controls. One fairly well-known example is rent control. The inflation of the late 1970s meant rapidly rising rents; and some communities, such as Santa Monica, California, decided to do something about it. In response, they limited how much landlords could charge for rental housing.

price ceiling
a legally established maximum price

price floor
a legally established minimum price

ECS

economic content standards

Government-enforced price ceilings set below the market clearing price and government enforced price floors set above the market clearing price distort price signals and incentives to producers and consumers. The price ceilings cause persistent shortages, while price floors cause persistent surpluses.

Price Ceilings: Rent Controls

Rent control experiences can be found in many cities across the country. San Francisco, Berkeley, and New York City all have had some form of rent control. Although the rules may vary from city to city and over time, generally the price (or rent) of an apartment remains fixed over the tenure of an occupant, except for allowable annual increases tied to the cost of living or some other price index. When an occupant moves out, the owners can usually, but not always, raise the rent to a near-market level for the next occupant. The controlled rents for existing occupants, however, are generally well below market rental rates.

Results of Rent Controls

Most people living in rent-controlled apartments are getting a good deal, one that they would lose by moving as their family circumstances or income changes. Tenants thus are reluctant to give up their governmentally granted right to a below-market-rent apartment. In addition, because the rents received by landlords are constrained and below market levels, the rate of return (roughly, the profit) on housing investments falls compared with that on other forms of real estate not subject to rent controls, such as office rents or mortgage payments on condominiums. Hence, the incentive to construct new housing is reduced.

Further, when landlords are limited in the rents they can charge, they have little incentive to improve or upgrade apartments—by putting in new kitchen appliances or new carpeting, for instance. In fact, rent controls give landlords some incentive to avoid routine maintenance, thereby lowering the cost of apartment ownership to a figure approximating the controlled rental price, although the quality of the housing stock will deteriorate over time.

Another impact of rent controls is that they promote housing discrimination. Where rent controls do not exist, prejudiced landlords might willingly rent to people they believe are undesirable simply because the undesirables are the only ones willing to pay the requested rents (and the landlords are not willing to lower their rents substantially to get desirable renters because of the possible loss of thousands of dollars in income). With rent controls, each rent-controlled apartment is likely to attract many possible renters, some desirable and

global watch Zimbabwe Price Controls Spark Food Shortages

ZIMBABWE'S government and the country's businesses have clashed over prices of basic commodities, now blamed for widespread shortages days after disputed polls won by President Robert Mugabe's ruling party.

Prices shot up by as much as 100 percent after the March 31 parliamentary elections in which Mugabe's ZANU-PF government defeated the opposition Movement for Democratic Change (MDC), but the government swiftly moved in, ordering businesses to reverse the increases.

"Increases were actually delayed to avoid harsh criticism of the government ahead of the elections but now the government is saying you can not increase prices without consulting us . . . that's not what we agreed," a spokesman for the Confederation of Zimbabwe Industries told Reuters.

The staple maize-meal, sugar and cooking oil have disappeared from most shops in Harare's city centre and suburbs while most pumps at fuel stations have run dry, forcing motorists to brace for long queues.

Maize-meal supplies were already erratic in the country in recent months with supermarkets out of stocks for days on end and long queues quickly form where the commodity is available.

AP PHOTO/KAREL PRINSLOO

consider this:

In July of 2007, Zimbabwe's government threatened to seize any business that did not roll their prices back. But many shop-keepers and manufacturers threatened to shut down and lay off workers rather than produce at a loss. Gasoline was disappearing from the pumps and many workers were forced to walk to work. Shoppers were told to queue (wait in line) for whatever products were left on the shelf. Police were sent in to enforce the price controls, which resulted in hundreds of shop owners being arrested for not lowering prices enough. In short, price controls and the resulting shortages can turn into social unrest. This is not the first time Zimbabwe has tried price controls; they are usually short-lived and poorly enforced. In 2009, the finance minister Patrick Chinamasa announced the government is abandoning price controls. Mr. Chinamasa told parliament "that price controls would be abandoned because they had 'unintentionally' harmed businesses and added to Zimbabwe's hyperinflation."

SOURCE: Macdonald Dzirutwe, newzimbabwe.com, retrieved 12/01/2008. © newzimbabwe.com.

some undesirable as judged by the landlord, simply because the rent is at a below-equilibrium price. Landlords can indulge in their "taste" for discrimination without any additional financial loss beyond that required by the controls. Consequently, they will be more likely to choose to rent to desirable people, perhaps a family without children or pets, rather than to undesirable ones, perhaps a family with lower income and so a greater risk of nonpayment.

Can rent controls promote housing discrimination?

Exhibit 1 shows the impact of rent controls. If the price ceiling (P_{RC}) is set below the equilibrium price (P_E), consumers are willing to buy Q_D, but producers are only willing to supply Q_S. The rent control policy will therefore create a persistent shortage, the difference between Q_D and Q_S.

Price Floors: The Minimum Wage

The argument for a minimum wage is simple: Existing wages for workers in some types of labor markets do not allow for a very high standard of living, and a minimum wage allows those workers to live better than before. Ever since 1938, when the first minimum wage was established (at 25 cents per hour), the federal government has, by legislation, made it illegal to pay most workers an amount below the current legislated minimum wage. As of July of 2009, the federal minimum wage was set at $7.25. A number of states also have minimum–wage laws. In cases where an employee is subject to both state and federal minimum–wage laws, the employee is entitled to the higher minimum wage.

Let's examine graphically the impact of a minimum wage on low-skilled workers. In Exhibit 2, suppose the government sets the minimum wage, W_{MIN}, above the market equilibrium wage, W_E. In Exhibit 2, we see that the price floor is binding. That is, there is a surplus of low-skilled workers at W_{MIN}, because the quantity of labor supplied is greater than the quantity of labor demanded. The reason for the surplus of low-skilled workers (unemployment) at W_{MIN} is that more people are willing to work than employers are willing and able to hire.

What does a binding price ceiling or binding price floor mean?

Notice that not everyone loses from a minimum wage. Workers who continue to hold jobs have higher incomes—those between 0 and Q_D in Exhibit 2. However, many low-skilled workers suffer from a minimum wage—those between Q_D and Q_S in Exhibit 2—because they either lose their jobs or are unable to get them in the first place. Although studies

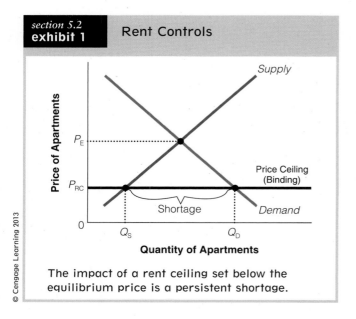

The impact of a rent ceiling set below the equilibrium price is a persistent shortage.

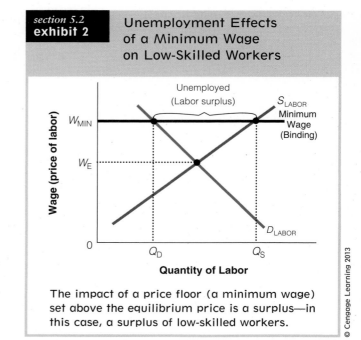

The impact of a price floor (a minimum wage) set above the equilibrium price is a surplus—in this case, a surplus of low-skilled workers.

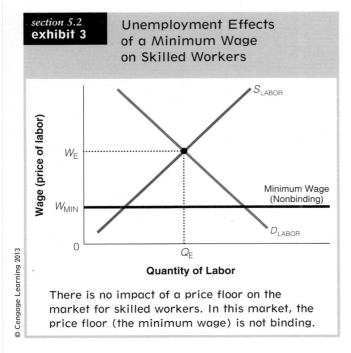

section 5.2
exhibit 3

Unemployment Effects of a Minimum Wage on Skilled Workers

There is no impact of a price floor on the market for skilled workers. In this market, the price floor (the minimum wage) is not binding.

Who loses and who wins with higher minimum wages?

Are consumers hurt by a higher minimum wage?

disagree somewhat on the precise magnitudes, they largely agree that minimum–wage laws do create some unemployment and that the unemployment is concentrated among teenagers—the least-experienced and least-skilled members of the labor force.

Most U.S. workers are not directly affected by the minimum wage because in the market for their skills, they earn wages that exceed the minimum wage. For example, a minimum wage will not affect the unemployment rate for physicians. In Exhibit 3, we see the labor market for skilled and experienced workers. In this market, the minimum wage (the price floor) is not binding because these workers are earning wages that far exceed the minimum wage—W_E is much higher than W_{MIN}.

This analysis does not "prove" that minimum–wage laws are "bad" and should be abolished. First, consider the empirical question of how much unemployment is caused by minimum wages. Economists David Card and Alan Kreuger published a controversial study on the increase in minimum wage in the fast-food industry in New Jersey and Pennsylvania. They found the effect on employment to be quite small. However, other researchers using similar data have found the effect on employment to be much larger. In fact, most empirical studies indicate that a 10 percent increase in the minimum wage would reduce employment of teenagers between 1 and 3 percent. Second, some might believe that the cost of unemployment resulting from a minimum wage is a reasonable price to pay for ensuring that those with jobs get a "decent" wage. However, opponents of minimum wage argue that it might induce teenagers to drop out of school. Less than one-third of minimum-wage earners are from families with incomes below the poverty line. In fact, many recipients of the minimum wage are part-time teenage workers from middle–income families. More efficient methods transfer income to low-wage workers, such as a wage subsidy like the earned income tax credit. This is a government program that supplements low–wage-workers. Of course, there are no free lunches so subsidies in the form of wages, income, or rent ultimately cost taxpayers. We will revisit this topic in upcoming chapters.

However, the analysis does point out there is a cost to having a minimum wage: The burden of the minimum wage falls not only on low-skilled workers and employers but also on consumers of products made more costly by the minimum wage.

Price Ceilings: Price Controls on Gasoline

Another example of price ceilings leading to shortages is the price controls imposed on gasoline in 1974. In 1973, the Organization of Petroleum Exporting Nations (OPEC) reduced the supply of oil. Because crude oil is the most important input in the production of gasoline, this reduction in the supply of oil caused a shift in the supply curve for gasoline leftward from S_1 to S_2 in Exhibit 4. In an effort to prevent sharply rising prices, the government imposed price controls

In 1974, the government imposed price ceilings on gasoline. The result was shortages. In some cities, such as Chicago, Portland, and New York, drivers waited over an hour to fill up their tanks. As you know, the value of your time has an opportunity cost.

on gasoline in 1974. The government told gasoline stations they could not charge more than P_C for gasoline. But people wanted to buy more gasoline than was available at the controlled price, P_C. That is, a shortage developed at P_C, as you can see in Exhibit 4. Some customers were lucky enough to get their gasoline at P_C (0 to Q_S), but others were left wanting (Q_S to Q_D). The price ceiling was binding. Consequently, people wasted hours waiting in line for gasoline. Some gas stations sold their gas on a first-come, first-served basis. Some states implemented an even/odd license plate system. If your license plate ended in an odd number, you could buy gas on only odd numbered days. In addition, quantity restrictions meant that some stations would only allow you to buy a few gallons a day; when they ran out of gas, they closed for the day. Many gas stations were closed in the evenings and on weekends.

A number of government officials wanted to put the blame on OPEC, but if prices were allowed to rise to their equilibrium at E_2, shortages would have been avoided. Instead, it would have meant higher prices at P_2 and a greater quantity sold, Q_2 rather than Q_S. Of course, not everybody was unhappy with the price ceiling. Recall our discussion of opportunity cost in Chapter 2. People place different values on their time. People with a low opportunity cost of time but who cannot as easily afford the higher price per gallon (e.g., poor retired senior citizens) would be more likely to favor the controls. Surgeons, lawyers, and others who have high hourly wages and salaries would view the controls less favorably, because the time spent waiting in line may be worth more to them than paying the higher price for gasoline.

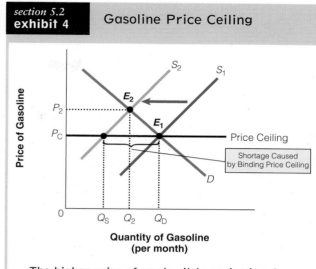

section 5.2 exhibit 4   Gasoline Price Ceiling

The higher price of crude oil (a major input for gasoline) caused the supply curve to shift leftward from S_1 to S_2. Without price controls, the price would have risen to P_2. However, with the binding price ceiling consumers were able and willing to buy Q_D but producers were able and willing to sell Q_S. Therefore, a shortage of Q_D-Q_S occurred at P_C.

© Cengage Learning 2013

Unintended Consequences

When markets are altered for policy reasons, it is wise to remember that actions do not always have the results that were initially intended—in other words, actions can have **unintended consequences**. As economists, we must always look for the secondary effects of an action, which may occur along with the initial effects. For example, the government is often well intentioned when it adopts price controls to help low-skilled workers or tenants in search of affordable housing; however, such policies may also cause unintended consequences that could completely undermine

What do you think would happen to the number of teenagers getting jobs if we raised the minimum wage to $50 an hour?

DOUG MENUEZ/GETTY IMAGES

the intended effects. For example, rent controls may have the immediate effect of lowering rents, but secondary effects may well include low vacancy rates, discrimination against low-income and large families, deterioration of the quality of rental units, and black markets. Similarly, a sizable increase in the minimum wage may help many low-skilled workers or apprentices but may also result in higher unemployment and/or a reduction in fringe benefits, such as vacations and discounts to employees. Society has to make tough decisions, and if the government subsidizes some programs or groups of people in one area, then something must always be given up somewhere else. The "law of scarcity" cannot be repealed!

unintended consequences
the secondary effects of an action that may occur as well as the initial effects

use what you've learned — Binding Price Controls

Q If binding price controls are imposed by the government at levels that are either above or below the equilibrium price, is the quantity of goods bought (and sold) less than the equilibrium quantity?

A If a price ceiling (a legally established maximum price) is set below the equilibrium price, quantity demanded will be greater than quantity supplied, resulting in a shortage at that price. Because producers will only increase the quantity supplied at higher prices, *ceteris paribus,* only Q_1 will be bought and sold. Alternatively, if a price floor (a legally established minimum price) is set above the equilibrium price, quantity supplied will be greater than quantity demanded, causing a surplus at that price. Because consumers will only increase their quantity demanded, *ceteris paribus,* at lower prices, only Q_1 will be bought and sold.

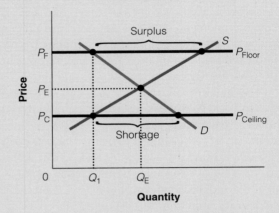

ⓠ SECTION QUIZ

1. If the equilibrium price of wheat is $3 per bushel and then a price floor of $2.50 per bushel is imposed by the government,

   a. there will be no effect on the wheat market.

   b. there will be a shortage of wheat.

   c. there will be a surplus of wheat.

   d. the price of wheat will decrease.

2. Which of the following is true?

   a. A price ceiling reduces the quantity exchanged in the market, but a price floor increases the quantity exchanged in the market.

   b. A price ceiling increases the quantity exchanged in the market, but a price floor decreases the quantity exchanged in the market.

   c. Both price floors and price ceilings reduce the quantity exchanged in the market.

   d. Both price floors and price ceilings increase the quantity exchanged in the market.

3. If a price floor was set at the current equilibrium price, which of the following would cause a surplus as a result?

   a. an increase in demand

   b. a decrease in demand

   c. an increase in supply

   d. a decrease in supply

   e. either (b) or (c)

(*continued*)

4. A current shortage is due to a price ceiling. If the price ceiling is removed,
   a. price would increase, quantity supplied would increase, and quantity demanded would decrease.
   b. price would increase, quantity supplied would decrease, and quantity demanded would increase.
   c. price would decrease, quantity supplied would increase, and quantity demanded would decrease.
   d. price would decrease, quantity supplied would decrease, and quantity demanded would increase.

5. A current surplus is due to a price floor. If the price floor is removed,
   a. price would increase, quantity demanded would increase, and quantity supplied would increase.
   b. price would increase, quantity demanded would decrease, and quantity supplied would decrease.
   c. price would decrease, quantity demanded would increase, and quantity supplied would decrease.
   d. price would decrease, quantity demanded would decrease, and quantity supplied would increase.

6. Which of the following will most likely occur with a 20 percent increase in the minimum wage?
   a. higher unemployment rates among experienced and skilled workers
   b. higher unemployment rates among young and low-skilled workers
   c. lower unemployment rates for young and low-skilled workers
   d. the price floor (minimum wage) will be binding in the young and low-skilled labor market but not in the experienced and skilled labor market
   e. both (b) and (d)

---

1. How is rent control an example of a price ceiling?
2. What predictable effects result from price ceilings such as rent control?
3. How is the minimum–wage law an example of a price floor?
4. What predictable effects result from price floors such as the minimum wage?
5. What may happen to the amount of discrimination against groups such as families with children, pet owners, smokers, or students when rent control is imposed?
6. Why does rent control often lead to condominium conversions?
7. What is the law of unintended consequences?
8. Why is the law of unintended consequences so important in making public policy?

Answers: 1. a   2. c   3. e   4. a   5. c   6. e

Interactive Summary

Fill in the blanks:

1. An increase in demand results in a(n) _____ equilibrium price and a(n) _____ equilibrium quantity.

2. A decrease in supply results in a(n) _____ equilibrium price and a(n) _____ equilibrium quantity.

3. If demand decreases and supply increases, but the decrease in demand is greater than the increase in supply, the equilibrium quantity will _____.

4. If supply decreases and demand increases, the equilibrium price will _____ and the equilibrium quantity will be _____.

5. A price _____ is a legally established maximum price; a price _____ is a legally established minimum price.

6. Rent controls distort market signals and lead to _____ of rent-controlled apartments.

7. The quality of rent-controlled apartments would tend to _____ over time.

8. An increase in the minimum wage would tend to create _____ unemployment for low-skilled workers.

9. The secondary effects of an action that may occur after the initial effects are called _____.

Answers: 1. greater; greater 2. higher; lower 3. lower 4. increase; indeterminate 5. ceiling; floor 6. shortages 7. decline 8. additional 9. unintended consequences

Key Terms and Concepts

price ceiling 145   price floor 145   unintended consequences 149

Section Quiz Answers

5.1   Changes in Market Equilibrium

1. **Does an increase in demand create a shortage or surplus at the original price?**
An increase in demand increases the quantity demanded at the original equilibrium price, but it does not change the quantity supplied at that price, meaning that it would create a shortage at the original equilibrium price.

2. **What happens to the equilibrium price and quantity as a result of a demand increase?**
Frustrated buyers unable to buy all they would like at the original equilibrium price will compete the market price higher, and that higher price will induce suppliers to increase their quantity supplied. The result is a higher market price and a larger market output.

3. **Does an increase in supply create a shortage or surplus at the original price?**
An increase in supply increases the quantity supplied at the original equilibrium price, but it does not change the quantity demanded at that price, meaning that it would create a surplus at the original equilibrium price.

4. **Assuming the market is already at equilibrium, what happens to the equilibrium price and quantity as a result of a supply increase?**
Frustrated sellers unable to sell all they would like at the original equilibrium price will compete the market price lower, and that lower price will induce demanders to increase their quantity demanded. The result is a lower market price and a larger market output.

5. **Why do heating oil prices tend to be higher in the winter?**
The demand for heating oil is higher in cold weather winter months. The result of this higher winter heating oil demand, for a given supply curve, is higher prices for heating oil in the winter.

6. **What would have to be true for both supply and demand to shift in the same time period?**
For both supply and demand to shift in the same time period, one or more of both the supply curve shifters and the demand curve shifters would have to change in that same time period.

7. **When both supply and demand shift, what added information do we need to know in order to determine in which direction the indeterminate variable changes?**
When both supply and demand shift, we need to know which of the shifts is of greater magnitude, so we can know which of the opposing effects in the indeterminate variable is larger; whichever effect is larger will determine the direction of the net effect on the indeterminate variable.

8. **If both buyers and sellers of grapes expect grape prices to rise in the near future, what will happen to grape prices and sales today?**
If grape buyers expect grape prices to rise in the near future, it will increase their current demand to

buy grapes, which would tend to increase current prices and increase the current quantity of grapes sold. If grape sellers expect grape prices to rise in the near future, it will decrease their current supply of grapes for sale, which would tend to increase current prices and decrease the current quantity of grapes sold. Because both these effects tend to increase the current price of grapes, grape prices will rise. However, the supply and demand curve shifts tend to change current sales in opposing directions, so without knowing which of these shifts was of a greater magnitude, we do not know what will happen to current grape sales. They could go up, go down, or even stay the same.

9. If demand for peanut butter increases and supply decreases, what will happen to equilibrium price and quantity?

An increase in the demand for peanut butter increases the equilibrium price and quantity of peanut butter sold. A decrease in the supply of peanut butter increases the equilibrium price and decreases the quantity of peanut butter sold. The result is an increase in peanut butter prices and an indeterminate effect on the quantity of peanut butter sold.

5.2 Price Controls

1. How is rent control an example of a price ceiling?

A price ceiling is a maximum price set below the equilibrium price by the government. Rent control is an example because the controlled rents are held below the market equilibrium rent level.

2. What predictable effects result from price ceilings such as rent control?

The predictable effects resulting from price ceilings include shortages, reduced amounts of the controlled good being made available by suppliers, reductions in the quality of the controlled good, and increased discrimination among potential buyers of the good.

3. How is the minimum–wage law an example of a price floor?

A price floor is a minimum price set above the equilibrium price by the government. The minimum–wage law is an example because the minimum is set above the market equilibrium wage level for some low-skill workers.

4. What predictable effects result from price floors such as the minimum wage?

The predictable effects resulting from price floors include surpluses, reduced amounts of the controlled good being purchased by demanders, increases in the quality of the controlled good, and increased discrimination among potential sellers of the good.

5. What may happen to the amount of discrimination against groups such as families with children, pet owners, smokers, or students when rent control is imposed?

Rent control laws prevent prospective renters from compensating landlords through higher rents for any characteristic landlords find less attractive, whether it is bothersome noise from children or pets, odors from smokers, increased numbers of renters per unit, risks of nonpayment by lower income tenants such as students, and so on. As a result, it lowers the cost of discriminating against anyone with what landlords consider unattractive characteristics, because other prospective renters without those characteristics are willing to pay the same controlled rent.

6. Why does rent control often lead to condominium conversions?

Rent control applies to rental apartments, but not to apartments owned by their occupants. Therefore, one way to get around rent control restrictions on apartment owners' ability to receive the market value of their apartments is to convert those apartments to condominiums by selling them to tenants instead (what was once a controlled rent becomes part of an uncontrolled mortgage payment).

7. What is the law of unintended consequences?

The law of unintended consequences is the term used to indicate that the results of actions are not always as clear as they appear. The secondary effects of an action may cause its results to include many consequences that were not part of what was intended.

8. Why is the law of unintended consequences so important in making public policy?

It is impossible to change just one incentive to achieve a particular result through a government policy. A policy will change the incentives facing multiple individuals making multiple decisions, and changes in all those affected choices will result. Sometimes, the unintended consequences can be so substantial that they completely undermine the intended effects of a policy.

Problems

1. Using supply and demand curves, show the effect of each of the following events on the market for wheat.
   a. The midwestern United States (a major wheat-producing area) suffers a flood.
   b. The price of corn decreases (assume that many farmers can grow either corn or wheat).
   c. The Midwest has great weather.
   d. The price of fertilizer declines.
   e. More individuals start growing wheat.

2. Beginning from an initial equilibrium, draw the effects of the changes in the following list in terms of the relevant supply and demand curves.
   a. an increase in the price of hot dogs on the hamburger market
   b. a decrease in the number of taxicab companies in New York City on cab trips
   c. effect of El Niño rain storms destroying the broccoli crop in two California counties

3. Use supply and demand curves to show:
   a. simultaneous increases in supply and demand, with a large increase in supply and a small increase in demand.
   b. simultaneous increases in supply and demand, with a small increase in supply and a large increase in demand.
   c. simultaneous decreases in supply and demand, with a large decrease in supply and a small decrease in demand.
   d. simultaneous decrease in supply and demand, with a small decrease in supply and a large decrease in demand.

4. What would be the impact of a rental price ceiling set above the equilibrium rental price for apartments? below the equilibrium rental price?

5. What would be the impact of a price floor set above the equilibrium price for dairy products? below the equilibrium price?

6. Giving in to pressure from voters who charge that local theater owners are gouging their customers with ticket prices as high as $10 per movie, the city council of a Midwestern city imposes a price ceiling of $2 on all movies. What effect is this likely to have on the market for movies in this particular city? What will happen to the quantity of tickets demanded? What will happen to the quantity supplied? Who gains? Who loses?

7. Why do price floors and price ceilings both reduce the quantity of goods traded in those markets?

8. Why do 10 A.M. classes fill up before 8 A.M. classes during class registration? Use supply and demand curves to help explain your answer.

9. What would happen to the equilibrium price and quantity exchanged in the following cases?
   a. an increase in income and a decreasing price of a complement, for a normal good
   b. a technological advance and lower input prices
   c. an increase in the price of a substitute and an increase in income, for an inferior good
   d. producers' expectations that prices will soon fall, and increasingly costly government regulations

10. Refer to the following supply and demand curve diagram.

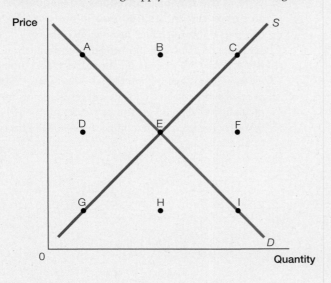

a. Starting from an initial equilibrium at E, what shift or shifts in supply and/or demand could move the equilibrium price and quantity to each of points A through I?

b. Starting from an initial equilibrium at E, what would happen if both a decrease in the price of a substitute in production and an increase in income occurred, if it is a normal good?

c. Starting from an initial equilibrium at E, what would happen if both an increase in the price of an input and an advance in technology occurred?

d. If a price floor is imposed above the equilibrium price, which of A through I would tend to be the quantity supplied, and which would tend to be the quantity demanded? Which would be the new quantity exchanged?

e. If a price ceiling is imposed below the equilibrium price, which of A through I would tend to be the quantity supplied, and which would tend to be the quantity demanded? Which would be the new quantity exchanged?

Elasticities

If a rock band increases the price it charges for concert tickets, what impact will that have on ticket sales? More precisely, will ticket sales fall a little or a lot? Will the band make more money by lowering the price or by raising the price? This chapter will allow you to answer these types of question and more.

Some of the results in this chapter may surprise you. A huge flood in the Midwest that destroyed much of this year's wheat crop would leave some wheat farmers better off. Ideal weather that led to a bountiful crop of wheat everywhere would leave wheat farmers worse off. As you will soon find out, these issues hinge importantly on the tools of elasticity.

In this chapter, we will also see the importance of elasticity in determining the effects of taxes. If a tax is levied on the seller, will the seller pay all of the taxes? If the tax were levied on the buyer—who pays the larger share of taxes? We will see that elasticity is critical in the determination of tax burden. Elasticities will also help us to more fully understand many policy issues—from illegal drugs to luxury taxes. For example, Congress were to impose a large tax on yachts, what do you think would happen to yacht sales? What would happen to employment in the boat industry?

Price Elasticity of Demand   6.1

📂 What is price elasticity of demand?

📂 How do we measure consumers' responses to price changes?

📂 What determines the price elasticity of demand?

In learning and applying the law of demand, we have established the basic fact that quantity demanded changes inversely with change in price, *ceteris paribus*. But how much does quantity demanded change? The extent to which a change in price affects quantity demanded may vary considerably from product to product and over the various price ranges for the same product. The **price elasticity of demand** measures the responsiveness of quantity demanded to a change in price. Specifically, price elasticity is defined as the percentage change in quantity demanded divided by the percentage change in price, or

price elasticity of demand
the measure of the responsiveness of quantity demanded to a change in price

$$\text{Price elasticity of demand } (E_\text{D}) = \frac{\text{Percentage change in quantity demanded}}{\text{Percentage change in price}}$$

Note that, following the law of demand, price and quantity demanded show an inverse relationship. For this reason, the price elasticity of demand is, in theory, always negative. But in practice and for simplicity, this quantity is always expressed in absolute value terms—that is, as a positive number.

Is the Demand Curve Elastic or Inelastic?

It is important to understand the basic intuition behind elasticities, which requires a focus on the percentage changes in quantity demanded and price.

Think of elasticity as an elastic rubber band. If the quantity demanded is responsive to even a small change in price, we call it elastic. On the other hand, if even a huge change in price results in only a small change in quantity demanded, then the demand is said to be inelastic. For example, if a 10 percent increase in the price leads to a 50 percent reduction in the quantity demanded, we say that demand is elastic because the quantity demanded is sensitive to the price change.

© BLUE JEAN IMAGES/ALAMY

Think of price elasticity like an elastic rubber band. When small price changes greatly affect, or "stretch," quantity demanded, the demand is elastic, much like a very stretchy rubber band. When large price changes can't "stretch" demand, however, then demand is inelastic, more like a very stiff rubber band.

$$E_\text{D} = \frac{\%\Delta Q_\text{D}}{\%\Delta P} = \frac{50\%}{10\%} = 5$$

Demand is elastic in this case because a 10 percent change in price led to a larger (50 percent) change in quantity demanded.

Alternatively, if a 10 percent increase in the price leads to a 1 percent reduction in quantity demanded, we say that demand is *inelastic* because the quantity demanded did not respond much to the price reduction.

$$E_D = \frac{\%\Delta Q_D}{\%\Delta P} = \frac{1\%}{10\%} = 0.10$$

Demand is inelastic in this case because a 10 percent change in price led to a smaller (1 percent) change in quantity demanded.

Types of Demand Curves

Economists refer to a variety of demand curves based on the magnitude of their elasticity. A demand curve, or a portion of a demand curve, can be elastic, inelastic, or unit elastic.

elastic when the percentage change in quantity demanded is greater than the percentage change in price ($E_D > 1$)

Demand is **elastic** when the elasticity is greater than 1 ($E_D > 1$)—the quantity demanded changes proportionally more than the price changes. In this case, a given percentage increase in price, say 10 percent, leads to a larger percentage change in quantity demanded, say 20 percent, as seen in Exhibit 1(a). If the curve is *perfectly elastic*, the demand curve is horizontal. The elasticity coefficient is infinity because even the slightest change in price will lead to a huge change in quantity demanded—for example, a tiny increase in price will cause the quantity demanded to fall to zero. In Exhibit 1(b), a *perfectly elastic* demand curve (horizontal) is illustrated.

inelastic when the percentage change in quantity demanded is less than the percentage change in price ($E_D < 1$)

Demand is **inelastic** when the elasticity is less than 1; the quantity demanded changes proportionally less than the price changes. In this case, a given percentage (for example, 10 percent) change in price is accompanied by a smaller (for example, 5 percent) reduction in quantity demanded, as seen in Exhibit 2(a). If the demand curve is *perfectly inelastic*, the quantity demanded is the same regardless of the price. The elasticity coefficient is zero because the quantity demanded does not respond to a change in price. This relationship is illustrated in Exhibit 2(b).

unit elastic demand demand with a price elasticity of 1; the percentage change in quantity demanded is equal to the percentage change in price

Goods for which E_D equals one ($E_D = 1$) are said to have **unit elastic demand**. In this case, the quantity demanded changes proportionately to price changes. For example, a 10 percent

---

section 6.1 exhibit 1   Elastic Demand

a. Elastic Demand ($E_D > 1$)

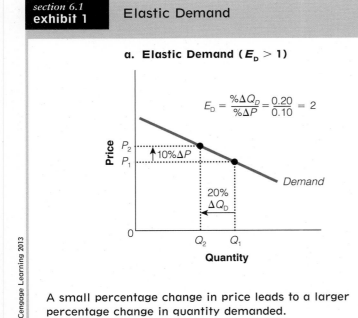

$$E_D = \frac{\%\Delta Q_D}{\%\Delta P} = \frac{0.20}{0.10} = 2$$

A small percentage change in price leads to a larger percentage change in quantity demanded.

b. Perfectly Elastic Demand ($E_D = \infty$)

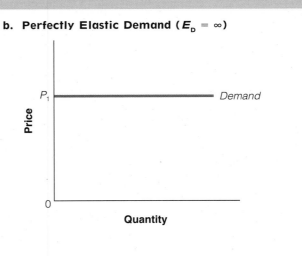

A small percentage change in price will change quantity demanded by an infinite amount.

section 6.1 exhibit 2 — Inelastic Demand

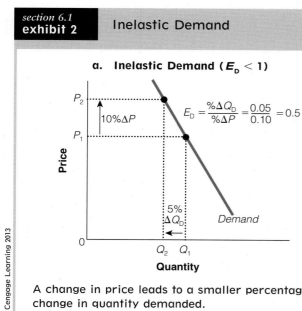

a. Inelastic Demand ($E_D < 1$)

$$E_D = \frac{\%\Delta Q_D}{\%\Delta P} = \frac{0.05}{0.10} = 0.5$$

A change in price leads to a smaller percentage change in quantity demanded.

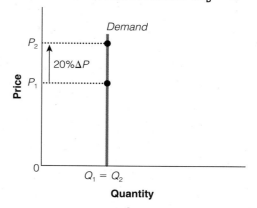

b. Perfectly Inelastic Demand ($E_D = 0$)

The quantity demanded does not change regardless of the percentage change in price.

increase in price will lead to a 10 percent reduction in quantity demanded. This relationship is illustrated in Exhibit 3.

The price elasticity of demand is closely related to the slope of the demand curve. Generally speaking, the flatter the demand curve passing through a given point, the more elastic the demand. The steeper the demand curve passing through a given point, the less elastic the demand.

Calculating the Price Elasticity of Demand: The Midpoint Method

To get a clear picture of exactly how the price elasticity of demand is calculated, consider the case for a hypothetical pizza market. Say the price of pizza increases from $19 to $21. If we take an average between the old price, $19, and the new price, $21, we can calculate an average price of $20. Exhibit 4 shows that as a result of the increase in the price of pizza, the quantity demanded has fallen from 82 million pizzas to 78 million pizzas per year. If we take an average between the old quantity demand, 82 million, and the new quantity demanded, 78 million, we have an average quantity demanded of 80 million pizzas per year. That is, the $2 increase in the price of pizza has led to a 4-million pizza reduction in quantity demanded. How can we figure out the price elasticity of demand?

You might ask why we are using the average price and average quantity. The answer is that if we did not use the average amounts, we would come up with different values for the elasticity of demand depending on whether we moved up or down the demand curve. When the change in price and quantity are of significant magnitude, the exact meaning of the term *percentage change* requires clarification, and the terms *price* and *quantity* must be defined more precisely. The issue thus is, should the percentage change be figured on the basis of price and quantity before or after the change has occurred? For example, a price rise from $10 to $15 constitutes a 50 percent change if the original price ($10) is used in figuring

section 6.1 exhibit 3 — Unit Elastic Demand

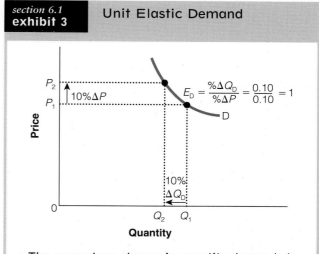

$$E_D = \frac{\%\Delta Q_D}{\%\Delta P} = \frac{0.10}{0.10} = 1$$

The percentage change in quantity demanded is the same as the percentage change in price that caused it ($E_D = 1$).

Does it matter whether we move up or down the demand curve when we calculate the price elasticity of demand?

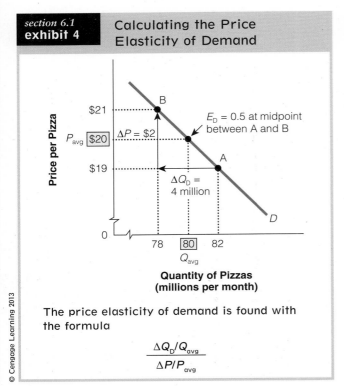

section 6.1
exhibit 4

Calculating the Price Elasticity of Demand

$E_D = 0.5$ at midpoint between A and B

The price elasticity of demand is found with the formula

$$\frac{\Delta Q_D / Q_{avg}}{\Delta P / P_{avg}}$$

the percentage ($5/$10), or a 33 percent change if the price after the change ($15) is used ($5/$15). For small changes, the distinction is not important, but for large changes, it is. To avoid this confusion, economists often use this average technique. Specifically, we are actually calculating the elasticity at a midpoint between the old and new prices and quantities.

Now to figure out the price elasticity of demand, we must first calculate the percentage change in price. To find the percentage change in price, we take the change in price (ΔP) and divide it by the average price (P_{avg}). (Note: The Greek letter delta, Δ, means "change in.")

Percentage change in price = $\Delta P / P_{avg}$

In our pizza example, the original price was $19, and the new price is $21. The change in price (ΔP) is $2, and the average price (P_{avg}) is $20. The percentage change in price can then be calculated as

Percentage change in price = $2/$20
$$= 1/10 = 0.10 = 10\%$$

Next, we must calculate the percentage change in quantity demanded. To find the percentage change in quantity demanded, we take the change in quantity demanded (ΔQ_D) and divide it by the average quantity demanded (Q_{avg}).

Percentage change in quantity demanded = $\Delta Q_D / Q_{avg}$

In our pizza example, the original quantity demanded was 82 million, and the new quantity demanded is 78 million. The change in quantity demanded (ΔQ_D) is 4 million, and the average quantity demanded (Q_{avg}) is 80 million. The percentage change in quantity demanded can then be calculated as

Percentage change in quantity demanded = 4 million/80 million = 1/20 = 0.05 = 5%

Because the price elasticity of demand is equal to the percentage change in quantity demanded divided by the percentage change in price, the price elasticity of demand for pizzas between point A and point B can be shown as

$$E_D = \frac{\text{Percentage change in quantity demanded}}{\text{Percentage change in price}}$$

$$= \frac{\Delta Q_D / Q_{avg}}{\Delta P / P_{avg}} = \frac{4 \text{ million}/80 \text{ million}}{\$2/\$20}$$

$$= \frac{1/20}{1/10} = \frac{5\%}{10\%} = 0.5$$

The Determinants of the Price Elasticity of Demand

Why are demand curves for goods with close substitutes more elastic?

As you have learned, the elasticity of demand for a specific good refers to movements along its demand curve as its price changes. A lower price will increase quantity demanded, and a higher price will reduce quantity demanded. But what factors will influence the magnitude of the change in quantity demanded in response to a price change? That is, what will make the demand curve relatively more elastic (where Q_D is responsive to price changes), and what will make the demand curve relatively less elastic (where Q_D is less responsive to price changes)?

For the most part, the price elasticity of demand depends on three factors: (1) the availability of close substitutes, (2) the proportion of income spent on the good, and (3) the amount of time that has elapsed since the price change.

Availability of Close Substitutes

Goods *with* close substitutes tend to have more elastic demands. Why? Because if the price of such a good increases, consumers can easily switch to other now relatively lower-priced substitutes. In many examples, such as one brand of root beer as opposed to another, or different brands of gasoline, the ease of substitution will make demand quite elastic for most individuals. Goods *without* close substitutes, such as insulin for diabetics, cigarettes for chain smokers, heroin for addicts, or emergency medical care for those with appendicitis or broken legs, tend to have inelastic demands.

The degree of substitutability can also depend on whether the good is a necessity or a luxury. Goods that are necessities, such as food, have no ready substitutes and thus tend to have lower elasticities than do luxury items, such as jewelry.

When the good is broadly defined, it tends to be less elastic than when it is narrowly defined. For example, the elasticity of demand for food, a broad category, tends to be inelastic over a large price range because few substitutes are available for food. But for a certain type of food, such as pizza, a narrowly defined good, it is much easier to find a substitute—perhaps tacos, burgers, salads, burritos, or chili fries. That is, the demand for a particular type of food is more elastic because more and better substitutes are available than for food as an entire category.

Proportion of Income Spent on the Good

The smaller the proportion of income spent on a good, the lower its elasticity of demand. If the amount spent on a good relative to income is small, then the impact of a change in its price on one's budget will also be small. As a result, consumers will respond less to price changes for small-ticket items than for similar percentage changes in large-ticket items, where a price change could potentially have a large impact on the consumer's budget. For example, a 50 percent increase in the price of salt will have a much smaller impact on consumers' behavior than a similar percentage increase in the price of a new automobile. Similarly, a 50 percent increase in the cost of private university tuition will have a greater impact on students' (and sometimes parents') budgets than a 50 percent increase in textbook prices.

Time

For many goods, the more time that people have to adapt to a new price change, the greater the elasticity of demand. Immediately after a price change, consumers may be unable to locate good alternatives or easily change their consumption patterns. But as time passes, consumers have more time to find or develop suitable substitutes and to plan and implement changes in their patterns of consumption. For example, drivers may not

If bus fares increase, will ridership fall a little or a lot? It all depends on the price elasticity of demand. If the price elasticity of demand is elastic, a 50-cent price increase will lead to a relatively large reduction in bus travel as riders find viable substitutes. If the price elasticity of demand is inelastic, a 50-cent price increase will lead to a relatively small reduction in bus ridership as riders are not able to find good alternatives to bus transportation.

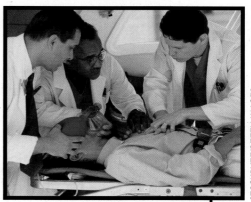

Unlike most tangible items (such as specific types of food or cars), there are few substitutes for a physician and medical care when you have an emergency. Because the number of available substitutes is limited, the demand for emergency medical care is relatively inelastic.

What impact does time have on elasticity?

Some studies show that a 10 percent increase in the price of cigarettes will lead to a 7 percent reduction in the quantity demanded of youth smoking. In this price range, however, demand is still inelastic at –0.7. Of course, proponents of higher taxes to discourage underage smoking would like to see a more elastic demand, where a 10 percent increase in the price of cigarettes would lead to a reduction in quantity demanded of more than 10 percent. However, compared to adults, younger people are more likely to smoke fewer cigarettes in response to a price change (a tax increase). The elasticity of demand for cigarettes for 24- to 26-year-olds is –0.20 and for 27- to 29-year-olds it is –0.09.

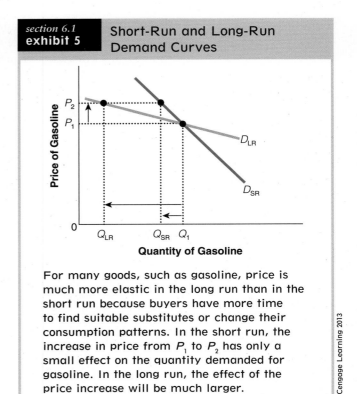

section 6.1
exhibit 5

Short-Run and Long-Run Demand Curves

For many goods, such as gasoline, price is much more elastic in the long run than in the short run because buyers have more time to find suitable substitutes or change their consumption patterns. In the short run, the increase in price from P_1 to P_2 has only a small effect on the quantity demanded for gasoline. In the long run, the effect of the price increase will be much larger.

respond immediately to an increase in gas prices, perhaps believing it to be temporary. However, if the price persists over a longer period, we would expect people to drive less, buy more fuel-efficient cars, move closer to work, carpool, take the bus, or even bike to work. So for many goods, especially nondurable goods (goods that do not last a long time), the short-run demand curve is generally less elastic than the long-run demand curve, as illustrated in Exhibit 5.

Estimated Price Elasticities of Demand

Because of shifts in supply and demand curves, researchers have a difficult task when trying to estimate empirically the price elasticity of demand for a particular good or service. Despite this difficulty, Exhibit 6 presents some estimates for the price elasticity of demand for certain goods. As you would expect, certain goods like medical care, air travel, and gasoline are all relatively price inelastic in the short run because buyers have fewer substitutes. On the other hand, air travel in the long run is much more sensitive to price (elastic) because the available substitutes are much more plentiful. Exhibit 6 shows that the price elasticity of demand for air travel is 2.4, which means that a 1 percent increase in price will lead to a 2.4 percent reduction in quantity demanded. Notice, in each case where the data are available, the estimates of the long-run price elasticities of demand are greater than the short-run price elasticities of demand. In short, the price elasticity of demand is greater when the price change persists over a longer time periods.

section 5.1 exhibit 6	Price Elasticities of Demand for Selected Goods	
Good	**Short Run**	**Long Run**
Salt	—	0.1
Air travel	0.1	2.4
Gasoline	0.2	0.7
Medical care and hospitalization	0.3	0.9
Jewelry and watches	0.4	0.7
Physician services	0.6	—
Alcohol	0.9	3.6
Movies	0.9	3.7
China, glassware	1.5	2.6
Automobiles	1.9	2.2
Chevrolets	—	4.0

© Cengage Learning 2013

SOURCES: Adapted from Robert Archibald and Robert Gillingham, "An Analysis of the Short-Run Consumer Demand for Gasoline Using Household Survey Data," *Review of Economics and Statistics* 62 (November 1980): 622–628; Hendrik S. Houthakker and Lester D. Taylor, *Consumer Demand in the United States: Analyses and Projections* (Cambridge, Mass.: Harvard University Press, 1970), pp. 56–149; Richard Voith, "The Long-Run Elasticity of Demand for Commuter Rail Transportation," *Journal of Urban Economics* 30 (November 1991): 360–372.

⑦ SECTION QUIZ

1. Price elasticity of demand is defined as the _____ change in quantity demanded divided by the _____ change in price.

   a. total; percentage

   b. percentage; marginal

   c. marginal; percentage

   d. percentage; percentage

   e. total; total

2. Demand is said to be _____ when the quantity demanded is not very responsive to changes in price.

   a. independent

   b. inelastic

   c. unit elastic

   d. elastic

3. When demand is inelastic,

   a. price elasticity of demand is less than 1.

   b. consumers are not very responsive to changes in price.

   c. the percentage change in quantity demanded resulting from a price change is less than the percentage change in price.

   d. all of the above are correct.

4. Which of the following will not tend to increase the elasticity of demand for a good?

   a. an increase in the availability of close substitutes

   b. an increase in the amount of time people have to adjust to a change in the price

   c. an increase in the proportion of income spent on the good

   d. all of the above will increase the elasticity of demand for a good

(*continued*)

② S E C T I O N   Q U I Z (Cont.)

5. Which of the following would tend to have the most elastic demand curve?

   a. automobiles

   b. Chevrolet automobiles

   c. (a) and (b) would be the same

   d. none of the above

6. Price elasticity of demand is said to be greater

   a. the shorter the period of time consumers have to adjust to price changes.

   b. the longer the period of time consumers have to adjust to price changes.

   c. when there are fewer available substitutes.

   d. when the elasticity of supply is greater.

7. The long-run demand curve for gasoline is likely to be

   a. more elastic than the short-run demand curve for gasoline.

   b. more inelastic than the short-run demand curve for gasoline.

   c. the same as the short-run demand curve for gasoline.

   d. more inelastic than the short-run supply of gasoline.

8. Demand curves for goods tend to become more inelastic

   a. when more good substitutes for the good are available.

   b. when the good makes up a larger portion of a person's income.

   c. when people have less time to adapt to a given price change.

   d. when any of the above is true.

   e. in none of the above situations.

---

1. What question is the price elasticity of demand designed to answer?

2. How is the price elasticity of demand calculated?

3. What is the difference between a relatively price elastic demand curve and a relatively price inelastic demand curve?

4. What is the relationship between the price elasticity of demand and the slope at a given point on a demand curve?

5. What factors tend to make demand curves more price elastic?

6. Why would a tax on a particular brand of cigarettes be less effective at reducing smoking than a tax on all brands of cigarettes?

7. Why is the price elasticity of demand for products at a 24-hour convenience store likely to be lower at 2 A.M. than at 2 P.M.?

8. Why is the price elasticity of demand for turkeys likely to be lower, but the price elasticity of demand for turkeys at a particular store at Thanksgiving likely to be greater than at other times of the year?

Answers: 1. d 2. b 3. d 4. d 5. b 6. b 7. a 8. c

6.2

Total Revenue and the Price Elasticity of Demand

☞ What is total revenue?

☞ What is the relationship between total revenue and the price elasticity of demand?

☞ Does the price elasticity of demand vary along a linear demand curve?

How Does the Price Elasticity of Demand Impact Total Revenue?

The price elasticity of demand for a good also has implications for total revenue. **Total revenue (TR)** is the amount sellers receive for a good or service. Total revenue is simply the price of the good (P) times the quantity of the good sold (Q): $TR = P \times Q$. The elasticity of demand will help to predict how changes in the price will impact total revenue earned by the producer for selling the good. Let's see how this works.

In Exhibit 1, we see that when the demand is price elastic ($E_D > 1$), total revenues will rise as the price declines, because the percentage increase in the quantity demanded is greater than the percentage reduction in price. For example, if the price of a good is cut in half (say from $10 to $5) and the quantity demanded more than doubles (say from 40 to 100), total revenue will rise from $400 ($10 × 40 = $400) to $500 ($5 × 100 = $500). Equivalently, if the price rises from $5 to $10 and the quantity demanded falls from 100 to 40 units, then total revenue will fall from $500 to $400. As this example illustrates, if the demand curve is relatively elastic, total revenue will vary inversely with a price change.

You can see from the following what happens to total revenue when demand is price elastic. (*Note:* The size of the price and quantity arrows represents the size of the percentage changes.)

When Demand Is Price Elastic

$$\downarrow TR = \uparrow P \times \downarrow Q$$

or

$$\uparrow TR = \downarrow P \times \uparrow Q$$

total revenue (TR)
the amount sellers receive for a good or service, calculated as the product price times the quantity sold

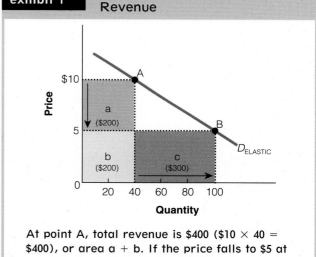

section 6.2
exhibit 1   **Elastic Demand and Total Revenue**

At point A, total revenue is $400 ($10 × 40 = $400), or area a + b. If the price falls to $5 at point B, the total revenue is $500 ($5 × 100 × $500), or area b + c. Total revenue increased by $100. We can also see in the graph that total revenue increased, because the area b + c is greater than area a + b, or c > a.

On the other hand, if demand for a good is relatively inelastic ($E_D < 1$), the total revenue will be lower at lower prices than at higher prices because a given price reduction will be accompanied by a proportionately smaller increase in quantity demanded. For example, as shown in Exhibit 2, if the price of a good is cut (say from $10 to $5) and the quantity demanded less than doubles (say it increases from 30 to 40), then total revenue will fall from $300 ($10 × 30 = $300) to $200 ($5 × 40 = $200). Equivalently, if the price increases from $5 to $10 and the quantity demanded falls from 40 to 30, total revenue will increase from $200 to $300. To summarize, then: If the demand curve is inelastic, total revenue will vary directly with a price change.

Can the relationship between price and total revenue tell you whether a good is elastic or inelastic?

section 6.2
exhibit 2   Inelastic Demand and Total Revenue

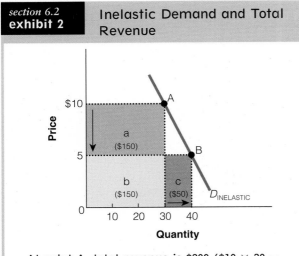

At point A, total revenue is $300 ($10 × 30 = $300), or area a + b. If the price falls to $5 at point B, the total revenue is $200 ($5 × 40 = $200), or area b + c. Total revenue falls by $100. We can also see in the graph that total revenue decreases, because area a + b is greater than area b + c, or a > c.

How is it possible that elasticity changes along a straight lined demand curve when the slope is constant?

When Demand Is Price Inelastic

$$\uparrow TR = \uparrow P \times \downarrow Q$$

or

$$\downarrow TR = \downarrow P \times \uparrow Q$$

In this case, the "net" effect on total revenue is reversed but easy to see. (Again, the size of the price and quantity arrows represents the size of the percentage changes.)

Price Elasticity Changes along a Linear Demand Curve

As already shown (Section 6.1, Exhibit 1), the slopes of demand curves can be used to estimate their *relative* elasticities of demand: The steeper one demand curve is relative to another, the more inelastic it is relative to the other. However, except for the extreme cases of perfectly elastic and perfectly inelastic curves, great care must be taken when trying to estimate the degree of elasticity of one demand curve from its slope. In fact, as we will soon see, a straight-line demand curve with a constant slope will change elasticity continuously as you move up or down it. It is because the slope is the ratio of changes in the two variables (price and quantity) while the elasticity is the ratio of percentage changes in the two variables.

We can easily demonstrate that the elasticity of demand varies along a linear demand curve by using what we already know about the interrelationship between price and total

use what you've learned   **Elasticities and Total Revenue**

Q Is a poor wheat harvest bad for all farmers and is a great wheat harvest good for all farmers? (Hint: Assume that demand for wheat is inelastic—the demand for food is generally inelastic.)

A Without a simultaneous reduction in demand, a reduction in supply from a poor harvest results in higher prices. With that, if demand for the wheat is inelastic over the pertinent portion of the demand curve, the price increase will cause farmers' total revenues to rise. As shown in Exhibit 3(a), if demand for the crop is inelastic, an increase in price will cause farmers to lose the revenue indicated by area c. They will, however, experience an increase in revenue equal to area a, resulting in an overall increase in total revenue equal to area

a – c. Clearly, if some farmers lose their entire crop because of, say, bad weather, they will be worse

(continued)

USE
what you've learned   Elasticities and Total Revenue (Cont.)

off; but collectively, farmers can profit from events that reduce crop size—and they do, because the demand for most agricultural products is inelastic. Interestingly, if all farmers were hurt equally, say losing one-third of their crop, each farmer would be better off. Of course, consumers would be worse off, because the price of agricultural products would be higher. Alternatively, what if phenomenal weather led to record wheat harvests or a technological advance led to more productive wheat farmers? Either event would increase the supply from S_1 to S_2 in Exhibit 3(b). The increase in supply leads to a decrease in price, from P_1 to P_2. Because the demand for wheat is inelastic, the quantity sold of wheat rises less than proportionately to the fall in the price. That is, in percentage terms, the price falls more than the quantity

demanded rises. Each farmer is selling a few more bushels of wheat, but the price of each bushel has fallen even more, so collectively wheat farmers will experience a decline in total revenue despite the good news.

The same is also true for the many government programs that attempt to help farmers by reducing production—crop restriction programs. These programs, like droughts or floods, tend to help farmers because the demand for food is relatively inelastic. But it hurts consumers who now have to pay a higher price for less food. Farm technology may be good for consumers because it shifts the supply curve to the right and lowers prices. However it may be bad for some small farmers because it could put them out of business. See Exhibit 3(b).

---

section 6.2
exhibit 3   Elasticities and Total Revenue

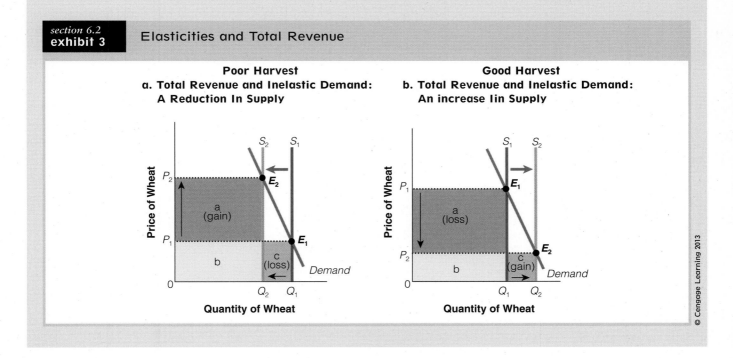

Poor Harvest
a. Total Revenue and Inelastic Demand: A Reduction In Supply

Good Harvest
b. Total Revenue and Inelastic Demand: An increase Iin Supply

© Cengage Learning 2013

---

revenue. Exhibit 4 shows a linear (constant slope) demand curve. In Exhibit 4(a), we see that when the price falls on the upper half of the demand curve from P_1 to P_2, and quantity demanded increases from Q_1 to Q_2, total revenue increases. That is, the new area of total revenue (area b + c) is larger than the old area of total revenue (area a + b). It is also true that if price increased in this region (from P_2 to P_1), total revenue would fall, because b + c is greater than a + b. In this region of the demand curve, then, there is a negative relationship between price and total revenue. As we discussed earlier, this is characteristic of an elastic demand curve ($E_D > 1$).

section 6.2
exhibit 4   Price Elasticity along a Linear Demand Curve

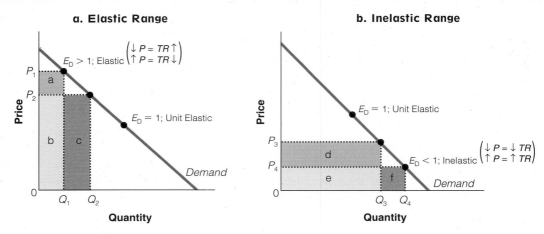

The slope is constant along a linear demand curve, but the elasticity varies. Moving down along the demand curve, the elasticity is elastic at higher prices and inelastic at lower prices. It is unit elastic between the inelastic and elastic ranges.

Is a good wheat harvest always good for all wheat farmers?

Exhibit 4(b) illustrates what happens to total revenue on the lower half of the same demand curve. When the price falls from P_3 to P_4 and the quantity demanded increases from Q_3 to Q_4, total revenue actually decreases, because the new area of total revenue (area e + f) is less than the old area of total revenue (area d + e). Likewise, it is clear that an increase in price from P_4 to P_3 would increase total revenue. In this case, there is a positive relationship between price and total revenue, which, as we discussed, is characteristic of an inelastic demand curve ($E_D < 1$). Together, parts (a) and (b) of Exhibit 4 illustrate that, although the slope remains constant, the elasticity of a linear demand curve changes along the length of the curve—from relatively elastic at higher price ranges to relatively inelastic at lower price ranges.

use what you've learned   Elasticity Varies along a Linear Demand Curve

Q Why do economists emphasize elasticity at the current price?

A Because for most demand (and supply) curves, the price elasticity varies along the curve. Thus, for most goods we usually refer to a particular point or a section of the demand (or supply) curves. In Exhibit 5, we see that the upper half of the straight-line demand curve is elastic and the lower half is inelastic. Notice on the lower half of the demand curve, a higher (lower) price increases (decreases) total revenue—that is, in this lower region, demand is inelastic. However, on the top half of the demand curve, a lower (higher) price increases (decreases) total revenue—that is, in this region demand is elastic.

For example, when the price increases from $2 to $3, the total revenue increases from $32 to $42—an increase in price increases total revenue, so demand is inelastic in this portion of the demand curve.

(continued)

use what you've learned   **Elasticity Varies along a Linear Demand Curve (Cont.)**

section 6.2
exhibit 5   Elasticity Varies along a Linear Demand Curve

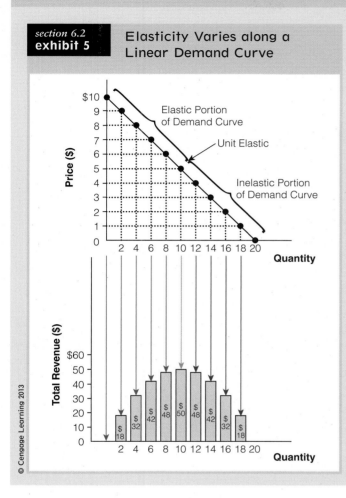

But when the price increases from $8 to $9, the total revenue falls from $32 to $18—an increase in price lowers total revenue, so demand is elastic in this portion of the demand curve.

Specifically, when the price is high and the quantity demanded is low, this portion of the demand curve is elastic. Why? It is because a $1 reduction in price is a smaller percentage change when the price is high than when it is low. Similarly, an increase in 2 units of output is a larger percentage change when quantity demanded is lower. So we have a relatively small change in price leading to a proportionately greater change in quantity demanded—that is, demand is elastic on this portion of the demand curve. Of course, the opposite is true when the price is low and the quantity demanded is high. Why? It is because a $1 change in price is a larger percentage change when the price is low and an increase in 2 units of output is a smaller percentage change when the quantity demanded is larger. That is, a relatively larger percentage change in price will lead to a relatively smaller change in quantity demanded—demand is relatively inelastic on this portion of the demand curve.

© Cengage Learning 2013

ⓘ SECTION QUIZ

1. When the local symphony recently raised the ticket price for its summer concerts in the park, the symphony was surprised to see that its total revenue had actually decreased. The reason was that the elasticity of demand for tickets was

   a. unit elastic.

   b. unit inelastic.

   c. inelastic.

   d. elastic.

2. A straight-line demand curve would

   a. have the same elasticity along its entire length.

   b. have a higher elasticity of demand near its top than near its bottom.

   c. have a lower elasticity of demand near its bottom than near its top.

   d. be relatively inelastic at high prices, but relatively elastic at low prices.

(*continued*)

⟨?⟩ SECTION QUIZ (Cont.)

3. Which of the following is a true statement?

   a. Total revenue is the price of the good times the quantity sold.

   b. If demand is price elastic, total revenue will vary inversely with a change in price.

   c. If demand is price inelastic, total revenue will vary in the same direction as a change in price.

   d. A linear demand curve is more price elastic at higher price ranges and more price inelastic at lower price ranges, and it is unit elastic at the midpoint.

   e. All of the above are true statements.

4. If demand was relatively inelastic in the short run, but elastic in the long run, a price increase would _____ total revenue in the short run and _____ total revenue in the long run.

   a. increase; increase

   b. increase; decrease

   c decrease; increase

   d. decrease; decrease

1. Why does total revenue vary inversely with price if demand is relatively price elastic?

2. Why does total revenue vary directly with price if demand is relatively price inelastic?

3. Why is a linear demand curve more price elastic at higher price ranges and more price inelastic at lower price ranges?

4. If demand for some good was perfectly price inelastic, how would total revenue from its sales change as its price changed?

5. Assume that both you and Art, your partner in a picture-framing business, want to increase your firm's total revenue. You argue that in order to achieve this goal, you should lower your prices; Art, on the other hand, thinks that you should raise your prices. What assumptions are each of you making about your firm's price elasticity of demand?

Answers: 1. d 2. b 3. e 4. b

6.3

Other Types of Demand Elasticities

▭ What is the cross-price elasticity of demand?   ▭ What is the income elasticity of demand?

The Cross-Price Elasticity of Demand

cross-price elasticity of demand
the measure of the impact that a price change of one good will have on the demand of another good

The price of a good is not the only factor that affects the quantity consumers will purchase. Sometimes the quantity of one good demanded is affected by the price of a related good. For example, if the price of potato chips falls, what is the impact, if any, on the demand for soda (a complement)? Or if the price of soda increases, to what degree will the demand for iced tea (a substitute) be affected? The cross-price elasticity of demand measures both the direction and magnitude of the impact that a price change for one good will have on the demand for another good. Specifically, the **cross-price elasticity of demand** is defined as the percentage change in the demand of one good (good A) divided by the percentage change in price of another good (good B), or

$$\text{Cross-price elasticity demand} = \frac{\%\ \Delta\ \text{in the demand for Good A}}{\%\ \Delta\ \text{in the price for Good B}}$$

The cross-price elasticity of demand indicates not only the degree of the connection between the two variables but also whether the goods in question are substitutes or complements for one another.

Calculating the Cross-Price Elasticity of Demand

Let's calculate the cross-price elasticity of demand between soda and iced tea, where a 10 percent increase in the price of soda results in a 20 percent increase in the demand for iced tea. In this case, the cross-price elasticity of demand would be +2 (+20% ÷ +10% = +2).

Consumers responded to the soda price increase by buying less soda (moving along the demand curve for soda) and increasing the demand for iced tea (shifting the demand curve for iced tea). In general, if the cross-price elasticity is positive, we can conclude that the two goods are substitutes because the price of one good and the demand for the other move in the same direction.

As another example, let's calculate the cross-price elasticity of demand between potato chips and soda, where a 10 percent decrease in the price of potato chips results in a 30 percent increase in the demand for soda. In this case, the cross-price elasticity of demand is −3 (+30% ÷ −10% = −3). The demand for chips increases as a result of the price decrease, as consumers then purchase additional soda to wash down those extra bags of salty chips. Potato chips and soda, then, are complements. In general, if the cross-price elasticity is negative, we can conclude that the two goods are complements because the price of one good and the demand for the other move in opposite directions.

Cross-Price Elasticity and Sodas

According to economist Jean-Pierre Dube, Coca-Cola is a good substitute for Pepsi—the cross-price elasticity is a 0.34. In other words, a 10 percent increase in the price of a Pepsi 12-pack will lead to an increase in the sales of Coca-Cola 12-packs by 3.4 percent. But six-packs of Coca-Cola and Diet Coke are even a better substitute with a cross-price elasticity of 1.15; a 10 percent increase in the price of a six-pack of Diet Coke will lead to a 11.5 percent increase in the sales of six-packs of Coca-Cola. And a 10 percent increase in the price of a 12-pack of Mountain Dew will lead to a 7.7 percent increase in the sales of 12-packs of Pepsi.

ISTOCKPHOTO.COM/JO UNRUH

A 10 percent increase in the price of a six-pack of Diet Coke will lead to a 11.5 percent increase in the sales of six-packs of Coca-Cola. That is a cross-price elasticity of 1.15.

The Income Elasticity of Demand

Sometimes it is useful to measure how responsive demand is to a change in income. The income elasticity of demand is a measure of the relationship between a relative change in income and the consequent relative change in demand, *ceteris paribus*. The income elasticity of demand coefficient not only expresses the degree of the connection between the two variables, but it also indicates whether the good in question is normal or inferior. Specifically, the income elasticity of demand is defined as the percentage change in the demand divided by the percentage change in income, or

income elasticity of demand
the percentage change in demand divided by the percentage change in consumer's income

$$\text{Income elasticity of demand} = \frac{\%\Delta \text{ in demand}}{\%\Delta \text{ in income}}$$

Calculating the Income Elasticity of Demand

Let's calculate the income elasticity of demand for lobster, where a 10 percent increase in income results in a 15 percent increase in the demand for lobster. In this case, the income elasticity of demand is +1.5 (+15% ÷ +10% = +1.5). Lobster, then, is a normal good because an increase in income results in an increase in demand. In general, if the income elasticity is positive, then the good in question is a normal good because income and demand move in the same direction.

In comparison, let's calculate the income elasticity of demand for beans, where a 10 percent increase in income results in a 15 percent decrease in the demand for beans. In this case, the income elasticity of demand is -1.5 ($-15\% \div +10\% = -1.5$). In this example, then, beans are an inferior good because an increase in income results in a decrease in the demand for beans. If the income elasticity is negative, then the good in question is an inferior good because the change in income and the change in demand move in opposite directions.

ⓘ SECTION QUIZ

1. If the cross-price elasticity of demand between two goods is negative, we know that
   a. they are substitutes.
   b. they are complements.
   c. they are both inferior goods.
   d. they are both normal goods.

2. If the income elasticity of demand for good A is 0.5 and the income elasticity of demand for good B is 1.5, then
   a. both A and B are normal goods.
   b. both A and B are inferior goods.
   c. A is a normal good, but B is an inferior good.
   d. A is an inferior good, but B is a normal good.

3. If good X has a negative cross-price elasticity of demand with good Y and good X also has a negative income elasticity of demand, then
   a. X is a substitute for Y, and X is a normal good.
   b. X is a substitute for Y, and X is an inferior good.
   c. X is a complement for Y, and X is a normal good.
   d. X is a complement for Y, and X is an inferior good.

4. Which of the following statements is true?
   a. The cross-price elasticity of demand is the percentage change in the demand of one good divided by the percentage change in the price of another good.
   b. If the sign on the cross-price elasticity is positive, the two goods are substitutes; if it is negative, the two goods are complements.
   c. The income elasticity of demand is the percentage change in demand divided by the percentage change in consumer's income.
   d. If the income elasticity is positive, then the good is a normal good; if it is negative, the good is an inferior good.
   e. All of the above are true statements.

---

1. How does the cross-price elasticity of demand tell you whether two goods are substitutes? Complements?

2. How does the income elasticity of demand tell you whether a good is normal? Inferior?

3. If the cross-price elasticity of demand between potato chips and popcorn was positive and large, would popcorn makers benefit from a tax imposed on potato chips?

4. As people's incomes rise, why will they spend an increasing portion of their incomes on goods with income elasticities greater than 1 (DVDs) and a decreasing portion of their incomes on goods with income elasticities less than 1 (food)?

5. If people spent three times as much on restaurant meals and four times as much on DVDs as their incomes doubled, would restaurant meals or DVDs have a greater income elasticity of demand?

Answers: 1. a   2. a   3. d   4. e

Price Elasticity of Supply

☐ What is the price elasticity of supply?

☐ How does time affect the supply elasticity?

☐ How does the relative elasticity of supply and demand determine the tax burden?

What Is the Price Elasticity of Supply?

According to the law of supply, there is a positive relationship between price and quantity supplied, *ceteris paribus*. But by how much does quantity supplied change as price changes? It is often helpful to know the degree to which a change in price changes the quantity supplied. The **price elasticity of supply** measures how responsive the quantity sellers are willing and able to sell is to changes in price. In other words, it measures the relative change in the quantity supplied that results from a change in price. Specifically, the price elasticity of supply (E_s) is defined as the percentage change in the quantity supplied divided by the percentage change in price, or

price elasticity of supply
the measure of the sensitivity of the quantity supplied to changes in price of a good

$$E_s = \frac{\%\Delta \text{ in the quantity supplied}}{\%\Delta \text{ in price}}$$

Calculating the Price Elasticity of Supply

The price elasticity of supply is calculated in much the same manner as the price elasticity of demand. Consider, for example, the case in which it is determined that a 10 percent increase in the price of artichokes results in a 25 percent increase in the quantity of artichokes supplied after, say, a few harvest seasons. In this case, the price elasticity is +2.5 (+25% ÷ +10% = +2.5). This coefficient indicates that each 1 percent increase in the price of artichokes induces a 2.5 percent increase in the quantity of artichokes supplied.

Types of Supply Curves

As with the elasticity of demand, the ranges of the price elasticity of supply center on whether the elasticity coefficient is greater than or less than 1. Goods with a supply elasticity that is greater than 1 ($E_s > 1$) are said to be relatively elastic in supply. With that, a 1 percent change in price will result in a greater than 1 percent change in quantity supplied. In our example, artichokes were elastic in supply because a 1 percent price increase resulted in a 2.5 percent increase in quantity supplied. An example of an *elastic supply curve* is shown in Exhibit 1(a).

Goods with a supply elasticity that is less than 1 ($E_s < 1$) are said to be inelastic in supply. In other words, a 1 percent change in the price of these goods will induce a proportionately smaller change in the quantity supplied. An example of an *inelastic supply curve* is shown in Exhibit 1(b).

Finally, two extreme cases of price elasticity of supply are perfectly inelastic supply and perfectly elastic supply. In a condition of *perfectly inelastic supply,* an increase in price will not change the quantity supplied. In this case the elasticity of supply is zero. For example, in a sports arena in the short run (that is, in a period too brief to adjust the structure), the number of seats available will be almost fixed, say at 20,000 seats. Additional portable seats might be available, but for the most part, even if a higher price is charged, only 20,000 seats will be available. We say that the elasticity of supply is zero, which describes a perfectly inelastic supply curve. Famous paintings, such as Van Gogh's *Starry Night,* provide another example: Only one original exists; therefore, only one can be supplied, regardless of price. An example of this condition is shown in Exhibit 1(c).

What does it mean if the supply of elasticity is less than 1? greater than 1?

Immediately after harvest season is over, the supply of pumpkins is inelastic. That is, even if the price for pumpkins rises, say 10 percent, the amount of pumpkins produced will change hardly at all until the next harvest season. Some pumpkins may be grown in greenhouses (at a much higher price to consumers), but most farmers will wait until the next growing season.

At the other extreme is a perfectly elastic supply curve, where the elasticity equals infinity, as shown in Exhibit 1(d). In a condition of *perfectly elastic supply,* the price does not change at all. It is the same regardless of the quantity supplied, and the elasticity of supply is infinite. Firms would supply as much as the market wants at the market price (P_1) or above. However, firms would supply nothing below the market price because they would not be able to cover their costs of production. Most cases fall somewhere between the two extremes of perfectly elastic and perfectly inelastic.

How Does Time Affect Supply Elasticities?

Time is usually critical in supply elasticities (as well as in demand elasticities), because it is more costly for sellers to bring forth and release products in a shorter period. For example, higher wheat prices may cause farmers to grow more wheat, but big changes cannot occur until the next growing season. That is, immediately after harvest season, the supply of wheat is relatively inelastic, but over a longer time extending

---

section 6.4
exhibit 1   The Price Elasticity of Supply

a. Elastic Supply ($E_s > 1$)

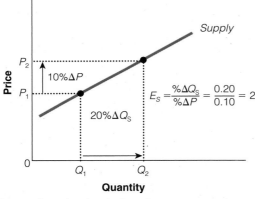

A change in price leads to a larger percentage change in quantity supplied.

b. Inelastic Supply ($E_s < 1$)

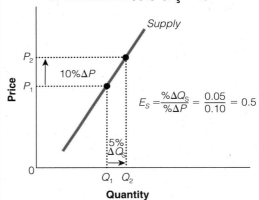

A change in price leads to a smaller percentage change in quantity supplied.

c. Perfectly Inelastic Supply ($E_s = 0$)

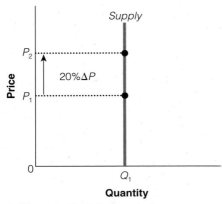

The quantity supplied does not change regardless of the change in price.

d. Perfectly Elastic Supply ($E_s = \infty$)

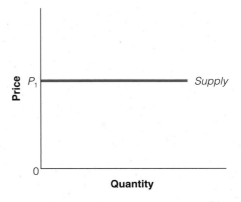

Even a small percentage change in price will change quantity supplied by an infinite amount.

over the next growing period, the supply curve becomes much more elastic. Thus, supply tends to be more elastic in the long run than in the short run, as shown in Exhibit 2.

In the short run, firms can increase output by using their existing facilities to a greater capacity, paying workers to work overtime, and hiring additional workers. However, firms will be able to change output much more in the long run when firms can build new factories or close existing ones. In addition, some firms can enter as others exit. In other words, the quantity supplied will be much more elastic in the long run than in the short run.

Elasticities and Taxes: Combining Supply and Demand Elasticities

Who pays the tax? Someone may be legally required to send the check to the government but that is not necessarily the party that bears the burden of the tax.

The relative elasticity of supply and demand determines the distribution of the tax burden for a good. As we will see, if demand is relatively less elastic than supply in the relevant tax region, the largest portion of the tax is paid by the consumer. However, if demand is relatively more elastic than supply in the relevant tax region, the largest portion of the tax is paid by the producer.

In Exhibit 3(a), the pretax equilibrium price is $1.00 and the pretax equilibrium quantity is Q_{BT}—the quantity before tax. If the government imposes a $0.50 tax on the seller, the supply curve shifts vertically by the amount of the tax (just as if an input price rose $0.50).

When demand is relatively less elastic than supply in the relevant region, the consumer bears more of the burden of the tax. For example, in Exhibit 3(a), the demand curve is relatively less elastic than the supply curve. In response to the tax, the consumer pays $1.40 per unit, $0.40 more than the consumer paid before the tax increase. The producer, however, receives $0.90 per unit, which is $0.10 less than the producer received before the tax.

In Exhibit 3(b), demand is relatively more elastic than the supply in the relevant region. Here we see that the greater burden of the same $0.50 tax falls on the producer. That is, the producer is now responsible for $0.40 of the tax, while the consumer only pays $0.10. In general, then, the tax burden falls on the side of the market that is relatively less elastic.

section 6.4 exhibit 2 — Short-Run and Long-Run Supply Curves

For most goods, supply is more elastic in the long run than in the short run. For example, if the price of a certain good increases, firms have an incentive to produce more but are constrained by the size of their plants. In the long run, they can increase their capacity and produce more.

© Cengage Learning 2013

Why does supply tend to be more elastic in the long run than in the short run?

Yachts, Taxes, and Elasticities

In 1991, Congress levied a 10 percent luxury tax. The tax applied to the "first retail sale" of luxury goods with sales prices above the following thresholds: automobiles $30,000; boats, $100,000; private planes, $250,000; and furs and jewelry, $10,000. The Congressional Budget Office forecasted that the luxury tax would raise about $1.5 billion over five years. However, in 1991, the luxury tax raised less than $30 million in tax revenues. Why? People stopped buying items subject to the luxury tax.

Let's focus our attention on the luxury tax on yachts. Congress passed this tax thinking that the demand for yachts was relatively inelastic and that the tax would have only a small impact on the sale of new yachts. However, the people in the market for new boats had plenty of substitutes—used boats, boats from other countries, new houses, vacations, and so on. In short, the demand for new yachts was more elastic

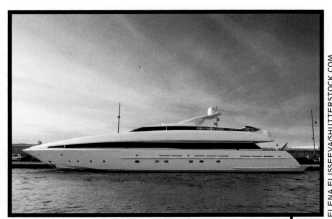

ELENA ELISSEEVA/SHUTTERSTOCK.COM

If the demand for yachts is elastic, will most of a luxury tax on yachts get passed on to producers of yachts? And if so, how will that impact employment in the boat-building industry?

section 6.4
exhibit 3   Elasticity and the Burden of Taxation

a. Demand Is Relatively Less Elastic Than Supply

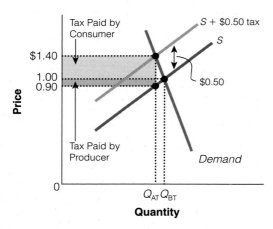

b. Demand Is Relatively More Elastic Than Supply

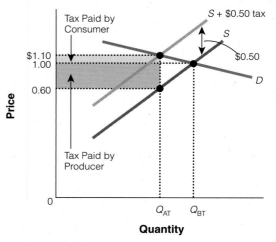

When demand is less elastic (or more inelastic) than supply, the tax burden falls primarily on consumers, as shown in (a). When demand is more elastic than supply, as shown in (b), the tax burden falls primarily on producers.

© Cengage Learning 2013

than Congress thought. Remember, when demand is relatively more elastic than supply, most of the tax is passed on to the seller—in this case, the boat industry (workers and retailers). And supply was relatively inelastic because boat factories are not easy to change in the short run. So sellers received a lower price for their boats, and sales fell. In the first year after the tax, yacht retailers reported a 77 percent drop in sales, and approximately 25,000 workers were laid off. The point is that incorrectly predicting elasticities can lead to huge social, political, and economic problems. After intense lobbying by industry groups, Congress repealed the luxury tax on boats in 1993, and on January 1, 2003, the tax on cars finally expired.

use what you've learned   Farm Prices Fall over the Last Half-Century

Q In the last half-century, farm prices experienced a steady decline—roughly 2 percent per year. Why?

A The demand for farm products grew more slowly than supply. Productivity advances in agriculture caused large increases in supply. And because of the inelastic demand for farm products, farmers' incomes fell considerably. That is, the total revenues ($P \times Q$) that farmers collected at the higher price, P_1, was much greater, area $0P_1E_1Q_1$, than the total revenue collected by farmers now when prices are lower, P_2, at area $0P_2E_2Q_2$.

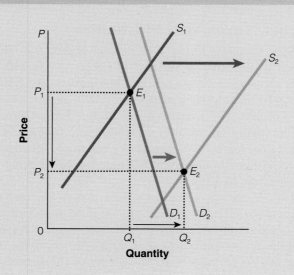

in the news   Drugs across the Border

The United States spends billions of dollars a year to halt the importation of illegal drugs across the border. Although these efforts are clearly targeted at suppliers, who really pays the higher enforcement and evasion costs? The government crackdown has increased the probability of apprehension and conviction for drug smugglers. That increase in risk for suppliers increases their cost of doing business, raising the cost of importing and distributing illegal drugs. This would shift the supply curve for illegal drugs to the left, from S_1 to S_2, as seen in Exhibit 4. For most drug users—addicts, in particular—the price of drugs such as cocaine and heroin lies in the highly inelastic region of the demand curve. Because the demand for drugs is relatively inelastic in this region, the seller would be able to shift most of this cost onto the consumer (think of it as similar to the tax shift just discussed). The buyer now has to pay a much higher price, P_B, and the seller receives a slightly lower price, P_S. That is, enforcement efforts increase the price of illegal drugs, but only a small reduction in quantity demanded results from this price increase. Increased enforcement efforts may have unintended consequences due to the fact that buyers bear the majority of the burden of this price increase. Tighter smuggling controls may, in fact, result in higher levels of burglary, muggings, and white-collar crime, as more cash-strapped buyers search for alternative ways of funding their increasingly expensive habit. In addition, with the huge financial rewards in the drug trade, tougher enforcement and higher illegal drug prices could lead to even greater corruption in law enforcement and the judicial system.

These possible reactions do not mean we should abandon our efforts against illegal drugs. Illegal drugs can impose huge personal and social costs— billions of dollars of lost productivity and immeasurable personal tragedy. However, solely targeting the supply side can have unintended consequences. Policy makers may get their best results by focusing on a reduction in demand—changing user preferences. For example, if drug education leads to a reduction in the demand for drugs, the demand curve will shift to the left—reducing the price and the quantity of illegal drugs exchanged, as shown in Exhibit 5. The remaining drug users, at Q_2, will now pay a lower price, P_2. This lower price for drugs will lead to fewer drug-related crimes, *ceteris paribus*.

It is also possible that the elasticity of demand for illegal drugs may be more elastic in the long run than the short run. In the short run, as the price rises, the quantity demanded falls less than proportionately because of the addictive nature of illegal drugs (this relationship is also true for goods such as tobacco and alcohol). However, in the long run, the demand for illegal drugs may be more elastic; that is, the higher price may deter many younger, and poorer, people from experimenting with illegal drugs.

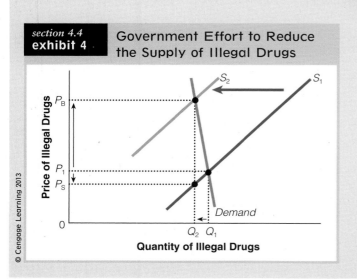

section 4.4 exhibit 4 Government Effort to Reduce the Supply of Illegal Drugs

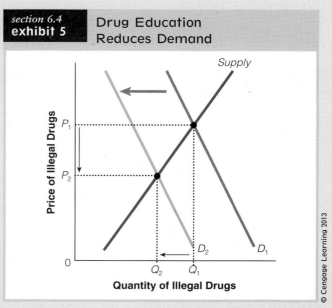

section 6.4 exhibit 5 Drug Education Reduces Demand

use *what you've learned* Oil Prices

One reason that small changes in supply (or demand) lead to large changes in oil prices and small changes in quantity is because of the inelasticity of demand (and supply) in the short run. Because bringing the production of oil to market takes a long time, the elasticity of supply is relatively low—supply is inelastic. Few substitutes for oil products (e.g., gasoline) are available in the short run, as seen in Exhibit 6(a).

However, in the long run, demand and supply are more elastic. At higher prices, consumers will replace gas guzzlers with more fuel-efficient cars, and non-OPEC oil producers will expand exploration and production. Thus, in the long run, when supply and demand are much more elastic, the same size reduction in supply will have a smaller impact on price, as seen in Exhibit 6(b).

section 6.4
exhibit 6

a. Oil Prices in the Short Run

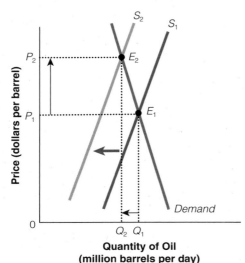

b. Oil Prices in the Long Run

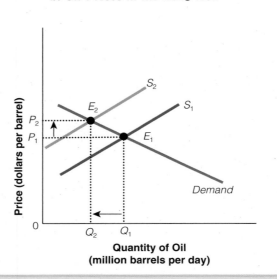

© Cengage Learning 2013

---

② SECTION QUIZ

1. For a given increase in price, the greater the elasticity of supply, the greater the resulting
   a. decrease in quantity supplied.
   b. decrease in supply.
   c. increase in quantity supplied.
   d. increase in supply.

2. If the demand for gasoline is highly inelastic and the supply is highly elastic, and then a tax is imposed on gasoline, it will be paid
   a. largely by the sellers of gasoline.
   b. largely by the buyers of gasoline.
   c. equally by the sellers and buyers of gasoline.
   d. by the government.

(*continued*)

? S E C T I O N Q U I Z (Cont.)

3. Which of the following statements is true?

   a. The price elasticity of supply measures the relative change in the quantity supplied that results from a change in price.

   b. If the supply price elasticity is greater than 1, it is elastic; if it is less than 1, it is inelastic.

   c. Supply tends to be more elastic in the long run than in the short run.

   d. The relative elasticity of supply and demand determines the distribution of the tax burden for a good.

   e. All of the statements above are true.

4. Which of the following statements is true?

   a. The price elasticity of supply measures the relative change in the quantity supplied that results from a change in price.

   b. When supply is relatively elastic, a 10 percent change in price will result in a greater than 10 percent change in quantity supplied.

   c. Goods with a supply elasticity that is less than 1 are called relatively inelastic in supply.

   d. Who bears the burden of a tax has nothing to do with who actually pays the tax at the time of the purchase.

   e. All of the statements above are true.

_____

1. What does it mean to say the elasticity of supply for one good is greater than that for another?

2. Why does supply tend to be more elastic in the long run than in the short run?

3. How do the relative elasticities of supply and demand determine who bears the greater burden of a tax?

Answers: 1. c 2. b 3. e 4. e

Interactive Summary

Fill in the blanks:

1. The price elasticity of demand measures the responsiveness of quantity _____ to a change in price.

2. The price elasticity of demand is defined as the percentage change in _____ divided by the percentage change in _____.

3. If the price elasticity of demand is elastic, it means the quantity demanded changes by a relatively _____ amount than the price change.

4. If the price elasticity of demand is inelastic, it means the quantity demanded changes by a relatively _____ amount than the price change.

5. A demand curve or a portion of a demand curve can be relatively _____, _____, or relatively _____.

6. For the most part, the price elasticity of demand depends on the availability of _____, the _____ spent on the good, and the amount of _____ people have to adapt to a price change.

7. The elasticity of demand for a Ford automobile would likely be _____ elastic than the demand for automobiles, because there are more and better substitutes for a certain type of car than for a car itself.

8. The smaller the proportion of income spent on a good, the _____ its elasticity of demand.

9. The more time that people have to adapt to a new price change, the _____ the elasticity of demand. The more time that passes, the more time consumers have to find or develop suitable _____ and to plan and implement changes in their patterns of consumption.

10. When demand is price elastic, total revenues will _____ as the price declines because the percentage increase in the _____ is greater than the percentage reduction in price.

11. When demand is price inelastic, total revenues will _____ as the price declines because the percentage increase in the _____ is less than the percentage reduction in price.

12. When the price falls on the _____ half of a straight-line demand curve, demand is relatively

_____. When the price falls on the lower half of a straight-line demand curve, demand is relatively _____.

13. The cross-price elasticity of demand is defined as the percentage change in the _____ _____ of good A divided by the percentage change in _____ of good B.

14. The income elasticity of demand is defined as the percentage change in the _____ by the percentage change in _____.

15. The price elasticity of supply measures the sensitivity of the quantity _____ to changes in the price of the good.

16. The price elasticity of supply is defined as the percentage change in the _____ divided by the percentage change in _____.

17. Goods with a supply elasticity that is greater than 1 are called relatively _____ in supply.

18. When supply is inelastic, a 1 percent change in the price of a good will induce a _____ 1 percent change in the quantity supplied.

19. Time is usually critical in supply elasticities because it is _____ costly for sellers to bring forth and release products in a shorter period of time.

20. The relative _____ determines the distribution of the tax burden for a good.

21. If demand is relatively _____ elastic than supply in the relevant region, the largest portion of a tax is paid by the producer.

Answers: 1. demanded 2. quantity demanded; price 3. larger 4. smaller 5. elastic; unit elastic; inelastic 6. close substitutes; proportion of income; time 7. more 8. lower 9. greater; substitutes 10. rise; quantity demanded 11. fall; quantity demanded 12. upper; elastic; inelastic 13. demand; price 14. demand; income 15. supplied 16. quantity supplied; price 17. elastic 18. less than 19. more 20. elasticity of supply and demand 21. more

Key Terms and Concepts

price elasticity of demand 157
elastic 158
inelastic 158

unit elastic demand 158
total revenue (TR) 165
cross-price elasticity of demand 170

income elasticity of demand 171
price elasticity of supply 173

Section Quiz Answers

6.1   Price Elasticity of Demand

1. What question is the price elasticity of demand designed to answer?
The price elasticity of demand is designed to answer the question: How responsive is quantity demanded to changes in the price of a good?

2. How is the price elasticity of demand calculated?
The price elasticity of demand is calculated as the percentage change in quantity demanded, divided by the percentage change in the price that caused the change in quantity demanded.

3. What is the difference between a relatively price elastic demand curve and a relatively price inelastic demand curve?
Quantity demanded changes relatively more than price along a relatively price elastic segment of a demand curve, while quantity demanded changes relatively less than price along a relatively price inelastic segment of a demand curve.

4. What is the relationship between the price elasticity of demand and the slope at a given point on a demand curve?
At a given point on a demand curve, the flatter the demand curve, the more quantity demanded changes for a given change in price, so the greater is the elasticity of demand.

5. What factors tend to make demand curves more price elastic?
Demand curves tend to become more elastic, the larger the number of close substitutes available for the good, the larger proportion of income spent on the good, and the greater the amount of time that buyers have to respond to a change in the good's price.

6. **Why would a tax on a particular brand of cigarettes be less effective at reducing smoking than a tax on all brands of cigarettes?**

A tax on one brand of cigarettes would allow smokers to avoid the tax by switching brands rather than by smoking less, but a tax on all brands would raise the cost of smoking any cigarettes. A tax on all brands of cigarettes would therefore be more effective in reducing smoking.

7. **Why is the price elasticity of demand for products at a 24-hour convenience store likely to be lower at 2 A.M. than at 2 P.M.?**

Fewer alternative stores are open at 2 A.M. than at 2 P.M., and with fewer good substitutes, the price elasticity of demand for products at 24-hour convenience stores is greater at 2 P.M.

8. **Why is the price elasticity of demand for turkeys likely to be lower, but the price elasticity of demand for turkeys at a particular store at Thanksgiving likely to be greater than at other times of the year?**

For many people, far fewer good substitutes are acceptable for turkey at Thanksgiving than at other times, so that the demand for turkeys is more inelastic at Thanksgiving. But grocery stores looking to attract customers for their entire large Thanksgiving shopping trip also often offer and heavily advertise turkeys at far better prices than normally. This means shoppers have available more good substitutes and a more price elastic demand curve for buying a turkey at a particular store than usual.

6.2   Total Revenue and the Price Elasticity of Demand

1. **Why does total revenue vary inversely with price if demand is relatively price elastic?**

Total revenue varies inversely with price if demand is relatively price elastic, because the quantity demanded (which equals the quantity sold) changes relatively more than price along a relatively elastic demand curve. Therefore, total revenue, which equals price times quantity demanded (sold) at that price, will change in the same direction as quantity demanded and in the opposite direction from the change in price.

2. **Why does total revenue vary directly with price, if demand is relatively price inelastic?**

Total revenue varies in the same direction as price, if demand is relatively price inelastic, because the quantity demanded (which equals the quantity sold) changes relatively less than price along a relatively inelastic demand curve. Therefore, total revenue, which equals price times quantity demanded (and sold) at that price, will change in the same direc-

tion as price and in the opposite direction from the change in quantity demanded.

3. **Why is a linear demand curve more price elastic at higher price ranges and more price inelastic at lower price ranges?**

Along the upper half of a linear (constant slope) demand curve, total revenue increases as the price falls, indicating that demand is relatively price elastic. Along the lower half of a linear (constant slope) demand curve, total revenue decreases as the price falls, indicating that demand is relatively price inelastic.

4. **If demand for some good was perfectly price inelastic, how would total revenue from its sales change as its price changed?**

A perfectly price inelastic demand curve would be one where the quantity sold did not vary with the price. In such an (imaginary) case, total revenue would increase proportionately with price—a 10 percent increase in price with the same quantity sold would result in a 10 percent increase in total revenue.

5. **Assume that both you and Art, your partner in a picture-framing business, want to increase your firm's total revenue. You argue that in order to achieve this goal, you should lower your prices; Art, on the other hand, thinks that you should raise your prices. What assumptions are each of you making about your firm's price elasticity of demand?**

You are assuming that a lower price will increase total revenue, which implies you think the demand for your picture frames is relatively price elastic. Art is assuming that an increase in your price will increase your total revenue, which implies he thinks the demand for your picture frames is relatively price inelastic.

6.3   Other Types of Demand Elasticities

1. **How does the cross-price elasticity of demand tell you whether two goods are substitutes? Complements?**

Two goods are substitutes when an increase (decrease) in the price of one good causes an increase (decrease) in the demand for another good. Substitutes have a positive cross-price elasticity. Two goods are complements when an increase (decrease) in the price of one good decreases (increases) the demand for another food. Complements have a negative cross-price elasticity.

2. How does the income elasticity of demand tell you whether a good is normal? Inferior?

If demand for a good increases (decreases) when income rises (falls), it is a normal good and has a positive income elasticity. If demand for a good decreases (increases) when income rises (falls), it is an inferior good and has a negative income elasticity.

3. If the cross-price elasticity of demand between potato chips and popcorn was positive and large, would popcorn makers benefit from a tax imposed on potato chips?

A large positive cross-price elasticity of demand between potato chips and popcorn indicates that they are close substitutes. A tax on potato chips, which would raise the price of potato chips as a result, would also substantially increase the demand for popcorn, increasing the price of popcorn and the quantity of popcorn sold, increasing the profits of popcorn makers.

4. As people's incomes rise, why will they spend an increasing portion of their incomes on goods with income elasticities greater than 1 (DVDs) and a decreasing portion of their incomes on goods with income elasticities less than 1 (food)?

An income elasticity of 1 would mean people spent the same fraction or share of their income on a particular good as their incomes increase. An income elasticity greater than 1 would mean people spent an increasing fraction or share of their income on a particular good as their incomes increase, and an income elasticity less than 1 would mean people spent a decreasing fraction or share of their income on a particular good as their incomes increase.

5. If people spent three times as much on restaurant meals and four times as much on DVDs as their incomes doubled, would restaurant meals or DVDs have a greater income elasticity of demand?

DVDs would have a higher income elasticity of demand (4) in this case than restaurant meals (3).

6.4 Price Elasticity of Supply

1. What does it mean to say the elasticity of supply for one good is greater than that for another?

For the elasticity of supply for one good to be greater than for another, the percentage increase in quantity supplied that results from a given percentage change in price will be greater for the first good than for the second.

2. Why does supply tend to be more elastic in the long run than in the short run?

Just as the cost of buyers changing their behavior is lower the longer they have to adapt, which leads to long-run demand curves being more elastic than short-run demand curves, the same is true of suppliers. The cost of producers changing their behavior is lower the longer they have to adapt, which leads to long-run supply curves being more elastic than short-run supply curves.

3. How do the relative elasticities of supply and demand determine who bears the greater burden of a tax?

When demand is more elastic than supply, the tax burden falls mainly on producers; when supply is more elastic than demand, the tax burden falls mainly on consumers.

Problems

1. In each of the following cases, indicate which good you think has a relatively *more* price elastic demand and identify the most likely reason, in terms of the determinants of the elasticity of demand (more substitutes, greater share of budget, or more time to adjust).
   a. cars or Chevrolets
   b. salt or housing
   c. going to a New York Mets game or a Cleveland Indians game
   d. natural gas this month or over the course of a year

2. How might your elasticity of demand for copying and binding services vary if your work presentation is next week versus in two hours?

3. The San Francisco Giants want to boost revenues from ticket sales next season. You are hired as an economic consultant and asked to advise the Giants whether to raise or lower ticket prices next year. If the elasticity of demand for Giants game tickets is estimated to be −1.6, what would you advise? If the elasticity of demand equals −0.4?

4. For each of the following pairs, identify which one is likely to exhibit more elastic demand.
   a. shampoo; Paul Mitchell Shampoo
   b. air travel prompted by an illness in the family; vacation air travel
   c. paper clips; an apartment rental
   d. prescription heart medication; generic aspirin

5. Using the midpoint formula for calculating the elasticity of demand, if the price of a good fell from $42 to $38, what would be the elasticity of demand if the quantity demanded changed from:
   a. 19 to 21?
   b. 27 to 33?
   c. 195 to 205?

6. Explain why using the midpoint formula for calculating the elasticity of demand gives the same result whether price increases or decreases, but using the initial price and quantity instead of the average does not.

7. Why is a more narrowly defined good (pizza) likely to have a greater elasticity of demand than a more broadly defined good (food)?

8. If the elasticity of demand for hamburgers equals −1.5 and the quantity demanded equals 40,000, predict what will happen to the quantity demanded of hamburgers when the price increases by 10 percent. If the price falls by 5 percent, what will happen?

9. Evaluate the following statement: "Along a downward-sloping linear demand curve, the slope and therefore the elasticity of demand are both 'constant.'"

10. If the midpoint on a straight-line demand curve is at a price of $7, what can we say about the elasticity of demand for a price change from $12 to $10? What about from $6 to $4?

11. Assume the following weekly demand schedule for Sunshine DVD Rentals in Cloverdale.

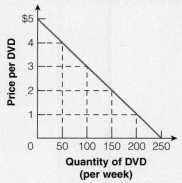

   a. When Sunshine DVD Rentals lowers its rental price from $4 to $3, what happens to its total revenue?
   b. Between a price of $4 and a price of $3, is the demand for Sunshine DVD Rentals in Cloverdale elastic or inelastic?
   c. Between a price of $2 and a price of $1, is the demand for Sunshine DVD Rentals in Cloverdale elastic or inelastic?

12. The Cowtown Hotel is the only first-class hotel in Fort Worth, Texas. The hotel owners hired economics advisors for advice about improving the hotel's profitability. They suggested the hotel could increase this year's revenue by raising prices. The owners asked, "Won't raising prices reduce the quantity of hotel rooms demanded and increase vacancies?" What do you think the advisors replied? Why would they suggest increasing prices?

13. A movie production company faces a linear demand curve for its film, and it seeks to maximize total revenue from the film's distribution. At what level should the price be set? Where is demand elastic, inelastic, or unit elastic? Explain.

14. Isabella always spends $50 on red roses each month and simply adjusts the quantity she purchases as the price changes. What can you say about Isabella's elasticity of demand for roses?

15. If taxi fares in a city rise, what will happen to the total revenue received by taxi operators? If the fares charged for subway rides, a substitute for taxi rides, do not change, what will happen to the total revenue earned by the subway as a result?

16. Mayor George Henry has a problem. He doesn't want to anger voters by taxing them because he wants to be reelected, but the town of Gapville needs more revenue for its schools. He has a choice between taxing tickets to professional basketball games or taxing food. If the demand for food is relatively inelastic while the supply is relatively elastic, and if the demand for professional basketball games is relatively elastic while the supply is relatively inelastic, in which case would the tax burden fall primarily on consumers? In which case would the tax burden fall primarily on producers?

17. Indicate whether a pair of products are substitutes, complements, or neither based on the following estimates for the cross-price elasticity of demand:
    a. 0.5.
    b. −0.5.

18. Using the midpoint formula for calculating the elasticity of supply, if the price of a good rose from $95 to $105, what would be the elasticity of supply if the quantity supplied changed from:
    a. 38 to 42?
    b. 78 to 82?
    c. 54 to 66?

19. Why is an increase in price more likely to decrease the total revenue of a seller in the long run than in the short run?

20. If both supply curves and demand curves are more elastic in the long run than in the short run, how does the incidence of a tax change from the short run to the long run as a result? What happens to the revenue raised from a given tax over time, *ceteris paribus*?

21. Assume you had the following observations on U.S. intercity rail travel: Between 1990 and 1993 rail travel increased from 17.5 passenger miles per person to 19 passenger miles per person. At the same time, neither per-mile railroad price or incomes changed but the per-mile price of intercity airline travel increased by 7.5 percent. Between 1995 and 1998 per capita incomes rose by approximately 13 percent while the price of travel by rail and plane stayed constant. Intercity rail travel was 20 passenger miles per person in 1995 and 19.5 in 1998. Assuming the demand for travel didn't change between these periods,
    a. calculate the income elasticity of demand for intercity rail travel.
    b. calculate the cross-price elasticity of demand for intercity rail travel.
    c. Indicate whether air travel and rail travel are substitutes or complements. Is intercity rail travel a normal or an inferior good?

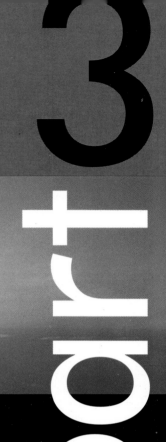

part 3

© SIMON McCOMB/STONE/GETTY IMAGES, INC.

Market Efficiency, Market Failure, and the Public System

Market Efficiency and Welfare

We can use the tools of consumer and producer surplus to study the welfare effects of government policy—rent controls, taxes, and agricultural support prices. To economists, welfare does not mean a government payment to the poor; rather, it is a way that we measure the impact of a policy on a particular group, such as consumers or producers. By calculating the changes in producer and consumer surplus that result from government intervention, we can measure the impact of such policies on buyers and sellers. For example, economists and policy makers may want to know how much a consumer or producer might benefit or be harmed by a tax or subsidy that alters the equilibrium price and quantity of a good or service. Take the the price support programs for farmers. The intent is to help poor farmers, not to hurt consumers and taxpayers. However, most

of the farm subsidies go to large corporations, not poor farmers. Between 2002 and 2009, U.S. farmers received an average of $16.4 billion of direct government subsidies per year. In earlier chapters, we saw how the market forces of supply and demand allocate society's scarce resources. However, we did not discuss whether this outcome was desirable or to whom. Are the price and output that result from the equilibrium of supply and demand right from society's standpoint?

Using the tools of consumer and producer surplus, we can demonstrate the *efficiency* of a competitive market. In other words, we can show that the equilibrium price and quantity in a competitive market maximize the economic welfare of consumers and producers. Maximizing total surplus (the sum of consumer and producer surplus) leads to an efficient allocation of resources. Efficiency makes the size of the economic pie as large as possible. How we distribute that economic pie (equity) is the subject of future chapters. Efficiency can be measured on objective, positive grounds while equity involves normative analysis.

Let's begin by presenting the most widely used tool for measuring consumer and producer welfare.

Consumer Surplus and Producer Surplus   7.1

📂 What is consumer surplus?

📂 What is producer surplus?

📂 How do we measure the total gains from trade?

Consumer Surplus

In a competitive market, consumers and producers buy and sell at the market equilibrium price. However, some consumers will be willing and able to pay more for the good than they have to. But they would never knowingly buy something that is worth less to them. That is, what a consumer actually pays for a unit of a good is usually less than the amount she is *willing* to pay. For example, would you be willing to pay more than the market price for a rope ladder to get out of a burning building? Would you be willing to pay more than the market price for a tank of gasoline if you had run out of gas on a desolate highway in the desert? Would you be willing to pay more than the market price for an anti-venom shot if you had been bitten by a rattlesnake? **Consumer surplus** is the monetary difference between the amount a consumer is willing and able to pay for an additional unit of a good and what the consumer actually pays—the market price. Consumer surplus for the whole market is the sum of all the individual consumer surpluses for those consumers who have purchased the good.

Imagine it is 115 degrees in the shade. Do you think you would get more consumer surplus from your first glass of iced tea than you would from a fifth glass?

consumer surplus the difference between the price a consumer is willing and able to pay for an additional unit of a good and the price the consumer actually pays; for the whole market, it is the sum of all the individual consumer surpluses

Marginal Willingness to Pay Falls as More Is Consumed

Suppose it is a hot day and iced tea is going for $1 per glass, but Julie is willing to pay $4 for the first glass (point a), $2 for the second glass (point b), and $0.50 for the third glass (point c), reflecting the law of demand. How much consumer surplus will Julie receive? First,

What happens to marginal willingness to pay as greater quantities are consumed in a given period?

it is important to note the general fact that if the consumer is a buyer of several units of a good, the earlier units will have greater marginal value and therefore create more consumer surplus, because *marginal willingness to pay* falls as greater quantities are consumed in any period. In fact, you can think of the demand curve as a marginal benefit curve—the additional benefit derived from consuming one more unit. Notice in Exhibit 1 that Julie's demand curve for iced tea has a step-like shape. This is demonstrated by Julie's willingness to pay $4 and $2 successively for the first two glasses of iced tea. Thus, Julie will receive $3 of consumer surplus for the first glass ($4 − $1) and $1 of consumer surplus for the second glass ($2 − $1), for a total consumer surplus of $4, as seen in Exhibit 1. Julie will not be willing to purchase the third glass, because her willingness to pay is less than its price ($0.50 versus $1.00).

In Exhibit 2, we can easily measure the consumer surplus in the market by using a market demand curve rather than an individual demand curve. In short, the market consumer surplus is the area under the market demand curve and above the market price (the shaded area in Exhibit 2). The market for chocolate contains millions of potential buyers, so we will get a smooth demand curve. That is, each of the million of potential buyers has their own willingness to pay. Because the demand curve represents the *marginal benefits* consumers receive from consuming an additional unit, we can conclude that all buyers of chocolate receive at least some consumer surplus in the market because the marginal benefit is greater than the market price—the shaded area in Exhibit 2.

Price Changes and Changes in Consumer Surplus

What happens to consumer surplus if there is a decrease in supply?

Imagine that the price of your favorite beverage fell because of an increase in supply. Wouldn't you feel better off? An increase in supply and a lower price will increase your consumer surplus for each unit you were already consuming and will also increase your consumer surplus from additional purchases at the lower price. Conversely, a decrease in supply and increase in price will lower your consumer surplus.

Exhibit 3 shows the gain in consumer surplus associated with, say, a technological advance that shifts the supply curve to the right. As a result, equilibrium price falls (from

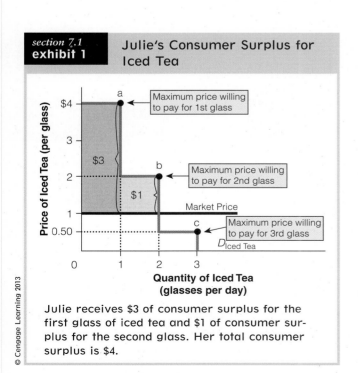

section 7.1 exhibit 1   Julie's Consumer Surplus for Iced Tea

Julie receives $3 of consumer surplus for the first glass of iced tea and $1 of consumer surplus for the second glass. Her total consumer surplus is $4.

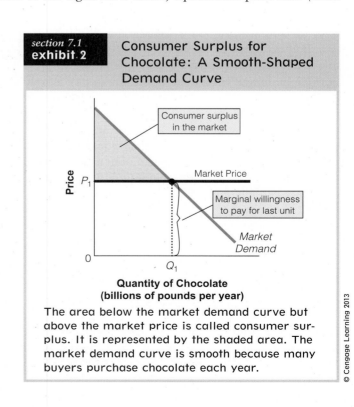

section 7.1 exhibit 2   Consumer Surplus for Chocolate: A Smooth-Shaped Demand Curve

The area below the market demand curve but above the market price is called consumer surplus. It is represented by the shaded area. The market demand curve is smooth because many buyers purchase chocolate each year.

P_1 to P_2) and quantity rises (from Q_1 to Q_2). Consumer surplus then increases from area P_1AB to area P_2AC, or a gain in consumer surplus of P_1BCP_2. The increase in consumer surplus has two parts. First, there is an increase in consumer surplus, because Q_1 can now be purchased at a lower price; this amount of additional consumer surplus is illustrated by area P_1BDP_2 in Exhibit 3. Second, the lower price makes it advantageous for buyers to expand their purchases from Q_1 to Q_2. The net benefit to buyers from expanding their consumption from Q_1 to Q_2 is illustrated by area BCD.

Producer Surplus

As we have just seen, the difference between what a consumer would be willing and able to pay for a given quantity of a good and what a consumer actually has to pay is called consumer surplus. The parallel concept for producers is called producer surplus. **Producer surplus** is the difference between what a producer is paid for a good and the cost of producing one unit of that good. Producers would never knowingly sell a good that is worth more to them than the asking price. Imagine selling coffee for half of what it cost to produce—you won't be in business very long with that pricing strategy. The supply curve shows the minimum amount that sellers must receive to be willing to supply any given quantity; that is, the supply curve reflects the marginal cost to sellers. The **marginal cost** is the cost of producing one more unit of a good. In other words, the supply curve is the marginal cost curve, just like the demand curve is the marginal benefit curve. Because some units can be produced at a cost that is lower than the market price, the seller receives a surplus, or a net benefit, from producing those units. For each unit produced, the producer surplus is the difference between the market price and the marginal cost of producing that unit. For example, in Exhibit 4, the market price is $4.50. Say the firm's marginal cost is $2 for the first unit, $3 for the second unit, $4 for the third unit, and $5 for the fourth unit. Because producer surplus for a particular unit is the difference between the market price and the seller's cost of producing that unit, producer surplus would be as follows: The first unit would yield $2.50; the second unit would yield $1.50; the third unit would yield $.50; and the fourth unit would add nothing to producer surplus, because the market price is less than the seller's cost.

When there are a lot of producers, the supply curve is more or less smooth, like in Exhibit 5. Total producer surplus for the market is obtained by summing all the producer surpluses of all the sellers—the area above the market supply curve and below the market price up to the quantity actually produced—the shaded area in Exhibit 5. Producer surplus is a measurement of how much sellers gain from trading in the market. Producer surplus represent the benefits that lower costs producers receive by selling at the market price.

Suppose an increase in market demand causes the market price to rise, say from P_1 to P_2; the seller now receives a higher price per unit, so additional producer surplus is generated. In Exhibit 6, we see the additions to producer surplus. Part of the added surplus (area P_2DBP_1) is due to a higher price for the quantity already being produced (up to Q_1) and part (area DCB) is due to the expansion of output made profitable by the higher price (from Q_1 to Q_2).

© Cengage Learning 2013

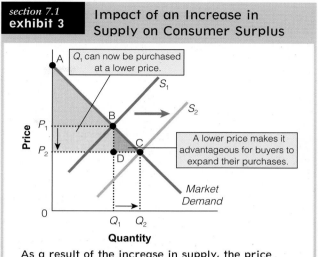

section 7.1
exhibit 3
Impact of an Increase in Supply on Consumer Surplus

Q_1 can now be purchased at a lower price.

A lower price makes it advantageous for buyers to expand their purchases.

As a result of the increase in supply, the price falls from P_1 to P_2. The initial consumer surplus at P_1 is the area P_1AB. The increase in the consumer surplus from the fall in price is from P_1 to P_2.

producer surplus
the difference between what a producer is paid for a good and the cost of producing that unit of the good; for the market, it is the sum of all the individual sellers' producer surpluses—the area above the market supply curve and below the market price

marginal cost
the cost of producing one more unit of a good

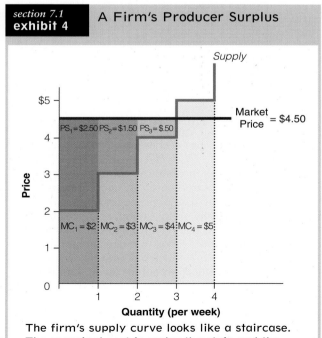

section 7.1
exhibit 4
A Firm's Producer Surplus

$PS_1=$2.50$ $PS_2=$1.50$ $PS_3=$.50$

$MC_1=$2$ $MC_2=$3$ $MC_3=$4$ $MC_4=$5$

Market Price $= $4.50

The firm's supply curve looks like a staircase. The marginal cost is under the stair and the producer surplus is above the red stair and below the market price for each unit.

© Cengage Learning 2013

section 7.1
exhibit 5 · Market Producer Surplus

The market producer surplus is the shaded area above the supply curve and below the market price up to the quantity produced, 50,000 units.

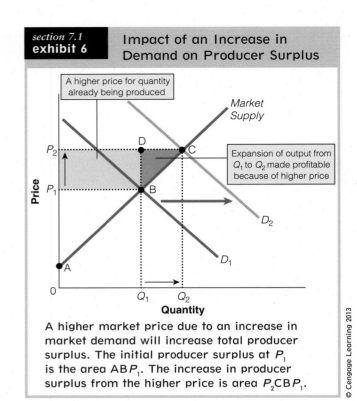

section 7.1
exhibit 6 · Impact of an Increase in Demand on Producer Surplus

A higher market price due to an increase in market demand will increase total producer surplus. The initial producer surplus at P_1 is the area ABP_1. The increase in producer surplus from the higher price is area P_2CBP_1.

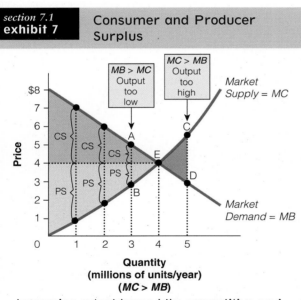

section 7.1
exhibit 7 · Consumer and Producer Surplus

Increasing output beyond the competitive equilibrium output, 4 million units, decreases welfare, because the cost of producing this extra output exceeds the value the buyer places on it ($MC > MB$)—producing 5 million units rather than 4 million units leads to a deadweight loss of area ECD. Reducing output below the competitive equilibrium output level, 4 million units, reduces total welfare, because the buyer values the extra output by more than it costs to produce that output—producing 3 million units rather than 4 million units leads to a deadweight loss of area EAB, $MB > MC$, only at equillibrium, E, is $MB = MC$.

Market Efficiency and Producer and Consumer Surplus

With the tools of consumer and producer surplus, we can better analyze the total gains from exchange. The demand curve represents a collection of maximum prices that consumers are willing and able to pay for additional quantities of a good or service. It also shows the marginal benefits derived by consumers. The supply curve represents a collection of minimum prices that suppliers require to be willing and able to supply each additional unit of a good or service. It also shows the marginal cost of production. Both are shown in Exhibit 7. For example, for the first unit of output, the buyer is willing to pay up to $7, while the seller would have to receive at least $1 to produce that unit. However, the equilibrium price is $4, as indicated by the intersection of the supply and demand curves. It is clear that the two would gain from getting together and trading that unit, because the consumer would receive $3 of consumer surplus ($7 – $4), and the producer would receive $3 of producer surplus ($4 – $1). Both would also benefit from trading the second and third units of output—in fact, both would benefit from trading every unit up to the market equilibrium output. That is, the buyer purchases the good, except for the very last unit, for less than the maximum amount she would have been willing to pay; the seller receives for the good, except for the last unit, more than the minimum amount for which he would have been willing to supply the good. Once the equilibrium output is reached at the equilibrium price, all the mutually beneficial trade opportunities between the demander and supplier will have taken place, and the sum of consumer surplus and producer surplus is maximized. This is where the marginal benefit to buyers is equal to the marginal cost to producers. Both buyer and seller are better off from each of the units traded than they would have been if they had not exchanged them.

It is important to recognize that, in this case, the **total welfare gains** to the economy from trade in this good is the sum of the consumer and producer surpluses created. That is, consumers benefit from additional amounts of consumer surplus, and producers benefit from additional amounts of producer surplus. Improvements in welfare come from additions to both consumer and producer surpluses. In competitive markets with large numbers of buyers and sellers, at the market equilibrium price and quantity, the net gains to society are as large as possible.

Why would it be inefficient to produce only 3 million units? The demand curve in Exhibit 7 indicates that the buyer is willing to pay $5 for the 3 millionth unit. The supply curve shows that it only costs the seller $3 to produce that unit. That is, as long as the buyer values the extra output by more than it costs to produce that unit, total welfare would increase by expanding output. In fact, if output is expanded from 3 million units to 4 million units, total welfare (the sum of consumer and producer surpluses) will increase by area AEB in Exhibit 7.

What if 5 million units are produced? The demand curve shows that the buyer is only willing to pay $3 for the 5 millionth unit. However, the supply curve shows that it would cost about $5.50 to produce that 5 millionth unit. Thus, increasing output beyond equilibrium decreases total welfare, because the cost of producing this extra output is greater than

total welfare gains the sum of consumer and producer surpluses

Why is total welfare maximized at the competitive equilibrium output?

in the news   Gift Giving and Deadweight Loss

Only about 15 percent of gifts during the holiday are money. Money fits the description as an efficient gift. An efficient gift is one that the recipient values at least as much as it costs the giver.

There are a lot of unwanted gifts that recipients receive during the holidays. What do people do with their unwanted gifts? Many people exchange or repackage unwanted gifts. Gift cards are becoming more popular. While they provide less flexibility to recipients than cash, gift cards might be seen as less "tacky" than cash. So why don't more people give cash and gift cards?

Over the past 20 years, University of Minnesota Professor Joel Waldfogel has done numerous surveys asking gift recipients about the items they've received: Who bought it? What did the buyer pay? What's the most you would have been willing to pay for it? Based on these surveys, he's concluded that we value items we receive as gifts 20 percent less, per dollar spent, than items we buy for ourselves. Given the $65 billion in U.S. holiday spending per year, that means we get $13 billion less in satisfaction than we would receive if we spent that money the usual way on ourselves. That is, deadweight loss

is about $13 billion a year, the difference between the price of the gifts and the value to their recipients.

Of course, people may derive satisfaction from trying to pick "the perfect gift." If that is the case, then the deadweight loss would be smaller. In addition, gift giving can provide a signal. If you really love a person, you will try to get enough information and spend enough time to get the right gift. This sends a strong signal that a gift card or money does not provide. If the recipients are adult children, they may already know of your affection for them so sending a gift card or cash might be less offensive.

the value the buyer places on it. If output is reduced from 5 million units to 4 million units, total welfare will increase by area ECD in Exhibit 7.

Not producing the efficient level of output, in this case 4 million units, leads to what economists call a **deadweight loss**. A deadweight loss is the reduction in both consumer and producer surpluses—it is the net loss of total surplus that results from the misallocation of resources.

In a competitive equilibrium, supply equals demand at the equilibrium. This means that the buyers value the last unit of output consumed by exactly the same amount that it cost to produce. If consumers valued the last unit by more than it cost to produce, welfare could be increased by expanding output. If consumers valued the last unit by less than it cost to produce, then welfare could be increased by producing less output.

In sum, *market efficiency* occurs when we have maximized the sum of consumer and producer surplus, when the margin of benefits of the last unit consumed is equal to the marginal cost of productivity, $MB = MC$.

deadweight loss net loss of total surplus that results from an action that alters a market equilibrium

How do we know when we have achieved market efficiency?

great economic thinkers — Alfred Marshall (1842–1924)

Alfred Marshall was born outside of London in 1842. His father, a domineering man who was a cashier for the Bank of England, wanted nothing more than for Alfred to become a minister. But the young Marshall enjoyed math and chess, both of which were forbidden by his authoritarian father. When he was older, Marshall turned down a theological scholarship to Oxford to study at Cambridge, with the financial support of a wealthy uncle. Here he earned academic honors in mathematics. Upon graduating, Marshall set upon a period of self-discovery. He traveled to Germany to study metaphysics, later adopting the philosophy of agnosticism, and moved on to studying ethics. He found within himself a deep sorrow and disgust over the condition of society. He resolved to use his skills to lessen poverty and human suffering, and in wanting to use his mathematics in this broader capacity, Marshall soon developed a fascination with economics.

Marshall became a fellow and lecturer in political economy at Cambridge. He had been teaching for nine years when, in 1877, he married a former student, Mary Paley. Because of the university's celibacy rules, Marshall had to give up his position at Cambridge. He moved on to teach at University College at Bristol and at Oxford. But in 1885, the rules were relaxed and Marshall returned to Cambridge as the Chair in Political Economy, a position that he held until 1908, when he resigned to devote more time to writing.

Before this point in time, economics was grouped with philosophy and the "moral sciences." Marshall fought all of his life for economics to be set apart as a field all its own. In 1903, Marshall finally succeeded in persuading Cambridge to establish a separate economics course, paving the way for the discipline as it exists today. As this event clearly demonstrates, Marshall exerted a great deal of influence on the development of economic thought in his time. Marshall popularized the heavy use of illustration, real-world examples, and current events in teaching, as well as the modern diagrammatic approach to economics. Relatively early in his career, it was being said that Marshall's former students occupied half of the economic chairs in the United Kingdom. His most famous student was John Maynard Keynes.

Marshall is most famous for refining the marginal approach. He was intrigued by the self-adjusting and self-correcting nature of economic markets, and he was also interested in time—how long did it take for markets to adjust? Marshall coined the analogy that compares the tools of supply and demand to the blades on a pair of scissors—that is, it is fruitless to talk about whether it was supply or demand that determined the market price; rather, one should consider both in unison. After all, the upper blade is not of more importance than the lower when using a pair of scissors to cut a piece of paper. Marshall was also responsible for refining some of the most important tools in economics—elasticity and consumer and producer surplus. Marshall's book *Principles of Economics* was published in 1890; immensely popular, the book went into eight editions. Much of the content in *Principles* is still at the core of microeconomics texts today.

ⓠ SECTION QUIZ

1. In a supply and demand graph, the triangular area under the demand curve but above the market price is

   a. the consumer surplus.

   b. the producer surplus.

   c. the marginal cost.

   d. the deadweight loss.

   e. the net gain to society from trading that good.

2. Which of the following is not true about consumer surplus?

   a. Consumer surplus is the difference between what consumers are willing to pay and what they actually pay.

   b. Consumer surplus is shown graphically as the area under the demand curve but above the market price.

   c. An increase in the market price due to a decrease in supply will increase consumer surplus.

   d. A decrease in market price due to an increase in supply will increase consumer surplus.

3. Which of the following is not true about producer surplus?

   a. Producer surplus is the difference between what sellers are paid and their cost of producing those units.

   b. Producer surplus is shown graphically as the area under the market price but above the supply curve.

   c. An increase in the market price due to an increase in demand will increase producer surplus.

   d. All of the above are true about producer surplus.

4. At the market equilibrium price and quantity, the total welfare gains from trade are measured by

   a. the total consumer surplus captured by consumers.

   b. the total producer surplus captured by producers.

   c. the sum of consumer surplus and producer surplus.

   d. the consumer surplus minus the producer surplus.

5. In a supply and demand graph, the triangular area under the demand curve but above the supply curve is

   a. the consumer surplus.

   b. the producer surplus.

   c. the marginal cost.

   d. the deadweight loss.

   e. the net gain to society from trading that good.

6. Which of the following are true statements?

   a. The difference between how much a consumer is willing and able to pay and how much a consumer has to pay for a unit of a good is called consumer surplus.

   b. An increase in supply will lead to a lower price and an increase in consumer surplus; a decrease in supply will lead to a higher price and a decrease in consumer surplus.

   c. Both (a) and (b) are true.

   d. None of the above is true.

7. Which of the following are true statements?

   a. Producer surplus is the difference between what a producer is paid for a good and the cost of producing that good.

   b. An increase in demand will lead to a higher market price and an increase in producer surplus; a decrease in demand will lead to a lower market price and a decrease in producer surplus.

   c. We can think of the demand curve as a marginal benefit curve and the supply curve as a marginal cost curve.

   d. Total welfare gains from trade to the economy can be measured by the sum of consumer and producer surpluses.

   e. All of the above are true statements.

(*continued*)

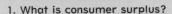

⑦SECTION QUIZ (Cont.)

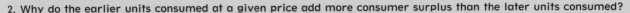

1. What is consumer surplus?

2. Why do the earlier units consumed at a given price add more consumer surplus than the later units consumed?

3. Why does a decrease in a good's price increase the consumer surplus from consumption of that good?

4. Why might the consumer surplus from purchases of diamond rings be less than the consumer surplus from purchases of far less expensive stones?

5. What is producer surplus?

6. Why do the earlier units produced at a given price add more producer surplus than the later units produced?

7. Why does an increase in a good's price increase the producer surplus from production of that good?

8. Why might the producer surplus from sales of diamond rings, which are expensive, be less than the producer surplus from sales of far less expensive stones?

9. Why is the efficient level of output in an industry defined as the output where the sum of consumer and producer surplus is maximized?

10. Why does a reduction in output below the efficient level create a deadweight loss?

11. Why does an expansion in output beyond the efficient level create a deadweight loss?

Answers: 1. a 2. c 3. d 4. c 5. a 6. c 7. e

7.2

The Welfare Effects of Taxes, Subsidies, and Price Controls

📂 What are the welfare effects of a tax?

📂 What is the relationship between a deadweight loss and price elasticities?

📂 What are the welfare effects of subsidies?

📂 What are the welfare effects of price controls?

In the previous section we used the tools of consumer and producer surplus to measure the efficiency of a competitive market—that is, how the equilibrium price and quantity in a competitive market lead to the maximization of aggregate welfare (for both buyers and sellers). Now we can use the same tools, consumer and producer surplus, to measure the welfare effects of various government programs—taxes and price controls. When economists refer to the **welfare effects** of a government policy, they are referring to the gains and losses associated with government intervention. This use of the term should not be confused with the more common reference to a welfare recipient who is getting aid from the government.

welfare effects the gains and losses associated with government intervention in markets

Using Consumer and Producer Surplus to Find the Welfare Effects of a Tax

To simplify the explanation of elasticity and the tax incidence, we will not complicate the illustration by shifting the supply curve (tax levied on sellers) or demand curve (tax levied on buyers) as we did in Section 6.4. We will simply show the result a tax must cause. The tax is illustrated by the vertical distance between the supply and demand curves at the new after-tax output—shown as the bold vertical line in Exhibit 1. After the tax, the buyers pay a higher price, P_B, and the sellers receive a lower price, P_S; and the equilibrium quantity of the good (both bought and sold) falls from Q_1 to Q_2. The tax revenue collected is measured by multiplying the amount of the tax times the quantity of the good sold after the tax is imposed ($T \times Q_2$).

In Exhibit 2, we can now use consumer and producer surpluses to measure the amount of welfare loss associated with a tax. First, consider the amounts of consumer and producer surplus before the tax. Before the tax is imposed, the price is P_1 and the quantity is Q_1; at that price and output, the amount of consumer surplus is area a + b + c, and the amount of producer surplus is area d + e + f. To get the total surplus, or total welfare, we add consumer and producer surpluses, area a + b + c + d + e + f. Without a tax, tax revenues are zero.

After the tax, the price the buyer pays is P_B, the price the seller receives is P_S, and the output falls to Q_2. As a result of the higher price and lower output from the tax, consumer surplus is smaller—area a. After the tax, sellers receive a lower price, so producer surplus is smaller—area f. However, some of the loss in consumer and producer surpluses is transferred in the form of tax revenues to the government, which can be used to reduce other taxes, fund public projects, or be redistributed to others in society. This transfer of society's resources is not a loss from society's perspective. The net loss to society can be found by measuring the difference between the loss in consumer surplus (area b + c) plus the loss in producer surplus (area d + e) and the gain in tax revenue (area b + d). The reduction in total surplus is area c + e, or the shaded area in Exhibit 2. This deadweight loss from the tax is the reduction in producer and consumer surpluses minus the tax revenue transferred to the government.

Deadweight loss occurs because the tax reduces the quantity exchanged below the original output level, Q_1, reducing the size of the total surplus realized from trade. The problem is that the tax distorts market incentives: The price to buyers is higher than before the tax, so they consume less; and the price to sellers is lower than before the tax, so they produce less. These effects lead to deadweight loss, or market inefficiencies—the waste associated with not producing the efficient level of output. That is, the tax causes a deadweight loss because it prevents some mutual beneficial trade between buyers and sellers.

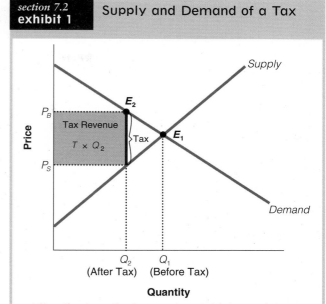

section 7.2
exhibit 1   Supply and Demand of a Tax

After the tax, the buyers pay a higher price, P_B, and the sellers receive a lower price, P_S; and the equilibrium quantity of the good (both bought and sold) falls from Q_1 to Q_2. The tax revenue collected is measured by multiplying the amount of the tax times that quantity of the good sold after the tax is imposed ($T \times Q_2$).

© Cengage Learning 2013

How do taxes distort market incentives?

use **what you've learned**   # Should We Use Taxes to Reduce Dependency on Foreign Oil?

Q What if we placed a $0.50 tax on gasoline to reduce dependence on foreign oil and to raise the tax revenue?

A If the demand and supply curves are both equally elastic, as in Exhibit 2, both consumers and

producers will share the burden equally. The tax collected would be b + d, but total loss in consumer surplus (b + c) and producer surplus (d + e) would be greater than the gains in tax revenue. Not surprisingly, both consumers and producers fight such a tax every time it is proposed.

section 7.2
exhibit 2   Welfare Effects of a Tax

The net loss to society due to a tax can be found by measuring the difference between the loss in consumer surplus (area b + c) plus the loss in producer surplus (area d + e) and the gain in tax revenue (area b + d). The deadweight loss from the tax is the reduction in the consumer and producer surpluses minus the tax revenue transferred to the government, area c + e.

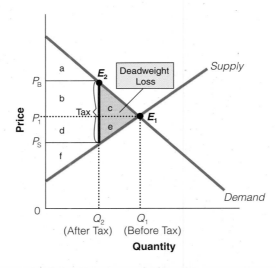

	Before Tax	After Tax	Change
Consumer Surplus	a + b + c	a	−b − c
Producer Surplus	d + e + f	f	−d − e
Tax Revenue ($T \times Q_2$)	zero	b + d	b + d
Total Welfare	a + b + c + d + e + f	a + b + d + f	−c − e

All taxes lead to deadweight loss. The deadweight loss is important because if the people are to benefit from the tax, then more than $1 of benefit must be produced from $1 of government expenditure. For example, if a gasoline tax leads to $100 million in tax revenues and $20 million in deadweight loss, then the government needs to provide a benefit to the public of more than $120 million with the $100 million revenues.

Elasticity and the Size of the Deadweight Loss

Does the elasticity affect the size of the deadweight loss?

The size of the deadweight loss from a tax, as well as how the burdens are shared between buyers and sellers, depends on the price elasticities of supply and demand. In Exhibit 3(a) we can see that, other things being equal, the less elastic the demand curve, the smaller the deadweight loss. Similarly, the less elastic the supply curve, other things being equal, the smaller the deadweight loss, as shown in Exhibit 3(b). However, when the supply and/or demand curves become more elastic, the deadweight loss becomes larger, because a given tax reduces the quantity exchanged by a greater amount, as seen in Exhibit 3(c). Recall that elasticities measure how responsive buyers and sellers are to price changes. That is, the more elastic the curves are, the greater the change in output and the larger the deadweight loss.

Elasticity differences can help us understand tax policy. Goods that are heavily taxed, such as alcohol, cigarettes, and gasoline, often have a relatively inelastic demand curve in the short run, so the tax burden falls primarily on the buyer. It also means that the deadweight

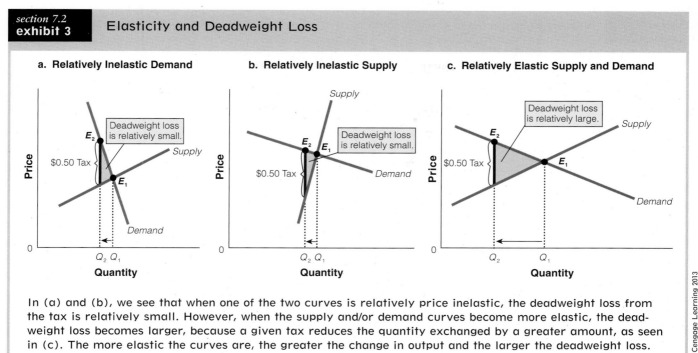

section 7.2
exhibit 3   Elasticity and Deadweight Loss

a. Relatively Inelastic Demand

b. Relatively Inelastic Supply

c. Relatively Elastic Supply and Demand

In (a) and (b), we see that when one of the two curves is relatively price inelastic, the deadweight loss from the tax is relatively small. However, when the supply and/or demand curves become more elastic, the deadweight loss becomes larger, because a given tax reduces the quantity exchanged by a greater amount, as seen in (c). The more elastic the curves are, the greater the change in output and the larger the deadweight loss.

loss to society is smaller for the tax revenue raised than if the demand curve were more elastic. In other words, because consumers cannot find many close substitutes in the short run, they reduce their consumption only slightly at the higher after-tax price. Even though the deadweight loss is smaller, it is still positive, because the reduced after-tax price received by sellers and the increased after-tax price paid by buyers reduces the quantity exchanged below the previous market equilibrium level.

The Welfare Effects of Subsidies

If taxes cause deadweight or welfare losses, do subsidies create welfare gains? For example, what if a government subsidy (paid by taxpayers) was provided in a particular market? Think of a subsidy as a negative tax. Before the subsidy, say the equilibrium price was P_1 and the equilibrium quantity was Q_1, as shown in Exhibit 4. The consumer surplus is area a + b, and the producer surplus is area c + d. The sum of producer and consumer surpluses is maximized (a + b + c + d), with no deadweight loss.

In Exhibit 4, we see that the subsidy lowers the price to the buyer to P_B and increases the quantity exchanged to Q_2. The subsidy results in an increase in consumer surplus from area a + b to area a + b + c + g, a gain of c + g. And producer surplus increases from area c + d to area c + d + b + e, a gain of b + e. With gains in both consumer and producer surpluses, it looks like a gain in welfare, right? Not quite. Remember that the government is paying for this subsidy, and the cost to government (taxpayers) of the subsidy is area b + e + f + c + g (the subsidy per unit times the number of units subsidized). That is, the cost to government (taxpayers), area b + e + f + c + g, is greater than the gains to consumers, c + g, and the gains to producers, b + e, by area f. Area f is the deadweight or welfare loss to society from the subsidy because it results in the production of more than the competitive market equilibrium, and the market value of that expansion to buyers is less than the marginal cost of producing that expansion to sellers. In short, the market overproduces relative to the efficient level of output, Q_1.

If taxes cause deadweight loss, why don't subsidies cause welfare gains?

section 7.2
exhibit 4   Welfare Effects of a Subsidy

With a subsidy, the price producers receive (P_s) is the price consumers pay (P_B) plus the subsidy ($\$S$). Because the subsidy leads to the production of more than the efficient level of output Q_1, a deadweight loss results. For each unit produced between Q_1 and Q_2, the supply curve lies above the demand curve, indicating that the marginal benefits to consumers are less than society's cost of producing those units.

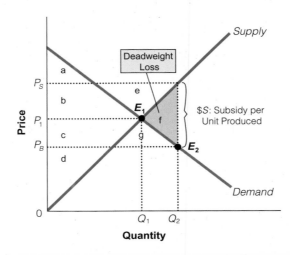

	Before Tax Subsidy	After Tax Subsidy	Change
Consumer Surplus (CS)	a + b	a + b + c + g	c + g
Producer Surplus (PS)	c + d	c + d + b + e	b + e
Government (Taxpayers, G)	zero	−b − e − f − c − g	−b − e − f − c − g
Total Welfare (CS + PS − G)	a + b + c + d	a + b + c + d − f	−f

Price Ceilings and Welfare Effects

Do consumers and producers both gain with a subsidy if it lowers the price to consumers and raises the price to producers? How about taxpayers?

As we saw in Chapter 5, price controls involve the use of the power of the government to establish prices different from the equilibrium market price that would otherwise prevail. The motivations for price controls vary with the markets under consideration. A maximum, or ceiling, is often set for goods deemed important, such as housing. A minimum price, or floor, may be set on wages because wages are the primary source of income for most people, or on agricultural products, in order to guarantee that producers will get a certain minimum price for their products.

If a price ceiling (that is, a legally established maximum price) is binding and set below the equilibrium price at P_{MAX}, the quantity demanded will be greater than the quantity supplied at that price, and a shortage will occur. At this price, buyers will compete for the limited supply, Q_2.

We can see the welfare effects of a price ceiling by observing the change in consumer and producer surpluses from the implementation of the price ceiling in Exhibit 5. Before the price ceiling, the buyer receives area a + b + c of consumer surplus at price P_1 and quantity Q_1. However, after the price ceiling is implemented at P_{MAX}, consumers can buy the good at a lower price but cannot buy as much as before (they can only buy Q_2 instead of Q_1). Because consumers can now buy Q_2 at a lower price, they gain area d of consumer surplus after the price ceiling. However, they lose area c of consumer surplus because they can only purchase Q_2 rather than Q_1 of output. Thus, the change in consumer surplus is d − c. In this case, area d is larger than area e and area c and the consumer gains from the price ceiling.

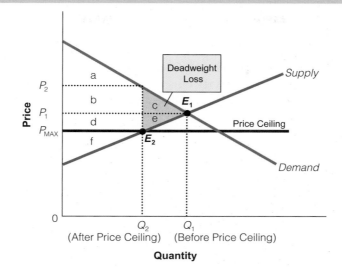

section 7.2
exhibit 5   Welfare Effects of a Price Ceiling

	Before Price Ceiling	After Price Ceiling	Change
Consumer Surplus (CS)	a + b + c	a + b + d	d − c
Producer Surplus (PS)	d + e + f	f	−d − e
Total Welfare (CS + PS)	a + b + c + d + e + f	a + b + d + f	−c − e

If area d is larger than area c, consumers in the aggregate would be better off from the price ceiling. However, any possible gain to consumers will be more than offset by the losses to producers, area d + e. Price ceiling causes a deadweight loss of c + e.

The price the seller receives for Q_2 is P_{MAX} (the ceiling price), so producer surplus falls from area d + e + f before the price ceiling to area f after the price ceiling, for a loss of area d + e. That is, any possible gain to consumers will be more than offset by the losses to producers. The price ceiling has caused a deadweight loss of area c + e.

There is a deadweight loss because less is sold at Q_2 than at Q_1; and consumers value those units between Q_2 and Q_1 by more than it cost to produce them. For example, at Q_2, consumers will value the unit at P_2, which is much higher than it cost to produce it—the point on the supply curve at Q_2.

Applications of Consumer and Producer Surplus

Rent Controls

If consumers use no additional resources, search costs, or side payments for a rent controlled unit, the consumer surplus is equal to a + b + d in Exhibit 5. If landlords were able to extract P_2 from renters, consumer surplus would be reduced to area a. Landlords are able to collect higher "rent" using a variety of methods. They might have the tenant slip them a couple hundred dollars each month; they might charge a high rate for parking in the garage; they might rent used furniture at a high rate; or they might charge an exorbitant key price—the price for changing the locks for a new tenant. These types of arrangements take place in so-called black markets—markets where goods are transacted outside the boundaries of the law. One problem is that law-abiding citizens will be among those least likely to find a rental

Who gains and who loses with rent controls? Is there a difference between a rent controlled price in the short run versus the long run?

unit. Other problems include black market prices that are likely to be higher than the price would be if restrictions were lifted and the inability to use legal means to enforce contracts and resolve disputes.

If the landlord is able to charge P_2, then the area b + d of consumer surplus will be lost by consumers and gained by the landlord. This redistribution from the buyer to the seller does not change the size of the deadweight loss; it remains area c + e.

The measure of the deadweight loss in the price ceiling case may underestimate the true cost to consumers. At least two inefficiencies are not measured. One, consumers may spend a lot of time looking for rental units because vacancy rates will be very low—only Q_2 is available and consumers are willing to pay as much as P_2 for Q_2 units. Two, someone may have been lucky to find a rental unit at the ceiling price, P_{MAX}, but someone who values it more, say at P_2, may not be able to find a rental unit.

It is important to distinguish between deadweight loss, which measures the overall efficiency loss, and the distribution of the gains and losses from a particular policy. For example, as a rent control tenant, you may be pleased with the outcome—a lower price than you would ordinarily pay (a transfer from landlord to tenant) providing that you can find a vacant rent-controlled unit.

Rent Controls—Short Run versus Long Run

In the absence of rent control (a price ceiling), the equilibrium price is P_1 and the equilibrium quantity is Q_1, with no deadweight loss. However, a price ceiling leads to a

Is it possible that removing rent controls in New York City is good economics but bad politics?

---

section 7.2 exhibit 6   Deadweight Loss of Rent Control: Short Run vs. Long Run

a. Deadweight Loss of Rent Control—Short Run

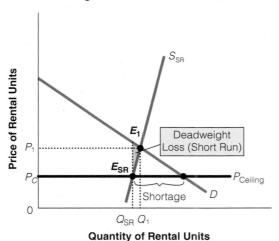

b. Deadweight Loss of Rent Control—Long Run

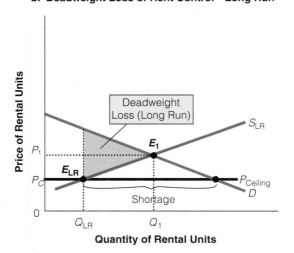

The reduction in rental units in response to the rent ceiling price P_C is much smaller in the short run (Q_1 to Q_{SR}) than in the long run (Q_1 to Q_{LR}). The deadweight loss is also much greater in the long run than in the short run, as indicated by the shaded areas in the two graphs. In addition, the size of the shortage is much greater in the long run than in the short run.

deadweight loss, but the size of the deadweight loss depends on elasticity: The deadweight loss is greater in the short run (less elastic supply) than the long run (more elastic supply). Why? A city that enacts a rent control program will not lose many rental units in the next week. That is, even at lowered legal prices, roughly the same number of units will be available this week as last week; thus, in the short run the supply of rental units is virtually fixed—relatively inelastic, as seen in Exhibit 6(a). In the long run, however, the supply of rental units is much more elastic; landlords respond to the lower rental prices by allowing rental units to deteriorate and building fewer new rental units. In the long run, then, the supply curve is much more elastic, as seen in Exhibit 6(b). It is also true that demand becomes more elastic over time as buyers respond to the lower prices by looking for their own apartment (rather than sharing one) or moving to the city to try to rent an apartment below the equilibrium rental price. What economic implications do these varying elasticities have on rent control policies?

In Exhibit 6(a), only a small reduction in rental unit availability occurs in the short term as a result of the newly imposed rent control price—a move from Q_1 to Q_{SR}. The corresponding deadweight loss is small, indicated by the shaded area in Exhibit 6(a). However, the long-run response to the rent ceiling price is much larger: The quantity of rental units falls from Q_1 to Q_{LR}, and the size of the deadweight loss and the shortage are both larger, as seen in Exhibit 6(b). Hence, rent controls are much more harmful in the long run than the short run, from an efficiency standpoint.

ECS

economic content standards

Price controls are often advocated by special interest groups. Price controls reduce the quantity of goods and services produced, thus depriving consumers of some goods and services whose value would exceed their cost.

Price Floors

Since the Great Depression, several agricultural programs have been promoted as assisting small-scale farmers. Such a price-support system guarantees a minimum price—promising a dairy farmer a price of $4 per pound for cheese, for example. The reasoning is that the equilibrium price of $3 is too low and would not provide enough revenue for small-volume farmers to maintain a "decent" standard of living. A price floor sets a minimum price that is the lowest price a consumer can legally pay for a good.

The Welfare Effects of a Price Floor When the Government Buys the Surplus

In the United States, price floors have been used to increase the price of dairy products, tobacco, corn, peanuts, soybeans and many other goods since the Great Depression. The government sets a price floor that guarantees producers will get a certain price. To ensure the support price, the government buys as much output as necessary to maintain the price at that level.

Who gains and who loses under price-support programs? In Exhibit 7, the equilibrium price and quantity without the price floor are at P_1 and Q_1, respectively. Without the price floor, consumer surplus is area a + b + c, and producer surplus is area e + f, for a total surplus of area a + b + c + e + f.

To maintain the price support, the government must buy up the excess supply at P_S; that is, the quantity $Q_S - Q_2$. As shown in Exhibit 7, the government purchases are added to the market demand curve (D + government purchases). This additional demand allows the price to stay at the support level. After the price floor is in effect, price rises to P_S; output falls to Q_2; consumer surplus falls from area a + b + c to area a, a loss of b + c; Some of the loss of consumer

In an effort to help producers of the cheese commonly grated over spaghetti, fettuccine and other pastas, the Italian government is buying 100,000 wheels of Parmigiano Reggiano and donating them to charity. This is similar to the price floors where the government buys up the surplus.

surplus occurs because at the higher price, P_s, some consumers will buy less of the good or not buy the good at all. Consumers also lose area b because they now have to pay a higher price, P_s, for Q_2 output. However, the policy was not intended to help the consumer, but to help the producer. And it does. Producer surplus increases from area e + f to area b + c + d + e + f, a gain of area b + c + d. If those changes were the end of the story, we would say that producers gained (area b + c + d) more than consumers lost (area b + c), and, on net, society would benefit by area d from the implementation of the price support. However, those changes are *not* the end of the story. The government (taxpayers) must pay for the surplus it buys, area c + d + f + g + h + i. That is, the cost to government is area c + d + f + g + h + i. The total welfare cost of the program is found by adding the change in consumer surplus (lost area b + c) and the change in producer surplus (gained area b + c + d) and then subtract the government costs. After adding the change in consumer surplus to the change in producer surplus we end up with a + d than we subtract the government costs c + d + f + g + h + i. Assuming no alternative use of the surplus the government purchases, the result is a deadweight loss from the price floor of area c + f + g + h + i. Why? Consumers are consuming less than the previous market equilibrium output, eliminating mutually beneficial exchanges, while sellers are producing more than is being consumed, with the excess production stored, destroyed, or exported. If the objective is to help the farmers, wouldn't it be less costly to just give them the money directly rather than through price supports? Then the program would only cost b + c + d. However, price supports may be more palatable from a political standpoint than an outright handout.

Wouldn't it cost less to give farmers money directly rather than through price supports?

---

section 7.2 **exhibit 7**	Welfare Effects of a Price Floor When Government Buys the Surplus

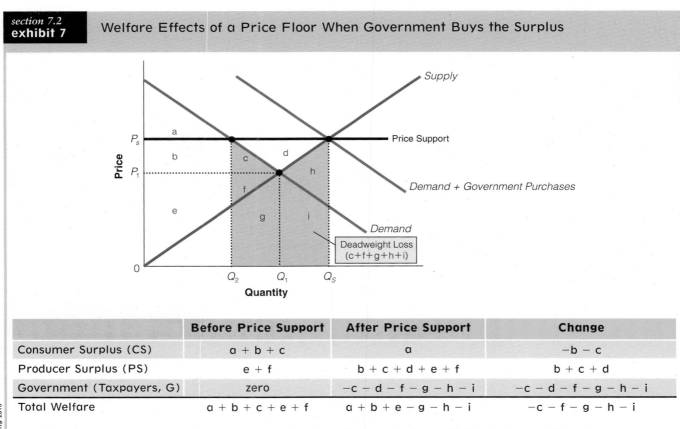

	Before Price Support	After Price Support	Change
Consumer Surplus (CS)	a + b + c	a	−b − c
Producer Surplus (PS)	e + f	b + c + d + e + f	b + c + d
Government (Taxpayers, G)	zero	−c − d − f − g − h − i	−c − d − f − g − h − i
Total Welfare	a + b + c + e + f	a + b + e − g − h − i	−c − f − g − h − i

After the price support is implemented, the price rises to Q_s and output falls to Q_2; the result is a loss in consumer surplus of area b + c but a gain in producer surplus of area b + c + d. However, these changes are not the end of the story, because the cost to the government (taxpayers), area c + d + f + g + h + i, is greater than the gain to producers, area d, so the deadweight loss is area c + f + g + h + i.

Deficiency Payment Program

Another possibility is the deficiency payment program. In Exhibit 8, if the government sets the support price at P_S, producers will supply Q_2 and sell all they can at the market price, P_M. The government then pays the producers a deficiency payment (DP)—the vertical distance between the price the producers receive, P_M, and the price they were guaranteed, P_S. Producer surplus increases from area c + d to area c + d + b + e, which is a gain of area b + e, because producers can sell a greater quantity at a higher price. Consumer surplus increases from area a + b to area a + b + c + g, which is a gain of area c + g, because consumers can buy a greater quantity at a lower price. The cost to government ($Q_2 \times$ DP), area b + e + f + c + g, is greater than the gains in producer and consumer surpluses (area b + e + c + g), and the deadweight loss is area f. The deadweight loss occurs because the program increases the output beyond the efficient level of output, Q_1. From Q_1 to Q_2, the marginal cost to sellers for producing the good (the height of the supply curve) is greater than the marginal benefit to consumers (the height of the demand curve).

Are deficiency payment programs more efficient than traditional price supports?

Compare area f in Exhibit 8 with the much larger deadweight loss for price supports in Exhibit 7. The deficiency payment program does not lead to the production of crops that will not be consumed, or to the storage problem we saw with the previous price-support program in Exhibit 7.

The purpose of these farm programs is to help poor farmers. However, large commercial farms (roughly 10 percent of all farms) receive the bulk of the government subsidies. Small farms receive less than 20 percent of the farm subsidies. Many other countries around the world also provide subsidies to their farmers.

---

section 7.2
exhibit 8   Welfare Effects of a Deficiency Payment Plan

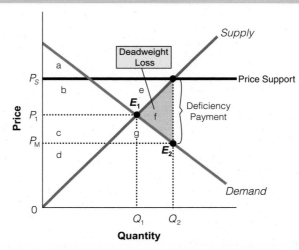

	Before Plan	After Plan	Change
Consumer Surplus (CS)	a + b	a + b + c + g	c + g
Producer Surplus (PS)	c + d	c + d + b + e	b + e
Government (Taxpayers, G)	zero	−b − e − f − c − g	−b − e − f − c − g
Total Welfare (CS + PS − G)	a + b + c + d	a + b + c + d − f	−f

The cost to government (taxpayers), area b + e + f + c + g, is greater than the gains to producer and consumer surplus, area b + e + c + g. The deficiency payment program increases the output level beyond the efficient output level of Q_1. From Q_1 to Q_2, the marginal cost of producing the good (the height of the supply curve) is greater than the marginal benefit to the consumer (the height of the demand curve)—area f.

⊙ SECTION QUIZ

1. In a supply and demand graph, the triangular area between the demand curve and the supply curve lost because of the imposition of a tax, price ceiling, or price floor is

   a. the consumer surplus.

   b. the producer surplus.

   c. the marginal cost.

   d. the deadweight loss.

   e. the net gain to society from trading that good.

2. After the imposition of a tax,

   a. consumers pay a higher price, including the tax.

   b. consumers lose consumer surplus.

   c. producers receive a lower price after taxes.

   d. producers lose producer surplus.

   e. all of the above occur.

3. With a subsidy,

   a. the price producers receive is the price consumers pay plus the subsidy.

   b. the subsidy leads to the production of more than the efficient level of output.

   c. there is a deadweight loss.

   d. all of the above are true.

4. In the case of a price floor, if the government buys up the surplus,

   a. consumer surplus decreases.

   b. producer surplus increases.

   c. a greater deadweight loss occurs than with a deficiency payment system.

   d. all of the above are true.

5. The longer a price ceiling is left below the equilibrium price in a market, the _____ is the reduction in the quantity exchanged and the _____ is the resulting deadweight loss.

   a. greater; greater

   b. greater; smaller

   c. smaller; greater

   d. smaller; smaller

6. With a deficiency payment program,

   a. the government sets the target price at the equilibrium price.

   b. producer and consumer surplus falls.

   c. there is a deadweight loss because the program increases the output beyond the efficient level of output.

   d. all of the above are true.

---

1. Could a tax be imposed without a welfare cost?

2. How does the elasticity of demand represent the ability of buyers to "dodge" a tax?

3. If both supply and demand were highly elastic, how large would the effect be on the quantity exchanged, the tax revenue, and the welfare costs of a tax?

4. What impact would a larger tax have on trade in the market? What will happen to the size of the deadweight loss?

5. What would be the effect of a price ceiling?

6. What would be the effect of a price floor if the government does not buy up the surplus?

7. What causes the welfare cost of subsidies?

8. Why does a deficiency payment program have the same welfare cost analysis as a subsidy?

Answers: 1. d 2. e 3. d 4. d 5. a 6. c

Interactive Summary

Fill in the blanks:

1. The monetary difference between the price a consumer is willing and able to pay for an additional unit of a good and the price the consumer actually pays is called _____.

2. We can think of the demand curve as a _____ curve.

3. Consumer surplus for the whole market is shown graphically as the area under the market _____ (willingness to pay for the units consumed) and above the _____ (what must be paid for those units).

4. A lower market price due to an increase in supply will _____ consumer surplus.

5. A(n) _____ is the difference between what a producer is paid for a good and the cost of producing that unit of the good.

6. We can think of the supply curve as a(n) _____ curve.

7. Part of the added producer surplus when the price rises as a result of an increase in demand is due to a higher price for the quantity _____ being produced, and part is due to the expansion of _____ made profitable by the higher price.

8. The demand curve represents a collection of _____ prices that consumers are willing and able to pay for additional quantities of a good or service, while the supply curve represents a collection of _____ prices that suppliers require to be willing to supply additional quantities of that good or service.

9. The total welfare gain to the economy from trade in a good is the sum of the _____ and _____ created.

10. In competitive markets, with large numbers of buyers and sellers at the market equilibrium price and quantity, the net gains to society are _____ as possible.

11. After a tax is imposed, consumers pay a(n) _____ price and lose the corresponding amount of consumer surplus as a result. Producers receive a(n) _____ price after tax and lose the corresponding amount of producer surplus as a result. The government _____ the amount of the tax revenue generated, which is transferred to others in society.

12. The size of the deadweight loss from a tax, as well as how the burdens are shared between buyers and sellers, depends on the relative _____.

13. When there is a subsidy, the market _____ relative to the efficient level of output.

14. Because the _____ leads to the production of more than the efficient level of output, a(n) _____ results.

15. With a(n) _____, any possible gain to consumers will be more than offset by the losses to producers.

16. With a price floor where the government buys up the surplus, the cost to the government is _____ than the gain to _____.

17. With no alternative use of the government purchases from a price floor, a(n) _____ will result because consumers are consuming _____ than the previous market equilibrium output and sellers are producing _____ than is being consumed.

18. With a deficiency payment program, the deadweight loss is _____ than with an agricultural price support program when the government buys the surplus.

Answers: 1. consumer surplus 2. marginal benefit 3. demand curve; market price 4. increase 5. producer surplus 6. marginal cost 7. already; output 8. maximum; minimum 9. consumer surplus; producer surplus 10. as large 11. higher; lower; gains 12. elasticities of supply and demand 13. overproduces 14. subsidy; deadweight loss 15. price ceiling 16. greater; producers 17. deadweight loss; less; more 18. smaller

Key Terms and Concepts

consumer surplus 187
producer surplus 189

marginal cost 189
total welfare gains 191

deadweight loss 192
welfare effects 194

Section Quiz Answers

7.1   Consumer Surplus and Producer Surplus

1. What is consumer surplus?

Consumer surplus is defined as the monetary difference between what a consumer is willing to pay for a good and what the consumer is required to pay for it.

2. Why do the earlier units consumed at a given price add more consumer surplus than the later units consumed?

Because what a consumer is willing to pay for a good declines as more of that good is consumed, the difference between what he is willing to pay and the price he must pay also declines for later units.

3. Why does a decrease in a good's price increase the consumer surplus from consumption of that good?

A decrease in a good's price increases the consumer surplus from consumption of that good by lowering the price for those goods that were bought at the higher price and by increasing consumer surplus from increased purchases at the lower price.

4. Why might the consumer surplus from purchases of diamond rings be less than the consumer surplus from purchases of far less expensive stones?

Consumer surplus is the difference between what people would have been willing to pay for the amount of the good consumed and what they must pay. Even though the marginal value of less expensive stones is lower than the marginal value of a diamond ring to buyers, the difference between the total value of the far larger number of less expensive stones purchased and what consumers had to pay may well be larger than that difference for diamond rings.

5. What is producer surplus?

Producer surplus is defined as the monetary difference between what a producer is paid for a good and the producer's cost.

6. Why do the earlier units produced at a given price add more producer surplus than the later units produced?

Because the earlier (lowest cost) units can be produced at a cost that is lower than the market price, but the cost of producing additional units rises, the earlier units produced at a given price add more producer surplus than the later units produced.

7. Why does an increase in a good's price increase the producer surplus from production of that good?

An increase in a good's price increases the producer surplus from production of that good because it results in a higher price for the quantity already being produced and because the expansion in output in response to the higher price also increases profits.

8. Why might the producer surplus from sales of diamond rings, which are expensive, be less than the producer surplus from sales of far less expensive stones?

Producer surplus is the difference between what a producer is paid for a good and the producer's cost. Even though the price, or marginal value, of a less expensive stone is lower than the price, or marginal value of a diamond ring to buyers, the difference between the total that sellers receive for those stones in revenue and the producer's cost of the far larger number of less expensive stones produced may well be larger than that difference for diamond rings.

9. Why is the efficient level of output in an industry defined as the output where the sum of consumer and producer surplus is maximized?

The sum of consumer surplus plus producer surplus measures the total welfare gains from trade in an industry, and the most efficient level of output is the one that maximizes the total welfare gains.

10. Why does a reduction in output below the efficient level create a deadweight loss?

A reduction in output below the efficient level eliminates trades whose benefits would have exceeded their costs; the resulting loss in consumer surplus and producer surplus is a deadweight loss.

11. Why does an expansion in output beyond the efficient level create a deadweight loss?

An expansion in output beyond the efficient level involves trades whose benefits are less than their costs; the resulting loss in consumer surplus and producer surplus is a deadweight loss.

7.2   The Welfare Effects of Taxes, Subsidies, and Price Controls

1. Could a tax be imposed without a welfare cost?

A tax would not impose a welfare cost only if the quantity exchanged did not change as a result—only when supply was perfectly inelastic or in the non-existent case where the demand curve was perfectly inelastic. In all other cases, a tax would create a welfare cost by eliminating some mutually beneficial trades (and the wealth they would have created) that would otherwise have taken place.

2. How does the elasticity of demand represent the ability of buyers to "dodge" a tax?

The elasticity of demand represents the ability of buyers to "dodge" a tax, because it represents how easily buyers could shift their purchases into other goods. If it is relatively low cost to consumers to shift out of buying a particular good when a tax is imposed on it—that is, demand is relatively elastic—they can dodge much of the burden of the tax by shifting their purchases to other goods. If it is relatively high cost to consumers to shift out of buying a particular good when a tax is imposed on it—that is, demand is relatively inelastic—they cannot dodge much of the burden of the tax by shifting their purchases to other goods.

3. If both supply and demand were highly elastic, how large would the effect be on the quantity exchanged, the tax revenue, and the welfare costs of a tax?

The more elastic are supply and/or demand, the larger the change in the quantity exchanged that would result from a given tax. Given that tax revenue equals the tax per unit times the number of units traded after the imposition of a tax, the smaller after-tax quantity traded would reduce the tax revenue raised, other things equal. Because the greater change in the quantity traded wipes out more mutually beneficial trades than if demand and/or supply was more inelastic, the welfare cost in such a case would also be greater, other things equal.

4. What impact would a larger tax have on trade in the market? What will happen to the size of the deadweight loss?

A larger tax creates a larger wedge between the price including tax paid by consumers and the price net of tax received by producers, resulting in a greater increase in prices paid by consumers and a greater decrease in price received by producers, and the laws of supply and demand imply that the quantity exchanged falls more as a result. The number of mutually beneficial trades eliminated will be greater and the consequent welfare cost will be greater as a result.

5. What would be the effect of a price ceiling?

A price ceiling reduces the quantity exchanged, because the lower regulated price reduces the quantity sellers are willing to sell. This lower quantity causes a welfare cost equal to the net gains from those exchanges that no longer take place. However, that price ceiling would also redistribute income, harming sellers, increasing the well-being of those who remain able to buy successfully at the lower price, and decreasing the well-being of those who can no longer buy successfully at the lower price.

6. What would be the effect of a price floor if the government does not buy up the surplus?

Just as in the case of a tax, a price floor where the government does not buy up the surplus reduces the quantity exchanged, thus causing a welfare cost equal to the net gains from the exchanges that no longer take place. However, that price floor would also redistribute income, harming buyers, increasing the incomes of those who remain able to sell successfully at the higher price, and decreasing the incomes of those who can no longer sell successfully at the higher price.

7. What causes the welfare cost of subsidies?

Subsidies cause people to produce units of output whose benefits (without the subsidy) are less than the costs, reducing the total gains from trade.

8. Why does a deficiency payment program have the same welfare cost analysis as a subsidy?

Both tend to increase output beyond the efficient level, so that units whose benefits (without the subsidy) are less than the costs, reducing the total gains from trade in the same way; further, the dollar cost of the deficiency payments are equal to the dollar amount of taxes necessary to finance the subsidy, in the case where each increases production the same amount.

Problems

1. Refer to the following exhibit.

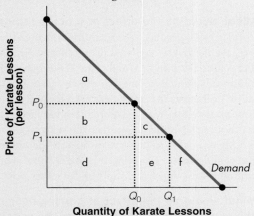

a. If the price of each karate lesson is P_0, the consumer surplus is equal to what area?
b. If the price falls from P_0 to P_1, the change in consumer surplus is equal to what area?

2. Steve loves potato chips. His weekly demand curve is shown in the following exhibit.

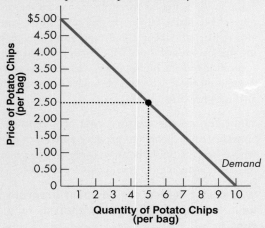

a. How much is Steve willing to pay for one bag of potato chips?
b. How much is Steve willing to pay for a second bag of potato chips?
c. If the actual market price of potato chips is $2.50, and Steve buys five bags as shown, what is the value of his consumer surplus?
d. What is Steve's total willingness to pay for five bags?

3. If a freeze ruined this year's lettuce crop, show what would happen to consumer surplus.

4. If demand for apples increased as a result of a news story that highlighted the health benefits of two apples a day, what would happen to producer surplus?

5. How is total surplus (the sum of consumer and producer surpluses) related to the efficient level of output? Using a supply and demand curve, demonstrate that producing less than the equilibrium output will lead to an inefficient allocation of resources—a deadweight loss.

6. If the government's goal is to raise tax revenue, which of the following are good markets to tax?
   a. luxury yachts
   b. alcohol
   c. movies
   d. gasoline
   e. grapefruit juice

7. Which of the following do you think are good markets for the government to tax if the goal is to boost tax revenue? Which will lead to the least amount of deadweight loss? Why?
   a. luxury yachts
   b. alcohol
   c. motor homes
   d. cigarettes
   e. gasoline
   f. pizza

8. Elasticity of demand in the market for one-bedroom apartments is 2.0, elasticity of supply is 0.5, the current market price is $1,000, and the equilibrium number of one-bedroom apartments is 10,000. If the government imposes a price ceiling of $800 on this market, predict the size of the resulting apartment shortage.

9. Use the diagram to answer the following questions (a–d).

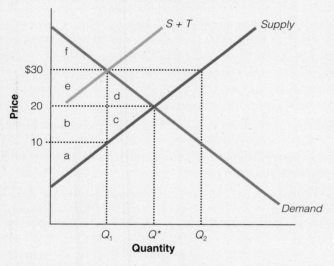

   a. At the equilibrium price before the tax is imposed, what area represents consumer surplus? What area represents producer surplus?
   b. Say that a tax of $T per unit is imposed in the industry. What area now represents consumer surplus? What area represents producer surplus?
   c. What area represents the deadweight cost of the tax?
   d. What area represents how much tax revenue is raised by the tax?

10. Use consumer and producer surplus to show the deadweight loss from a subsidy (producing more than the equilibrium output). (*Hint:* Remember that taxpayers will have to pay for the subsidy.)

11. Use the diagram to answer the following questions (a)–(c).

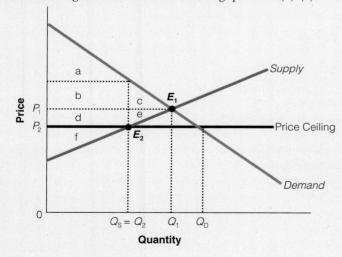

a. At the initial equilibrium price, what area represents consumer surplus? What area represents producer surplus?
b. After the price ceiling is imposed, what area represents consumer surplus? What area represents producer surplus?
c. What area represents the deadweight loss cost of the price ceiling?

12. Use the diagram to answer the following questions (a)–(c).

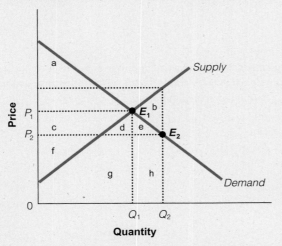

a. At the competitive output, Q_1, what area represents the consumer surplus? What area represents the producer surplus?
b. At the larger output, Q_2, what area represents the consumer surplus? What area represents the producer surplus?
c. What area represents the deadweight loss of producing too much output?

13. The 2000–2001 California energy crisis produced brownouts, utility company bankruptcies, and worries about high prices. The California electric power regulatory program imposed price ceilings on electricity sold to consumers. The following exhibit describes the California situation with P_S as the price ceiling. Answer the following questions referring to this exhibit.

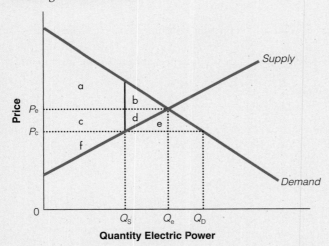

a. What was the loss imposed on consumers by this price ceiling?
b. What was the loss imposed on producers by this price ceiling?
c. What was the total loss imposed on California by this price ceiling?
d. Using this exhibit, explain the brownouts in California.
e. What would have to be true for consumers to support market set prices? Use the exhibit to explain why there might not be support among consumers for raising prices.

Market Failure

8

If a road is crowded, it creates a negative externality. That is, when one more car enters a roadway, all the other drivers must go a little more slowly. Highway space can be overused because we pay so little for it. At some particular times, such as at rush hours, if we charge a zero money price, a shortage of road space will result. Many big cities, such as London, have set up tolls to charge higher prices to travel downtown during the weekdays; the higher price brings the market closer to equilibrium.

In the last several chapters, we concluded that markets are efficient. But we made some assumptions about how markets work. If these assumptions do not hold, our conclusion about efficiency may be flawed. What are the assumptions?

First, in our model of supply and demand, we assumed that markets are perfectly competitive—many buyers and sellers exchanging similar goods in an environment where buyers and sellers can easily enter and exit the market. This is not always true. In some markets, few firms may have control over the market price. When firms can control the market price, we say that they have market power. This market power can cause inefficiency because it will lead to higher prices and lower quantities than the competitive solution.

Sometimes the market system fails to produce efficient outcomes because of side effects economists call *externalities*. Another possible source of market failure is that competitive markets provide less than the efficient quantity of public goods. A public good is a good or service that someone can consume simultaneously with everyone else, even if he or she doesn't pay for it. For example, everyone enjoys the benefits of national defense and yet it would be difficult to exclude anyone from receiving these benefits. The problem is that if consumers know it is too difficult to exclude them, then they could avoid paying their share of the public good (take a free ride), and producers would find it unprofitable to provide the good. Therefore, the government provides important public goods such as national defense.

Many economists believe that asymmetric information can cause market failures. *Asymmetric information* is a situation where some people know what other people don't know. This can lead to adverse selection where an informed party benefits in an exchange by taking advantage of knowing more than the other party.

8.1

Externalities

📁 **What is a negative externality?**   📁 **What is a positive externality?**

📁 **How are negative externalities internalized?**   📁 **How are positive externalities internalized?**

externality a benefit or cost from consumption or production that spills over onto those who are not consuming or producing the good

positive externality when benefits spill over to an outside party who is not involved in producing or consuming the good

negative externality when costs spill over to an outside party who is not involved in producing or consuming the good

Even if the economy is competitive, it is still possible that the market system fails to produce the efficient level of output because of side effects economists call **externalities**. With **positive externalities**, the private market supplies too little of the good in question (such as education). In the case of **negative externalities** (such as pollution), the market supplies too much. Both types of externalities are caused by economic agents—producers and consumers—receiving the wrong signals. That is, the free market works well in providing most goods but does less well without regulations, taxes, and subsidies in providing others.

Negative Externalities in Production

The classic example of a negative externality in production is air pollution from a factory, such as a steel mill. If the firm uses clean air in production and returns dirty air to the atmosphere, it creates a negative externality. The polluted air "spills over" to outside parties. Now people in the neighboring communities may experience higher incidences of disease, dirtier houses, and other property damage. Such damages are real costs; but because no one owns the air, the firm does not have to pay for its use, unlike the other resources the firm uses in production. A steel mill pays for labor, capital, energy, and raw materials because it must compensate the owners of those inputs for their use. If a firm can avoid paying the costs it imposes on others—the external costs—it has lowered its own costs of production, but not the true costs to society.

Examples of negative externalities are numerous: the roommate who plays his stereo too loud at 2:00 A.M., the neighbor's dog that barks all night long or leaves "messages" on your front lawn, or the gardener who runs the leaf blower on full power at 7:00 A.M. on the weekend. Driving our cars may be another area in which people don't bear the full costs of their choices. We pay the price to purchase cars, as well as to maintain, insure, and fuel them—those are the private costs. But do we pay for all of our external costs such as emissions, congestion, wear and tear on our highways, and the possible harm to those driving in cars smaller than ours?

Graphing Negative External Costs in Production

Let's take a look at the steel industry. In Exhibit 1, we see the market for steel. Notice that at each level of output, the first supply curve, $S_{Private}$, is lower than the second, S_{Social}. The reason is simple: $S_{Private}$ only includes the private costs to the firm—the capital, entrepreneurship, land, and labor for which it must pay. However, S_{Social} includes all of these costs, plus the external costs that production imposes on others. If the firm could somehow be required to compensate society for the damage it causes, the cost of production for the firm would increase and would shift the supply curve to the left. That is, the true social cost of producing steel is represented by S_{Social} in Exhibit 1. The equilibrium at P_2 and Q_2 is efficient. The market equilibrium is not efficient because the true supply curve is above the demand curve at Q_1. At Q_1 the marginal benefits (point a) are less than the marginal cost (point b) and society would be better off if the firm produced less steel. The deadweight loss from overproduction is measured by the shaded area in Exhibit 1. From society's standpoint, Q_2 is the efficient level of output because it represents all the costs (private plus external costs) associated with the production of this good. If the suppliers of steel are not aware of or not responsible for the external costs, they will tend to produce too much, Q_1 from society's standpoint and efficiency would be improved if less were produced and consumed.

What Can the Government Do to Correct for Negative Externalities?

The government can intervene in market decisions in an attempt to take account of these negative externalities. It may do this by estimating the amount of those external costs and then taxing the manufacturer by that amount, forcing the manufacturer to internalize (bear) the costs.

Pollution Taxes

Pollution taxes are designed to internalize negative externalities. If government could impose a pollution tax equal to the exact size of the external cost, then the firm would produce the efficient level of output, Q_2. That is, the tax would shift the supply curve for steel leftward to S_{Social} and would provide an incentive for the firm to produce at the socially optimum level of output. Additionally, tax revenues would

What are externalities? Are they always bad?

ECS
economic content standards

Externalities exist when some of the costs or benefits associated with production and/or consumption of a good or service falls on someone other than the producers or consumers of the product or service.

When a price fails to reflect all the costs of a product, too much of it is produced and/or consumed.

section 8.1 exhibit 1 **Negative Externalities in Production**

When a negative externality in production is present, firms do not bear the full cost of their actions, and they will produce more than the efficient level of output: Q_1 rather than Q_2. $S_{Private}$ reflects the private cost of the firm. S_{Social} reflects the private costs plus the external (or spillover) costs that the steel production imposes on others. If the supply curve is $S_{Private}$, the market equilibrium is at P_1 and Q_1. This level is not efficient and leads to a deadweight loss—the shaded area. However, when the supply curve is S_{Social}, then the equilibrium occurs at P_2 and Q_2, which is the efficient equilibrium.

be generated that could be used to compensate those who had suffered damage from the pollution or in some other productive way.

Regulation

Alternatively, the government could use regulation. The government might simply prohibit certain types of activities that cause pollution or force firms to adopt a specific technology to reduce their emissions. However, regulators would have to know the best available technology for each and every industry. The purchase and use of new pollution-control devices will increase the cost of production and shift the supply curve to the left, from $S_{Private}$ to S_{Social}.

Which Is Better—Pollution Tax or Regulation?

Most economists agree that a pollution tax, or a corrective tax, is more efficient than regulation. The pollution tax is good because it gets rid of the externality and moves society closer to the efficient level of output. The tax also gives firms an incentive to find and apply new technology to further reduce pollution levels in their plant and consequently lower the tax they would have to pay. Under regulation, a firm has little incentive to further reduce emissions once it reaches the predetermined level set by the regulated standard.

For example, a gas tax is a form of pollution tax: It helps reduce the externalities of pollution and congestion. The higher the tax, then fewer vehicles are on the road, fewer miles are driven, and more fuel efficient vehicles are purchased, each of which leads to less congestion and pollution. Therefore, the pollution tax, unlike other taxes, can enhance economic efficiency while generating revenue for the government.

Many economists like the gas tax because it is easy to collect, difficult for users to avoid, and encourages fuel economy. It puts the tax on highway users but completely internalizing the externality may cost much more than U.S. drivers are currently charged. In Europe, the gas tax is over $4 per gallon.

In the United States, people deposit large amounts of solid waste as litter on beaches, campgrounds, highways, and vacant lots. Some of this litter is removed by government agencies, and some of it biodegrades over many years. Several solutions are possible for the litter problem. Stiffer fines and penalties and more aggressive monitoring could be employed. Alternatively, through education and civic pride, individuals and groups could be encouraged to pick up trash.

Secondhand smoke is a negative externality. According to the U.S. Surgeon General, the health effects of secondhand smoke are more pervasive than previously thought. A recent report claims that exposure to secondhand smoke at home or the office increases the nonsmokers' risk of developing heart disease by 25 to 30 percent and lung cancer by 20 to 30 percent over their lifetimes. It is especially dangerous for children living with smokers.

Positive Externalities in Consumption

Unlike negative externalities, positive externalities benefit others. For some goods, the individual consumer receives all the benefits. If you buy a hamburger, for example, you get all its benefits. On the other hand, consider education. This is a positive externality in consumption whose benefits extend beyond the individual consumer of education. Certainly, when you "buy" an education, you receive many of its benefits: greater future income, more choice of future occupations, and the consumption value of knowing more about life as a result of learning. However, these benefits, great as they may be, are not all the benefits associated with your education. You may be less likely to be unemployed or commit crimes; you may end up curing cancer or solving some other social problem. These nontrivial benefits are the positive external benefits of education.

The government frequently subsidizes education. Why? Presumably because the private market does not provide enough. It is argued that the education of a person benefits not only that person but all society, because a more informed citizenry can make more intelligent collective decisions, which benefits everyone.

Public health departments sometimes offer "free" inoculations against certain communicable diseases, such as influenza, because by protecting one group of citizens, everyone gets some protection; if one citizen is prevented from getting the disease, that person cannot pass it on to others. Many governmental efforts in the field of health and education are justified on the basis of positive externalities. Of course, because positive externalities are often difficult to measure, it is hard to demonstrate empirically whether many governmental education and health programs achieve their intended purposes.

In short, the presence of positive externalities interferes with reaching economic efficiency because of the tendency for the market to underallocate (produce too little) of this good.

Graphing Positive External Benefits of Consumption

Let's take the case of a new vaccine against the common cold. The market for the vaccine is shown in Exhibit 2. The demand curve, $D_{Private}$, represents the prices and quantities that buyers would be willing to pay in the private market to reduce their probability of catching the common cold. The supply curve shows the amounts that suppliers would offer for sale at different prices. However, at the equilibrium market output, Q_1, the output of vaccinations falls far short of the efficient level, Q_2. Why? Many people benefit from the vaccines, including those who do not have to pay for them; they are now less likely to be infected because others took the vaccine. If we could add the benefits derived by nonpaying consumers, the demand curve would shift to the right, from $D_{Private}$ to D_{Social}. The greater level of output, Q_2, that would result if D_{Social} were the observed demand reflects the efficient output level.

The market equilibrium at P_1 and Q_1 is not efficient because D_{Social} is above $D_{Private}$ for all levels of output between Q_1 and Q_2. That is, at Q_1 the marginal benefits (D_{Social}) at point b are greater than the marginal cost (S_{Social}) at point a. Consequently, a deadweight loss is associated with the underproduction. In short, too little of the good is produced. Because producers are unable to collect payments from all those who benefit from the good or service, the market has a tendency to underproduce. In this case, the market is not producing enough vaccinations from society's standpoint and an *underallocation* of resources occurs.

Technology Spillover

Another potentially important positive externality is called a technology spillover. One firm's research and production can spill over to increase another firm's access to technological advances. For example, in technology industries like semiconductors, bioengineering and software design, one firm's innovations are often imitated and improved on by other firms. The firm benefits from the new knowledge, but that knowledge also generates positive externalities that spill over to other firms. That is one reason why many technology firms are clustered together in California's Silicon Valley. That clustering allows workers to more easily share knowledge and collaborate in a rapidly changing industry.

economic content standards

Government can use taxes or regulation to correct for excessive output of a good whose production generates external costs.

When a price fails to reflect all the benefits of a product, too little of the product is produced and consumed.

The government can use subsidies to help correct for insufficient output of a good that generates external benefits, or it can regulate output directly to correct for underproduction or underconsumption of a good.

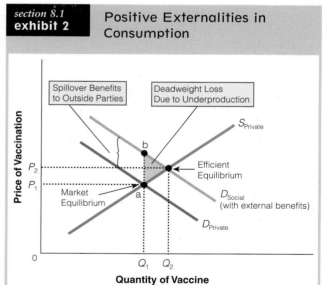

section 8.1 exhibit 2 | Positive Externalities in Consumption

The private demand curve plus external benefits is presented as the demand curve D_{Social}. This demand curve is to the right of the private demand curve, $D_{Private}$. At Q_1 the marginal benefits (point b) are greater than the marginal cost (point a) leading to a deadweight loss—the shaded area. The market equilibrium output, Q_1, falls short of the efficient level of output, Q_2. The market produces too little of the good or service.

© Cengage Learning 2013

Did you know that according to the NHTSA, 20 percent of injury crashes in 2009 involved reports of distracted driving. And of those killed in distracted driving-related crashes, 995 involved reports a cell phone as a distraction (18% of fatalities in distraction-related crashes). The age group with the greatest proportion of distracted drivers was the under-20 age group. In an insurance industry study, drivers who use handheld devices are four times as likely to get into crashes serious enough to injure themselves. According to a University of Utah study, using a cell phone while driving, whether it's handheld or hands-free, delays a driver's reactions as much as having a blood alcohol concentration at the legal limit of .08 percent. That is, driving while texting can create a serious negative externality.

What Can the Government Do to Correct for Positive Externalities?

How could society correct for this market failure? Two particular methods of achieving the higher preferred output are subsidies and regulation.

Subsidies

Government could provide a subsidy—either give refunds to individuals who receive an inoculation or provide an incentive for businesses to give their employees "free" inoculations at the office. If the subsidy was exactly equal to the external benefit of inoculation, the demand curve would shift from D_{Private} to D_{Social}, resulting in an efficient level of output, Q_2.

Regulation

The government could also pass a regulation requiring each person to get an inoculation. This approach would also shift the demand curve rightward toward the efficient level of output.

In summary, with positive externalities, the private market supplies too little of the good in question (such as education or inoculations for communicable diseases). In the case of negative externalities, the market supplies too much. In either case, buyers and sellers are receiving the wrong signals. The producers and consumers are not doing what they do because they are evil; rather, whether well-intentioned or ill-intentioned, they are behaving according to the incentives they face. The free market, then, works fine in providing most goods, but it functions less well without regulations, taxes, and subsidies in providing others.

Nongovernmental Solutions to Externalities

Sometimes externality problems can be handled by individuals without the intervention of government, where people may decide to take steps on their own to minimize negative externalities. Moral and social codes may prevent some people from littering, driving gas-guzzling cars, or using gas-powered mowers and log-burning fireplaces. The same self-regulation also applies to positive externalities. Philanthropists, for example, frequently donate money to public and private schools. In part, this must be because they view the positive externalities from education as a good buy for their charitable dollars.

⑦ SECTION QUIZ

1. The presence of negative externalities leads to a misallocation of societal resources because

   a. whenever external costs are imposed on outside parties, the good should not be produced at all.

   b. less of the good than is ideal for society is produced.

   c. some costs are associated with production that the producer fails to take into consideration.

   d. the government always intervenes in markets when negative externalities are present, and the government is inherently inefficient.

2. A tax equal to the external cost on firms that emit pollutants would

   a. provide firms with the incentive to increase the level of activity creating the pollution.

   b. provide firms with the incentive to decrease the level of activity creating the pollution.

   c. provide firms with little incentive to search for less environmentally damaging production methods.

   d. not reduce pollution levels at all.

3. In the case of a good whose production generates negative externalities,

   a. those not directly involved in the market transactions are harmed.

   b. internalizing the externality would tend to result in a greater output of the good.

   c. too little of the good tends to be produced.

   d. a subsidy would be the appropriate government corrective action.

   e. all of the above are true.

4. If firms were required to pay the full social costs of the production of goods, including both private and external costs, other things being equal, there would probably be a(n)

   a. increase in production.

   b. decrease in production.

   c. greater misallocation of resources.

   d. decrease in the market price of the product.

5. Which of the following will most likely generate positive externalities of consumption?

   a. a hot dog vendor

   b. public education

   c. an automobile

   d. a city bus

   e. a polluting factory

6. Assume that production of a good imposes external costs on others. The market equilibrium price will be _____ and the equilibrium quantity _____ for efficient resource allocation.

   a. too high; too high

   b. too high; too low

   c. too low; too high

   d. too low; too low

7. Assume that production of a good generates external benefits of consumption. The market equilibrium price of the good will be _____ and the equilibrium quantity _____ for efficient resource allocation.

   a. too high; too high

   b. too high; too low

   c. too low; too high

   d. too low; too low

(*continued*)

ⓘ SECTION QUIZ (Cont.)

8. In the case of externalities, appropriate government corrective policy would be

   a. taxes in the case of external benefits and subsidies in the case of external costs.

   b. subsidies in the case of external benefits and taxes in the case of external costs.

   c. taxes in both the case of external benefits and the case of external costs.

   d. subsidies in both the case of external benefits and the case of external costs.

   e. none of the above; the appropriate thing to do would be to do nothing.

---

1. Why are externalities also called spillover effects?
2. How do external costs affect the price and output of a polluting activity?
3. How can the government intervene to force producers to internalize external costs?
4. How do external benefits affect the output of an activity that causes them?
5. How can the government intervene to force external benefits to be internalized?
6. Why do most cities have more stringent noise laws for the early morning and late evening hours than for during the day?

Answers: 1. c 2. b 3. a 4. b 5. b 6. c 7. d 8. b

8.2

Public Policy and the Environment

🗀 What is the "best" level of pollution? 🗀 What is a pollution tax?

🗀 What are command and control regulations? 🗀 What are transferable pollution rights?

Why Is a Clean Environment Not Free?

In many respects, a clean environment is no different from any other desirable good. In a world of scarcity, we can increase our consumption of a clean environment only by giving up something else. The problem that we face is choosing the combination of goods that does the most to enhance human well-being. Few people would enjoy a perfectly clean environment if they were cold, hungry, and generally destitute. On the other hand, an individual choking to death in smog is hardly to be envied, no matter how great his or her material wealth.

Only by considering the additional cost as well as the additional benefit of increased consumption of all goods, including clean air and water, can decisions on the desirable combination of goods to consume be made properly.

The Costs and Benefits of Pollution Control

It is possible, even probable, that pollution elimination, like nearly everything else, is subject to diminishing returns. Initially, a large amount of pollution can be eliminated fairly inexpensively, but getting rid of still more pollution may prove more costly. Likewise, it is also possible that the marginal benefits from eliminating "crud" from the air might decline as more and more pollution is eliminated. For example, perhaps some pollution elimination initially would have a profound impact on health costs, home repair expenses, and so on, but as pollution levels fall, further elimination of pollutants brings fewer marginal benefits.

The cost-benefit trade-off just discussed is illustrated in Exhibit 1, which examines the marginal social benefits and marginal social costs associated with the elimination of air pollution. In the early 1960s, as a nation we had few regulations on pollution control, and as a result, private firms had little incentive to eliminate the problem. In the context of Exhibit 1, we may have spent Q_1 on controls, meaning that the marginal social benefits of greater pollution control expenditures exceeded the marginal costs associated with having the controls. Investing more capital and labor to reduce pollution is efficient in such a situation.

Optimum pollution control occurs when Q^* of pollution is eliminated. Up to that point, the benefits from the elimination of pollution exceed the marginal costs, both pecuniary and nonpecuniary, of the pollution control. Overly stringent compliance levels force companies to control pollution to the level indicated by Q_2 in Exhibit 1, where the additional costs from the controls far outweigh the environmental benefits. It should be stated, however, that increased concerns about pollution have probably caused the marginal social benefit curve to shift to the right over time, increasing the optimal amount of pollution control. Because of measurement problems, however, it is difficult to state whether we are generally below, at, or above the optimal pollution level.

---

section 8.2 **exhibit 1**	**Marginal Costs and Benefits of Pollution Controls**

Marginal Social Benefits and Marginal Social Costs (dollars)

Marginal Social Cost

$MSB > MSC$ $MSC > MSB$

Marginal Social Benefit

0 Q_1 Q^* Q_2

Amount of Pollutants Eliminated

Pollution has costs and benefits. At output Q_1, pollution control is inadequate; on the other hand, elimination of Q_2 pollution will entail marginal costs that exceed the marginal benefits. Only at Q^* is pollution control expenditure at an optimum level. Of course, in practice, it is difficult to know exactly the position and slope of these curves.

© Cengage Learning 2013

Measuring Externalities

How much damage, at the margin, does a steel mill's air pollution do to nonconsumers of the steel? No one really knows because no market fully measures those costs. Indeed, the costs are partly nonpecuniary, meaning that no outlay of money occurs. Even though we pay dollars to see the doctor for respiratory ailments and pay dollars to repaint pollution-caused peeling on buildings, we do not make explicit money payments for the visual pollution and undesirable odors that the mill might produce as a byproduct of making steel. Nonpecuniary costs are real costs and potentially have a monetary value that can be associated with them, but assessing that value in practical terms is immensely difficult. You might be able to decide how much you would be willing to pay to live in a pollution-free world, but no current mechanism allows anyone to express the perceived monetary value of having clear air to breathe and smell. Even some pecuniary, or monetary, costs are difficult to truly measure: How much respiratory disease is caused by pollution and how much by other factors? Environmental economists continue to make progress in valuing these difficult to measure damages.

Even though measuring externalities, both negative and positive, is often nearly impossible, it does not necessarily mean that it is better to ignore the externality and allow the market solution to operate. As already explained, the market solution will almost certainly result in excessive output by polluters unless some intervention occurs. What form should the intervention take?

COURTESY OF ROBERT L. SEXTON

Can skyscrapers be good for the environment? People who live in the city drive less, use more public transportation, and also use less electricity and home heating because they tend to live in smaller living spaces compared to suburbanites. As a result, central city residents may emit less carbon into the atmosphere than suburbanites.

At the turn of the 20th century, horses and carriages were the predominant form of transportation in New York City. During inclement weather, the city was knee high in mud and manure. Horses that died on the job had to be dealt with as well. Ironically, the solution to the pollution problem was the horseless carriage—the automobile.

Command and Control Policies: Regulation

One approach to dealing with externalities is to require private enterprise to produce their outputs in a manner that would reduce negative externalities below the amounts that would persist in the absence of regulation. For example, the Environmental Protection Agency (EPA) was established by the Clean Air Act of 1970 to serve as a watchdog over the production of goods and services in areas where externalities, especially negative externalities, exist. The EPA's main duty is to enforce environmental standards.

However, the EPA might also require a firm to use a certain technology to reduce emissions. In order to design good policies, the government regulators need information on specific industries and the technologies they could employ. This is not easy information for the government to obtain.

For example, the EPA may identify and then enforce a standard equal to the maximum amount of pollution that firms can produce per unit of output per year. To be effective in pollution reduction, of course, these standards must result in less pollution than would exist in the absence of regulation. The regulations, then, force companies to find less pollution-intensive ways of producing goods and services. Or in the case of consumer products that pollute—such as automobiles, for example—manufacturers have been forced to reduce the emissions from the products themselves. In 1984, the federal government required that auto producers install catalytic converters in new cars to reduce auto emissions.

How can we determine the optimum level of pollution control?

Pollution Taxes: A Market-Based Policy

Using taxes to internalize external costs is appealing because it allows the relatively efficient private sector to operate according to market forces in a manner that takes socially important spillover costs into account. A major objection to the use of such taxes and subsidies is that, in most cases, it is difficult to measure externalities with any precision. Choosing a tax rate involves some guesswork, and poor guessing might lead to a solution that is far from optimal. But it is likely to be better than ignoring the problem. In spite of the severe difficulties in measurement, however, many economists would like to see greater effort made to force internalization of externalities through taxes rather than using alternative approaches. Why? We know that firms will seek out the least-expensive (in terms of using society's scarce resources) approaches to cleanup because they want more profits.

transferable pollution rights
a right given to a firm to discharge a specified amount of pollution; its transferable nature creates incentive to lower pollution levels

What is the advantage to the pollution rights approach?

Transferable Pollution Rights

Economists see an opportunity to control pollution through a government-enforced system of property rights. In this system, the government issues transferable pollution rights that give the holder the right to discharge a specified amount (smaller than the uncontrolled amount) of pollution into the air. In this plan, firms have an incentive to lower their levels of pollution because they can sell their permits if they go unused. Specifically, firms that can lower their emissions at the lowest costs will do so and trade their pollution rights to firms that cannot reduce their pollution levels as easily. That is, each polluter—required either to reduce pollution to the level allowed by the number of rights it holds or buy more rights—will be motivated to eliminate all pollution that is cheaper than the price of pollution rights. The crucial advantage to the pollution rights approach comes from the fact that the rights are private property and can be sold.

It is worth emphasizing that this least-cost pattern of abatement does not require any information about the techniques of pollution abatement on the part of the government—more specifically, the EPA. The EPA does not need to know the cheapest abatement strategy for each and every polluter. Faced with a positive price for pollution rights, each polluter has every motivation to discover and use the cheapest way to reduce pollution. Nor does the EPA need to know anything about the differences in abatement costs among polluters. Each polluter is motivated to reduce pollution as long as the cost of reducing one more unit is less than the price of pollution rights. The information and incentives generated by private ownership and market exchange of these pollution rights automatically leads to the desirable pattern of pollution.

The pollution rights approach also creates an incentive for polluters to develop improved pollution abatement technologies.

The prospect of buying and selling pollution permits would allow firms to move into an area that is already as polluted as allowed by EPA standards. Under the tradeable permits policy, the firm can set up operation by purchasing pollution permits from an existing polluter in the area. This type of exchange allows the greatest value to be generated with a given amount of pollution. It also encourages polluters to come up with cheaper ways of reducing pollution, because the firm that reduces pollution is able to sell its pollution credits to others, making pollution reduction profitable.

Pulp and paper mills pollute our environment. The pulp and paper industry is one of the largest and most polluting industries in North America. One of the primary environmental concerns is the use of chlorine-based bleaches and resultant toxic emissions to air, water, and soil.

⑦ SECTION QUIZ

1. Taxes on the emissions of polluting firms are primarily intended to

   a. encourage firms to reduce product prices.

   b. encourage firms to increase production of output.

   c. raise revenue for general spending needs.

   d. encourage firms to pollute less.

2. An ideal pollution tax

   a. does not affect the quantity of the good produced.

   b. forces a firm to internalize the externality.

   c. causes a polluting firm to increase production to the socially efficient level of output.

   d. leads to a reduction in price to the consumer of the polluting firm's output.

3. If compliance standards are too stringent,

   a. the marginal social benefit of pollution reduction may outweigh the marginal social cost of pollution reduction.

   b. the marginal social cost of pollution reduction may outweigh the marginal social benefit of pollution reduction.

   c. the marginal social cost of pollution reduction will just equal the marginal social benefit from pollution reduction.

   d. none of the above is correct.

4. An advantage that emission taxes and tradable emissions permits have over compliance standards is that the former

   a. work well even if pollution output cannot be accurately measured.

   b. result in equal levels of pollution abatement across all firms.

   c. make it in the interests of firms to reduce pollution in the most efficient manner possible.

   d. reduce pollution to zero.

(*continued*)

8.3

Property Rights and the Environment

📂 What is the relationship between externalities and property rights?

📂 What is the Coase theorem?

The existence of externalities and the efforts to deal with them in a manner that will enhance the social good can be considered a question of the nature of property rights. If the EPA limits the soot that a steel company emits from its smokestack, then the property rights of the steel company with respect to its smokestack have been altered or restricted. Similarly, zoning laws restrict how property owners can use their property. Sometimes, to deal with externalities, governments radically alter arrangements of property rights.

Indeed, the entire matter of dealing with externalities ultimately evolves into a question of how property rights should be altered. If no externalities existed in the world, reasons for prohibiting property owners from using their property in any manner they voluntarily chose would be few. Ultimately, then, externalities involve an evaluation of the legal arrangements under which we operate our economy and thus illustrate one area where law and economics merge.

What is the Coase theorem?

Coase theorem
where property rights are defined in a clear-cut fashion, and externalities are internalized if transaction costs are low

The Coase Theorem

In a classic paper, Nobel laureate Ronald Coase observed that when the benefits are greater than the costs for some course of action (say, environmental cleanup), potential transactions can make some people better off without making anyone worse off. This idea is known as the **Coase theorem**. To appreciate this important insight, consider the following problem: A cattle rancher lives downstream from a paper mill. The paper mill dumps waste into the stream, which injures the rancher's cattle. If the rancher is not compensated, an externality exists.

Suppose the courts have established (perhaps because the paper mill was there first) that the property rights to use (or abuse) the stream reside with the mill. If the benefits of cleanup are greater than the costs, the rancher should be willing to pay the mill owner to stop polluting. Let's assume that the rancher's benefits (say $10,000) from the cleanup undertaken by the mill are greater than the cost (say $5,000). If the rancher were to offer $7,500 to the mill owner to clean up the stream, both the rancher and the mill owner would be better off than with continued pollution. If, on the other hand, the rancher had the property rights to the stream, and the mill owner received a sufficiently high benefit from polluting the river, then it would be rational for the mill owner to pay the rancher up to the point where the marginal benefit to the mill owner of polluting equaled the marginal damage to the rancher from pollution.

COURTESY OF ROBERT L. SEXTON

Transaction Costs and the Coase Theorem

The mill owner and rancher example hinges critically on low transaction costs. Transaction costs are the costs of negotiating and executing an exchange, excluding the cost of the good or service bought. For example, when buying a car, it is usually rational for the buyer to spend some time searching for the "right" car and negotiating a mutually agreeable price.

If a rancher lives downstream from a polluting factory and the courts have given the rights to the factory to pollute, economists say that the property rights to pollute are well defined. However, the rancher may be able to negotiate privately and pay the polluting firm to reduce the amount of pollution—and make both parties better off.

Suppose instead that the situation involved 1,000 ranchers and 10 mill owners. Trying to coordinate the activity between the ranch owners and mill owners would be almost impossible. Now imagine the complexities of more realistic cases: 12 million people live within 60 miles of downtown Los Angeles. Each of them is damaged a little by a large number of firms and other individuals (for example, automobile drivers) in Los Angeles.

It thus becomes apparent why the inefficiencies resulting from pollution control are not eliminated by private negotiations. First is the issue of ambiguity regarding property rights in air, water, and other environmental media. Firms that have historically polluted resent controls, giving up their rights to pollute only if bribed, yet consumers feel they have the right to breathe clean air and use clean bodies of water. These conflicting positions must be resolved in court, with the winner being, of course, made wealthier. Second, transaction costs increase greatly with the number of transactors, making it next to impossible for individual firms and citizens to negotiate private agreements. Finally, the properties of air or water quality (and similar public goods) are such that additional people can enjoy the benefits at no additional cost and cannot be excluded from doing so. Hence, in practice, private agreements are unlikely to solve many problems of market failure.

It is, however, too easy to jump to the conclusion that governments should solve any problems that cannot be solved by private actions. No solution may be possible, or all solutions may involve costs that exceed benefits. In any event, the ideas developed in this chapter should enable you to think critically about such problems and the difficulties in formulating appropriate policies.

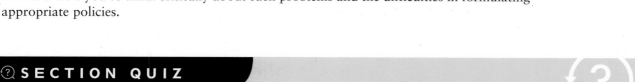

⊘ SECTION QUIZ

1. According to the Coase theorem, one way to deal with an externality problem when transaction costs are low is

   a. for the government to impose pollution taxes.

   b. for the government to make certain that property rights are well-defined.

   c. for the government to issue transferable pollution permits.

   d. for the government to impose compliance standards.

(continued)

8.4

Public Goods

📂 What is a public good?

📂 What is the free-rider problem?

📂 Why does the government provide public goods?

📂 What is a common resource good?

📂 What is the tragedy of the commons?

What is a public good? Is it any good that is purchased by the government?

public good
a good that is nonrivalrous in consumption and nonexcludable

Private Goods versus Public Goods

Externalities are not the only culprit behind resource misallocation. A **public good** is another source of market failure. As used by economists, this term refers not to how these particular goods are purchased—by a government agency rather than some private economic agent—but to the properties that characterize them. In this section, we learn the difference between private goods, public goods, and common resources.

Private Goods

private good
a good with rivalrous consumption and excludability

A private good such as a cheeseburger has two critical properties in this context; it is rival and excludable. First, a cheeseburger is rival in consumption because if one person eats a particular cheeseburger, nobody else can eat the same cheeseburger. Second, a cheeseburger is excludable. It is easy to keep someone from eating your cheeseburger by not giving it to him. Most goods in the economy, like food, clothing, cars, and houses are private goods that are rival and excludable.

Public Goods

The consumption of public goods, unlike private goods, is neither rival nor excludable. A public good is not rival because everyone can consume the good simultaneously; that is, one person's use of it does not diminish another's ability to use it. A public good is likewise *not excludable* because once the good is produced, it is prohibitively costly to exclude anyone from consuming the good. Consider national defense. Everyone enjoys the benefits of national defense (not rival) and it would be too costly to exclude anyone from those benefits (not excludable). That is, once the military has its defense in place, everyone is protected simultaneously (not rival) and it would be prohibitively costly to exclude anyone from consuming national defense (not excludable).

Another example of a public good is a flood control project. A flood control project would allow all the people who live in the flood plain area to enjoy the protection of the new program simultaneously (not rival). It would also be very difficult to exclude someone who lived in the middle of the project who said she did not want to pay (not excludable).

Voters may disagree on whether we have too much or too little, but most agree that we must have national defense. If national defense were provided privately and people were asked to pay for the use of national defense, many would be free riders, knowing they could derive the benefits of the good without paying for it. For this reason, the government provides important public goods, such as national defense.

Public Goods and the Free-Rider Problem

The fact that a public good is not rival and not excludable makes the good difficult to produce privately. Some would know they could derive the benefits from the good without paying for it, because once it is produced, it is too difficult to exclude them. Some would try to take a *free ride*—derive benefits from something they did not pay for. Let's return to the example of national defense. Suppose the private protection of national defense is actually worth $100 to you. Assume that 100 million households in the United States are willing to make a $100 contribution for national defense. These contributions would add up to $10 billion. You might write a check for $100, or you might reason as follows: "If I don't give $100 and everybody else does, I will be equally well protected plus derive the benefits of $100 in my pocket." Taking the latter course represents a rational attempt to be a **free rider**. The rub is that if everyone attempts to take a free ride, the ride will not exist.

The free-rider problem prevents the private market from supplying the efficient amounts of public goods. That is, no private firm would be willing to supply national defense because people can consume it without paying for it—the free rider problem. Therefore, the government provides important public goods such as national defense.

The Government and Benefit-Cost Analysis

Everything the government provides has an opportunity cost. What is the best level of national defense? More national defense means less of something else that society may value more, like

ECS
economic content standards

Public goods provide benefits to more than one person at a time, and their use cannot be restricted to only those people who have paid to use them.

free rider
deriving benefits from something not paid for

Is busking, or street entertaining, a public good? The nonpaying public can benefit so you have a free rider problem. It is difficult to exclude someone from the pitch (where buskers play). However, if the street entertainers are really good, it is possible that local vendors will pay them because they may attract customers. Did you know busking has been around since the Roman Empire?

If an outdoor firework program is not rival, and not excludable, is it a public good? How about a tornado siren in a small town?

health care or Social Security. To be efficient, additional goods from the public sector must also follow the rule of rational choice—pursue additional government activities if and only if the expected marginal benefits exceed the expected marginal costs. It all comes back to the adage—there are no free lunches.

In addition, there is also the problem of assessing the value of these goods. Consider the case of a new highway. Before it builds the highway, the appropriate government agency will undertake a benefit-cost analysis of the situation. In this case, it must evaluate consumers' willingness to pay for the highway against the costs that will be incurred for construction and maintenance. However, those individuals who want the highway have an incentive to exaggerate their desire for it. At the same time, individuals who will be displaced or otherwise harmed by the highway have an incentive to exaggerate the harm that will be done to them. Together, these elements make it difficult for the government to accurately assess benefits and costs. Ultimately, their evaluations are reduced to educated guesses about the net impact, weighing both positive and negative effects, of the highway on all parties concerned.

Common Resources and the Tragedy of the Commons

In many cases we do not have exclusive private property rights to things such as the air around us or the fish in the sea. They are common resources—goods that are owned by everyone and therefore not owned by anyone. When a good is not owned by anyone, individuals feel little incentive to conserve or use the resource efficiently.

common resource
a good that is rival in consumption and non excludable

A **common resource** is a rival good that is nonexcludable; that is, nonpayers cannot be easily excluded from consuming the good, and when one unit is consumed by one person, it means that it cannot be consumed by another. Fish in the vast ocean waters are a good example of a common resource. They are rival because fish are limited—a fish taken by one person is not available for others. They are nonexcludable because it is prohibitively costly to keep anyone from catching them—almost anyone with a boat and a fishing rod could catch one. Common resources can lead to the tragedy of the commons. This is the case of private incentives failing to provide adequate maintenance of of public resources.

Other examples of common resources where individuals have relatively free access and the resources can be easily exploited are congested roads and the Internet. "Free" way is a misnomer. No one owns the space on the freeway. Because there are no property rights to the freeway, you cannot exclude others from driving on and sharing the freeway. When you occupy a part of the freeway, you are keeping others from using that portion. So, all drivers compete for limited space, causing a negative externality in the form of congestion.

The Internet poses a similar problem. If everyone attempts to access the same website at the same time, overcrowding occurs and congestion can cause the site to slow down.

There are two possible solutions to the common property rights problem. First, the government, through taxes and fees, can attempt to internalize the externality. To prevent road congestion, the government could charge drivers a toll—a corrective tax on congestion—or it could charge higher tolls on bridges during rush hour. A gasoline tax would be an inferior policy solution because while it would reduce driving, it would not necessarily reduce driving during peak periods. Similarly, the government can charge fees to reduce congestion in national parks during peak periods. They can have restrictions through licensing on hunting and fishing to control animal populations.

Second, the government could assign assign private property rights to common resources. For example, private fish farms have become more profitable as overfishing depletes the stock of fish in open waters.

ECS

economic content standards

Governments provide an alternative method to markets for supplying goods and services when it appears that the benefits to society of doing so outweigh the costs to society. Not all individuals will bear the same costs or share the same benefits of those policies.

A government policy to correct a market imperfection is not justified economically if the cost of implementing it exceeds its expected benefits.

ERIC ISSELÉE/SHUTTERSTOCK.COM

Poachers in Africa hunt elephants for their tusks. Where no one owns them, allowing owners to capture both the benefits and the costs from them, elephants roam free and they are treated as a common resource. Poachers are numerous in those places and each poacher has an incentive to kill as many elephants as possible to get their tusks before someone else does. Kenya is one example, where, since 1975, the elephant population in Kenya has fallen from 170,000 to 30,000. On the other hand, the elephant population in Zimbabwe has increased from 20,000 to over 100,000 over the same period. Why? Zimbabwe allows safari hunting on private property, allowing effective ownership of the elephants on that property and providing the ability to protect its herds against poachers and the incentive to efficiently manage its herds.

⊘ SECTION QUIZ

1. The market system fails to provide the efficient output of public goods because

   a. people place no value on public goods.

   b. private firms cannot restrict the benefits from those goods to consumers who are willing to pay for them.

   c. public enterprises can produce those goods at lower cost than private firms.

   d. public goods create widespread spillover costs.

2. Public goods, like national defense, are usually funded through government because

   a. no one cares about them, because they are public.

   b. it is prohibitively difficult to withhold national defense from someone unwilling to pay for it.

   c. they cost too much for private firms to produce them.

   d. they provide benefits only to individuals, and not firms.

3. A public good is both _____ in consumption and _____.

   a. nonrivalrous; exclusive

   b. nonrivalrous; nonexclusive

   c. rivalrous; exclusive

   d. rivalrous; nonexclusive

4. Public goods

   a. do not need to be produced by government.

   b. are subject to the free rider problems.

   c. tend to be underproduced in the marketplace.

   d. All of the above are true.

5. A common resource

   a. is rivalrous in consumption.

   b. is nonexcludable.

   c. can lead to the tragedy of the commons.

   d. All of the above are true.

(*continued*)

8.5

Asymmetric Information

📁 What is asymmetric information?   📁 What is moral hazard?

📁 What is adverse selection?

What Is Asymmetric Information?

asymmetric information
when the available information is initially distributed in favor of one party relative to another in an exchange

When the available information is initially distributed in favor of one party relative to another, **asymmetric information** is said to exist. Suppose you just bought a used car that had 3,000 miles on the odometer. The car was in pristine shape—no dents, no scratches, good tires and so on. Would you be willing to pay close to the same price for this car as you would for a new car (same model, same accessories) from the dealer? Probably not, because you are going to suspect that something is wrong with the car.

Sellers are at an information advantage over potential buyers when selling a used car because they have more information about the car than does the potential buyer. However, potential buyers know that sellers are more likely to sell a lemon. As a result, potential buyers will offer a lower price than they would if they could be certain of the quality. This is known as the lemon problem. Without incurring significant quality detection costs, such as having it inspected by a mechanic, the potential buyer is at an informational disadvantage relative to the seller. It is rational for the seller to claim that the car is in good shape and has no known defects, but the potential buyer cannot detect whether the car is a lemon or not without incurring costs. If the quality detection costs are sufficiently high, a solution is to price all used cars as if they are average quality. That is, used cars of the same year, make, and model generally will be offered at the same price, regardless of their known conditions. The seller of a lemon will then receive a payment that is more than the car is worth, and the seller of a relatively high-quality car will receive less than the car is worth. However, if a seller of a high-quality car does *not* receive what the car would sell for if the potential buyer knew its quality, the seller will rationally withdraw the offer to sell the car. Given the logical response of sellers of higher-than-average quality

ISTOCKPHOTO.COM/BRIAN BEHUNIN

Because the seller of a car has more information than the buyer has, the potential buyer does not know whether the car is a cherry or a lemon. So the buyer guesses the car is average quality and consequently he offers an average price. The owner of a carefully maintained, good used car will be unable to get a high enough price to make selling that car worthwhile. Consequently, owners of good cars will not place their cars on the used car market. But those with cars of less than average quality will dump their cars on the market. Hence, the lemon problem.

cars, the average quality of used cars on the market will fall, and consequently, many people will avoid buying in the used-car market. In other words, the bad cars will drive the good cars out of the market. Thus, fewer used cars are bought and sold because fewer good cars are offered for sale. That is, information problems reduce economic efficiency. A situation where an informed party benefits in an exchange by taking advantage of knowing more than the other party is called **adverse selection**.

> **adverse selection**
> a situation where an informed party benefits in an exchange by taking advantage of knowing more than the other party

This distortion in the used-car market resulting from adverse selection can be reduced by the buyer acquiring more information so that the buyer and seller have equal information. In the used-car example, it might mean that an individual buyer would demand that an independent mechanic do a detailed inspection of the used car or that the dealership provide an extended warranty. A warranty provides a credible signal that this dealer is not selling lemons. In addition, new services such as carfax.com allow you to pay to find the history of a used car before you buy it. These services help eliminate the adverse selection problem because buyers have more information about the product they are buying.

The least-cost solution would have sellers reveal their superior information to potential buyers. The problem is that it is not individually rational for the seller to provide a truthful and complete disclosure, a point that is known by a potential buyer. Only if the seller is punished for not truthfully revealing exchange-relevant information will a potential buyer perceive the seller's disclosure as truthful.

Adverse selection also occurs in the insurance market. Imagine an auto insurance company that has a one-size-fits-all policy for its insurance premiums. Careful drivers would be charged the same premium as careless drivers. The company would assess the average risk of accidents for all drivers and then set the premium. Of course, this would be very appealing to careless drivers, who are more likely to get in an accident, but not very appealing to careful drivers, who have a much lower probability of getting in an accident. Under this pricing scheme, the bad drivers would drive the good drivers out of the market. Good drivers would be less likely to buy a policy, thinking that they are paying too much, since they are less likely to get in an accident than a careless driver. Many good drivers would exit the market, leaving a disproportionate share of bad drivers—exactly what the insurance companies do not want—people with a higher risk of getting in accidents. So what do they do?

Insurance companies set premiums according to the risk associated with particular groups of drivers, so good drivers do not exit the market. One strategy they use for dealing with adverse selection is called *screening,* where they use observable information about people to reveal private information. For example, a 17-year-old male driving a sports car will be charged a much higher premium than a 40-year-old female driving a minivan, even if he is a careful driver. Or someone with a good driving record or good grades gets a discount on his insurance. Insurance companies have data on different types of drivers and the probability of those drivers being in accidents, and they use these data to set insurance premiums. They may be wrong on an individual case (the teenager may be accident-free for years), but they are likely to be correct on average.

When players get traded from one team to another, a potential asymmetric information and adverse selection problem occurs—especially with pitchers. The team that is trading the pitcher knows more about his medical past, his pitching mechanics, his demeanor on and off the field, and so on, than the team that is trading for him. Even though trades are not finalized until the player passes a physical, many ailments or potential problems may go undetected.

Reputation and Standardization

Asymmetric information is also present in other markets like rare stamps, coins, paintings, and sports memorabilia where the dealer (seller) knows more about the product than does the potential buyer. Potential buyers want to be assured that these items are authentic, not counterfeits. Unless the seller can successfully provide evidence of the quality of the product, bad products will tend to drive good products out of the market, resulting in a market failure.

© STEVE HAMBLIN/ALAMY

When confronted with the choice between a little known motel and a reputable hotel chain, like Holiday Inn or Hilton, you may pick the national chain because of its reputation.

One method that sellers can use to convince potential buyers that their products are high quality is *reputation*. For example, if a supermarket has a reputation of selling fresh produce, you are more likely to shop there. The same is true when you choose an electrician, plumber, or physician. In the used car market, the dealer might advertise how long he has been in business. This provides a signal that he has many satisfied customers. Therefore, he is likely to sell more used cars. In short, if there is a reputation of high quality, it will minimize the market failure problem.

However, there may be cases where it is difficult to develop a reputation. For example, take a restaurant or a motel on a desolate highway. These establishments may not receive repeat customers. Customers have little idea of the quality of food, the probability of bedbugs, and so on. In this case, *standardization* is important.

Asymmetric Information and Job Market Signaling

Why does non-job-related schooling raise your income? Why would salaried workers work longer hours—putting in 60 to 70 hours a week? The reason is this behavior provides a useful signal to the employer about the person's intelligence and work ethic.

Signaling is important because it reduces information costs associated with asymmetric information; the seller of labor (potential employee) has more information about her work ethic and reliability than the buyer of labor (potential employer). Imagine how costly it would be to try out 150 potential employees for a job. In short, signals provide a measure that can help reduce asymmetric information and lower hiring costs.

There are strong signals and weak signals. Wearing a nice suit to work would be a weak signal because it does not necessarily distinguish a highly productive worker from a less productive worker—a less productive worker can dress well too. To provide a strong signal, it must be harder for a low productivity worker to give the signal than a high productivity worker. Education is a strong signal in labor markets because it requires achievements that many low productivity workers may find too difficult to obtain. The education signal is also relatively easy to measure—years of education, grade point average, highest degree attained, reputation of the university of college, rigor of courses attempted, and so on. Education can clearly improve a person's productivity; even if it did not, however, it would be a useful signal because more productive people find it easier to obtain education than lazy people. Furthermore, productive people are more likely to attain more education in order to signal to their employer that they are productive. So it may not just be the knowledge obtained from a college education, it may be the effort that you are signaling—something you presumably already had before you entered college. So according to the signaling model, workers go to college, not for the knowledge gained, but to send the important signal that they are highly productive.

In all likelihood, education provides knowledge and enhances productivity. However, it also sends an important signal. For example, many firms will not hire managers without an MBA because of the knowledge potential employees gained in courses like finance and economics, but also because an MBA sends a powerful signal that the worker is disciplined and hard working.

Durable Goods, Signals, and Warranties

Why are people reluctant to buy durable goods like televisions, refrigerators, and cameras without a warranty? Warranties are a signal. Honest and reliable firms find it less expensive to provide a warranty than dishonest firms do. The dilemma for consumers is that they are trying to distinguish the good brands from the bad brands. One way to do this is to see what kind of warranty the producer offers. Low-quality items would require more frequent and expensive servicing than high-quality items. Thus, producers of low-quality items will tend to not offer extensive warranties. In short, extensive warranties signal high quality, while low-quality items without extensive warranties signal poor quality. With this knowledge, consumers will pay more for high-quality products with good warranties.

What Is Moral Hazard?

Another information problem is associated with the insurance market and is called moral hazard. If an individual is fully insured for fire, theft, auto, life, and so on, what incentives will this individual have to take additional precautions from risk? For example, a person with auto insurance may drive less cautiously than would a person without auto insurance.

Insurance companies do, however, try to remedy the adverse selection problem by requiring regular checkups, discounts for nonsmokers, charging different deductibles and different rates for different age and occupational groups, and so on.

Additionally, those with health insurance may devote less effort and resources to staying healthy than those who are not covered. The problem, of course, is that if the insured are behaving more recklessly than they would if they were not insured, the result might be much higher insurance rates. The moral hazard arises from the fact that it is costly for the insurer to monitor the behaviors of the insured party. Suppose an individual knew that his car was protected with a "bumper-to-bumper" warranty. He might have less incentive to take care of the car, despite the manufacturer's contract specifying that the warranty was only valid under "normal wear and tear." It would be too costly for the manufacturer to detect if a product failure was the consequence of a manufacturing defect or the abuse of the owner-user.

moral hazard
taking additional risks because you are insured, thus lowering the cost to you of taking those risks

Does the winner's curse apply to all auctions?

Adverse Selection versus Moral Hazard

Don't confuse adverse selection and moral hazard. Adverse selection is the phenomenon that occurs when one party in the exchange takes advantage of knowing more than the other party. Moral hazard involves the action taken *after* the exchange, such as if you were a nonsmoker who had just bought a life insurance policy and then started smoking heavily.

winner's curse
a situation that arises in certain auctions where the winner is worse off than the loser because of an overly optimistic value placed on the good

Winner's Curse

Suppose you and five other classmates were asked to bid on a jar of pennies. Nobody knows how many pennies are in the jar and you are not allowed to open the jar. The winner gets the jar of pennies. Let's say there are 500 pennies ($5) in the jar and you win by bidding $7. You are happy you won the bid until they count the pennies and you realize you just paid $7 for $5 worth of pennies. A common-value auction is where the auctioned item has the same value for all buyers but the value is unknown prior to the bidding. We call this a winner's curse because in this case the "winner" is overly optimistic and bids more for an item than its worth. Therefore, the winner could end up being worse off (cursed) than the loser.

The problem also occurs because value is subjective. In some cases bidders have a difficult time establishing an item's value. Without complete information, participants with limited skill in establishing valuation may overpay for an item. Historically, we have seen this when speculative bubbles in the stock or real estate markets occur. In such cases, investors with little skill in valuation and incomplete information tend to push prices beyond their true value.

However, an actual overpayment will generally occur only if the winner fails to account for the winner's curse when bidding. So despite its dire-sounding name, the winner's curse does not necessarily have ill effects.

The severity of the winner's curse tends to increase with the number of bidders. This is because the more bidders, the more likely it is that some of them have overestimated the auctioned item's value. The more serious your

Bid on this jar of pennies and you may get it. Winners will often be overeager to win and overbid. In the winner's curse, the most optimistic buyer wins, but may overpay as a result, leaving the winner worse off.

error of overbidding, the more likely you are to win. However, if you win you probably made a serious error. The best strategy may be to underbid. If the winner normally over-estimates the true value by 20 percent then you might offer 80 percent of what you think the item is worth. That way, if you happen to win by overbidding you won't "get taken to the cleaners." You might also choose not to participate in auctions likely to generate a winner's curse.

There is often confusion that winner's curse applies to the winners of all auctions. However, it is worth repeating here that for auctions based on the private value someone places on a good (i.e., when the item is desired independent of its value in the market), the winner's curse does not arise.

The winner's curse can also occur with underbidding, where people offer to do a job for less than other bidders. Imagine you need to hire a landscaper, so you get estimates from various landscapers. Who is likely to win? Probably, the landscaper with the lowest estimate. However, he may not think he won if he underestimated the amount of work required in your yard.

ⓘ SECTION QUIZ

1. Adverse selection refers to

   a. the phenomenon that occurs when one party in an exchange takes advantage of knowing more than another party.

   b. the tendency for individuals to alter their behavior once they are insured against loss.

   c. the tendency for individuals to engage in insurance fraud.

   d. both (b) and (c).

2. If, after you buy a car with air bags, you start to drive recklessly, it would be an illustration of

   a. the moral hazard problem.

   b. the free-rider problem.

   c. the adverse selection problem.

   d. the "lemon" problem.

3. In the market for insurance, the moral hazard problem leads

   a. those most likely to collect on insurance to buy it.

   b. those who buy insurance to take fewer precautions to avoid the insured risk.

   c. those with more prior insurance claims to be charged a higher premium.

   d. to none of the above.

4. The winner's curse

   a. is more likely the fewer the bidders.

   b. is more likely the more frequently a good is purchased.

   c. is more likely when a good is being purchased because of its expected future market value.

   d. is a myth.

---

1. How do substantial warranties offered by sellers of used cars act to help protect buyers from the problem of asymmetric information and adverse selection? Why might too extensive a warranty lead to a moral hazard problem?

2. If where you got your college degree acted as a signaling device to potential employers, why would you want the school from which you graduated to raise its academic standards after you leave?

3. Why might withdrawals in several classes send a poor signal to potential employers?

4. Why is the winner's curse less likely for repeat-purchase items?

Answers: 1. a 2. a 3. b 4. c

Interactive Summary

Fill in the blanks:

1. Sometimes the market system fails to produce efficient outcomes because of side effects economists call _____.

2. Whenever an activity has physical impacts on individuals not directly involved in the activity, if the impact on the outside party is negative, it is called a _____; if the impact is positive, it is called a _____.

3. If a firm can avoid paying the external costs it imposes on others, it _____ its own costs of production but not the _____ cost to society.

4. If the government taxed a manufacturer by the amount of those external costs it imposes on others, it would force the manufacturer to _____ the costs.

5. The benefits of a product or service that spill over to an outside party not involved in producing or consuming the good are called _____.

6. If suppliers are unaware of or not responsible for the external costs created by their production, the result is a(n) _____ of scarce resources to the production of the good.

7. Because producers are unable to collect payments from all who are benefiting from the good or service, the market has a tendency to _____ goods with external benefits.

8. In the case of either external benefits or external costs, buyers and sellers are receiving the wrong signals: The apparent benefits or costs of some actions differ from the _____ benefits or costs.

9. Unlike the consumption of private goods, the consumption of public goods is both _____ and _____.

10. Pollution reduction, like other forms of production, is subject to _____ returns.

11. The marginal cost of pollution abatement _____ with increasing levels of abatement.

12. The optimal quantity of pollution is where the _____ of pollution abatement equals the _____ from pollution abatement.

13. Compliance standards should be stricter where the marginal benefit from pollution reduction is _____.

14. Eliminating nearly all pollution would be economically _____, because the marginal _____ would exceed the marginal _____.

15. The economically ideal tax to impose on a polluter would be _____ the marginal external costs imposed on others by its production.

16. Compared to compliance standards, pollution taxes lead to abatement by firms who can do so at the _____ cost.

17. The imposition of per-unit pollution taxes would likely be _____ costly than compliance standards for the same degree of pollution abatement.

18. Firms buy and sell rights to pollute under a system of _____ rights.

19. Transferable pollution rights _____ work when the EPA does not know the cheapest way for polluters to reduce their emissions, because they make it in polluters' interests to reduce pollution the cheapest way.

20. Under a system of transferable pollution rights, firms with high costs of abatement would likely be _____, and firms with low costs of abatement would be _____.

21. Problems of external costs are largely a question of how _____ should be assigned.

22. _____, the costs of negotiating and executing exchanges, must be low for well-defined property rights to allow externalities to be internalized.

23. According to the Coase theorem, markets can internalize externalities as long as _____ are well-defined and _____ costs are low.

24. When large numbers of individuals are affected by an external cost, the transaction costs of using voluntary negotiation to internalize it is likely to be _____.

25. If once a good is produced it is prohibitively costly to exclude anyone from consuming the good, consumption of that good is called _____.

26. If everyone can consume a good simultaneously, it is _____.

27. When individuals derive the benefits of a good without paying for it, it is called a(n) _____.

28. The government may be able to overcome the free-rider problem by _____ the public good and imposing taxes to pay for it.

29. Goods that are owned by everyone and therefore not owned by anyone are called _____ resources.

30. A common resource is a(n) _____ good that is _____.

31. Fish in the vast ocean are a good example of a(n) _____ resource.

32. The failure of private incentives to provide adequate maintenance of public resources is known to economists as the _____.

33. When the available information is initially distributed in favor of one party relative to another, _____ is said to exist.

34. The existence of _____ may give rise to signaling behavior.

35. When one party enters into an exchange with another party that has more information, we call it _____ selection.

36. A college education can provide a(n) _____ about a person's intelligence and perseverance.

37. Good warranties are an example of _____ behavior that takes place because the _____ may know the actual quality of durable goods better than the _____.

38. _____ arises from the cost involved for the insurer to monitor the behaviors of the insured party.

39. The _____ occurs when the winner of an auction overpays.

40. The winner's curse is less likely for items that are purchased _____/infrequently and where there is a larger/_____ number of bidders.

Answers: 1. externalities 2. negative externality; positive externality 3. lowers; true 4. internalize (bear) 5. positive externalities 6. overallocation 7. underproduce 8. true social 9. nonexcludable; nonrivalous 10. diminishing 11. rises 12. marginal cost 13. greater 14. inefficient; costs; benefits 15. equal to 16. lowest 17. less 18. transferable pollution 19. can 20. buyers; sellers 21. property rights 22. Transaction costs 23. property rights; transaction 24. large 25. nonexcludable 26. nonrivalous 27. free ride 28. providing 29. common 30. rival; nonexcludable 31. common 32. tragedy of the commons 33. asymmetric information 34. asymmetric information 35. adverse 36. signal 37. signaling; sellers; buyers 38. Moral hazard 39. winner's curse 40. frequently; smaller

Key Terms and Concepts

externality 212
positive externality 212
negative externality 212
transferable pollution rights 220
Coase theorem 222

public good 224
private good 224
free rider 225
common resource 226
asymmetric information 228

adverse selection 229
moral hazard 231
winner's curse 231

Section Quiz Answers

8.1   Externalities

1. Why are externalities also called spillover effects?

An externality exists whenever the benefits or costs of an activity impact individuals outside the market mechanism. That is, some of the effects spill over to those who have not voluntarily agreed to bear them or compensate others for them, unlike the voluntary exchange of the market.

2. How do external costs affect the price and output of a polluting activity?

If the owner of a firm that pollutes does not have to bear the external costs of pollution, she can ignore those real costs of pollution to society. The result is that the private costs she must pay are less than the true social costs of production, so that the market output of the polluting activity is greater, and the resulting market price less, than it would be

if producers did have to bear the external costs of production.

3. How can the government intervene to force producers to internalize external costs?

If the government could impose a tax or fee on producers equal to the external costs imposed on people without their consent, producers would have to take those costs into account. The result would be that those costs would no longer be external costs, but internalized by producers.

4. How do external benefits affect the output of an activity that causes them?

External benefits are benefits that spill over to others, because the party responsible need not be paid for those benefits. Therefore, some of the benefits of an activity to society will be ignored by the relevant decision makers in this case, and the result will be a smaller output and a higher price for goods that generate external benefits to others.

5. How can the government intervene to force external benefits to be internalized?

Just as taxes can be used to internalize external costs imposed on others, subsidies can be used to internalize external benefits generated for others.

6. Why do most cities have more stringent noise laws for the early morning and late evening hours than for during the day?

The external costs to others from loud noises in residential areas early in the morning and late in the evening are higher, because most residents are home and trying to sleep, than when many people are gone at work or are already awake in the daytime. Given those higher potential external costs, most cities impose more restrictive noise laws for nighttime hours to reduce them.

8.2   Public Policy and the Environment

1. How does pollution control lead to both rising marginal costs and falling marginal benefits?

The marginal costs of pollution control rise for the same reason it is true of other goods. Pollution will be reduced in the lowest cost manner first. Once lower cost pollution control methods are exhausted, if we wish to reduce pollution further, we will have to turn to progressively more costly methods. The marginal benefits from pollution controls will fall, because the value of reducing crud in the atmosphere is higher, the more crud there is. As controls reduce the level of crud in the air, the marginal benefit of further crud reductions will fall.

2. How is the optimal amount of pollution control determined, in principle?

In principle, the optimal amount of pollution control is the amount at which the marginal social benefit of pollution reduction equals the marginal cost of pollution reduction. But there is no clear agreement about what those marginal benefits or costs are, leading to disagreements about the optimal amount of pollution.

3. How do command and control policies act to internalize external costs?

By forcing companies to find less pollution-intensive ways of production rather than imposing the costs of additional pollution on others, they are forced to internalize those costs formerly imposed on others.

4. How could transferable pollution rights lead to pollution being reduced at the lowest possible opportunity cost?

Transferable pollution rights would create a market for pollution reduction. Every polluter would then find it profitable to reduce pollution as long as they could do it more cheaply than the price of a pollution right. Therefore, producers would employ the lowest-cost pollution control methods for a given amount of pollution reduction.

5. What are the objectives of an ideal pollution control policy from the perspective of economists interested in resource allocation?

An ideal pollution control strategy from the perspective of economists interested in resource allocation would reduce pollution to the efficient level, it would do so at the lowest possible opportunity cost, and it would create incentives to motivate advances in pollution abatement technology.

8.3   Property Rights and the Environment

1. Why can externalities be considered a property rights problem?

If the rights to clean air, water, and so on, were clearly owned, those that infringe on those rights would be forced to compensate the owners. Such costs would be internalized, rather than external, to the relevant decision makers. Therefore, externalities are the result of the absence of clear and enforceable property rights in certain goods.

2. Why, according to the Coase theorem, will externalities tend to be internalized when property rights are clearly defined and information and transaction costs are low?

When property rights are clearly defined and information and transaction costs are low, whoever wants to exercise their right faces an opportunity cost of what others would pay for that right. That opportunity cost, represented by the potential payment from others to sell the right, is what forces decision makers to internalize what would otherwise be an externality.

3. How do transaction costs limit the market's ability to efficiently solve externality problems?

Transaction costs limit the ability of the market mechanism to internalize externalities, because trading becomes more difficult. The free-rider problem—where those who benefit from some action cannot be forced to pay for it—also hinders the ability for voluntary trade across markets to generate efficient levels of goods such as cleaner air.

8.4   Public Goods

1. How are public goods different from private goods?

Private goods are rival in consumption (we can't both consume the same unit of a good) and exclusive (nonpayers can be prevented from consuming the good unless they pay for it). Public goods are nonrival in consumption (more than one person can consume the same good) and nonexclusive (nonpayers can't be effectively kept from consuming the good, even if they don't voluntarily pay for it).

2. Why does the free-rider problem arise in the case of public goods?

The free-rider problem arises in the case of public goods because people cannot be prevented from enjoying the benefits of public goods once they are provided. Therefore, people have an incentive not to voluntarily pay for those benefits, making it difficult or even impossible to finance the efficient quantity of public goods through voluntary market arrangements.

3. In what way can government provision of public goods solve the free-rider problem?

The government can overcome the free-rider problem by forcing people to pay for the provision of a public good through taxes.

4. What is a common resource?

A common resource good is rival in consumption but nonexcludable.

5. What is the tragedy of the commons?

Common resource goods often lead to overuse because if no one owns the resource, they are not likely to consider the cost of their use of the resource on others. This is the so-called tragedy of the commons. This problem has led to overfishing. Of course, you could remove the common and make the resource private property, but assigning private property rights to a vast ocean area would be virtually impossible.

8.5   Asymmetric Information

1. How do substantial warranties offered by sellers of used cars act to help protect buyers from the problem of asymmetric information and adverse selection? Why might too extensive a warranty lead to a moral hazard problem?

In the used car market, the seller has superior information about the car's condition, placing the buyer at an information disadvantage. It also increases the chance that the car being sold is a "lemon." A substantial warranty can provide the buyer with valuable additional information about the condition of the car, reducing both asymmetric information and adverse selection problems.

Too extensive a warranty (e.g., an unlimited "bumper-to-bumper" warranty) will give the buyer less incentive to take care of the car because the buyer is effectively insured against the damage that lack of care would cause.

2. If where you got your college degree acted as a signaling device to potential employers, why would you want the school from which you graduated to raise its academic standards after you leave?

If an employer used your college's academic reputation as a signal of your likely "quality" as a potential employee, you want the school to raise its standards after you graduate, because it would improve the average quality of its graduates, improving the quality it signals about you to an employer.

3. Why might withdrawals in several classes send a poor signal to potential employers?

It would indicate a failure to stick to difficult tasks relative to other students.

4. Why is the winner's curse less likely for repeat-purchase items?

Repeat purchases reveal good information on the actual value of items.

Problems

1. Indicate which of the following activities create a positive externality, a negative externality, or no externality at all.
   a. During a live theater performance, an audience member's cell phone loudly rings.
   b. You are given a flu shot.
   c. You purchase and drink a soda during a break from class.
   d. A college fraternity and sorority clean up trash along a two-mile stretch on the highway.
   e. A firm dumps chemical waste into a local water reservoir.
   f. The person down the hall in your dorm plays loud music while you are trying to sleep.

2. Draw a standard supply-and-demand diagram for televisions, and indicate the equilibrium price and output.
   a. Assuming that the production of televisions generates external costs, illustrate the effect of the producers being forced to pay a tax equal to the external costs generated, and indicate the equilibrium output.
   b. If instead of generating external costs, television production generates external benefits, illustrate the effect of the producers being given a subsidy equal to the external benefits generated, and indicate the equilibrium output.

3. For each of the following goods, indicate whether they are nonrival and/or nonexclusive. Indicate whether they are private or public goods.
   a. hot dogs
   b. cable TV
   c. broadcast TV
   d. automobiles
   e. national defense
   f. pollution control
   g. parking in a parking structure
   h. a sunset
   i. admission to a theme park

4. Is a lighthouse a public good if it benefits many ship owners? What if it primarily benefits ships going to a port nearby?

5. Why do you think buffaloes became almost completely extinct on the Great Plains but cattle did not? Why is it possible that you can buy a buffalo burger in a store or diner today?

6. What kind of problems does the government face when trying to perform a cost-benefit analysis of whether or how much of a public project to produce?

7. How does a TV broadcast have characteristics of a public good? What about cable services such as HBO?

8. In order to get a license to practice in the United States, foreign-trained veterinarians must take an exam given by the American Veterinary Association. Only 48 people per year are allowed to take the exam, which is administered at only two universities. The fee for the exam, which must be booked at least 18 months in advance, was recently raised from $2,500 to $6,000. What effects does this clinical competency exam have on the number of veterinarians practicing in the United States? Do you think it improves the quality of veterinary services?

9. How would the adverse selection problem arise in the insurance market? How is it like the "lemon" used-car problem?

10. In terms of signaling behavior:
    a. Why is wearing a suit a weaker signal of ability than higher educational achievement?
    b. Why do some majors in college provide more powerful signals to future employers than others?
    c. Why could double-majoring provide a more powerful labor market signal than having a single major?
    d. How would you explain why students might be said to "overinvest" in grades as opposed to learning course material?

11. In terms of winner's curse:
    a. Why is the winner's curse unlikely for frequently purchased goods?
    b. Why would the winner's curse be more likely as the number of bidders increases?
    c. Why would we except there to be no winner's curse for goods desired for their own private value, unlike the case of purchases based on a good's market value to others?

12. In terms of moral hazard:
    a. Why does someone's willingness to pay a large deductible on an insurance policy tell an insurer something valuable about the seriousness of the moral hazard problem they might expect from the policyholder?
    b. Why does car insurance that explicitly excludes insuring the car for commercial use act to reduce moral hazard?
    c. Why does vehicle insurance based in part on miles driven reduce moral hazard problems?
    d. Why would a GPS monitor that can record the location and the speed a rental car is driven help reduce the moral hazard problem that rental companies are exposed to?

Public Finance and Public Choice

You just took your first job after graduating from college, and it pays $36,000 a year. You had expected to receive a check for roughly $3,000 this month but you check online and your company has deposited much less than the $3,000 into your bank account. What happened? Taxes. There are federal income taxes, state income taxes, and also FICA taxes (Federal Insurance Corporation Act) for programs such as Social Security and Medicare. You will also have to pay sales taxes in most states. And if you inherit money from your grandparents, you will have to pay tax on that, too. The bottom line is,

if you are working, or consuming, you are paying taxes and supporting the work the government does.

In the last chapter, we discussed the role of government in the case of externalities and public goods. We argued that the government can sometimes improve economic well-being by remedying externalities through pollution taxes, regulation and subsidies, and providing public goods.

In this chapter, we will see how the government obtains revenues through taxation to provide these goods and services. We also examine the different types of taxation. The last section of the chapter is on public choice economics, the application of economic principles to politics.

Public Finance: Government Spending and Taxation

9.1

- How does government finance its spending?
- On what does the public sector spend its money?
- What are progressive and regressive taxes?
- What is a flat tax?
- What is the ability to pay principle?
- What is vertical equity?
- What is the benefits received principle?
- What is a value-added tax?

Growth in Government

Government plays a large role in the economy; and its role increased markedly during World War II. From 1950–1975, government expenditures grew slowly from about 25 percent of GDP to 33 percent GDP. However, government expenditures increased sharply with the recession that began in 2008. By 2009, government expenditures reached a peacetime record of 39 percent of GDP, as seen in Exhibit 1.

National defense spending fluctuates with international tension. The aftermath of the terrorist attacks of September 11, 2001, and the wars in Iraq and Afghanistan, led to increases in defense spending. Consequently, defense spending, as a percentage of total federal spending, rose from 17 percent in 2001 to 20 percent in 2010. Terrorism is probably not going away anytime soon, so defense expenditures will most likely remain high. The global recession of 2008–2009 also expanded the size of government further. In addition, the Obama administration has created a greater role for government in the health care and energy sectors. Finally, as baby boomers age, there will be an even greater demand on public pensions and health care. Government spending will probably not be shrinking any time soon. Areas of government growth can be identified at least in part by looking at statistics on the types of government spending.

Exhibit 2(a) shows that 38 percent of federal government spending in 2010 went to Social Security and income security programs. Another 24 percent was spent on health care and Medicare (for the elderly). The remaining federal expenditures were national defense, 20 percent; interest on the national debt, 6 percent; and miscellaneous items such as foreign aid, agriculture, transportation, and housing, 12 percent.

Exhibit 2(b) shows that state and local spending differs greatly from federal spending. Education and public welfare account for 51 percent of state and local expenditures. Other significant areas of state and local spending include highways, utilities, and police and fire protection.

ECS

economic content standards

Most federal government tax revenue comes from individual income and payroll taxes. Payments to social security recipients, the costs of national defense, medical expenditures, and interest payments on the national debt constitute the bulk of federal government spending.

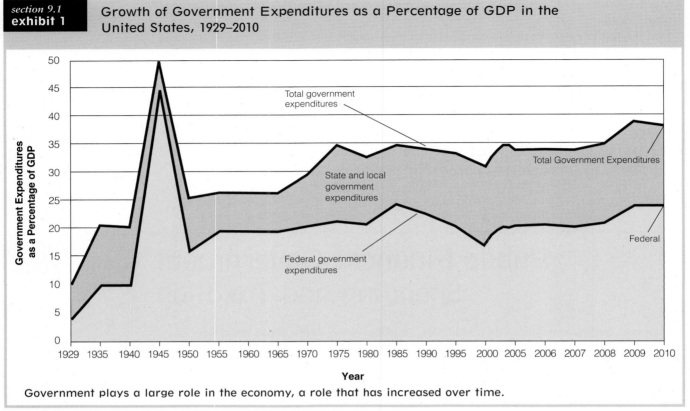

section 9.1
exhibit 1

Growth of Government Expenditures as a Percentage of GDP in the United States, 1929–2010

Government plays a large role in the economy, a role that has increased over time.

SOURCE: *Economic Report of the President*, 2011.

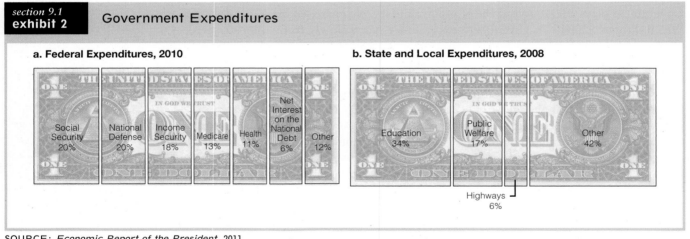

section 9.1
exhibit 2

Government Expenditures

a. Federal Expenditures, 2010

Social Security 20%   National Defense 20%   Income Security 18%   Medicare 13%   Health 11%   Net Interest on the National Debt 6%   Other 12%

b. State and Local Expenditures, 2008

Education 34%   Public Welfare 17%   Other 42%   Highways 6%

SOURCE: *Economic Report of the President*, 2011.

Generating Government Revenue

Governments have to pay their bills like any person or institution that spends money. But how do they obtain revenue? In most years, a large majority of government activity is financed by taxation. What kinds of taxes are levied on the American population?

At the federal level, most taxes or levies are on income. Exhibit 3 shows that 51 percent of tax revenues come in the form of income taxes on individuals and corporations, Most of

**section 9.1
exhibit 3**   Tax Revenues

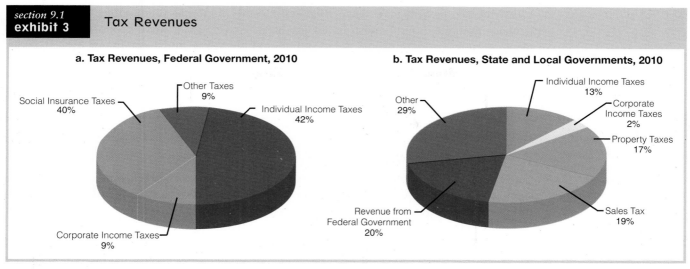

a. Tax Revenues, Federal Government, 2010

Other Taxes
9%

Social Insurance Taxes
40%

Individual Income Taxes
42%

Corporate Income Taxes
9%

b. Tax Revenues, State and Local Governments, 2010

Individual Income Taxes
13%

Other
29%

Corporate Income Taxes
2%

Property Taxes
17%

Revenue from Federal Government
20%

Sales Tax
19%

SOURCE: *Economic Report of the President and Bureau of Economic Analysis*, 2011.

the remaining revenues come from social insurance taxes (payroll taxes), which are levied on work-related income, that is, payrolls. These taxes are used to pay for Social Security and compulsory insurance plans such as Medicare. Payroll taxes are split between employees and employers. The Social Security share of federal taxes has steadily risen as the proportion of the population over age 65 has grown and as Social Security benefits have been increased.

policy watch   Social Security: How Can We Save It?

What are the options for saving Social Security?

1. Increase the payroll taxes to a rate closer to 15 percent. It is currently 10.4 percent.

2. Increase the age of full-time benefits to age 70. The problem is that seniors already have a difficult time finding employment and may not be able to do the physical work expected of them.

3. Implement "means testing." Means testing would reduce the benefits to retirees who have "sufficient means" for retirement.

4. Increase the return to Social Security funds. The government might be interested in investing part of Social Security in the stock market. The historical returns are much greater in the stock market. The real rate of return (indexed for inflation) has been roughly 7 percent in the stock market compared with only 2 percent for government bonds. However, one of the drawbacks of government investment in the stock market is the potential for political abuse. With such a large amount of funds, the temptation emerges for the government to favor some firms and punish others.

5. Put some of the payroll tax in an individual retirement plan and let individuals manage their own funds—perhaps choosing from a list of mutual funds.

6. Let individuals choose to continue with the current Social Security system or contribute a minimum of, say, 10 percent or 20 percent of their wages to a private investment fund. This option has been tried in a number of Central and South American countries. In Chile, almost 90 percent of workers choose to leave the government Social Security program to invest privately.

Critics of the private plan argue that it is risky, individuals might make poor investment decisions, and the government might ultimately have to pay for their mistakes. That is, the stock market may have a good long-term track record, but it is still inherently uncertain and risky because of economic fluctuations. This may not be consistent with a guaranteed stream of retirement income.

ECS
economic
content
standards

Most federal government tax revenue comes from personal income and payroll taxes. Payments to Social Security recipients, the costs of national defense, Medicare/Medicaid expenditures, and interest payments on the national debt constitute the bulk of federal government spending.

Most state and local government revenues come from sales taxes, grants from the federal government, personal income taxes, and property taxes. The bulk of state and local government revenue is spent is for education, public welfare, road construction and repair, and public safety.

© Flying Colours Ltd/Jupiterimages

What is a progressive income tax?

Consequently, payroll taxes have risen significantly in recent years. Other taxes, on such items as gasoline, liquor, and tobacco products, provide for a small proportion of government revenues, as do customs duties, estate and gift taxes, and some minor miscellaneous taxes and user charges.

The U.S. federal government relies more heavily on income-based taxes than nearly any other government in the world. Most other governments rely more heavily on sales taxes, excise taxes, and customs duties.

A Progressive Tax

One effect of substantial taxes on income is that the "take home" income of Americans is significantly altered by the tax system. Progressive taxes, of which the federal income tax is one example, are designed so that those with higher incomes pay a greater proportion of their income in taxes. A progressive tax is one tool that the government can use to redistribute income. It should be noted, however, that certain types of income are excluded from income for taxation purposes, such as interest on municipal bonds and income in kind—food stamps or Medicare, for example.

A Regressive Tax

Payroll taxes, the second most important source of income for the federal government, are actually regressive taxes, when considered alone. That is, they take a greater proportion of the income of lower-income groups than of higher-income groups. The reasons for this are simple. Social Security, for example, is imposed as a fixed proportion of wage and salary income up to $106,800 as of 2011. Also, wealthy persons have relatively more income from sources such as dividends and interest that are not subject to payroll taxes.

The Tax Relief, Unemployment Insurance Reauthorization, and Job Creation Act of 2010 changed this to an unequal split: 6.2 employers, 4.2 employees.

An Excise Tax

Some consider an excise tax—a sales tax on individual products such as alcohol, tobacco, and gasoline—to be the most unfair type of tax because it is generally the most regressive. Excise taxes on specific items impose a far greater burden, as a percentage of income, on the poor and middle classes than on the wealthy, because low-income families generally spend a greater proportion of their income on these items than do high-income families.

In addition, excise taxes may lead to economic inefficiencies. By isolating a few products and subjecting them to discriminatory taxation, excise taxes subject economic choices to political manipulation, and leads to inefficiency.

Financing State and Local Government Activities

Historically, the primary source of state and local revenue has been property taxes. In recent decades, state and local governments have relied increasingly on sales and income taxes for revenues (see Exhibit 3). Today, sales taxes account for roughly 22 percent of revenues, property taxes account for

AP PHOTO/THE OAKLAND PRESS, JOSE JUAREZ

If a person who earns $20,000 a year spends $2,000 of it on lottery tickets, he will spend 10 percent of his income. However, if a person who earns $200,000 a year spends $2,000 of it on lottery tickets, she will only pay 1 percent. They both have the same chance of winning. But if people in different income brackets spend the same amount on the lottery, then the lottery acts as a regressive tax because it places a heavier burden on the rich than the poor. Studies show that lottery sales tend to be higher in zip codes where per capita income is lower. Thus, non-winning lottery tickets may act like a regressive tax for the state.

21 percent, and personal and corporate income taxes account for another 18 percent. Approximately 20 percent of state and local revenues come from the federal government as grants. The remaining share of revenues comes from license fees and user charges (e.g., payment for utilities, occupational license fees, tuition fees) and other taxes.

Should We Have a Flat Tax?

Some politicians and individuals believe that we should scrap the current progressive income tax and replace it with a **flat tax**. A flat tax, also called a proportional tax, is designed so that everybody would be charged the same percentage of their income. How would a flat tax work? What do you think would be the advantages and disadvantages of a flat tax?

With a flat tax, a household could simply report its income, multiply it by the tax rate, and send in the money. Because no deductions are involved, the form could be a simple page! But most flat tax proposals call for exempting income to a certain level—say, the poverty line.

Actually, if the flat tax plan allowed individuals to deduct a standard allowance of, say, $20,000 from their wages, the tax would still be progressive. Here's how it would work: If you were earning less than $20,000 a year, you would not have to pay any income taxes. However, if you earned $50,000 a year, and the flat tax rate was 15 percent, after subtracting your $20,000 allowance you would be paying taxes on $30,000. In this system, you would have to pay $4,500 in taxes (0.15 × $30,000) and your average tax rate would be 9 percent ($4,500/$50,000 = 0.09). Now, say you made $100,000 a year. After taking your $20,000 allowance, you would have to pay a 15 percent tax on $80,000, and you would owe the government $12,000. Notice, however, that your average tax rate would be higher: 12 percent ($12,000/$100,000 = 0.12) as opposed to 9 percent. So if the flat tax system allows individual taxpayers to take a standard allowance, like most flat tax proposals, then the tax is actually progressive. That is, lower- and middle-income families will pay, on average, a smaller average tax rate, even though everyone has the same marginal tax rate over the stipulated allowance.

The advantages of the flat tax are that all of the traditional exemptions, like entertainment deductions, mortgage interest deductions, business travel expenses, and charitable contribution deductions, would be out the door, along with the possibilities of abuses and misrepresentations that go with tax deductions. Taxpayers could fill out tax returns in the way they did in the old days, in a space about the size of a postcard. Advocates argue that the government could collect the same amount of tax revenues, but the tax would be much more efficient, as many productive resources would be released from looking for tax loopholes to doing something productive from society's standpoint.

Of course, some versions of the flat tax will hurt certain groups. Not surprisingly, realtors and home owners, who like the mortgage interest deductions, and tax accountants, who make billions every year preparing tax returns, will not be supportive of a flat tax with no deductions. And, of course, many legitimate questions would inevitably arise, such as: What would happen to the size of charitable contributions if the charitable contribution deduction was eliminated? And how much will the housing sector be hurt if the mortgage interest deduction was eliminated or phased out? After all, the government's intent of the tax break was to increase home ownership. And the deductions for hybrid cars are intended to get drivers into cleaner, more fuel-efficient cars. These deductions could be gone in most flat tax proposals. In addition, the critics of the flat tax believe that the tax is not progressive

Excise taxes are sales taxes on goods like cigarettes and alcohol. This type of tax can impose a greater burden on the middle and lower class if they spend a greater proportion of their income on these items compared to higher income families.

progressive tax
a tax designed so that a larger percentage of taxable income is taken as taxable income increases.

regressive tax
a tax designed so that a smaller percentage of taxable income is taken as taxable income increases.

excise tax
a sales tax on individual products such as alcohol, tobacco, and gasoline

flat tax
a tax that charges all income earners the same percentage of their income

enough to eliminate the inequities in income and are skeptical of the tax-revenue–raising capabilities of a flat tax.

Some flat-tax proposals exclude taxing income from saving and investment like interest, dividends, and capital gains. This exemption is intended to encourage investment, saving, and economic growth. However, it raises some equity issues. Under this proposal, a family earning $70,000 a year would have to pay taxes while a wealthy retiree, living on his or her interest and dividends, might pay zero taxes. Is that fair?

In short, many people like the appeal of a flat tax but may not like the particulars. For example, think of middle-income households that would lose their mortgage interest deduction. Eliminating this exemption could lead to falling home values. Reworking the tax code might provide a better alternative.

Taxes: Efficiency and Equity

Why are most taxes inefficient?

In the last few chapters, we talked about efficiency—getting the most out of our scarce resources. However, taxes for the most part are *not* efficient (except for internalizing externalities and providing public goods) because they change incentives and distort the values that buyers and sellers place on goods and services. That is, decisions made by buyers and sellers are different from what they would be without the tax. Taxes can be inefficient because they may lead to less work, less saving, less investment, and lower output.

Economists spend a lot of time on issues of efficiency, but policy makers (and economists) are also concerned about other goals, such as fairness. Income redistribution through taxation may also lead to greater productivity for low-income workers through improvements in health and education. Even though what is fair to one person may not be fair to another, most people would agree that we should have a fair tax system based on either ability to pay or benefits received.

ability-to-pay principle
the belief that those with the greatest ability to pay taxes should pay more than those with less ability to pay

vertical equity
the concept that people with different levels of income should be treated differently

Ability-to-Pay Principle and Vertical Equity The **ability-to-pay principle** is simply that those with the greatest ability to pay taxes (richer people) should pay more than those with the least ability to pay taxes (poorer people). This concept is known as **vertical equity**—people with different levels of income should be treated differently. The federal income tax is a good example of the ability-to-pay principle because the rich pay a larger percentage of their income in taxes. That is, high-income individuals will pay a higher percentage of their income in taxes than low-income individuals. Sales taxes are not a good example of the ability-to-pay principle, because low-income individuals pay a larger percentage of their income in such taxes.

Benefits-Received Principle

The *benefits-received principle* means that the individuals receiving the benefits are those who pay for them. Take the gasoline tax: the more miles one drives on the highway, the more gasoline used and the more taxes collected. The tax revenues are then used to maintain the highways. Or those who benefit from a new airport or an opera house should be the ones who pay for such public spending. Although this principle may work for some private goods, it does not work well for public goods such as national defense and the judicial system. Because we collectively consume national defense, it is not possible to find out who benefits and by exactly how much.

Administration Burden of Taxation

The administration burden of the income tax also leads to another deadweight loss. Imagine if everyone filled out a one-page tax form that took no more than 5 minutes. Instead the opportunity cost of the hours of time and services used in tax preparation is in the billions

policy application Taxing Sin

Economists have long known that there is a tension between the dual goals of taxing sin (alcohol, tobacco, gambling, etc.), because the more successful the tax is at discouraging the sinful activity, the less revenue the government raises. This problem was highlighted recently by Russian Finance Minister Alexei Kudrin. After announcing plans to raise taxes on cigarettes and liquor, he nevertheless urged Russians to keep smoking and drinking, saying the activities are good for the state by helping finance social services and programs to raise the birth rate.

Taxing sin is nothing new, of course. Among the earliest federal taxes were those on alcohol, tobacco, and playing cards, and they remained mainstays of the federal revenue system until the creation of the corporate and individual income taxes in 1909 and 1913, respectively. In 1900, 50 percent of all federal revenue came from taxing alcohol, tobacco, and playing cards; the rest mostly came from customs duties. Today, taxes on alcohol and tobacco constitute just 1 percent of federal receipts.

Related to taxes on sin are taxes on luxuries—things people could easily do without or are consumed almost exclusively by the rich. Over the years, the federal government has had special taxes on carriages, refined sugar, watches, yachts, billiard tables, gold and silver plate, furs, jewelry, electrical appliances, luggage, phonographs and recordings, cameras and film, and many other items.

Sin taxes represent a somewhat more important revenue source at the state and local level. According to the Census Bureau, taxes on alcohol and tobacco constitute 1.8 percent of total state and local government revenue, a percentage that has been about the same for at least 20 years, despite significant increases in tax rates on both products. The higher rates have been offset by lower consumption.

In recent years, there have been many efforts to expand sin taxes to include other activities that are thought to be socially harmful—or perhaps just not socially favored. These include taxing sugary drinks, strip clubs, fast food, firearms, pornography, escort services, cosmetic surgery, plastic shopping bags, tanning salons, and many others.

Of course, it's not just a puritanical desire to encourage people to live better lives that underlies the expansion of sin taxes. Clearly, the pressing budgetary needs of governments at all levels are driving a desperate search for revenue. And given voters' strong opposition to increases in broad-based taxes, sin taxes are one of the few areas potentially available for additional revenue. That's partly because those not engaging in the allegedly sinful activities targeted for taxation usually don't care, and because those who do often feel guilty about their indulgences and view sin taxes as a sort of penance.

The drive to raise revenue isn't limited to imposing new taxes and raising rates on sinful activities. It also has led to the legalization of previously illegal activities such as gambling and the relaxation of so-called blue laws. Sunday closing laws have been abolished or liberalized in many states partially because legislatures hoped that additional opportunities for shopping would raise sales tax revenue.

Historically, efforts to abolish smoking and drinking ended in large part because they prevented governments from taxing those activities and imposed additional costs in the form of law enforcement and incarceration. . . .

. . . Perhaps the lesson to be drawn from the historical experience is that prohibiting nonviolent activities and substances that people are going to insist on doing or using anyway will never stamp them out. But if they are legalized, controlled, and taxed, society may be able to keep them within acceptable bounds while raising significant government revenue exclusively on the backs of those who insist on engaging in the behavior. That's about as close to a win-win situation as one is going to find in the public policy arena.

SOURCE: Bruce Bartlett, "Taxing Sin: A Win-Win for Everyone?" *Tax Notes*, Vol. 128, No. 12, p. 1289, September 20, 2010. Reprinted by permission of the author.

use what you've learned — The Burden of the Corporate Income Tax

Corporate income taxes are generally popular among voters because they think the tax comes from the corporation. Of course, it does write the check to the IRS, but that does not mean that the corporation (and its stockholders) bears the burden of the tax. Some of the tax burden (perhaps a great deal) is passed on to consumers in the form of higher prices. It will also impact investors' rates of return. Less investment leads to less capital for workers which lowers workers' productivity and wages. The key here is to be careful to distinguish between who pays the tax and who incurs the burden of the tax.

of dollars. The government also spends a great deal to enforce these taxes. A simplified tax system would reduce the deadweight loss.

Social Policy of Taxes

Taxes and subsidies can be efficiency enhancing when used to correct for externalities. For example, the government may view it as good social policy to subsidize cleaner, more efficient hybrid vehicles. Or they may want to put a high tax on cigarettes in an attempt to reduce teen smoking. In other words, taxes on alcohol and cigarettes may be used to discourage these activities—sometimes we call these "sin taxes."

policy application — Should We Have a Consumption Tax?

In Chapter 8, we discussed the deadweight loss associated with taxes. A higher marginal tax rate on income may discourage people from working as hard as they otherwise would. In addition, the individual income tax might discourage people from saving.

Consequently, many economists favor the idea of replacing the individual income tax with a consumption tax. A consumption tax would tax the amount that is spent rather than what is earned. In that sense, people are taxed based on what they take out of the economy, not on what they earn (in exchange for the benefits provided to others).

Under a consumption tax, saved income is not taxed. As a result, people would save more. That would provide increased funds for investment, which would expand the capital stock over time,

increasing worker productivity, economic output, and real wages.

Unfortunately, there are issues with transitioning from an income tax to a consumption tax. Some argue that low-income individuals spend a large fraction of their income, and therefore save little, so they would benefit little from a consumption tax. The transition from an income tax to a consumption tax would also shift tax burdens to older generations that would have to pay a consumption tax on spending, in addition to the income taxes they already had to pay when that income was earned. And equity issues might require a phase-in period, which would increase tax complexity during that period. Furthermore, people can already invest in individual retirement accounts (IRAs), which allow them to defer paying taxes until after retirement, much like with a consumption tax.

② SECTION QUIZ

1. Which of the following are important roles of the government?

   a. protecting property rights

   b. providing a legal system

   c. intervention when insufficient competition occurs in the marketplace

   d. promoting stability and economic growth

   e. all of the above

2. Social Security and Medicare are financed by

   a. personal income taxes.

   b. payroll taxes.

   c. excise taxes.

   d. corporation income taxes.

   e. none of the above taxes.

3. Who must legally pay Social Security and Medicare taxes?

   a. employers

   b. employees

   c. both employers and employees

   d. neither employers nor employees

4. Expenditures on _____ comprise the largest component of state and local government budgets.

   a. education

   b. public safety

   c. public infrastructure (such as roads and water works)

   d. public welfare (such as food stamps and income supplemental programs)

5. _____ taxes are designed to take a larger percentage of high incomes as compared to lower incomes.

   a. Progressive

   b. Regressive

   c. Proportional

   d. Negative

6. An example of a proportional tax would be

   a. a state sales tax.

   b. a local property tax.

   c. a flat rate income tax.

   d. the current U.S. income tax.

7. The largest single source of revenue for the federal government is the

   a. corporate income tax.

   b. federal excise tax.

   c. personal income tax.

   d. Social Security tax.

8. The U.S. federal income tax is an example of a

   a. progressive tax.

   b. proportional tax.

   c. regressive tax.

   d. value-added tax.

(*continued*)

② SECTION QUIZ (Cont.)

9. The ability-to-pay principle states:

   a. Those with the greatest ability to pay taxes should pay more.

   b. Those with the least ability to pay taxes should pay more.

   c. Individuals receiving the benefits should pay for them.

   d. All of the above are true.

---

1. Has federal government spending as a fraction of GDP changed much since the 1960s?

2. What finances the majority of federal government spending?

3. What happens to the proportion of income paid as taxes when income rises, for a progressive tax? What is an example of such a progressive tax?

4. Why are excise taxes on items such as alcohol, tobacco, and gasoline considered regressive taxes?

5. How could a flat tax also be a progressive tax?

6. Why is the federal income tax an example of the ability to pay principle?

7. How is a gas tax an example of the benefits received principle?

Answers: 1. e   2. b   3. a   4. a   5. a   6. c   7. c   8. a   9. a

---

9.2

Public Choice

📂 What is public choice theory?

📂 What is the median voter model?

📂 What is rational ignorance?

📂 Why do special interest groups arise?

ECS

economic content standards

Costs of government policies sometimes exceed benefits. This may occur because voters, government officials and government employees have opposing incentives, actions by special interest groups can impose costs on the general public, or social goals other than economic efficiency are being pursued.

When the market fails, as in the case of an externality or public good, it may be necessary for the government to intervene and make public choices. However, it is possible for government actions in response to externalities to make matters worse. Our discussion of public goods considered what goods the government should provide, like national defense or flood control programs, but it did not specify how much of the public good the government would provide. How many new jet fighters, missiles, or aircraft carriers? The same is true with law enforcement and environmental protection: how much should the government provide? In addition, as we discussed in the section on public goods, we do not know the true demand for public services. A vote does not signal how much an individual values that good or service. What if 51 percent of the voters are going to vote for a new highway but do not have very strong preferences while 49 percent fell very strongly that the highway should not get built? The highway is built. The political system uses majority rules. The market system uses a proportional rule; so if 20 percent of the dollar votes want hybrid vehicles, 20 percent of the money would go to purchase hybrids. That is, just because markets have failed to generate efficient results does not necessarily mean that government can do a better job—see Exhibit 1. One explanation for this outcome is presented by public choice theory.

What Is Public Choice Theory?

Public choice theory is the application of economic principles to politics. Public choice economists believe that government actions are an outgrowth of individual behavior. Specifically, they assume that the behavior of individuals in politics, as in the marketplace, will be

section 9.2 exhibit 1	Do People in Government Waste Tax Money? 1970–2008 (percent of population agreeing)																			
	'70	'72	'74	'76	'78	'80	'82	'84	'86	'88	'90	'92	'94	'96	'98	'00	'02	'04	'08
A Lot	69	66	74	74	77	78	66	65	**	63	67	67	70	59	61	59	48	61	72
Some	26	30	22	20	19	18	29	29	**	33	30	30	27	39	34	38	49	37	26
Not Very Much	4	2	1	3	2	2	2	4	**	2	2	2	2	1	4	3	3	2	1
Don't Know		2	2	3	2	2	3	2	**	2	1	1	1	0	1	1	0	1	1

**No data available for 1986 and 2006.

SOURCE: The American National Election Studies, 2009, http://www.electionstudies.org.

influenced by self-interest. Bureaucrats, politicians, and voters make choices that they believe will yield them expected marginal benefits that will be greater than their expected marginal costs. Of course, the private sector and the public sector differ when it comes to the "rules of the game" that they must follow. The self-interest assumption is, however, central to the analysis of behavior in both arenas.

Scarcity and the Public Sector

The self-interest assumption is not the only similarity between the market and public sectors. For example, scarcity is present in the public sector as well as in the private sector. Public schools and public libraries come at the expense of something else. While the cost to the consumer of a new park may seem free—zero price—like everything else, it has an opportunity cost. What else could that land been used for? Competition is also present in the public sector, as different government agencies compete for government funds and lobbyists compete with each other to get favored legislation through Congress.

The Individual Consumption-Payment Link

In private markets, when a shopper goes to the supermarket to purchase groceries, the shopping cart is filled with many different goods that the consumer presumably wants and is willing to pay for; the shopping cart reflects the individual consumption-payment link. The link breaks down when an assortment of political goods is decided on by majority rule. These political goods might include such items as additional national defense, additional money for the space program, new museums, new public schools, increased foreign aid, and so on. Even though an individual may be willing to pay for some of these goods, it is unlikely that she will want to consume or pay for everything placed in the political shopping cart. However, if the majority decides that these political goods are important, the individual will have to purchase the goods through higher taxes, whether she values the goods or not.

Majority Rule and the Median Voters

In a two-party system, the candidate with the most votes wins the election. Because voters are likely to vote for the candidate who holds views similar to theirs, candidates must pay close attention to the preferences of the majority of voters.

For example, in Exhibit 2, we assume a normal distribution, with a continuum of voter preferences from the liberal left to the conservative right. We can see from the figure that

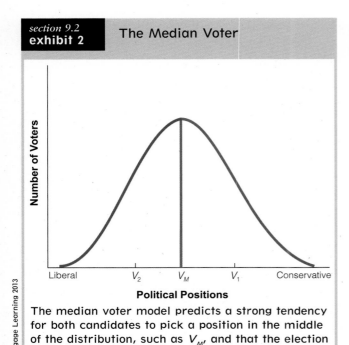

section 9.2
exhibit 2   The Median Voter

The median voter model predicts a strong tendency for both candidates to pick a position in the middle of the distribution, such as V_M, and that the election will be close.

© Cengage Learning 2013

median voter model
a model that predicts candidates will choose a position in the middle of the distribution

only a few are extremely liberal or extremely conservative. A successful campaign would have to address the concerns of the median voters (those in the middle of the distribution in Exhibit 2), resulting in moderate policies. For example, if one candidate ran a fairly conservative campaign, attracting voters at and to the right of V_1, an opponent could win by a landslide by taking a fairly conservative position just to the left of this candidate. Alternatively, if the candidate takes a liberal position, say V_2, then the opponent can win by campaigning just to the right of that position. In this case, it is easy to see that the candidate who takes the median position, V_M, is least likely to be defeated. Of course, the distribution does not have to be normal or symmetrical; it could be skewed to the right or left. Regardless of the distribution, however, the successful candidate will still seek out the median voters. In fact, the **median voter model** predicts a strong tendency for both candidates to choose a position in the middle of distribution, and therefore the election will be close. If the model predicts correctly, then the median voter will determine the outcome of the election, because those voters whose preferences are in the tails—the two extremes—will prefer the middle position rather than the other extreme position.

Of course, this model does not mean that all politicians will find or even attempt to find the median. Politicians, for example, may take different positions because they have arrived at different predictions of voter preferences or have merely misread public sentiment; or they may think they have the charisma to change voter preferences.

Voters and Rational Ignorance

Representative democracy provides a successful mechanism for making social choices in many countries. But some important differences are evident in the way democracy is ideally supposed to work and how it actually works.

One of the keys to an efficiently working democracy is a concerned and informed electorate. Everyone is supposed to take time to study the issues and candidates and then carefully weigh the relevant information before deciding how to vote. Although an informed citizenry is desirable from a social point of view, it is not clear that individuals will find it personally desirable to become politically informed.

Obtaining detailed information about issues and candidates is costly. Many issues are complicated, and a great deal of technical knowledge and information is necessary to make an informed judgment on them. To find out what candidates are really going to do requires a lot more than listening to their campaign slogans. It requires studying their past voting records, reading a great deal that has been written either by or about them, and asking them questions at public meetings. Taking the time and trouble to do these things—and more—is the cost that each eligible voter has to pay personally for the benefits of being politically informed. These costs may help to explain why the majority of Americans cannot identify their congressional representatives and are unlikely to be acquainted with their representatives' views on Social Security, health care, tariffs, and agricultural policies.

For many people, the costs of becoming politically informed are high, whereas the benefits are low. As a result, they limit their quest for political information to listening to the radio on the way to work, talking with friends, casual reading, and other things they would normally do anyway. Even though most people in society might be better off if every-

Are political goals and economic goals always the same?

one became more informed, it isn't worth the cost for most individuals to make the requisite effort to become informed themselves. Public choice economists refer to this lack of incentive to become informed as rational ignorance. People will generally make much more informed decisions as buyers than as voters. For example, you are likely to gather more information when making a decision on a car purchase than when you are deciding between candidates in an upcoming election. An uninformed decision on a car purchase will most likely affect your life much more than an uninformed decision on a candidate, especially when your vote will most likely not alter the outcome of the election. Because you cannot disbundle, you are voting for a candidate who takes a stand on many issues—that is, you are voting on a bundle of issues that are difficult to assess.

Can we predict what would happen to voter turnout on a day like this? Some potential voters might rationally decide to stay home if they perceive the cost of going to the polls outweighs the benefit.

The fact that one vote, especially in a state or national election, is highly unlikely to affect the outcome of the election may explain why some citizens choose not to vote. Many factors may determine the net benefits for voting, including candidates and issues on the ballot, weather, and distance to the polling booths. For example, we would certainly expect fewer voters to turn out at the polls on the day of a blizzard; the blizzard would change the net benefits. We would also expect more voters at the polls if the election were predicted to be a close one, with emotions running higher and voters perceiving their individual votes as more significant.

rational ignorance
lack of incentive to be informed

If the cost of being an informed voter is high and the benefits low, why do people vote? Many people vote for reasons other than to affect the outcome of the election. They vote because they believe in the democratic process and because of civic pride. In other words, they perceive that the benefits they derive from being involved in the political process outweigh the costs.

Furthermore, rational ignorance does not imply that people should not vote; it is merely one explanation for why some people do not vote. The point that public choice economists are making is that some people will vote only if they think that their vote will make a difference; otherwise, they will not vote.

Special Interest Groups

special interest groups
groups with an intense interest in particular voting issues that may be different from that of the general public

Even though many voters may be uninformed about specific issues, others may feel a strong need to be politically informed. Such individuals may be motivated to organize a special interest group. These groups may have intense feelings about and a degree of interest in particular issues that is at variance with the general public. However, as a group these individuals are more likely to influence decision makers and have a far greater impact on the outcome of a political decision than they would with their individual votes.

ECS
economic content standards

Incentives exist for political leaders to favor programs that entail immediate benefits and deferred costs; few incentives favor programs promising immediate costs and deferred benefits, even though they are sometimes economically more effective.

There are incentives for political leaders to implement policies that disperse costs widely over large groups of people and benefit small and politically powerful groups of people.

If a special interest group is successful in getting everyone else to pay for a project that benefits them, the cost will be spread over so large a number of taxpayers that the amount any one person will have to pay is negligible. Hence, the motivation for an individual citizen to spend the necessary time and effort to resist an interest group is minimal, even if she had a guarantee that this resistance would be effective.

Public choice economists believe that if government becomes a vehicle for promoting special interests, it fails in its primary responsibility of expanding opportunities for all. That is, instead of creating opportunities to benefit through productive cooperation with each other, government will have created the illusion that people can benefit at the the expense of each other. Public choice economists are not callously indifferent to the the social benefits that government can provide. In fact, the difference between public choice economists and those who see every social ill as justification for expanding government is not a difference in moral vision. Instead, it is a difference in their interpretation of how government works. Public choice economists lean toward less government not because they want less from government, but because they, like many others, want less waste from government.

Politicians and Logrolling

logrolling
exchanging votes to get support for legislation

Sometimes members of Congress engage in logrolling. Logrolling involves politicians trading votes for their legislation. For example, Representative A may tell Representative B that he will vote for her water bill if she votes for his new highway bill. Of course, if Representative B does not go along with Representative A's legislation, she runs the risk of not getting support for her legislation at a later date. Local projects such as federally funded dams, bridges, highways, housing projects, VA hospitals, job-training centers, and military bases are often pushed through Congress and state legislatures by logrolling.

The trading of votes could lead to an outcome where the majority of Congress now supports the economic interests of a few at the economic expense of many. This is especially true if the cost to the many is so low that they are rationally ignorant to the effects of rent-seeking behavior. Rent seeking occurs when individuals and firms use resources, like money and lobbyists, to influence government to grant them special privileges.

Why Is It Difficult to Reduce the Size of Government Programs?

It is very difficult politically to reduce government spending, even if the majority of the voters favor such a reduction. The reason is when people argue for cutting government spending, they invariably have in mind government programs other than the ones that benefit them. So any attempt to reduce government spending by reducing one program at a time generally meets strong resistance from those benefitting from the program under review and receives little support from the millions of taxpayers who will save but a few dollars each if the program were eliminated.

The best hope for controlling spending is presenting a political package that calls for a simultaneous reduction in many programs. If government has grown to a point that people feel they are not getting their money's worth from their taxes, many groups may be willing to see their programs reduced if it means some savings on the taxes paid to support everyone else's programs.

ECS
economic
content
standards

It is important to realize that governments, like markets, also have shortcomings and imperfections. Citizens should understand the sources of these imperfections, including the distribution of costs and benefits of some programs that lead to special-interest problems, the costs involved in gathering and using information about different candidates and government programs, and the incentives that can induce government leaders and employees to act in ways that do not promote the general national interest. Understanding this allows citizens to compare actual with ideal government performance and to decide about the appropriate role for federal, state, and local government.

⑦ SECTION QUIZ

1. The amount of information that is necessary to make an efficient choice is generally _____ in the public sector than in the private sector.

   a. less

   b. more

   c. the same

   d. None of the above is true.

2. Voters will tend to be _____ informed about their political choices than their private market choices, other things being equal.

   a. more

   b. equally

   c. less

   d. Any of the above are equally likely to be true.

(continued)

② SECTION QUIZ (Cont.)

3. The median voter result implies that

    a. elections will often be very close.

    b. elections will usually be landslides for the same party year after year.

    c. elections will usually be landslides, with victories alternating between parties each year.

    d. when the preferences of most voters change substantially, winning political positions will also tend to change.

    e. both (a) and (d) are true.

4. For a voter to become more informed on a political issue is likely to have _____ benefits and _____ costs than for similar market decisions, other things being equal.

    a. smaller; larger

    b. smaller; smaller

    c. larger; larger

    d. larger; smaller

5. Which of the following would tend to raise voter turnout?

    a. a blizzard or heavy rainstorm on election day

    b. an election that is expected to be a landslide

    c. the longer the wait is expected to be at the voting locations

    d. a feeling that the candidates are basically running on the same platforms

    e. None of the above would tend to raise voter turnout.

6. If there are far fewer sugar growers than sugar consumers,

    a. the growers are likely to be more informed and influential on policy than voters.

    b. the consumers are likely to be more informed and influential on policy than voters.

    c. individual sugar growers are likely to have more at stake than individual sugar consumers.

    d. individual sugar consumers are likely to have more at stake than individual sugar growers.

    e. Because (c) is likely to be true, (a) is also likely to be true.

---

1. What principles does the public choice analysis of government behavior share with the economic analysis of market behavior?

2. Why is the tendency strong for candidates to choose positions in the middle of the distribution of voter preferences?

3. Why is it rational to be relatively less informed about most political choices than about your own market choices?

4. Why can't the majority of citizens effectively counter the political power of special interest groups?

Answers: 1. b 2. c 3. e 4. a 5. d 6. e

Interactive Summary

Fill in the blanks:

1. Governments obtain revenue through two major avenues: _____ and _____.

2. The government share of GDP changed _____ between 1970 and 2000, but its composition has changed _____.

3. From 1968 to 2005, national defense spending as a fraction of GDP _____.

4. By the mid-1970s, for the first time in history, roughly half of government spending in the United States was for _____.

5. Income transfer payments _____ in the 1980s and 1990s.

6. _____ and _____ account for roughly half of state and local government expenditures.

7. At the federal level, _____ half of taxes are from personal income taxes and corporate income taxes.

8. The United State relies _____ heavily on income-based taxes than most other developed countries in the world.

9. If a higher-income person paid the same taxes as a lower-income person, that tax would be considered _____.

10. Excise taxes are considered regressive because lower-income people spend a(n) _____ fraction of their incomes on such taxes than do higher-income people.

11. Sales taxes account for _____ state and local tax revenue than property taxes.

12. Most people agree that the tax system should be based on either _____ or _____.

13. When people with different levels of income are treated differently, it is called _____ equity.

14. Federal income tax is a good example of the _____ principle.

15. The _____ principle means that the individuals receiving the benefits are those who pay for them.

16. The _____ burden of a tax leads to a dead-weight loss.

17. With a(n) _____ tax, individuals are taxed on what they take out of the economy, not on what they put in.

18. Public choice theory is the application of _____ principles to politics.

19. Public choice economists believe that the behavior of individuals in politics, as in the marketplace, will be influenced by _____.

20. The amount of information that is necessary to make an efficient decision is much _____ in political markets than in private markets.

21. In private markets, an individual _____ link indicates that the goods consumers get reflect what they are willing to pay for.

22. Even though actors in both the private and public sectors are _____, the _____ are different.

23. A successful political campaign would have to address the concerns of the _____ voters.

24. _____ implies that most private-sector buyers will tend to be more informed than voters on a given issue.

25. If voters were _____ informed, special-interest groups would have less influence on political results, other things being equal.

26. Compared to private-sector decisions, acquiring information to make public-sector decisions will tend to have _____ benefits and _____ costs.

27. _____ positions tend to win in elections decided by majority votes.

Answers: 1. taxation; borrowing 2. little; considerably 3. fell 4. social concerns 5. increased 6. Education; public welfare 7. more than 8. more 9. regressive 10. larger 11. more 12. ability to pay; benefits received 13. vertical 14. ability to pay 15. benefits received 16. administrative 17. consumption 18. economic 19. self-interest 20. greater 21. consumption-payment 22. self-interested; "rules of the game" 23. median 24. Rational ignorance 25. more 26. smaller; larger 27. Middle-of-the-road

Key Terms and Concepts

progressive tax 243
regressive tax 243
excise tax 243
flat tax 243

ability-to-pay principle 244
vertical equity 244
median voter model 250
rational ignorance 251

special interest groups 251
logrolling 252

Section Quiz Answers

9.1 Public Finance: Government Spending and Taxation

1. Has federal government spending as a fraction of GDP changed much since the 1960s?
Overall federall government spending as a fraction of GDP has not changed much since the 1960s. However, the composition of federal government spending has changed, with substantial decreases in national defense spending and substantial increases in income security spending, such as for Social Security and Medicare.

2. What finances the majority of federal government spending?
The majority of federal government spending is financed by taxes on personal and corporate incomes, although payroll taxes have risen substantially in recent years.

3. What happens to the proportion of income paid as taxes when income rises, for a progressive tax? What is an example of such a progressive tax?
A progressive tax is one that takes an increasing proportion of income as income rises. The personal income tax is an example because higher-income earners pay a larger proportion of their incomes than lower-income earners.

4. Why are excise taxes on items such as alcohol, tobacco, and gasoline considered regressive taxes?
Lower-income people pay a larger fraction of their incomes for such items, so that they pay a larger fraction of their incomes for taxes on those items, even though all users pay the same tax rate on them.

5. How could a flat tax also be a progressive tax?
With a standard allowance or deduction amount, a proportional tax on taxable income would represent

a larger fraction of total income for a high-income earner than for a low-income earner.

6. Why is the federal income tax an example of the ability to pay principle?
Higher-income people, with a greater ability to pay, pay a larger fraction of their income in taxes.

7. How is a gas tax an example of the benefits received principle?
Those who drive more benefit more from the highway system, but they also pay more in total gasoline taxes.

9.2 Public Choice

1. What principles does the public choice analysis of government behavior share with the economic analysis of market behavior?
Public choice analysis of government behavior is based on the principle that the behavior of individuals in politics, just like that in the marketplace, is influenced by self-interest. That is, it applies basic economic theory to politics, looking for differences in incentives to explain people's behavior.

2. Why is the tendency strong for candidates to choose positions in the middle of the distribution of voter preferences?
This is what we would predict from the median voter model, because the candidate closer to the median is likely to attract a majority of the votes.

3. Why is it rational to be relatively less informed about most political choices than about your own market choices?
It is rational to be relatively less informed about most political choices because the costs of becoming more informed about political issues tend to be higher and the benefits of becoming more informed about political choices tend to be lower than for your own market choices.

4. Why can't the majority of citizens effectively counter the political power of special interest groups?

The majority of citizens can't effectively counter the political power of special interest groups because even if a special interest group is successful in getting everyone else to pay for a project that benefits that group, the cost to each citizen will be small. In fact, this cost is very likely to be far smaller than the cost to a member of the majority of becoming sufficiently informed and active to successfully oppose it.

Problems

1. Why would means-tested transfer payments (such as food stamps, in which benefits are reduced as income rises) act like an income tax facing recipents?

2. Why are income taxes more progressive than excise taxes such as those on alcohol, tobacco, and gasoline?

3. Why is the Social Security payroll tax considered regressive?

4. Could the burdens of a regulation be either progressive or regressive, like the effects of a tax?

5. Is a gas tax better described as reflecting the ability-to-pay principle or the benefits-received principle? What about the federal income tax?

6. Why would the benefits-received principle be difficult to apply to national defense and the provision of the justice system?

7. Illustrate the median voter model graphically and explain it.

8. Why would a candidate offering "a choice, not an echo," run a risk of losing in a landslide?

9. Why might the party favorites at a political convention sometimes be harder to elect than more moderate candidates?

10. How can you be forced to pay for something you do not want to "buy" in the political sector? Is this sometimes good?

11. Why does the creation of a government program create a special interest group, which makes it difficult to reduce or eliminate it in the future?

12. Why are college students better informed about their own teachers' and schools' policies than about national education issues?

13. Why do you think news reporters are more informed than average citizens about public policy issues?

© SIMON McCOMB/STONE/GETTY IMAGES, INC.

part 4

Macroeconomic Foundations

Introduction to Macroeconomics: Unemployment, Inflation, and Economic Fluctuations

AP PHOTO

Now we focus our attention on macroeconomics and, in particular, on two key concepts that are at the heart of macroeconomics and economic policymaking—unemployment and inflation. To those who have just lost a job, unemployment ranks high on the stress meter. To an elderly person who is living on a fixed income, inflation and the loss of purchasing power may be just as threatening.

In this chapter, we see how economists define unemployment and inflation and consider the problems associated with each. In the last section of the chapter, we examine the short-run fluctuations in the economy—the so-called business cycle.

Macroeconomic Goals 10.1

📂 What are the most important macro economic goals in the United States?

📂 How has the United States shown its commitment to these goals?

Three Major Macroeconomic Goals

Recall from Chapter 1 that macroeconomics is the study of the whole economy—the study of the forest, not the trees. Nearly every society has been interested in three major macroeconomic goals: (1) maintaining employment of human resources at relatively high levels, meaning that jobs are relatively plentiful and financial suffering from lack of work and income is relatively uncommon; (2) maintaining prices at a relatively stable level so that consumers and producers can make better decisions; and (3) achieving a high rate of economic growth, meaning a growth in output per person over time. We use the term **real gross domestic product (RGDP)** to measure output or production. The term *real* is used to indicate that the output is adjusted for the general increase in prices over time. Technically, gross domestic product (GDP) is defined as the total value of all final goods and services produced in a given period of time, such as a year or a quarter. Accomplishing smooth, rapid economic growth in an environment of stable prices and low unemployment is no easy task. Sometimes the cure for one problem comes at the expense of another. In the coming chapters we will discuss the causes and possible remedies for high inflation, high unemployment, and sluggish economic growth.

© Flying Colours Ltd/Jupiterimages

What do economists mean by "real" in real gross domestic product?

real gross domestic product (RGDP)
the total value of all final goods and services produced in a given period, such as a year or a quarter, adjusted for inflation

Acknowledging Our Goals: The Employment Act of 1946

Many economic problems—particularly those involving unemployment, price instability, and economic stagnation—are pressing concerns for the U.S. government. The **Employment Act of 1946** and the Full Employment and Balanced Growth Act of 1978 (the Humphrey–Hawkins Act) commit the U.S. government to pursue policies that will lead to full employment and stable prices. This legislation was the first formal acknowledgment of these primary macroeconomic goals.

Employment Act of 1946
a commitment by the federal government to pursue both full employment and stable prices

---

②SECTION QUIZ

1. Which is *not* one of society's major economic goals?

   a. maintaining employment at high levels

   b. maintaining prices at a stable level

   c. maintaining a high rate of economic growth

   d. All of the above are major economic goals of society.

   (continued)

② SECTION QUIZ (Cont.)

2. The three major macroeconomic goals of nearly every society are

   a. maintaining stable prices, reducing interest rates, and achieving a high rate of economic growth.

   b. maintaining high levels of employment, increasing the supply of money, and achieving a high rate of economic growth.

   c. maintaining stable prices, maintaining high levels of employment, and achieving high rates of economic growth.

   d. achieving high rates of economic growth, reducing unemployment, and reducing interest rates.

3. Economic growth is measured by changes in

   a. nominal GDP.

   b. the money supply.

   c. real GDP per capita.

   d. the rate of unemployment.

   e. none of the above.

4. High rates of unemployment

   a. can lead to increased tensions and despair.

   b. result in the loss of some potential output in society.

   c. reduce the possible level of consumption in society.

   d. represent a loss of efficiency in society.

   e. All of the above are true.

1. What are the three major economic goals of most societies?

2. What is the Employment Act of 1946? Why was it significant?

Answers: 1. d 2. c 3. c 4. e

10.2

Employment and Unemployment

🗁 What are the consequences of unemployment?

🗁 What is the unemployment rate?

🗁 Does unemployment affect everyone equally?

🗁 What causes unemployment?

🗁 How long are people typically unemployed?

The Consequences of High Unemployment

Unemployment figures are reported by the U.S. Department of Labor on a monthly basis. News of lower unemployment usually sends stock prices higher; and the news of higher unemployment usually sends stock prices lower. Politicians are also concerned about the unemployment figures because elections often hinge precariously on whether unemployment has been rising or falling.

Nearly everyone agrees that it is unfortunate when a person who wants a job cannot find one. A loss of a job can mean financial insecurity and a great deal of anxiety. High rates of unemployment in a society can increase tensions and despair. A family without income from work undergoes great suffering; as a family's savings fade, family members wonder

What are some of the political and social implications of high unemployment?

where they are going to obtain the means to survive. Society loses some potential output of goods when some of its productive resources—human or nonhuman—remain idle, and potential consumption is reduced. Clearly, then, a loss in efficiency occurs when people willing to work and equipment able to produce remain idle. That is, other things being equal, relatively high rates of unemployment are viewed almost universally as undesirable.

What Is the Unemployment Rate?

When discussing unemployment, economists and politicians refer to the **unemployment rate**. To calculate the unemployment rate, you must first understand another important concept— the **labor force**. The labor force is the number of people over the age of 16 who are available for employment, as shown in Exhibit 1. The civilian labor force figure excludes people in the armed services and those in prisons or mental hospitals. Other people regarded as outside the labor force include homemakers, retirees, and full-time students. These groups are excluded from the labor force because they are not considered currently available for employment.

When we say that the unemployment rate is 5 percent, we mean that 5 percent of the population over the age of 16 who are willing and able to work are unable to get jobs. This 5 percent means that 5 out of 100 people in the total labor force are unemployed. To calculate the unemployment rate, we simply divide the number of unemployed by the number in the civilian labor force:

$$\text{Unemployment rate} = \frac{\text{Number of unemployed}}{\text{Civilian labor force}}$$

In August 2011, the number of civilians unemployed in the United States was 14 million, and the civilian labor force totaled 153.6 million. Using these data, we can calculate that the unemployment rate in August 2011 was 9.1 percent:

$$\text{Unemployment rate} = 14 \text{ million}/153.6 \text{ million}$$
$$= 0.091 \times 100 = 9.1 \text{ percent}$$

The Worst Case of U.S. Unemployment

By far, the worst employment downturn in U.S. history occurred during the Great Depression, which began in late 1929 and continued until 1941. Unemployment rose from only 3.2 percent of the labor force in 1929 to more than 20 percent in the early 1930s,

unemployment rate
the percentage of the population aged 16 and older who are willing and able to work but are unable to obtain a job

labor force
the number of people aged 16 and over who are available for employment

How do you calculate the unemployment rate?

ECS
economic content standards

The unemployment rate is the percentage of the labor force that is willing and able to work, does not currently have a job, and is actively looking for work.

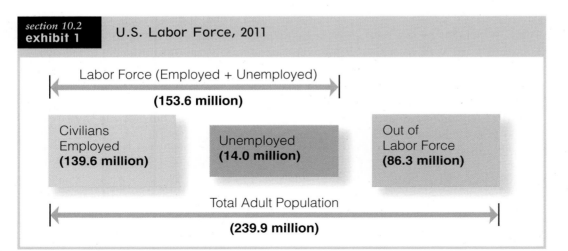

section 10.2
exhibit 1   U.S. Labor Force, 2011

Labor Force (Employed + Unemployed)
(153.6 million)

| Civilians Employed **(139.6 million)** | Unemployed **(14.0 million)** | Out of Labor Force **(86.3 million)** |

Total Adult Population
(239.9 million)

SOURCE: Bureau of Labor Statistics, August 2011.

in the news   Joblessness and Hopelessness

. . . Researchers have long sought to understand the possible link between unemployment and suicide. As layoffs surged late in 2008, the *Suicide Prevention Resource Center*, a group based in D.C. and Massachusetts that helps organizations develop suicide prevention programs, reviewed two decades' worth of research on the question. It found that a "strong relationship exists between unemployment, the economy, and suicide."

But, the group cautioned, it's never just one factor that drives people to the edge.

"Economic circumstances themselves are insufficient to cause a suicide; in fact, we do not know of any single factor that is sufficient on its own to 'cause' a suicide," says an SPRC memo based on the research. "Stressors such as the loss of a job, a home, or retirement security can result in shame, humiliation or despair, and in that context, can precipitate suicide attempts in those who are already vulnerable or do not have sufficient resources to draw on for support."

A new *study by the Centers for Disease Control and Prevention* finds that the suicide rate from 1928 to 2007 has risen and fallen in tandem with the business cycle. It spiked at the onset of the Great Depression, rising to its all-time high in 1933. It fell during the expansionary World War II period from 1939 to 1945. It rose during the oil crisis of the early '70s and the double-dip recession of the early '80s, and fell to its lowest level ever during the booming '90s.

"Economic problems can impact how people feel about themselves and their futures as well as their relationships with family and friends. Economic downturns can also disrupt entire communities," the study's author, Feijun Luo, an economist in the CDC's Division of Violence Prevention, says in a statement. "We know suicide is not caused by any one factor—it is often a combination of many that lead to suicide."

Has suicide spiked during the worst recession since the Great Depression started in 2007? The government's official numbers lag, so it's too early to answer that question. According to the most recent data—a preliminary estimate the CDC released in March—suicide ticked up slightly in 2009, becoming the 10th leading cause of death in the United States. Suicides accounted for 11.7 of every 100,000 deaths in 2009, up from 11.6 deaths the previous year and 11.3 in 2007.

A recent paper by Timothy J. Classen of Loyola University Chicago and Richard A. Dunn of Texas A&M found that mass layoffs and long spells of unemployment specifically were associated with increased suicide risk. That study relied on data from 1996 to 2005.

In this recession, the long-term unemployment rate (defined by the government as jobless spells lasting at least six months) has soared to unprecedented levels. More than 6 million people—nearly half the total unemployed in March—had been out of work that long. And more than a million people have been out of work for 99 weeks or longer, passing the maximum limit for unemployment insurance. The ranks of the long-term jobless keep growing even as the unemployment rate goes down.

"Given our findings for a slightly earlier time period, I would be concerned that the increasing rate of long-term unemployment in the United States is having important consequences on the mental health of many American workers, and I would be concerned that we are going to see increased rate of suicide because of it," Dunn says. "We won't be able to study this until the latest data comes out, but we won't have that data for another two or three years."

Comment: Good economic policies can save lives.

SOURCE: "Joblessness and Hopelessness: The Link Between Unemployment and Suicide," Arthur Delaney, *The Huffington Post*, April 15, 2011. Reprinted by permission of *The Huffington Post*.

and double-digit unemployment persisted through 1941. The debilitating impact of having millions of productive people out of work led Americans (and people in other countries as well) to say, "Never again." Some economists would argue that modern macroeconomics, with its emphasis on the determinants of unemployment and its elimination, truly began in the 1930s.

Variations in the Unemployment Rate

Exhibit 2 shows U.S. unemployment rates over the last 49 years. Unemployment since 1960 ranged from a low of 3.5 percent in 1969 to a high of 10.8 percent in 1982. The financial crisis of 2008 led to unemployment rates of 9.4 percent by mid-2009. Unemployment in the worst years is two or more times what it is in good years. Before 1960, variations in unemployment were more pronounced.

Are Unemployment Statistics Accurate Reflections of the Labor Market?

In periods of prolonged recession, some individuals think that the chances of landing a job are so bleak that they quit looking. These people are called **discouraged workers.** Individuals who have not actively sought work for four weeks are not counted as unemployed; instead, they fall out of the labor force. Also, people looking for full-time work who grudgingly settle for part-time jobs are counted as "fully" employed, even though they are only "partly" employed. At least partially balancing these two biases in government employment statistics, however, is the number of people who are overemployed—that is, working overtime or at more than one job. Also, a number of jobs in the underground economy (e.g., drug dealing, prostitution, gambling, and so on) are not reported. In addition, many people may claim they are seeking work when, in fact, they may just be going through the motions so they can continue to collect unemployment compensation or receive other government benefits.

discouraged worker
an individual who has left the labor force because he or she could not find a job

Are discouraged workers unemployed?

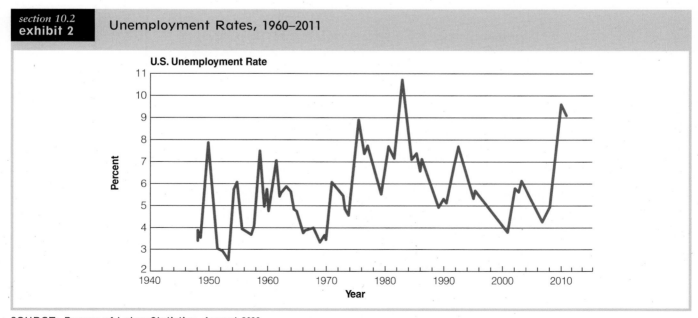

section 10.2
exhibit 2   Unemployment Rates, 1960–2011

U.S. Unemployment Rate

SOURCE: Bureau of Labor Statistics, August 2011.

Teenagers have the highest rates of unemployment. Do you think it would be easier for them to find jobs if they had more experience and higher skill levels?

ECS

economic content standards

The unemployment rate is an imperfect measure of unemployment. Reasons for this are that (1) it doesn't include workers whose job prospects are so poor that they are discouraged from seeking jobs, and (2) it fails to reflect part-time workers who are looking for full-time work.

job loser
an individual who has been temporarily laid off or fired

job leaver
a person who quits his or her job

reentrant
an individual who worked before and is now reentering the labor force

new entrant
an individual who has not held a job before but is now seeking employment

Who Are the Unemployed?

Unemployment usually varies greatly across different segments of the population and over time.

Education as a Factor in Unemployment

According to the Bureau of Labor Statistics, the unemployment rate across the sexes and races among college graduates is significantly lower than for those who do not complete high school. In August 2011, the unemployment rate for individuals without high school diplomas was 14.3 percent, compared with 4.3 percent for those with bachelor's degrees and higher. Further, college graduates have lower unemployment rates than people who have some college education but did not complete their bachelor's degrees (8.2 percent).

Age, Sex, and Race as Factors in Unemployment

The incidence of unemployment varies widely among the population. Unemployment tends to be greater among the very young, among blacks and other minorities, and among workers with few skills. The unemployment rate for adult females tends to be higher than that for adult males.

Considering the great variations in unemployment for different groups in the population, we calculate separate unemployment rates for groups classified by sex, age, race, family status, and type of occupation. Exhibit 3 shows unemployment rates for various groups. Note that the variation around the average unemployment rate for the total population of 9.1 percent was considerable. The unemployment rate for blacks was much higher than the rate for whites, a phenomenon that has persisted throughout the post–World War II period. Unemployment among teenagers was much higher than adult unemployment, at 25.4 percent.

Categories of Unemployed Workers

According to the Bureau of Labor Statistics, the four main categories of unemployed workers are **job losers** (those who have been temporarily laid off or fired), **job leavers** (those who have quit their jobs), **reentrants** (those who worked before and are reentering the labor force), and **new entrants** (those entering the labor force for the first time—primarily teenagers). It is a common misconception that most workers are unemployed because they have lost their jobs. Although job losers may typically account for 50 to 60 percent of the unemployed, a sizable fraction is due to job leavers, new entrants, and reentrants, as seen in Exhibit 4.

How Much Unemployment?

Even though unemployment is painful to those who have no source of income, reducing unemployment is not costless. In the short run, a reduction in unemployment may come at the expense of a higher rate of inflation, especially if the economy is close to full capacity, where resources are almost fully employed. Moreover, trying to match employees with jobs can quickly lead to significant inefficiencies, because of mismatches between a worker's skill level and the level of skill required for a job. For example, the economy would be wasting

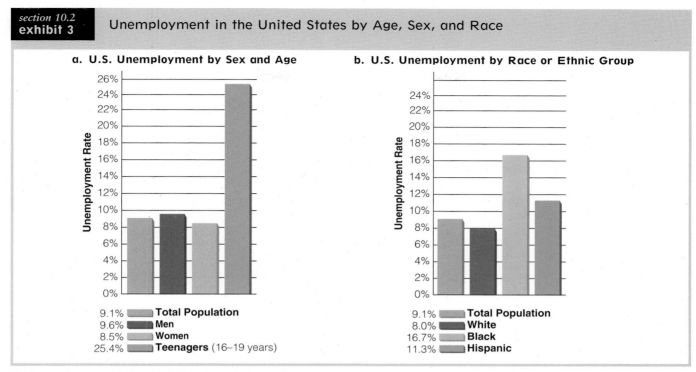

section 10.2
exhibit 3   Unemployment in the United States by Age, Sex, and Race

a. U.S. Unemployment by Sex and Age

Unemployment Rate

9.1% ▭ Total Population
9.6% ▰ Men
8.5% ▰ Women
25.4% ▰ Teenagers (16–19 years)

b. U.S. Unemployment by Race or Ethnic Group

Unemployment Rate

9.1% ▭ Total Population
8.0% ▰ White
16.7% ▰ Black
11.3% ▰ Hispanic

SOURCE: Bureau of Labor Statistics, August 2011.

resources subsidizing education if people with PhDs in bio-chemistry were driving taxis or tending bars. That is, the skills of the employee may be higher than those necessary for the job, resulting in what economists call **underemployment**. Another source of inefficiencies is placing employees in jobs beyond their abilities.

Because of the problems associated with accurately measuring the unemployment rate the Bureau of Labor Statistics (BLS) calculates alternative measures of labor underutilization, as shown in Table 1.

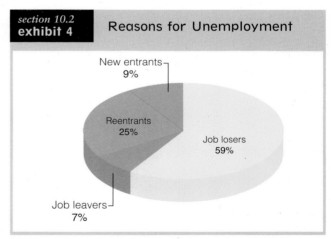

section 10.2
exhibit 4   Reasons for Unemployment

New entrants 9%
Reentrants 25%
Job losers 59%
Job leavers 7%

SOURCE: Bureau of Labor Statistics, August 2011.

How Long Are People Usually Unemployed?

The duration of unemployment is equally as important as the amount of unemployment. The financial consequences of a head of household being unemployed for four or five weeks are usually not extremely serious, particularly if the individual is covered by an unemployment compensation system. The impact becomes much more serious if that person is unemployed for several months. Therefore, it is useful to look at the average duration of unemployment to discover what percentage of the labor force is unemployed longer than a certain period, say 15 weeks. Exhibit 5 presents data on the duration of unemployment. As you can see in this table, 19.6 percent of the unemployed were out of work less than five weeks, and 42.9 percent of the total unemployed were out of work for more than six months. The duration of unemployment tends to be greater when the amount of unemployment is high and smaller when the amount of unemployment is low. For example, in 2000 when the economy had low levels of unemployment, 45 percent

underemployment
a situation in which a worker's skill level is higher than necessary for a job

Which groups tend to have the highest rate of unemployment?

Table 1	Alternative Measures of Labor Underutilization	
Measure and Description		**Rate**
U-1 Persons unemployed 15 weeks or longer, as a percent of the civilian labor force		5.4
U-2 Job losers and persons who completed temporary jobs, as a percent of the civilian labor force		5.3
U-3 Total unemployed, as a percent of the civilian labor force (official unemployment rate)		9.1
U-4 Total unemployed plus discouraged workers, as a percent of the civilian labor force plus discouraged workers		9.7
U-5 Total unemployed, plus discouraged workers, plus all other persons marginally attached to the labor force, as a percent of the civilian labor force plus all persons marginally attached to the labor force		10.6
U-6 Total unemployed, plus all persons marginally attached to the labor force, plus total employed part time for economic reasons, as a percent of the civilian labor force plus all persons marginally attached to the labor force		16.2

Bureau of Labor Statistics definitions:

Marginally attached workers: persons who currently are neither working nor looking for work but indicate that they want and are available for a job and have looked for work sometime in the past 12 months.

Discouraged workers: a subset of the marginally attached. These are persons who have given a job-market-related reason for not currently looking for work.

Persons employed part time for economic reasons: those who want and are available for full-time work but have had to settle for a part-time schedule.

SOURCE: U.S. Bureau of Labor Statistics, August 2011.

What has been the trend in the gender make-up of labor force participation?

of the unemployed had been unemployed for less than 5 weeks and 77 percent less than 15 weeks. Unemployment of any duration, of course, means a potential loss of output. This loss of current output is permanent; it is not made up when unemployment starts falling again.

Labor Force Participation Rate

The percentage of the working age (over 16 years of age) population that is in the labor force is what economists call the **labor force participation rate**. Since 1950, the labor force participation rate has increased from 59.2 percent to 64 percent today. During this time, the gender makeup of the labor force participation rate has changed significantly. For example, the number of women working shifted dramatically, reflecting the changing role of women in the workforce. Some factors contributing to this dramatic change are technological advances in household appliances and the decline in average household size. In addition, throughout this period, women have increasingly attained higher levels of education and experienced an increase in their earnings as a proportion of men's earnings. In Exhibit 6, we see that in 1950 less than 34 percent of women were working or looking for work. In 2011 that figure was roughly 60 percent. In 1950, more than 85 percent of men were working or looking for work. In 2011 the labor force participation rate for men fell to roughly 70 percent, as many men stay in school longer and opt to retire earlier.

labor force participation rate
the percentage of the working age population in the labor force

section 10.2 exhibit 5	Duration of Unemployment
Duration	**Percent Unemployed**
Less than 5 weeks	19.6%
5 to 14 weeks	21.7
15 to 26 weeks	15.9
27 weeks and over	42.9

SOURCE: Bureau of Labor Statistics, September 2011.

section 10.2 exhibit 6	Labor Force Participation Rates for Men and Women						
	1950	**1960**	**1970**	**1980**	**1990**	**2000**	**2011**
Total	59.2%	59.4%	60.4%	63.8%	66.4%	67.1%	64.0%
Men	86.4	83.3	79.7	77.4	76.1	64.8	70.4
Women	33.9	37.7	43.3	51.5	57.5	59.9	58.0

SOURCE: Bureau of Labor Statistics, August 2011.

⑦ SECTION QUIZ

1. The unemployment rate is the number of people officially unemployed divided by
   a. the civilian labor force.
   b. the noninstitutional population.
   c. the total population.
   d. the number of people employed.
   e. none of the above.

2. The labor force consists of
   a. discouraged workers, employed workers, and those actively seeking work.
   b. all persons over the age of 16 who are working or actively seeking work.
   c. all persons over the age of 16 who are able to work.
   d. all persons over the age of 16 who are working, plus those not working.
   e. discouraged workers, part-time workers, and full-time workers.

3. Discouraged workers are considered
   a. unemployed.
   b. not in the labor force.
   c. in the labor force.
   d. both unemployed and in the labor force.
   e. unemployed but not in the labor force.

4. Which of these groups tends to have the lowest unemployment rate?
   a. teenagers
   b. those with some college education
   c. college graduates
   d. those with a high school diploma but no college experience

5. The largest fraction of those counted as unemployed is due to
   a. job losers.
   b. job leavers.
   c. new entrants.
   d. reentrants.

6. The official unemployment rate may overstate the extent of unemployment because
   a. it excludes discouraged workers.
   b. it counts part-time workers as fully employed.
   c. it does not count those with jobs in the underground economy as employed.
   d. it includes those who claim to be looking for work as unemployed, even if they are just going through the motions in order to get government benefits.
   e. of both (c) and (d).

(*continued*)

ⓆSECTION QUIZ(Cont.)

7. If unemployment benefits increase and encourages more people to claim they are looking for work when they really are not, then the measured unemployment rate will

   a. rise.

   b. fall.

   c. be unaffected.

   d. change in an indeterminate direction.

8. After looking for a job for more than eight months, Kyle became frustrated and stopped looking. Economists view Kyle as

   a. unemployed.

   b. part of the labor force, but neither employed nor unemployed.

   c. a discouraged worker.

   d. cyclically unemployed.

   e. both (b) and (c).

1. What happens to the unemployment rate when the number of unemployed people increases, *ceteris paribus*? When the labor force grows, *ceteris paribus*?

2. How might the official unemployment rate understate the "true" degree of unemployment? How might it overstate it?

3. Why might the fraction of the unemployed who are job leavers be higher in a period of strong labor demand?

4. Suppose you live in a community of 100 people. If 80 people are over 16 years old and 72 people are willing and able to work, what is the unemployment rate in this community?

5. What would happen to the unemployment rate if a substantial group of unemployed people started going to school full time? What would happen to the size of the labor force?

6. What happens to the unemployment rate when officially unemployed people become discouraged workers? Does anything happen to employment in this case?

Answers: 1. a 2. b 3. b 4. c 5. a 6. e 7. a 8. c

10.3

Types of Unemployment

🗀 What are the three types of unemployment?   🗀 What is cyclical unemployment?

🗀 What is frictional unemployment?   🗀 What is the natural rate of unemployment?

🗀 What is structural unemployment?

In examining the status of and changes in the unemployment rate, it is important to recognize that unemployment can take several forms. In this section, we will examine the three types of unemployment—frictional, structural, and cyclical—and evaluate the relative effects of each on the overall unemployment rate.

Is all unemployment the same?

frictional unemployment
the unemployment that results from workers searching for suitable jobs and firms looking for suitable workers

Frictional Unemployment

In a dynamic economy where people are constantly losing or leaving their jobs, some frictional unemployment is always present. **Frictional unemployment** is the temporary unemployment that results from the search time that occurs when people are searching for suitable jobs and firms are looking for suitable workers. People seeking work do not usually take the first job offered to them. Likewise, firms do not usually take the first person they interview. People and firms engage in a search to match up skills and interests. While the unemployed are looking, they are frictionally unemployed.

For example, consider an advertising executive who was fired in Chicago on March 1 and is now actively looking for similar work in San Francisco. Of course, not all unemployed workers were fired; some may have voluntarily quit their jobs. In either case, frictional unemployment is short term and results from normal turnover in the labor market, as when people change from one job to another.

Should We Worry about Frictional Unemployment?

A certain amount of frictional unemployment may be good for the economy, because workers who are temporarily unemployed may find jobs that are better suited to their skill level. Even though the amount of frictional unemployment varies somewhat over time, it is unusual for it to be much less than 2 percent of the labor force. Actually, frictional unemployment tends to be somewhat greater in periods of low unemployment, when job opportunities are plentiful. This high level of job opportunity stimulates mobility, which, in turn, creates some frictional unemployment.

Structural Unemployment

A second type of unemployment is structural unemployment. Like frictional unemployment, **structural unemployment** is related to occupational movement or mobility—in this case, to a lack of mobility. Structural unemployment occurs when workers lack the necessary skills for jobs that are available or have particular skills that are no longer in demand. For example, if a machine operator in a manufacturing plant loses his job, he could still remain unemployed despite the openings for computer programmers in his community. The quantity of unemployed workers conceivably could equal the number of job vacancies, with the unemployment persisting because the unemployed lack the appropriate skills. Given the existence of structural unemployment, it is wise to look at both unemployment and job vacancy statistics in assessing labor market conditions. Structural unemployment, like frictional unemployment, reflects the dynamic dimension of a changing economy. Over time, new jobs open up that require new skills, while old jobs that required different skills disappear. It is not surprising, then, that many people advocate government-subsidized retraining programs as a means of reducing structural unemployment.

Another reason for structural unemployment is that low-skilled workers are frequently unable to find desirable long-term employment. Some of these low-skilled jobs do not last long and involve little job training, so a worker may soon be looking for a new job. Because they acquired no new skill from the old job, they may be stuck without long-term secure work. That is, structural workers cannot be said to be "in-between jobs" like those who are frictionally unemployed. Structural unemployment is more long term and serious than frictional unemployment because these workers do not have marketable skills.

The dimensions of structural unemployment are debatable, in part because of the difficulty in precisely defining the term in an operational sense. Structural unemployment

ECS
economic content standards

Unemployment can be caused by people changing jobs, by seasonal fluctuations in demand, by changes in the skills needed by employers, or by cyclical fluctuations in the level of national spending.

How can a certain amount of unemployment be good for the economy?

structural unemployment the unemployment that results from workers not having the skills to obtain long-term employment

© KAREN KASMAUSKI/CORBIS

What type of unemployment would occur if these coal miners lost their jobs as a result of a permanent reduction in demand for coal and needed retraining to find other employment? Usually, structural unemployment occurs because of workers' lack of skills or long-term changes in demand. Consequently, it generally lasts for a longer period than does frictional unemployment.

varies considerably—sometimes it is low and at other times, as in the 1970s and early 1980s, it is high. To some extent, in the latter period, jobs in the traditional sectors such as automobile manufacturing and oil production were giving way to jobs in the computer and biotechnology sectors. Consequently, structural unemployment was higher.

Some Unemployment Is Unavoidable

How are structurally unem-ployed workers different from frictionally unemployed workers?

Some unemployment is actually normal and important to the economy. Frictional and structural unemployment are simply unavoidable in a vibrant economy. To a considerable extent, we can view both frictional and structural unemployment as phenomena result-ing from imperfections in the labor market. For example, if individuals seeking jobs and employers seeking workers had better information about each other, the amount of frictional unemployment would be considerably lower. It takes time for suppliers of labor to find the demanders of labor services, and it takes time and money for labor resources to acquire the necessary skills. But because information and job search are costly, bringing together demanders and suppliers of labor services does not occur instantaneously.

Cyclical Unemployment

cyclical unemployment
unemployment due to short-term cyclical fluctuations in the economy

Often, unemployment is composed of more than just frictional and structural unemploy-ment. In years of relatively high unemployment, some joblessness may result from short-term cyclical fluctuations in the economy. We call this type **cyclical unemployment**. Whenever the unemployment rate is greater than normal, such as during a recession, it is due to cyclical unemployment. Most attempts to solve the cyclical unemployment problem emphasized increasing aggregate demand to counter recession.

The Cost of Cyclical Unemployment

When the unemployment rate is high, numerous economic and social hardships result. The economic costs are the forgone output when the economy is not producing at its potential level. According to Okun's Law (really, a rule of thumb), a 1 percent increase in cyclical unemployment reduces output by 2 percentage points. Thus, we can actually estimate the eco-nomic costs of not producing at our potential output. The costs are particularly high for those groups with the least skills—the poorly educated and teenagers with little work experience.

The Natural Rate of Unemployment

What is the natural rate of unemployment? Can the natural rate of unemploy-ment change?

natural rate of unemployment
the median, or "typical," unemployment rate, equal to the sum of frictional and structural unemployment when they are at a maximum

It is interesting to observe that over the period in which annual unemployment data are avail-able, the median, or "typical," annual unemployment rate has been at or slightly above 5 per-cent. Some economists call this typical unemployment rate the **natural rate of unemployment**.

The current rate of unemployment (October 2011) is 9.1 percent, which is well above the natural rate of 5 percent. The natural rate does not necessarily mean that is the desirable rate; it merely refers to the rate that the economy normally experiences. The unemploy-ment rate will never be zero. There will always be some people without jobs even when the economy is performing well. Some will be transitioning between jobs, others will have lost jobs, and still others may quit to look for better jobs.

When unemployment rises well above 5 percent, we have abnormally high unemploy-ment; when it falls well below 5 percent, we have abnormally low unemployment. The natu-ral rate of unemployment of approximately 5 percent roughly equals the sum of frictional and structural unemployment when they are at their maximums. Thus, we can view unem-ployment rates below the natural rate as reflecting the existence of below-average levels of frictional and structural unemployment. When unemployment rises above the natural rate, however, it reflects the existence of cyclical unemployment. In short, the natural rate of unemployment is the unemployment rate when the economy is experiencing neither a recession nor a boom. The natural rate of unemployment is also called the *full-employment rate of unemployment*.

The natural rate of unemployment can change over time as technological, demographic, institutional, and other conditions vary. For example, as baby boomers age, the natural rate falls because middle-aged workers generally experience lower unemployment rates than do younger workers. In addition, the Internet and job placement agencies have improved access to employment information and allowed workers to find jobs more quickly. Also, the new work requirements of the welfare laws increased the number of people with jobs. Thus, the natural rate is not fixed, because it can change with demographic changes over time.

Full Employment and Potential Output

When all the resources of an economy—labor, land, and capital—are fully employed, the economy is said to be producing its **potential output**. Literally, *full employment of labor* means that the economy is providing employment for all who are willing and able to work

ECS

economic content standards

Why are some people unemployed when the economy is said to be functioning at full employment?

potential output
the amount of real output the economy would produce if its labor and other resources were fully employed, that is, at the natural rate of unemployment

---

use what you've learned Cyclical Unemployment

Q Are layoffs more prevalent during a recession than a recovery? Do most resignations occur during a recovery?

A Layoffs are more likely to occur during a recession. When times are bad, employers are often forced to let workers go. Resignations are relatively more prevalent during good economic times because more job opportunities are available to those seeking new jobs.

---

global watch Unemployment around the Globe, 2010

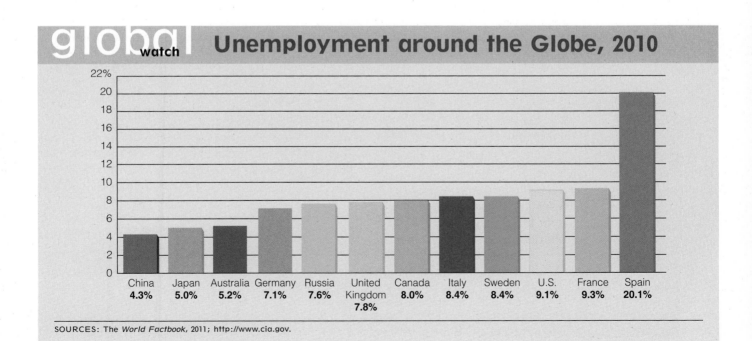

Country	China	Japan	Australia	Germany	Russia	United Kingdom	Canada	Italy	Sweden	U.S.	France	Spain
Rate	4.3%	5.0%	5.2%	7.1%	7.6%	7.8%	8.0%	8.4%	8.4%	9.1%	9.3%	20.1%

SOURCES: The *World Factbook*, 2011; http://www.cia.gov.

with no cyclical unemployment. It also means that capital and land are fully employed. That is, at the natural rate of unemployment, all resources are fully employed, the economy is producing its potential output, and no cyclical unemployment is present. It does not mean the economy will always be producing at its potential output of resources. For example, when the economy is experiencing cyclical unemployment, the unemployment rate is greater than the natural rate. It is also possible for the economy to temporarily exceed the natural rate, as workers put in overtime or moonlight by taking on extra jobs.

POLICY application   The Job Market

While the job market is improving slightly, one particular challenge faces labor markets: long-term unemployment. Long-term unemployment has reached nearly every segment of the population, but some groups have been hit particularly hard. The typical long-term unemployed worker is a white man with a high school education or less. Older unemployed workers also tend to be out of work longer. "The longer folks are out of a job, the longer it takes them to find a new one." What is particularly troubling for the long-term unemployed is that their skill levels deteriorate. Consequently, they are more likely to stop looking—becoming discouraged workers.

Education has not been a cure-all. More college graduates have become long-term unemployed. They represent 15.9 percent of the long-term jobless, compared with 14.9 percent of all unemployed workers. Those with high school degrees who haven't been to college comprise 40.7 percent of long-term unemployed, compared with 37.8 percent of all unemployed workers.

Worker mobility has fallen sharply. That is, the number of job seekers who successfully relocate for new positions has hit historically low levels. "What's unique in this job cycle is hires and fires are very low, and fewer people are quitting jobs," says Jeffrey Cleveland, senior economist at the investment firm Payden & Rygel. In addition, taking jobs in other cities is harder in this housing market, as more and more people decide to keep their homes.

In short, employers are frequently finding that job candidates don't have the right skills to match the jobs they have to offer.

One reason why corporations aren't hiring is the absence of clarity about the costs of financial and health-care regulations and the weakness of global growth. Austan Goolsbee, former White House Council of Economic Advisers chair, stated: "We've got to rely on government policies that are trying to leverage the private sector and give incentives to the private sector to be doing the growth." University of Chicago economist Raghuram Rajan says, "The truth is, there aren't many short-term fixes. The real answers to the jobs problem will take more time." And that means chronically high unemployment may persist.

The silver lining is that chronically high joblessness won't last forever. As incomes and wages in emerging markets rise, demand will rise, leading globally focused companies to begin increasing hiring in the United States.

SOURCES: Roya Wolverson, "Why Is Chronic Joblessness on the Rise?" *Time*, June 8, 2011. "http://curiouscapitalist.blogs.time.com/2011/06/08/is-chronic-joblessness-here-to-stay/"\l "ixzz1VUFUICdZ" http://curiouscapitalist.blogs.time.com/2011/06/08/is-chronic-joblessness-here-to-stay/#ixzz1VUFUICdZ.

Ben Tracy, "Chronic Unemployment Highest Since Great Depression," June 5, 2011, *CBS News.* http://www.cbsnews.com/stories/2011/06/05/eveningnews/main20069136.shtml.

Sara Murray, "Chronic Joblessness Bites Deep: Long-Term Unemployment Hits New High, Cuts Across Income Levels, Demographics," *The Wall Street Journal*, June 2, 2010. http://online.wsj.com/article/SB100014240527487039612 04575280753219161046.html?mod=WSJ_hpp_MIDDLENexttoWhatsNewsThird.

② SECTION QUIZ

1. Frictional unemployment is

   a. unemployment that is due to normal turnover in the labor market.

   b. unemployment caused by automation in the workplace.

   c. unemployment caused by lack of training and education.

   d. unemployment that is due to the friction of competing ideological systems.

   e. all of the above.

2. Unemployment caused by a contraction in the economy is called

   a. frictional unemployment.

   b. cyclical unemployment.

   c. structural unemployment.

   d. seasonal unemployment.

3. A federal program aimed at retraining the unemployed workers of the declining auto and steel industries is designed to reduce which type of unemployment?

   a. seasonal

   b. cyclical

   c. structural

   d. frictional

4. When unemployment rises above the natural rate, it reflects the existence of _____ unemployment.

   a. frictional

   b. structural

   c. seasonal

   d. cyclical

5. When an economy is operating at full employment,

   a. the unemployment rate will equal zero.

   b. frictional unemployment will equal zero.

   c. cyclical unemployment will equal zero.

   d. structural unemployment will equal zero.

   e. both (b) and (d) are correct.

6. The natural rate of unemployment would increase when which of the following increases?

   a. frictional unemployment

   b. structural unemployment

   c. cyclical unemployment

   d. any of the above

   e. either frictional or structural unemployment

7. If a nation's labor force receives a significant influx of young workers,

   a. the natural rate of unemployment is likely to increase.

   b. the natural rate of unemployment is likely to decrease.

   c. the natural rate of unemployment is unlikely to change.

   d. frictional unemployment will likely decrease to zero.

---

1. Why do we want some frictional unemployment?

2. Why might a job retraining program be a more useful policy to address structural unemployment than to address frictional unemployment?

(*continued*)

10.4

Reasons for Unemployment

📁 How does a higher minimum wage lead to greater unemployment among the young and unskilled?

📁 Can unions cause higher rates of unemployment?

📁 How does an efficiency wage cause a higher rate of unemployment?

📁 How do changes in job search costs affect the unemployment rate?

📁 Does unemployment insurance increase the unemployment rate?

In this section, we look at the causes of frictional and structural unemployment. In later chapters, we discuss the causes of cyclical unemployment.

Why Does Unemployment Exist?

Why do wages fail to balance the quantity of labor demanded with the quantity of labor supplied?

In many markets, prices adjust to the market equilibrium price and quantity, and no prolonged periods of shortage or surplus occur. However, in labor markets, obstacles prevent wages from adjusting and balancing the quantity of labor supplied and the quantity of labor demanded. In Exhibit 1, we see that W_1 is higher than the market equilibrium wage that equates the quantity demanded of labor with the quantity supplied of labor. At W_1, the quantity of labor supplied is greater than the quantity of labor demanded, resulting in an excess quantity supplied of labor—unemployment. That is, more people want to work at the going (nonequilibrium) wage than employers want to hire, and those who are seeking and not able to find work are "unemployed." Why? Economists cite three reasons for the failure of wages to balance the labor demand and labor supply equilibrium—minimum wages, unions, and the efficiency wage theory.

Minimum Wages and Unemployment

minimum-wage rate
an hourly wage floor set above the equilibrium wage

Many different types of labor markets exist for different types of workers. The labor market for workers with little experience and job skills is called the unskilled labor market. Suppose the government decided to establish a **minimum-wage rate** (an hourly wage floor) for unskilled workers above the equilibrium wage, W_E. At the minimum wage, the quantity of labor supplied grows because more people are willing to work at a higher wage. However, the quantity of labor demanded falls because some employers would find it unprofitable to hire low-skilled workers at the higher wage. At W_1, a gap exists between the quantity of labor demanded and the quantity supplied, representing a surplus of unskilled workers—unemployment, as seen in Exhibit 1. That is, workers are waiting for jobs to open up.

Because minimum wage-earners, a majority of whom are 25 years or younger, are a small portion of the labor force, most economists believe the effect of minimum wage on unemployment is small.

The Impact of Unions on the Unemployment Rate

Unions negotiate their wages and benefits collectively through their union officials, a process called collective bargaining. If, through this process of collective bargaining, union officials are able to increase wages, then unemployment will rise in the union sector. If the bargaining raises the union wage above the equilibrium level, the quantity of union labor demanded will decrease, and the quantity of union labor supplied will increase—that is, union workers will be unemployed. The union workers who still have their jobs will be better off, but some who are equally skilled will be unemployed and will either seek nonunion work or wait to be recalled in the union sector. Many economists believe that is why wages are approximately 15 percent higher in union jobs, even when nonunion workers have comparable skills. On the other hand, even though wages in the union sector are typically higher than the market wage, the presence of unions does not necessarily lead to greater unemployment because workers can find jobs in the nonunion sector. Less than 10 percent of private sector jobs are unionized.

section 10.4
exhibit 1   Wages Above Equilibrium Lead to Greater Unemployment

The labor market is in equilibrium where the quantity demanded of labor is equal to the quantity supplied of labor, at W_E and Q_E. If the wage persists above the equilibrium wage, a surplus of labor or unemployment of $Q_S \times Q_D$ exists. That is, at W_1, the quantity of labor supplied is greater than the quantity of labor demanded; we can think of this surplus of labor as unemployment.

© Cengage Learning 2013

Efficiency Wage

In economics, it is generally assumed that as productivity rises, wages rise, and workers can raise their productivity through investments in human capital like education and on-the-job training. However, some economists follow the **efficiency wage model**, which is based on the belief that *higher wages lead to greater productivity*.

In the efficiency wage model, employers pay their employees more than the equilibrium wage to be more efficient. Proponents of this theory suggest that it may lead to attracting the most productive workers, fewer job turnovers, and higher morale, which in turn can lead to lower hiring and training costs. In addition, higher paid workers may be healthier (better diets) and therefore more productive. This is particularly true in developing countries. In Exhibit 1, suppose workers are paid W_E. Why wouldn't they shirk at their current job if someone else will hire them almost immediately at the same wage? In short, there are few adverse consequences to shirking. One option for firms is to pay an efficiency wage. However, if all firms pay an efficiency wage, like W_1 in Exhibit 1, then why can't they just shirk and if fired, find another firm that will pay them W_1? The reason is because at W_1, firms are paying higher than the equilibrium wage, reducing the number of jobs, so fired workers might face a prolonged period of unemployment.

In 1914, Henry Ford increased his workers' wages from $3 to $5 per day—roughly twice the going wage rate for unskilled workers. This wage rate led to long lines of workers seeking jobs at the Ford plant—that is, quantity supplied greatly exceeded quantity demanded at the efficiency wage rate. Ford knew that assembly line work was boring,

efficiency wage model
theory stating that higher wages lead to greater productivity

and to overcome the problem he was having with morale and absenteeism, he decided to increase daily wages to $5 a day. At the time, many business leaders were skeptical because this put Ford's labor costs at nearly twice that of his rivals. However, Ford profits continued to mount. Historical records suggest that the efficiency wage led to lower turnover, less absenteeism, better hires, and less shirking—in short, greater worker productivity. Even though the higher wages led to higher labor costs, the costs were more than offset by the increase in worker productivity.

Some scholars have argued that the positive effects of the efficiency wage are unique to assembly line production and its high degree of worker interdependence. Furthermore, it is costly for firms to pay an efficiency wage, and firms must monitor their workers' efforts. If enough firms resort to paying the efficiency wage rate it leads to a surplus of workers who want jobs and cannot find them. This, like a binding minimum wage, leads to unemployment.

Job Search

When should a worker stop looking for a job and accept the best offer so far?

Another reason for unemployment has to do with the nature of labor markets. Because of frictional unemployment, some unemployment would exist even if labor supply and labor demand were balanced. Different firms offer different compensation packages (salary, fringe benefits, working conditions), and workers are sometimes unaware of these packages when they seek the "best" job available. It takes time and money to locate the best available opportunities. Also, not all job seekers are the same: They have different tastes and preferences about types of jobs and job locations. Sometimes it is difficult to get the information about particular jobs to the right job candidate. These search activities prolong the duration of unemployment. However, the search goes on because the job seeker hopes to find a better offer.

The labor demand and supply curves are constantly shifting. That is, labor markets are constantly in flux—people losing jobs, leaving jobs, reentering jobs. In a growing and dynamic economy, jobs are constantly being destroyed and created, leading to temporary unemployment as workers search for the best jobs for their skills.

Unemployment Insurance

Can unemployment insurance lead to prolonged unemployment? Does it reduce income uncertainty? Can it help workers find better matches for their skill set?

Losing a job can lead to considerable hardships, and unemployment insurance is designed to partially offset the severity of the unemployment problem. That is, unemployment insurance allows unemployed workers to maintain some income and spending, reducing hardships and the severity of a recession. The program does not cover those who were fired or quit their jobs. To qualify, recipients must have worked a certain length of time and lost their jobs because the employer no longer needed their skills. The typical compensation is half salary for 26 weeks. Although the program is intended to ease the pain of unemployment, it also leads to prolonged periods of unemployment, as job seekers stay unemployed for longer periods searching for new jobs.

For example, some unemployed people may show little drive in seeking new employment, because unemployment insurance lowers the opportunity cost of being unemployed. Say a worker making $600 a week when employed receives $300 in compensation when unemployed; as a result, the cost of losing the job is not $600 a week in forgone income but $300. It has been estimated that the existence of unemployment compensation programs may raise overall unemployment rates by as much as 1 percent.

Without unemployment insurance, a job seeker would be more likely to take the first job offered, even if the job did not match the job seeker's preferences or skill levels. A longer job search might mean a better match, but it comes at the expense of lost production and greater amounts of tax dollars.

Of course, that does not mean that unemployment insurance is necessarily a bad program. It still serves its desired goal of reducing income uncertainty. Workers that turn down unattractive jobs have an opportunity to find better jobs that may be better suited for their

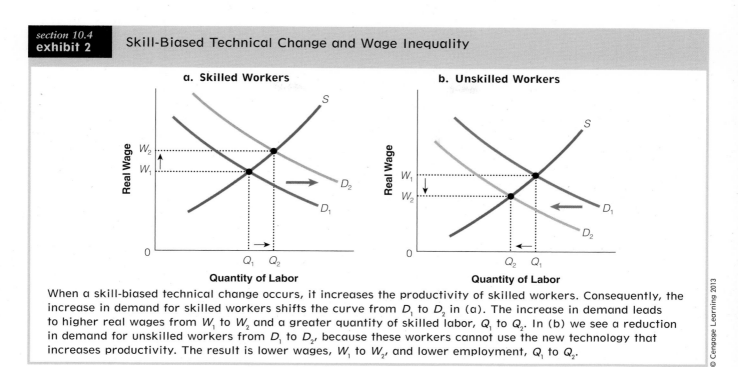

section 10.4
exhibit 2   **Skill-Biased Technical Change and Wage Inequality**

a. Skilled Workers

b. Unskilled Workers

(Real Wage axis, Quantity of Labor axis; curves S, D₁, D₂ with points W₂, W₁, Q₁, Q₂)

When a skill-biased technical change occurs, it increases the productivity of skilled workers. Consequently, the increase in demand for skilled workers shifts the curve from D_1 to D_2 in (a). The increase in demand leads to higher real wages from W_1 to W_2 and a greater quantity of skilled labor, Q_1 to Q_2. In (b) we see a reduction in demand for unskilled workers from D_1 to D_2, because these workers cannot use the new technology that increases productivity. The result is lower wages, W_1 to W_2, and lower employment, Q_1 to Q_2.

tastes and skills. In summary, most economists believe that eliminating unemployment insurance could reduce unemployment, but they disagree on whether economic well-being is reduced or enhanced by a change in the policy.

Does New Technology Lead to Greater Unemployment?

The widespread belief that technological advances inevitably result in the displacement of workers is not necessarily true. Generally, new inventions are cost saving, and these cost savings usually generate higher incomes for producers and lower prices and better products for consumers—benefits that ultimately result in the growth of other industries. If the new equipment is a substitute for labor, it might displace workers. For example, many fast-food restaurants installed self-service beverage bars to replace workers. However, new capital equipment requires new workers to manufacture and repair the new equipment. The most famous example of this trade-off is the computer, which was supposed to displace thousands of workers. Instead, the computer generated a whole new growth industry that created jobs. The problem is that it is easy to see only the initial effect of technological advances (displaced workers) but difficult to recognize the implications of that invention throughout the whole economy over time.

If jobs become more skill oriented, will this increase the wage inequality between low-skilled and high-skilled workers?

Some economists believe that some of the real wage differentials between skilled and unskilled workers in the last couple of decades are due to technical changes that are biased toward skilled workers. New machines, with highly sophisticated computerization, require highly skilled workers. Consequently, the new machines make these workers more productive and therefore they receive higher real wages. In Exhibit 2(a), we graph the labor market for skilled workers. Because of the increase in demand for skilled labor—skilled workers can produce more with the new machines—their real wages and employment are higher. At the same time, the demand is lower for workers who do not have the technical training to work with specialized machinery, and the demand for unskilled workers falls as seen in Exhibit 2(b). As a result of the decrease in demand for unskilled workers, real wages and employment fall. Thus, skill-biased technical change tends to create even greater disparities between the wages of skilled and unskilled workers. The message: stay in school (vocational or traditional).

⑦ SECTION QUIZ

1. Which of the following are reasons why wages may fail to bring the quantity of labor demanded into balance with the quantity of labor supplied?

    a. the minimum wage

    b. unions

    c. efficiency wage theory

    d. all of the above

2. Which of the following statements is true?

    a. At the minimum wage, the quantity of labor supplied grows because more people are willing to work at a higher wage.

    b. At the minimum wage, the quantity of labor demanded falls because some employers would find it unprofitable to hire low-skilled workers at the higher wage.

    c. Both (a) and (b) are true.

    d. None of the above is true.

3. Efficiency wages

    a. can lead to greater unemployment if the quantity of labor supplied is greater than the quantity of labor demanded.

    b. may attract the most productive workers.

    c. may lead to less turnover.

    d. may reduce morale problems.

    e. All of the above are true.

4. Unemployment insurance

    a. leads to lower rates of unemployment.

    b. may reduce the drive for workers to find jobs and thereby prolong unemployment.

    c. Both (a) and (b) are true.

    d. None of the above is true.

5. If unions are able to increase wages through collective bargaining, then

    a. some union workers will become unemployed.

    b. more union workers will be employed in the union sector.

    c. some union workers will be better off.

    d. both (a) and (c).

---

1. What are the three reasons for wages to fail to balance labor supply and labor demand?

2. What is an efficiency wage?

3. How do search costs lead to prolonged periods of unemployment?

4. Why would higher unemployment compensation in a country like France lead to higher rates of unemployment?

5. Does new technology increase unemployment?

Answers: 1. d 2. c 3. e 4. b 5. d

Inflation   10.5

📁 Why is the overall price level important?

📁 How did the price level behave during the previous century?

📁 What is the purpose of a price-level index?

📁 What problems are inherent with a price-level index?

📁 Who are the winners and losers during inflation?

📁 Can wage earners avoid the consequences of inflation?

Stable Price Level as a Desirable Goal

Just as full employment brings about one kind of economic security, an overall stable price level increases another form of economic security. Most prices in the U.S. economy tend to rise over time. The continuing rise in the overall price level is called **inflation**. Even when the level of prices is stable, some prices will be rising while others are falling. However, when inflation is present, the goods and services with rising prices will outweigh the goods and services with lower prices. Without stability in the price level, consumers and producers will experience more difficulty in coordinating their plans and decisions. When the *overall* price level is falling, it is called **deflation**. The average price level in the U.S. economy fell throughout the late nineteenth century.

A reduction in the rate of inflation is called *disinflation*. In the United States, we saw disinflation from 1981–1986, 1991–1994, and 2001–2003. It is difficult and costly to bring the inflation rate down once it has become expected. Most economists believe that the inflation rates of the 1970s were finally brought under control by the 1980–1981 recession, when the unemployment rate reached 10.7 percent. Thus, most believe the best policy is to not let inflation get out of control in the first place—one of the primary jobs of the Federal Reserve System.

In general, the only thing that can cause a *sustained* increase in the rate of inflation is a high rate of growth in money, a topic we will discuss thoroughly in upcoming chapters.

price level
the average level of prices in the economy

inflation
a rise in the overall price level, which decreases the purchasing power of money

deflation
a decrease in the overall price level, which increases the purchasing power of money

Measuring Inflation

We often use the term *purchasing power* when we discuss how much a dollar can buy of goods and services. In times of inflation, a dollar cannot buy as many goods and services. Thus, the higher the inflation rate, the greater the rate of decline in purchasing power.

In periods of high and variable inflation, households and firms have a difficult time distinguishing between changes in the **relative price** of individual goods and services (the price of a specific good compared to the prices of other goods) and changes in the general price level of all goods and services. Suppose the price of milk rises by 5 percent between 2010 and 2011, but the overall price level (inflation rate) increases by only 2 percent during that period. Then we could say that between 2010 and 2011, the relative price of milk rose only 3 percent (5 − 2 percent). The next year, the price of milk might increase 5 percent again, but the general inflation rate might be 6 percent. That is, between 2013 and 2014, the relative price of milk might actually fall by 1 percent (5 − 6 percent). Remember, the relative price is the price of a good relative to all other goods and services. Because of this difficulty in establishing relative prices, inflation distorts the information that flows from price signals. Does the good have a higher price because it has become relatively more scarce and therefore more valuable relative to other goods, or did the price rise along with all other prices because of inflation? This muddying of price information undermines good decision making.

Thus, we need a method to measure inflation. We adjust for the changing purchasing power of the dollar by constructing a **price index**. Essentially, a price index attempts to provide a measure of the prices paid for a certain bundle of goods and services over time.

relative price
the price of a specific good compared to the price of other goods

price index
a measure of the trend in prices paid for a certain bundle of goods and services over a given period

use what you've learned   Babe Ruth's Salary Adjusted for Inflation

AP PHOTO

Q To many baseball purists, Babe Ruth was the greatest player of the game, but how does his salary compare with the highest salary in baseball today? When Babe Ruth made $80,000 a year in 1931, he was asked by the press if he knew that his salary exceeded that of President Herbert Hoover. Ruth said, "Yes, I know. But I had a better year than President Hoover did."

A The Bureau of Labor Statistics computes CPI all the way back to 1913. The average CPI for 1931, the year Babe Ruth made $80,000, was 15.2. The average CPI for 2011 was 224. We can easily convert the Babe's salary into current dollars by performing the following calculation:

Babe Ruth's salary in 1931

$$\$80,000 \times \frac{\text{Price level in 2011}}{\text{Price level in 1931}}$$

$$= \$80,000 \times \frac{224}{15.2} = \$1,178,947$$

Therefore, the Babe would be making $1,178,947 a year if he were paid the same in 2011 as he was paid in 1931. Not bad, but not even close to what today's stars of the game are paid. At $27 million a year, Alex Rodriguez makes roughly 25 times Babe Ruth's adjusted salary.

---

section 10.5 exhibit 1   The Typical CPI Shopping Basket of Goods and Services

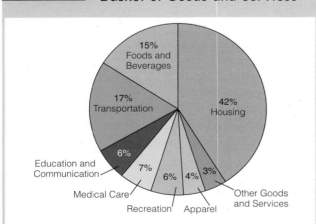

- 15% Foods and Beverages
- 17% Transportation
- 6% Education and Communication
- 7% Medical Care
- 6% Recreation
- 4% Apparel
- 3% Other Goods and Services
- 42% Housing

The Bureau of Labor Statistics divides the typical consumer's spending among various categories of goods and services.

SOURCE: U.S. Bureau of Labor Statistics.

consumer price index (CPI)
a measure of the cost of a market basket that represents the consumption of a typical household

The Consumer Price Index and the GDP Deflator

There are many different types of price indices. The most well-known index, the **consumer price index (CPI)**, measures the trend in the prices of certain goods and services purchased for consumption purposes—see Exhibit 1.

The **GDP deflator** corrects for changing prices in even broader terms. The GDP deflator measures the average level of prices of all final goods and services produced in the economy.

How Is a Price Index Created?

Constructing a price index is complicated. First, literally thousands of goods and services are in our economy; attempting to include all of them in an index would be cumbersome and make the index expensive to compute, and it would take a long time to gather the necessary data. Therefore, a "bundle" or "basket" of representative goods and services is selected by the index calculators (the Bureau of Labor Statistics of the U.S. Department of Labor for consumer and wholesale price indices; the Office of Business Economics of the Department of Commerce for the GDP deflator).

Calculating a Simple Price Index

Suppose a consumer typically buys 24 loaves of bread and 12 gallons of milk in a year. The following table lists the prices of bread and milk and the cost of the consumer's typical market basket in the years 2010–2012.

Year	Price of Bread	Price of Milk	Cost of Market Basket
2010	$1.00	$2.00	(24 × $1.00) + (12 × $2.00) = $48.00
2011	1.15	2.10	(24 × $1.15) + (12 × $2.10) = $52.80
2012	1.40	2.20	(24 × $1.40) + (12 × $2.20) = $60.00

Using the numbers from the table and the following formula, we can calculate a price index to measure the inflation rate.

$$\text{Price index} = \frac{\text{Cost of market basket in current year}}{\text{Cost of market basket in base year}} \times 100$$

The year 2010 is designated as the base year, so its value is set equal to 100.

Year	Price Index
2010	$48/$48 × 100 = 100
2011	$52.80/$48 × 100 = 110
2012	$60/$48 × 100 = 125

A comparison of the price indices shows that between 2010 and 2011, prices increased an average of 10 percent. In addition, between 2010 and 2012, prices rose 25 percent.

$$\text{Price index} = \frac{\text{Cost of market basket in 2012}}{\text{Cost of market basket in 2010}} \times 100$$
$$= \frac{\$60}{\$48} \times 100 = 125$$

That is, the price index for 2012 compared with 2010 is 125. Therefore, using the price index formula, we can say that prices are 25 percent higher in 2012 than they were in 2010, the base year.

Unfortunately, not all prices move by the same amount or in the same direction. Consequently, we need to calculate an average of the many price changes. This calculation is complicated by several factors. First, goods and services change in quality over time, so the observed price change may, in reality, reflect a quality change in the product rather than the purchasing power of the dollar. A $300 television set today is dramatically better than a television set in 1950. Second, new products come on the market and old products occasionally disappear. For example, color TV sets did not exist in 1950 but are a major consumer item now. How can we calculate changes in prices over time when some products did not even exist in the earlier period?

Clearly, calculating a price index is not a simple, direct process. As you can see from the *In the News* article ("A Better CPI"), many factors can potentially distort the CPI.

Producer Price Index

Economists also calculate the **producer price index**—a measure of the cost of goods and services bought by firms. Because firms often pass on part of their costs to consumers, this measure is useful in predicting changes in the CPI.

GDP deflator
a price index that helps measure the average price level of all final consumer goods and services produced

producer price index
a measure of the cost of goods and services bought by firms

Which price index—CPI or GDP deflator—is more volatile?

GDP Deflator Versus CPI

Is the CPI or the GDP deflator a better indicator of inflation? Or does it not really matter which one we use? The two measures tend to move in the same direction, but the CPI tends to be much more volatile—it bounces around more than the GDP deflator. Divergences between the two measures are rare—during the 1970s, both measures showed high rates of inflation. During the late 1980s, the 1990s, and the decade of 2000, both showed low rates of inflation. One important difference between them that can yield different results is that the GDP deflator measures the price of all goods and services that are *produced domestically,* while the CPI measures the goods and services *bought by consumers.* For example, a Porsche produced in Stuttgart, Germany, will show up in the CPI, but it will not show up in the GDP deflator because it was not produced in the U.S. economy. More important, the same is true for the price of oil, because much of U.S. oil is imported. Consequently, oil price increases are fully captured in the CPI but only partially captured in the GDP deflator—partially captured because those increases do add to the cost of production.

However, suppose the price of an airplane or aircraft carrier being produced domestically for the military increases. Because it is produced domestically, its price will show up in the GDP deflator but not in the typical consumer basket—the CPI. In summary, all three of these measures of prices would yield different inflation rates which could be substantial over a long period of time. The important point is that all three of these measures tend to move together.

The Price Level over the Years

Unanticipated and sharp changes in the price level are almost universally considered to be "bad" and to require a policy remedy. What is the historical record of changes in the overall U.S. price level? Exhibit 2 shows changes in the consumer price index (CPI), the standard measure of inflation, from 1914 to 2010. Can you believe that in 1940, stamps were 3 cents per letter, postcards were a penny, the median price of a house was $2,900, and the price of a new car was $650? However, the problem with comparing prices today with prices in the past is that it focuses on the number of dollars it takes to buy something rather than the

in the news   Top-Grossing U.S. Films of All Time Adjusted for Inflation

Movie	Year	Gross Domestic Receipts (millions)	Inflation-Adjusted Gross Receipts (millions)
1. *Gone with the Wind*	1939	$198.7	$1,560.1
2. *Star Wars*	1977	460.9	1,348.6
3. *The Sound of Music*	1965	163.2	1,082.4
4. *E.T. The Extra-Terrestrial*	1982	434.9	1,070.4
5. *The Ten Commandments*	1956	80.0	995.7
6. *Titanic*	1997	600.8	981.7
7. *Jaws*	1975	260.0	973.5
8. *Doctor Zhivago*	1965	111.7	920.4
9. *Jungle Book*	1967	141.8	823.3
10. *Snow White and the Seven Dwarfs*	1937	184.9	808.1

SOURCE: The Movie Times, http://www.the-movie-times.com/thrsdir/alltime.mv?adjusted+ByAG+1, 2011.

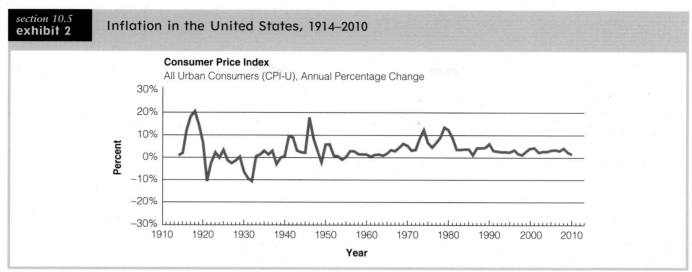

section 10.5
exhibit 2   Inflation in the United States, 1914–2010

SOURCE: Bureau of Labor Statistics, 2009.

in the news A Better CPI

The monthly consumer price index (CPI) is the most oft-cited measure of inflation and one of the most important and closely watched statistics in the U.S. economy. It is an indicator of how well the Federal Reserve is doing in achieving and maintaining low inflation, and it also is used to determine cost-of-living adjustments for many government programs, collective bargaining contracts, and individual income tax brackets.

Since 1995, the Bureau of Labor Statistics (BLS) has been eliminating biases that cause the index to overstate inflation. . . . These changes are expected to create a more reliable index. . . . Although this may seem like a small change, the effect of these changes is permanent so that measured inflation will be lower by this amount in all future years.

It is important that the CPI should measure inflation accurately or that the degree of bias be known. Macroeconomic policymakers such as the Fed then can take appropriate steps to keep inflation low, and the public can be informed about their successes and failures in achieving their goal. Also, if the CPI does not measure inflation correctly, cost-of-living adjustments based on it will have different effects from those desired when the commitments to make these adjustments were made. For example, adjusting Social Security benefits based on an

upwardly biased CPI may shift spending power from the young toward the old.

The BLS has been studying possible biases in the CPI for a long time. The issue gained national prominence in 1996 when the Congress commissioned a panel of experts on price measurement issues, chaired by Michael Boskin of Stanford University, to examine biases in the CPI. Their report, "Toward a More Accurate Measure of the Cost of Living," identified four major sources of bias and estimated that they caused the CPI to overstate inflation by 1.1 percentage points per year at that time.

Substitution Bias

Substitution bias occurs because the CPI measures the price changes of a fixed basket of goods and services and thus does not capture the savings that households enjoy when they change their spending in response to relative price changes of goods and services. For example, a rise in the price of beef leads people to buy more chicken in order to keep their food costs down. . . .

Outlet Bias

This type of bias is similar to substitution bias, but refers to where households shop rather than to what they purchase. Over the past 15 years, for example, the growth of discount stores has helped consumers lower their expenditures by offering high-volume

(*continued*)

in the news   A Better CPI (Cont.)

If people prefer buying in bulk at discount stores, will the CPI accurately measure inflation? The success of discount stores has grown over the last few years, indicating that for some customers, the reduction in customer service often associated with these megastores does not offset the lower prices, introducing an upward bias into the index.

REUTERS/MOLLY RILEY/LANDOV

purchases at reduced prices. The expansion of these establishments has not been adequately represented in the CPI, thus creating an upward bias of prices estimated at 0.1 percentage point per year. A similar problem may arise in the future as shopping online becomes more widespread.

New Product Bias

This bias occurs because new products, such as iPhones or IPads, are not introduced into the index until they are commonplace items. This means that the substantial price decreases and quality increases that occur during the early years following introduction are not captured by the index. A problem of dealing with this bias is that the BLS can never know in advance which of the many new products introduced each year will be successful and hence worthy of inclusion in the CPI. . . .

Quality Bias

This bias arises because some of any increase in the price of an item may be due to an improvement in quality, rather than being a pure price increase. For example, take the personal computer where greater speeds and more features have become available, without substantial increase in price. If the CPI only looks at the price of a computer, they will miss the quality changes from these features. Quality improvements in other areas—such as medical care—are more difficult to measure so that bias is more likely to occur. And features of a product that become mandatory—such as seat belts, which buyers are forced to purchase even if they would prefer not to—are particularly difficult to handle.

Ongoing research is necessary to identify biases in the CPI. Changes to this index are ongoing as the BLS strives to maintain an accurate measure of inflation in our dynamic economy. The BLS has reduced the size of the substitution bias and the new product bias by updating the market basket every 2 years rather than every 10 years. Other improvements have also been implemented. Many economists believe that the BLS improvements have cut the inflationary bias in half and it is now less than 1 percent.

SOURCE: Reprinted from the Federal Reserve Bank of San Francisco, Economic Letter, 99-05, February 5, 1999 (http://www.frbsf.org/econrsrch/wklyltr/wklyltr99/el99-05.html). The opinions expressed in this article do not necessarily reflect the views of the management of the Federal Reserve Bank of San Francisco, or of the Board of Governors of the Federal Reserve System.

purchasing power of the dollar. For example, if prices and wages both doubled overnight, raising the price of a quart of milk from $1 to $2, you would be no worse off because you would still work the same number of minutes to buy a quart of milk.

Anticipated Versus Unanticipated Inflation

Before we can determine the effects of inflation, we must distinguish between anticipated and unanticipated inflation. If the annual inflation rate has been 3 percent for several years and people anticipate the inflation rate to remain at 3 percent, then there is anticipated inflation. Anticipated inflation causes few problems. For the most part, people see it coming and prepare for it.

Unanticipated inflation occurs when people don't see it coming and have failed to prepare for it. Suppose people anticipate a 3 percent inflation rate, but the inflation rate unexpectedly jumps to 10 percent. When inflation is unanticipated, people are less able to protect themselves from its costs. But that does not mean that everybody is worse off. Unanticipated inflation leads to arbitrary gains and losses as wealth and income are redistributed from one group to another. In addition, it makes it more difficult to make long-term plans, and forces people to focus more on money and prices and less on efficient choices about production and consumption in order to protect themselves from eroding purchasing power.

Who Loses with Inflation?

Inflation brings about changes in peoples' purchasing power, and these changes may be either desirable or undesirable. Suppose you retire on a fixed pension of $2,000 per month. Over time, that $2,000 will buy less and less if prices generally rise. Your real income—your income adjusted to reflect changes in purchasing power—falls. Inflation lowers income in real terms for people on fixed-dollar incomes. Likewise, inflation can hurt creditors. For example, suppose a bank loaned someone money for a house, at a 4 percent fixed rate for 20 years, in the early 1960s (a period of low inflation). However, the 1970s was a period of high inflation rates (roughly 10 percent per year). Under this scenario, because the lender did not correctly anticipate the higher rate of inflation, the lender is the victim of unanticipated inflation. That is, the borrower is paying back with dollars that have much less purchasing power than those dollars they borrowed in the early 1960s. Another group that sometimes loses from inflation, at least temporarily, are people whose incomes are tied to long-term contracts. If inflation begins shortly after a labor union signs a three-year wage agreement, it may completely eat up the wage gains provided by the contract. The same applies to businesses that agree to sell quantities of one thing, say coal, for a fixed price for a given number of years.

If some people lose because of unanticipated inflation, others must gain. Debtors pay back dollars worth less in purchasing power than those borrowed. Corporations that can quickly raise the prices on their goods may have revenue gains greater than their increases in costs, providing additional profits. Wage earners sometimes lose from inflation because wages may rise at a slower rate than the price level. The redistributional impact of inflation is not the result of conscious public policy; it just happens.

Can high and variable rates of unanticipated inflation reduce investment?

Some economists believe that significant costs are incurred when individuals and firms devote resources to protecting themselves against expected future inflation. This could include working out long-term contracts with automatic adjustments for employment or purchases of raw materials and other goods.

The uncertainty that unanticipated inflation creates can also discourage investment and economic growth. When inflation rates are high, they also tend to vary considerably, which creates a lot of uncertainty. This uncertainty complicates planning for businesses and households, which is vital to capital formation, as well as adding an inflation risk premium to long-term interest rates.

Moreover, inflation can raise one nation's price level relative to price levels in other countries. In turn, this shift can make financing the purchase of foreign goods difficult, or it can decrease the value of the national currency relative to that of other countries.

Costs of High Inflation

Predictably low rates of inflation, while still a problem, are considerably better than high and variable inflation rates. A slow, predictable rate of inflation makes predicting future price increases relatively easy. Consequently, setting interest rates will be an easier task and the redistribution effects of inflation will be minimized. In addition, high and variable inflation rates make it almost impossible to set long-term contracts because prices and interest rates may be changing by the day, or even by the hour in the case of **hyperinflation**—extremely high rates of inflation for sustained periods of time.

hyperinflation
extremely high rates of inflation for sustained periods of time

In its extreme form, inflation can lead to a complete erosion of faith in the value of the pieces of paper we commonly call money. In Germany, after both world wars, prices rose so fast that people in some cases finally refused to take paper money, insisting instead on payment in goods or metals, whose prices tend to move predictably with inflation. Unchecked inflation can feed on itself and may ultimately lead to hyperinflation of 300 percent or more per year. We saw these rapid rates of inflation in Argentina and Brazil in the early 1990s when the inflation rate topped 2,000 percent per year. Most economists believe we can live quite well in an environment of low, steady inflation, but no economist believes we can prosper with high, variable inflation.

Unanticipated Inflation Distorts Price Signals

We often use the term *purchasing power* when we discuss how many goods and services a dollar can buy. In times of inflation, a dollar buys fewer goods and services. Thus, the higher the inflation rate, the greater the rate of decline in purchasing power. In periods of high and variable inflation, households and firms have a difficult time distinguishing between changes in the relative prices of individual goods and services and changes in the general price level. Suppose the price of milk rises by 5 percent between 2012 and 2013, but the overall price level increases by only 2 percent during that period. Then we could say that between 2012 and 2013, the relative price of milk rose only 3 percent (5 percent minus 2 percent). The next year, the price of milk might increase 5 percent again, but the general inflation rate might be 6 percent. Then, between 2013 and 2014, the relative price of milk would actually have fallen by 1 percent (5 percent minus 6 percent). Remember, the relative price is the price of a good relative to all other goods and services.

Because of the difficulty in determining relative prices, inflation distorts the information that flows from price signals. Does the good have a higher price because it has become relatively more scarce, and therefore more valuable relative to other goods, or did the price rise along with the average of all other prices, because of inflation? The muddying of price information undermines good decision making.

Other Costs of Anticipated and Unanticipated Inflation

Whether inflation is perfectly anticipated or not, firms as incur costs a result of the need to change prices more frequently. For example, a restaurant might have to print new menus, or a department or mail-order store may have to print new catalogs, to reflect the new higher prices. These costs are called **menu costs**; they are the costs of changing posted prices. In some South American economies in the 1980s, inflation increased at more than 300 percent per year, with prices changing on a daily, or even hourly, basis in some cases. Imagine how large the menu costs could be in an economy such as that!

Another problem with inflation is that, even when inflation is fully anticipated, some people will experience a cost from holding money. Firms and households have to hold some money for daily transactions. People holding on to money will find its purchasing power is eroded each year by the the rate of inflation.

The **shoe-leather cost** of inflation is the cost of going to and from the bank to check on your assets (so often that you wear out the leather on your shoes). Specifically, high rates of inflation erode the value of a currency, which means that people will want to hold less currency—perhaps going to the ATM once a week rather than twice a month. That is, the higher inflation rates lead to higher nominal interest rates, which may induce more individuals to put money in the bank rather than allowing it to depreciate in their pockets. So, the cost is really the time and convenience sacrificed to keep less money on hand than you would if

ECS

economic
content
standards

The costs of inflation are different for different groups of people. Unexpected inflation hurts savers and people on fixed incomes; it helps people who have already borrowed money at a fixed rate of interest.

Inflation imposes costs on people beyond its effects on wealth distribution, because people devote resources to protect themselves from expected inflation.

menu costs
the costs imposed on a firm from changing listed prices

What are menu costs?

What are shoe leather costs?

shoe-leather cost
the time and inconvenience cost incurred when individuals reduce their money holdings because of inflation

inflation were not a factor. The effects of shoe-leather costs of inflation, like those of menu costs, are modest in countries with low inflation rates but can be quite large in countries where inflation is anticipated and substantial.

nominal interest rate
the reported interest rate that is not adjusted for inflation

real interest rate
the nominal interest rate minus the inflation rate; also called the inflation-adjusted interest rate

Inflation and Interest Rates

The interest rate is usually reported as the **nominal interest rate**, which means it is not adjusted for inflation. We determine the **real interest rate** by taking the nominal rate of interest and subtracting the inflation rate:

Real interest rate = Nominal interest rate − Inflation rate

For example, if the nominal interest rate was 5 percent, and the inflation rate was 3 percent, the real interest rate would be 2 percent.

If people can correctly anticipate inflation, they will behave in a manner that will largely protect them against loss. However, if the inflation is not correctly anticipated (it is not an easy task to predict inflation), inflation will still redistribute income. Consider the creditor who believes that the overall price level will rise 6 percent a year, based on experience in the immediate past. Would that creditor lend money to someone at a 5 percent rate of interest? No. A 5 percent rate of interest means that a person borrowing $1,000 now will pay back $1,050 ($1,000 plus 5 percent of $1,000) one year from now. But if prices go up 6 percent, it will take $1,060 to buy what $1,000 does today ($1,060 is 6 percent more than $1,000). Thus, the creditor lending at 5 percent will get paid back an amount ($1,050) less than the purchasing power of the original loan ($1,060) at the time it was paid back. The real interest rate would actually be negative. To protect themselves, creditors will demand a rate of interest large enough to compensate for the deteriorating value of money.

Understanding the difference between nominal and real interest rates is critical. In most economic decisions, it is the real rate of interest that matters because it is this rate that shows how much borrowers pay and lenders receive in terms of purchasing power—goods and services money can buy. Investors and lenders will do best when the real interest rates are high.

© WORLD HISTORY ARCHIVE/ALAMY

German woman using money as fuel in her wood burning stove. During the 1923–24 hyperinflation in Germany, it took less paper money to generate needed heat in the stove by burning the money than it did to use it to buy wood to burn (photo courtesy of wikipedia commons, © Adsd der Friedrich-Ebert-Stiftung)

global **watch** Average Annual Inflation Rates, Selected Countries, 2010

Inflation Rate (annual percent change)

Venezuela	Argentina	Jamaica	Russia	Indonesia	Brazil	Mexico	U.K.	China	Iraq	Canada	U.S.
28.2%	22%	12.6%	6.9%	5.1%	5.0%	4.2%	3.3%	3.2%	2.4%	1.8%	1.5%

SOURCES: The *World Factbook*, 2011; http://www.cia.gov.

When the nominal interest rate is high, the inflation rate tends to be high; and when the nominal interest rate is low, the inflation rate tends to be low. Why? The reason is that when inflation is high, borrowers offer and lenders demand higher nominal interest rates to compensate for the falling value of money in the future. When the inflation rate is low, borrowers offer and lenders demand lower nominal interest rates because the value of money (purchasing power) is falling less quickly. Therefore, the tendency is for nominal interest rates and inflation rates to move together—high inflation rates mean high nominal interest rates, and low inflation rates mean low nominal interest rates.

Do Creditors Always Lose During Inflation?

economic
content
standards

Expectations of inflation may lead to higher interest rates.

Usually, lenders are able to anticipate inflation with reasonable accuracy. For example, in the late 1970s, when the inflation rate was more than 10 percent a year, nominal interest rates on a 90-day Treasury bill were relatively high. In 2002, with low inflation rates, the nominal interest rate was relatively low. If the inflation rate is anticipated accurately, new creditors will not lose nor will debtors gain from a change in the inflation rate. However, nominal interest rates and real interest rates do not always run together. For example, in periods of high *unexpected* inflation, the nominal interest rates can be high when the real interest rates are low or even negative.

Protecting Ourselves from Inflation

How does a COLA contract protect someone from unexpected changes in inflation?

Increasingly, groups try to protect themselves from inflation by means of cost-of-living clauses in contracts. Many long-term contracts between firms and unions include a cost of living allowance (COLA) that automatically increases when the consumer price index (CPI) increases. With these clauses, laborers automatically get wage increases that reflect rising prices. The same is true of many pensioners, including those on Social Security. Personal income taxes likewise are now indexed (adjusted) for inflation. However, some of the tax code is still not indexed for inflation. These factors affect the incentives to work, save, and invest. Also, adjustable mortgage rates adjust to market conditions, reducing the chance that there will be winners and losers with changes in the unanticipated inflation rate.

---

use what you've learned   Inflation and Capital Gains Taxes

In an environment of inflation, the tax code can distort market signals and may lead to a reduction in saving, lending, and investment. To many economists, the problem stems from *capital gains tax* (a tax on a person's assets) being taxed in nominal terms rather than in real terms (adjusted for inflation). For example, suppose you sold a stock in 1980 for $50,000 that you bought in 1970 for $40,000. In real terms, adjusted for inflation, you would have lost money because the 25 percent increase in the stock price would be less than the percentage change in

the inflation rate (over 100). In fact, inflation was so high in the 1970s that you would have lost money on your stock in real terms and then have to pay capital gains tax on the nominal gains—$10,000 ($50,000 – $40,000)—ouch! Thus, many economists believe capital gains should be taxed on real gains. In this case, you could write off capital losses because you actually lost money on your investment in real terms. These costs are not just a redistribution cost but can impact economic growth if the taxes are discouraging saving and investment.

⊘ SECTION QUIZ

1. When would consumers and producers experience increased difficulty in coordinating their plans and decisions?

   a. in a period of inflation

   b. in a period of deflation

   c. in a period of either inflation or deflation

   d. none of the above

2. The CPI is a measure of

   a. the overall cost of goods and services produced in the economy.

   b. the overall cost of inputs purchased by a typical producer.

   c. the overall cost of buying a market basket of goods and services purchased by a typical consumers.

   d. the overall cost of stocks on the New York Stock Exchange.

3. If the consumer price index was 100 in the base year and 110 in the following year, the inflation rate was

   a. 110 percent.

   b. 100 percent.

   c. 11 percent.

   d. 10 percent.

4. The CPI overestimates changes in the cost of living because

   a. the growth of discount stores where consumers can obtain goods at discount prices has not been adequately represented in the construction of the CPI.

   b. the CPI does not adequately deal with changes in the quality of products over time.

   c. the CPI deals with a fixed market basket and doesn't capture the savings households enjoy when they substitute cheaper alternatives in response to a price change.

   d. of all of the above.

5. Which measures of inflation tend to overstate it?

   a. the CPI, but not the GDP deflator

   b. the GDP deflator, but not the CPI

   c. both the GDP deflator and the CPI

   d. neither the GDP deflator nor the CPI

6. Inflation can harm

   a. retirees on fixed pensions.

   b. borrowers who have long-term fixed interest rate loans.

   c. wage earners whose incomes grow slower than inflation.

   d. either (a) or (c).

   e. all of the above.

7. Inflation will be least harmful if

   a. interest rates are not adjusted accordingly when inflation occurs.

   b. worker wages are set by long-term contracts.

   c. it is correctly anticipated and interest rates adjust accordingly.

   d. it is not fully anticipated.

(*continued*)

? SECTION QUIZ (Cont.)

8. Unexpected inflation generally benefits

   a. lenders.

   b. borrowers.

   c. the poor.

   d. people on fixed incomes.

9. The costs of inflation include

   a. menu costs.

   b. shoe-leather costs.

   c. a distortion of price signals.

   d. all of the above.

10. If the nominal interest rate is 9 percent and the inflation rate is 3 percent, the real interest rate is

   a. 3 percent.

   b. 6 percent.

   c. 9 percent.

   d. 12 percent.

   e. 27 percent.

---

1. How does price level stability reduce the difficulties buyers and sellers have in coordinating their plans?

2. Why does the consumer price index tend to overstate inflation if the quality of goods and services is rising over time?

3. Why would the CPI take into account some goods imported from other countries, but not take into account some goods produced domestically, unlike the GDP deflator?

4. Why doesn't the consumer price index accurately adjust for the cost-of-living effects of a tripling in the price of bananas relative to the prices of other fruits?

5. What will happen to the nominal interest rate if the real interest rate rises, *ceteris paribus?* What if inflation increases, *ceteris paribus?*

6. Say you owe money to Big River Bank. Will you gain or lose from an unanticipated decrease in inflation?

7. How does a variable interest rate loan "insure" the lender against unanticipated increases in inflation?

8. Why will neither creditors nor debtors lose from inflation if it is correctly anticipated?

9. How could inflation make people turn to exchange by barter?

Answers: 1. c   2. c   3. d   4. d   5. c   6. e   7. c   8. b   9. d   10. b

Economic Fluctuations   10.6

📁 What are short-term economic fluctuations?

📁 What are the four stages of a business cycle?

📁 What is the difference between a recession and a depression?

Short-Term Fluctuations in Economic Growth

The aggregate amount of economic activity in the United States and most other nations has increased markedly over time, even on a per capita basis, indicating economic growth. Short-term fluctuations in the level of economic activity also occur. We sometimes call these short-term fluctuations **business cycles**. Exhibit 1 illustrates the distinction between long-term economic growth and short-term economic fluctuations. Over a long period, the line representing economic activity slopes upward, indicating increasing real output. Over short periods, however, downward, as well as upward, output changes occur. Business cycles refer to the short-term ups and downs in economic activity, not to the long-term trend in output, which in modern times has been upward.

The Phases of a Business Cycle

A business cycle has four phases—expansion, peak, contraction, and trough—as illustrated in Exhibit 2. The period of **expansion** is when output (real GDP) is rising significantly. Usually, during the expansion phase, unemployment is falling and both consumer and business confidence are high. Thus, investment is rising, as are expenditures for expensive durable consumer goods, such as automobiles and household appliances. The **peak** is the point in time when the expansion comes to an end, when output is at the highest point in the cycle. The **contraction** is a period of falling real output and is usually accompanied by rising unemployment and declining business and consumer confidence. The contraction phase is measured from the peak to the **trough**—the point in time when output stops declining and business activity is at its lowest point in the cycle. Investment spending and expenditures on consumer durable goods fall sharply in a typical contraction. The contraction phase is also called **recession**, a period of significant decline in output and employment (lasting more than a few months). Unemployment is relatively high at the trough, although the actual maximum amount of unemployment may not occur exactly at the trough. Often, unemployment remains fairly high well into the expansion phase. The expansion phase is measured from the trough to the peak.

How Long Does a Business Cycle Last?

The length of any given business cycle is not uniform. Because it does not have the regularity that the term *cycle* implies, economists often use the term *economic fluctuation* rather than *business cycle*. In addition, economic fluctuations are almost impossible to predict. In both the 1980s and the 1990s, expansions were quite long by historical standards. The contraction phase is one of recession, a decline in

What are business cycles?

business cycles
short-term fluctuations in the economy relative to the long-term trend in output

expansion
when output (real GDP) is rising significantly—the period between the trough of a recession and the next peak

peak
the point in time when expansion comes to an end, that is, when output is at the highest point in the cycle

contraction
when the economy is slowing down—measured from the peak to the trough

trough
the point in time when output stops declining, that is, when business activity is at its lowest point in the cycle

recession
a period of significant decline in output and employment

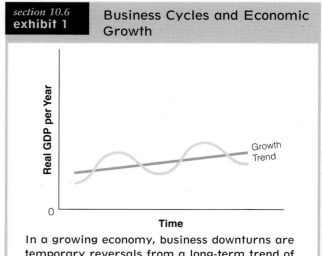

| section 10.6 **exhibit 1** | **Business Cycles and Economic Growth** |

Graph: Real GDP per Year (vertical axis) vs. Time (horizontal axis) showing business cycle curve fluctuating around an upward-sloping Growth Trend line.

In a growing economy, business downturns are temporary reversals from a long-term trend of economic growth.

© Cengage Learning 2013

section 10.6
exhibit 2   Four Phases of a Business Cycle

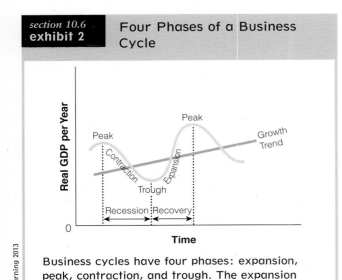

Business cycles have four phases: expansion, peak, contraction, and trough. The expansion phase usually is longer than the contraction; and in a growing economy, output (real GDP) will rise from one business cycle peak to the next.

business activity. A severe recession is called a **depression**. Likewise, a prolonged expansion in economic activity is sometimes called a **boom**. Exhibit 3 shows the record of U.S. business cycles since 1854. Notice that contractions seem to be getting shorter over time. The National Bureau of Economic Research (NBER) Business Cycle Dating Committee determined that a recession began in March 2001, ending an expansion that lasted from March 1991 to March 2001. The attacks of September 11, 2001, clearly deepened the contraction and may have been instrumental in turning a contraction into a recession. The committee met in November of 2008 and determined that the economy peaked in December 2007, marking the end of a 73-month expansion and the beginning of an 18-month recession that ended in June of 2009. There is a delay before the NBER announces the beginning or end of a recession, because of the complexities involved in gathering and evaluating the data. So the official beginning and end dates of a recession are not known until many months later.

depression
severe recession or contraction in output

boom
period of prolonged economic expansion

Seasonal Fluctuations Affect Economic Activity

The determinants of cyclical fluctuations in the economy are the major thrust of the next several chapters, and some fluctuation in economic activity reflects seasonal patterns. Business activity, whether measured by production or by the sale of goods, tends to be high in the two months before the winter holidays and somewhat lower in summertime, when many families are on vacation. Within individual industries, of course, seasonal fluctuations in output often are extremely pronounced, agriculture being the best example. Often, key economic statistics, such as unemployment rates, are seasonally adjusted, meaning the numbers are modified to account for normal seasonal fluctuations. Thus, seasonally adjusted unemployment rates in summer months are below actual unemployment rates, because employment is normally high in summertime due to the inflow of school-age workers into the labor force.

section 10.6
exhibit 3   A Historical Record of U.S. Recessions, 1921–2008

Peak	Trough	Length of Recession
January 1920	July 1921	18
May 1923	July 1924	14
October 1926	November 1927	13
August 1929	March 1933	43
May 1937	June 1938	13
February 1945	October 1945	8
November 1948	October 1949	11
July 1953	May 1954	10
August 1957	April 1958	8
April 1960	February 1961	10
December 1969	November 1970	11
November 1973	March 1975	16
January 1980	July 1980	6
July 1981	November 1982	16
July 1990	March 1991	8
March 2001	November 2001	8
December 2007	June 2009	18

SOURCES: National Bureau of Economic Research, Inc., http://www.nber.org/cycles.html; and U.S. Department of Commerce.

Forecasting Cyclical Changes

The farmer and the aviator rely heavily on weather forecasters for information on climatic conditions in planning their activities. Similarly, businesses, government agencies, and, to a lesser extent, consumers rely on economic forecasts to learn of forthcoming developments in the business cycle. If it looks as if the economy will continue in an expansionary phase, businesses may expand production to meet a perceived forthcoming need; if it looks as if contraction is coming, businesses may decide to be more cautious.

Forecasting Models

Using theoretical models, which will be discussed in later chapters, economists gather statistics on economic activity in the immediate past, including, for example, consumer expenditures, business inventories, the supply of money, governmental expenditures, tax revenues, and so on. Using past historical relationships between these factors and the overall level of economic activity (which form the basis of the economic theories), they formulate *econometric models*. Statistics from the immediate past are plugged into the model, and forecasts are made. Because human behavior changes, and our assumptions about certain future developments may not be correct, our numbers are imperfect, and our econometric models are not always accurate. But like the weather forecasts, although the econometric models are not perfect, they are helpful.

Economic Indicators

The media also publish data on business cycle indicators that fall into three main categories: leading economic indicators, coincident economic indicators, and lagging economic indicators.

leading economic indicators
factors that economists at the Commerce Department have found typically change before changes in economic activity

The index of leading economic indicators are designed to predict activity in the U.S. economy six to nine months in the future and can be useful as short-term predictors of the economy. The stock market, measured by the S&P 500 index, is one of the leading economic indicators. For example, the stock market often turns downward before a recession and usually begins to improve before the economy recovers from a slump. Another leading indicator is new consumer goods orders; often consumers reduce their spending on big-ticket items like homes and automobiles before a recession begins. Interest rates are also an important economic indicator because they have strong effects on consumer and business spending. Other leading economic indicators include the length of the average workweek, initial claims for unemployment, new building permits, new orders for plant and equipment, the extent of delayed deliveries, and the money supply (M2). The Department of Commerce combines all these into an index of leading indicators. If the index rises sharply for two or three months, it is likely (but not certain) that increases in the overall level of activity will follow.

However, using leading economic indicators to predict future trends can be unreliable. For example, if the federal government responds with policies to combat the recession as soon as the leading economic indicators begin predicting it, then a recession that would have occurred may fail to materialize. On the other hand, a self-fulfilling prophecy may result if businesses respond with cutbacks in orders for plants and equipment as soon as the leading economic indicators begin predicting a recession.

In addition to leading economic indicators, there are coincident economic indicators, which help to predict peaks and troughs. In other words, they change with real GDP. For example, as real GDP increases we would expect an increase in total employment, personal income, industrial production, and sales.

Lagging economic indicators follow economic activity. That is, they change after real GDP changes. For example, the duration of unemployment is a lagging economic indicator. As real GDP rises and the economy begins to recover, it may take many months before the average time unemployed workers remain unemployed falls. Other lagging indicators include interest rates, the unemployment rate, and the consumer price index.

ⓠ SECTION QUIZ

1. A business cycle reflects changes in economic activity, particularly real GDP. The stages of a business cycle in order are

   a. expansion, peak, contraction, and trough.

   b. expansion, trough, contraction, and peak.

   c. contraction, recession, expansion, and boom.

   d. trough, expansion, contraction, and peak.

(continued)

ⓘ SECTION QUIZ (Cont.)

2. In the contraction phase of the business cycle,

   a. output is rising.

   b. unemployment is falling.

   c. consumer and business confidence are high.

   d. investment is rising.

   e. none of the above is true.

3. The contractionary phase of the business cycle is characterized by

   a. reduced output and increased unemployment.

   b. reduced output and reduced unemployment.

   c. increased output and increased unemployment.

   d. increased output and reduced unemployment.

4. Which of the following is true?

   a. In an expansion, investment is rising, but expenditures for expensive durable consumer goods are falling.

   b. A contraction is a period of falling real output and is usually accompanied by rising unemployment and declining business and consumer confidence.

   c. Unemployment falls substantially as soon as the economy enters the expansion phase of the business cycle.

   d. Since the development of the index of leading economic indicators, it has never failed to give some warning of an economic downturn.

1. Why would you expect unemployment to fall during an economy's expansionary phase and to rise during a contractionary phase?

2. Why is the output of investment goods and durable consumer goods more sensitive to the business cycle than that of most goods?

3. Why might the unemployment rate fall after output starts recovering during the expansion phase of the business cycle?

Answers: 1. a 2. e 3. a 4. b

Interactive Summary

Fill in the blanks:

1. Three major macroeconomic goals are maintaining employment at _____ levels; maintaining prices at a(n) _____ level; and achieving a(n) _____ rate of economic growth.

2. Concern over both unemployment and price instability led to the passage of the _____, in which the United States committed itself to policies designed to reduce unemployment in a manner consistent with price stability.

3. With high rates of unemployment, society loses some potential _____ of goods and services.

4. The unemployment rate is the number of people officially _____ divided by _____.

5. The labor force is the number of people over the age of 16 who are either _____ or _____.

6. _____ workers, who have not actively sought work for four weeks, are not counted as unemployed; instead, they fall out of the _____.

7. Some people working overtime or extra jobs might be considered to be _____ employed.

8. The four main categories of unemployed workers include job _____ (temporarily laid off or fired), job _____ (quit), _____ (worked before and now reentering the labor force), and _____ (entering the labor force for the first time).

9. _____ typically account for the largest fraction of those unemployed.

10. In the short run, a reduction in unemployment may come at the expense of a higher rate of _____, especially if the economy is close to full capacity.

11. Trying to match employees with jobs quickly may lead to significant inefficiencies because of _____ between a worker's skill level and the level of skill required for a job.

12. The duration of unemployment tends to be greater when the amount of unemployment is _____ and smaller when the amount of unemployment is _____.

13. The percentage of the population that is in the labor force is called the _____ rate.

14. Frictional unemployment is _____ term and results from the _____ turnover in the labor market.

15. Frictional unemployment tends to be somewhat _____ in periods of low unemployment, when job opportunities are plentiful.

16. If individuals seeking jobs and employers seeking workers had better information about each other, the amount of frictional unemployment would be considerably _____.

17. _____ unemployment reflects the existence of persons who lack the necessary skills for jobs that are available.

18. _____ unemployment is the most volatile form of unemployment.

19. Most of the attempts to solve the unemployment problem have placed an emphasis on increasing _____.

20. Job retraining programs have the potential to reduce _____ unemployment.

21. The natural rate of unemployment roughly equals the sum of _____ and _____ unemployment when they are at a maximum.

22. One can view unemployment rates below the _____ rate as reflecting the existence of a below-average level of frictional and structural unemployment.

23. The natural rate of unemployment is the median, or "typical," unemployment rate, equal to the sum of _____ and _____ unemployment when they are at a maximum.

24. The natural rate of unemployment may change over time as _____, _____, _____, and other conditions vary.

25. When all of the economy's labor resources and other resources, such as capital, are fully employed, the economy is said to be producing its _____ level of output.

26. When the economy is experiencing cyclical unemployment, the unemployment rate is _____ than the natural rate.

27. The economy can _____ exceed potential output as workers put in overtime or moonlight by taking on extra employment.

28. Without price stability, consumers and producers will experience more difficulty in _____ their plans and decisions.

29. In general, the only thing that can cause a sustained increase in the rate of inflation is a(n) _____ rate of growth in money.

30. The _____ is the standard measure of inflation.

31. We must adjust for the changing purchasing power of the dollar by constructing a price _____.

32. The best-known price index is the _____, which provides a measure of the trend in the prices of goods and services purchased for consumption purposes.

33. The GDP deflator measures the average level of prices of all _____ goods and services produced in the economy.

34. The CPI is the price index that is most relevant to _____ trying to evaluate their changing financial position over time.

35. A price index is equal to the cost of the chosen market basket in the _____ year, divided by the cost of the same market basket in the _____ year, times 100.

36. While the CPI and the GDP deflator move together, the CPI tends to be _____ volatile.

37. Retirees on fixed pensions, creditors, and those whose incomes are tied to long-term contracts can be hurt by inflation because inflation _____ the purchasing power of the money they receive.

38. The _____ that inflation creates can discourage investment and economic growth.

39. Inflation can _____ one nation's price level relative to price levels in other countries, which can lead to difficulties in financing the purchase of foreign goods or to a decline in the value of the national currency relative to that of other countries.

40. In periods of high and variable inflation, households and firms have a difficult time distinguishing changes in _____ prices from changes in the general price level, distorting the information that flows from price signals.

41. _____ costs are the costs of changing posted prices.

42. _____ costs are the costs of checking on your assets.

43. The real interest rate equals the _____ interest rate minus the _____ rate.

44. In most economic decisions, it is the _____ rate of interest that matters, because it shows how much borrowers pay and lenders receive in terms of purchasing power.

45. The _____ the interest rate, the greater the quantity of funds people will demand, *ceteris paribus;* the _____ the interest rate, the greater the quantity of loanable funds supplied, *ceteris paribus.*

46. When creditors start expecting future inflation, there will be a(n) _____ shift in the supply curve of loanable funds. Likewise, demanders of funds (borrowers) are more anxious to borrow because they think they will pay their loans back in dollars of lesser purchasing power than the dollars they borrowed. Thus, the demand for funds increases.

47. If the inflation rate is _____ anticipated, new creditors do not lose, nor do debtors gain, from inflation.

48. Groups try to protect themselves from inflation by using _____ clauses in contracts.

49. The tendency is for nominal interest rates and inflation rates to move in the _____ direction.

50. Business cycles refer to the _____ fluctuations in economic activity, not to the _____ trend in output.

51. A business cycle has four phases: _____, _____, _____, and _____.

52. Expansion occurs when output is _____ significantly, unemployment is _____, and both consumer and business confidence are _____.

53. The _____ is when an expansion comes to an end, that is, when output is at the highest point in the business cycle; while the _____ is the point in time when output stops declining, that is, when business activity is at its lowest point in the business cycle.

54. Seasonally adjusted unemployment rates in summer months are _____ actual unemployment rates because unemployment is normally _____ in summertime as a result of the inflow of school-age workers into the labor force.

55. Businesses, government agencies, and, to a lesser extent, consumers rely on economic _____ to learn of forthcoming developments in the business cycles.

56. If the index of _____ increases sharply for two or three months, it is likely (but not certain) that increases in the overall level of activity will follow.

57. Even though the leading economic indicators do provide a warning of a likely downturn, they do not provide accurate information on the _____ or _____ of the downturn.

Answers: 1. high; stable 2. Employment Act of 1946 3. output 4. unemployed; the civilian labor force 5. employed; unemployed 6. Discouraged; labor force 7. over 8. losers; leavers; reentrants; new entrants 9. Job losers 10. inflation 11. mismatches 12. high; low 13. labor force participation 14. short; normal 15. greater 16. lower 17. Structural 18. Cyclical 19. aggregate demand 20. structural 21. frictional; structural 22. natural 23. frictional; structural 24. technological; demographic; institutional 25. potential 26. greater 27. temporarily 28. coordinating 29. high 30. consumer price index 31. index 32. consumer price index 33. final 34. households 35. current; base 36. more 37. erodes 38. uncertainty 39. raise 40. relative 41. Menu 42. Shoe-leather 43. nominal; inflation 44. real 45. lower; higher 46. leftward 47. accurately 48. cost-of-living 49. same 50. short-term; long-term 51. expansion; peak; contraction; trough 52. rising; falling 53. peak; trough 54. below; high 55. forecasts 56. leading indicators 57. depth; duration

Key Terms and Concepts

Section Quiz Answers

10.1 Macroeconomic Goals

1. What are the three major economic goals of most societies?

The three major economic goals of most societies are (1) maintaining employment at high levels, so that jobs are relatively plentiful and financial suffering from lack of income is relatively uncommon; (2) price stability, so consumers and producers can make better decisions; and (3) achieving a high rate of economic growth, so output, and therefore income and consumption, increases over time.

2. What is the Employment Act of 1946? Why was it significant?

The Employment Act of 1946 was a law that committed the federal government to policies designed to reduce unemployment in a manner consistent with price stability. It was significant as the first formal government acknowledgment of these primary macroeconomic goals.

10.2 Employment and Unemployment

1. What happens to the unemployment rate when the number of unemployed people increases, *ceteris paribus*? When the labor force grows, *ceteris paribus*?

The unemployment rate is defined as the number of people officially unemployed divided by the labor force. Therefore, the unemployment rate rises as the number of unemployed people increases and it falls when the labor force grows, *ceteris paribus*.

2. How might the official unemployment rate understate the "true" degree of unemployment? How might it overstate it?

The official unemployment rate understates the "true" degree of unemployment by not including discouraged workers as unemployed, by counting part-time workers who cannot find full-time jobs as "fully" employed, and by counting those employed in jobs that underutilize worker skills as "fully" employed. It overstates the "true" degree of unemployment by not counting those working overtime or multiple jobs as "overemployed," by counting those employed in the underground economy as unemployed, and by including those just "going through the motions" of job search to maintain unemployment benefits or other government benefits as unemployed.

3. Why might the fraction of the unemployed who are job leavers be higher in a period of strong labor demand?

In a period of strong labor demand, people would be more confident of their ability to find other jobs, and therefore they would be more likely to leave (quit) their current jobs.

4. Suppose you live in a community of 100 people. If 80 people are over 16 years old and 72 people are willing and able to work, what is the unemployment rate in this community?

The unemployment rate in this community is the number unemployed (8) divided by the labor force (80), or 10 percent.

5. What would happen to the unemployment rate if a substantial group of unemployed people started going to school full time? What would happen to the size of the labor force?

Full-time students are not considered part of the labor force, so the labor force, the number officially unemployed, and the unemployment rate would all fall if a substantial group of unemployed people became full-time students.

6. What happens to the unemployment rate when officially unemployed people become discouraged workers? Does anything happen to employment in this case?

When officially unemployed workers become discouraged workers, they stop seeking jobs and are no longer counted as either part of the labor force or as unemployed, reducing the unemployment rate. However, since they do not find jobs, there is no effect on employment as a result.

10.3 Types of Unemployment

1. Why do we want some frictional unemployment?

We want some frictional unemployment because we want human resources employed in areas of higher productivity, and some period of job search (frictional unemployment), rather than taking the first job offered, can allow workers to find more productive employment.

2. Why might a job retraining program be a more useful policy to address structural unemployment than to address frictional unemployment?

Structural unemployment reflects people who lack the necessary skills for the jobs available, rather than a temporary period of search between jobs. A job retraining program to develop skills to match the jobs available addresses such structural unemployment, not frictional unemployment.

3. What is the traditional government policy "cure" for cyclical unemployment?

The traditional government policy "cure" for cyclical unemployment is to adopt policies designed to increase aggregate demand for goods and services.

4. What types of unemployment are present at full employment (at the natural rate of unemployment)?

At full employment (at the natural rate of unemployment), both frictional and structural unemployment, but not cyclical unemployment, are present.

5. Why might frictional unemployment be higher in a period of plentiful jobs (low unemployment)?

In a period of plentiful jobs, frictional unemployment can be higher because job opportunities are plentiful, which stimulates mobility between jobs, which, in turn, increases frictional unemployment.

6. If the widespread introduction of the automobile caused a productive buggy whip maker to lose his job, would he be frictionally, structurally, or cyclically unemployed?

If the buggy whip maker's skills were not in demand in other industries and he had no new transferable skills from the old job, this would result in structural unemployment.

7. If a fall in demand for domestic cars causes auto workers to lose their jobs in Michigan, while plenty of jobs are available for lumberjacks in Montana, what kind of unemployment results?

This would be an example of structural unemployment, resulting from skills mismatched to the jobs available.

10.4 Reasons for Unemployment

1. What are the three reasons for wages to fail to balance labor supply and labor demand?

Minimum wages, unions, and efficiency wages can each lead to a failure to balance labor supply and demand, by leading to wages for some workers that are above their opportunity costs, and increasing unemployment.

2. What is an efficiency wage?

An efficiency wage is a wage that is greater than the equilibrium wage. Its intent is to reduce the costs of turnover, absenteeism, and shirking, and increase worker quality and morale, thereby increasing productivity and reducing costs. If the increased productivity and reduced costs that result outweigh the higher wage costs, producers' profits will rise.

3. How do search costs lead to prolonged periods of unemployment?

Because employers offer different jobs, compensation packages, and working conditions, and workers differ in skills and preferences, matching up workers to appropriate jobs requires a great deal of information. The search for this information entails frictional unemployment, which can also be thought of as employment in gathering information, which, in some cases, can lead to prolonged periods of unemployment.

4. Why would higher unemployment compensation in a country like France lead to higher rates of unemployment?

Unemployment insurance lowers the opportunity cost to a worker from being unemployed, increasing the duration of unemployment and the unemployment rate. Higher unemployment insurance payments will decrease the opportunity cost of remaining unemployed, tending to induce the duration of unemployment and raise the unemployment rate.

5. Does new technology increase unemployment?

New technology can increase unemployment among those whose skills are replaced by that technology. However, it also creates new jobs manufacturing, servicing, and repairing the new equipment, and, by lowering costs, new technology frees up more income to demand other goods and services, creating jobs in those industries.

10.5 Inflation

1. How does price level stability reduce the difficulties buyers and sellers have in coordinating their plans?

Price level instability increases the difficulties buyers and sellers have in coordinating their plans by reducing their certainty about what price changes mean—do they reflect changes in relative prices or changes in inflation? Eliminating this uncertainty makes the meaning of price changes clearer, allowing buyers and sellers to better coordinate their plans through the price system. High and variable rates of inflation also interact with the tax code in ways which distort incentives and lead people to invest resources trying to protect themselves against inflation rather than in socially productive activities.

2. Why does the consumer price index tend to overstate inflation if the quality of goods and services is rising over time?

The consumer price index does not adjust for most quality increases that take place in goods and services. Therefore, higher prices that actually reflect increased quality are counted as higher prices for a given quality, and as a result the consumer price index overstates increases in the cost of living.

3. Why would the CPI take into account some goods imported from other countries, but not take into account some goods produced domestically, unlike the GDP deflator?

The CPI measures the prices of goods and services bought by U.S. consumers, and some goods consumed by U.S. consumers are imported from other countries. The CPI also fails to take into account those goods produced domestically that are not purchased by U.S. consumers, such as investment goods purchased by businesses and military goods bought by the government. The GDP deflator, on the other hand, takes into account all the goods produced in the United States, whether purchased directly by consumers or not.

4. Why doesn't the consumer price index accurately adjust for the cost-of-living effects of a tripling in the price of bananas relative to the prices of other fruits?

The consumer price index assumes that people continue to consume the same number of bananas as in the base year (survey period). Therefore, the cost of the banana component of the consumer price index triples when the price of bananas triples. However, in fact, consumers will substitute other fruits that become relatively cheaper as a result of the banana price increase; so this component of their cost of living has not actually increased as fast as banana prices.

5. What will happen to the nominal interest rate if the real interest rate rises, *ceteris paribus*? What if inflation increases, *ceteris paribus*?

The real interest rate is the nominal interest rate minus the inflation rate. Alternatively, the nominal interest rate is the sum of the desired real interest rate and the expected inflation rate. If either the real interest rate or the rate of inflation increases, nominal interest rates will also increase.

6. Say you owe money to Big River Bank. Will you gain or lose from an unanticipated decrease in inflation?

An unanticipated decrease in inflation will mean that the dollars you must pay back on your loan will be worth more than you expected, raising the real interest rate you must pay on that loan, which makes you worse off.

7. How does a variable interest rate loan "insure" the lender against unanticipated increases in inflation?

With a variable interest rate loan, an unanticipated increase in inflation does not reduce the real interest rate received by the lender, but instead increases the nominal interest rate on the loan to compensate for the increased inflation.

8. Why will neither creditors nor debtors lose from inflation if it is correctly anticipated?

Correctly anticipated inflation will be accurately reflected in the terms creditors and debtors agree to, so that neither will lose from inflation. Only unexpected rates of inflation can redistribute wealth between debtors and creditors.

9. How could inflation make people turn to exchange by barter?

If inflation is very rapid, people lose faith in the value of their monetary unit, and this can lead to exchange by barter, because goods can then have a more predictable value than their country's money.

10.6 Economic Fluctuations

1. Why would you expect unemployment to fall during an economy's expansionary phase and to rise during a contractionary phase?

Output increases during an economy's expansion phase. To produce that increased output in the short term requires more workers, which increases employment and reduces the unemployment rate, other things equal.

2. Why is the output of investment goods and durable consumer goods more sensitive to the business cycle than that of most goods?

When output is growing and business confidence is high, investment rises sharply because it appears highly profitable; when incomes and consumer confidence are high, durable goods, whose purchases are often delayed in less prosperous times, rise sharply in demand. In recessions, investment and consumer durables purchases fall sharply, as such projects no longer appear profitable, and plans are put on hold until better times.

3. **Why might the unemployment rate fall after output starts recovering during the expansion phase of the business cycle?**

Often unemployment remains fairly high well into the expansion phase, because it takes a period of recovery before businesses become convinced that the increasing demand for their output is going to continue, making it profitable to hire added workers.

Problems

1. What would be the labor force participation rate if:
   a. The _____ population = 200 million, the labor force = 160 million, and employment = 140 million?
   b. The _____ population = 200 million, the labor force = 140 million, and employment = 120 million?
   c. Starting from the situation in (a), what would happen to the labor force participation rate if 30 million people lost their jobs and all of them exited the labor force?
   d. Starting from the situation in (a), what would happen to the labor force participation rate if employment rose from 140 million to 150 million?

2. Answer the following questions about unemployment.
   a. If a country has a noninstitutional population of 200 million and a labor force of 160 million, and 140 million people were employed, what is its labor force participation rate and its unemployment rate?
   b. If 10 million new jobs were created in the country, and it attracted 20 million of the people previously not in the labor force into the labor force, what would the new labor force participation rate and new unemployment rate be?
   c. Beginning with the situation in part (a), if 10 million unemployed people became discouraged and stopped looking for work, what would the new labor force participation rate and new unemployment rate be?
   d. Beginning with the situation in part (a), if 10 million current workers retired but their jobs were filled by others still in the labor force, what would the new labor force participation rate and new unemployment rate be?

3. Which of the following individuals would economists consider unemployed?
   a. Sam looked for work for several weeks but has now given up his search and is going back to college.
   b. A 14-year-old wants to mow lawns for extra cash but is unable to find neighbors willing to hire her.
   c. A factory worker is temporarily laid off but expects to be called back to work soon.
   d. A receptionist, who works only 20 hours per week, would like to work 40 hours per week.
   e. A high school graduate is spending the summer backpacking across the country rather than seeking work.

4. Identify whether each of the following reflects seasonal, structural, frictional, or cyclical unemployment.
   a. A sales employee is laid off due to slow business after consumer spending falls.
   b. An automotive worker is replaced by robotic equipment on the assembly line.
   c. A salesperson quits a job in California and seeks a new sales position after moving to New York.
   d. An employee is fired due to poor job performance and searches the want ads each day for work.

5. Which type of unemployment would be affected with the following changes? Would it go up or down?
   a. Employment benefits are increased.
   b. Minnesota has heavy snowfall.
   c. Online job searches become more effective.
   d. Coal has a large, permanent decrease in the demand.
   e. More people have been retrained to develop new skills.
   f. Demand for goods and services in the economy falls sharply.

6. Answer the following questions about reasons for unemployment.
   a. In a severe recession, what would tend to happen to the number of people in each of the following categories?
      job losers   reentrants
      job leavers   new entrants
   b. In good economic times, why might the number of job leavers, reentrants, and new entrants all increase?

7. a. What is the relationship between the natural rate of unemployment and frictional, structural, and cyclical unemployment?

b. What would happen to both unemployment and the normal rate of unemployment if:
   i. cyclical unemployment increases.
   ii. frictional unemployment increases.
   iii. structural unemployment falls and cyclical unemployment rises by the same amount.
   iv. structural unemployment increases and cyclical unemployment decreases by a larger amount.
   v. frictional unemployment decreases and structural unemployment increases by the same amount.

8. Unemployment benefits in many European countries tend to be both more generous and available for longer periods than those in the United States. What impact do you think this is likely to have on the unemployment rate in a European country? Why?

9. How can unions result in higher unemployment rates? How would the results differ for someone who wants to be employed in the union sector as compared with someone who currently has a job in the union sector?

10. Why isn't the belief that technological advances inevitably displace workers true?

11. Answer the following questions about inflation.
    a. What would be the effect of unexpected inflation on each of the following?

retirees on fixed incomes	creditors
workers	shoe-leather costs
debtors	menu costs

    b. How would your answers change if the inflation was expected?

12. Does anticipated inflation or unanticipated inflation discourage economic growth? Why?

13. Answer the following questions about the nominal and real interest rates.
    a. What would be the real interest rate if the nominal interest rate were 14 percent and the inflation rate were 10 percent? If the nominal interest rate were 8 percent and the inflation rate were 1 percent?
    b. What would happen to the real interest rate if the nominal interest rate went from 9 percent to 15 percent when the inflation rate went from 3 percent to 10 percent? If the nominal interest rate went from 11 percent to 7 percent when the inflation rate went from 8 percent to 4 percent?

14. You borrow money at a fixed rate of interest to finance your college education. If the rate of inflation unexpectedly slows down between the time you take out the loan and the time you begin paying it back, is there a redistribution of income? Do you gain or lose? What if you already expected the inflation rate to slow at the time you took out the loan? Explain.

15. How does an adjustable rate mortgage agreement protect lenders against inflation? Who bears the inflation risk?

16. In 2000, a proposal was made in Santa Monica, California, to raise the minimum wage in the hotel and shopping district to a "living" wage of $10.69 per hour. Predict the effect of such legislation on unemployment in the hotel and shopping industries in Santa Monica. What would you expect to happen to the unemployment rate in neighboring areas?

17. Calculate a price index for 2010, 2011, and 2012 using the following information about prices. Let the market basket consist of one pizza, two sodas, and three video rentals. Let the year 2010 be the base year (with an index value of 100).

Year	Price of a Pizza	Price of a Soda	Price of a Video Rental
2010	$ 9.00	$0.50	$2.00
2011	9.50	0.53	2.24
2012	10.00	0.65	2.90

How much inflation occurred between 2010 and 2011? Between 2010 and 2012?

18. Say that the bundle of goods purchased by a typical consumer in the base year consisted of 20 gallons of milk at a price of $1 per gallon and 15 loaves of bread at a price of $2 per loaf. What would the price index be in a year in which
    a. milk cost $2 per gallon and bread cost $1 per loaf?
    b. milk cost $3 per gallon and bread cost $2 per loaf?
    c. milk cost $2 per gallon and bread cost $4 per loaf?

19. Indicate which of the following are true of the CPI and the GDP deflator:

	CPI	GDP Deflator
Tends to overstate inflation	_____	_____
More volatile	_____	_____
Will reflect the cost of building an aircraft carrier domestically	_____	_____
Reflects the cost of imported consumer goods	_____	_____
Reflects prices charged in the underground economy	_____	_____

Measuring Economic Performance

How is it that, between 1997 and 2007, Venezuela's nominal GDP was one of the most rapid in the world yet its real GDP growth was similar to other countries, at around 3 percent per year? The key was that most of the growth in its nominal GDP came from the high inflation that Venezuela had been facing. In other words, when we are measuring the performance of the economy, we must be careful to incorporate price changes. In this chapter, we will study this and other important factors to consider when measuring an economy.

The desire to measure the success, or performance, of our national economy is significant. Is it getting "bigger" (and, we hope, better) or "smaller" (and worse) over time? Aside from intellectual curiosity, the need to evaluate the magnitude of the country's economic performance is important to macroeconomic policymakers, who want to know how well the economy is performing so that they can set goals and develop policy recommendations.

Measurement of the economy's performance is also important to private businesses because inaccurate measurement can lead to bad decision making. Traders in stocks and bonds are continually checking economic statistics—buying and selling in response to the latest economic data.

national income accounting
a uniform means of measuring economic performance

To fulfill the need for a reliable method of measuring economic performance, national income accounting was born early in the twentieth century. The establishment of a uniform means of accounting for economic performance was such an important accomplishment that one of the first Nobel prizes in economics was given to the late Simon Kuznets, a pioneer of national income accounting in the United States.

Several measures of aggregate national income and output have been developed, the most important of which is gross domestic product (GDP). We will examine GDP and other indicators of national economic performance in detail in this chapter.

11.1

National Income Accounting: A Standardized Way to Measure Economic Performance

⌂ What is gross domestic product?   ⌂ Why must expenditures equal income?

What Is Gross Domestic Product?

gross domestic product (GDP)
the measure of economic performance based on the value of all final goods and services produced within a country during a given period

The measure of aggregate economic performance that gets the most attention in the popular media is gross domestic product (GDP), which is defined as the value of all final goods and services produced within a country during a given period. By convention, that period is almost always one year. But let's examine the rest of this definition. What is meant by "final good or service" and "value"?

Measuring the Value of Goods and Services

Value is determined by the market prices at which goods and services sell. Underlying the calculations, then, are the various equilibrium prices and quantities for the multitude of goods and services produced.

What Is a Final Good or Service?

double counting
adding the value of a good or service more than once by mistakenly counting the intermediate goods and services in GDP

The word *final* means that the good is ready for its designated ultimate use. Many goods and services are intermediate goods or services—that is, used in the production of other goods. For example, suppose U.S. Steel Corporation produces some steel that it sells to General Motors Corporation for use in making an automobile. If we counted the value of steel used in making the car as well as the full value of the finished auto in the GDP, we would be engaging in double counting—adding the value of the steel in twice, first in its raw form and second in its final form, the automobile.

Production, Income, and the Circular Flow Model

When we calculate GDP in the economy, we are measuring the value of total production—our total expenditures, on the economy's output of goods and services. However, we are also measuring the total income of everyone in the economy. Why? Because every dollar of spending by some buyer ends up being a dollar of income for some seller. In short, for the economy as a whole, expenditures (spending) must equal income. And this is true whether it is a household, firm, or the government that buys the good or service. The main point is that when we spend (the value of total expenditure) it ends up as someone's income (the value of total income). Buyers have sellers.

Why does total expenditure have to equal total income?

In Exhibit 1, we reintroduce the circular flow model to show the flow of money in the economy. For example, households use some of their income to buy domestic goods and services and some to buy foreign goods and services (imports). Households also use some of their income to pay taxes and invest in financial markets (stocks, bonds, saving accounts, and other financial assets). When income flows into the financial system as saving, it makes it possible for consumers, firms, and government to borrow. This market for saving and borrowing is vital to a well-functioning economy.

Firms sell their goods and services to domestic and foreign consumers and foreign firms and government. Firms use their factors of production (labor, land, capital, and entrepreneurship) to produce goods and services. Firms pay wages to workers, interest for the use of capital, and rent for land. Profits are the return to entrepreneurs for taking the risk

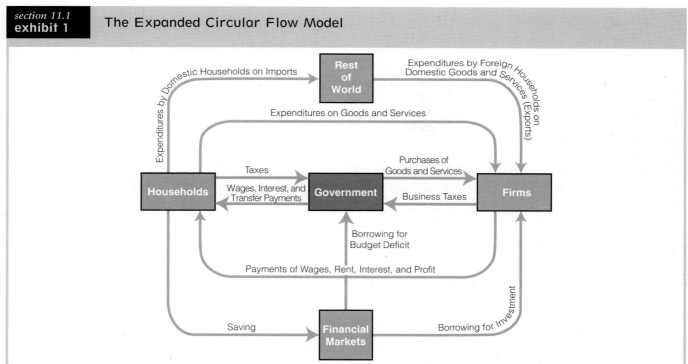

section 11.1
exhibit 1   The Expanded Circular Flow Model

In the circular flow model of income and expenditures, we can measure GDP either by calculating the total value of expenditures or the total value of aggregate income because, for the economy as a whole, expenditures must equal income. GDP equals the total amount spent by households in the market—to buy goods and services, to pay taxes, and to save. To produce goods and services, the firm uses the factors of production (labor, land, capital, and entrepreneurship), and it pays these factors wages, rent, interest, and profit. These payments are total income, which is also equal to GDP. The government and firms borrow the funds that flow into the financial system from households.

Why doesn't GDP include the value of intermediate goods?

of producing the goods and services. Wages, rent, interest, and profit comprise aggregate income in the economy. Government provides transfer payments such as Social Security and unemployment insurance payments. Whether we add up the aggregate expenditure on final goods and services, or the value of aggregate income, we get the same GDP. For an economy as a whole, expenditures and income are the same. Actually, while the two should be exactly the same—there may be a slight variation because of data issues.

ⓘ SECTION QUIZ

1. GDP is defined as the

   a. value of all final goods and services produced in a country in a period of time.

   b. value of all final goods produced in a country in a period of time.

   c. value of all goods and services produced in a country in a period of time.

   d. value of all final services produced in a country in a period of time.

2. An example of an intermediate product is

   a. the purchase of tires by Ford Motor Company to put on its Ford Explorers.

   b. the purchase of wood by a home construction firm.

   c. the purchase of leather by a shoe manufacturer.

   d. All of the above are examples of intermediate products.

3. GDP is calculated including

   a. intermediate products but not final products.

   b. manufactured goods but not services.

   c. final products but not intermediate products.

   d. only goods purchased by consumers in a given year.

4. Which of the following is false?

   a. Measuring the performance of our economy is important to private businesses and to macroeconomic policy makers in setting goals and developing policy recommendations.

   b. All goods and services exchanged in the current period are included in this year's GDP.

   c. The value of a good or service is determined by the market prices at which goods and services sell.

   d. If we counted the value of intermediate goods as well as the full value of the final products in GDP, we would be double counting.

5. Which of the following will be counted as part of this year's U.S. GDP?

   a. goods produced last year but not sold until this year

   b. goods produced this year by an American working in Paris

   c. purchases of Cisco Systems stock (not issued this year) that take place this March

   d. sales of used lawn mowers that take place this year

   e. none of the above

---

1. Why does GDP measure only final goods and services produced rather than all goods and services produced?

2. Why aren't all of the expenditures on used goods in an economy included in current GDP?

3. Why do GDP statistics include real estate agents' commissions from selling existing homes and used car dealers' profits from selling used cars, but not the value of existing homes or used cars when they are sold?

4. Why are sales of previously existing inventories of hula hoops not included in the current year's GDP?

Answers: 1. a 2. d 3. c 4. b 5. e

Measuring Total Production   11.2

- What are the four categories of purchases included in the expenditure approach?
- What are durable and nondurable goods?
- What are fixed investments?
- What types of government purchases are included in the expenditure approach?
- How are net exports calculated?

The Expenditure Approach to Measuring GDP

One approach to measuring GDP is the **expenditure approach**. With this method, GDP is calculated by adding how much market participants spend on final goods and services over a specific period of time. For convenience and for analytical purposes, economists usually group spending into four categories: consumption, designated by the letter C; investment, I; government purchases, G; and net exports, which equals exports (X) minus imports (M), or $X - M$. According to the expenditure method, then,

$$GDP = C + I + G + (X - M)$$

expenditure approach
calculation of GDP by adding the expenditures by market participants on final goods and services over a given period

Consumption (C)

Consumption refers to the purchase of consumer goods and services by households. For most of us, a large percentage of our income in a given year goes for consumer goods and services. The consumption category does not include purchases by business or government. As Exhibit 1 indicates, in 2011, U.S. consumption expenditures totaled more than $10 trillion ($10,676 billion) or 71 percent of GDP. In this respect, the 2011 data were fairly typical. In every year since 1929, when GDP accounts began to be calculated annually, consumption has been more than half of total expenditures on goods and services (even during World War II). Consumption spending, in turn, is usually broken down into three subcategories: nondurable goods, durable consumer goods, and services.

consumption
purchases of final goods and services

How much of GDP is consumption expenditures?

What Are Nondurable and Durable Goods?

Nondurable goods include tangible consumer items that are typically consumed or used up in a relatively short period. Food and clothing are examples, as are such quickly consumable items as drugs, toys, magazines, soap, razor blades, and so on. Nearly everything purchased in a supermarket or drug store is a nondurable good.

Durable goods include longer-lived consumer goods, the most important single category of which is automobiles and other consumer vehicles. Appliances, stereos, and furniture are

nondurable goods
tangible items consumed in a short period of time, such as food

durable goods
longer-lived consumer goods, such as automobiles

section 11.2 **exhibit 1**	GDP: The Expenditure Approach	
Category	**Amount (billions of current dollars)**	**Percent of GDP**
Consumption (*C*)	$10,676.0	71%
Investment (*I*)	1,895.3	13
Government purchases (*G*)	3,038.6	20
Net exports of goods and services (*X – M*)	−597.1	−4
Gross domestic product	$15,012.8	100%

SOURCE: U.S. Bureau of Economic Analysis, October 2011.

also included in the durable goods category. On occasion, it is difficult to decide whether a good is durable or nondurable; the definitions are, therefore, somewhat arbitrary.

The distinction between durables and nondurables is important because consumers' buying behavior is somewhat different for each of these categories of goods. In boom periods, when GDP is rising rapidly, expenditures on durables often increase dramatically, while in years of stagnant or falling GDP, sales of durable goods often plummet. By contrast, sales of nondurables such as food tend to be more stable over time because purchases of such goods are more difficult to shift from one period to another. You can "make do" with your car for another year but not your lettuce.

What Are Services?

services
intangible items of value provided to consumers, such as education

Services are intangible items of value, as opposed to physical goods. Education, health care, domestic housekeeping, professional football, legal help, automobile repair, haircuts, airplane transportation—all these items are services. In recent years, U.S. service expenditures grew faster than spending on goods; the share of total consumption of services increased from 35 percent in 1950 to 66 percent by 2008. As incomes rise, service industries such as health, education, financial, and recreation grow dramatically.

Investment (I)

investment
the creation of capital goods to augment future production

Investment, according to economists, refers to the creation of capital goods—inputs such as machines and tools whose purpose is to produce other goods. This definition of *investment* differs from the popular use of that term. It is common for people to say that they have invested in stocks, meaning that they have traded money for pieces of paper, called stock certificates, that say they own shares in certain companies. Such transactions are not investments as defined by economists (i.e., increases in capital goods), even though they might provide the enterprises selling the stocks the resources to buy new capital goods, which *would* be counted as investment purchases by economists.

The two categories of investment purchases measured in the expenditures approach are fixed investment and inventory investment.

Fixed Investment

fixed investment
all new spending on capital goods by producers

producer goods
capital goods that increase future production capabilities

Fixed investment includes all spending on capital goods—sometimes called **producer goods**—such as machinery, tools, and factory buildings. All these goods increase future production capabilities. Residential construction is also included as an investment expenditure in GDP calculations. The construction of a house allows for a valuable consumer service—shelter—to be provided and is thus considered an investment. Residential construction is the only part of investment tied directly to household expenditure decisions.

Inventory Investment

inventory investment
purchases that add to the stocks of goods kept by the firm to meet consumer demand

Inventory investment includes all purchases by businesses that add to their inventories—stocks of goods kept on hand by businesses to meet customer demands. Every business needs inventory and, other things being equal, the greater the inventory, the greater the amount of goods and services that can be sold to a consumer in the future. Thus, inventories are considered a form of investment. For example, if a grocery store expands and increases the quantity and variety of goods on its shelves, future sales can rise. An increase in inventories, then, is presumed to increase the firm's future sales, which is why we say it is an investment.

How Stable Are Investment Expenditures?

In recent years, investment expenditures generally hovered around 15 percent of gross domestic product. Investment spending is the most volatile category of GDP, however, and tends to fluctuate considerably with changing business conditions. When the economy is booming, investment purchases tend to increase dramatically. In downturns, the reverse happens. In the first year of the Great Depression, investment purchases declined by 37 percent. In recent years, expenditures on capital goods have been a smaller proportion of GDP in the United States than in many other developed nations. This fact worries some people who are concerned about GDP growth in the United States compared to that in other countries, because investment in capital goods is directly tied to a nation's future production capabilities.

Government Purchases (G)

The portion of government purchases included in GDP is expenditures on goods and services. For example, a government must pay the salaries of its employees, and it must also make payments to the private firms with which it contracts to provide various goods and services, such as highway construction companies and weapons manufacturers. All these payments would be included in GDP. However, *transfer payments* (such as Social Security, farm subsidies, and welfare) are not included in government purchases, because this spending does not go to purchase newly produced goods or services but is merely a transfer of income among the country's citizens (which is why such expenditures are called transfer payments).

Exports (X – M)

Some of the goods and services produced in the United States are exported for use in other countries. The fact that these goods and services were made in the United States means that they should be included in a measure of U.S. production. Thus, we include the value of exports when calculating GDP. At the same time, however, some of our expenditures in other categories (consumption and investment, in particular) were for foreign-produced goods and services. These imports must be excluded from GDP to obtain an accurate measure of U.S. production. Thus, GDP calculations measure net exports, which equals total exports (X) minus total imports (M). Net exports are a small proportion of GDP and are often negative for the United States.

Why are transfer payments not included as part of government purchases?

ⓘ SECTION QUIZ

1. The expenditure measure of GDP accounting *is the total of*

   a. consumption, interest, government purchases, and net exports.

   b. consumption, government purchases, wages and salaries, and net exports.

   c. consumption, investment, government purchases, and net exports.

   d. wages and salaries, rent, interest, and profits.

   e. wages and salaries, rent, investment, and profits.

2. Investment includes

   a. fixed investment.

   b. fixed investment plus government investment.

   c. fixed investment plus additions to business inventories.

   d. fixed investment plus subtractions from business inventories.

   e. fixed investment plus government investment plus additions to business inventories.

(*continued*)

? SECTION QUIZ (Cont.)

3. Which of the following is not included in government purchases?

   a. government purchases of investment goods

   b. transfer payments

   c. government spending on services

   d. None of the above is included in government purchases.

   e. Neither (b) nor (c) is included in government purchases.

4. A negative amount of net exports in the GDP expenditures accounting means

   a. exports are less than imports.

   b. imports are less than exports.

   c. the sum of this period's exports and imports has declined from the previous period.

   d. net exports have declined from the previous period.

   e. none of the above.

5. The largest category of GDP is _____, and the most unstable category of GDP is _____.

   a. consumption, consumption

   b. government, investment

   c. consumption, investment

   d. consumption, government purchases

   e. investment, consumption

1. What would happen to GDP if consumption purchases (C) and net exports (X – M) both rose, holding other things equal?

2. Why do you think economic forecasters focus so much on consumption purchases and their determinants?

3. Why are durable goods purchases more unstable than nondurable goods purchases?

4. Why does the investment component of GDP include purchases of new capital goods but not purchases of company stock?

5. If Mary received a welfare check this year, would that transfer payment be included in this year's GDP? Why or why not?

6. Can inventory investment or net exports ever be negative?

Answers: 1. c 2. c 3. b 4. a 5. c

11.3

Other Measures of Total Production and Total Income

📂 How is national income calculated?   📂 What does personal income measure?

In addition to computing the gross domestic product, the Bureau of Economic Analysis (BEA) also computes five additional measures of production and income: gross national product, net national product, national income, personal income, and disposable personal income.

Incomes received by people providing goods and services are actually payments to the owners of productive resources. These payments are sometimes called **factor payments.** Factor payments include wages for the use of labor services, rent for land, payments for the

factor payments
wages (salaries), rent, interest payments, and profits paid to the owners of productive resources

use of capital goods in the form of interest, and profits for entrepreneurs who put labor, land, and capital together. Before we can measure national income, we must make three adjustments to GDP. First, we must look at the net income of foreigners—that is, we add any income earned abroad by U.S. citizens or firms and we subtract any income earned in the United States by foreign firms and citizens. This difference between net income of foreigners and GDP is called **gross national product (GNP)**. For example, we would add to GDP the profits sent back to the United States from Walmart stores in Canada and Mexico. However, the profits Toyota earns in the United States are sent back to Japan and are subtracted from U.S. GDP, so GNP becomes the income earned worldwide by U.S. firms and residents. In the United States, the difference between GDP and GNP is small because net income of foreigners is a small percentage of GDP.

The second adjustment we make to find national income is to deduct depreciation from GNP. **Depreciation** payments are annual allowances set aside for the replacement of worn-out plant and equipment. After we subtract depreciation, we have **net national product (NNP)**.

The final adjustment is to subtract **indirect business taxes**. The best example of an indirect business tax is a sales tax. For example, a compact disc might cost $14.95 plus a tax of $1.20 for a total of $16.15. The retail distributor (record store), record producer, and others will share $14.95 in proceeds, even though the actual equilibrium price is $16.15. In other words, the output (compact disc) is valued at $16.15, even though recipients only get $14.95 in income. Besides sales taxes, other important indirect business taxes include excise taxes (e.g., taxes on cigarettes, automobiles, and liquor) and gasoline taxes.

Now we can measure **national income (NI)**, which is a measure of the income earned by owners of resources—factor payments. Accordingly, national income includes payments for labor services (wages, salaries, and fringe benefits), payments for use of land and buildings (rent), money lent to finance economic activity (interest), and payments for use of capital resources (profits). To obtain GDP, we add indirect business taxes, depreciation, and net income of foreigners.

We should keep in mind that not all income can be used by those who earn it. **Personal income (PI)** measures the amount of income received by households (including transfer payments) before income taxes. **Disposable personal income** is the personal income available to individuals after taxes.

What do factor payments include?

gross national product (GNP)
the difference between net income of foreigners and GDP

depreciation
annual allowance set aside to replace worn-out capital

net national product (NNP)
GNP minus depreciation

indirect business taxes
taxes, such as sales tax, levied on goods and services sold

national income (NI)
a measure of income earned by owners of the factors of production

personal income (PI)
the amount of income received by households before personal taxes

disposable personal income
the personal income available after personal taxes

ⓘ SECTION QUIZ

1. In the income approach to measuring GDP, factor payments do *not* include

   a. wages and salaries for the use of labor services.

   b. rent for land.

   c. interest payments for the use of capital goods.

   d. profits for entrepreneurs.

   e. All of the above are included as factor payments.

2. Which of the following is *not* considered a factor payment?

   a. wages

   b. interest

   c. rent

   d. profit

   e. transfer payments

(*continued*)

⑦ SECTION QUIZ (Cont.)

3. What is *not* subtracted from GDP to get national income?

   a. the net income of foreigners

   b. depreciation

   c. indirect business taxes

   d. personal income taxes

   e. All of the above are subtracted from GDP to get national income.

4. Disposable income is

   a. a measure of the market value of total output.

   b. a measure of the income households have to spend before paying taxes.

   c. a measure of the income households have to spend after paying taxes.

   d. a measure of household income from investment income, such as dividends and capital gains.

5. Disposable personal income will increase when

   a. taxes rise and transfer payments rise.

   b. taxes rise and transfer payments fall.

   c. taxes fall and transfer payments rise.

   d. taxes fall and transfer payments fall.

1. How is personal income different from national income?

2. What is the difference between GDP and national income?

Answers: 1. e 2. e 3. d 4. c 5. c

11.4

Problems in Calculating an Accurate GDP

📂 What are the problems with using GDP to measure output?

📂 What is per capita GDP?

Problems in Calculating an Accurate GDP

The primary problem in calculating accurate GDP statistics becomes evident when attempts are made to compare the GDP over time. Between 1970 and 1978, a period of relatively high inflation, GDP in the United States rose more than 100 percent. What great progress! Unfortunately, however, the "yardstick" used in adding the values of different products, the U.S. dollar, also changed in value over this period. A dollar in 1979, for example, would certainly not buy as much as a dollar in 1970, because the *overall* price level for goods and services increased.

How Do We Solve This Problem?

One solution to this problem would be to use physical units of output—which, unlike the dollar, do not change in value from year to year—as the measure of total economic activity. The major problem with this approach is that different products have different units of measurement. How can anyone add tons of steel to bushels of wheat, kilowatts of electricity, gallons of paint, cubic feet of natural gas, miles of air passenger travel, and number of magazines sold? To compare GDP values over time, the calculations must use a common, or standardized, unit of measure, which only money can provide.

A Price-Level Index

The dollar, then, is the yardstick of value we can use to correct the inflation-induced distortion of the GDP. We must adjust for the changing purchasing power of the dollar by using a price index. As we discussed in the last chapter, a price index attempts to provide a measure of the prices paid for a certain bundle of goods and services over time. The price index can be used to deflate the nominal or current dollar GDP values to a real GDP expressed in dollars of constant purchasing power.

Real GDP

Once the price index has been calculated, the actual procedure for adjusting nominal, or current dollar, GDP to get real GDP is not complicated. For convenience, an index number of 100 is assigned to some base year. The base year is arbitrarily chosen—it can be any year. The Bureau of Economic Analysis (BEA) currently uses 2005 as a base year.

The formula for converting any year's nominal GDP into real GDP (in base year dollars) is as follows:

$$\text{Real GDP} = \frac{\text{Nominal GDP}}{\text{Price index}} \times 100$$

Suppose the GDP deflator (price index) was expressed in terms of 2005 prices (2005 = 100), and the GDP price deflator for 2010 is 110.992 as seen in Exhibit 1. The increase in the figure means that prices were roughly 11 percent higher in 2010 than they were in 2005.

section 11.4 **exhibit 1**	Real GDP: Correcting GDP for Price Index Changes 2000–2010		
(1) Year	**(2)** Nominal GDP (billions of dollars per year)	**(3)** GDP Deflator (2005 = 100)	**(4) [(2) ÷ (3)] × 100** Real GDP (billions of dollars per year, 2005 dollars)
2000	$ 9,951.5	88.723	$11,216.4
2001	10,286.2	90.727	11,337.5
2002	10,642.3	92.196	11,543.1
2003	11,142.2	94.135	11,836.4
2004	11,853.3	96.786	12,246.9
2005	12,623.0	100	12,623.0
2006	13,377.2	103.231	12,958.5
2007	14,028.7	106.227	13,206.4
2008	14,291.5	108.552	13,165.6
2009	13,939.0	109.727	12,703.1
2010	14,526.5	110.992	13,088.0

SOURCE: U.S. Bureau of Economic Analysis, 2011.

To correct the 2011 nominal GDP, we take the nominal GDP figure for 2010—$14,526.5 billion and divide it by the GDP deflator 110.992, which results in a quotient of 130.88 billion. We then multiply this number by 100, giving us $13,088 billion, which would be the 2010 GDP in 2005 dollars (that is, 2010 real GDP, in terms of the 2005 base year). Or to correct the 2000 nominal GDP into real GDP, take the nominal GDP figure for 2000, $9,951.5 billion and divide it by the GDP deflator (88.723), which results in a quotient of 112.164 billion. We then multiply this number by 100, giving us $11,216.4 billion, which would be the 2000 GDP in 2005 dollars (that is, 2000 real GDP, in terms of the 2005 base year).

In Exhibit 2, notice that in years after the base year (2005), real GDP is greater than nominal GDP. This means the price level has risen since 2005, lowering the purchasing power of the dollar. Prior to 2005, nominal GDP was less than real GDP; the purchasing power of the dollar was higher relative to the base year (2005). Also, notice that nominal GDP rises more rapidly than real GDP because inflation is included in the nominal GDP figures.

Is Real GDP Always Less Than Nominal GDP?

In modern times, inflation has been prevalent. For many readers of this book, the price level (as measured by the consumer price index and the GDP deflator) has risen in every year of their lifetime, because the last year with a negative price level was 1955. Therefore, the adjustment of nominal (money) GDP to real GDP will tend to reduce the growth in GDP suggested by nominal GDP figures. Given the distortions introduced by inflation, most news reports about GDP today speak of real GDP changes, although this distinction is not always made explicit.

Real GDP per Capita

real gross domestic product per capita
real output of goods and services per person

The measure of economic well-being, or standard of living, most often used is **real gross domestic product per capita.** We use a measure of real GDP for reasons already cited. To calculate real GDP per capita, we divide the real GDP by the total population to get the value of real output of final goods and services per person. *Ceteris paribus,* people prefer more goods to fewer, so a higher GDP per capita would seemingly make people better off, improving their standard of living. Economic growth, then, is usually considered to have occurred anytime the real GDP per capita has risen. In Exhibit 2, we see that in the United States the real gross domestic product per capita grew sharply from 1958 to 2010. Real GDP per capita is almost three times larger in 2010 than it was in 1958. However, the growth in real GDP per capita is not steady, as seen by the shaded areas that represent recessions in Exhibit 2. Falling real GDP per capita can bring on many human hardships, such as rising unemployment, lower profits, stock market losses, and bankruptcies.

Why Is the Measure of per Capita Real GDP So Important?

Because one purpose of using GDP as a crude welfare measure is to relate output to human desires, we need to adjust for population change. If we do not take population growth into account, we can be misled by changes in real GDP values. For example, in some less-developed countries in some periods, real GDP has risen perhaps 2 percent a year, but the population has grown just as fast. In these cases, the real output of goods and services per person has remained virtually unchanged, but this would not be apparent in an examination of real GDP trends alone.

section 11.4
exhibit 2   Real GDP per Capita

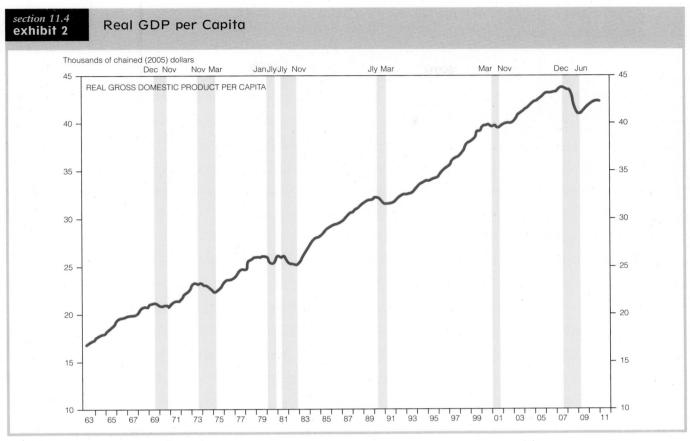

NOTE: Shaded areas represent recessions.
SOURCE: U.S. Bureau of Economic Analysis, August 2011.

⊘ SECTION QUIZ

1. Nominal GDP is

   a. the base year market value of all final goods and services produced domestically during a given period.

   b. the current year market value of all final goods and services produced domestically during a given period.

   c. usually less than real GDP.

   d. the current year market value of domestic production of intermediate goods.

   e. none of the above.

2. Nominal GDP differs from real GDP in that

   a. nominal GDP tends to increase when total production of output in the economy increases, while real GDP does not.

   b. nominal GDP is measured in base year prices, while real GDP is measured in current year prices.

   c. nominal GDP is measured in current year prices, while real GDP is measured in base year prices.

   d. real GDP excludes taxes paid to the government, while nominal GDP does not.

3. Real GDP in base year dollars equals

   a. nominal GDP divided by the price index, times 100.

   b. nominal GDP divided by the price index.

   c. nominal GDP times the price index.

   d. nominal GDP times the price index, divided by 100.

   e. none of the above.

(continued)

4. If real GDP increases and population increases, then real GDP per capita

   a. will rise.

   b. will fall.

   c. will remain unchanged.

   d. could either rise, fall, or remain unchanged.

1. If we overestimated inflation over time, would our calculations of real GDP growth be over- or underestimated?

2. Why would the growth in real GDP overstate the growth of output per person in a country with a growing population?

Answers: 1. b 2. c 3. a 4. d

11.5

Problems with GDP as a Measure of Economic Welfare

📁 What are some of the deficiencies of GDP as a measure of economic welfare?

📁 What is the underground economy?

📁 What are nonmarket transactions?

As we noted throughout this chapter, real GDP is often used as a measure of the economic welfare of a nation. The accuracy of this measure for that purpose is questionable, however, because several important factors are excluded from its calculation. These factors include nonmarket transactions, the underground economy, leisure, externalities, and the quality of the goods purchased.

Nonmarket Transactions

Are nonmarket transactions excluded from GDP because they are unimportant?

Nonmarket transactions include the provision of goods and services outside traditional markets for which no money is exchanged. We simply do not have reliable enough information on this output to include it in the GDP. The single most important nonmarket transaction omitted from the GDP is the services of housewives (or househusbands). These services are not sold in any market, so they are not entered into the GDP; but they are nonetheless performed. For example, if a single woman hires a tax accountant, those payments enter into the calculation of GDP. Suppose, though, that the woman marries her tax accountant. Now the woman no longer pays her husband for his accounting services. Reported GDP falls after the marriage, although output does not change.

In less-developed countries, where a significant amount of food and clothing output is produced in the home, the failure to include nonmarket economic activity in GDP is a serious deficiency. Even in the United States, homemade meals, housework, and the vegetables and flowers produced in home gardens are excluded, even though they clearly represent an output of goods and services.

The Underground Economy

It is impossible to know for sure the magnitude of the underground economy, which includes unreported income from both legal and illegal sources. For example, illegal gambling and prostitution are not included in the GDP, leading to underreporting of an unknown magnitude. The reason these activities are excluded, however, has nothing to do with the morality of the services performed; rather, the cause of the exclusion is that most payments made for these services are neither reported to government authorities nor go through normal credit channels. Likewise, cash payments made to employees "under the table" slip through the GDP net. Estimates of the size of the underground economy vary from less than 4 percent to more than 20 percent of GDP. It also appears that a significant portion of this unreported income comes from legal sources, such as self-employment.

What is the underground economy?

Measuring the Value of Leisure

The value that individuals place on leisure is omitted in calculating GDP. Most of us could probably get a part-time job if we wanted to, earning some additional money by working in the evening or on weekends. Yet we choose not to do so. Why? The opportunity cost is too high—we would have to forgo some leisure. If you work on Saturday nights, you cannot see your friends, go to parties, attend concerts, watch television, or go to the movies. The opportunity cost of leisure is the income forgone by not working. For example, if people start taking more three-day weekends, GDP will surely fall, but can we necessarily say that the standard of living will fall? GDP will fall, but economic well-being may rise.

Leisure, then, has a positive value that does not show up in the GDP accounts. To put leisure in the proper perspective, ask yourself whether you would rather live in Country A, which has a per capita GDP of $25,000 a year and a 30-hour work week, or Country B, with a $25,000 per capita GDP and a 50-hour work week. Most people would choose Country A. The problem that this omission in GDP poses can be fairly significant in international comparisons or observations of one nation over time.

DOUG MENUEZ/GETTY IMAGES

GDP and Externalities

As we have discussed in earlier chapters, positive and negative externalities may result from the production of some goods and services. As a result of these externalities, the equilibrium prices of these goods and services—the figures used in GDP calculations—do not reflect their true values to society (unless, of course, the externalities have been internalized). For example, if a steel mill produces 100,000 more tons of steel, GDP increases; GDP does not, however, decrease to reflect damages from the air pollution that results from the production of that additional steel. Likewise, additional production of a vaccine would be reflected in the GDP, but the positive benefit to members of society—other than the purchaser—would not be included in the calculation. In other words, while GDP measures the goods and services produced, it does not adequately measure the "goods" and "bads" that result from the production processes.

GDP doesn't measure everything that contributes to or detracts from our well-being; it is difficult to measure the value of those effects. Environmentalists believe that national income accounts should adjust for changes in the environment. But this leads to many conceptual problems, such as how to measure the marginal values of goods and services not sold in markets and how to adjust for geographical differences in environmental damage. The critical issue is whether important trends in "uncounted" goods and services result in questionable conclusions about whether we are becoming better or worse off.

in the news   The Underground Economy

Here is the brief, unremarkable story of how I recently came to participate in the underground economy: Mid-afternoon on the iciest day this past winter, a man knocked at my front door. "Shovel your walk?" he asked. "Only $5." Outside, it was a bone-chilling 15 degrees. "Sold," I said. A half hour later I handed over a five-dollar bill and thanked him for saving me the trouble. Officially, this was an unofficial transaction—off the books, with no taxes paid or safety regulations followed. (At least, I assume this hired hand didn't bother to report that income or register with the proper authorities.) As such, it was technically illegal. And, of course, it's the sort of thing that happens all the time. The size of the official U.S. economy, as measured by Gross Domestic Product (GDP), was almost $12 trillion in 2004. Measurements of the unofficial economy—not including illegal activities like drug dealing and prostitution—differ substantially. But it's generally agreed to be significant, somewhere between 6 percent and 20 percent of GDP. At the midpoint, this would be about $1.5 trillion a year.

Broadly defined, the underground, gray, informal, or shadow economy involves otherwise legal transactions that go unreported or unrecorded. That's a wide net, capturing everything from baby-sitting fees, to bartering home repairs with a neighbor, to failing to report pay from moonlighting gigs. The "underground" label tends to make it sound much more sinister than it really is. Criminal activities make up a large portion of what could be termed the total underground economy. Many studies have been done on the economics of drug dealing, prostitution, and gambling. But because money from crime is almost never recovered, many policymakers are more interested in portions of the underground economy that otherwise would be legal if not hidden from authorities. Things like shoveling walks.

. . . Without knowing the precise size, scope, and causes of the underground economy, how can they decide what—if anything—to do about it? Was the man who shoveled my walk engaging in a socially positive or negative activity? Was I? Suffice it to say, some economists have dedicated their entire careers to answering questions about the underground economy—and still there is nothing close to a consensus about its size or description. In Schneider's latest study, the U.S. informal economy—or "shadow economy," as he calls it—is pegged at 8.4 percent of GDP. . . .

. . . [E]conomists generally agree that the shadow economy is worse in developing nations, whose webs of bureaucratic red tape and corruption are notorious. For instance, Schneider in 2003 published "shadow economy" estimates (defined broadly as all market-based, legal production of goods and services deliberately concealed from the authorities) for countries including: Zimbabwe, estimated at a whopping 63.2 percent of GDP, Thailand's at 54.1 percent, and Bolivia's at 68.3 percent. Among former Soviet bloc nations, Georgia led the way with a 68 percent of GDP shadow economy, and together those nations had an average 40.1 percent of GDP underground. This contrasts with an average of 16.7 percent among Western nations.

Some of Schneider's estimates of the size of the underground economy are controversial; critics say that he has jumbled different definitions of the underground economy in his estimates and sometimes not matched measurement methods, thus making comparisons less meaningful. But few quibble with his reasons for paying attention to the underground. . . . Official statistics—like GDP—may be rendered less useful if they don't really capture the breadth of economic activity.

SOURCE: Doug Campbell, "Searching for the Hidden Economy," Region Focus, Federal Reserve Bank of Richmond, Spring 2005.

Quality of Goods

GDP can also miss important changes in the improvements in the *quality* of goods and services. For example, the quality of a computer bought today differs significantly from one that was bought 10 years ago, but it will not lead to an increase in measured GDP. The same is true of many other goods, from cellular phones to automobiles to medical care.

Other Measures of Economic Well-Being

Even if we included some of these statistics that are difficult to measure, such as nonmarket transactions, the underground economy, leisure, externalities, and the quality of products, GDP would still not be a precise measure of economic well-being. Many other indices of well-being should be considered: life expectancies, infant mortality rates, education and environmental quality, levels of discrimination and fairness, health care, low crime rates, and minimum traffic congestion, just to name a few. GDP is a measure of economic production, *not* a measure of economic well-being. However, greater levels of GDP can lead to improvements in economic well-being, because society will now be able to afford better education and health care and a cleaner, safer environment.

⑦ SECTION QUIZ

1. Important factors that are excluded from GDP measurements include
   a. leisure.
   b. the underground economy.
   c. nonmarket transactions.
   d. the value of changes in the environment.
   e. all of the above.

2. If country A has a bigger underground economy than country B, and country A's citizens work fewer hours per week than the citizens of country B, other things being equal, then
   a. GDP comparisons between the countries would overstate the economic welfare of country A compared to B.
   b. GDP comparisons between the countries would understate the economic welfare of country A compared to B.
   c. it is impossible to know which direction GDP comparisons between the countries would be biased as measures of the economic welfare of the two countries.
   d. it would not introduce any bias in using GDP to compare economic welfare between the countries.
   e. none of the above would be true.

3. Which of the following is true?
   a. Real GDP is a highly accurate measure of the economic welfare of a nation.
   b. In less-developed countries, where a significant amount of food and clothing output is produced in the home, the failure to include non-market economic activity in GDP is a serious deficiency.
   c. Almost all of the underground economy represents income from illegal sources, such as drug dealing.
   d. GDP is decreased to reflect pollution resulting from production.

1. Why do GDP measures omit nonmarket transactions?

2. How would the existence of a high level of nonmarket activities in one country impact real GDP comparisons between it and other countries?

3. If we choose to decrease our hours worked because we value the additional leisure time more, will the resulting change in real GDP accurately reflect the change in our well-being? Why or why not?

4. How do pollution and crime affect GDP? How do pollution- and crime-control expenditures impact GDP?

Answers: 1. e 2. b 3. b

Interactive Summary

Fill in the blanks:

1. _____ accounting was created to provide a reliable, uniform method of measuring economic performance.

2. _____ is defined as the value of all final goods and services produced in a country in a period of time, almost always one year.

3. A(n) _____ good or service is one that is ready for its designated ultimate use, in contrast to _____ goods or services, which are used in the production of other goods.

4. The two primary ways of calculating economic output are the _____ approach and the _____ approach.

5. With the _____ approach, GDP is calculated by adding up the expenditures of market participants on final goods and services over a period of time.

6. For analytical purposes, economists usually categorize expenditures into four categories: _____, _____, _____, and _____.

7. Consumption spending is usually broken down into three subcategories: _____ goods, _____ consumer goods, and _____.

8. Consumption refers to the purchase of consumer goods and services by _____.

9. The most important single category of consumer durable goods is consumer _____.

10. Sales of nondurable consumer goods tend to be _____ stable over time than sales of durable goods.

11. Investment, as used by economists, refers to the creation of _____ goods, whose purpose is to _____.

12. The two categories of investment purchases measured in the expenditures approach are _____ investment and _____ investment.

13. When the economy is booming, investment purchases tend to _____ dramatically.

14. _____ payments are not included in government purchases because that spending does not go to purchase newly produced goods or services.

15. Imports must be _____ from GDP in order to obtain an accurate measure of domestic production.

16. The _____ approach to measuring GDP involves summing the incomes received by producers of goods and services.

17. Output creates _____ of equal value.

18. Factor payments include _____ for the use of labor services, _____ for land, _____ payments for the use of capital goods, and _____ for entrepreneurs, who put labor, land, and capital together.

19. The incomes received by persons providing goods and services are actually payments to the owners of _____ resources and are sometimes called _____ payments.

20. _____ must be subtracted from gross domestic product to get net national product (NNP).

21. _____ income is the personal income available to individuals after taxes.

22. The formula for converting any year's nominal GDP into real GDP (in base year dollars) is real GDP equals _____ divided by the _____, times 100.

23. To calculate real per capita GDP, we divide _____ GDP by the _____ to get the value of real output of final goods and services per person.

24. We do not have _____ enough information on the output of nonmarket transactions to include it in the GDP.

25. The most important nonmarket transactions omitted from GDP are services provided directly _____.

26. The value that individuals place on leisure is _____ in calculating GDP.

Key Terms and Concepts

national income accounting 304
gross domestic product (GDP) 304
double counting 304
expenditure approach 307
consumption 307
nondurable goods 307
durable goods 307
services 308

investment 308
fixed investment 308
producer goods 308
inventory investment 308
factor payments 310
gross national product (GNP) 311
depreciation 311
net national product (NNP) 311

indirect business taxes 311
national income (NI) 311
personal income (PI) 311
disposable personal income 311
real gross domestic product
   per capita 314

Section Quiz Answers

11.1 National Income Accounting: A Standardized Way to Measure Economic Performance

1. Why does GDP measure only final goods and services produced rather than all goods and services produced?

If the market value of every good and service sold were included in GDP, the same output would be counted more than once in many circumstances (as when the sales price of, say, bread includes the value of the flour that was used in making the bread, and the flour, in turn, includes the value of the wheat that was used to make the flour). Only final goods and services are included in GDP to avoid such double counting.

2. Why aren't all of the expenditures on used goods in an economy included in current GDP?

Current GDP does not include expenditures on used goods because GDP is intended to measure the value of currently produced goods and services in the economy. Used goods are not currently produced and have already been counted for the year they were newly produced.

3. Why do GDP statistics include real estate agents' commissions from selling existing homes and used car dealers' profits from selling used cars, but not the value of existing homes or used cars when they are sold?

Existing homes and used cars were both produced in the past and therefore aren't counted as part of current GDP. However, the services provided this year by real estate agents and used car dealers are currently produced, so the market value of those services, measured by real estate agent commis-sions and the profits earned by used car dealers, are included in GDP.

4. Why are sales of previously existing inventories of hula hoops not included in the current year's GDP?

Previously existing inventories of any product are not newly produced and are therefore not included in current year GDP. They were already produced and counted in an earlier period.

11.2 Measuring Total Production

1. What would happen to GDP if consumption purchases (C) and net exports (X – M) both rose, holding other things equal?

Since GDP is the sum of consumption purchases (C), investment purchases (I), government purchases (G), and net exports (X – M), an increase of any of these components of GDP will increase GDP, other things being equal. Since either an increase in consumption (C) or an increase in net exports (X – M) increases GDP, both changing in the same time period will also increase GDP, other things being equal.

2. Why do you think economic forecasters focus so much on consumption purchases and their determinants?

Economic forecasters focus so much on consumption purchases and their determinants because consumption purchases are by far the largest component (roughly two-thirds) of GDP; what happens to consumption purchases is therefore crucial to what happens to GDP.

3. Why are durable goods purchases more unstable than nondurable goods purchases?

Durable goods purchases are more unstable than nondurable goods purchases because nondurable goods are used up in a relatively short period of time; hence, their purchase is hard to shift from one time period to another. Durable goods, on the other hand, provide service for long periods of time, so consumer durable purchases can be significantly delayed to "make do" during economic hard times and significantly accelerated during good times.

4. Why does the investment component of GDP include purchases of new capital goods but not purchases of company stock?

New capital goods are newly produced goods, by definition, so they are included in GDP. However, sales of company stock do not involve a newly produced good or service (although the services of the broker, measured by the transaction fee, are included as a newly produced service). When someone buys shares of stock from someone else, no goods are being newly produced. Instead, already existing ownership claims on the future income of the company are simply being transferred from one person to another.

5. If Mary received a welfare check this year, would that transfer payment be included in this year's GDP? Why or why not?

GDP includes only currently produced goods and services. But since transfer payments are not payments in exchange for newly produced goods and services, they are not included in GDP.

6. Can inventory investment or net exports ever be negative?

Yes. If end-of-the-year inventories are smaller than beginning-of-the-year inventories, inventory investment is negative, and if the value of exports is smaller than the value of imports, net exports are negative.

11.3 Other Measures of Total Production and Total Income

1. How is personal income different from national income?

Personal income, the amount of income available to spend by consumers, is not the same as national income, because owners of productive resources do not receive all of the income that they earn and they receive "unearned" transfer payments. Undistributed corporate profits and social insurance taxes, which are not received by the factors of production, must be subtracted from, and transfer payments must be added to, national income to get personal income.

2. What is the difference between GDP and national income?

To find national income, we must subtract from GDP: (1) indirect business taxes, such as sales taxes;

(2) depreciation—payments set aside for the replacement of worn-out capital; and (3) net income of foreigners in the United States.

11.4 Problems in Calculating an Accurate GDP

1. If we overestimated inflation over time, would our calculations of real GDP growth be over- or underestimated?

Nominal GDP is deflated by the measure of inflation being used to calculate real GDP and real GDP growth. Therefore, for a given nominal GDP growth rate, overestimating inflation over time would result in underestimating real GDP growth over time.

2. Why would the growth in real GDP overstate the growth of output per person in a country with a growing population?

Real GDP growth measures what happens to output for the economy as a whole. But if the population is growing, real GDP is being split among an increasing number of people, and thus real GDP growth exceeds per capita real GDP growth.

11.5 Problems with GDP as a Measure of Economic Welfare

1. Why do GDP measures omit nonmarket transactions?

GDP measures omit nonmarket transactions because there is no accurate way to measure the values of those transactions, unlike for normal market transactions, where market prices can be used to measure the values involved.

2. How would the existence of a high level of nonmarket activities in one country impact real GDP comparisons between it and other countries?

Since nonmarket activities are not included in GDP, GDP would understate the true value of total output more for a country with a relatively high level of nonmarket activities than for a country with a smaller proportion of nonmarket activities, making countries with smaller shares of nonmarket activities look more productive relative to countries with larger shares of nonmarket activities.

3. If we choose to decrease our hours worked because we value the additional leisure time more, will the resulting change in real GDP accurately reflect the change in our well-being? Why or why not?

Decreasing hours worked will reduce real GDP, other things being equal. But if we choose to do so voluntarily, that would mean we place a higher value on the leisure time (which is not counted in GDP) than on the market output (which is counted in GDP) forgone by reducing hours worked, so the change in real GDP would not accurately reflect the change in our well-being.

4. How do pollution and crime affect GDP? How do pollution- and crime-control expenditures impact GDP?

Neither pollution nor crime are included (as "bads" to be subtracted) in GDP calculations. However, market expenditures for pollution and crime control are included in GDP, as currently produced goods and services.

Problems

1. Answer the following questions about GDP.
   a. What is the definition of GDP?
   b. Why does GDP measure only the final value of goods and services?
   c. Why does GDP measure only the value of goods and services produced within a country?
   d. How does GDP treat the sales of used goods?
   e. How does GDP treat sales of corporate stock from one stockholder to another?

2. Which of the following are included in GDP calculations?
   a. cleaning services performed by Molly Maid Corporation
   b. lawn-mowing services performed by a neighborhood child
   c. drugs sold illegally on a local street corner
   d. prescription drugs manufactured in the United States and sold at a local pharmacy
   e. a rug woven by hand in Turkey
   f. air pollution that diminishes the quality of the air you breathe
   g. toxic-waste cleanup performed by a local company
   h. car parts manufactured in the United States for a car assembled in Mexico
   i. a purchase of 1,000 shares of IBM stock
   j. monthly Social Security payment received by a retiree

3. To which category of U.S. GDP expenditure does each of the following correspond?
   a. Department of Motor Vehicles services
   b. automobiles exported to Europe
   c. a refrigerator
   d. a newly constructed four-bedroom house
   e. a restaurant meal
   f. additions to inventory at a furniture store
   g. F-16 fighter jets built by a U.S. aerospace corporation and contracted for by the government
   h. a new steel mill

4. The expenditures on tires by the Ford Motor Company are not included directly in GDP statistics while consumer expenditures on replacement tires are included. Why?

5. Using any relevant information below, calculate GDP using the expenditure approach.

Inventory investment	$ 50 billion
Fixed investment	120 billion
Consumer durables	420 billion
Consumer nondurables	275 billion
Interest	140 billion
Indirect business taxes	45 billion
Government wages and salaries	300 billion
Government purchases of goods and services	110 billion
Imports	80 billion
Exports	40 billion
Profits	320 billion
Services	600 billion

6. Fill in the missing data for the following table (in billions):

Consumption: _____
Consumption of durable goods: $1,200
Consumption of nondurable goods: $1,800
Consumption of services: $2,400
Investment: _____
Fixed investment: $800
Inventory investment: $600
Government expenditures on goods and services: $1,600
Government transfer payments: $500
Exports: $500
Imports: $650
Net exports: _____
GDP: _____

7. Answer these questions about durable goods and GDP:
   a. Do consumer nondurable or durable goods tend to change more over the course of a business cycle?
   b. How are consumer durables like investments?
   c. Can either fixed investment or inventory be negative in a given year?
   d. Why isn't all of government spending part of GDP?

8. How does GNP compare to GDP when:
   a. earnings of foreigners and foreign firms in the United States equal earnings of American citizens and firms overseas?
   b. earnings of foreigners and foreign firms in the United States exceed earnings of American citizens and firms overseas?
   c. earnings of foreigners and foreign firms in the United States are less than earnings of American citizens and firms overseas?

9. List, from the largest magnitude to the smallest, the following categories: disposable personal income, gross national product, national income, net national product, personal income.

10. Nominal GDP in Nowhereland in 2008 and 2009 is as follows:

NGDP 2008	NGDP 2009
$4 trillion	$4.8 trillion

Can you say that the production of goods and services in Nowhereland has increased between 2008 and 2009? Why or why not?

11. Answer these questions about GDP.
   a. Could next year's real GDP exceed next year's nominal GDP?
   b. Could real GDP grow at the same time that real GDP per capita falls?
   c. Could people's real consumption possibilities expand at the same time that real GDP per capita falls?
   d. How does changing amounts of leisure complicate comparisons of real well-being over time?

12. Fill in the missing data for the following table:

Year	GDP Deflator	Nominal GDP (in billions)	Real GDP (in billions)
1997	90.9	$7,000	_____
1998	100	_____	$8,000
1999	_____	$10,000	$8,000
2000	140	$14,000	_____
2001	150	_____	$12,000

Economic Growth in the Global Economy

The average U.S. citizen is at least 40 times wealthier than the average North Korean or Ethiopian. Why is the globe divided between the haves and the have nots? Is it institutions and incentives? If this is it, how do poor countries implement those changes?

John Maynard Keynes, one of the most influential economic thinkers of all time, once said that "in the long run, we are all dead." He made this statement because he was primarily concerned with explaining and reducing

short-term fluctuations in the level of business activity. He wanted to smooth out the business cycle, largely because of the implications that cyclical fluctuations had for buyers and sellers in terms of unemployment and price instability. No one would deny that Keynes's concerns were important and legitimate.

At the same time, however, Keynes's flippant remark about the long run discounts the fact that human welfare is greatly influenced by long-term changes in a nation's capacity to produce goods and services. Emphasis on short-run economic fluctuations ignores the longer-term dynamic changes that affect output, leisure, real income, and lifestyle.

What are the determinants of long-run economic change in our ability to produce goods and services? What are some of the consequences of rapid economic change? Why are some nations rich while others are poor? Does growth in output improve our economic welfare? We will explore these questions in this chapter.

12.1 | Economic Growth

📁 What is economic growth?   📁 What is productivity?

📁 What is the Rule of 70?

Defining Economic Growth

economic growth
an upward trend in the real per capita output of goods and services

How do we generally measure economic growth?

Economic growth is usually measured by the annual percentage change in real output of goods and services per capita (real GDP per capita), reflecting the expansion of the economy over time. We focus on per capita because we want to isolate the effect of increased population on economic growth. That is, an increase in population, *ceteris paribus*, will lower the standard of living because more people will be sharing a fixed real GDP. It is also important to note that our economic growth rate does not say anything about the distribution of output and income. For example, a country could have extraordinary growth in per capita output and yet the poor might make little or no improvement in their standard of living. That is, it is possible that income group made little or no gain.

In Chapter 3, we introduced the production possibilities curve. Along the production possibilities curve, the economy is producing at its potential output. How much the economy will produce at its potential output, sometimes called its *natural rate of output*, depends on the quantity and quality of its resources, including labor, capital (factories, machinery, tools, productive skills, etc.), and natural resources (land, coal, timber, oil, iron, etc.). In addition, technology can increase the economy's production capabilities. As shown in Exhibit 1, improvements in and greater stocks of land, labor, capital, and entrepreneurial activity will shift the production possibilities curve outward. Another way of saying that economic growth has shifted the production possibilities curve outward is to say that it has increased potential output.

The Rule of 70

If Nation A and Nation B start off with the same population and the same level of real GDP, will a slight difference in their growth rates over a long period of time make much of a difference? Yes. In the first year or two, the difference will be small, after a decade the difference will be large, and after 50 to 100 years it will be huge. The final effect will be a much higher standard of living in the nation with the greater economic growth, *ceteris paribus*.

ECS

economic content standards

Economic growth is a sustained rise in a nation's production of goods and services. It results from investments in human and physical capital, research and development, technological advances, and improved institutional arrangements and incentives.

A simple formula, called the Rule of 70, shows roughly how many years it will take a nation to double its output at various growth rates. If you take a nation's growth rate and divide it into 70, you will have the approximate time it will take to double the income level. For example, if a nation grows at 3.5 percent per year, then its real output will double every 20 years (70/3.5). However, if an economy only grows at 2 percent per year, the economy will double every 35 years (70/2), and at a 1 percent annual growth rate, it will take 70 years to double income (70/1). So even a small change in the growth rate of a nation will have a large impact over a lengthy period.

In Exhibit 2, we see the growth in real GDP for the United States since 1978. The exhibit shows that U.S. real GDP per capita (measured in 2005 dollars) grew from $25,503 in 1978 to $42,205 in 2010. Since the depth of the Great Depression in 1932, Americans today, on average, can purchase roughly nine times the amount of goods and services.

In Exhibit 3, we see a comparison of selected industrial countries. Because of differences in growth rates, some countries will become richer than others over time. With relatively slower economic growth, today's richest countries will not be the richest for very long. On the other hand, with even slight improvements in economic growth, today's poorest countries will not remain poor for long. China and India have both experienced spectacular economic growth over the past 20 years. Because of this economic growth, much of the world is now poorer than these two heavily populated countries.

Because of past economic growth, the "richest" or "most-developed" countries today have many times the market output of the "poorest" or "least-developed" countries. Put differently, the most-developed countries produce and market more output in a day than the least-developed countries do in a year. The international differences in income, output, and wealth are indeed striking and have caused a great deal of friction between developed and

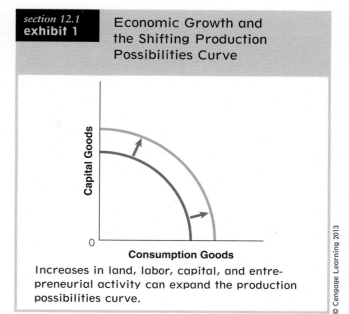

section 12.1
exhibit 1

Economic Growth and the Shifting Production Possibilities Curve

Increases in land, labor, capital, and entrepreneurial activity can expand the production possibilities curve.

© Cengage Learning 2013

ECS

economic content standards

Historically, economic growth has been the primary vehicle for alleviating poverty and raising standards of living.

What is the Rule of 70?

section 12.1
exhibit 2

U.S. Real GDP per Capita (Year 2005 Dollars)

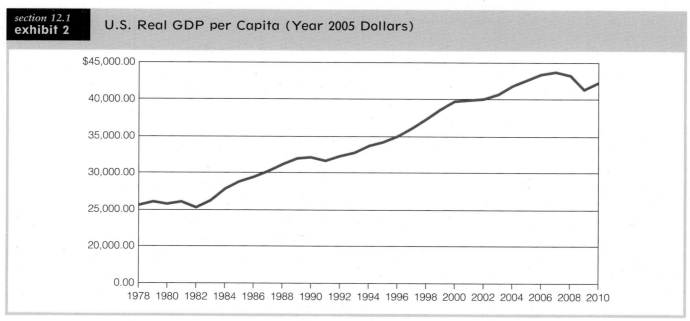

SOURCE: http://www.measuringgrowth.org.

section 12.1 exhibit 3	Average Annual Growth Rates in Real GDP per Capita in Selected Industrial Countries

	2003–2012
United States	1.5%
Japan	0.6
Germany	0.4
France	1.4
Italy	0.5
United Kingdom	1.1
Canada	2.9

SOURCE: International Monetary Fund, http://imf.org.

ECS

economic content standards

Investment in factories, machinery, new technology, and in the health, education, and training of people stimulates economic growth and can raise future standards of living.

How does the circular flow model help us understand the link between productivity and the standard of living?

ECS

economic content standards

Standards of living increase as productivity improves.

less-developed countries. The United States and the nations of the European Union experienced sizable increases in real output over the past two centuries. Even in 1800 most of these nations were better off in terms of market output than many impoverished present-day countries such as Ethiopia, India, and Nepal. See the U.S. real GDP per capita from 1978–2010 in Exhibit 2.

China and India

Both China and India have per capita real GDP levels that are far less than the United States. The power of compound interest could well change this ranking in the future. As Nobel laureate Robert Lucas once said, "Once one starts to think about differences in growth rates among countries, it is hard to think about anything else." But the current rate of economic growth in these two countries will change things in the future. India experienced an average annual growth rate almost 9 percent per year from 2003 to 2008. The economic growth rate slowed in 2008 to 2009 as India felt the effect of the global financial crisis. India has a highly educated English-speaking population and is a major exporter of software services and software workers. In 2010, India's real GDP growth rate was 10.4 percent per year.

China is growing at about 10 percent per year. Foreign investment in China has helped spur output of both domestic and export goods. China grew at only 9 percent annually in 2008, its slowest growth rate since 2001. However, by 2010 China's real GDP growth rate was back to 10.3 percent per year. The global financial crisis had a larger impact on China than India because China's economy is more heavily reliant on exports. Exports account for about one-third of China's GDP. Since economic liberalization began in 1978, China's investment and export-led economy has grown 70 times bigger and is the fastest-growing major economy in the world. China has the world's third-largest nominal GDP, although its per capita income is still low, behind roughly a hundred countries.

The rapid economic growth in both countries has pulled millions out of poverty.

Productivity: The Key to a Higher Standard of Living

Will the standard of living in the United States rise, level off, or decline over time? For a large part, the answer depends on productivity growth. Productivity measures how efficiently resources are used. When productivity rises, more can be produced from a given amount of resources. A country's standard of living rises when it can produce goods and services more efficiently. All resources can become more productive—capital, labor, or natural resources. However, labor is the resource most often used to measure productivity because it accounts for roughly 70 percent of production costs.

The link between productivity and the standard of living may be understood most easily by recalling the circular flow model, where we show that aggregate expenditures are equal to aggregate income. In other words, the aggregate value of all goods and services produced in the economy must equal the payments made to the factors of production—wages and salaries paid to workers, rental payments to capital, profits to owners, and so on. That is, the only way an economy can increase its rate of consumption in the long run is by increasing the amount it produces. But why are some countries so much better than others at producing goods and services? We will answer this question in the next section as we examine the determinants of productivity—physical capital, human capital, natural resources, and technology.

⑦ SECTION QUIZ

1. Economic growth refers to a(n) _____ in the output of goods and services in an economy. The greater the economic growth, the _____ goods citizens and their descendants will have to consume.

   a. decrease; less

   b. decrease; more

   c. increase; more

   d. increase; less

2. Economic growth is usually measured by the annual percent change in

   a. nominal GDP.

   b. nominal GDP per capita.

   c. real GDP.

   d. real GDP per capita.

3. How much the economy can produce at its natural rate of output depends on

   a. technology.

   b. the quantity of available natural resources.

   c. the productivity of labor.

   d. the stock of available capital.

   e. all of the above.

4. An economy's production possibilities curve will shift outward over time if

   a. technological progress occurs.

   b. the stock of available capital decreases.

   c. emigration results in a decrease in the supply of available labor.

   d. the productivity of labor increases.

   e. either (a) or (d) occurs.

5. According to the Rule of 70, if a nation grows at a rate of 5 percent per year, it will take roughly _____ for national income to double.

   a. 10 years

   b. 7 years

   c. 70 years

   d. 14 years

   e. none of the above

---

1. Why does the production possibilities curve shift outward with economic growth?

2. Even if "in the long run, we are all dead," are you glad earlier generations of Americans worked and invested for economic growth?

3. If long-run consequences were not important, would many students go to college or participate in internship programs without pay?

4. When the Dutch "created" new land with their system of dikes, what did it do to their production possibilities curve? Why?

Answers: 1. c   2. d   3. e   4. e   5. d

Determinants of Economic Growth

📂 What factors contribute to economic growth?

📂 What is human capital?

Why are there vastly different standards of living around the world? The answer can be found in a single concept: labor productivity. For the most part, real GDP per capita depends on increases in **labor productivity**. Labor productivity is defined as output per unit of worker. Sustained economic growth can only occur if the amount of output by the average worker increases. As we explained earlier, a nation's standard of living ultimately depends on its ability to produce goods and services.

labor productivity
output per unit of worker

What are the four main factors that contribute to productivity growth?

Factors that Contribute to Productivity Growth

We will look at four major factors that contribute to growth in productivity. These include physical capital, human capital, natural resources, and technology. Today's workers generally produce more output than workers in the past. Of today's workers, those in some countries, like the United States, generally produce more output than do workers in most other countries. Workers with higher productivity usually have more physical capital like buildings and computers, are more educated than their counterparts, and have benefited from tremendous technological advancements.

Now that we know how productivity leads to long-run economic growth, let's look at the factors that lead to greater productivity.

Physical Capital

Recall that physical capital includes goods such as tools, machinery, and factories that have already been produced and are now producing other goods and services. Combining workers with more capital makes workers more productive. Thus, capital investment can lead to increases in labor productivity.

Even in primitive economies, workers usually have some rudimentary tools to further their productive activity. Consider the farmer who needs to dig a ditch to improve drainage in his fields. If he used just his bare hands, it might take a lifetime to complete the job. If he used a shovel, he could dig the ditch in hours or days. But with a big earth-moving machine, he could do it in minutes. Most economists agree that capital formation has played a significant role in the economic development of nations. Physical capital increases labor productivity.

Per-Worker Production Function

In Chapter 2, we found that by increasing the rate of saving, we can produce a greater amount of new capital goods and increase the stock of productive capital for the future. Because resources are scarce, in order to invest in new capital, society must sacrifice some current consumption. To save more now, we need to consume less now. Ultimately, this will allow society to consume more in the future.

In Exhibit 1, we see how the amount of capital per worker influences the amount of output per worker. This positively sloped curve is called the per-worker production function. Holding the other determinants of output constant (human capital, natural resources, and technology), we see that moving up along the production function, when the quantity of capital per worker rises, so does the amount of output per worker, but at a diminishing rate—the curve eventually becomes flatter as more capital per worker is added. That is, capital is subject to diminishing marginal returns. If the economy has a very low level of capital, an extra unit of capital leads to a relatively large increase in output—a movement from point A to point B in Exhibit 1. If the economy already has a great deal of capital, an extra unit of capital leads to a relatively smaller increase in output—a movement from point C to point D in Exhibit 1. Imagine that you owned a small store and you had 10 employees and one computer. As you added more computers, output per worker rose, but only up to a point. What if you added 20 computers to you work force of 10? Adding more computers (capital) still adds to output but by smaller and smaller additional amounts. This is what is called diminishing marginal returns to capital. Thus, in the long run, other things equal, the benefits of a higher saving rate and additional capital stock become smaller and the rate of growth slows.

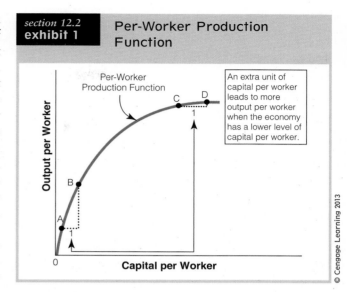

section 12.2 **exhibit 1**   **Per-Worker Production Function**

An extra unit of capital per worker leads to more output per worker when the economy has a lower level of capital per worker.

Some economists believe diminishing marginal returns to capital can help explain the variation in growth rates between rich and poor countries. In poor countries, where there is little capital, small increases in capital investment can lead to relatively large increases in productivity. In rich countries, where workers already have large amounts of capital, increases in capital investment may have a very small additional effect on productivity. Economists call this the catch-up effect.

Human Capital

When workers acquire qualitative improvements (learning new skills, for example), output increases. Workers with a large stock of human capital are more productive than those with small stocks of human capital. Indeed, it has become popular to view labor skills as human capital that can be augmented or improved by education and on-the-job training. Like physical capital, human capital must be produced, usually by means of teachers, schoolrooms, libraries, computer labs, and time devoted to studying. Human capital may be more important than physical capital as a determinant of labor productivity. Human capital also includes improvements in health. Better health conditions allow workers to be more productive. In fact, University of Chicago economist and Nobel laureate Robert Fogel has shown that improved health from better nutrition has a significant impact on long-run economic growth.

Natural Resources

An abundance of natural resources, such as fertile soil, and other raw materials, such as timber and oil, can enhance output. Many scholars cite the abundance of natural resources in the United States as one reason for its historical success. Canada and Australia are endowed with a large natural resource base and high per capita incomes. Resources are, however, not the whole story; for example, Japan and Hong Kong have had tremendous economic success despite having relatively few natural resources. In addition, Kuwait and Saudi Arabia are rich because they sit on top of large pools of oil. On the other hand, Brazil has a large and varied natural resource base, yet its income per capita is relatively low compared with many developed countries. It appears that a natural resource base can affect the initial development process, but sustained growth is influenced by other factors. However, most economists would agree that a limited resource base does pose an important obstacle to economic growth.

Technology

Most economists believe that it is the progress in technology that drives productivity. It is technology that allows workers to produce more even with the same amount of physical

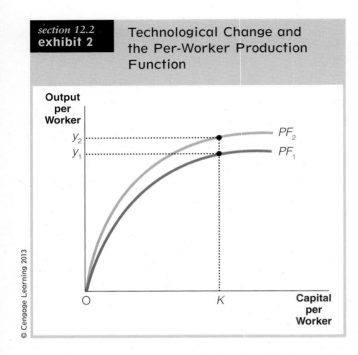

section 12.2 exhibit 2

Technological Change and the Per-Worker Production Function

and human capital. Technological change can lead to better machinery and equipment, increases in capital, and better organization and production methods. Technological advances stem from human ingenuity and creativity in developing new ways of combining the factors of production to enhance the amount of output from a given quantity of resources. The process of technological advance involves invention and innovation. **Innovation** is the adoption of the product or process. For example, in the United States, the invention and innovation of the cotton gin, the Bessemer steel-making process, and the railroad were important stimuli to economic growth. New technology, however, must be introduced into productive use by managers or entrepreneurs who weigh the perceived estimates of benefits of the new technology against estimates of costs. Thus, the entrepreneur is also an important economic factor in the growth process.

Technological advances permit us to economize on one or more inputs used in the production process. They can permit savings of labor. For example, when a new machine does the work of many workers, technology is said to be embodied in capital and to be labor saving. Technology, however, can also be land (natural resource) saving or even capital saving. For example, nuclear fission has permitted us to build power plants that economize on the use of coal, a natural resource. The reduction in transportation time that accompanied the invention and innovation of the railroad allowed businesses to reduce the capital they needed in the form of inventories. Because goods could be obtained more quickly, businesses could reduce the stock kept on their shelves.

innovation
applications of new knowledge that create new products or improve existing products

And inventions can come in all sizes. Obviously, the semiconductor chip made a huge impact on productivity and growth, but so did the Post-it note that was introduced in the early 1980s, the laptop computer, or barcode scanners, which were first introduced in Walmart stores. We have also seen huge advances in communication (the Internet) and medicine.

In short, better methods of organization and production can lead to increases in labor productivity. When fewer workers are needed in a grocery store or a department store due to better methods of organization, or new machinery and equipment, labor productivity rises.

In Exhibit 2, we see that technological change can shift the per-worker production curve upward, producing more output per worker with the same amount of capital per worker.

Technological change allows the economy to escape the full impact of diminishing marginal returns to capital. Thus, in the long run, *ceteris paribus*, an economy must experience technological advance in order to improve its standard of living and overcome the diminishing marginal returns to capital.

New Growth Theory

The greater the reward for new technology, the more research and technology will occur. According to Paul Romer, a new growth economist, economic growth can continue unimpeded as long as we keep coming up with new ideas. And there is a role for government, too—encouraging the creation of new ideas. While the market is a great engine for economic growth, it can be "turbocharged" with strong institutional support for education and science. Romer believes that it is ideas that drive economic growth. To Romer, economic growth comes from increases in value—rearranging fixed amounts of matter and making new combinations that are more valuable. "There are zillions of combinations that we can use to make new goods and services we value."

⊙ SECTION QUIZ

1. Which of the following will lead to productivity growth?

   a. technology

   b. natural resources

   c. physical capital

   d. human capital

   e. all of the above

2. In the long run, the most important determinant of a nation's standard of living is

   a. its rate of productivity growth.

   b. its ability to export cheap labor.

   c. its ability to control the nation's money supply.

   d. its endowment of natural resources.

3. Which of the following is true?

   a. In poor countries where there is little capital, small increases in capital investment can lead to relatively large increases in productivity.

   b. In rich countries, where workers already have large amounts of capital, increases in capital investment may have a very small additional effect on productivity.

   c. Economists call (a) and (b) the catch-up effect.

   d. All of the above are true.

4. According to Paul Romer, a new growth economist,

   a. economic growth can continue unimpeded, as long as we keep coming up with new ideas.

   b while the market is a great engine for economic growth, it can be "turbocharged" with strong institutional support for education and science.

   c. economic growth comes from increases in value—rearranging fixed amounts of matter and making new combinations that are more valuable.

   d. all of the above are true.

---

1. Why is no single factor capable of completely explaining economic growth patterns?

2. Why might countries with relatively scarce labor be leaders in labor-saving innovations? In what area would countries with relatively scarce land likely be innovative leaders?

3. Why could an increase in the price of oil increase real GDP growth in oil-exporting countries such as Saudi Arabia and Mexico, while decreasing growth in oil-importing countries such as the United States and Japan?

4. How is Hong Kong a dramatic example of why abundant natural resources are not necessary for rapid economic growth?

Answers: 1. e   2. a   3. d   4. d

global watch   Why Are Some Countries Rich?

In the beginning of this chapter, we asked why is the average citizen of the United States 40 times richer than those of Ethiopa and North Korea? But perhaps the question we should have been asking is how did particular countries prosper while others did not? Nations are not inherently rich or poor. Government policies can make the difference.

According to Professor Daron Acemoglu of MIT, the reason why some nations succeed and others don't comes down to the soundness and transparency of their government institutions—the ability of a nation's citizens to own property, freely elect representatives, and live without fear of crime and corruption.

COURTESY OF KATHERINE SEXTON

SOURCE: Daron Acemoglu, "What Makes a Nation Rich? One Economist's Big Answer," Esquire, November 18, 2009, http://www.esquire.com/features/ best-and-brightest-2009/ world-poverty-map-1209.

12.3   Public Policy and Economic Growth

📁 Why is the saving rate so important for increasing economic growth?

📁 Why is research and development so important for economic growth?

📁 Why are property rights so important for increasing economic growth?

📁 What impact will free trade have on economic growth?

📁 Why is education so important for economic growth?

The Impact of Economic Growth

Economic growth means more than an increase in the real income (output) of the population. A number of other important changes accompany changes in output. Claims that economic growth stimulates political freedom or democracy have even been made, but evidence for that correlation is far from conclusive. Even though some democratic societies are rich and some authoritarian ones are poor, the opposite also holds. That is, some features of democracy, such as majority voting and special interest groups, may actually be growth retarding. For example, if the majority decides to vote for large land reforms and wealth transfers, the consequences will be higher taxes and market distortions that will reduce incentives for work, investment, and ultimately economic growth. However, a nation can pursue a number of policies that will increase economic growth.

Saving Rates, Investment, Capital Stock, and Economic Growth

One of the most important determinants of economic growth is the saving rate. To consume more in the future, we must save more now. Generally, higher levels of saving will lead to higher rates of investment and capital formation and, therefore, greater economic growth.

Individuals can either consume or save their income. If individuals choose to consume all their income, they will have nothing left for saving, which businesses could use for investment purposes to build new plants or replace worn-out or obsolete equipment. With little investment in capital stock, there will be little economic growth. Capital can also increase as a result of injections of capital from abroad (foreign direct investments), but the role of national saving rates in economic growth is of particular importance.

Does added investment guarantee economic growth?

However, investment alone does not guarantee economic growth. Economic growth hinges on the quality and type of investment as well as on investments in human capital and improvements in technology.

Infrastructure

Infrastructure (e.g., highways, ports, bridges, power lines, airports, and information technology) is critical to economic coordination and activity. Some infrastructure is private and some is public. In the past several decades, the amount of government investment in U.S. infrastructure has fallen. Some economists argue that improvements in infrastructure could lead to higher productivity. Others argue the causality runs in the other direction, that higher productivity leads to greater infrastructure. In addition, a special interest problem concerns favored districts with political clout that end up as the recipients of improved infrastructure—which may not be an efficient solution. Most would agree, however, that poor infrastructure is a major deterrent to economic growth.

Research and Development

Some scholars believe that the importance of **research and development (R&D)** is understated. Research and development consists of the activities undertaken to create new products and processes that will lead to technological progress. The concept of R&D is broad indeed—it can include new products, management improvements, production innovations, or simply learning by doing. However, it is clear that investing in R&D and rewarding innovators with patents have paid big dividends in the past 50 to 60 years. Some would argue that even larger rewards for research and development would spur even more rapid economic growth. Some types of scientific research may have far-reaching benefits that cannot be captured by a private firm. Such a case presents a compelling argument for government support of basic research. GPS satellite systems in cars, for example, were originally designed for military purposes. In addition, an important link exists between R&D and capital investment. As already noted, when capital depreciates over time, it is replaced with new equipment that embodies the latest technology. Consequently, R&D may work hand in hand with investment to improve growth and productivity. Lastly, R&D may benefit foreigners as they import goods from technologically advanced countries to make their firms more efficient.

research and development (R&D)
activities undertaken to create new products and processes that will lead to technological progress

How can R&D and investment work together to improve economic growth?

The Protection of Property Rights Impacts Economic Growth

Economic growth rates tend to be higher in countries where the government enforces property rights. Property rights give owners the legal right to keep or sell their properties—land, labor, or capital. Without property rights, life would be a huge "free-for-all" where people could take whatever they wanted. Economists call the government's ability to protect private property rights and enforce contracts the *rule of law*.

People living in developed countries take property rights for granted but those living in developing countries know the difficulties associated with a lack of property rights. In most developed countries, property rights are effectively protected by the government. However, in developing countries, such protection is not usually the case. If the government does not enforce property rights, the private sector must respond in costly ways that stifle economic growth. For example, an unreliable judiciary system means that entrepreneurs must often rely on informal agreements that are difficult to enforce. As a result, they may have to pay bribes to get things done, and even then, they may not get the promised services. Individuals may have to buy private security or pay "organized crime" for protection against crime and corruption. In addition, landowners and business owners may be fearful of coups or takeovers from a new government, which might confiscate their property altogether. In short, if government is not adequately protecting property rights, the incentive to invest will be hindered, and political instability, corruption, and lower rates of economic growth will be likely. However, it may well be a two-way street. In the words of former U.N. Secretary-General Kofi Annan, "There will be no development without security and no security without development."

Free Trade and Economic Growth

Allowing free trade can also lead to greater output because of the principle of comparative advantage. Essentially, the principle of comparative advantage suggests that if two nations or individuals with different resource endowments and production capabilities specialize in

policy application   Institutional Economics

Douglass C. North, an economic historian, was the recipient of the Nobel Prize in Economics in 1993. One of North's contributions is his analysis of the linkage between institutional changes and economic growth. According to North, "the sources of sustained economic growth and the determinants of income distribution are to be found in the institutional structure of a society. Economic historians can no longer write good economic history without explicitly taking into account the institutional structure of the system, both economic and political. We can't avoid the political aspect because decisions made outside the marketplace have had, and will continue to have, a fundamental influence upon growth and welfare."

Institutions matter because they affect the choices open to people, shape incentives, and are an important determinant of human action. The institutional structure of a society (or the "rules of the game," as Mr. North calls it) includes formal rules (such as constitutions, property rights, laws of contract), informal constraints (conventions, customs, codes of conduct), and the means of enforcing both formal and informal standards of behavior (courts, social ostracism, personal beliefs). As in sports, the way the game is played and its outcome depend on the nature of the rules, the character of the players, and the fairness (impartiality) of the referee. Moreover, the choice of the rules and the enforcement mechanisms will be affected by prevailing ideology and culture.

According to North, rules must be credible if they are to be effective. That is, they must be enforced. Private enforcement is possible, but as economic life becomes more complex, political institutions become the major instrument for defining and enforcing property rights. The history of economic performance cannot be separated from the history of political performance. The New Institutional Economics studies both.

North has shown that those countries that (1) adopt a rule of law that limits the power of government over economic life and protects the rights of persons and property and (2) maintain open markets and freedom of contract are more likely to achieve long-run economic prosperity than those who do not.

According to North, economic change is "path dependent": The future depends on the past and present choices. History is not predetermined or based on some grand design; it is the sum of human actions. How we act will depend on the rules we inherit and formulate, as well as on our cultural and moral heritage. But ultimately, it is individuals who must choose.

SOURCES: See Douglass C. North, *Growth and Welfare in the American Past*, 2nd ed., Englewood Cliffs, NJ: Prentice Hall, 1974; and James Dorn, "North Wins Nobel for New Institutional Economics," *The Margin* (Spring 1994): 56.

producing a smaller number of goods and services and engage in trade, both parties will benefit. Total output will rise. This concept will be discussed in greater detail in the chapter on International Trade.

Education

Education, investment in human capital, may be just as important as improvements in physical capital. At any given time, an individual has a choice between current work and investment activities such as education that can increase future earning power. An individual will usually accept reduction in current income to devote effort to education and training. In turn, a certain return on the investment is expected because in later years, the individual will earn a higher wage rate (the amount of the increase depending on the nature of the education and training as well as natural ability). For example, in the United States, a person with a college education can be expected to earn almost twice as much per year as a high-school graduate.

© VIVIANE MOOS/CORBIS

Improving education is a relatively inexpensive way to enrich the lives of people living in poorer countries. Education allows these countries to produce more advanced goods and services and enjoy the wealth created from trading in the global economy. Taiwan, India, and South Korea are now part of the high-tech global economy, but most of Africa, with the lowest levels of education, has been left behind.

One argument for government subsidizing education is that the investment can increase the skill level of the population and raise the standard of living. However, even if the individual does not benefit financially from increased education, society may benefit culturally and in other respects from having its members highly educated. For example, more education can lead to lower crime rates, new ideas that may benefit society, and more informed voters.

With economic growth, illiteracy rates fall and formal education grows. The correlation between per capita output and the proportion of the population that is able to read or write is striking. Improvements in literacy stimulate economic growth by reducing barriers to the flow of information; when information costs are high, out of ignorance, many resources flow to or remain in uses that are unproductive. Moreover, education imparts skills that are directly useful in raising labor productivity, whether it is mathematics taught to a sales clerk, engineering techniques taught to a college graduate, or just good ideas that facilitate production and design.

Many economists believe that the tremendous growth in East Asia (South Korea, Taiwan, Hong Kong, and Singapore) in the last half of the twentieth century was a result of good basic education for many of their citizens. This reason was one of many factors that contributed to growth, including high rates of saving and a large increase in labor force participation.

global watch   Education: A Vital Component of Economic Growth

The Organization for Economic Co-operation and Development (OECD) recently released the results of a survey examining the performance of international education systems. It found that even a small improvement in ability can have a significant impact on the future of a nation's economy, as measured by gains in the growth rates of real gross domestic product per capita.

The report found that it was the quality of education, not the quantity or "seat time." Eric Hanushek, an economist at Stanford and one of the authors of the study, found that indiscriminately throwing money at education isn't effective. The educational systems that perform the best are able to target funds where they're needed most. One factor that was particularly significant was the teaching quality. Even replacing ineffective teachers with "average" ones was beneficial.

SOURCE: "New Study Links Education to Economic Growth," Education-Portal.com, June 16, 2011, http://education-portal.com/articles/New_Study_ Links_Education_to_Economic_Growth.html.

However, in poorer developing countries, the higher opportunity costs of education present an obstacle. Children in developing countries are an important part of the labor force starting at a young age. If they attend school, children cannot help in the fields—planting, harvesting, fence building, and many other tasks—which many households depend on in the rural areas of developing countries. A child's labor contribution to the family is far less important in a developed country. Thus, the higher opportunity cost of education in developing countries is one of the reasons that school enrollments are lower.

Education may also be a consequence of economic growth, because as incomes rise, people's tendency to consume education increases. People increasingly look to education for more than the acquisition of immediately applicable skills. Education becomes a consumption good as well as a means of investing in human capital. There are also a number of factors that can lead to slower economic growth. Countries that fail to enforce the rule of law, experience wars and revolutions, have poor education and health systems and low rates of saving and investment are not likely to grow very rapidly.

Do Economies Converge?

Many economists believe that, holding other things equal, countries with lower real GDP per capita will grow faster than countries with higher real GDP per capita. However, other things, including infrastructure, the extent to which the rule of law is followed and the level of education are not equal. Adjusting for such additional variables, there is a tendency for poorer countries to grow faster. This has certainly been true of South Korea, Taiwan, and Singapore, which have invested in technology and human resources, but many poor countries of Africa and Latin America continue to be poor. So, there is no guarantee that being poorer leads to greater economic growth.

Why is it easier for developing countries to grow faster than advanced ones? First, they can adopt existing technology from developed countries. Second, developed economies may be subject to diminishing marginal returns to capital—a concept we discussed earlier in the chapter. Third, population growth is higher in developing counties, leading to lower levels of per capita consumption for a given level of economic output. For example, in Western Europe and the United States, population growth rates are currently roughly 1 percent per year, while in some of the poorer African countries, they can approach 3 percent per year or more. In addition, while technology is portable, the ability to use that technology is not. With low literacy rates and educational attainment, as in sub-Saharan African nations, countries can lack the human capital to adopt and use the new technology.

---

⑦ SECTION QUIZ

1. If a country increased its saving rate,

   a. its current consumption would have to fall.

   b. its current consumption would have to rise.

   c. its future consumption possibilities will fall.

   d. its future consumption possibilities will rise.

   e. both (a) and (d) will occur.

2. Which of the following statements is incorrect?

   a. One of the most important determinants of economic growth is a nation's saving rate.

   b. Injections of foreign capital from abroad may contribute to a nation's economic growth.

   c. Economic growth depends on the quality and type of investments made.

   d. Economic growth rates tend to be lower in countries where property rights are better enforced by government.

(continued)

⑦ SECTION QUIZ (Cont.)

3. High rates of saving and investment in a country

   a. guarantee rapid economic growth.

   b. tend to increase economic growth but do not guarantee it.

   c. will result in greater economic growth if they are accompanied by advances in technology than if they are not.

   d. will result in greater economic growth if they are accompanied by more investment in human capital than if they are not.

   e. will result in all of the above except (a).

4. Economic growth tends to be greater in countries where

   a. the government effectively protects property rights.

   b. more resources are devoted to research and development.

   c. there is greater freedom to trade freely.

   d. any of the above is true.

5. In a country that has an unstable government or judiciary, would you expect to see more or less entrepreneurial activity?

   a. less, because an unstable economy has fewer entrepreneurs

   b. less, because of an unreliable infrastructure for protecting property rights

   c. more, because of fewer governmental restrictions

   d. more, because of less taxation of commercial and research activities

---

1. Why does knowing what factors are correlated with economic growth not tell us what causes economic growth?

2. How does increasing the capital stock lead to economic growth?

3. How do higher saving rates affect long-run economic growth?

4. Why would you expect an inverse relationship between self-sufficiency and real GDP per capita?

5. If a couple was concerned about their retirement, why could that lead them to have more children if they lived in an agricultural society, but fewer children if they were in an urban society?

6. Why is the effective use of land, labor, capital, and entrepreneurial activities dependent on the protection of property rights and the rule of law?

Answers: 1. e   2. d   3. e   4. d   5. b

Population and Economic Growth   12.4

📁 When is population growth beneficial to per capita economic growth?

📁 When is population growth detrimental to per capita economic growth?

📁 Why are rising expectations detrimental to the desirability of economic growth?

📁 How do environmental concerns affect the desirability of economic growth?

Population Growth and Economic Growth

At the beginning of the English Industrial Revolution (c. 1750), the world's population was perhaps 700 million. It took 150 years (to 1900) for that population to slightly more than double to 1.6 billion. Just 64 years later (in 1964), it had doubled again to 3.2 billion.

After another 41 years (in 2005), the population doubled yet again to more than 6.4 billion. According to estimates by the United Nations, the world population should reach approximately 9 billion by 2050 and than level off. And most of this population growth will occur in developing countries. Industrialized countries will see very little growth in population. Economic development occurred amidst all this growth in population, but what role does population play in economic growth?

Why is the effect of population growth on per capita growth unclear?

The effect of population growth on per capita economic growth is far from obvious. If population were to expand faster than output, per capita output would fall; population growth would inhibit growth with a larger population. With a larger population, however, comes a larger labor force. Also, economies of large-scale production may exist in some forms of production, so larger markets associated with greater populations lead to more efficient-sized production units. Certainly, rapid population growth—more than 3 percent a year—did not seem to impede U.S. economic growth in the mid-nineteenth century. U.S. economic growth until at least World War I was accompanied by population growth that was among the highest in the world for the time.

The general feeling, however, is that in many of the developing countries today, rapid population growth threatens the possibility of attaining sustained economic growth. These countries are predominantly agricultural with modest natural resources, especially land. The land-labor ratio is low. Why is population growth a threat in these countries? One answer was provided nearly two centuries ago by an English economist, the Reverend Thomas Malthus.

The Malthusian Prediction

Malthus formulated a theoretical model that predicted that per capita economic growth would eventually become negative and that wages would ultimately reach equilibrium at a subsistence level, or just large enough to provide enough income to stay alive. To create this model, Malthus made three assumptions: (1) the economy was agricultural, with goods produced by two inputs, land and labor; (2) the supply of land was fixed; and (3) human sexual desires worked to increase population.

The Law of Diminishing Marginal Returns

How does Malthus's analysis rely on the law of diminishing marginal returns?

As population increases, the number of workers increases, and with greater labor inputs available, output also goes up. At some point, however, output will increase by diminishing amounts because of the law of diminishing returns, which states that if you add variable amounts of one input (in this case, labor) to fixed quantities of another input (in this case, land), output will rise but by diminishing amounts (because as the land-labor ratio falls, less land is available per worker). For example, a rapid growth in the labor force might make it more difficult to equip each worker with sufficient capital, and lower amounts of capital per worker lead to lower productivity and a lower real GDP per capita. In short, the increase in the one factor of production, labor, might cause the other factors of production to be spread too thinly.

Avoiding Malthus's Prediction

Fortunately, Malthus's theory proved spectacularly wrong for much of the world. Although the law of diminishing returns is a valid concept, Malthus's other assumptions were unrealistic. The quantity or quality of tillable land is not completely fixed. Irrigation, fertilizer, and conservation techniques effectively increase arable land. More important, Malthus implicitly neglected the potential for technological advances and ignored the real possibility that improved technology, often embodied in capital, could overcome the impact of the law of diminishing returns.

Malthus did not envision a world of greater agricultural productivity through fertilizers, pesticides, and mechanization of farm equipment. A world where fewer farmers could produce more food. Further, the Malthusian assumption that sexual desire would necessarily lead to population increase is not accurate. True, sexual desire will always be with us, but the number of births can be reduced by birth control techniques.

As we discussed earlier, some economists believe that population growth can lead to greater economic growth. In some countries, a larger population may lead to more entrepreneurs, engineers, and scientists who will contribute to even greater economic growth through technological progress. Furthermore, a larger labor force is created by a larger population. A larger labor force can produce more goods and services. However, that does not necessarily mean a higher standard of living for the typical citizen, which requires that real output grows faster than population. One size does not fit all: Countries with small populations and countries with large populations can experience high standards of living. These factors turn Malthus's theory on its head; instead of population being the villain, it could actually turn out to be the hero.

Could added capital and technology overcome the effects of diminishing returns?

Do Some Developing Countries Still Fit Malthus's Prediction Today?

Unfortunately, the Malthusian assumptions don't vary widely from reality for several developing countries today. Some developing nations of the world are having substantial population increases, with a virtually fixed supply of land, slow capital growth, and few technological advances. For example, in some African nations, the population growth rate is 3 percent per year, while food output is growing at only 2 percent per year. In these cases, population growth causes a negative effect on per capita output because the added output derived from having more workers on the land is small.

Some economists worry about population growth and the capital stock. The greater the production growth rate, the lower the capital stock per worker. This could lead to lower labor productivity, a reduction in one's standard of living, and slower economic growth.

In fact, some developing countries have tried to reduce the rate of population growth to achieve greater economic growth per capita and higher standards of living. For example, China tried to reduce its population growth rate through laws regulating the number of children a family may have. It is true that in many poor countries, the population growth rate is much higher, nearly 3 percent per year, than in richer countries, about 1 percent per year. High population growth rates may be one explanation for lower standards of living, but many non-Malthusian explanations help explain the recurring poverty that exists in developing countries today, such as political instability, the lack of defined and enforceable property rights, and inadequate investment in human capital.

Economic Growth and Fertility

Economists have also found that as countries become richer, family sizes tend to become smaller. This has been the case in the United States, Western Europe and the Soviet Union. As a nation becomes richer, families have access to better medical care and do not require as many children to provide for them as they age. Another reason that birth rates fall as nations become richer is that, as women achieve better access to education and jobs, their opportunity costs of raising children rise and fertility rates fall. So one possible policy approach for developing countries struggling with an exploding population is to provide more equal treatment for women.

⑦ SECTION QUIZ

1. Which of the following is true?

   a. If population expands faster than real output, per capita real GDP will fall.

   b. If real GDP expands faster than population, per capita real GDP will rise.

   c. With economies of large scale production, larger populations can result in more efficient production.

   d. All of the above are true.

2. Thomas Malthus's model assumed that

   a. the economy was agricultural, using land and labor.

   b. the supply of land was fixed.

   c. sexual desire worked to increase population.

   d. all of the above are true.

3. Malthus

   a. predicted that per capita economic growth would eventually become negative.

   b. predicted that wages would ultimately reach equilibrium at a subsistence level.

   c. relied heavily on the law of diminishing returns.

   d. ignored the potential for technological advances.

   e. All of the above are true.

---

1. What happens to per capita real output if population grows faster than output? If population grows more slowly than output?

2. How can economies of large-scale production allow per capita output to rise as population rises?

3. How did Malthus's prediction on population growth follow from the law of diminishing returns?

4. Why is population control a particularly important issue in countries with very low levels of per capita income?

Answers: 1. d 2. d 3. e

Interactive Summary

Fill in the blanks:

1. John Maynard Keynes was primarily concerned with explaining and reducing _____ fluctuations in the level of business activity.

2. Many would argue that in the long run, economic growth is a(n) _____ determinant of people's well-being.

3. Economic growth is usually measured by the annual percent change in _____.

4. How much the economy will produce at its potential output depends on the _____ and _____ of an economy's resources.

5. _____ in technology can increase the economy's production capabilities.

6. A nation with _____ economic growth will end up with a much higher standard of living, *ceteris paribus*.

7. The Rule of 70 says that the number of years necessary for a nation to double its output is approximately equal to the nation's _____ rate divided into 70.

8. Several factors have contributed to economic growth in some or all countries: (1) growth in the quantity and quality of _____ resources used (human capital); (2) increase in the use of inputs provided by the _____ (natural resources); (3) growth in physical _____ inputs (machines, tools, buildings, inventories); and (4) _____ advances (new ways of combining given quantities of

labor, natural resources, and capital inputs) allowing greater output than previously possible.

9. If the labor force participation rate in a country _____ or if workers put in _____ hours, output per capita will tend to increase.

10. It has become popular to view labor as _____ capital that can be augmented or improved by education and on-the-job training.

11. _____ formation has played a significant role in the economic development of nations.

12. _____ is the adoption of a new product or process.

13. Technological advance permits us to economize on _____, _____, or even _____.

14. Generally speaking, higher levels of saving will lead to _____ levels of investment and capital formation and, therefore, to _____ economic growth.

15. Investment alone does not guarantee economic growth, which hinges on the _____ and the _____ of investment as well.

16. Research and development can result in _____ products, management

_____, production _____, or learning by _____.

17. Economic growth rates tend to be higher in countries where the government enforces _____.

18. If a country's government is not enforcing property rights, the private sector must respond in _____ ways that _____ economic growth.

19. _____ can lead to greater output because of the principle of comparative advantage.

20. Accepting a(n) _____ in current income to acquire education and training can _____ future earning ability, which can raise the standard of living.

21. With economic growth, illiteracy rates _____ and formal education _____.

22. Improvements in literacy stimulate economic growth by _____ barriers to the flow of information and _____ labor productivity.

23. One problem in providing enough education in poorer countries is that children in developing countries are an important part of the labor force at a young age; therefore, a(n) _____ opportunity cost of education is involved in terms of forgone contributions to family income.

Answers: 1. short-term 2. crucial 3. real GDP per capita 4. quantity; quality 5. Increases 6. greater 7. growth 8. labor; land; capital; technological 9. rises; longer 10. human 11. Capital 12. Innovation 13. labor; land (natural resources); capital 14. higher; greater 15. quality; type 16. new; improvements; innovations; doing 17. property rights 18. costly; stifle 19. Free trade 20. reduction; increase 21. fall; grows 22. reducing; raising 23. higher

---

economic growth 326
labor productivity 330

innovation 332

research and development (R&D) 335

12.1   Economic Growth

1. Why does the production possibilities curve shift outward with economic growth?

Economic growth means that an economy is able to produce more goods and services than before. An outward shift in a country's production possibilities curve simply illustrates this fact graphically.

2. Even if "in the long run, we are all dead," are you glad earlier generations of Americans worked and invested for economic growth?

The fact that earlier generations of Americans worked and invested for economic growth means that there is currently a greater stock of capital in the United States than there would have been otherwise. With more tools to work with, you are more productive, resulting in a higher income and greater consumption possibilities.

3. **If long-run consequences were not important, would many students go to college or participate in internship programs without pay?**

No. These are two of many examples where people sacrifice in the short run in order to benefit in the long run. Saving and research and development are other obvious examples.

4. **When the Dutch "created" new land with their system of dikes, what did it do to their production possibilities curve? Why?**

Building dikes in Holland increased the quantity of usable land the Dutch had to work with; an increase in the amount of usable natural resources shifts a country's production possibilities curve outward.

12.2   Determinants of Economic Growth

1. **Why is no single factor capable of completely explaining economic growth patterns?**

No single factor is capable of completely explaining economic growth patterns because economic growth is a complex process involving many important factors, no one of which completely dominates.

2. **Why might countries with relatively scarce labor be leaders in labor-saving innovations? In what area would countries with relatively scarce land likely be innovative leaders?**

Those in countries with relatively scarce and therefore more costly labor would benefit more from labor-saving innovations and so would be likely to be leaders in such innovations. Similarly, those in countries with relatively scarce and therefore more costly land would likely be leaders in innovative ways to conserve land.

3. **Why could an increase in the price of oil increase real GDP growth in oil-exporting countries such as Saudi Arabia and Mexico, while decreasing growth in oil-importing countries such as the United States and Japan?**

Since GDP measures the market value of goods and services produced, an increase in prices for what a country exports adds to its GDP. However, an increase in the price of imported oil will raise costs and reduce output in that country, other things being equal.

4. **How is Hong Kong a dramatic example of why abundant natural resources are not necessary for rapid economic growth?**

Hong Kong has virtually no natural resources, yet has long been among the fastest-growing economies in the world, proving that abundant natural resources are not necessary for rapid economic growth.

12.3   Public Policy and Economic Growth

1. **Why does knowing what factors are correlated with economic growth not tell us what causes economic growth?**

Knowing what factors are correlated with economic growth does not tell us what causes economic growth because correlation does not prove causation. A factor may cause changes in economic growth, or economic growth could cause changes in it, or changes in both the factor and economic growth may be caused by yet another variable.

2. **How does increasing the capital stock lead to economic growth?**

Increasing the capital stock adds to the tools workers have to work with, increasing their productivity over time, which in turn increases output over time.

3. **How do higher saving rates affect long-run economic growth?**

Higher savings rates provide more funds for capital investment, and greater capital investment (which often also embodies advances in technology) increases productivity and output growth.

4. **Why would you expect an inverse relationship between self-sufficiency and real GDP per capita?**

Because of different endowments and abilities, both people and countries have different opportunity costs of production for large numbers of goods and services (different comparative advantages). Specialization and large-scale production, combined with domestic and international trade, allow an expansion of productive and consumption possibilities by taking advantage of lower cost production, while self-sufficiency sacrifices those potential gains.

5. **If a couple was concerned about their retirement, why could that lead them to have more children if they lived in an agricultural society, but fewer children if they were in an urban society?**

In an agricultural society, children can typically "earn their own keep," making them financially "profitable" investments, as well as helping to provide for parents' retirement. In an urban society, however, children are a substantial financial liability to their parents.

6. **Why is the effective use of land, labor, capital, and entrepreneurial activities dependent on the protection of property rights and the rule of law?**

Without protected property rights and the rule of law, both production and exchange become far more difficult, costly, and uncertain, undermining the ability of market incentives to induce the effective use of the factors of production. Similarly, the rewards to investors and those who seek new and better ways of doing things are also more uncertain, reducing the incentives to make such investments and innovations.

12.4 Population and Economic Growth

1. What happens to per capita real output if population grows faster than output? If population grows more slowly than output?

If population grows faster than real output, per capita real output falls, while if population grows more slowly than real output, per capita real output rises.

2. How can economies of large-scale production allow per capita output to rise as population rises?

Economies of large-scale production mean that output can expand more than proportionately to an increase in inputs. The increasing labor force that accompanies a larger population may increase output enough, through more efficient-sized production units, that per capita real output rises as population rises.

3. How did Malthus's prediction on population growth follow from the law of diminishing returns?

Malthus's prediction that population growth results in a subsistence level of wages was based on the assumption of an agricultural society with land and labor as the only factors of production. Assuming that the amount of land was fixed, population and the labor force would grow to where production exhibited the law of diminishing returns, with output growing more slowly than increases in the variable input, labor, which would reduce per capita incomes, eventually to the point of subsistence.

4. Why is population control a particularly important issue in countries with very low levels of per capita income?

In countries with a fixed supply of land and little if any technological advance, Malthus's assumptions are not far from the reality. Population control is one way to hold down the rate of population increase, to prevent the Malthusian subsistence wage result.

Problems

1. a. According to the Rule of 70, how many years will it take a country to double its output at each of the following annual growth rates?

    0.5 percent   _____ years
    1 percent   _____ years
    1.4 percent   _____ years
    2 percent   _____ years
    2.8 percent   _____ years
    3.5 percent   _____ years
    7 percent   _____ years

   b. If a country has $100 billion of real GDP today, what will its real GDP be in 50 years if it grows at an annual growth rate of
      1.4 percent?   _____
      2.8 percent?   _____
      7 percent?   _____

2. Answer these questions about GDP.
   a. How could real GDP grow while, over the same period, real GDP per capita falls?
   b. If Country A has a 4 percent annual growth rate of real GDP and a 2 percent annual rate of population growth, while Country B has a 6 percent annual growth rate of real GDP and a 5 percent annual rate of population growth, which country will have a higher growth rate of real GDP per capita?

3. In which direction would the following changes alter GDP growth and per capita GDP growth in a country (increase, decrease, or indeterminate), other things being equal?

	Real GDP Growth	Real GDP Growth per Capita
An increase in population	_____	_____
An increase in labor force participation	_____	_____
An increase in population and labor force participation	_____	_____
An increase in current consumption	_____	_____
An increase in technology	_____	_____
An increase in illiteracy	_____	_____
An increase in tax rates	_____	_____
An increase in productivity	_____	_____
An increase in tariffs on imported goods	_____	_____
An earlier retirement age in the country	_____	_____
An increase in technology and a decrease in labor force participation	_____	_____
An earlier retirement age and an increase in the capital stock	_____	_____

4. Answer the following questions about real GDP per capita.
   a. If Country A had four times the initial level of real GDP per capita of Country B and it was growing at 1.4 percent a year, while real GDP was growing at 2.3 percent in Country B, how long would it take before the two countries had the same level of real GDP per capita?
   b. If two countries had the same initial level of real GDP per capita, and Country A grows at 2.8 percent, while Country B grows at 3.5 percent, how will their real per capita GDP levels compare at the end of a century?

5. Suppose that two poor countries experience different growth rates over time. Country A's real GDP per capita grows at a rate of 7 percent per year on average, and Country B's real GDP per capita grows at an average annual rate of only 3 percent. Predict how the standard of living will vary between these two countries over time as a result of divergent growth rates.

6. Could a country experience a fall in population and a rise in real GDP at the same time? Could an increase in labor force participation allow that?

7. What is the difference between labor and human capital? How can human capital be increased?

8. Would a shift from investment in capital goods to investment in education increase or decrease the growth rate of real GDP per capita?

9. Which of the following are likely to improve the productivity of labor and thereby lead to economic growth? Why?
   a. on-the-job experience
   b. vocational school
   c. a decrease in the amount of capital per worker
   d. improvements in management of resources

10. What is the implication about economic growth for an economic system with weak enforcement of patent and copyright laws? Why does weak property rights enforcement create an incentive problem?

11. How could permanently lower marginal tax rates increase the capital stock, the level of education, the level of technology, and the amount of developed natural resources over time?

Financial Markets, Saving, and Investment

According to *The Economist*, "Ten experts are brought together to solve a mystery, but they can't get along and reach three different conclusions." Unfortunately, that was the story of the America's Financial Crisis Inquiry Commission that reported their findings in January 2011. Reports on the cause of the crisis split along party lines. The Democrats pointed to failures of the financial industry, greed, sloppy risk management, and predatory mortgage lenders. Republicans claimed that it was politicians, regulators, and bankers and home buyers who were too unconcerned about leverage.

A rebuttal of the report put the blame squarely on government policies aimed at increasing home ownership among the poor. Because this was arguably the worst downturn since the Great Depression, we will discuss the financial crisis in this chapter and throughout the macroeconomic section.

In this chapter, we discuss how the financial system works. We begin with an introduction to financial institutions and financial intermediaries. The two most important financial institutions are the stock market and the bond market.

We also discuss financial intermediaries, including banks, savings and loans, mutual funds, and insurance companies. We then develop equations to connect the financial system to our macroeconomic model. In the rest of this section we present the supply and demand for loanable funds. Using this framework, we can examine a number of potential policy prescriptions that could alter real interest rates and, as a result, the amount of saving, investment, and capital formation—the foundation of growth in the economy. In the last section, we examine the causes of the financial crisis that officially started in December of 2007.

13.1   Financial Institutions and Intermediaries

📂 **What are financial institutions?**

📂 **What are bonds?**

📂 **What are stocks?**

📂 **What are retained earnings?**

📂 **How do expected business conditions affect the price of a stock?**

📂 **What are financial intermediaries?**

© Flying Colours Ltd/Jupiterimages

Why does economic growth depend on investment?

What is the difference between saving and savings?

As we saw in the previous chapter, potential real GDP and economic growth depend on productive resources and the growth of these resources. In order for an economy to grow, there must be investment; firms invest in new capital (machines and factories) and new production techniques, often incorporating new technology. This makes labor more productive, leading to increases in real incomes and living standards.

Some people in the economy are seeking to save some of their income for the future, whereas others are seeking to borrow in order to finance investments that would grow their businesses. How do we get these two groups together?

Financial institutions exist to facilitate the channeling of saving into investment. The financial system is composed of both financial markets and financial intermediaries. Firms can obtain resources to invest in capital by using retained earnings; (the profits that are reinvested in the firm rather than distributed as dividends to shareholders). But there are several other methods they can use as well, including selling stocks or bonds in the financial markets or borrowing from financial intermediaries such as banks.

The loanable funds market is where households make their saving available to those who desire to borrow additional funds. Note that we said saving rather than savings. Saving without an s at the end refers to a flow concept—your rate of saving (how much you save per day, per week, per month, or per year). Savings with an s at the end, however, refers to how much you have accumulated at a particular moment in time—your stock of savings. When you save, you can put the funds in a bank, buy stocks or bonds, or invest in a variety of other financial assets, such as treasury bills or mutural funds. We begin by discussing two of the most important financial institutions—the bond market and the stock market.

Corporations obtain financial capital (dollars used to buy capital goods) by borrowing money in exchange for bonds, by selling stock or by reinvesting profits that are earned in the business.

Bonds

Although corporate borrowing takes different forms, corporations primarily borrow by issuing **bonds**. The holder of a bond is not a part owner of a corporation. Rather, a bondholder is a creditor to whom the corporation has a debt obligation. The obligation to bondholders is of higher legal priority than that of stockholders. Before any dividends can be paid, even to owners of preferred stock, the interest obligations to bondholders must be met. If a company is liquidated, bondholders must be paid the full face value of their bond holding before any disbursements can be made to stockholders. Bondholders have greater financial security than stockholders, but receive a fixed annual interest payment, with no possibility to receive increased payments as the company prospers. The possibility of the value of a bond increasing greatly—a capital gain—is limited compared to that of stocks.

However, there are some risks involved with holding bonds, such as from corporate bankruptcy or higher market interest rates. For example, suppose you buy a bond that pays 5 percent interest and the market interest rate rises, so that newly issued bonds are now paying, say, 7 percent. The value of your bond has now declined.

bonds
obligations issued by the corporation that promise the holder to receive fixed annual interest payments and payment of the principal upon maturity

How are bondholders different from stockholders?

What is the difference between common stock and preferred stock?

Stocks

The owners of corporations own shares of stock in the company and are called **stockholders**. Each stockholder's ownership of the corporation and voting rights in the selection of corporate management are proportionate to the number of shares owned. Suppose a corporation has 1,000 shares of stock outstanding. If you own 10 shares, you own a 1 percent interest in the corporation (10 is 1 percent of 1,000). Another stockholder may only own one share and have but one-tenth the interest you do. Therefore, she earns one-tenth the dividend income from the stock that you do and has one-tenth the number of votes that you do in annual shareowner meetings to select members of the board of directors. (The board provides overall supervision of the business and hires the management.) Individuals and institutions buy shares of stock in the stock market, usually on one of the organized stock exchanges. The price that shares sell for will fluctuate (often many times a day) with changes in demand or supply. Corporations sometimes use proceeds from new sales of stock to finance expansion of their activities.

stockholders
entities that hold shares of stock in a corporation

The two primary types of stock are preferred stock and common stock. Owners of **preferred stock** receive a regular, fixed dividend payment; the payment does not vary with the profits of the corporation. No dividends can generally be paid to holders of common stock until the preferred stockholders receive a specified fixed amount per share of stock, assuming that funds are available after the debts of the corporation are paid.

preferred stock
a stock that pays fixed, regular dividend payments that do not vary with the profits of the corporation

Owners of **common stock** are the residual claimants on the resources of the corporation. They share in all profits remaining *after* expenses are paid, including interest payments to owners of debt obligations of the corporation and dividend payments to owners of preferred stock. Dividends in common stock frequently vary with profits, often going up in years of prosperity and down in less prosperous years. If the corporation is sold or liquidated, the common stockholders receive all the corporate assets after all debts are paid and preferred stockholders are paid a fixed amount per share. Owners of common stock assume greater risks than preferred stockholders, because the potential rewards are greater if the company is in fact successful.

common stock
residual claimants of corporate resources who receive a proportion of profits based upon the ratio of shares held

Who Owns Stock in U.S. Corporations?

Individuals as well as institutions such as insurance companies, pension funds, mutual funds, trust departments of banks, and university and foundation endowment funds, all hold corporate stocks. To provide a perspective on the ease with which one can share in the ownership of a company, Ford, IBM, and Microsoft have millions of individual stockholders. Indirectly, millions more are involved in stocks through their mutual funds, ownership of life insurance, vested rights in private pension funds, and so on.

Retained Earnings

retained earnings
the practice of using
corporate profits for capital
investment rather than
dividend payouts

*What is the most important
source of business funding?*

*How do expectations
influence the price of
securities?*

securities
stocks and bonds

A third way a company can get money is through **retained earnings**. Instead of using its profits to pay out dividends, a firm might take some of its profits and plow them back into the company for new capital equipment. A company may decide, for example, to take its $10 million of after-tax profit and pay $3 million in dividends and plow back the $7 million into the firm. Reinvestment is by far the most important source of funding, accounting for almost 65 percent of a firm's finances. One reason firms find reinvestment an attractive source of funds is that issuing new stocks and bonds can be an expensive and lengthy process.

The Value of Securities

The two most important financial markets where savers can provide funds to borrowers are the stock market and the bond market. The values of **securities** (stocks and bonds) sold in financial markets change with expectations of benefits and costs. For example, if people expect corporate earnings to rise, prospective stockholders increase what they would be willing to pay for the fixed amount of securities, while existing stockholders become more reluctant to sell, leading to increased prices. If present business conditions or expectations about future profits worsen, stock prices will fall. A variety of other concerns, such as the economic policies of the government, business conditions in foreign countries, and concern over inflation, also influence the price of stocks (and, to a lesser extent, bonds). During periods of rising securities markets, optimism is generally great, and businesses are more likely to invest in new capital equipment, perhaps financing it by selling new shares of stock at current high prices.

During periods of pessimism, stock prices fall, and businesses reduce expenditures on new capital equipment, partly because financing such equipment by stock sales is more costly. More shares have to be sold to get a given amount of cash, seriously diluting the ownership interest of existing stockholders.

Can You Consistently Pick Stock Winners?

*What is the random walk
theory of the stock market?*

Economists have a theory about the stock market. They call it a *random walk*. That is, it is difficult, without illegal inside information or a lot of luck, to consistently pick winners in the stock market. The fact remains that hot tips are only hot if you are one of only a few to know whether a company's stock is going to rise. Once that news hits the street, it will cease to be a source of profit. In sum, if markets are operating efficiently, the current stock prices will reflect all available information, and consistent, extraordinary profit opportunities will not exist. Many financial analysts think that the best stock market strategy is to diversify, buying several different stocks, and holding them for long periods. At least that way you don't have to continue to pay commissions on additional trades. Besides, over the long run the stock market has historically outperformed other financial assets.

Reading Stock Tables

Most newspapers (and many Web sites) provide a financial section that covers the prices of stocks so investors can have some of the information they need to make their decisions to buy and sell stocks. Some investors (day traders) watch these data by the second as they trade in and out of stocks a number of times during the day. At the other extreme, some investors pick a good company and hold the stock for a long time hoping that it will give them a better return than other assets—such as saving accounts. Exhibit 1 is a reproduction

section 13.1
exhibit 1   Reading a Stock Table

52-WEEK							
HI	**LO**	**STOCK (DIV)**	**YLD %**	**PE**	**VOL**	**CLOSE**	**NET CHG**
46.88	28.14	HOG .50	1.38	22.44	3,090,000	34.33	−1.79

in the news Lusha the Chimpanzee Outperforms 94 Percent of Russia Bankers with Her Investment Portfolio

They are paid a fortune for their ability to make complex decisions about where to invest millions of pounds every single day.

But perhaps the job of an investment banker is not quite as difficult as it might seem.

A chimpanzee in Russia has outperformed 94 percent of the country's investment funds with her portfolio growing by three times in the last year.

Moscow TV reported how circus chimp Lusha chose eight companies from a possible 30 to invest her one million rubles—around £21,000.

"She bought successfully and her portfolio grew almost three times. She did better than almost the whole of the rest of the market," said editor of Russian Finance magazine Oleg Anisimov.

He questioned why so-called financial whizz-kids are still receiving hefty perks for their expertise.

"Everyone is shocked. What are they getting their bonuses for? Maybe it's worth sending them all to the circus."

The money-wise mape was given cubes representing different companies and asked: "Lusha where would you like to invest your money this year?"

Pausing briefly to think, she then picked out her eight cubes.

Lusha's top picks included banks where shares soon rose a stunning 600 percent after large-scale support from the Kremlin to weather the crisis.

She missed out on telecommunications which scored a 240 percent profit, but went for mining companies, up 150 percent.

The Russian media heaped more scorn on the investment experts saying: "Lusha made all serious analysts look like clowns."

One broker hit back: "If the experiment had taken place a year earlier, the monkey would not have had enough money to pay for her bananas."

And her trainer Svetlana Maksimova admitted: "Money questions should be decided by financiers and politicians. If monkeys get into it, our economy will collapse at once."

But Pavel Trunin, the head of monetary policy department at the Institute for the Economy in Transition in Moscow, said enviously: "It shows that financial knowledge does not play a great role in giving forecasts to how the market will change.

It is usually a matter of more or less successful guessing. And the monkey got lucky." The monkey, owned by legendary Russian trainer Lev Dorov, split her investments between state-owned corporations and private companies.

SOURCE: Will Stewart, "Lusha the Chimpanzee Outperforms 94% of Russia Banks with Her Investment Portfolio," *The Daily Mail,* January 13, 2010, http://www.dailymail.co.uk/news/worldnews/article-1242575/Lusha-monkey-outperforms-94-Russia-bankers-investment-portfolio.html.

of *The Wall Street Journal* on September 28, 2011. Let's look at the key indicators for one stock—Harley-Davidson—a company that makes motorcycles and accessories.

The first two columns show the stock's performance over the last 52 weeks—the highest price in the first column and the lowest price in the second column. We see that Harley-Davidson has been as high as $46.88 per share and as low as $28.14.

In column three we see the name of the stock—Harley-Davidson; the symbol for this stock is HOG. Also in column three is the **dividend**—this number indicates the annual amount the company has paid over the preceding year on each share of stock. Harley-Davidson paid $0.50 per share. If we divide the dividend by the price of the stock, we get the figure in the fourth column called the yield—1.38 percent.

The fifth column has the **price-earnings ratio (PE)**, found by taking the price of the stock and dividing it by the amount the company earned per share over the past year. The price-earnings ratio is a measure of how highly a stock is valued. A typical price-earnings ratio is about 15; Harley-Davidson's PE is 22.44. If the PE ratio is higher, it means that the stock is relatively expensive in terms of its recent earnings; the stock might be overvalued or investors are expecting share prices to rise in the future. A lower PE ratio means either that the stock is undervalued or that investors may expect future earnings to fall.

The last three columns measure the performance of the stock on the last trading day—the stock's volume for the day, closing price, and net change from the closing price of the previous day.

Financial Intermediaries

Financial intermediaries are financial institutions that accept funds from households and make them available to firms. They are the intermediary between savers and borrowers. The most important financial intermediaries are banks, mutual funds, savings and loans, and insurance companies.

A bank is a financial intermediary that takes in deposits from customers who want to save and makes loans available to those who want to borrow. Banks make a profit by charging borrowers a higher interest rate than what they pay their depositors.

Banks also provide a medium of exchange—that is, they facilitate transactions. For example, by allowing people to write checks against their deposits, banks lower transaction costs. Imagine the difficulty of trying to trade a share of stock for groceries. Banks have also introduced debit cards, prepaid cards, smart cards and credit cards to facilitate transactions and smooth consumption spending.

Another important financial intermediary is mutual funds. Mutual fund companies sell portfolios of stocks and bonds. The advantage of a mutual fund is that it allows an individual with even a small amount of income to spread risk across hundreds of different companies, adhering to the sage advice "do not put all your eggs in one basket." A far riskier strategy would be to invest in one stock. There are also the services of "expert" money managers who watch your portfolio. If a stock is underperforming, it can be sold. If a stock looks promising, it can be purchased. Perhaps, this is expertise a small individual investor could not afford. However, it is not clear that the expert will do any better than someone picking stocks randomly. In fact, index funds are a type of fund that includes all the stocks in a given market, like the Dow Jones Industrial average or the S&P 500. These index funds tend to outperform those managed by money managers. It costs less to run an index fund because there are no highly paid stock pickers or analysts.

Saving and loans are also financial intermediaries. They accept deposits in savings accounts and pay interest for these funds. The most important purpose of these institutions is to make mortgage loans on residential property.

Another financial intermediary, insurance companies, will invest your premiums in financial markets. They can make a profit if their investment income is greater than their losses on insurance claims.

---

dividend
the annual per share payment to shareholders based on realized profits

price-earnings ratio (PE)
a measure of stock value that is determined by dividing the price of the stock by the amount of annual corporate earnings per share

⟲ SECTION QUIZ

1. A firm can acquire financial resources through
   a. retained earnings.
   b. selling stocks.
   c. issuing bonds.
   d. all of the above.

2. You could invest your savings in
   a. treasury bills
   b. mutual funds.
   c. bank deposits.
   d. stocks and bonds.
   e. any of the above.

3. Corporations can finance their growth
   a. by issuing bonds.
   b. by issuing new shares of stock.
   c. through plowbacks.
   d. by all of the above.

4. Which of the following entities do not hold corporate stocks?
   a. university and nonprofit foundation endowment funds
   b. insurance companies
   c. other corporations
   d. pension funds
   e. All of the above entities hold corporate stocks.

5. Ownership of a share of stock in a corporation is different from ownership of a corporate bond in that
   a. the owner of a share of stock receives payment before a bondholder in the event of a corporation's liquidation.
   b. a bondholder receives a fixed interest payment plus a lump sum payment at maturity, whereas a stockholder may receive income in the form of dividends and capital gains.
   c. a bondholder has voting rights, a shareholder does not.
   d. a bondholder bears greater business risk than does a shareholder.

6. Preferred stockholders
   a. assume greater risks than do common stockholders.
   b. receive payment before common stockholders in the event of liquidation.
   c. receive payment before bondholders in the event of liquidation.
   d. are characterized by all of the above.

7. Stock prices are influenced by
   a. concern over inflation.
   b. the economic policies of the government.
   c. business conditions in foreign economies.
   d. expectations about corporate earnings.
   e. all of the above.

(*continued*)

② SECTION QUIZ (Cont.)

8. The random walk theory suggests

   a. that stock prices fluctuate in highly predictable ways.

   b. that it is extremely difficult without inside information to consistently pick winners in the stock market.

   c. that if stock price fluctuations are scrutinized carefully, one can consistently pick winners in the stock market.

   d. that information filters sufficiently slowly that one can consistently profit by trading on newly released information.

---

1. If you believed a company's profitability was about to jump sharply, would you rather own bonds, preferred stock, or common stock in that company?

2. If almost all investors expected the profits of a company to jump sharply, would that make purchasing the stock today unusually profitable?

3. Why are issues of new stocks to finance business investments more common in periods of high and rising stock prices?

4. What are some of the reasons that stock prices rise and fall?

5. What is the random walk?

6. What is a dividend?

7. How do you calculate a price-earnings ratio?

Answers: 1. d   2. e   3. c   4. e   5. b   6. b   7. e   8. b

---

13.2

Saving, Investment, and the Financial System

- 📂 What is the demand for loanable funds curve?
- 📂 What is the supply of loanable funds curve?
- 📂 How is the real interest rate determined?

- 📂 How are shortages and surpluses eliminated in the loanable funds market?
- 📂 What is private saving? Public saving?

As we have discussed, saving and investment are critical components of long-run economic growth and living standards. We will now begin discussing how we can use national income accounting to understand the relationship between total saving and total investment.

The Macroeconomics of Saving and Investment

What is the relationship between saving and investment for the entire economy?

The key point that we will develop in this section is that for the entire economy, the total value of saving must equal the total value of investment, $S = I$. Recall from our discussion of national income accounts that GDP (or Y) $= C + I + G + (X - M)$. That is, aggregate expenditures (Y) must equal the sum of its four components, $C + I + G + (X - M)$. For simplicity, we begin by working in a closed economy, without the complications introduced by the international, or net export $(X - M)$, component. In a closed economy, net exports are zero, because there is no international trade—that is, exports are zero and imports are zero. So we can now write:

(1) $$Y = C + I + G$$

That is, GDP (Y) is the sum of consumption plus investment plus government purchases. If we subtract C and G from both sides of the equation, we have

(2) $$I = Y - C - G$$

The right hand side $(Y - C - G)$ is what is left over from total income (Y) when you subtract consumption and government purchases. Thus, in a closed economy, investment spending (I) is equal to total income (Y) minus consumption spending (C) minus government purchases (G).

We can also derive an expression for national (total) saving. There are two types of saving—private saving and public saving. Private saving is the amount of income households have left over after consumption and taxes, plus any transfer payments (social security and unemployment insurance payments) the household may receive. So private saving can be written then as:

What is private saving? What is public saving?

(3) $$S_{private} = Y - C - T + TR$$

Public saving is the amount of income the government has left over after paying for its spending. So public saving (S_{public}) is equal to the amount of tax revenues (T) government has left over after paying for government purchases (G) and transfer payments (TR):

(4) $$S_{public} = T - G - TR$$

National (total) saving in an economy is the sum of private saving and public saving:

(5) $$S = S_{private} + S_{public}$$

or:

(6) $$S = (Y - C - T + TR) + (T - G - TR)$$

or simplifying:

(7) $$S = Y - C - G$$

Since from equation (2) we know that $I = Y - C - G$, we can then conclude that:

(8) $$S = I$$

That is, national (total) saving equals total investment.

Most people are familiar with the idea that households and firms can save, but are less familiar with the idea that the government can also save. If the government collects the same amount in taxes as it spends, we say there is a balanced budget. If the government collects more in taxes than it spends $(T > G + TR)$, it runs a budget surplus and public saving is positive. If the government spends more than it collects in taxes $(T < G + TR)$, it runs a deficit and public saving is negative. That is, the government has to borrow the money to fund the difference between taxes and spending.

When is public saving positive? negative?

In sum, for the economy as a whole, total saving must equal total investment. However, this equation need not hold for any individual household or firm. In the next section, we develop the market for loanable funds that brings saving and investment together.

The Market for Loanable Funds

As we have seen, potential GDP and economic growth depend on the extent of productive resources and the rate at which they increase. In order for an economy to grow, there must be investment. Firms invest in new capital (machines and factories) and new production techniques, often incorporating new technology. These investments make labor more productive, leading to increases in real incomes and living standards.

For simplicity, let us assume the loanable funds market is a single big financial market. All savers deposit their saving there and all borrowers go there to take out loans. Savers are spending less than they are earning and borrowers are spending more than they are earning. If there is one big market, there is just one interest rate, which represents both the cost to borrow and the return to saving. In the market for loanable funds, the market interest rate and the quantity of loanable funds is determined by the interaction of borrowers and lenders.

What determines the market interest rate and the quantity of loanable funds exchanged?

The Demand for Loanable Funds

The demand for loanable funds comes from households and firms. Households and firms borrow in the loanable funds market. Households often take out loans to invest in new houses or cars. Firms borrow to invest in new capital equipment, such as factories. Thus, both firms and households borrow in the loanable funds market to make investments. The demand for loanable funds curve is negatively sloped. That is, a higher interest rate makes it more expensive to borrow, so the quantity of loanable funds demanded falls; a lower interest rate makes it less expensive to borrow, so the quantity of loanable funds demanded rises. For example, firms must compare the return they expect to make with the real interest rate they must pay to borrow. At a high real interest rate, firms will only pursue those investment activities that have an even higher expected rate of return. As the real interest rate falls, additional projects with lower expected rates of returns become profitable for firms and the quantity of loanable funds demanded rises. The idea that lower real interest rates stimulate investment is the reason that government often tries to combat recessions by lowering the interest rate.

Why is the demand for loanable funds curve negatively sloped?

The Supply of Loanable Funds

The loanable funds market is where households make their saving available to those who need to borrow funds. Households supply loanable funds because they earn interest in exchange. The higher the interest rate, the greater the reward for saving. With their saving, a household may buy stocks or bonds from firms, or save in banks that will use the new funds to make loans. Thus, saving provides the supply of loanable funds. The interest rate can be understood as the price of a loan. It is the price that borrowers pay for a loan and it is the price lenders receive for their saving.

Why is the supply of loanable funds curve positively sloped?

The supply of loanable funds curve is positively sloped. The supply of loanable funds is determined by the willingness of households to save and the amount of government saving or dissaving (which we will discuss later). Households can either save or consume. The amount households consume or save depends to some extent on the interest rate. A higher interest rate makes saving more attractive, so that the quantity of loanable funds supplied rises; a lower interest rate makes saving less attractive, so that the quantity of loanable funds supplied falls.

The Equilibrium Adjusts to Balance the Demand and Supply of Loanable Funds

The interest rate adjusts to generate equilibrium in the loanable funds market. In equilibrium, the quantity of loanable funds demanded is equal to the quantity of loanable funds supplied at the equilibrium real interest rate, r^*, as seen in Exhibit 1. At a real interest rate that is higher than equilibrium, the quantity of loanable funds supplied is greater than the quantity of loanable funds demanded—a surplus of loanable funds at the current real interest rate. As lenders (savers) compete against each other to attract borrowers (investors), the real interest rate falls. Alternatively, if the real interest rate is below the equilibrium real interest rate, the quantity of loanable funds demanded is greater than the quantity of loanable funds supplied—a shortage of loanable funds at the current real interest rate. As a result of the shortage, lenders will raise their interest rates. A higher interest rate would encourage saving (increase the quantity of loanable funds supplied) and discourage borrowing (decrease the quantity of loanable funds demanded), eliminating the shortage when the interest rate hits the equilibrium level at r^*.

Recall that there is a difference between the nominal interest rate and the real interest rate. The stated interest rate on a loan is the nominal interest rate. However, we can calculate the real interest rate by subtracting the inflation rate from the nominal interest rate. The real interest rate is important because it shows how much borrowers pay and lenders receive in terms of purchasing power. Since inflation tends to erode the value of money over time, the real interest rate is a more accurate gauge of the return to savers and the cost to borrowers. Remember that the interest rate determined in the loanable funds market is the real interest rate, not the nominal interest rate.

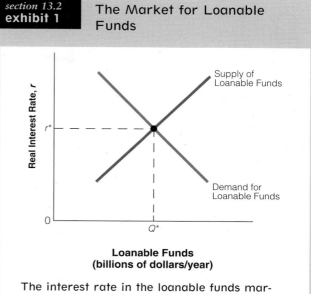

section 13.2 **exhibit 1**   **The Market for Loanable Funds**

The interest rate in the loanable funds market adjusts to balance the quantity of loans demanded with the quantity of loans supplied. The supply of national saving is the sum of private saving and public saving. The demand for loanable funds comes from firms and households that want to borrow for investment purposes. At the equilibrium interest rate, the quantity of loanable funds demanded equals the quantity of loanable funds supplied.

© Cengage Learning 2013

Analyzing the Market for Loanable Funds

In this section we use the tools of supply and demand to examine how certain changes will impact real interest rates and the equilibrium quantity of loanable funds exchanged.

Saving Incentives

As we have discussed, saving is an important long-run determinant of real economic growth and the standard of living. Therefore, policy makers might want to encourage saving by changing the tax code—perhaps making Individual Retirement Accounts (IRAs) more attractive. This would encourage people to save more of their income, because it would not be taxed. How would this new tax law affect the market for saving and investment? It would shift the loanable funds supply curve to the right, from S_1 to S_2, leading to a lower equilibrium real interest rate and a higher equilibrium quantity of loanable funds exchanged—as seen in Exhibit 2. The increased supply of saving causes the interest rate to fall, which stimulates investment. Thus, the change in the tax law would increase saving and investment.

An Investment Tax Credit

The passage of a new investment tax credit would give a tax advantage to any firm that invested in new equipment or plant. Because firms would want to invest more, it would shift out (increase) the demand curve for loanable funds from D_1 to D_2, in Exhibit 3 leading to a higher real interest rate and a greater equilibrium quantity of loanable funds exchanged—greater levels of both saving and investment. That is, an investment tax

ECS
economic content standards

Higher real interest rates reduce business investment spending and consumer spending on housing, cars, and other major purchases. Policies that raise real interest rates can be used to reduce these kinds of spending, while policies that decrease real interest rates can be used to increase these kinds of spending.

What process moves real interest rates toward equilibrium when they begin out of equilibrium?

What would happen in the loanable funds market if the supply of saving increased? Or if the demand for loanable funds increased?

credit would encourage investment and lead to a higher interest rate and greater saving. Of course, eliminating or reducing the investment tax credit would have the opposite effect: shifting the demand for loanable funds to the left, leading to a higher real interest rate and a lower equilibrium quantity of saving and investment.

Technological Change

Suppose a technological change causes an increase in demand for loanable funds, as firms see a new profitable opportunity for investment. The increase in the demand for loanable funds from D_1 to D_2 raises the real interest rate from r_1 to r_2 and leads to an increase in the equilibrium quantity of loanable funds from Q_1 to Q_2, as seen in Exhibit 3. At Q_2, there is greater levels of both saving and investment. This will ultimately lead to an increase in capital formation, more capital per worker, higher productivity, higher wages, and enhanced economic growth.

Budget Deficits and Surpluses

When the government spends more than it receives in tax revenues, it experiences a budget deficit. Not including the effects of foreign saving, a budget deficit will lower national saving in the economy, causing a decrease in the supply of loanable funds from S_1 to S_2 in Exhibit 4. That is, the government is actually dissaving (borrowing), decreasing national saving. At the new equilibrium, there is a higher real interest rate and lower equilibrium quantity of loanable funds exchanged—less saving and investment. When the real interest rate rises as a result of the government budget deficit, it causes a decrease in

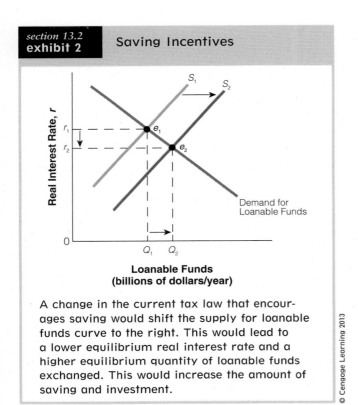

A change in the current tax law that encourages saving would shift the supply for loanable funds curve to the right. This would lead to a lower equilibrium real interest rate and a higher equilibrium quantity of loanable funds exchanged. This would increase the amount of saving and investment.

© Cengage Learning 2013

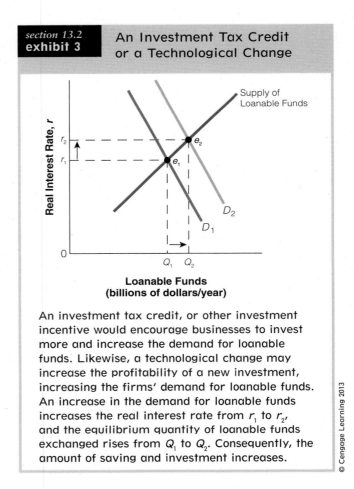

An investment tax credit, or other investment incentive would encourage businesses to invest more and increase the demand for loanable funds. Likewise, a technological change may increase the profitability of a new investment, increasing the firms' demand for loanable funds. An increase in the demand for loanable funds increases the real interest rate from r_1 to r_2, and the equilibrium quantity of loanable funds exchanged rises from Q_1 to Q_2. Consequently, the amount of saving and investment increases.

© Cengage Learning 2013

use what you've learned   What I Like About Scrooge

Here's what I like about Ebenezer Scrooge: His meager lodgings were dark because darkness is cheap, and barely heated because coal is not free. His dinner was gruel, which he prepared himself. Scrooge paid no man to wait on him.

Scrooge has been called ungenerous. I say that's a bum rap. What could be more generous than keeping your lamps unlit and your plate unfilled, leaving more fuel for others to burn and more food for others to eat? Who is a more benevolent neighbor than the man who employs no servants, freeing them to wait on someone else?

Oh, it might be slightly more complicated than that. Maybe when Scrooge demands less coal for his fire, less coal ends up being mined. But that's fine, too. Instead of digging coal for Scrooge, some would-be miner is now free to perform some other service for himself or someone else.

Dickens tells us that the Lord Mayor, in the stronghold of the mighty Mansion House, gave orders to his 50 cooks and butlers to keep Christmas as a Lord Mayor's household should—presumably for a houseful of guests who lavishly praised his generosity. The bricks, mortar, and labor that built the Mansion House might otherwise have built housing for hundreds; Scrooge, by living in three sparse rooms, deprived no man of a home. By employing no cooks or butlers, he ensured that cooks and butlers were available to some other household where guests reveled in ignorance of their debt to Ebenezer Scrooge.

In this whole world, there is nobody more generous than the miser—the man who could deplete the world's resources but chooses not to. The only difference between miserliness and philanthropy is that the philanthropist serves a favored few while the miser spreads his largess far and wide.

If you build a house and refuse to buy a house, the rest of the world is one house richer. If you earn a dollar and refuse to spend a dollar, the rest of the world is one dollar richer—because you produced a dollar's worth of goods and didn't consume them.

Who exactly gets those goods? That depends on how you save. Put a dollar in the bank and you'll bid down the interest rate by just enough so someone somewhere can afford an extra dollar's worth of vacation or home improvement. Put a dollar in your mattress and (by effectively reducing the money supply) you'll drive down prices by just enough so someone somewhere can have an extra dollar's worth of coffee with his dinner. Scrooge, no doubt a canny investor, lent his money at interest. His less conventional namesake Scrooge McDuck filled a vault with dollar bills to roll around in. No matter. Ebenezer Scrooge lowered interest rates. Scrooge McDuck lowered prices. Each Scrooge enriched his neighbors as much as any Lord Mayor who invited the town in for a Christmas meal.

Saving is philanthropy, and—because this is both the Christmas season and the season of tax reform—it's worth mentioning that the tax system should recognize as much. If there's a tax deduction for charitable giving, there should be a tax deduction for saving. What you earn and don't spend is your contribution to the world, and it's equally a contribution whether you give it away or squirrel it away.

Of course, there's always the threat that some meddling ghosts will come along and convince you to deplete your savings, at which point it makes sense (insofar as the taxation of income ever makes sense) to start taxing you. Which is exactly what individual retirement accounts are all about: They shield your earnings from taxation for as long as you save (that is, for as long as you let others enjoy the fruits of your labor), but no longer.

Great artists are sometimes unaware of the deepest meanings in their own creations. Though Dickens might not have recognized it, the primary moral of *A Christmas Carol* is that there should be no limit on IRA contributions. This is quite independent of all the other reasons why the tax system should encourage saving (e.g., the salutary effects on economic growth).

crowding-out effect
theory that government borrowing drives up the interest rate, lowering consumption by households and investment spending by firms

private investment—households buy fewer homes and firms invest in fewer new factories. Economists call this the **crowding-out effect**, a topic we will return to in the chapter on fiscal policy. That is, the budget deficit reduces investment spending and long-term economic growth.

You might ask why didn't we shift the demand curve for loanable funds when the government entered the loanable funds market. That's a legitimate question. The answer is that we are interpreting the loanable fund model to mean the flow of resources available to fund private investment. So the government budget deficit reduces the supply of loanable funds.

Now consider how a budget surplus (or a reduction in the budget deficit) will impact the real interest rate and the amount of saving and investment. In Exhibit 5, suppose that when the government has a balanced budget, the supply of loanable funds curve is S_1, the demand for loanable funds curve is D_1, the equilibrium real interest rate is r_1, and the equilibrium quantity of loanable funds exchanged is Q_1. If the government begins running a budget surplus—receiving more in tax revenues than it spends—there is an increase in public saving. Because national saving is the sum of private saving and public saving, national saving has now increased, shifting the supply of loanable funds curve right from S_1 to S_2. What impact does this budget surplus (government saving) have on the real interest rate, saving, and investment? The increase in the supply of loanable funds from S_1 to S_2 leads to a decrease in the real interest rate to r_2 and an increase in equilibrium of loanable funds exchanged from Q_1 to Q_2. The budget surplus has increased the supply of loanable funds, lowered the real interest rate, and increased the equilibrium quantity of loanable funds exchanged—that is, more saving and investment. This will ultimately lead to increases in capital formation and economic growth.

What do government budget surpluses do to national saving? To the supply of loanable funds?

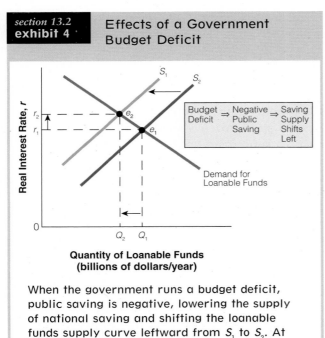

© Cengage Learning 2013

**section 13.2
exhibit 4**

Effects of a Government Budget Deficit

Quantity of Loanable Funds
(billions of dollars/year)

When the government runs a budget deficit, public saving is negative, lowering the supply of national saving and shifting the loanable funds supply curve leftward from S_1 to S_2. At the new equilibrium, the result is a higher real interest rate and a lower equilibrium quantity of loanable funds—that is, less saving and investment. When the real interest rate rises as a result of the government budget deficit, it causes a decrease in private investment, known as the crowding-out effect.

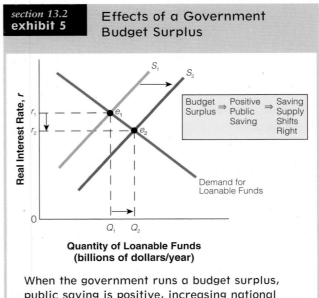

© Cengage Learning 2013

**section 13.2
exhibit 5**

Effects of a Government Budget Surplus

Quantity of Loanable Funds
(billions of dollars/year)

When the government runs a budget surplus, public saving is positive, increasing national saving and causing the saving supply curve to shift rightward from S_1 to S_2. This shift leads to a decrease in the real interest rate to r_2 and an increase in equilibrium saving and investment from Q_1 to Q_2. The budget surplus results in an increase in the supply of loanable funds, a lower real interest rate, and larger amounts of saving and investment. These factors cause increases in the capital formation and economic growth.

Tax Laws, Government Programs, and the Saving Rate When the saving rate increases, there are more resources available for investment. Investment in capital (plant and equipment) raises labor productivity, wages, and national income. So, should we reform the tax laws to encourage a higher rate of saving? Currently, saving is taxed at a relatively high rate. Investors who save some of their wealth in stock are taxed twice—the corporation (shareholders) is taxed and then dividends are taxed again. Inheritance taxes can also discourage saving because it taxes a percentage of the wealth that many have saved to pass on to their children. Taxes on interest, dividends, capital gains, and estates raise the cost of saving versus consumption and drain capital from the economy.

Do some government policies discourage saving?

Government programs, especially Social Security, discourage saving. Individuals use to save more for their retirement and health care but now rely more heavily on Medicare and other government health programs. Also means-tested government programs and colleges and universities have benefits and scholarships that are linked to wealth—which may discourage some from saving.

However, there are the equity effects of tax reform. High income families tend to save more—so the rich may benefit more from a tax policy aimed to encourage saving. There are also other ways to encourage saving like reducing the deficit—that is, increasing public saving. In fact, policy makers must be careful when they pass tax reform to encourage private saving because it may lead to less government revenue and higher deficits—a decrease in public saving. Policy makers face difficult choices.

② SECTION QUIZ

1. A lower real interest rate will

   a. increase the loanable funds demand curve.

   b. decrease the loanable funds demand curve.

   c. increase the dollar amount of loanable funds exchanged but not change the loanable funds demand curve.

   d. decrease the dollar amount of loanable funds exchanged but not change the loanable funds demand curve.

2. A higher real interest rate will

   a. increase the supply of loanable funds.

   b. decrease the supply of loanable funds.

   c. increase the dollar amount of loanable funds exchanged, but not shift the supply of loanable funds curve to the right.

   d. decrease the dollar amount of loanable funds exchanged, but not shift the supply of loanable funds curve to the left.

3. At a given interest rate if the quantity of loanable funds supplied is less than the quantity of loanable funds demanded,

   a. there is a surplus of loanable funds and real interest rates will rise.

   b. there is a surplus of loanable funds and real interest rates will fall.

   c. there is a shortage of loanable funds and real interest rates will rise.

   d. there is a shortage of loanable funds and real interest rates will fall.

4. At a higher than equilibrium real interest rate, the quantity of loanable funds supplied would be _____ than the quantity of loanable funds demanded; there would be a _____ of loanable funds at this real interest rate.

   a. greater; shortage

   b. greater; surplus

   c. less than; shortage

   d. less than; surplus

(*continued*)

⊘ S E C T I O N   Q U I Z (Cont.)

5. An increase in the supply of loanable funds would

   a. increase real interest rates.

   b. decrease real interest rates.

   c. increase the dollar amount of loanable funds exchanged.

   d. do both (a) and (c).

   e. do both (b) and (c).

6. An increase in the loanable funds demand curve would

   a. increase real interest rates.

   b. decrease real interest rates.

   c. increase the dollar amount of loanable funds exchanged.

   d. decrease the dollar amount of loanable funds exchanged.

   e. do both (a) and (c).

7. Other things equal, if the government runs a budget surplus, it will tend to

   a. increase national saving.

   b. decrease the real interest rate.

   c. increase the amount of investment.

   d. increase economic growth.

   e. do all of the above.

---

1. Why does $Y - C - G = S$ in a simple, closed economy?

2. If net taxes rise, what happens to private saving? To public saving?

3. Why does the demand for loanable funds curve slope downward?

4. Why does the supply of loanable funds curve slope upward?

5. How is the real interest rate determined?

6. How are shortages and surpluses eliminated in the loanable funds market?

7. What factors can shift the demand for loanable funds curve?

8. What factors can shift the supply of loanable funds curve?

9. What would happen to the equilibrium interest rate and quantity of loanable funds exchanged if both the loanable funds demand and supply curves shifted right? What if the loanable funds demand curve shifted right and the loanable funds supply curve shifted left?

10. Other things equal, which direction will an increasing budget surplus change the equilibrium interest rate, the loanable funds supply curve, the level of investment in the economy, and the likely rate of economic growth?

Answers: 1. c 2. c 3. b 4. b 5. e 6. e 7. e

The Financial Crisis of 2008

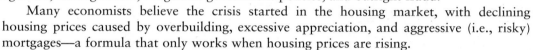

👉 What role did the housing market play in the financial crisis?

👉 What impact did low short-term interest rates have on the housing market?

👉 What role did relaxed standards for mortgage loans have on the housing market?

👉 What impact did the higher interest rate of 2005 have on the housing market?

The best word to sum up the financial crisis of 2008 is DEBT. In technical terms, it is called excessive leverage. In short, too many homeowners and financial firms had assumed too much debt and taken on too much risk. Why did this happen? There is plenty of blame to go around—poorly informed borrowers, predatory mortgage lenders, incompetent rating agencies, lax regulators, misguided government policies, and outright fraud.

Many economists believe the crisis started in the housing market, with declining housing prices caused by overbuilding, excessive appreciation, and aggressive (i.e., risky) mortgages—a formula that only works when housing prices are rising.

Housing prices were rising at an extraordinary rate from 2000–2006. Housing prices peaked in 2006 and fell sharply in 2007, with the worst of the housing decline concentrated in California, Florida, Arizona, and Nevada.

Why do risky mortgages only work when housing prices are rising?

Low Interest Rates (2002–2004) Led to Aggressive Borrowing

After the 2001 recession, the Fed pursued an expansionary monetary policy that pushed interest rates down to historically low levels. The federal funds rate was maintained at 2 percent or lower for almost three years. Economists disagree on whether this was the correct government policy. Some argue that the Fed pursued the appropriate policy to stimulate economic growth and employment after the 2001 recession and terrorist attacks in order to head off potential deflation. Once deflation sets in, it is very difficult to successfully use expansionary monetary policy. In addition, worldwide interest rates were very low at this time due to the large amount of savings in emerging markets. Because the U.S. financial markets appeared relatively safe, many of these global funds flowed into the United States, lowering the interest rate and eventually helping to fuel the housing bubble.

Why could the Fed's low interest rate policy lead to excessive debt?

Critics of the Fed argue that it lowered interest rates too much, for too long, in a growing economy, as shown in Exhibit 1. Most would agree that monetary policy was "too loose for too long" in the United States and around the world.

But whatever the reason for the low interest rates, there is common agreement that the low interest rates increased aggressive borrowing that encouraged less qualified buyers to purchase houses. The low interest rates set off a housing boom, especially in California, Florida, and the Northeast.

Deregulation in the Housing Market and Subprime Mortgages

In the last several decades the federal government encouraged the mortgage industry, especially Fannie Mae and Freddy Mac, to lower lending standards for low-income families in an effort to increase home ownership. Fannie Mae and Freddy Mac are the government-sponsored enterprises that fund or guarantee the majority of mortgage loans in the United States.

Specifically, lenders devised innovative adjustable-rate mortgages with extremely low "teaser" rates, making it possible for many new higher risk buyers to purchase houses, often

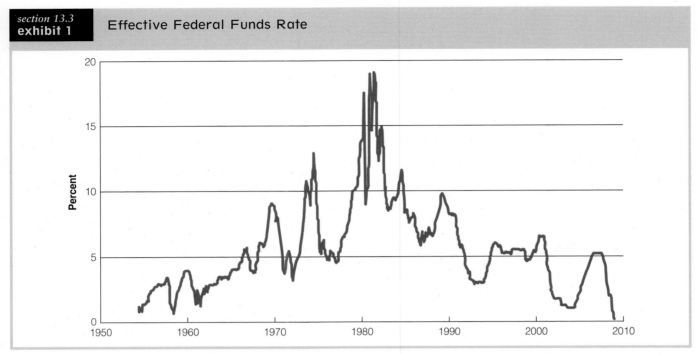

SOURCE: Board of Governors of the Federal Reserve System.

How did low interest rates fuel the housing bubble?

with little or no money as a down payment and, in some cases, no documentation of income. Most of these loans ended up in the hands of high-risk borrowers. These loans were called subprime loans because the borrower had less than a prime credit rating and many would not have qualified for a conventional loan.

In 2006, almost 70 percent of the subprime loans were in the form of a new innovative product called a hybrid. These loans started at a very low fixed rate for the initial period, say three to seven years, and then reset to a much higher rate for the remainder of the loan. Many subprime borrowers just expected to refinance later—thinking their property would continue to appreciate and interest rates would remain low. In retrospect, borrowers and lenders focused too much on the borrower's ability to cover the low initial payment and not enough on risk.

Speculators flipped (quickly bought and sold) properties with inflated appraisals and outright lying on loan applications. In addition, excessive credit provided to subprime borrowers (individuals who may not have qualified for conventional loans) fueled the housing bubble. Mortgage originators were not worried about making risky loans because they could pass on the risk to others (particularly Fannie Mae and Freddy Mac, who were aggressively buying such loans). Because origination fees on loans were due up front, and others would buy the loans, lenders were less concerned if the loan was ever repaid. It is safe to say that if mortgage companies had given loans only to safe investors, the United States would not have had a financial crisis.

Subprime mortgages jumped from 8 percent of the total in 2001 to 13.5 percent in 2005, as shown in Exhibit 2. These new buyers pushed housing prices higher. The increase in the lending to "subprime" borrowers helped inflate the housing bubble. The rising housing prices then led to overly optimistic expectations, with both borrowers and lenders thinking that with housing prices increasing, the risks were minimal. (After all, housing prices jumped almost 10 percent a year nationally from 2000–2006, as shown in Exhibit 3.)

Lenders were eager to make loans to anyone because they thought the prices for housing would continue to rise and, if borrowers defaulted, lenders would be left with an asset worth more than they were owed.

In short, the relaxed lending standards, backed by the government, put many low-income families into homes they could not afford. Unscrupulous mortgage brokers even

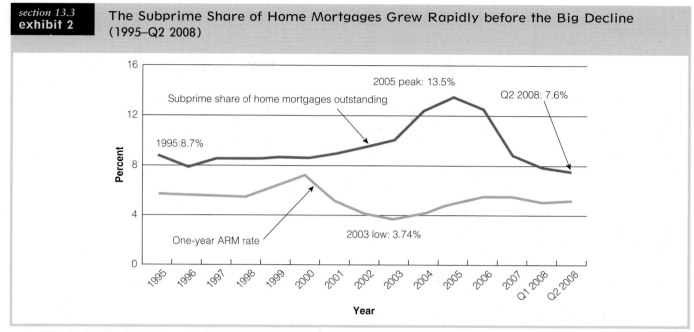

section 13.3 exhibit 2 The Subprime Share of Home Mortgages Grew Rapidly before the Big Decline (1995–Q2 2008)

SOURCES: Inside Mortgage Finance; Federal Reserve; Milken Institute.

falsified loan application forms so clients could qualify for larger loans. Many borrowers also did not completely understand the terms of their loan.

Who Bought These Risky Subprime Mortgages?

Many of these risky subprime mortgages were sold to investors such as Bear Stearns and Merrill Lynch. They pooled them with other securities into packages and sold them all over the world. Part of the impetus for them was the great demand for mortgage-backed securities in the global market. A mortgage-backed security (MBS) is a package of mortgages bundled together and then sold to an investor, like a bond. Foreign investors were hungry to invest in these securities, because the U.S. housing market traditionally has been strong and stable. These mortgage-backed securities were also thought to have minimal risk because of the diversity of mortgages in each portfolio and because they had high security ratings. Security rating agencies gave their highest ratings to these securities—AAA (Standard and Poor's) and Aaa (Moody's). High ratings encouraged investors to buy securities backed by subprime mortgages, helping finance the housing boom. The rating agencies clearly underestimated the risk of these securities. The risk was spread among many different investment institutions, but no one knew exactly where the bad loans had ended up.

Consumers Borrowing against Their Equity

To complicate matters further, consumers borrowed hundreds of billions of dollars against the equity from the appreciation in their homes, fueling consumption spending and an increase in household debt, both combined with a fall in personal saving. The low interest rates subsidized massive borrowing, and credit market debt soared as well.

The Fed Raises Interest Rates and the Housing Bust

The low interest rates of the 2002–2004 period and other factors led to the Fed becoming concerned about rising prices. In 2005–2006, therefore, the Fed reversed course and pushed short-term interest rates up, as shown in Exhibit 1. For those holding new adjustable-rate

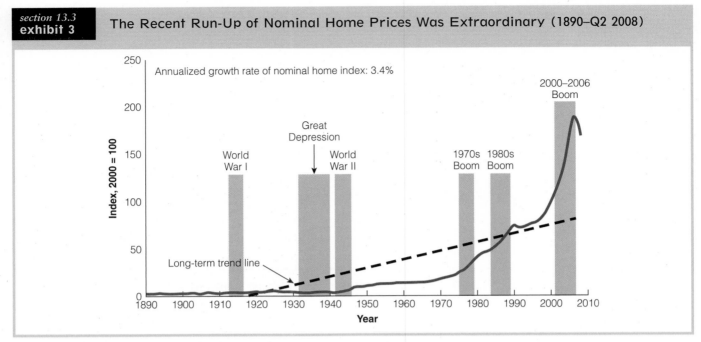

NOTE: The annualized growth rate is the geometric mean.
SOURCES: Shiller (2002); Milken Institute.

mortgages (ARMs), it meant their monthly payments rose. Higher interest rates and falling housing prices were a recipe for disaster. Consequently, many homes went into default and foreclosure—both subprime borrowers and prime borrowers lost their homes. (The default rate was much lower on those holding fixed mortgage rates.)

When housing prices crashed, not only did too many homeowners find themselves over their heads, but there was also a huge excess inventory of new homes. From 2006–2008, housing construction fell by a whopping $350 billion—a huge hit on the economy. And by December of 2007, the United States was officially in a recession.

What caused the housing foreclosures?

Why did the banking *industry get hit so hard?*

As housing prices fell and interest rates rose, foreclosures jumped. Once home prices fell below loan values, borrowers could not qualify to refinance and many were forced into foreclosure. When houses turn "upside down"—people owe more on their loan than the house is worth—many walk away from their houses. If a homeowner had put 20 percent down and had an appreciable amount of equity, she would have a greater incentive to make it work. Zero-down mortgages meant more defaults, especially when given to someone with a poor credit rating and little documentation of income. There was a major mispricing of risk in the mortgage markets.

When housing prices fell and mortgage delinquencies soared, the securities-backed subprime mortgages lost most of their value. When subprime borrowers defaulted, it resulted in a large decline in the capital of many banks and financial institutions, tightening credit around the world. Three investment banks either went bankrupt (Lehman Brothers) or were sold at fire-sale prices to other banks (Bear Stearns and Merrill Lynch) during September 2008. The failures of three of the five largest investment banks augmented the instability in the global financial system. The remaining two investment banks, Morgan Stanley and Goldman Sachs, opted to become commercial banks, thereby subjecting themselves to more stringent regulation.

Banks ended up receiving a double hit. Their securities investors started demanding money and their borrowers were failing to pay their loans. And troubled banks were not able to raise more money because other banks and investors sensed that they were in trouble and refused to lend to them.

It is also easy to see why the government-sponsored financial intermediaries, Freddy Mac and Fannie Mae, collapsed. Many economists believe it had to do with moral hazard, when individuals take additional risks because they are insured. Investors knew that the government supported Freddy and Fannie mortgage-backed securities, so they considered them very low risk. With the government behind them, Freddy and Fannie had an incentive to issue risky securities and buy risky mortgages from banks. Banks knew that Freddy and Fannie would buy almost any mortgage they created. However, when people stopped paying their mortgages, the two giant intermediaries lost billions of dollars. Their stocks became worthless and the government had to take control of both Fannie Mae and Freddy Mac.

What makes risky loans less risky?

Financial markets depend on lenders making funds available to borrowers. However, when lenders become reluctant to make loans, it becomes difficult to assess credit risk. This happened in 2008, which led the Federal Reserve and other central banks around the world to pour hundreds of billions of dollars (euros, pounds, etc.) into credit markets to ease the pain of the financial crisis. In addition, the government has enacted large fiscal stimulus packages of close to $1 trillion. The borrowing and spending is intended to offset the reduction in private sector demand caused by the crisis. We will return to this topic in the chapter entitled "Fiscal Policy." In sum, we saw several factors that contributed to the financial crisis. First, there was a decline in asset prices. In the case of the financial crisis of 2007 to 2008, the asset was housing, which had its worse downturn in over 70 years. Second, many financial institutions became insolvent as a result of investments in the real estate market. When housing prices fell, some homeowners stopped paying their loans, and financial institutions that were holding those loans were compromised. Third, the financial crisis led to a decline in confidence and a credit crunch. Because a number of financial institutions were in trouble, many borrowers had a difficult time securing a loan, even for promising investment projects. This led to a reduction in overall demand for goods and services in the economy. The good news is that financial crises do eventually end.

⊘ SECTION QUIZ

1. Which of the following was not a factor in the financial crisis of 2008?

   a. poorly informed borrowers

   b. credit rating agencies

   c. fraud

   d. misguided government policies

   e. All of the above were factors in the financial crisis of 2008.

2. Which of the following is true of the financial crisis of 2008?

   a. The financial crisis had multiple causes.

   b. Fannie Mae and Freddy Mac's willingness to buy subprime loans reduced the perceived risk others felt in issuing or buying them.

   c. Home loan standards were lowered contributing to the housing boom.

   d. Fed policy helped cause the housing boom, and a change in Fed policy helped trigger the bust.

   e. All of the above are true.

3. Which of the following is true?

   a. Subprime loans became much more common leading up to the financial crisis.

   b. In 2006, more than half of subprime loans were hybrids.

   c. Hybrid home loans were often taken out on the assumption that home prices would continue to rise and the borrower expected to refinance when the teaser rates ended.

   d. Securities rating agencies gave high rating to securities backed by subprime mortgages.

   e. All of the above are true.

(*continued*)

1. Why would history and the role of Fannie Mae and Freddy Mac have made investors consider mortgage-backed securities to be safe?

2. Why were those who took out hybrid loans at far greater risk of foreclosure when the Fed began raising interest rates?

Answers: 1. e   2. e   3. e

Interactive Summary

Fill in the blanks:

1. Investment cannot occur unless someone in the economy is _____.

2. The _____ market is where households make their saving available to those who desire to borrow additional funds.

3. Saving refers to a(n) _____ concept, while savings refers to a(n) _____ concept.

4. The two most important financial institutions are the _____ market and the _____ market.

5. An economy that invests a(n) _____ fraction of its GDP tends to grow faster.

6. Owners of preferred stock receive a(n) _____ dividend payment, whereas owners of _____ stock do not.

7. A(n) _____ is an owner of a corporation, whereas a(n) _____ is a creditor of a corporation.

8. The obligation to _____ is of higher legal priority than that to _____.

9. _____ is the most important source of funding for firms.

10. Better business conditions would tend to make the value of stocks _____.

11. The reason it is difficult, without inside information, to consistently pick winners in the stock market is because the value of a stock is a(n) _____ _____.

12. Many financial analysts think that the best stock market strategy is to _____ and to hold stocks for _____ periods of time.

13. The _____ interest rate is determined by investment demand and national savings.

14. The loanable funds _____ curve for the economy is downward sloping.

15. As the real interest rate falls, _____ investment projects become profitable, _____ the dollar amount of investment.

16. The supply of national saving comprises both _____ saving and _____ saving.

17. At a(n) _____ real interest rate, a greater quantity of loanable funds will be supplied.

18. Desired loanable funds demanded equals desired _____ at the equilibrium real interest rate.

19. If the real interest rate was above equilibrium, the quantity of loanable funds _____ would exceed the quantity of loanable funds _____.

20. At a real interest rate below equilibrium, a(n) _____ for loanable funds would occur.

21. In a(n) _____ economy, GDP is the sum of consumption plus investment plus government purchases.

22. Public saving is positive as the government _____ more in taxes than it _____.

23. Starting from a balanced budget, a government's move to a budget _____ would increase public saving and increase national saving, other things equal.

24. If the government moved into a budget _____, it would result in negative public saving, reduced national saving, a higher real interest rate, and reduced levels of investment.

25. If the government runs a budget _____, other things equal, it will tend to increase national saving, decrease the real interest rate, increase the amount of investment, and increase economic growth.

26. When foreigners supply more funds than they demand, a capital _____ occurs.

27. Capital inflows from foreign countries _____ to the supply of loanable funds.

28. When the domestic real interest rate is _____, capital will tend to flow out to foreign countries.

29. Too much _____, or excessive _____, was a major cause of the financial crisis of 2008.

30. Many economists think the financial crisis of 2008 began in the _____ market.

31. The worst of the housing market decline after 2006 was in _____, _____, _____, and _____.

32. After the 2001 recession, the Fed funds rate was maintained at _____ or lower for over three years.

33. In order to maintain investment yields as market interest rates decline requires an investor to take more _____.

34. In 2006, a majority of subprime loans were _____ loans, with a(n) _____ fixed rate for the first few years, which then reset to a(n) _____ rate for the rest of the term.

35. After several years of maintaining _____ real interest rates, the Fed reversed course and pushed short-term interest rates _____.

36. The default rate on home loans was much lower on those holding _____ interest rate mortgage loans.

Answers: 1. saving 2. loanable funds 3. flow; stock 4. stock; common 7. stockholder; bondholder 8. bondholders; stockholders 9. Reinvestment 10. rise 11. random walk 12. diversify; substantial 13. real 14. demand 15. more; increasing 16. private; public 17. higher 18. loanable funds supplied 19. supplied; demanded 20. shortage 21. closed 22. collects; spends 23. surplus 24. deficit 25. surplus 26. inflow 27. add 28. low 29. debt; leverage 30. housing 31. California; Florida; Arizona; Nevada 32. 2 percent 33. risk 34. hybrid; low; higher 35. low; up 36. fixed.

Key Terms and Concepts

Section Quiz Answers

13.1 Financial Institutions and Intermediaries

1. **If you believed a company's profitability was about to jump sharply, would you rather own bonds, preferred stock, or common stock in that company?**

   You would rather own common stock because owners of common stock are the residual claimants on the resources of the corporation. If profits were about to jump sharply, common stock owners would benefit because that residual will get substantially larger. Preferred stocks, which pay regular, fixed dividends, and bonds, which pay fixed interest payments, would not benefit nearly as much from increased future profitability.

2. **If almost all investors expected the profits of a company to jump sharply, would that make purchasing the stock today unusually profitable?**

   No. Generally shared expectations of higher future profits will result in higher current prices that capitalize those expected profits. Once those expected profits are reflected in current stock prices, buyers of that stock will not earn unusually high profits as a result.

3. **Why are issues of new stocks to finance business investments more common in periods of high and rising stock prices?**

   In periods of high and rising stock prices, a firm can raise more money for a given number of new ownership shares issued.

4. What are some of the reasons that stock prices rise and fall?

Stock prices rise and fall with expectations of corporate earnings, business conditions, economic policies of the government, business conditions in foreign countries, concern over inflation, and more. Anything that changes expectations of benefits or costs from holding securities will change stock prices.

5. What is the random walk?

The random walk idea is that if markets are operating efficiently, the current stock prices will reflect all available information, so that consistent, extraordinary profit opportunities will not exist. That is, without illegal inside information or consistent good luck, one should not expect to be able to consistently pick winners in the stock market.

6. What is a dividend?

The dividend reported on financial pages is the annual amount the company in question has paid over the preceding year on each share of stock.

7. How do you calculate a price-earnings ratio?

The price-earnings ratio reported on financial pages is found by taking the price of the stock and dividing it by the amount the company earned per share over the past year.

13.2 Saving, Investment, and the Financial System

1. Why does $Y - C - G = S$ in a simple, closed economy?

$Y - C - G$ is what is left over from income after spending on consumption and government purchases, which is what is available for investment. But in equilibrium, investment must equal saving.

2. If net taxes rise, what happens to private saving? To public saving?

Increased net taxes reduce disposable income, which, in turn reduces private saving. However, increased net taxes move the government budget toward surplus, increasing public saving.

3. Why does the demand for loanable funds curve slope downward?

As the real interest rate falls, additional investment projects with lower expected rates of return become profitable for firms, and the quantity of loanable funds demanded rises.

4. Why does the supply of loanable funds curve slope upward?

At a higher real interest rate, the reward for saving and supplying funds to financial markets is greater, leading to an increased quantity of loanable funds supplied.

5. How is the real interest rate determined?

The real interest rate is determined by the intersection of the loanable funds demand curve and the supply curve.

6. How are shortages and surpluses eliminated in the loanable funds market?

If the real interest rate was above the equilibrium real interest rate, the quantity of loanable funds supplied would be greater than the quantity of loanable funds demanded—there would be a surplus of loanable funds. As lenders compete against each other to attract borrowers, the real interest rate will fall toward the equilibrium level. If the real interest rate was below the equilibrium real interest rate, the quantity of loanable funds supplied would be less than the quantity of loanable funds demanded—there would be a shortage of loanable funds. As borrowers compete against each other to attract lenders, the real interest rate will rise toward the equilibrium level.

7. What factors can shift the demand for loanable funds curve?

The investment demand curve would increase (shift to the right) if firms expect higher rates of return on their investments; if profitable new products are developed; or if business taxes are lowered. The loanable funds demand curve would decrease (shift to the left) in the opposite situations.

8. What factors can shift the supply of loanable funds curve?

The saving supply curve would increase (shift to the right) if disposable (after-tax) income rose (say, because taxes were reduced). The saving supply curve would decrease (shift to the left) if disposable (after-tax) income fell.

9. What would happen to the equilibrium interest rate and quantity of loanable funds exchanged if both the loanable funds demand and supply curves shifted right? What if the loanable funds demand curve shifted right and the loanable funds supply curve shifted left?

Whenever both the supply and demand curves shift in any market, we add up the separate effects on price (interest rate) and quantity (of loanable funds) exchanged. When both the loanable funds demand and supply curves shift right, each would increase the quantity of loanable funds exchanged, but would have opposing effects on the interest rate, making that change indeterminate without knowing about the relative magnitudes of the changes.

When the loanable funds demand curve shifted right and the loanable funds supply curve shifted left, both effects would tend to increase the interest rate, but have opposing effects on the quantity of loanable funds exchanged, making that change indeterminate without knowing about the relative magnitudes of the changes.

10. **Other things equal, which direction will an increasing budget surplus change the equilibrium interest rate, the loanable funds supply curve, the level of investment in the economy, and the likely rate of economic growth?**
    An increasing budget surplus would increase the saving supply curve, which would decrease the equilibrium interest rate and increase the equilibrium level of investment in the economy, which would tend to increase economy growth.

13.3 The Financial Crisis of 2008

1. **Why would history and the role of Fannie Mae and Freddy Mac have made investors consider mortgage-backed securities to be safe?**
   Historically, home loans in the United States had been very safe investments. In addition, both Fannie Mae and Freddy Mac were willing to buy large amounts of mortgage-backed securities and to guarantee others. Both made investors think mortgage-backed securities were not unduly risky.

2. **Why were those who took out hybrid loans at far greater risk of foreclosure when the Fed began raising interest rates?**
   Hybrid loans began, with a low fixed rate for the first few years, which then reset to a higher rate for the rest of the term. Borrowers with hybrid loans also had far smaller down payments than traditional home borrowers. As a result, the combination of falling home prices and increasing interest rates hit those homeowners and their lenders particularly hard.

Problems

1. Why are firms less likely to issue new shares of stock when consumers or businesses are pessimistic about economic conditions?

2. In the event of a corporate bankruptcy, would you rather be a bondholder, a preferred stockholder, or a common stockholder in the ailing corporation? Explain.

3. Why might governments sometimes try to combat recessions by lowering interest rates?

4. What would happen to the loanable funds demand curve if new potentially profitable technologies arise and business taxes are raised at the same time?

5. What would happen to the loanable funds supply curve if there was both an increase in current disposable income and a decrease in new technologies creating investment opportunities?

6. Starting from equilibrium in the loanable funds market, what changes in loanable funds supply or demand would tend to cause a surplus of funds at the current interest rate? What changes in loanable funds supply or demand would tend to cause a shortage of funds at the current interest rate?

7. What happens to net taxes when transfer payments increase? When both taxes and transfer payments increase?

8. Which direction will an increasing budget deficit change the equilibrium interest rate, the loanable funds supply curve, the level of loanable funds in the economy, and the likely rate of economic growth, *ceteris paribus*?

9.

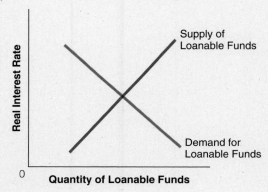

    a. What happens to the loanable funds supply and demand curves if business expectations and disposable income both increase?

    b. What happens to the loanable funds supply and demand curves if profitable new technologies are invented and disposable income decreases?

    c. What happens to the loanable funds supply and demand curves if taxes on investment increase and taxes on savings decrease?

    d. What happens to the loanable funds supply and demand curves if increasingly costly business regulations are imposed, along with increased taxes on current earnings?

10. In retrospect, what should have been the Federal Reserve's monetary policy during the 2008 financial crisis?

11. If housing prices had continued to rise during the 2008 financial crisis, would we still have had the same problem with subprime borrowers? Or would it have just been delayed?

12. Why was home building such an important factor in this crisis?

13. If the government had not encouraged a goal of homeownership with easy credit, would we have the current housing market problem?

Future Evaluation

One of the most important decisions a firm makes is investment in new capital. A lot of money will be invested in factory equipment and machines expected to last for many years. The firm making the investment decision must consider the price that it must pay *now* for the new capital compared with the additional revenue the capital should generate *over time*. That is, the firm must compare current costs with future benefits. To figure out how much those future benefits are worth today, economists use a concept called present value.

present value
the value in today's dollars of some future benefit

How Do We Determine the Present Value?

One of the most useful formulas in economics is the formula for present value. The present value of future income is the value of having that future income now. That is, a dollar today is worth more than a dollar in the future. People prefer to have money now rather than later, which is why they are willing to pay interest to borrow it. The present value of receiving $1,000 a year from now can be calculated by using the present value equation:

$$PV = \$X/(1 + r)^t$$

where $X = \$1,000$; r = current market interest rate; and t = years from now. So the present value of $1,000

Present Value Table

Year	3%	6%	8%	10%	15%
1	0.9709	0.9434	0.9259	0.9091	0.8696
2	1.9135	1.8334	1.7833	1.7355	1.6257
3	2.8286	2.6730	2.5771	2.4869	2.2832
4	3.7171	3.4651	3.3121	3.1699	2.8550
5	4.5797	4.2124	3.9927	3.7908	3.3522
6	5.4172	4.9173	4.6229	4.3553	3.7845
7	6.2303	5.5824	5.2064	4.8684	4.1604
8	7.0197	6.2098	5.7466	5.3349	4.4873
9	7.7861	6.8017	6.2469	5.7590	4.7716
10	8.5302	7.3601	6.7101	6.1446	5.0188
11	9.2526	7.8869	7.1390	6.4951	5.2337
12	9.9540	8.3838	7.5361	6.8137	5.4206
13	10.6350	8.8527	7.9038	7.1034	5.5831
14	11.2961	9.2950	8.2442	7.3667	5.7245
15	11.9379	9.7122	8.5595	7.6061	5.8474
16	12.5611	10.1059	8.8514	7.8237	5.9542
17	13.1661	10.4773	9.1216	8.0216	6.0472
18	13.7535	10.8276	9.3719	8.2014	6.1280
19	14.3238	11.1581	9.6036	8.3649	6.1982
20	14.8775	11.4699	9.8181	8.5136	6.2593
30	19.6004	13.7648	11.2578	9.4269	6.5660

one year from now at the current market interest rate of 5 percent is

$$\$1,000/(1.05)^1 = \$952.38$$

The present value of $1,000 two years from now at a current market interest rate of 5 percent is

$$\$1,000/(1.05)^2 = \$907.03$$

To illustrate, suppose a company is contemplating the purchase of a new factory that it thinks will produce additional annual earnings of $100,000 a year for 10 years, at which time it will be obsolete (worthless). In this case, let us assume that we can get 10 percent annually on the use of our funds in some comparable alternative investment; a good proxy for this "comparable investment" is the market rate of interest. We can now calculate the present value of earnings to be received in each year (first, second, third, and so on) and sum them. Because these multiyear computations can be tedious, a present value table is given on the previous page. For example, $100,000 per year over 10 years at 10 percent interest yields a present value of $614,460 ($100,000 × 6.1446). If the price of the factory were only $500,000, we would invest; if the price were $700,000, however, the marginal cost of $700,000 would exceed the present value, $614,460, so we would not invest in the new factory.

However, if interest rates were to fall to 6 percent, the present value of the flow of future earnings would grow to $736,010 ($1,000,000 × 7.3601), and we probably would make the investment even if the factory cost $700,000. Thus, falling interest rates lead to greater investment. In short, we see that an investor will buy capital (the factory) if the expected discounted present value of the capital exceeds the current price.

Thus, the company's decision whether or not to invest in a new factory depends on the interest rate. We can see from the example how the quantity of loanable funds demanded and investment is related to the interest rate. At a higher interest rate, the quantity of loanable funds demanded (and investments) falls and at a lower interest rate the quantity of loanable funds demanded (and investments) rises.

Key Terms and Concepts

present value 373

Problems

1. Why is money worth more now than at some future date?

   Answer

   You can use the money that you have right now. You could save it and get interest on it or you can buy goods and services with that money. If you are receiving money a year from now—you can't use that money right now to save or consume. There is also a risk associated with lending the money. If you lend the money to a friend, he or she may not be able to pay it back in a year like you had expected.

2. How does the interest rate affect the present value payments?

   Answer

   The interest rate connects the present value with the future. The interest rate reflects *how much more* a person values a dollar today versus a dollar in the future.

3. If you won $10 million in the lottery and were given a choice of a lump sum payment or payment over a 20-year period, which would you choose?

   Answer

   First compute the actual present value of the $10 million lottery prize. Using a 10 percent interest rate, the present value over a 20-year period is $4,256,800. That is, using the present value tables, we multiply $500,000 × 8.5136 = $4,256,800. If you want it up front, it is certainly less than $10 million.

part 5

The Macroeconomic Models

Aggregate Demand and Aggregate Supply

CHRIS HONDROS/GETTY IMAGES

In this chapter, we develop the aggregate demand and aggregate supply model. The AD/AS model is a variable price model; that is, it allows us to see changes in the price level and changes in real GDP simultaneously. We explain changes in the price level and real GDP in both the short run and long run. This model will help us understand such key macroeconomic variables as inflation, unemployment, and economic growth. In the following chapters, we will also use this model to help us understand how stabilization policies can help with problems that result from recession and inflationary expansion.

The Determinants of Aggregate Demand 14.1

- What is aggregate demand?
- What is consumption?
- What is investment?
- What are government purchases?
- What are net exports?

What Is Aggregate Demand?

Aggregate demand (*AD*) is the sum of the demand for all final goods and services in the economy. It can also be seen as the quantity of real gross domestic product demanded at different price levels. The four major components of aggregate demand are consumption (*C*), investment (*I*), government purchases (*G*), and net exports (*X − M*). Aggregate demand, then, is equal to $C + I + G + (X - M)$.

aggregate demand (AD)
the total demand for all the final goods and services in the economy

What are four major components of aggregate demand?

Consumption (C)

Consumption is by far the largest component in aggregate demand. Expenditures for consumer goods and services typically absorb almost 70 percent of total economic activity, as measured by GDP. Understanding the determinants of consumption, then, is critical to an understanding of the forces leading to changes in aggregate demand, which, in turn, changes total output and income.

Investment (I)

Because investment spending (purchases of investment goods) is an important component of aggregate demand, which in turn is a determinant of the level of GDP, changes in investment spending are often responsible for changes in the level of economic activity. If consumption is determined largely by the level of disposable income, what determines the level of investment expenditure? As you may recall, investment expenditure is the most unstable category of GDP; it is sensitive to changes in economic, social, and political variables.

What is the most unstable component of GDP?

Many factors are important in determining the level of investment. Good business conditions "induce" firms to invest because a healthy growth in demand for products in the future seems likely, based on current experience. We will consider the key variables that influence investment spending in the next section.

Government Purchases (G)

Government purchases, another component of aggregate demand, include spending by federal, state, and local governments for the purchase of new goods and services produced. For example, an increase in highway or other transportation projects will increase aggregate demand, holding other factors like interest rates and taxes constant.

Net Exports (X − M)

The interaction of the U.S. economy with the rest of the world is becoming increasingly important. Up to this point, for simplicity, we have not included the foreign sector. However, international trade must be incorporated into the framework. Models that include the effects of international trade are called **open economy** models.

open economy
a type of model that includes international trade effects

net exports
the difference between the value of exports and the value of imports

Remember, exports are goods and services that we sell to foreign customers, such as movies, wheat, and Ford Mustangs; imports are goods and services that we buy from foreign companies, such as BMWs, French wine, and Sony TVs. Exports and imports can alter aggregate demand. Exports minus imports is what we call **net exports**. If exports are greater than imports $(X > M)$, we have positive net exports. If imports are greater than exports $(X < M)$, net exports are negative.

The impact of net exports $(X - M)$ on aggregate demand is similar to the impact of government purchases on aggregate demand. Suppose that the United States has no trade surplus and no trade deficit—zero net exports. What would happen if foreign consumers started buying more U.S. goods and services, while U.S. consumers continued to buy imports at roughly the same rate? The result would be *positive net exports* $(X > M)$ and greater demand for U.S. goods and services—a higher level of aggregate demand. What if a country has a trade deficit? Assuming, again, that the economy initially has zero net exports, a trade deficit, or *negative net exports* $(X < M)$, would lower U.S. aggregate demand, *ceteris paribus*.

ⓘ SECTION QUIZ

1. The largest component of aggregate demand is
   a. government purchases.
   b. net exports.
   c. consumption.
   d. investment.

2. A reduction in personal income taxes, other things being equal, will
   a. leave consumers with less disposable income.
   b. decrease aggregate demand.
   c. leave consumers with more disposable income.
   d. increase aggregate demand.
   e. do both (c) and (d).

3. Aggregate demand is the sum of _____.
   a. $C + I + G$
   b. $C + I + G + X$
   c. $C + I + G + (X - M)$
   d. $C + I + G + (X + M)$

4. Empirical evidence suggests that consumption _____ with any _____.
   a. decreases; increase in income
   b. decreases; tax cut
   c. increases; decrease in consumer confidence
   d. increases; increase in income
   e. Both (a) and (b) are true.

5. Investment (I) includes
   a. the amount spent on new factories and machinery.
   b. the amount spent on stocks and bonds.
   c. the amount spent on consumer goods that last more than one year.
   d. the amount spent on purchases of art.
   e. all of the above.

(*continued*)

⟳ SECTION QUIZ (Cont.)

6. If our exports of final goods and services increase more than our imports, other things being equal, aggregate demand will

   a. increase.

   b. be negative.

   c. decrease by the change in net exports.

   d. stay the same.

   e. do none of the above.

---

1. What are the major components of aggregate demand?

2. How would an increase in personal taxes or a decrease in transfer payments affect consumption?

3. What would an increase in exports do to aggregate demand, other things being equal? An increase in imports? An increase in both imports and exports, where the change in exports was greater in magnitude?

Answers: 1. c 2. e 3. c 4. d 5. a 6. a

The Aggregate Demand Curve   14.2

📁 How is the aggregate demand curve different from the demand curve for a particular good?

📁 Why is the aggregate demand curve downward sloping?

The **aggregate demand curve** reflects the total amount of real goods and services that all groups together want to purchase in a given period. In other words, it indicates the quantities of real gross domestic product demanded at different price levels. Note that this is different from the demand curve for a particular good presented in Chapter 4, which looked at the relationship between the relative price of a good and the quantity demanded. Because we are dealing with the economy as a whole, we need an explanation for why the aggregate demand curve is downward sloping and why the short-run aggregate supply curve is upward sloping.

How Is the Quantity of Real GDP Demanded Affected by the Price Level?

The aggregate demand curve slopes downward, which means an inverse (or opposite) relationship exists between the price level and real gross domestic product (RGDP) demanded. Exhibit 1 illustrates this relationship, where the quantity of RGDP demanded is measured on the horizontal axis and the overall price level is measured on the vertical axis. As we move from point A to point B on the aggregate demand curve, we see that an increase in the price level causes RGDP demanded to fall. Conversely, if a reduction in the price level occurs—a movement from B to A—RGDP demanded increases. Why do purchasers in the economy demand less real output when the price level rises and more real output when the price level falls?

aggregate demand curve
graph that shows the inverse relationship between the price level and RGDP demanded

How is the aggregate demand curve different than the demand curve for a particular good?

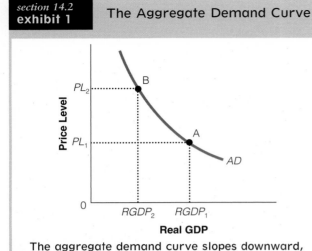

section 14.2
exhibit 1   The Aggregate Demand Curve

The aggregate demand curve slopes downward, reflecting an inverse relationship between the overall price level and the quantity of real GDP demanded. When the price level increases, the quantity of RGDP demanded decreases; when the price level decreases, the quantity of RGDP demanded increases.

Why Is the Aggregate Demand Curve Negatively Sloped?

Three complementary explanations exist for the negative slope of the aggregate demand curve: the wealth effect, the interest rate effect, and the open economy effect.

The Wealth Effect: Changes in Consumer Spending

If you had $1,000 in cash stashed under your bed while the economy suffered a serious bout of inflation, the purchasing power of your cash would be eroded by the extent of the inflation. That is, an increase in the price level reduces the real value of money and makes consumers poorer, encouraging them to spend less. A decrease in consumer spending means a decrease in quantity of RGDP demanded.

In the event that the price level falls, the reverse would hold true. A falling price level increases the real value of money and makes consumers wealthier, encouraging them to spend more. An increase in consumer spending means an increase in the quantity of RGDP demanded. This is called the wealth effect of a change in the price level. Because of the wealth effect, consumer spending, C, falls (rises) when the price level increases (decreases).

What is the wealth effect of a price level change?

How does a lower price level lead to lower interest rates?

The Interest Rate Effect: A Change in Investment

If the price level falls, households and firms will need to hold less money to conduct their day-to-day activities. Firms will need to hold less money for such inputs as wages and taxes; households will need to hold less money for such purchases as food, rent, and clothing. At a lower price level, households and firms will shift their "excess" money into interest-earning assets such as bonds or savings accounts. This will increase the supply of funds to the loanable funds market, leading to lower interest rates. As interest rates fall, households and firms will borrow more and buy more goods and services—thus, the quantity of RGDP demanded will increase.

If the price level rises, households and firms will need to hold more money to buy goods and services and conduct their daily activities. Households and firms will need to borrow money, and this increased demand for loanable funds will result in higher interest rates. At higher interest rates, consumers may give up plans to buy new cars or houses, and firms may delay investments in plant and equipment.

In sum, a higher price level raises the interest rate and discourages investment spending and decreases the quantity of RGDP demanded. A lower price level reduces the interest rate and encourages investment spending causing RGDP demanded to rise.

The Open Economy Effect

Many goods and services are bought and sold in global markets. If the price level in the United States rises relative to the price level in other countries, U.S. exports will become relatively more expensive and foreign imports will become relatively less expensive. Some U.S. consumers will shift from buying domestic goods to buying foreign goods (imports). Some foreign consumers will stop buying U.S. goods. U.S. exports will fall and U.S. imports will rise. Thus, net exports will fall, thereby reducing the amount of RGDP purchased in the United States. A lower price level makes U.S. exports less expensive and foreign imports more expensive. So U.S. consumers will buy more domestic goods, and foreign consumers will buy more U.S. goods. This will increase net exports, thereby increasing the amount of RGDP purchased in the United States.

⊘ SECTION QUIZ

1. The aggregate demand curve
   a. is negatively sloped.
   b. demonstrates an inverse relationship between the price level and real gross domestic product demanded.
   c. shows how real gross domestic product demanded changes with the changes in the price level.
   d. All of the above are correct.

2. As the price level increases, other things being equal,
   a. aggregate demand decreases.
   b. the quantity of real gross domestic product demanded increases.
   c. the quantity of real gross domestic product demanded decreases.
   d. aggregate demand increases.
   e. both (a) and (c) occur.

3. According to the real wealth effect, if you are living in a period of falling price levels on a fixed income (that is, not indexed), the cost of the goods and services you buy _____ and your real income _____.
   a. decreases; decreases
   b. increases; increases
   c. decreases; remains the same
   d. decreases; increases

4. As the price level decreases, real wealth _____, purchasing power _____, and the quantity of RGDP demanded _____.
   a. increases; decreases; increases
   b. increases; increases; increases
   c. decreases; decreases; decreases
   d. decreases; decreases; increases
   e. increases; decreases; decreases

5. As the price level increases, interest rates _____, investments _____, and the quantity of RGDP demanded _____.
   a. decrease; increase; decreases
   b. increase; increase; decreases
   c. decrease; decrease; increases
   d. decrease; increase; increases
   e. increase; decrease; decreases

6. What is the open economy effect?
   a. If prices of the goods and services in the domestic market rise relative to those in global markets as a result of a higher domestic price level, consumers and businesses will buy less from foreign producers and more from domestic producers.
   b. People are allowed to trade with anyone, anywhere, anytime.
   c. It is the ability of firms to enter or leave the marketplace—easy entry and exit with low entry barriers.
   d. If prices of the goods and services in the domestic market rise relative to those in global markets as a result of a higher domestic price level, consumers and businesses will buy more from foreign producers and less from domestic producers, other things being equal.

(*continued*)

7. Which of the following helps explain the downward slope of the aggregate demand curve?

   a. the real wealth effect

   b. the interest effect

   c. the open economy effect

   d. all of the above

   e. none of the above

8. Which of the following will result as part of the interest rate effect when the price level rises?

   a. Money demand will increase.

   b. Interest rates will increase.

   c. The dollar amount of investment will decrease.

   d. A lower quantity of real GDP will be demanded.

   e. All of the above will result.

---

1. Why is the aggregate demand curve downward sloping?

2. How does an increased price level reduce the quantities of investment goods and consumer durables demanded?

3. What is the wealth effect, and how does it imply a downward-sloping aggregate demand curve?

4. What is the interest rate effect, and how does it imply a downward-sloping aggregate demand curve?

5. What is the open economy effect, and how does it imply a downward-sloping aggregate demand curve?

Answers: 1. d 2. c 3. d 4. b 5. e 6. d 7. d 8. e

14.3   Shifts in the Aggregate Demand Curve

📁 What is the difference between a movement along and a shift in the aggregate demand curve?

📁 What variables shift the aggregate demand curve to the right?

📁 What variables shift the aggregate demand curve to the left?

Shifts versus Movements along the Aggregate Demand Curve

Like the supply and demand curves described in Chapter 4, the aggregate demand curve may experience both shifts and movements. In the previous section, we discussed three factors—the real wealth effect, the interest rate effect, and the open economy effect—that result in the downward slope of the aggregate demand curve. Each of these factors, then, generates a movement *along* the aggregate demand curve in reaction to changes in the general price level. In this section, we will discuss some of the many factors that can cause the aggregate demand curve to shift to the right or left.

The whole aggregate demand curve can shift to the right or left, as shown in Exhibit 1. Put simply, if some nonprice-level determinant causes total spending to increase, the aggregate demand curve will shift to the right. If a nonprice-level determinant causes the level of total spending to decline, the aggregate demand curve will shift to the left. Let's look at some specific factors that could cause the aggregate demand curve to shift.

Aggregate Demand Curve Shifters

Anything that changes the amount of total spending in the economy (holding price levels constant) will affect the aggregate demand curve. An increase in any component of GDP (C, I, G, or $X - M$) will cause the aggregate demand curve to shift rightward. Conversely, decreases in C, I, G, or $X - M$ will shift aggregate demand leftward.

Changing Consumption (C)

A whole host of changes could alter consumption patterns. For example, an increase in consumer confidence, an increase in wealth (not the wealth effect caused by the change in the price level), or a tax cut can increase consumption and shift the aggregate demand curve to the right. An increase in population will also increase the aggregate demand because more consumers will be spending more money on goods and services. A lower interest rate can also spur consumption spending.

Of course, the aggregate demand curve could shift to the left as a result of decreases in consumption demand. For example, if consumers sense that the economy is headed for a recession, if the government imposes a tax increase or if interest rates rise, the result will be a leftward shift of the aggregate demand curve. Because saving more is consuming less, an increase in saving, *ceteris paribus*, will shift aggregate demand to the left. Consumer debt may also cause some consumers to put off additional spending.

Changing Investment (I)

Investment is also an important determinant of aggregate demand. Increases in the demand for investment goods occur for a variety of reasons. For example, if business confidence increases or real interest rates fall, business investment will increase and aggregate demand will shift to the right. A reduction in business taxes would also shift the aggregate demand curve to the right, because businesses would now retain more of their profits to invest. However, if interest rates or business taxes rise, we would expect to see a leftward shift in aggregate demand.

Changing Government Purchases (G)

Government purchases are another part of total spending and therefore must have an impact on aggregate demand. An increase in government purchases, other things being equal, shifts the aggregate demand curve to the right, while a reduction shifts aggregate demand to the left. If state governments start building new highways, this will lead to a rightward shift in aggregate demand, too.

Changing Net Exports (X – M)

Global markets are also important in a domestic economy. For example, when major trading partners experience economic slowdowns, they will demand fewer U.S. imports. This causes U.S. net exports ($X - M$) to fall, shifting aggregate demand to the left. Alternatively, an economic boom in the economies of major trading partners may lead to an increase in our exports to them, causing net exports ($X - M$) to rise and aggregate demand to increase.

In addition, changes in the exchange rate can shift the aggregate demand curve. Suppose financial speculators lose confidence in foreign economies and want to put their wealth in the U.S. economy. As foreigners convert their weath into dollars, the dollar appreciates. This makes U.S. goods more expensive compared to foreign goods, which decreases net exports and shifts the aggregate demand curve to the left. Of course, speculation could also lead to a depreciation of the dollar. This would stimulate net exports and shift the aggregate demand curve to the right.

section 14.3 exhibit 1 — **Shifts in the Aggregate Demand Curve**

An increase in aggregate demand shifts the curve to the right (from AD_1 to AD_2). A decrease in aggregate demand shifts the curve to the left (from AD_1 to AD_3).

© Cengage Learning 2013

Do wealth increases and/or tax cuts increase the consumption component of aggregate demand?

How do foreign economies' growth rates affect a country's domestic aggregate demand?

use what you've learned Changes in Aggregate Demand

Q Any aggregate demand category that has the ability to change total purchases in the economy will shift the aggregate demand curve. That is, changes in consumption purchases, investment purchases, government purchases, or net export purchases shift the aggregate demand curve. For each component of aggregate demand (C, I, G, and $X - M$), list some changes that can increase aggregate demand. Then list some changes that can decrease aggregate demand.

A The following are some aggregate demand curve shifters.

INCREASES IN AGGREGATE DEMAND (RIGHTWARD SHIFT)	DECREASES IN AGGREGATE DEMAND (LEFTWARD SHIFT)
Consumption (C)	Consumption (C)
— lower personal taxes	— higher personal taxes
— a rise in consumer confidence	— a fall in consumer confidence
— greater stock market or real estate wealth	— reduced stock market or real estate wealth
— an increase in transfer payments or lower real interest rates	— a reduction in transfer payments or higher real interest rates
Investment (I)	Investment (I)
— lower real interest rates	— higher real interest rates
— optimistic business forecasts	— pessimistic business forecasts
— lower business taxes	— higher business taxes
Government purchases (G)	Government purchases (G)
— an increase in government purchases	— a reduction in government purchases
Net exports ($X - M$)	Net exports ($X - M$)
— income increases abroad, which will likely increase the sale of domestic goods (exports)	— income falls abroad, which leads to a reduction in the sale of domestic goods (exports)
— speculation that causes a depreciation of the dollar and stimulates net exports	— speculation that causes an appreciation of the dollar and depresses net exports

⑦ SECTION QUIZ

1. An economic bust or severe downturn in the Japanese economy will likely result in a(n)
   a. decrease in U.S. exports and U.S. aggregate demand.
   b. increase in U.S. exports and U.S. aggregate demand.
   c. decrease in U.S. imports and U.S. aggregate demand.
   d. increase in U.S. imports and U.S. aggregate demand.

2. Which of the following will cause consumption and, as a result, aggregate demand to decrease?
   a. a tax increase
   b. a fall in consumer confidence
   c. reduced stock market wealth
   d. rising levels of consumer debt
   e. all of the above

3. A massive increase in interstate highway construction will affect aggregate demand through which sector? Will this change increase or decrease aggregate demand?
   a. investment; increase
   b. government purchases; increase
   c. government purchases; decrease
   d. consumption; decrease

(continued)

4. An increase in government purchases, combined with a decrease in investment, would have what effect on aggregate demand?

   a. *AD* would increase.

   b. *AD* would decrease.

   c. *AD* would stay the same.

   d. *AD* could either increase or decrease, depending on which change was of greater magnitude.

5. An increase in consumption, combined with an increase in exports, would have what effect on aggregate demand?

   a. *AD* would increase.

   b. *AD* would decrease.

   c. *AD* would stay the same.

   d. *AD* could either increase or decrease, depending on which change was of greater magnitude.

6. What would happen to aggregate demand if the federal government increased military purchases and state and local governments decreased their road-building budgets at the same time?

   a. *AD* would increase because only federal government purchases affect *AD*.

   b. *AD* would decrease because only state and local government purchases affect *AD*.

   c. *AD* would increase if the change in federal purchases was greater than the change in state and local purchases.

   d. *AD* would decrease if the change in federal purchases was greater than the change in state and local purchases.

7. If exports and imports both decrease, but exports decrease more than imports,

   a. *AD* would decrease.

   b. *AD* would increase.

   c. *AD* would be unaffected.

   d. *AD* could either increase or decrease.

---

1. How is the distinction between a change in demand and a change in quantity demanded the same for aggregate demand as for the demand for a particular good?

2. What happens to aggregate demand if the demand for consumption goods increases, *ceteris paribus*?

3. What happens to aggregate demand if the demand for investment goods falls, *ceteris paribus*?

Answers: 1. a   2. e   3. b   4. d   5. a   6. c   7. a

The Aggregate Supply Curve   14.4

📂 What does the aggregate supply curve represent?

📂 Why do producers supply more as the price level increases in the short run?

📂 Why is the long-run aggregate supply curve vertical at the natural rate of real output?

What Is the Aggregate Supply Curve?

The **aggregate supply** (*AS*) **curve** is the relationship between the total quantity of final goods and services that suppliers are *willing* and *able* to produce and the overall price level. The aggregate supply curve represents how much RGDP suppliers are willing to produce

aggregate supply (*AS*) **curve** the total quantity of final goods and services suppliers are willing and able to supply at a given price level at different price levels. In fact, the two aggregate supply curves are a **short-run aggregate supply (*SRAS*) curve** and a **long-run aggregate supply (*LRAS*) curve**. The short-run relationship refers to a period when output can change in response to supply and demand, but input prices have not yet been able to adjust. For example, wages are assumed to adjust slowly in the short run. The long-run relationship refers to a period long enough for the prices of outputs and all inputs to fully adjust to changes in the economy.

Because the effects of the price level on aggregate supply is very different in the short run versus the long run, we have two aggregate supply curves—one for the long run and one for the short run.

Why Is the Short-Run Aggregate Supply Curve Positively Sloped?

In the short run, the aggregate supply curve is upward sloping, as shown in Exhibit 1. At a higher price level, then, producers are willing to supply more real output, and at lower price levels, they are willing to supply less real output. Why would producers be willing to supply more output just because the price level increases? Two possible explanations are the profit effect and the misperception effect.

The Profit Effect

For many firms, input costs—wages and rents, for example—are relatively constant in the short run. Workers and other material input suppliers often enter into long-term contracts with firms at prearranged prices. Thus, the slow adjustments of input prices are due to contracts that do not adjust quickly to output overall price level changes. So when the overall price level rises, output prices rise relative to input prices (costs), raising producers' short-run profit margins. That is, a higher price level leads to a higher profit per unit of output and higher RGDP supplied because wages and other input prices can be slow to adjust in the short run. With this short-run profit effect, the increased profit margins make it in producers' self-interest to expand production and sales at higher price levels.

If the price level falls, output prices fall and producers' profits tend to fall. That is, a lower price level leads to a lower profit per unit of output and lower RGDP supplied because wages and other input prices can be slow to adjust in the short run. Again, this is because many input costs, such as wages and other contracted costs, are relatively constant in the short run. When output price levels fall, producers find it more difficult to cover their input costs and, consequently, reduce their levels of output.

The Misperception Effect

The second explanation for the upward-sloping short-run aggregate supply curve is that producers can be fooled by price changes in the short run. That is, changes in the overall price level can temporarily mislead producers about what is taking place in their particular market. For example, suppose a wheat farmer sees the price of wheat rising. Thinking that the *relative price* of wheat is rising (i.e., that wheat is becoming more valuable in real terms), the wheat farmer supplies more. Suppose, however, that wheat was not the

What is the difference between the short-run aggregate supply curve and the long-run aggregate supply curve?

short-run aggregate supply (*SRAS*) curve
the graphical relationship between RGDP and the price level when output prices can change but input prices are unable to adjust

long-run aggregate supply (*LRAS*) curve
the graphical relationship between RGDP and the price level when output prices and input prices can fully adjust to economic changes

How do rising output prices change a firm's profit margins in the short run?

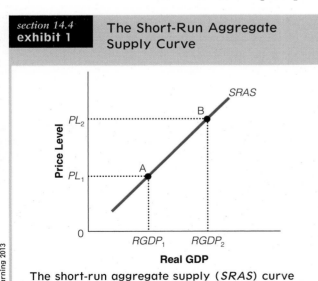

section 14.4
exhibit 1   The Short-Run Aggregate Supply Curve

The short-run aggregate supply (*SRAS*) curve is upward sloping. Suppliers are willing to supply more RGDP at higher price levels and less at lower price levels, other things being equal.

3 percent increase in wages for their members if they anticipate the price level to rise 3 percent next year. If they are successful in getting the wage increase for their members, this will cause the short-run aggregate supply curve to shift to the left.

Of course, firms and workers can make incorrect predictions about the future price level. For example, if workers expect a small increase in the price level and it turns out to be much larger, they will negotiate for even higher wages in the next contract—this will shift the *SRAS* curve leftward. The higher wages will increase the firm's costs, and it will need higher prices now to produce the same level of output. If most firms and workers are making the adjustment to a higher than expected price level, then the *SRAS* curve will shift left. If they are adjusting to the price level being lower than expected, then the *SRAS* curve will shift right.

Supply Shocks

Supply shocks are unexpected temporary events that can either increase or decrease the short-run aggregate supply. For example, negative supply shocks like major widespread flooding, earthquakes, droughts, and other natural disasters can increase the costs of production, causing the short-run aggregate supply curve to shift to the left, *ceteris paribus*. However, once the temporary effects of these disasters have been felt, no appreciable change in the economy's productive capacity has occurred, so the long-run aggregate supply doesn't shift as a result. Other temporary supply shocks, such as disruptions in trade due to war or labor strikes, will have similar effects on short-run aggregate supply. However, positive supply shocks such as favorable weather conditions or temporary price reductions of imported resources like oil can lower production costs and shift the short-run aggregate supply curve rightward. During the mid- to late 1990s, the United States experienced a positive supply shock as the Internet, and information technology in general, gave a huge boost to productivity.

Exhibit 4 presents a table that summarizes the factors that can shift the short-run aggregate supply curve, the long-run aggregate supply curve, or both, depending on whether the effects are temporary or permanent.

supply shocks
unexpected temporary events that can either increase or decrease aggregate supply

---

use

what you've learned   **Shifts in the Short-Run Aggregate Supply Curve**

Q Why do wage increases (and other input prices) affect the short-run aggregate supply but not the long-run aggregate supply?

A Remember, in the short run, wages and other input prices are assumed to be constant along the *SRAS* curve. If the firm has to pay more for its workers or any other input, its costs will rise. That is, the *SRAS* curve will shift to the left. This shift from *SRAS*₁ to *SRAS*₂ is shown in Exhibit 3. The reason the *SRAS* curve will not shift is that unless these input prices reflect permanent changes in input supply, those changes will only be temporary, and output will not be permanently or sustainedly different as a result. Other things being equal, if an input price is to be permanently higher, relative to other goods, its supply must have decreased; but

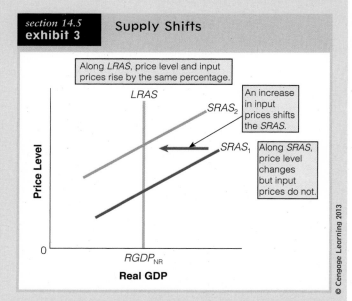

section 14.5 **exhibit 3**   **Supply Shifts**

Along *LRAS*, price level and input prices rise by the same percentage.

LRAS

*SRAS*₂

An increase in input prices shifts the *SRAS*.

*SRAS*₁

Along *SRAS*, price level changes but input prices do not.

Price Level

0   *RGDP*ₙᵣ

Real GDP

© Cengage Learning 2013

that would mean that potential real output, and hence long-run aggregate supply, would also shift left.

section 14.5
exhibit 4   Factors That May Shift the Aggregate Supply

An Increase in Aggregate Supply Curve (Rightward Shift)

Lower costs
- lower wages
- other input prices fall

Government policy
- tax cuts
- deregulation
- lower trade barriers

Economic growth
- improvements in human and physical capital
- technological advances
- an increase in labor

Favorable weather
A fall in the future expected price level

A Decrease in Aggregate Supply Curve (Leftward Shift)

Higher costs
- higher wages
- other input prices rise

Government policy
- overregulation
- waste and inefficiency
- higher trade barriers
- stagnation
- a decline in labor productivity
- capital deterioration

Unfavorable weather
Natural disasters and war
A rise in the future expected price level

These factors can shift the short-run aggregate supply curve, the long-run aggregate supply curve, or both, depending on whether the effects are temporary or permanent.

---

② SECTION QUIZ

1. The short-run aggregate supply curve will shift to the left, other things being equal, if

   a. energy prices fall.

   b. technology and productivity increase in the nation.

   c. an increase in input prices occurs.

   d. the capital stock of the nation increases.

2. An increase in input prices causes

   a. the short-run aggregate supply curve to shift outward, which means the quantity supplied at any price level declines.

   b. the short-run aggregate supply curve to shift inward, which means the quantity supplied at any price level declines.

   c. the short-run aggregate supply curve to shift inward, which means the quantity supplied at any price level increases.

   d. the short-run aggregate supply curve to shift outward, which means the quantity supplied at any price level increases.

3. Which of the following could be expected to shift the short-run aggregate supply curve rightward?

   a. a rise in the price of oil

   b. a natural disaster

   c. wage increases without increases in labor productivity

   d. all of the above

4. An unusual series of rainstorms washes out the grain crop in the upper plains states, severely curtailing the supply of corn and wheat, as well as soybeans. What effect would this situation have on aggregate supply?

   a. It would shift the *SRAS* left, but not the *LRAS*.

   b. It would shift both the *SRAS* and the *LRAS* left.

   c. It would shift the *SRAS* right, but not the *LRAS*.

   d. It would shift both the *SRAS* and the *LRAS* right.

(*continued*)

ⓘ S E C T I O N Q U I Z (Cont.)

5. Any permanent increase in the quantity of any of the factors of production—capital, land, labor, or technology—available will cause

   a. the *SRAS* to shift to the left and *LRAS* to remain constant.

   b. the *SRAS* to shift to the right and *LRAS* to remain constant.

   c. both *SRAS* and *LRAS* to shift to the right.

   d. both *SRAS* and *LRAS* to shift to the left.

6. Which of the following could be expected to shift the short-run aggregate supply curve upward?

   a. a rise in the price of oil

   b. a natural disaster

   c. wage increases without increases in labor productivity

   d. all of the above

7. A temporary positive supply shock will shift _____; a permanent positive supply shock will shift _____.

   a. *SRAS* and *LRAS* right; *SRAS* and *LRAS* right

   b. *SRAS* but not *LRAS* right; *SRAS* and *LRAS* right

   c. *SRAS* and *LRAS* right; *SRAS* but not *LRAS* right

   d. *SRAS* but not *LRAS* right; *SRAS* but not *LRAS* right

8. A year of unusually good weather for agriculture would

   a. increase *SRAS* but not *LRAS*.

   b. increase *SRAS* and *LRAS*.

   c. decrease *SRAS* but not *LRAS*.

   d. decrease *SRAS* and *LRAS*.

9. When the price of oil experiences a temporary sharp increase, which curve(s) will shift left?

   a. *SRAS*

   b. *LRAS*

   c. neither *SRAS* nor *LRAS*

   d. both *SRAS* and *LRAS*

---

1. Which of the aggregate supply curves will shift in response to a change in the expected price level? Why?

2. Why do lower input costs increase the level of RGDP supplied at any given price level?

3. What would discovering huge new supplies of oil and natural gas do to the short- and long-run aggregate supply curves?

4. What would happen to short- and long-run aggregate supply curves if the government required every firm to file explanatory paperwork each time a decision was made?

5. What would happen to the short- and long-run aggregate supply curves if the capital stock grew and available supplies of natural resources expanded over the same period of time?

6. How can a change in input prices change the short-run aggregate supply curve but not the long-run aggregate supply curve? How could it change both long- and short-run aggregate supply?

7. What would happen to short- and long-run aggregate supply if unusually good weather led to bumper crops of most agricultural produce?

8. If OPEC temporarily restricted the world output of oil, what would happen to short- and long-run aggregate supply? What would happen if the output restriction was permanent?

Answers: 1. c 2. b 3. d 4. a 5. c 6. d 7. b 8. a 9. a

14.6
Macroeconomic Equilibrium: The Short Run and the Long Run

- 📂 What is short-run macroeconomic equilibrium?
- 📂 What is the long-run macroeconomic equilibrium?
- 📂 What are recessionary and inflationary gaps?
- 📂 What is demand-pull inflation?
- 📂 What is cost-push inflation?
- 📂 How does the economy self-correct?
- 📂 What is wage and price inflexibility?

Determining Macroeconomic Equilibrium

ECS

economic content standards

Fluctuations of real GDP around its potential level occur when overall spending declines, as in a recession, or when overall spending increases rapidly, as in recovery from a recession or in an expansion.

recessionary gap
the output gap that occurs when the actual output is less than the potential output

inflationary gap
the output gap that occurs when the actual output is greater than the potential output

The short-run equilibrium level of real output and the price level are given by the intersection of the aggregate demand curve and the short-run aggregate supply curve. When this equilibrium occurs at the potential output level, the economy is operating at full employment on the long-run aggregate supply curve, as shown in Exhibit 1. Only a short-run equilibrium that is at potential output is also a long-run equilibrium. Short-run equilibrium can change when the aggregate demand curve or the short-run aggregate supply curve shifts rightward or leftward; the long-run equilibrium level of RGDP only changes when the *LRAS* curve shifts. Sometimes, these supply or demand changes are anticipated; at other times, however, the shifts occur unexpectedly. As we have seen, economists call these unexpected shifts *shocks*.

The economy can be either at a point where actual and potential *RGDP* are equal at $RGDP_{NR}$ or the economy can be at a point where the potential *RGDP* and actual *RGDP* are not equal. In Exhibit 2, we see that it is rare that actual and potential *RGDP* are equal. In other words, the economy can be in a boom, where actual *RGDP* is greater than potential *RGDP*, or in a recession, where actual *RGDP* is less than potential *RGDP*. However, notice that the economy does not often stray too far from potential *RGDP*—of course, the recent exception is the financial crisis of 2008.

section 14.6 exhibit 1 **Long-Run Macroeconomic Equilibrium**

Long-run macroeconomic equilibrium occurs at the level where short-run aggregate supply and aggregate demand intersect at a point on the long-run aggregate supply curve. At this level, real GDP will equal potential GDP at full employment ($RGDP_{NR}$).

Recessionary and Inflationary Gaps

As we have just seen, equilibrium will not always occur at full employment. In fact, equilibrium can occur at less than the potential output of the economy, $RGDP_{NR}$ (a **recessionary gap**), temporarily beyond $RGDP_{NR}$ (an **inflationary gap**), or at potential GDP. Exhibit 3 shows these three possibilities. In (a), we have a recessionary gap at the short-run equilibrium, E_{SR}, at $RGDP_1$. When *RGDP* is less than $RGDP_{NR}$, the result is a recessionary gap—aggregate demand is insufficient to fully employ all of society's resources, so unemployment will be above the normal rate. In (c), we have an inflationary gap at the short-run equilibrium, E_{SR}, at $RGDP_3$, where aggregate demand is so high that the economy is temporarily operating beyond full capacity ($RGDP_{NR}$); this gap will lead to inflationary pressure, and unemployment will be below the normal rate. In (b), the economy is just right where AD_2 and *SRAS* intersect at $RGDP_{NR}$—the long-run equilibrium position.

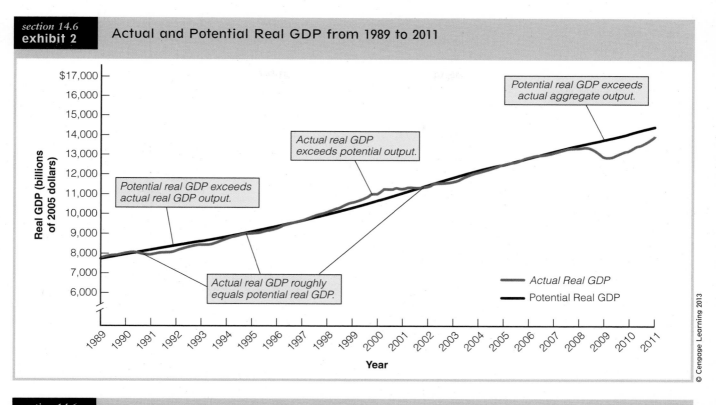

section 14.6
exhibit 2   Actual and Potential Real GDP from 1989 to 2011

section 14.6
exhibit 3   Recessionary and Inflationary Gaps

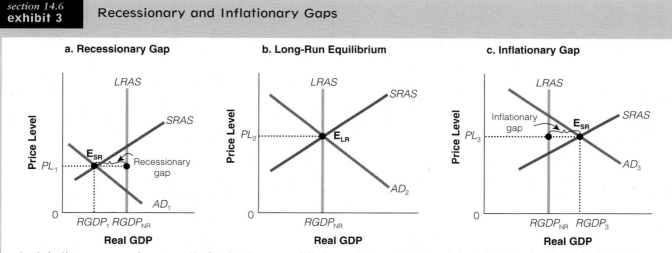

In (a), the economy is currently in short-run equilibrium at E_{SR}. At this point, $RGDP_1$ is less than $RGDP_{NR}$. That is, the economy is producing less than its potential output and is in a recessionary gap. In (c), the economy is currently in short-run equilibrium at E_{SR}. At this point, $RGDP_3$ is greater than $RGDP_{NR}$. The economy is temporarily producing more than its potential output, and we have an inflationary gap. In (b), the economy is producing its potential output at $RGDP_{NR}$. At this point, the economy is in long-run equilibrium and is not experiencing an inflationary or a recessionary gap.

Demand-Pull Inflation

What causes a recessionary gap?
What causes an inflationary gap?

demand-pull inflation
a price-level increase due to an increase in aggregate demand

Demand-pull inflation occurs when the price level rises as a result of an increase in aggregate demand. Consider the case in which an increase in consumer optimism results in a corresponding increase in aggregate demand. Exhibit 4 shows that an increase in aggregate demand causes an increase in the price level and an increase in real output. The movement

stagflation
a situation in which lower growth and higher prices occur together

cost-push inflation
a price-level increase due to a negative supply shock or increases in input prices

How can an economy operate beyond its potential output?

is along the *SRAS* curve from point E_1 to point E_2 and causes an inflationary gap. Recall that an increase in output occurs as a result of the increase in the price level in the short run, because firms have an incentive to increase real output when the prices of the goods they are selling are rising faster than the costs of the inputs they use in production.

Note that E_2 in Exhibit 4 is positioned beyond $RGDP_{NR}$—an inflationary gap. It seems strange that the economy can operate beyond its potential, but it is possible—temporarily—as firms encourage workers to work overtime, extend the hours of part-time workers, hire recently retired employees, reduce frictional unemployment through more extensive searches for employees, and so on. However, this level of output and employment *cannot* be sustained in the long run.

Cost-Push Inflation

The 1970s and early 1980s witnessed a phenomenon known as **stagflation**, where lower growth and higher prices occurred together. Some economists believe that this situation was caused by a leftward shift in the short-run aggregate supply curve, as shown in Exhibit 5. If the aggregate demand curve did not increase significantly but the price level did, then the inflation was caused by supply-side forces, which is called **cost-push inflation**.

The increase in oil prices was the primary culprit responsible for the leftward shift in the aggregate supply curve. As we discussed in the last section, an increase in input prices can cause the short-run aggregate supply curve to shift to the left, and this spelled big trouble for the U.S. economy—higher price levels, lower output, and higher rates of unemployment. The impact of cost-push inflation is illustrated in Exhibit 5.

In Exhibit 5, we see that the economy is initially at full-employment equilibrium at point E_1. A negative supply shock like a sudden increase in input prices, such as an increase in the price of oil, shifts the *SRAS* curve to the left—from $SRAS_1$ to $SRAS_2$. A negative supply shock like as a result of the shift in short-run aggregate supply, the price level rises to PL_2, and real output falls from $RGDP_{NR}$ to $RGDP_2$ (point E_2). Firms demand fewer workers as a result of higher input costs that cannot be passed on to consumers. This lower demand, in turn, leads to higher prices, lower real output, and more unemployment—and a recessionary gap. In the United States, these negative supply shocks occurred in 1974, 1979, 1990, 2005, and 2007–2008. These supply shocks can change *RGDP* significantly, but temporarily, away from

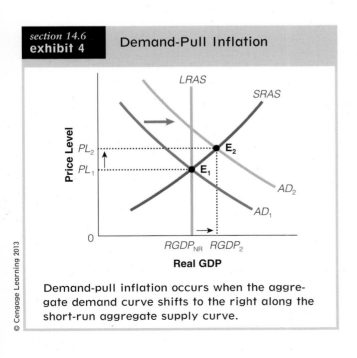

section 14.6 exhibit 4   **Demand-Pull Inflation**

Demand-pull inflation occurs when the aggregate demand curve shifts to the right along the short-run aggregate supply curve.

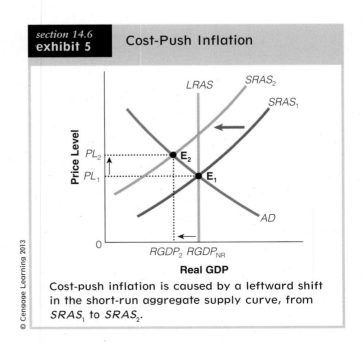

section 14.6 exhibit 5   **Cost-Push Inflation**

Cost-push inflation is caused by a leftward shift in the short-run aggregate supply curve, from $SRAS_1$ to $SRAS_2$.

potential aggregate output at $RGDP_{NR}$. In 2007, the price of many raw materials shot up globally—a global negative supply shock. Many countries around the world felt the effects of the negative supply shock.

However, recessions are not all bad—they can at least slow the rate of inflation. Two periods of serious inflation, 1974–1975 and 1979–1981, were followed by recessions and a slower rate of inflation.

What Helped the United States Recover in the 1980s?

Oil prices fell during the 1980s when OPEC lost some of its clout because of internal problems. In addition, many non-OPEC oil producers increased production. The net result in the short run was a rightward shift in the aggregate supply curve. Holding aggregate demand constant, this rightward shift in the aggregate supply curve leads to a lower price level, greater output, and lower rates of unemployment—moving the economy back toward E_1 in Exhibit 5.

A Decrease in Aggregate Demand and Recessions

What kind of shocks have caused most recessions?

Just as cost-push inflation may cause a recessionary gap, so may a decrease in aggregate demand. For example, consider the case in which consumer confidence plunges and the stock market "tanks." As a result, aggregate demand falls, shown in Exhibit 6 as the shift from AD_1 to AD_2, leaving the economy in a new short-run equilibrium at point E_2. Households, firms, and governments buy fewer goods and services at every price level. In response to this drop in demand, output falls from $RGDP_{NR}$ to $RGDP_2$, and the price level falls from PL_1 to PL_2. Therefore, in the short run, this fall in aggregate demand causes higher unemployment and a reduction in output—and it, too, can lead to a recessionary gap.

The recession of 2001 and the slow recovery that followed can be attributed to three shocks that affected aggregate demand: the end of the stock market boom, the terrorist attacks of September 11 (which had an impact on both stock market wealth and consumer confidence), and a series of corporate scandals that rocked the stock market. Corrective stabilizing measures were taken following these events to prevent even further damage. For example, the Federal Reserve continued to lower interest rates. Lower interest rates stimulate the economy by encouraging investment and consumption spending. Other stabilizing measures included a tax cut passed by Congress in 2001 and increased government spending to help rebuild New York City and provide financial assistance to the ailing airline industry. Both the 2001 tax cut and the war on terrorism led to an increase in government spending. Both of these policies shifted the aggregate demand curve to the right, reducing the magnitude of the 2001 recession. The recovery did not pick up steam until 2003.

Most of the post war recessions have been caused by negative demand shocks. Negative supply shocks have been relatively few, but quite severe, in terms of unemployment rates. The 2007–2008 recession appears to be the product of both negative demand and supply shocks.

During the financial crisis of 2008, both consumers and firms reduced their spending, and this caused the aggregate demand curve to shift to the left, in turn leading to a recessionary gap. In short, real estate and financial market wealth decreased, precautionary saving by consumers increased as confidence fell, obtaining credit became more difficult, and both households and firms adopted a wait and see attitude.

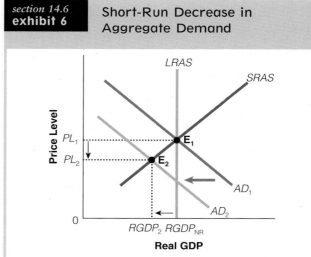

section 14.6 exhibit 6 Short-Run Decrease in Aggregate Demand

A fall in aggregate demand due to a drop in consumer confidence can cause a short-run change in the economy. The decrease in aggregate demand (shown in the movement from E_1 to E_2) causes lower output and higher unemployment in the short run.

section 14.6
exhibit 7

Adjusting to a
Recessionary Gap

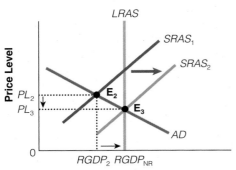

At point E_2, the economy is in a recessionary gap. However, the economy may self-correct because laborers and other input suppliers are willing to accept lower wages and prices for the use of their resources, resulting in a reduction in production costs that shifts the short-run supply curve from $SRAS_1$ to $SRAS_2$. Eventually, the economy returns to a long-run equilibrium at point E_3, the intersection of $RGDP_{NR}$ and a lower price level, PL_3. However, if wages and other input prices are sticky, the economy's adjustment mechanism might take many months to totally self-correct.

How can an economy self-correct if it is in a recessionary gap?

wage and price inflexibility
the tendency for prices and wages to only adjust slowly downward to changes in the economy

How can sticky prices (wages and other input prices) slow the economy's recovery from a recessionary gap?

The rate of inflation slowed and GDP fell over 2 percent in a year. It began with a boom-to-bust story in the housing market and then rippled into the stock market. In order to prop up aggregate demand, the Federal Reserve increased the money supply and lowered interest rates. In addition, Congress enacted a number of measures to stimulate consumption, investment, and government spending. This helped to shift the aggregate demand curve to the right and RGDP and the price level rose by the end of 2009. We will discuss this in much more detail in our chapters on monetary and fiscal policy.

Adjusting to a Recessionary Gap

Many recoveries from a recessionary gap occur because of increases in aggregate demand—perhaps consumer and business confidence picks up, or the government lowers taxes and/or lowers interest rates to stimulate the economy. That is, an eventual rightward shift in the aggregate demand curve takes the economy back to potential output—$RGDP_{NR}$.

However, it is possible for the economy to *self-correct* through declining wages and prices. In Exhibit 7, at point E_2, the intersection of PL_2 and $RGDP_2$, the economy is in a recessionary gap—that is, the economy is producing less than its potential output. At this lower level of output, firms lay off workers to avoid inventory accumulation. In addition, firms may cut prices to increase demand for their products. Unemployed workers and other input suppliers may also bid down wages and prices. That is, laborers and other input suppliers are now willing to accept lower wages and prices for the use of their resources, and the resulting reduction in production costs shifts the short-run supply curve from $SRAS_1$ to $SRAS_2$. Eventually, the economy returns to a long-run equilibrium at point E_3, the intersection of $RGDP_{NR}$ and a lower price level, PL_3.

Slow Adjustments to a Recessionary Gap

Many economists believe that wages and prices may be slow to adjust, especially downward. This downward wage and price inflexibility may prolong the duration of a recessionary gap.

For example, in Exhibit 7 we see that the economy is in a recession at E_2 and $RGDP_2$. The economy will eventually self-correct to $RGDP_{NR}$ at E_3, as workers and other input owners accept lower wages and prices for their inputs, shifting the $SRAS$ curve to the right from $SRAS_1$ to $SRAS_2$. However, if wages and other input prices are sticky, the economy's adjustment mechanism might take many months to totally self-correct.

Japan witnessed several recessionary gaps in the 1990s and even experienced deflation as the self-adjustment mechanism predicts. However, the adjustment out of the recessionary gap was slow and painful.

What Causes Wages and Prices to Be Sticky Downward?

Empirical evidence supports several explanations for the downward stickiness of wages and prices. Firms may not be able to legally cut wages because of long-term labor contracts (particularly with union workers) or a legal minimum wage. Efficiency wages may also limit a firm's ability to lower wage rates. Menu costs may cause price inflexibility as well.

Efficiency Wages

In economics, it is generally assumed that as productivity rises, wages will rise, and that workers can raise their productivity through investments in human capital such as education and on-the-job training. However, some economists believe that in some cases, *higher wages will lead to greater productivity*.

In the efficiency wage model, employers pay their employees more than the equilibrium wage as a means to increase efficiency. Proponents of this theory suggest that higher-than-equilibrium wages might attract the most productive workers, lower job turnover and training costs, and improve morale. Because the efficiency wage rate is greater than the equilibrium wage rate, the quantity of labor that would be willingly supplied is greater than the quantity of labor demanded, resulting in greater amounts of unemployment.

However, aside from creating some additional unemployment, the efficiency wage could also cause wages to be inflexible downward. For example, if aggregate demand decreases, firms that pay efficiency wages may be reluctant to cut wages, fearing that cuts could lead to lower morale, greater absenteeism, and general productivity losses. In short, if firms are paying efficiency wages, they may be reluctant to lower wages in a recession, leading to downward wage inflexibility.

How can efficiency wages slow wage adjustments due to a recessionary gap?

Menu Costs

Some costs are associated with changing prices in an inflationary environment. Thus, the higher price level in an inflationary environment is often reflected slowly, as restaurants, mail-order houses, and department stores change their prices gradually so as to incur fewer *menu costs* (the costs of changing posted prices) in printing new catalogs, new mailers, new advertisements, and so on. Because businesses are not likely to change all their prices immediately, we can say that some prices are sticky, or slow to change. For example, many outputs, such as steel, are inputs in the production of other products, such as automobiles. As a result, these prices are slow to change.

Suppose aggregate demand unexpectedly decreases. This change could lower the price level. Some firms may adjust to the change quickly. Others, however, may move more slowly because of menu costs, causing their prices to become too high (above equilibrium). Ultimately, the sales and outputs will fall, potentially causing a recession. Firms not responding quickly to changes in demand fail to do so for a reason; and to some economists, menu costs are at least part of that reason.

Adjusting to an Inflationary Gap

In Exhibit 8, the economy is in an inflationary gap at E_2, where $RGDP_2$ is greater than $RGDP_{NR}$. Because the price level, PL_2, is higher than the one workers anticipated, PL_1, workers become disgruntled with wages that have not adjusted to the new price level (if prices have risen but wages have not risen as much, real wages have fallen). Recall that along the *SRAS* curve, wages and other input prices are assumed to

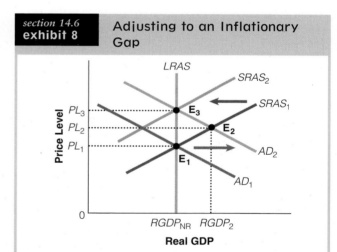

section 14.6 exhibit 8   **Adjusting to an Inflationary Gap**

The economy is in an inflationary gap at E_2, where $RGDP_2$ is greater than $RGDP_{NR}$. Because the price level is higher than workers anticipated (that is, it is PL_2 rather than PL_1), workers become disgruntled with wages that have not adjusted to the new price level. Consequently, workers and other nonlabor input suppliers demand higher prices to be willing to supply their inputs. As input prices respond to the higher level of output prices, the short-run aggregate supply curve shifts to the left, from $SRAS_1$ to $SRAS_2$. Suppliers will continually seek higher prices for their inputs until they reach long-run equilibrium, at point E_3. At that point, input suppliers' purchasing power is restored to the natural rate, $RGDP_{NR}$, at a new higher price level, PL_3.

be constant. Therefore, workers' and input suppliers' purchasing power falls as output prices rise. Real (adjusted for inflation) wages have fallen. Consequently, workers and other suppliers demand higher prices if they are to be willing to supply their inputs. As input prices respond to the higher level of output prices, the short-run aggregate supply curve shifts to the left, from $SRAS_1$ to $SRAS_2$. Suppliers will continue to seek higher prices for their inputs until they reach the long-run equilibrium, at point E_3 in Exhibit 8. At point E_3, input suppliers' purchasing power is restored at the long-run equilibrium, at $RGDP_{NR}$ and a new higher price level, PL_3.

Price Level and RGDP over Time

In Exhibit 9, we traced out the pattern of RGDP versus the price level. According to the Bureau of Economic Analysis, both the price level and RGDP have been rising over the last 38 years. So what is responsible for the changes? The answer is both aggregate demand and aggregate supply. Aggregate demand has risen because of growing population (which impacts consumption and investment spending), rising income, increases in government purchases, and increases in the money supply. Aggregate supply has been generally increasing as well, including increases in the labor force and improvements in labor productivity and technology.

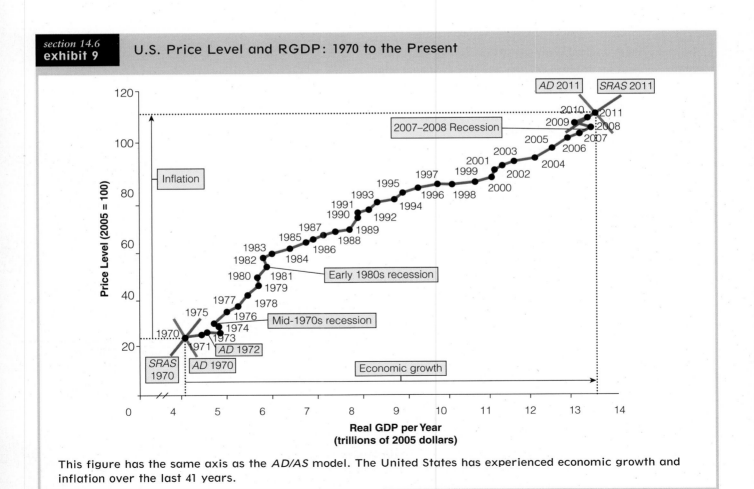

section 14.6
exhibit 9

U.S. Price Level and RGDP: 1970 to the Present

This figure has the same axis as the *AD/AS* model. The United States has experienced economic growth and inflation over the last 41 years.

SOURCE: Bureau of Economic Analysis.

in the news Recession Can Change a Way of Life

As job losses mount and bailout costs run into the trillions, the social costs of the economic downturn become clearer. The primary question, to be sure, is what can be done to shorten or alleviate these bad times. But there is also a broader set of questions about how this downturn is changing our lives, in ways beyond strict economics.

All recessions have cultural and social effects, but in major downturns the changes can be profound. The Great Depression, for example, may be regarded as a social and cultural era as well as an economic one. And the current crisis is also likely to enact changes in various areas, from our entertainment habits to our health.

First, consider entertainment. Many studies have shown that when a job is harder to find or less lucrative, people spend more time on self-improvement and relatively inexpensive amusements. During the Depression of the 1930s, that meant listening to the radio and playing parlor and board games, sometimes in lieu of a glamorous night on the town. These stay-at-home tendencies persisted through at least the 1950s.

In today's recession, we can also expect to turn to less expensive activities—and maybe to keep those habits for years. They may take the form of greater interest in free content on the Internet and the simple pleasures of a daily walk, instead of expensive vacations and N.B.A. box seats.

In any recession, the poor suffer the most pain. But in cultural influence, it may well be the rich who lose the most in the current crisis. This downturn is bringing a larger-than-usual decline in consumption by the wealthy.

The shift has been documented by Jonathan A. Parker and Annette Vissing-Jorgenson, finance professors at Northwestern University, in their recent paper, "Who Bears Aggregate Fluctuations and How? Estimates and Implications for Consumption Inequality." Of course, people who held much wealth in real estate or stocks have taken heavy losses. But most important, the paper says, the labor incomes of high earners have declined more than in past recessions, as seen in the financial sector.

Popular culture's catering to the wealthy may also decline in this downturn. We can expect a shift

away from the lionizing of fancy restaurants, for example, and toward more use of public libraries. Such changes tend to occur in downturns, but this time they may be especially pronounced.

Recessions and depressions, of course, are not good for mental health. But it is less widely known that in the United States and other affluent countries, physical health seems to improve, on average, during a downturn. Sure, it's stressful to miss a paycheck, but eliminating the stresses of a job may have some beneficial effects. Perhaps more important, people may take fewer car trips, thus lowering the risk of accidents, and spend less on alcohol and tobacco. They also have more time for exercise and sleep, and tend to choose home cooking over fast food.

In a 2003 paper, "Healthy Living in Hard Times," Christopher J. Ruhm, an economist at the University of North Carolina at Greensboro, found that the death rate falls as unemployment rises. In the United States, he found, a 1 percent increase in the unemployment rate, on average, decreases the death rate by 0.5 percent.

David Potts studied the social history of Australia in the 1930s in his 2006 book, "The Myth of the Great Depression." Australia's suicide rate spiked in 1930, but overall health improved and death rates declined; after 1930, suicide rates declined as well.

While he found in interviews that many people reminisced fondly about those depression years, we shouldn't rush to conclude that depressions are happy times.

Many of their reports are likely illusory, as documented by the Harvard psychologist Daniel Gilbert in his best-selling book "Stumbling on Happiness." According to Professor Gilbert, people often have rosy memories of very trying periods, which may include extreme poverty or fighting in a war.

In today's context, we are also suffering fear and anxiety for the rather dubious consolation of having some interesting memories for the distant future.

But this downturn will likely mean a more prudent generation to come. That is implied by the work of two professors, Ulrike Malmendier of the

(continued)

in the news Recession Can Change a Way of Life (Cont.)

University of California, Berkeley, and Stefan Nagel of the Stanford Business School, in a 2007 paper, "Depression Babies: Do acroeconomic Experiences Affect Risk-Taking?"

A generation that grows up in a period of low stock returns is likely to take an unusually cautious approach to investing, even decades later, the paper found. Similarly, a generation that grows up with high inflation will be more cautious about buying bonds decades later.

In other words, today's teenagers stand less chance of making foolish decisions in the stock market down the road. They are likely to forgo some good business opportunities, but also to make fewer mistakes.

When all is said and done, something terrible has happened in the U.S. economy, and no one should wish for such an event. But a deeper look at the downturn, and the social changes it is bringing, shows a more complex picture.

In addition to trying to get out of the recession—our first priority—many of us will be making do with less and relying more on ourselves and our families. The social changes may well be the next big story of this recession.

Tyler Cowen is a professor of economics at George Mason University.

⑦ SECTION QUIZ

1. Cost-push inflation occurs when
   a. the aggregate demand curve shifts right at a faster rate than short-run aggregate supply.
   b. the short-run aggregate supply curve shifts left, while aggregate demand is fixed.
   c. the aggregate demand curve shifts left and aggregate supply is fixed.
   d. the short-run aggregate supply curve shifts right.

2. Starting from long-run equilibrium, an increase in aggregate demand will cause
   a. an inflationary gap in the short run.
   b. a recessionary gap in the short run.
   c. an inflationary gap in the short run and long run.
   d. a recessionary gap in the short run and long run.
   e. neither an inflationary nor a recessionary gap in the short run or the long run.

3. When a recessionary gap occurs,
   a. real output exceeds the natural level of output, and unemployment exceeds its natural rate.
   b. real output exceeds the natural level of output, and unemployment is less than its natural rate.
   c. real output is less than the natural level of output, and unemployment exceeds its natural rate.
   d. real output is less than the natural level of output, and unemployment is less than its natural rate.

4. Which of the following could begin an episode of demand-pull inflation?
   a. an increase in consumer optimism
   b. a faster rate of economic growth for a major trading partner country
   c. expectations of higher rates of return in investment
   d. any of the above
   e. none of the above

(continued)

5. In the short run, demand-pull inflation
   a. increases both unemployment and the price level.
   b. increases unemployment but not the price level.
   c. increases the price level but not unemployment.
   d. decreases unemployment and increases the price level.

6. In a stagflation situation,
   a. unemployment increases and the price level increases.
   b. unemployment increases and the price level decreases.
   c. unemployment decreases and the price level increases.
   d. unemployment decreases and the price level decreases.

7. During the self-correction process after a fall in aggregate demand,
   a. the price level increases and real output increases.
   b. the price level increases and real output decreases.
   c. the price level decreases and real output increases.
   d. the price level decreases and real output decreases.

---

1. What is a recessionary gap?
2. What is an inflationary gap?
3. What is demand-pull inflation?
4. What is cost-push inflation?
5. Starting from long-run equilibrium on the long-run aggregate supply curve, what happens to the price level, real output, and unemployment as a result of cost-push inflation?
6. How would a drop in consumer confidence impact the short-run macroeconomy?
7. What would happen to the price level, real output, and unemployment in the short run if world oil prices fell sharply?
8. What are *sticky prices* and *wages?*
9. How does the economy self-correct?

Answers: 1. b 2. a 3. c 4. d 5. d 6. a 7. c

The Classical and the Keynesian Macroeconomic Model

14.7

▱ What is the classical school?

▱ What is Say's law?

▱ What was Keynes's criticism of the classical school?

▱ What is the full-employment classical school model?

▱ What is the Keynesian short-run supply curve?

▱ What is the modern Keynesian short-run supply curve?

The Classical School and Say's Law

Historically, the two primary approaches to macroeconomics have been the classical school and the Keynesian school. Let's begin with the classical school. The classical school of thought believed that wages and prices adjust quickly to changes in supply and demand.

   Writing at the beginning of the nineteenth century, the French economist Jean Baptiste Say formulated a notion since dubbed Say's law, which in its simplest form states that

What did the classical school believe about wages and prices?

What is Say's law?

"supply creates its own demand." More precisely, the production of goods and services creates income for owners of inputs (land, labor, capital, and entrepreneurship) used in production, which in turn creates a demand for goods. According to Say's law, we need not worry about output not being utilized; production creates income, which creates demand for goods, which leads to still more production. That is, Say's law establishes that full employment can be maintained because total spending will be great enough for firms to sell all the output a fully employed economy can produce. Say's ideas were incorporated into the teaching of economists of the late nineteenth century who were considered classical economists.

Before the 1930s, the problem of unemployment was considered one that could be analyzed using microeconomic analysis; indeed, macroeconomics as we know it today did not exist. The theory that evolved to analyze unemployment suggested that joblessness could be eliminated by market forces, in the same way that shortages and surpluses of goods and services are eliminated by movement in the relative prices of those goods, as we discussed in Chapter 5.

The Full-Employment Classical School Model

The macroeconomic models presented in this text draw from both the classical and Keynesian schools of thought and emphasize the commonality between the two schools. The classical school focuses on the economy at full employment, because both schools agree that in the long run both wages and prices adjust freely to changes in demand and supply and the economy moves back naturally to its potential, full-employment output level. That is, eventually (in the long run) all markets adjust to their equilibrium values. Recall that full employment does not mean zero unemployment; rather, it refers to zero cyclical unemployment. Some structural and frictional unemployment occurs naturally in a dynamic and vibrant economy.

The actual output that the economy produces need not be the same as potential output—what the economy can produce without leading to inflation. If the economy is producing at less than its potential output, unemployment is greater than the natural rate; if the economy is producing at greater than its potential output, unemployment is less than the natural rate, causing inflationary pressures. That is, it is possible on the peak of a business cycle that actual RGDP can exceed potential RGDP, but only for a short period of time. The problem is that the causal observer often confuses potential and actual output. When the economy is accelerating at a fast clip, some observers believe we are on a new growth trajectory. And when the economy slows, some observers confuse this change with doom and gloom.

Earlier in this chapter we discussed monetary and fiscal policy, using the *AS/AD* model to examine business cycles and short-run policy prescriptions that involve government intervention to help the economy get back to its long-run growth trajectory.

Changes in Aggregate Demand in the Classical Model

In Exhibit 1, we see the impact of either an increase or a decrease in aggregate demand in the classical model. According to Say's law, prolonged unemployment is impossible in the long-run classical model. Prices, wages, and interest rates all adjust quickly, which keeps workers and resources fully employed at the natural rate of real output, $RGDP_{NR}$. The classical school made very little distinction between the short run and the long run, so the only aggregate supply curve is the vertical long-run aggregate supply curve, *LRAS* in Exhibit 1. That is, there is no separate short-run aggregate supply curve in the classical model. Prices and wages adjust so quickly that the economy seldom remains far from $RGDP_{NR}$.

In Exhibit 1(a), if prices, wages, and interest rates were not completely and quickly flexible, an increase in aggregate demand from AD_1 to AD_2 might cause the economy to move toward point A beyond $RGDP_{AD}$. However, when the price level rises, input suppliers bid up input prices and the economy quickly adjusts to the new price level at PL_2, moving along the *LRAS*.

In Exhibit 1(b), there is a decrease in aggregate demand that could cause the economy to move toward point A, where resources (labor, factories, and other inputs) would be unemployed.

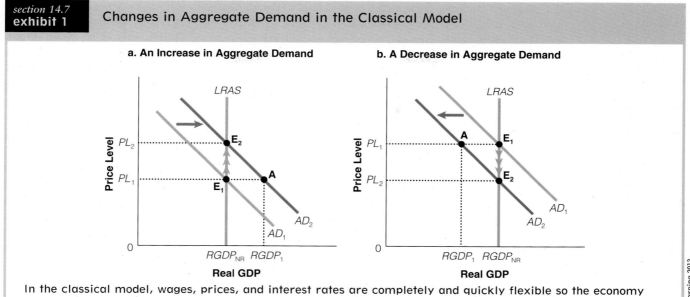

section 14.7
exhibit 1   Changes in Aggregate Demand in the Classical Model

a. An Increase in Aggregate Demand

b. A Decrease in Aggregate Demand

In the classical model, wages, prices, and interest rates are completely and quickly flexible so the economy will quickly adjust to an increase in *AD* moving from E_1 to E_2 as seen in 1(a) and quickly adjust to a decrease in *AD* moving from E_1 to E_2 as seen in 1(b). If wages and prices were not completely flexible the economy could move toward point A from E_1.

However, because input suppliers will compete against each other, it will drive input prices down. If this occurs quickly, as predicted in the classical model, the economy will not experience prolonged unemployment and will adjust to the new price level, PL_2, along the *LRAS*.

Keynes's Criticism of the Classical School

In 1936, John Maynard Keynes's book, *The General Theory of Employment, Interest and Money*, was published. Along with Adam Smith's *The Wealth of Nations* in the eighteenth century, *The General Theory of Employment, Interest and Money* was one of the most influential books in economics. In his book, Keynes attacked the classical economic theory. He pointed out the naiveté of Say's law: Not all income generated from output need be used to buy goods and services; it can also be saved, hoarded, or taxed away. Supply does not automatically create an adequate demand. Keynes's severest attacks were against classical ideas about unemployment. With unemployment rates at that time in the double digits, where did the classicists go wrong?

To begin with, when a recession begins, wages rarely fall quickly to a new equilibrium level consistent with full employment. Long-term labor contracts with unions, minimum wage laws, and other factors often prevent wages from falling as quickly as the classical model suggests. Thus, wage inflexibility prevents the market solution from working rapidly enough to avert a prolonged recession.

The Keynesian Short-Run Aggregate Supply Curve—Sticky Prices and Wages

Keynes and his followers argued that wages and price are inflexible downward. As we just discussed, wage stickiness can arise as a result of long-term labor and raw material contracts, unions, and minimum wage laws. If wages and prices are sticky and the economy has sufficient excess capacity, then the short-run aggregate supply curve is flat. That is, with so many resources idle, producers will not have to compete with each other for machinery or labor and input prices will tend to stay flat.

In Exhibit 2(a), we see what is called the Keynesian aggregate supply curve. When RGDP(Y) is below potential GDP and firms are operating with excess capacity, the short-run

What would make the short-run aggregate supply curve flat?

aggregate supply curve is horizontal over this range of output. For example, in Exhibit 2(a), we see that in the horizontal range of the *SRAS* curve an increase in *AD* from AD_1 to AD_2 has no impact on the price level but considerable impact on RGDP and employment. When AD_1 increases to AD_2, we see an increase in real gross domestic product from $RGDP_1$ to $RGDP_2$—a new equilibrium where resources are more fully utilized. Similarly, a reduction in *AD*, from AD_1 to AD_3, in this region will also leave the price level unchanged. Specifically, it means that the price level does not rise or fall in this situation, but RGDP does. This price and wage inflexibility when *AD* is falling played a significant part in the Keynesian theory. With stickiness of wages and other input costs, a reduction in aggregate demand will not lead to a lower price level if the economy has sufficient excess capacity—say at $RGDP_1$. Historically, the mid- to late 1930s seems to fit the Keynesian short-run aggregate supply curve quite well—increases in RGDP without simultaneous increases in the price level. It was a period of high unemployment of resources and double-digit unemployment—that is, sufficient level of excess capacity and little competition to bid up input prices.

However, most macroeconomists now believe that price and wages are not completely inflexible downward. Wages and prices tend to be less flexible when excess capacity is available—the slope of the *SRAS* is flatter the further it is below full employment. When the economy is temporarily operating beyond $RGDP_{NR}$, the *SRAS* is steep because higher output prices are necessary if firms are expanding output in this unsustainable region beyond full employment. That is, the firm can increase output by working labor and capital more intensively. When resources are idle, output will be more responsive to changes in *AD*, and the price level will not be as responsive—the *SRAS* is flatter—as it moves from AD_1 to AD_2 in Exhibit 2(b). And when resources are at full capacity, output is less responsive to changes in *AD* and the price level is highly responsive—the *SRAS* is steeper—as it moves from AD_5 to AD_6, as seen in Exhibit 2(b). That is, the steeper the SRAS curve, the greater the price level effect and the smaller the RGDP effect.

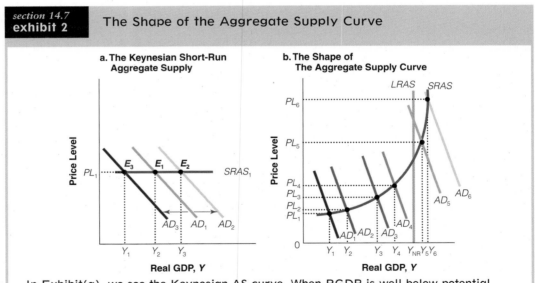

section 14.7
exhibit 2 The Shape of the Aggregate Supply Curve

a. The Keynesian Short-Run Aggregate Supply

b. The Shape of The Aggregate Supply Curve

In Exhibit(a), we see the Keynesian AS curve. When RGDP is well below potential output, an increase or decrease in aggregate demand has no impact on the price level but considerable impact on RGDP and employment. In Exhibit(b), we see the more usual case, the SRAS curve has an upward slope. Over the flatter range of the SRAS curve, a change in aggregate demand leads to a small change in the price level and a large change in RGDP(Y)—a move from AD_1 to AD_2. In the middle range of the SRAS curve, a change in aggregate demand leads to a appreciable change in both the price level and RGDP(Y)—a move from AD_3 to AD_4. In the steep portion of the SRAS curve, very little additional output can be produced as the economy is at, or temporarily beyond, capacity—a move from AD_5 to AD_6. Any change in aggregate demand in this range will lead to sharp changes in the price level and little or no change in RGDP(Y).

Economists continue to debate the actual shape of the short-run aggregate supply curve because the shape of the SRAS has important implications for changes in aggregate demand, as seen in Exhibit 2(b). Over the flatter range of the short-run aggregate supply curve, a change in aggregate demand leads to a small change in the price level and a large change in RGDP(Y)—AD_1 to AD_2. In the middle range, a change in aggregate demand leads to an appreciable change in both the price level and RGDP(Y)—AD_3 to AD_4. In the steep portion of the SRAS curve, very little additional output can be produced as the economy is at, or temporarily beyond, full capacity—AD_5 to AD_6. Any change in aggregate demand in this steep range will lead to sharp changes in the price level and little or no change in RGDP(Y).

In the chapters to come we will see that when the government uses expansionary monetary or fiscal policy to stimulate aggregate demand, it must be careful to assess where it is on the SRAS curve—if the economy is on the flat portion of the SRAS curve, stimulus works better than on the steep part.

② SECTION QUIZ

1. If the economy was operating on a completely flat segment of the short-run aggregate supply curve, an increase in aggregate demand would
   a. increase real output and increase the price level.
   b. increase real output and decrease the price level.
   c. decrease real output and increase the price level.
   d. decrease real output and decrease the price level.
   e. do none of the above.

2. "In the long run, both wages and prices adjust freely to changes in demand and supply, and the economy will be at its full-employment level of real output."
   a. Classical economists but not Keynesian economists would accept this statement.
   b. Keynesian economists but not classical economists would accept this statement.
   c. Both classical economists and Keynesian economists would accept this statement.
   d. Neither classical economists nor Keynesian economists would accept this statement.

3. Which of the following statements is true?
   a. The classical short-run aggregate supply curve gets steeper as real output increases.
   b. The Keynesian short-run aggregate supply curve gets steeper as real output increases.
   c. The classical long-run aggregate supply curve gets steeper as real output increases.
   d. The Keynesian long-run aggregate supply curve gets steeper as real output increases.

4. Which of the following is true?
   a. The extended high unemployment rate of the Great Depression was inconsistent with the conclusions of the classical economists.
   b. The extended high unemployment rate of the Great Depression was consistent with the conclusions of the Keynesian model
   c. The degree of wage and price flexibility decreases with the extent of excess capacity in the modern Keynesian model.
   d. All of the above are true.

1. What are the two primary approaches to macroeconomics?
2. Which school of thought emphasized that markets can rapidly adjust to changes?
3. Why was the double-digit unemployment of the Great Depression when Keynes wrote *The General Theory of Employment, Interest and Money* helpful in leading to its general acceptance?
4. What would keep wages from falling quickly in a recession?
5. If wages are sticky downward, why will a decrease in aggregate demand primarily reduce real output?

Answers: 1. e   2. c   3. b   4. d

Interactive Summary

Fill in the blanks:

1. Aggregate demand (*AD*) refers to the quantity of _____ at different price levels.

2. _____ is by far the largest component of *AD*.

3. Government purchases tend to be a(n) _____ volatile category of aggregate demand than investment.

4. Models that include international trade effects are called _____ models.

5. Exports minus imports equals _____.

6. The *AD* curve slopes _____, which means a(n) _____ relationship between the price level and real gross domestic product (RGDP) demanded.

7. Three complementary explanations exist for the negative slope of the aggregate demand curve: the _____ effect, the _____ effect, and the _____ effect.

8. As the price level decreases, the real value people's money_____ so that their planned purchases of goods and services _____.

9. The wealth effect can be summarized as follows: A higher price level → _____ the real value of money → _____ consumer spending → _____ RGDP demanded.

10. At higher interest rates, the opportunity cost of borrowing _____; and _____ interest-sensitive investments will be profitable, which will result in a(n) _____ quantity of RGDP demanded.

11. The interest rate effect process can be summarized as follows: A higher price level → _____ the demand for loanable funds → _____ the interest rate → _____ investments → _____ RGDP demanded.

12. If the prices of goods and services in the domestic market rise relative to those in global markets as a result of a higher domestic price level, consumers and businesses will buy _____ from foreign producers and _____ from domestic producers.

13. If the price level in the United States rises, U.S. exports will become _____ expensive, imports will become _____ expensive, and net exports will _____.

14. The real wealth effect, the interest rate effect, and the open economy effect all contribute to the _____ slope of the *AD* curve.

15. An increase in any component of GDP (*C*, *I*, *G*, or *X* − *M*) can cause the *AD* curve to shift _____.

16. If consumers sensed that the economy was headed for a recession or the government imposed a tax increase, this would result in a(n) _____ shift of the *AD* curve.

17. Because consuming less is saving more, an increase in savings, *ceteris paribus,* would shift *AD* to the _____.

18. A reduction in business taxes would shift *AD* to the _____, while an increase in real interest rates or business taxes would shift *AD* to the _____.

19. An increase in government purchases, other things being equal, shifts *AD* to the _____.

20. If major trading partners are experiencing economic slowdowns, then they will demand _____ imports from the United States, shifting *AD* to the _____.

21. The _____ curve is the relationship between the total quantity of final goods and services that suppliers are willing and able to produce and the overall price level.

22. The two aggregate supply curves are a(n) _____ aggregate supply curve and a(n) _____ aggregate supply curve.

23. The short-run relationship refers to a period when _____ can change in response to supply and demand, but _____ prices have not yet been able to adjust.

24. In the short run, the aggregate supply curve is _____ sloping.

25. In the short run, at a higher price level, producers are willing to supply _____ real output, and at lower price levels, they are willing to supply _____ real output.

26. The two explanations for why producers would be willing to supply more output when the price level increases are the _____ effect and the _____ effect.

27. When the price level rises in the short run, output prices _____ relative to input prices (costs), _____ producers' short-run profit margins.

28. If the price level falls, output prices _____, producers' profits will _____, and producers will _____ their level of output.

29. If the overall price level is rising, producers can be fooled into thinking that the _____ price of their output is rising and as a result supply _____ in the short run.

30. The long run is a period long enough for the price of _____ to fully adjust to changes in the economy.

31. Along the *LRAS* curve, two sets of prices are changing: the prices of _____ and the prices of _____.

32. The level of RGDP producers are willing to supply in the long run is _____ by changes in the price level.

33. The vertical *LRAS* curve will always be positioned at the _____ of output.

34. The long-run equilibrium level is where the economy will settle when undisturbed and all resources are _____ employed.

35. Long-run equilibrium will only occur where *AS* and *AD* intersect along the _____.

36. The underlying determinant of shifts in short-run aggregate supply is _____.

37. _____ production costs will motivate producers to produce less at any given price level, shifting the short-run aggregate supply curve _____.

38. A permanent increase in the available amount of capital, entrepreneurship, land, or labor can shift the *LRAS* curve to the _____.

39. A decrease in the stock of capital will _____ real output in the long run, *ceteris paribus*.

40. Investments in human capital would cause productivity to _____.

41. A(n) _____ in the amount of natural resources available would result in a leftward shift of the *LRAS* curve.

42. An increase in the number of workers in the labor force, ceteris paribus, tends to _____ wages and _____ short-run aggregate supply.

43. _____ output per worker causes production costs to rise and potential real output to fall, resulting in a(n) _____ shift in both *SRAS* and *LRAS*.

44. A(n) _____ in government regulations on businesses would lower the costs of production and expand potential real output, causing both *SRAS* and *LRAS* to shift to the right.

45. The most important of the factors that shift *SRAS* are changes in _____, _____, _____, and _____.

46. If the price of steel rises, it will shift *SRAS* _____.

47. A fall in input prices, which shifts *SRAS* right, shifts *LRAS* right only if _____ has risen, and this situation only occurs if the _____ of those inputs is increased.

48. _____ supply shocks, such as natural disasters, can increase the costs of production.

49. Only a short-run equilibrium that is at _____ output is also a long-run equilibrium.

50. The short-run equilibrium level of real output and the price level are determined by the intersection of the _____ curve and the _____ curve.

51. The long-run equilibrium level of RGDP changes only when the _____ curve shifts.

52. Economists call unexpected shifts in supply or demand _____.

53. When short-run equilibrium occurs at less than the potential output of the economy, it results in a(n) _____ gap.

54. _____ inflation occurs when the price level rises as a result of an increase in aggregate demand.

55. Demand-pull inflation causes a(n) _____ in the price level and a(n) _____ in real output in the short run, illustrated by a movement up along the *SRAS* curve.

56. Demand-pull inflation causes a(n) _____ gap.

57. When *AD* increases, real (adjusted for inflation) wages _____ in the short run.

58. In response to an inflationary gap in the short run, real wages and other real input prices will tend to _____, which is illustrated by a(n) _____ shift in the *SRAS* curve.

59. _____ is the situation in which lower economic growth and higher prices occur together.

60. An increase in input prices can cause the *SRAS* curve to shift to the _____, resulting in _____ price levels, _____ real output, and _____ rates of unemployment in the short run.

61. With the economy initially at full-employment equilibrium, a sudden increase in oil prices would result in _____ unemployment and in real output _____ than potential output in the short run.

62. Falling oil prices would result in a(n) _____ shift in the *SRAS* curve.

63. Holding *AD* constant, falling oil prices would lead to _____ prices, _____ output, and _____ rates of unemployment in the short run.

64. An economy can self-correct from a recessionary gap through _____ wages and prices.

65. The long-run result of a fall in aggregate demand is an equilibrium _____ potential output and a(n) _____ price level.

66. Wages and prices may be sticky downward because of _____ labor contracts, a legal _____ wage, employers paying _____ wages, and _____ costs.

67. If the economy is currently in an inflationary gap, with output greater than potential output, the price level is _____ than workers anticipated.

68. The _____ of the *AD* and *AS* curves makes the *AD/AS* analysis less than completely satisfactory.

69. Say's law could be stated as "_____ creates its own _____."

70. When real output is below potential real output, unemployment is _____ than its natural rate.

71. Unlike our modern understanding, the classical model has no separate _____ _____ curve.

72. The economy will not experience unemployment in the _____ model.

73. When resources are idle, output will be _____ responsive to changes in aggregate demand and the price level will be _____ responsive to changes in aggregate demand.

Answers: 1. real GDP demanded 2. Consumption 3. less 4. open economy 5. net exports 6. downward; inverse 7. wealth; interest rate; open economy 8. rises 9. reduced; reduced; reduced 10. rises; fewer; lower 11. increases; increases; reduces; reduces 12. more; less 13. more; less; fall 14. downward 15. rightward 16. leftward 17. left 18. right; left 19. right 20. fewer; left 21. aggregate supply 22. short-run; long-run 23. output; input 24. upward 25. more; less 26. profit; misperception 27. rise; raising 28. fall; fall 29. relative; reduce 30. all inputs 31. outputs; inputs 32. not affected 33. natural rate 34. fully 35. long-run aggregate supply curve 36. production costs 37. Higher; leftward 38. right 39. reduce; reduce 40. rise 41. decrease 42. depress; increase 43. Lower; leftward 44. reduction 45. wages; nonlabor input prices; labor productivity; supply shocks 46. left; not shift 47. potential output; supply 48. Adverse 49. potential 50. aggregate demand; short-run aggregate supply 51. *LRAS* 52. shocks 53. recessionary 54. Demand-pull 55. increase; increase 56. inflationary 57. fall 58. rise; leftward 59. Stagflation 60. left; higher; lower; higher 61. higher; less 62. rightward 63. lower; greater; lower 64. declining 65. at; lower 66. long-term; minimum; efficiency; menu 67. higher 68. interdependence 69. supply; demand 70. greater 71. short-run aggregate supply 72. classical 73. more; less

Key Terms and Concepts

Section Quiz Answers

14.1 The Determinants of Aggregate Demand

1. What are the major components of aggregate demand?

The major components of aggregate demand are consumption, planned investment, government purchases, and net exports.

2. How would an increase in personal taxes or a decrease in transfer payments affect consumption?

An increase in taxes or a decrease in transfer payments would decrease the disposable income of households, hence reducing their demand for consumption goods.

3. What would an increase in exports do to aggregate demand, other things being equal? An increase in imports? An increase in both imports and exports, where the change in exports was greater in magnitude?

An increase in exports would increase aggregate demand, other things being equal, since net exports are part of aggregate demand. An increase in imports would decrease aggregate demand, other things being equal, by reducing net exports (demand shifts from domestic producers to foreign producers). An increase in both imports and exports would increase aggregate demand if the increase in exports exceeded the increase in imports, other things being equal, because the combination would increase net exports.

14.2 The Aggregate Demand Curve

1. Why is the aggregate demand curve downward sloping?

Aggregate demand shows what happens to the total quantity of all real goods and services demanded in the economy as a whole (that is, the quantity of real GDP demanded) at different price levels. Aggregate demand is downward sloping because of the real wealth effect, the interest rate effect, and the open economy effect as the price level changes.

2. How does an increased price level reduce the quantities of investment goods and consumer durables demanded?

An increased price level increases the demand for money, which, in turn, increases interest rates. Higher interest rates increase the opportunity cost of financing both investment goods and consumer durables, reducing the quantities of investment goods and consumer durables demanded.

3. What is the wealth effect, and how does it imply a downward-sloping aggregate demand curve?

A reduced price level increases the real value of people's currency holdings; as their wealth increases, so does the quantity of real goods and services demanded, particularly consumption goods. Therefore, the aggregate demand curve, which represents the relationship between the price level and the quantity of real goods and services demanded, slopes downward as a result.

4. What is the interest rate effect, and how does it imply a downward-sloping aggregate demand curve?

A reduced price level reduces the demand for money, which lowers interest rates, thereby increasing the quantity of investment goods and consumer durable goods people are willing to purchase. Therefore, the aggregate demand curve, which represents the relationship between the price level and the quantity of real goods and services demanded, slopes downward as a result.

5. What is the open economy effect, and how does it imply a downward-sloping aggregate demand curve?

The open economy effect occurs when a higher domestic price level raises the prices of domestically produced goods relative to the prices of imported goods. This reduces the quantity of domestically produced goods demanded (by both citizens and foreigners) as relatively cheaper foreign-made goods are substituted for them. The result is a downward-sloping aggregate demand curve, as a higher price level results in a lower quantity of domestic real GDP demanded.

14.3 Shifts in the Aggregate Demand Curve

1. How is the distinction between a change in demand and a change in quantity demanded the same for aggregate demand as for the demand for a particular good?

Just as a change in the price of a particular good changes its quantity demanded but not its demand, a change in the price level changes the quantity of real GDP demanded but not aggregate demand. Just as a change in any of the demand-curve shifters (factors other than the price of the good itself) changes the demand for a particular good, a change in any of the $C + I + G + (X - M)$ components of aggregate demand not caused by a change in the price level changes aggregate demand.

2. What happens to aggregate demand if the demand for consumption goods increases, *ceteris paribus*?

Since consumption purchases are part of aggregate demand, an increase in the demand for consumption goods increases aggregate demand, *ceteris paribus*.

3. What happens to aggregate demand if the demand for investment goods falls, *ceteris paribus*?

Since planned investment purchases are part of aggregate demand, a falling demand for investment goods makes aggregate demand fall, *ceteris paribus*.

4. Why would an increase in the money supply tend to increase expenditures on consumption and investment, *ceteris paribus*?

An increase in the money supply would increase how many now relatively more plentiful dollars people would be willing to pay for goods in general. This would increase expenditures on consumption and investment, increasing aggregate demand, *ceteris paribus*.

14.4 The Aggregate Supply Curve

1. What relationship does the short-run aggregate supply curve represent?

The short-run aggregate supply curve represents the relationship between the total quantity of final goods and services that suppliers are willing and able to produce (the quantity of real GDP supplied) and the overall price level, before all input prices have had time to completely adjust to the price level.

2. What relationship does the long-run aggregate supply curve represent?

The long-run aggregate supply curve represents the relationship between the total quantity of final goods and services that suppliers are willing and able to produce (the quantity of real GDP supplied) and the overall price level, once all input prices have had time to completely adjust to the price level. (Actually, it shows there is no relationship between these two variables, once input prices have had sufficient time to completely adjust to the price level.)

3. Why is focusing on producers' profit margins helpful in understanding the logic of the short-run aggregate supply curve?

Profit incentives are the key to understanding what happens to real output as the price level changes in the short run (before input prices completely adjust to the price level). When the prices of outputs rise relative to the prices of inputs (costs), as when aggregate demand increases in the short run, profit margins increase, which increases the incentives to produce, which leads to increased real output. When the prices of outputs fall relative to the prices of inputs (costs), as when aggregate demand decreases in the short run, profit margins decrease, which decreases the incentives to produce, which leads to decreased real output.

4. Why is the short-run aggregate supply curve upward sloping, while the long-run aggregate supply curve is vertical at the natural rate of output?

The short-run aggregate supply curve is upward sloping because in the short run, before input prices have completely adjusted to the price level, an increase in the price level increases profit margins by increasing output prices relative to input prices, leading producers to increase real output. The long-run aggregate supply curve is vertical because in the long run, when input prices have completely adjusted to changes in the price level, input prices as well as output prices have adjusted to the price level; hence, profit margins in real terms do not change as the price level changes, and therefore there is no relationship between the price level and real output in the long run. The long-run aggregate supply curve is vertical at the natural rate of real output because that is the maximum output level allowed by capital, labor, and technological inputs at full employment (that is, given the determinants of the economy's production possibilities curve), which is therefore sustainable over time.

5. What would the short-run aggregate supply curve look like if input prices always changed instantaneously as soon as output prices changed? Why?

If input prices always changed instantaneously as soon as output prices changed, the short-run aggregate supply curve would look the same as the long-run aggregate supply curve—vertical at the natural rate of real output. This is because both input and output prices would then change proportionately, so that real profit margins (the incentives facing producers), and therefore real output, would not change as the price level changes.

6. If the price of cotton increased 10 percent when cotton producers thought other prices were rising 5 percent over the same period, what would happen to the quantity of RGDP supplied in the cotton industry? What if cotton producers thought other prices were rising 20 percent over the same period?

If the price of cotton increased 10 percent when cotton producers thought other prices were rising 5 percent over the same period, the quantity of RGDP supplied in the cotton industry would increase, because with other prices (including input prices) falling relative to cotton prices, the profitability of growing cotton would be rising. If the price of cotton increased 10 percent when cotton producers thought other prices were rising 20 percent over the same period, the quantity of RGDP supplied in the cotton industry would decrease, because with other prices (including input prices) rising relative to cotton prices, the profitability of growing cotton would be falling.

14.5 Shifts in the Aggregate Supply Curve

1. Which of the aggregate supply curves will shift in response to a change in the expected price level? Why?

The short-run aggregate supply curve shifts in response to a change in the expected price level by changing the expected production costs and therefore the expected profitability of producing output at any given output price level. Remember that the long-run aggregate supply curve assumes that people have had enough time to completely adjust to a changing price level, so a change in the expected price level does not change expected profit margins along the long-run aggregate supply curve.

2. Why do lower input costs increase the level of RGDP supplied at any given price level?

Lower input costs increase the level of RGDP supplied at any given (output) price level by increasing the profit margin for any given level of output prices.

3. What would discovering huge new supplies of oil and natural gas do to the short-run and long-run aggregate supply curves?

Discovering huge new supplies of oil and natural gas would increase both the short-run and long-run aggregate supply curves, because those additional resources would allow more to be produced in the short run, at any given output price level, as well as on a sustainable, long-run basis (since such a discovery would shift the economy's production possibilities curve outward).

4. What would happen to short-run and long-run aggregate supply curves if the government required every firm to file explanatory paperwork each time a decision was made?

This would shift both the short-run and long-run aggregate supply curves to the left. It would permanently raise producers' costs of producing any level of output, which would reduce how much producers would produce in the short run at any given price level, as well as on a sustainable, long-run basis (since such a requirement would shift the economy's production possibilities curve inward).

5. What would happen to the short-run and long-run aggregate supply curves if the capital stock grew and available supplies of natural resources expanded over the same period of time?

An increase in the capital stock together with increased available supplies of natural resources would shift both the short-run and long-run aggregate supply curves to the right (shifting the economy's production possibilities curve outward), increasing the short-run and sustainable levels of real output.

6. How can a change in input prices change the short-run aggregate supply curve but not the long-run aggregate supply curve? How could it change both long-run and short-run aggregate supply?

A temporary change in input prices can change the short-run aggregate supply curve by changing profit margins in the short run. However, when input prices return to their previous levels (reflecting a return to their previous relative scarcity) in the long run, the sustainable level of real output will be no different from before. If, on the other hand, input price changes reflect a permanently changed supply of inputs (lower input prices reflecting an increased supply), a change in input prices would increase both the long-run and short-run aggregate supply curves by increasing the real output producible both currently and on an ongoing basis (permanently shifting the economy's production possibilities curve outward).

7. What would happen to short- and long-run aggregate supply if unusually good weather led to bumper crops of most agricultural produce?

Since this would mean only a temporary change in output, it would increase the short-run aggregate supply curve but not the long-run aggregate supply curve.

8. If OPEC temporarily restricted the world output of oil, what would happen to short- and long-run aggregate supply? What would happen if the output restriction was permanent?

A temporary oil output restriction would temporarily increase oil (energy input) prices, reducing the short-run aggregate supply curve (shifting it left) but not the long-run aggregate supply curve. If the oil output restriction was permanent, the oil price increase would also reduce the level of real output producible on a sustainable basis, and so would shift both short-run aggregate supply and long-run aggregate supply to the left.

14.6 Macroeconomic Equilibrium: The Short Run and the Long Run

1. What is a recessionary gap?

A recessionary gap exists when the macroeconomy is in equilibrium at less than the potential output of the economy because aggregate demand is insufficient to fully employ all of society's resources.

2. What is an inflationary gap?

An inflationary gap exists when the macroeconomy is in equilibrium at more than the potential output of the economy because aggregate demand is so high that the economy is operating temporarily beyond its long-run capacity.

3. What is demand-pull inflation?

Demand-pull inflation reflects an increased price level caused by an increase in aggregate demand.

4. What is cost-push inflation?

Cost-push inflation is output price inflation caused by an increase in input prices (that is, by supply-side forces rather than demand-side forces). It is illustrated by a leftward or upward shift of the short-run aggregate supply curve for given long-run aggregate supply and demand curves.

5. Starting from long-run equilibrium on the long-run aggregate supply curve, what happens to the price level, real output, and unemployment as a result of cost-push inflation?

Starting from long-run equilibrium on the long-run aggregate supply curve, cost-push inflation causes the price level to rise, real output to fall, and unemployment to rise in the short run.

6. How would a drop in consumer confidence impact the short-run macroeconomy?

A drop in consumer confidence would decrease the demand for consumer goods, other things being equal, which would reduce (shift left) the aggregate demand curve, resulting in a lower price level, lower real output, and increased unemployment in the short run for a given short-run aggregate supply curve.

7. What would happen to the price level, real output, and unemployment in the short run if world oil prices fell sharply?

If world oil prices fell sharply, it would increase (shift right) the short-run aggregate supply curve, resulting in a lower price level, greater real output, and reduced unemployment in the short run for a given aggregate demand curve.

8. What are *sticky prices* and *wages*?

Sticky prices and *wages* are terms for input prices and wages that may be very slow to adjust in the downward direction, causing the economy's adjustment mechanism to take a substantial amount of time to self-correct from a recession.

9. How does the economy self-correct?

The economy self-corrects for a short-run recession through declining wages and prices, brought

on by reduced demand for labor and other inputs; the economy self-corrects for a short-run boom through increasing wages and prices, brought on by increased demand for labor and other inputs.

14.7 The Classical and the Keynesian Macroeconomic Model

1. What are the two primary approaches to macroeconomics?

The classical school and the Keynesian school are the two primary approaches to macroeconomics.

2. Which school of thought emphasized that markets can rapidly adjust to changes?

The classical school emphasized that markets can rapidly adjust to change.

3. Why was the double-digit unemployment of the Great Depression when Keynes wrote *The General Theory of Employment, Interest and Money* helpful in leading to its general acceptance?

The classical school held that persistent high unemployment would not occur in a market economy, so the high unemployment in the Great Depression—a central aspect of it—appeared to be something the classical approach could not explain.

4. What would keep wages from falling quickly in a recession?

The two reasons cited most often that prevent wages from falling quickly in a recession are long-term union contracts and minimum-wage laws.

5. If wages are sticky downward, why will a decrease in aggregate demand primarily reduce real output?

For a decrease in AD, if wages are sticky downward, the short-run aggregate supply curve will be nearly horizontal over the relevant range, and the fall in real output would be nearly as great as the fall in AD.

Problems

1. Describe what the effect on aggregate demand would be, other things being equal, if
   a. exports increase.
   b. both imports and exports decrease.
   c. consumption decreases.
   d. investment increases.
   e. investment decreases and government purchases increase.
   f. the price level increases.
   g. the price level decreases.

2. Fill in the blanks in the following explanations:
   a. The wealth effect is described by the following: An increase in the price level leads to a(n) _____ in real value of money, which leads to a(n) _____ in consumer spending, which leads to a(n) _____ in RGDP demanded.
   b. The interest rate effect is described by the following: A decrease in the price level leads to a(n) _____ in the interest rate, which leads to a(n) _____ in investments, which leads to a(n) _____ in RGDP demanded.
   c. The open economy effect is described by the following: An increase in the price level leads to a(n) _____ in the demand for domestic goods, which leads to a(n) _____ in RGDP demanded.

3. How will each of the following changes alter aggregate supply?

Change	Short-Run Aggregate Supply	Long-Run Aggregate Supply
An increase in aggregate demand	_____	_____
A decrease in aggregate demand	_____	_____
An increase in the stock of capital	_____	_____
A reduction in the size of the labor force	_____	_____
An increase in input prices (that does not reflect permanent changes in their supplies)	_____	_____
A decrease in input prices (that does reflect permanent changes in their supplies)	_____	_____
An increase in usable natural resources	_____	_____
A temporary adverse supply shock	_____	_____
Increases in the cost of government regulations	_____	_____

4. Use the accompanying diagram to answer questions a and b.

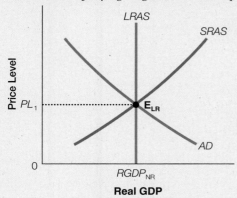

   a. On the exhibit provided, illustrate the short-run effects of an increase in aggregate demand. What happens to the price level, real output, employment, and unemployment?
   b. On the exhibit provided, illustrate the long-run effects of an increase in aggregate demand. What happens to the price level, real output, employment, and unemployment?

5. Use the accompanying diagram to answer questions a and b.

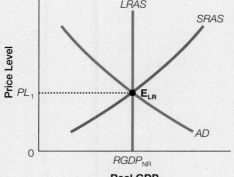

   a. On the exhibit provided, illustrate the short-run effects of a decrease in aggregate demand. What happens to the price level, real output, employment, and unemployment?
   b. On the exhibit provided, illustrate the long-run effects of a decrease in aggregate demand. What happens to the price level, real output, employment, and unemployment?

6. Use the accompanying diagram to answer questions a and b.

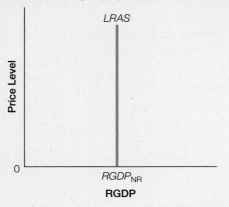

   a. Illustrate a recessionary gap on the diagram provided.
   b. Using the results in a, illustrate and explain the eventual long-run equilibrium in this case.

7. Use the accompanying diagram to answer questions a and b.

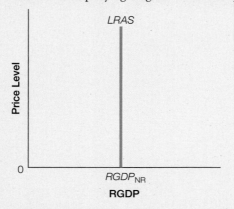

   a. Illustrate an inflationary gap on the diagram provided.
   b. Using the results in a, illustrate and explain the eventual long-run equilibrium in this case.

8. If retailers such as Walmart and Target find that inventories are rapidly being depleted, would it have been caused by a rightward or leftward change in the aggregate demand curve? What are the likely consequences for output and investment?

9. Evaluate the following statement: "A higher price level decreases the purchasing power of the dollar and reduces RGDP."

10. How does a higher price level in the U.S. economy affect purchases of imported goods? Explain.

11. Explain how a recession in Latin America might affect aggregate demand in the U.S. economy.

12. You operate a business in which you manufacture furniture. You are able to increase your furniture prices by 5 percent this quarter. You assume that the demand for your furniture has increased and begin increasing furniture production. Only later do you realize that prices in the macroeconomy are rising generally at a rate of 5 percent per quarter. This is an example of what effect? What does it imply about the slope of the short-run aggregate supply curve?

13. Distinguish cost-push from demand-pull inflation. Provide an example of an event or shock to the economy that would cause each.

14. Is it ever possible for an economy to operate above the full-employment level in the short term? Explain.

15. Evaluate the following statement: The Keynesian assumption of wage and price rigidity best corresponds to the steepest portion of the aggregate supply curve where factories are operating well below capacity.

16. Why do classical economists and Keynesian economists agree on the long-run effects of a fall in aggregate demand, but not agree on the short-run effects?

17. How does the slope of the Keynesian short-run aggregate supply curve depend on the degree of excess capacity in the economy?

18. Why does the effect of a given increase in aggregate demand have a larger effect on real output in the short run, the more excess capacity exists in the economy?

The Aggregate Expenditure Model

Keynes studied how unanticipated changes in investment spending affect aggregate spending and real GDP. The Keynesian expenditure model is based on the condition that the components of aggregate demand (consumption, investment, government purchases, and net exports) must equal total output. Keynes believed that total spending was the critical determinant of the overall level of economic activity. When total spending increases, firms increase their output and hire more workers. Even though Keynes ignored an important component—aggregate supply—his model still provides a great deal of information about aggregate demand.

The Simple Aggregate Expenditure Model

📖 Why do we assume a fixed price level?

📖 What economic variables influence aggregate demand?

📖 What are the autonomous factors that influence consumption spending?

In this chapter, we go into a more detailed description of the causes of short-run business cycles. We assume that we are in the Keynesian region of the aggregate supply curve, where the aggregate supply curve is horizontal and RGDP is completely determined by aggregate demand. Recall that Keynes believed that, in the short run, wages and prices were inflexible, so inflation is not a concern; real values and nominal values are equal in the aggregate expenditure model. Keynes focused on how unanticipated changes in expenditure, particularly investment expenditures, had an impact on real GDP. Keynes's model enlightens our understanding of the short-run business cycle. The model is called the aggregate expenditure model (sometimes the Keynesian cross model), because its focus is aggregate expenditures (aggregate demand), which has historically been especially important to the economy in the short run.

The key to the aggregate expenditure model is that the amount of goods and services (real GDP) depends on aggregate expenditures (total spending). When aggregate expenditures fall, it causes a decrease in output and employment. When aggregate expenditures rise, it causes an increase in output and employment. Thus, in the short run, the level of RGDP is determined by the level of aggregate expenditure.

Keynes pointed out the naiveté of Say's law. Not all income generated from output is used to buy goods and services; some is saved, hoarded, or taxed away. Supply does not automatically create an adequate demand. In other words, income is not always spent in the period that it is produced. Keynes recognized the volatility of investment spending. A decline in investment would lead to insufficient total spending—inventories would accumulate, and firms will cut production and lay off workers. To fully understand investment fluctuations, Keynes believed you had to study people's income and consumption spending patterns.

What do we assume in the the Keynesian region of the aggregate supply curve?

Why Do We Assume the Price Level Is Fixed?

Because Keynes believed wages and prices were inflexible in the short run, in this chapter we will assume that the price level is fixed or constant. If the price level is fixed, then changes in nominal income will be equivalent to changes in real income. That is, when we assume the price level is fixed, we do not have to distinguish real variable changes from nominal variable changes. Keynes believed that prices and wages were rigid or fixed until we reached full employment. But let us begin by looking at the most important aggregate demand determinant—consumption.

If the price level is fixed, what is the relationship between changes in nominal income and changes in real income?

The Simplest Aggregate Expenditure Model: Autonomous Consumption Only

It is useful to begin by considering consumption spending by households. Household spending on goods and services is the largest single component of the demand for final goods, accounting for more than 70 percent of GDP.

section 15.1 exhibit 1   Autonomous Changes in Consumption Spending

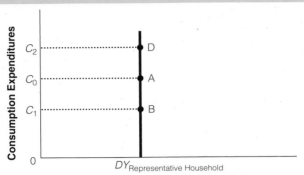

An increase in real wealth would raise consumption spending to C_2, at point D. A decrease in real wealth would tend to lower the level of consumption spending to C_1, at point B. A higher interest rate tends to cause a decrease in consumption spending from point A to point B. As household debt increases, other things equal, consumption spending would fall from point A to point B. In general, an increase in consumer confidence would act to increase household spending (a movement from point A to point D) and a decrease in consumer confidence would act to decrease household spending (a movement from point A to point B).

Why are some determinants of consumption called autonomous?

How do changes in interest rates affect consumption?

Numerous economic variables influence aggregate demand for consumer goods and services, and thus, aggregate consumption expenditures. Using you or your family as an example, you know that such things as family disposable income (after-tax income), credit conditions, the level of debt outstanding, the amount of financial assets, and expectations are important determinants of consumption purchases. Most economists believe that disposable income is one of the dominant factors.

Let's begin by simplifying things quite a bit. Imagine an economy in which only consumption spending exists (no investment, government purchases, or net exports; later, we'll add in these other sectors). To begin with the simplest situation possible, let's suppose that each household has the same level of disposable income. This kind of analysis that relies on averages is called a representative household analysis. On a graph of consumption spending (vertical axis) for our representative household and the household's representative disposable income (horizontal axis), we could represent average consumption of disposable income at point A in Exhibit 1. From point A, a horizontal dotted line to the vertical axis permits us to read the value of average consumption spending, C_0.

What Are the Autonomous Factors That Influence Spending?

Even though income is given for the representative household, other economic factors that influence consumption spending are not. When consumption (or any of the other components of spending, such as investment) does not depend on income, we call it *autonomous* (or independent). Let's look at some of these other autonomous factors and see how they would change consumption spending.

Real Wealth

The larger the value of a household's real wealth (the money value of wealth divided by the price level, which indicates the amount of consumption goods that the wealth could buy), the larger the amount of consumption spending, other things equal. Thus, in Exhibit 1, an increase in real wealth would raise consumption to C_2, at point D, for a given level of current income. Similarly, something that would lower the value of real wealth, such as a decline in property values or a stock market decline, would tend to lower the level of consumption to C_1, at point B in Exhibit 1.

The Interest Rate

A higher interest rate tends to make the consumption items that we buy on credit more expensive, which reduces expenditures on those items. An increase in the interest rate increases the monthly payments made to buy such things as automobiles, furniture, and major appliances and reduces our ability to spend out of a given income. This shift is shown as a decrease in consumption from point A to point B in Exhibit 1. Moreover, an increase in the interest rate provides a higher future return from reducing current spending, which motivates increasing savings. Thus, a higher interest rate in the current period would likely motivate an increase in savings today, which would permit households to consume more goods and services at some future date.

Household Debt

Remember when that friend of yours ran up his credit card obligations so high that he stopped buying goods except the basic necessities? Well, our average household might find itself in the same situation if its outstanding debt exceeds some reasonable level relative to its income. So, as debt increases, other things equal, consumption expenditure would fall from point A to point B in Exhibit 1.

Expectations

Just as in microeconomics, decisions to spend may be influenced by a person's expectations of future disposable income, employment, or certain world events. Based on monthly surveys conducted that attempt to measure consumer confidence, an increase in consumer confidence generally acts to increase household spending (a movement from point A to point D in Exhibit 1) and a decrease in consumer confidence would act to decrease spending (a movement from A to B in Exhibit 1). For example, a decline in the consumer confidence index after the financial crisis that begun in December of 2007 and a subsequent fall in household spending are considered factors in the recession in the United States.

Tastes and Preferences

Of course, each household is different. Some are young and beginning a working career; some are without children; others have families; still others are older and perhaps retired from the workforce. Some households like to save, putting dollars away for later spending, while others spend all their income, or even borrow to spend more than their current disposable income. These saving and spending decisions often vary over a household's life cycle.

As you can see, many economic factors affect consumption expenditures. The **factors** already listed represent some of the most important. All of these factors are considered **autonomous determinants of consumption expenditures**; that is, those expenditures that are not dependent on the level of current disposable income. Now let's make our model more complete and evaluate how changes in disposable income affect household consumption expenditures.

autonomous determinants of consumption expenditures
expenditures not dependent on the level of current disposable income that can result from factors such as real wealth, the interest rate, household debt, expectations, and tastes and preferences

---

⑦ SECTION QUIZ

1. Demand for consumer goods will be affected by which of the following?

   a. disposable income

   b. credit conditions

   c. the level of debt outstanding

   d. expectations about the future

   e. all of the above

2. Autonomous consumption will increase when

   a. real wealth increases.

   b. the interest rate increases.

   c. household debt increases.

   d. any of the above occur.

(*continued*)

3. If autonomous consumption fell, it could have been caused by

   a. falling interest rates.

   b. falling household debt.

   c. more optimistic expectations about future disposable income.

   d. increasing real wealth.

   e. none of the above.

1. How does the assumption of a fixed price level in the Keynesian expenditure model solve the problem of distinguishing between changes in the real value of a variable (such as GDP) and changes in its nominal value?

2. Would it be possible for some consumption expenditures to be autonomous and other parts of consumption expenditures not to be autonomous?

3. In what two ways does a higher interest rate tend to reduce current consumption?

4. What would happen to autonomous consumption expenditures if the value of a consumer's stock market investments rose and his household debt rose at the same time?

5. What would happen to your autonomous consumption if you expected to get a job next week paying 10 times your current salary?

6. Why do households headed by a 50-year-old tend to save a larger fraction of their incomes than those headed by either a 30-year-old or a 70-year-old?

Answers: 1. e 2. a 3. e

15.2 Finding Equilibrium in the Aggregate Expenditure Model

📂 What factors determine consumer spending?

📂 How do we find equilibrium in the aggregate expenditure model?

📂 Why does income equal output?

📂 Why does expenditure equal output?

In our first model, we looked at the economic variables that affected consumption expenditures when disposable income was fixed. This assumption is clearly unrealistic, but it allows us to develop some of the basic building blocks of the aggregate expenditure model. Now we'll look at a slightly more complicated model in which consumption also depends on disposable income.

If you think about what determines your own current consumption spending, you know that it depends on many factors previously discussed, such as your age, family size, interest rates, expected future disposable income, wealth, and, most importantly, your current disposable income. Recall from earlier chapters, disposable income is your after-tax income. Your personal consumption spending depends primarily on your current disposable income. In fact, empirical studies confirm that most people's consumption spending is closely tied to their disposable income.

Revisiting Marginal Propensity to Consume and Save

What happens to current consumption spending when a person earns some additional disposable income? Most people will spend some of their extra income and save some of it. The percentage of your extra disposable income that you decide to spend on consumption is what economists call your **marginal propensity to consume (MPC)**. That is, MPC is equal to the *change* in consumption spending (ΔC) divided by the *change* in disposable income (ΔDY).

$$MPC = \Delta C / \Delta DY$$

For example, suppose you won a lottery prize of $1,000. You might decide to spend $750 of your winnings today and save $250. In this example, your marginal propensity to consume is 0.75 (or 75 percent) because out of the extra $1,000, you decided to spend 75 percent of it ($0.75 \times \$1,000 = \$750$).

The term *marginal propensity to consume* has two parts: (1) *marginal* refers to the fact that you received an extra amount of disposable income—in addition to your income, not your total income; and (2) *propensity to consume* refers to how much you tend to spend on consumer goods and services out of your additional income.

What do economists mean by the term "marginal propensity to consume"?

marginal propensity to consume (MPC) the additional consumption that results from an additional dollar of income

Marginal Propensity to Save

The flip side of the marginal propensity to consume is the **marginal propensity to save (MPS)**, which is the proportion of an addition to your income that you would save or not spend on goods and services today. That is, MPS is equal to the *change* in savings (ΔS) divided by the change in disposable income (ΔDY).

$$MPS = \Delta S / \Delta DY$$

In the earlier lottery example, your marginal propensity to save is 0.25, or 25 percent, because you decided to save 25 percent of your additional disposable income ($0.25 \times \$1,000 = \$250$). Because your additional disposable income must be either consumed or saved, the marginal propensity to consume plus the marginal propensity to save must add up to 1, or 100 percent.

Let's illustrate the marginal propensity to consume in Exhibit 1. Suppose you estimated that you had to spend $16,000 a year, even if you earned no income for the year, for "necessities" such as food, clothing, and shelter. And suppose for every $1,000 of added disposable income you earn, you spend 75 percent of it and save 25 percent of it. So if your disposable income is $0, you spend $16,000 (that means you have to borrow or reduce your existing savings just to survive). If your disposable income is $40,000, you'll spend $16,000 plus 75 percent of $40,000 (which equals $30,000), for total spending of $46,000. If your disposable income is $80,000, you'll spend $16,000 plus 75 percent of $80,000 (which equals $60,000), for total spending of $76,000.

What's your marginal propensity to consume? In this case, if you spend 75 percent of every additional $1,000 you earn, your marginal propensity to consume is 0.75, or 75 percent. And if you save 25 percent of every additional $1,000 you earn, your marginal propensity to save is 0.25.

In Exhibit 1, the slope of the line represents the marginal propensity to consume. To better understand this concept, look at what happens when your disposable income rises from $36,000 to $40,000. At a disposable income of $36,000, you spend $16,000 plus 75 percent of $36,000 (which is $27,000), for total spending of $43,000. If your disposable income rises to $40,000, you spend $16,000 plus 75 percent of $40,000 (which is $30,000), for total spending of $46,000. So when your disposable income rises by $4,000 (from $36,000 to

marginal propensity to save (MPS) the additional saving that results from an additional dollar of income

What is the relationship between MPC and MPS?

Why is MPC the slope of the consumption function?

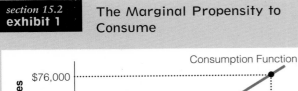

section 15.2 exhibit 1 The Marginal Propensity to Consume

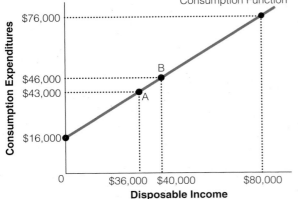

The slope of the line represents the marginal propensity to consume. At a disposable income of $36,000, you spend $16,000 plus 75 percent of $36,000 (which is $27,000), for total spending of $43,000. If your disposable income rises to $40,000, you spend $16,000 plus 75 percent of $40,000 (which is $30,000), for total spending of $46,000. So when your disposable income rises by $4,000 (from $36,000 to $40,000), your spending goes up by $3,000 (from $43,000 to $46,000). Your marginal propensity to consume is $3,000 (the increase in spending) divided by $4,000 (the increase in disposable income), which equals 0.75, or 75 percent. But notice that this MPC calculation is also the calculation of the slope of the line from point A to point B.

$40,000), your spending goes up by $3,000 (from $43,000 to $46,000). Your marginal propensity to consume is $3,000 (the increase in spending) divided by $4,000 (the increase in disposable income), which equals 0.75, or 75 percent. But notice that this calculation is also the calculation of the slope of the line from point A to point B in the exhibit. Recall that the slope of the line is the rise (the change on the vertical axis) over the run (the change on the horizontal axis). In this case, that's $3,000 divided by $4,000, which makes 0.75 the marginal propensity to consume. So the marginal propensity to consume is the same as the slope of the line in our graph of consumption and disposable income.

Now, let's take this same logic and apply it to the economy as a whole. If we add up, or aggregate, everyone's consumption and everyone's income, we'll get a line that looks like the one in Exhibit 1, but that applies to the entire economy. This line or functional relationship is called a *consumption function*. Let's suppose consumption spending in the economy is $1 trillion plus 75 percent of income.

Now, with consumption equal to $1 trillion plus 75 percent of income, consumption is partly autonomous (the $1 trillion part, which people would spend no matter what their income, which depends on the current interest rate, real wealth, debt, and expectations), and partly *induced*, which means it depends on income. The induced consumption is the portion that's equal to 75 percent of income.

What is the total amount of expenditure in this economy? Because we've assumed that investment, government purchases, and net exports are zero, aggregate expenditure is just equal to the amount of consumption spending represented by our consumption function.

Equilibrium in the Aggregate Expenditure Model

The next part of the aggregate expenditure model is to examine what conditions are needed for the economy to be in equilibrium. In order to determine equilibrium, we need to show (1) that income equals output in the economy, and (2) that in equilibrium, aggregate expenditure (or consumption in this example) equals output. First, income equals output because people earn income by producing goods and services. For example, workers earn wages because they produce some product that is then sold on the market, and owners of firms earn profits because the products they sell provide more income than the cost of producing them. So any income that is earned by anyone in the economy arises from the production of output in the economy. From now on, we'll use this idea and say that income equals output; we'll use the terms *income* and *output* interchangeably. Another way to remember this concept is to recall the circular flow diagram; the top half (output) is always equal to the bottom half (income—the sum of wages, rents, interest payments, and profits).

The second condition needed for equilibrium (aggregate expenditure in the economy equals output) is the distinctive feature of the aggregate expenditure model. Just as income must equal output (because income comes from selling goods and services), aggregate expenditure equals output because people can't earn income until the products they produce are sold to someone. Every good or service that is produced in the economy must be purchased by someone or added to inventories. Exhibit 2 plots aggregate expenditure against output. As you can see, it's a 45-degree line (slope = 1). The 45-degree line shows that the number

In the expenditure model, why must aggregate expenditure equal output in equilibrium?

on the horizontal axis, representing the amount of output in the economy, real GDP (Y), is equal to the number on the vertical axis, representing the amount of real aggregate expenditure (AE) in the economy. If output is $14 trillion, then in equilibrium, aggregate expenditure must equal $14 trillion. All points of macroeconomic equilibrium lie on the 45-degree line.

Disequilibrium in the Aggregate Expenditure Model

What would happen if, for some reason, output were lower than its equilibrium level, as would be the case if output were Y_1 in Exhibit 3?

Looking at the vertical dotted line, we see that when output is Y_1, aggregate expenditure (shown by the consumption function) is greater than output (shown by the 45-degree line). This amount is labeled the distance AB on the graph. So people would be trying to buy more goods and services (A) than were being produced (B), which would cause producers to increase the amount of production, which would increase output in the economy. This process would continue until output reached its equilibrium level, where the two lines intersect. Another way to think about this disequilibrium is that consumers would be buying more than is currently produced, causing a decrease in inventories on shelves and in warehouses from their desired levels. Clearly, profit-seeking businesspeople would increase production to bring their inventory stocks back up to the desired levels. In doing so, they would move production to the equilibrium level.

Similarly, if output were above its equilibrium level, as would occur if output were Y_2 in Exhibit 3, economic forces would act to reduce output. At this point, as you can see by looking at the graph, at point Y_2 on the horizontal axis aggregate expenditure (D) is less than output (C). People wouldn't want to buy all the output that is being produced, so producers would want to reduce their production. They would keep reducing their output until reaching the equilibrium level. Using the inventory adjustment process, inventories would be bulging from shelves and warehouses, and firms would reduce output and production until inventory stocks returned to the desired level. For example, automobile companies might close plants to reduce inventories.

This basic model—in which we've assumed that consumption spending is the only component of aggregate expenditure (that is, we've ignored investment, government spending, and net exports) and that some consumption spending is autonomous—is quite simple, yet it is the essence of the aggregate expenditure model. Equilibrium in this model, and in more complicated versions of the model, always occurs where one line representing aggregate expenditure crosses another line that represents the equilibrium condition where aggregate expenditure equals output (the 45-degree line).

Now let's put Exhibits 1 and 2 together to find the equilibrium in the economy, shown in Exhibit 3. As you might guess, the point where the two lines cross is the equilibrium point. Why? Because it is only at this point that aggregate expenditure is equal to output. Aggregate expenditure is shown by the flatter line (Aggregate Expenditure = Consumption). The equilibrium condition is shown by the 45-degree line ($Y = AE$). The only point for which consumption spending equals aggregate expenditure equals output is the point where those two lines intersect, labeled "Equilibrium." Because these points are on the 45-degree line, equilibrium output Y^*, equals equilibrium aggregate expenditure AE^*.

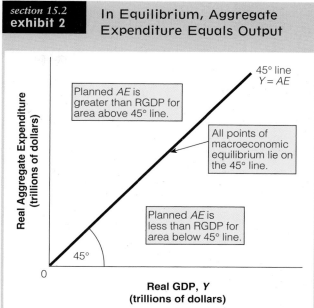

section 15.2 exhibit 2 — In Equilibrium, Aggregate Expenditure Equals Output

The 45-degree line shows that the number on the horizontal axis, representing the amount of output in the economy, is equal to the number on the vertical axis, representing the amount of aggregate expenditure in the economy. If output is $14 trillion, then in equilibrium, aggregate expenditure must equal $14 trillion.

© Cengage Learning 2013

In the aggregate expenditure model, why does output increase when expenditures exceed output?

section 15.2
exhibit 3   Disequilibrium and Equilibrium in the Aggregate Expenditure Model

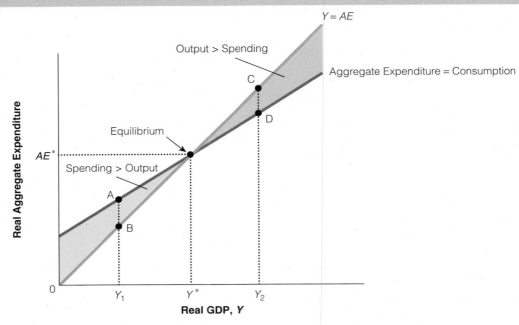

When RGDP is Y_1, aggregate expenditure is greater than output—distance AB on the graph. Consumers are trying to buy more goods and services (A) than are being produced (B), which causes producers to increase the amount of production, increasing output in the economy. This process continues until output reaches its equilibrium level, Y^*, where the two lines intersect. If RGDP is at Y_2, aggregate expenditure (D) is less than output (C). Consumers wouldn't want to buy all the output that is being produced, so producers would want to reduce their production. They would keep reducing their output until the equilibrium level of output was reached. The only point for which consumption spending equals real aggregate planned expenditure equals output is the point where those two lines intersect. Because these points are on the 45-degree line, equilibrium output, Y^* equals equilibrium aggregate expenditure AE^*.

⑦ SECTION QUIZ

1. If an economy's marginal propensity to consume was 0.75, which of the following is not true?

   a. The consumption function would have a slope of 0.75.

   b. The marginal propensity to save would be 0.25.

   c. Increases in disposable income would increase consumption spending by three times as much as it would increase saving.

   d. Consumption will always equal 75 percent of disposable income.

   e. All of the above would be true.

2. If the MPS is 0.25, which of the following is true?

   a. The slope of the consumption function would be 0.75.

   b. The MPC is 0.75.

   c. Consumption would not always be 75 percent of income.

   d. All of the above are true.

(*continued*)

SECTION QUIZ (Cont.)

3. Which of the following need not be equal at equilibrium in the aggregate expenditure model?
   a. income and output
   b. aggregate expenditures and output
   c. consumption and income
   d. All of the above must be equal at equilibrium in the aggregate expenditure model.
4. If output was less than the equilibrium level in the aggregate expenditure model, people would be trying to buy ______ goods and services than are being produced, so producers would _____ the amount of production.
   a. more; increase
   b. more; decrease
   c. less; increase
   d. less; decrease
5. If output was greater than the equilibrium level in the aggregate expenditure model, unplanned inventory investment would be _____, leading real output to ______.
   a. positive; increase
   b. positive; decrease
   c. negative; increase
   d. negative; decrease
6. Output equals income
   a. always.
   b. only in equilibrium.
   c. only when MPC equals MPS.
   d. unless inventories are changing.

---

1. If consumption purchases rise with disposable income, how would an increase in taxes affect consumption purchases?
2. If your marginal propensity to consume was 0.75, what would be your marginal propensity to save? If your marginal propensity to consume rose to 0.80, what would happen to your marginal propensity to save?
3. Could a student have a positive marginal propensity to save, and yet have negative savings (increased borrowing) at the same time?
4. What would happen to the slope of the consumption function if the marginal propensity to save fell?
5. Why would an increase in disposable income increase induced consumption but not autonomous consumption?
6. What tends to happen to inventories if aggregate expenditures exceed output? What tends to happen to output?
7. What tends to happen to inventories if output exceeds aggregate expenditures? What tends to happen to output?

Answers: 1. d 2. d 3. c 4. a 5. b 6. a

15.3

Adding Investment, Government Purchases, and Net Exports

📂 What is the impact of adding investment, government purchases, and net exports to aggregate expenditures?

📂 What is planned investment?

📂 What is unplanned investment?

📂 How does the aggregate expenditure model help explain the process of the business cycle?

Why does adding other autonomous expenditures to the consumption function not change its slope?

Now we can complicate our model in another important way by adding in the other three major components of expenditure in the economy: investment, government purchases, and net exports. As a first step, we'll add these components to the model but assume that they are autonomous, that is, they don't depend on the level of income or output in the economy. Later, we'll relax that assumption.

Suppose that consumption depends on the level of income or output in the economy, but investment, government purchases, and net exports don't; instead, they depend on other things in the economy, such as interest rates, political considerations, or the condition of foreign economies (we'll discuss these things in more detail later). Now, aggregate expenditure (*AE*) consists of consumption (*C*) plus investment (*I*) plus government purchases (*G*) plus net exports (*NX*):

$$AE \equiv C + I + G + NX$$

This equation is nothing more than a definition (indicated by the $\equiv$ rather than =): Aggregate expenditure equals the sum of its components.

When we add up all the components of aggregate expenditure, we'll get an upward-sloping line, as we did in the previous section, because consumption increases as income increases. But because we're now allowing for investment, government purchases, and net exports, the autonomous portion of aggregate expenditure is larger. Thus, the intercept of the aggregate expenditure line is higher, as shown in Exhibit 1.

What is the new equilibrium? As before, the equilibrium occurs where the two lines cross, that is, where the aggregate expenditure line intersects the equilibrium line, which is the 45-degree line.

Now that we've added in the other components of spending, especially investment spending, we can begin to discuss some of the more realistic factors related to the business cycle. This discussion of what happens to the economy during business cycles is a major element of Keynesian theory, which was designed to explain what happens in recessions.

If you look at historical economic data, you'll see that investment spending fluctuates much more than overall output in the economy. In recessions, output declines, and a major portion of the decline occurs because investment falls sharply. In expansions, investment is the major contributor to economic growth. The two major explanations for the volatile movement of investment over the business cycle involve planned investment and unplanned investment.

The first explanation for investment's strong business cycle movement is that *planned* investment responds dramatically to perceptions of future changes in economic activity. If business firms think that the economy will be good in the future, they'll build new factories, buy more computers, and hire more workers today, in anticipation of being able to sell more goods in the future. On the other hand, if firms think the economy will be weak in the future, they'll cut back on both investment and hiring. Economists find that planned investment is extremely sensitive to firms' perceptions about the future. And if firms desire to invest more today, it generates ripple effects that make the economy grow even faster.

The second explanation for investment's movement over the business cycle is that businesses encounter *unplanned* changes in investment as well. The idea here is that

How is unplanned inventory investment the key to future changes in output?

section 15.3
exhibit 1

Adding Investment, Government Purchases, and Net Exports to Aggregate Expenditures

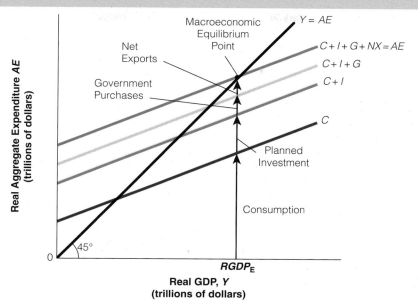

Adding $I + G + NX$ leads to a larger intercept of the aggregate expenditure line. Because consumption is the only component of aggregate expenditure that depends on income, the slope of the line is the same as the slope of the line in Exhibit 3 of Section 15.2.

recessions, to some extent, occur as the economy is making a transition, before it reaches equilibrium. We'll use Exhibit 2 to illustrate this idea. In the exhibit, equilibrium occurs at output of Y^*. Now consider what would happen if, for some reason, firms produced too many goods, bringing the economy to output level Y_2. At output level Y_2, aggregate expenditure is less than output because the aggregate expenditure line is below the 45-degree line at that point. When people aren't buying all the products that firms are producing, unsold goods begin piling up. In the national income accounts, unsold goods in firms' inventories are counted in a subcategory of investment—inventory investment. The firms didn't plan for this to happen, so the piling up of inventories reflects **unplanned inventory investment**. Of course, once firms realize that inventories are rising because they've produced too much, they cut back on production, reducing output below Y_2. This process continues until firms' inventories are restored to normal levels and output returns to Y^*.

Now let's look at what would happen if firms produced too few goods, as occurs when output is at Y_1. At output level Y_1, aggregate expenditure is greater than output because the aggregate expenditure line is above the 45-degree line at that point. People want to buy more goods than firms are producing, so firms' inventories begin to decline or become depleted. Again, this change in inventories shows up in the national income accounts, this time as a decline in firms' inventories and thus a decline in investment. Again, the firms didn't plan for this situation, so once they realize that inventories are

unplanned inventory investment
changes in inventories that firms did not anticipate

section 15.3
exhibit 2

Unplanned Inventory Investment

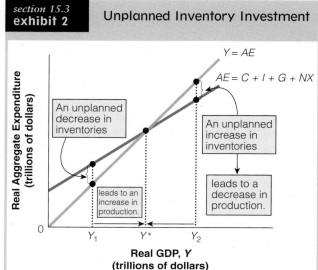

At Y_2, AE is less than output and unsold goods pile up. As unplanned inventory investment builds up, firms cut back on production until equilibrium output is restored at Y^*. At Y_1, AE is greater than output: Consumers want to buy more than firms are producing. Inventories become depleted, and firms increase production until inventories are restored and output returns to equilibrium at Y^*.

declining because they haven't produced enough, they'll increase production beyond Y_1. Equilibrium is reached when firms' inventories are restored to normal levels and output returns to Y^*.

So our Keynesian expenditure model helps to explain the process of the business cycle, working through investment. Next, let's see how other economic events can act to affect the equilibrium level of output in the economy. We'll begin by looking at how changes in autonomous spending (consumption, investment, government purchases, and net exports) can influence output.

ⓘ SECTION QUIZ

1. In addition to consumption, the major components of aggregate expenditures do not include
   a. investment.
   b. saving.
   c. government purchases.
   d. net exports.
   e. All of the above are included in aggregate expenditures.

2. When the autonomous level of investment increases,
   a. at first, inventories will fall below desired levels.
   b. output will rise.
   c. consumption spending will rise.
   d. all of the above will occur.

3. Equilibrium output will tend to increase when
   a. planned investment increases.
   b. unplanned investment is positive.
   c. either planned investment increases or unplanned investment is positive.
   d. either planned investment decreases or unplanned investment is negative.

---

1. When all the nonconsumption components of aggregate expenditures are autonomous, why does the aggregate expenditures line have the same slope as the consumption function?

2. If net exports are negative, what happens to the aggregate expenditures line, other things equal? What will happen to equilibrium income?

3. As the economy turns toward a recession, what happens to unplanned inventory investment? Why? What happens to planned investment? Why?

4. How does unplanned inventory investment signal which way real GDP will tend to change in the economy?

Answers: 1. b 2. d 3. a

Shifts in Aggregate Expenditure and the Multiplier

☞ How do changes in the components of aggregate expenditure affect the aggregate expenditure curve?

☞ How does the multiplier affect aggregate expenditures?

What happens if one of the components of aggregate expenditure increases for reasons other than an increase in income? Remember that we called these components or parts *autonomous*. Households' expectations might become more optimistic, or households may find credit conditions easier as interest rates decline, or their real wealth might increase as the stock market rises. All these factors increase autonomous consumption, and thus total consumption at every level of income increases. Firms might increase their investment (especially if their productivity rises or the interest rate declines), government might increase its spending, or net exports could rise as foreign economies improve their economic health. Any of these things would increase aggregate expenditure for any given level of income, shifting the aggregate expenditure curve up, as shown in Exhibit 1.

Why do increases in autonomous purchases increase equilibrium output in the Keynesian model?

Suppose that firms optimistic about their future profitability increase their planned investment spending on plants, factories, and machines by $100 billion. In Exhibit 1, we see that the increase in planned investment spending shifts the aggregate expenditure curve upward and results in a $400 billion gain in equilibrium real GDP; the difference between the equilibrium real GDP at point A and the equilibrium real GDP at point B. How did the $100 billion increase in autonomous investment raise real GDP demanded by $400 billion? This result might seem amazing—that an increase in planned investment spending of a $100 billion can result in a $400 billion increase in real GDP—but it merely reflects a well-understood process, known as the **expenditure multiplier**.

expenditure multiplier
the multiplier that only considers the impact of consumption changes on aggregate expenditures

A caution here: Do not assume that the multiplier applies only to changes in planned investment spending. Multipliers apply to any increase in autonomous expenditure. As an example, if the stock market went up to increase the amount of autonomous household spending by $100 billion, the level of output would go up the same $400 billion as found in the preceding example.

The idea of the multiplier is that permanent increases in spending in one part of the economy lead to increased spending by others in the economy as well. When firms increase investment spending private resource owners earn more wages, interest, rents, and profits, so they spend more. The higher level of economic activity encourages even more spending, until a new equilibrium with higher output is reached, Y_2 rather than Y_1. In this example, the increase in output is four times as big as the initial increase in investment spending that started the cycle. Let's see how this process works in more detail.

Exhibit 2 shows what happens along the way. We begin at point A, with output of $14 trillion. The increase in investment spending of $100 billion directly increases aggregate expenditure by that amount, represented by point B. Firms observe the increase in aggregate expenditure (perhaps because they see their inventories declining), so over the next few months

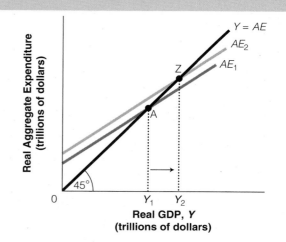

section 15.4
exhibit 1

Increases in the Autonomous Components of Aggregate Expenditure

If one of the "autonomous" components of aggregate expenditure increases for reasons other than an increase in income, like optimistic consumer or business expectations, a decrease in the interest rate, or real wealth increases, government might increase its spending, or net exports could rise as foreign economies improve their economic health. Any of these things would increase aggregate expenditure for any given level of income, shifting the aggregate expenditure curve up, as shown in Exhibit 1.

© Cengage Learning 2013

section 15.4 exhibit 2	Aggregate Expenditures and the Multiplier Process

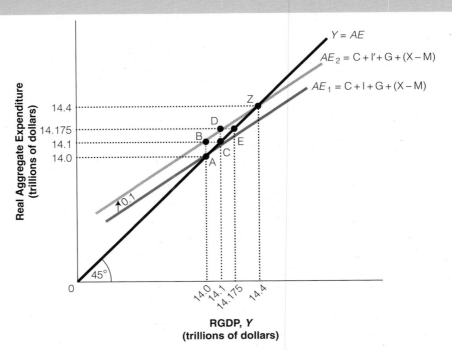

At point A, output is $14 trillion and the increase in investment spending of $100 billion directly increases aggregate expenditure by that amount, represented by point B. Firms observe the increase in aggregate expenditure and produce more output, moving the economy to point C, with output of $14.1 trillion. But now consumers have an extra $100 billion in income and they wish to spend three-fourths of it (the MPC is 0.75). Three-fourths of $100 billion is $75 billion, so consumers now spend an additional $75 billion, increasing aggregate expenditure to $14.175 trillion at point D. Again, firms observe the increase in expenditure and increase output, bringing the economy to point E. This process continues until the economy eventually reaches point Z, at which output is $14.4 trillion. The process is not accomplished immediately but over the course of several quarters.

Why does the multiplier depend on the MPC?

they produce more output, moving the economy to point C, with output of $14.1 trillion. But now consumers have an extra $100 billion in income and they wish to spend three-fourths of it (because the marginal propensity to consume is 0.75). Three-fourths of $100 billion is $75 billion, so consumers now spend an additional $75 billion, increasing aggregate expenditure to $14.175 trillion at point D. Again, firms observe the increase in expenditure, so over the next few months they increase output, bringing the economy to point E. This process continues until the economy eventually reaches point Z, at which output is $14.4 trillion.

You can see on the graph how the economy reaches its new equilibrium at point Z. We can also calculate it numerically by adding up an infinite series of numbers in the following way. The first increase in output was $100 billion, which comes directly from the increase in investment spending. Then consumers, with higher incomes of $100 billion, want to spend three-fourths of it, so they increase spending: $100 billion × 3/4 = $75 billion. Now, with incomes higher by $75 billion, consumers want to spend an additional three-fourths of it: $75 billion × 3/4 = $56 billion. Again, incomes are higher, so consumers will spend more, this time in the amount $56 billion × 3/4 = $42 billion. The process continues indefinitely. To find the total increase in output (or income), we simply need to add up all these amounts. It turns out that an infinite sum with this pattern is exactly $100 billion/(1 − 3/4) = $400 billion. So output increases by $400 billion from $14 trillion to $14.4 trillion.

This calculation of the sum of all the increases to output can be written in a convenient way. As you saw in this example, the multiplier depends on how much consumers spend out of any additions to their income. So in this model in which consumption spending is the only component of aggregate expenditure that depends on income, the multiplier is equal to 1/(1 − MPC), where MPC is the marginal propensity to consume. In the previous example,

MPC = 3/4, so the multiplier is 1/(1 − 3/4) = 4. The same multiplier holds whether the increase in aggregate expenditures arises from an increase in investment spending, as in the example, or from an increase in other autonomous elements of spending, such as government purchases, net exports, or the autonomous portion of consumption spending. The larger (smaller) the MPC the larger (smaller) the multiplier. For example, if the MPC is 0.8 (1/1 − 0.8 or 1/0.2 = 5) than the multiplier would be 5. If the MPC is 0.5 (1/1 − 0.5 or 1/0.5 = 2). The true multiplier is usually smaller because of complications that we will discuss in the chapter on fiscal policy.

The multiplier can operate in both directions. During the Great Depression, both consumption spending and planned investment fell, causing a decrease in aggregate expenditure. As sales fell, workers were laid off and falling levels of production and income led to further declines in consumption spending as the economy fell into a downward spiral. The downturn can also start in a certain sector and than spread via the multiplier to other sectors of the economy. Recall, the information technology recession of 2001. The initial impact of the decline in investment spending was felt in the computer and telecommunications industries but eventually the declines in production, income, and spending spread into other industries, such as automobiles, furniture, appliances, airlines, and restaurants. And the financial crisis of 2008 started in the housing and financial sectors and was quickly felt throughout the economy.

⍰ SECTION QUIZ

1. Which of the following would increase aggregate expenditures?

   a. Households become more optimistic about the future.

   b. Interest rates fall.

   c. Foreign economies improve.

   d. Government purchases increase.

   e. Any of the above would increase aggregate expenditures.

2. If the MPC equals 0.5,

   a. the expenditure multiplier will equal 2.

   b. a $5 billion increase in investment would tend to increase output by $10 billion.

   c. the expenditure multiplier is less than if the MPC = 0.8.

   d. all of the above are true.

3. Equilibrium output would tend to rise when

   a. autonomous expenditures increase.

   b. the MPC increases.

   c. either autonomous expenditures increase or the MPC increases.

   d. neither autonomous expenditures increase nor the MPC increases.

---

1. If autonomous expenditure rises and the marginal propensity to consume rises, what would happen to equilibrium income?

2. If autonomous expenditure rises and the marginal propensity to consume falls, what would happen to equilibrium income?

3. If the marginal propensity to consume was 0.75, what would happen to equilibrium income if government purchases increased by $500 billion and investment fell by $500 billion at the same time? What if government purchases increased by $500 billion and investment fell by $400 billion at the same time?

4. Why does a larger marginal propensity to consume lead to a larger multiplier?

5. If autonomous consumption was $300 billion, investment was $200 billion, government purchases were $400 billion, and net exports were a negative $100 billion, what would autonomous consumption be? What would equilibrium income be?

6. What would happen to equilibrium income if, other things equal, imports increased by $100 billion and the marginal propensity to consume was 0.9?

Answers: 1. e 2. d 3. c

15.5

From Aggregate Expenditures to Aggregate Demand

📂 Why do aggregate expenditures depend on the price level?

📂 How do we move from aggregate expenditures to aggregate demand?

How do changes in the price level affect the aggregate expenditure function?

To go from the Keynesian cross-aggregate expenditure model to aggregate demand, all we need to add is how the price level affects the components of aggregate demand.

The effect of different price levels can be seen in Exhibit 1. Let's consider three different price levels, $P = 90$, $P = 100$, and $P = 110$, where P is a price index like the GDP deflator. Suppose the price level is 100, and suppose at that level of prices, the aggregate expenditure curve is given as the curve labeled AE ($P = 100$), shown in the top diagram. The equilibrium in the Keynesian aggregate expenditure model occurs at point A. Now we plot point A in the bottom diagram, corresponding to a price level of 100 and output of $8 trillion.

What happens if the price level falls from 100 to 90? Recall from the previous chapter, that a lower price level will cause an increase in RGDP demanded through the real wealth, interest rate and open economy effects. The lower price level will (1) increase the real value of household's money holdings (part of their wealth) causing purchasing power to rise leading to greater consumption expenditures; (2) firms and households will reduce their holdings of money and save, more causing interest rates to fall and increasing investment and consumption expenditures; and (3) it leads to an increase in imports and a decrease in exports. As a consequence of the increase in RGDP demanded associated with the lower price level there is a higher level of planned expenditures, so the aggregate expenditure curve shifts up to (AE, $P = 90$) and the new equilibrium is at point B. So we plot B in the bottom diagram, corresponding to the price level 90 and output $15 trillion, as seen in Exhibit 1.

Finally, what happens if the price level rises to 110? The higher price level will (1) decrease the value of household's money holdings (part of their wealth), causing purchasing power to fall leading to reduced consumption expenditures; (2) firms and households will increase their holdings of money and increase the demand for loanable funds, causing interest rates to rise and decreasing consumption and investment expenditures; and (3) it leads to an increase in exports and a decrease in imports. As a consequence of the decrease in RGDP demanded associated with the higher price level, there is a lower level of planned expenditures (AE, $P = 110$) and a lower level, of output, $13 trillion, as seen in Exhibit 1. The higher price level means lower aggregate expenditure, so the aggregate expenditure curve shifts down to AE ($P = 110$), and the equilibrium in the Keynesian-cross diagram is at point C. We plot point C in the bottom diagram, corresponding to a price level of 110 and output of $13 trillion.

What is the relationship between the price level and equilibrium real GDP?

Notice that the higher the price level, the lower is aggregate demand. Imagine carrying out this same experiment for every possible price level. Then the points like A, B, and C in the lower diagram would trace out the entire aggregate demand curve.

Shifts in Aggregate Demand

In the previous section, we used the relationship between aggregate expenditure and the price level to derive the aggregate demand curve. Now we'll show that changes in any of the components of aggregate expenditure that occur for any reason other than a change in the price level or output lead to a shift of the aggregate demand curve. We'll start with Exhibit 1 (but to keep things readable we'll only draw in one of the aggregate expenditure lines in the top half of the exhibit), then consider what happens when the autonomous parts of consumption, investment, government purchases, or net exports change. Such a change would shift the aggregate expenditure curve upwards, as shown in Exhibit 2, where we denote the original aggregate expenditure curve AE_1 and the new aggregate expenditure curve AE_2.

Originally, we had equilibrium at point A with output of $14 trillion when the price level was 100. After the increase in government spending, the aggregate expenditure curve shifts up, and we get equilibrium at point D with output of $14.5 trillion when the price level is

How do changes in the aggregate expenditure function change aggregate demand?

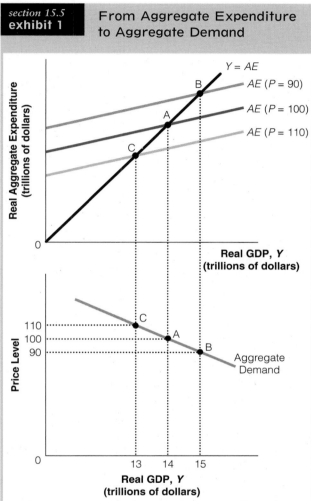

section 15.5 exhibit 1
From Aggregate Expenditure to Aggregate Demand

Suppose the price level is 100, and suppose at that level of prices, the aggregate expenditure curve is given as the curve labeled AE (P = 100), shown in the top diagram. The equilibrium in the aggregate expenditure model occurs at point A. Now we plot point A in the bottom diagram, corresponding to a price level of 100 and output of $14 trillion. If the price level falls from 100 to 90, the aggregate expenditure curve shifts up to AE (P = 90), and the equilibrium in the aggregate-cross diagram is at point B. So we plot point B in the bottom diagram, corresponding to price level 90 and output $15 trillion. If the price level rises to 110 the aggregate expenditure curve shifts down to AE (P = 110), and the equilibrium is at point C. We plot point C in the bottom diagram, corresponding to a price level of 110 and output of $13 trillion.

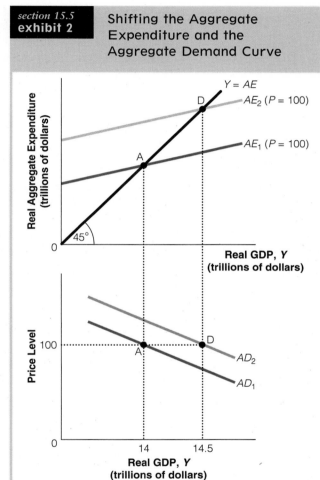

section 15.5 exhibit 2
Shifting the Aggregate Expenditure and the Aggregate Demand Curve

If the autonomous parts of consumption, investment, government purchases, or net exports increase, it shifts the aggregate expenditure curve upwards from AE_1 to AE_2. Originally, we had equilibrium at point A with output of $14 trillion when the price level was 100. Now suppose the government increased spending, the aggregate expenditure curve shifts up, and we get equilibrium at point D with output of $14.5 trillion when the price level is 100. Similarly, for any other given price level, equilibrium output would be higher. So, the new aggregate demand curve on the lower diagram has shifted to the right.

100. Similarly, for any other given price level, equilibrium output would be higher. So the new aggregate demand curve on the lower diagram has shifted to the right. In sum, changes in the price level create the real wealth, interest rate, and open economy effects, which shift the aggregate expenditure curve and change RGDP demanded; these price quantity combinations generate the aggregate demand curve. But at a given price level, changes in spending plans, C, I, G, or $(X - M)$, shift the aggregate demand curve.

If aggregate supply is vertical, how does an increase in aggregate demand affect real GDP?

Why is the aggregate expenditure model inconsistent with the stagflation of the 1970s?

Limitations of the Aggregate Expenditure Model

The aggregate expenditure model is helpful in explaining how short-run business cycles occur. However, the model fails to show price level changes, so there is no way to measure inflation. The model also fails to explain the stagflation of the 1970s—unemployment and inflation together—that is, it does not incorporate possible shifts in the aggregate supply curve. In other words, it cannot explain cost-push inflation. It also does not take into consideration the expectations of consumers and firms as they react to changes in policies designed to stabilize the economy. It does not take into account that an economy can *temporarily* produce beyond the natural rate of real output, $RGDP_{NR}$. It does not allow for the economy to self-correct.

great economic thinkers · John Maynard Keynes (1883–1946)

John Maynard Keynes was born in Cambridge, England, in 1883. Keynes's father was a political economist and logician; his mother was a justice of the peace who eventually became the mayor of Cambridge, England.

Many would argue that Keynes was one of the most brilliant minds of the twentieth century. He was educated at Eton and Cambridge, where he studied mathematics and philosophy. Keynes had a brief tutelage under Alfred Marshall who tried to convince Keynes to pursue economics. Keynes began his career in the India Office of the British government. He soon became bored and returned to King's College, Cambridge, to lecture in economics, a post he held until his death in 1946.

Keynes had many interests outside of economics, including mathematics, art, and theater. Keynes married a Russian ballerina, and for a time, he associated with a group of intellectuals known as Bloomsury Group (which included such notables as E. M. Forster and Virginia Wolff).

Keynes's contributions to the field of economics have influenced public policy since 1930. He is the father of discretionary fiscal policy—deliberating using government spending and taxes to stabilize the economy.

Keynes believed that the economy could stay in a period of unemployment for a long time and not self-correct. Specifically, Keynes emphasized the idea that wages and prices do not always adjust rapidly to bring about full employment in an economy. Keynes believed that government spending could stimulate the economy back to full employment.

Keynes was also a successful investor in the commodity and stock markets. His own net worth increased from a miniscule level in 1920 to over $2 million by the time of his death.

⑦ SECTION QUIZ

1. When the price level falls,

   a. consumption increases because real wealth increases.

   b. investment rises because interest rates decline.

   c. net exports rise because exchange rates decline.

   d. all of the above are true.

2. Which of the following would shift both the aggregate expenditure function and aggregate demand?

   a. an increase in consumption because disposable income rose

   b. an increase in consumption because the price level fell

   c. an increase in consumption because of increased consumer optimism

   d. All of the above would shift both the aggregate expenditure function and aggregate demand

3. If the economy was operating on a completely flat segment of the short-run aggregate supply curve, an increase in aggregate demand would

   a. increase output and increase the price level.

   b. increase output and decrease the price level.

   c. decrease output and increase the price level.

   d. decrease output and decrease the price level.

   e. do none of the above.

---

1. In the aggregate expenditure model, does a lower price level lead to an increase in the real quantity of goods and services demanded or an increase in demand?

2. If autonomous expenditures increased by $20 billion, what is the change in aggregate demand at a given price level if the marginal propensity to consume is 0.75?

3. If autonomous expenditures decreased by $50 billion, what is the change in aggregate demand at a given price level if the marginal propensity to consume is 0.8?

4. Along a vertical, long-run aggregate supply curve, what effect will a $10 billion increase in government expenditures have on real output?

5. If the short-run aggregate supply curve is upward sloping, why will the change in real output due to an increase in autonomous expenditures in the short run be less than that indicated by the change in aggregate demand?

6. If wages are sticky downward, why will a decrease in autonomous expenditures reduce real output much like the Keynesian expenditure model indicates?

Answers: 1. d 2. c 3. e

Interactive Summary

Fill in the blanks:

1. Keynes believed that _____ was the critical determinant of the overall level of economic activity.

2. In the simple Keynesian model, we assume that the price level is _____ as output changes.

3. _____ spending is the largest component of the demand for final goods and services.

4. The _____ factors affecting consumption are those that do not depend on income.

5. A(n) _____ in real wealth would decrease autonomous consumption.

6. A higher interest rate today tends to make items purchased on credit _____ expensive and _____ expenditures on those items.

7. Either lower interest rates or lower household debt would tend to _____ autonomous consumption.

8. An increase in consumer confidence would tend to _____ consumption spending.

9. Personal consumption spending depends most importantly on your current _____.

10. Your marginal propensity to consume is equal to the change in _____ divided by the change in _____.

11. The more you spend out of any given increase in income, the _____ your marginal propensity to consume.

12. Your marginal propensity to save is equal to the change in _____ divided by the change in _____.

13. The MPC and MPS must add up to _____.

14. The MPC is equal to the _____ of the consumption function.

15. Consumption spending is partly _____, or independent of income, and partly _____, or dependent on income.

16. Income and _____ are always the same in the economy.

17. Aggregate _____ equal _____ when the economy is in equilibrium.

18. In the Keynesian model, if output were lower than its equilibrium level, inventories would _____ desired levels and producers would _____ output.

19. When inventories rise above desired levels, output will _____.

20. When aggregate expenditures exceed output, output will _____.

21. In addition to consumption, the major components of aggregate expenditures are _____, _____, and _____.

22. Only in equilibrium do aggregate expenditures _____ output.

23. One reason that investment contributes to the business cycle is that _____ investment responds dramatically to perceptions about future changes in business activity.

24. When unplanned inventory investment is _____, output will tend to fall.

25. In equilibrium, unplanned business investment _____ zero.

26. An increase in autonomous government purchases by $2 billion will increase output by _____ $2 billion in the simple Keynesian model.

27. The expenditure multiplier is equal to 1 divided by _____, when consumption is the only component of aggregate expenditures.

28. When autonomous investment increases, the level of consumption will _____ as a result.

29. The _____ the MPC, the smaller is the expenditure multiplier.

30. To go from the aggregate expenditure model to aggregate demand, we need to add how the _____ affects each of the aggregate expenditure components.

31. Consumption, investment, and net exports all increase as a result of a(n) _____ in the price level.

32. In terms of the aggregate expenditure model, a fall in the price level shifts the aggregate expenditures curve _____.

33. Changes in any of the components of aggregate expenditures for any reason other than a change in the _____ or _____ will also shift the aggregate demand curve.

34. When the aggregate expenditure curve shifts up for reasons other than changes in the price level, the aggregate demand curve shifts _____.

35. The aggregate supply curve must be _____ in the long run.

36. If the short-run aggregate supply curve slopes upward, an increase in aggregate demand will increase real output _____ than aggregate expenditures in the short run.

37. The aggregate expenditure model could not explain the _____ of the 1970s.

Answers: 1. total spending 2. constant 3. Consumption 4. autonomous 5. decrease 6. more; reduces 7. increase 8. increase 9. disposable income 10. consumption spending; disposable income 11. greater 12. savings; disposable income 13. 1 14. slope 15. autonomous; induced 16. output 17. expenditures; output 18. fall below; increase 19. fall 20. rise 21. investment; government purchases; net exports 22. equal 23. planned 24. positive 25. equals 26. more than 27. (1 − MPC) 28. increase 29. smaller 30. price level 31. fall 32. up 33. price level; income 34. right 35. vertical 36. less 37. stagflation

Key Terms and Concepts

autonomous determinants of consumption expenditures 421
marginal propensity to consume (MPC) 423

marginal propensity to save (MPS) 423

unplanned inventory investment 429
expenditure multiplier 431

Section Quiz Answers

15.1 The Simple Aggregate Expenditure Model

1. **How does the assumption of a fixed price level in the Keynesian expenditure model solve the problem of distinguishing between changes in the real value of a variable (such as GDP) and changes in its nominal value?**

   If the price level is fixed, a change in nominal income is equivalent to a change in real income.

2. **Would it be possible for some consumption expenditures to be autonomous and other parts of consumption expenditure not to be autonomous?**

   Yes. Some consumption depends on income, but other consumption is autonomous (not changing with income), depending on variables such as real wealth, interest rates, and so on.

3. **In what two ways does a higher interest rate tend to reduce current consumption?**

   A higher interest rate reduces current consumption by (1) increasing the cost of consumption items bought on credit and (2) increasing the return to current saving, which increases savings, which in turn reduces consumption.

4. **What would happen to autonomous consumption expenditures if the value of a consumer's stock market investments rose and his household debt rose at the same time?**

   If the value of a consumer's stock market investments rose, it would increase autonomous consumption, but if household debt rose, it would reduce autonomous consumption. Since these effects are in opposite directions, the net effect would be indeterminate without more information.

5. **What would happen to your autonomous consumption if you expected to get a job next week paying 10 times your current salary?**

   Since your expected future income will rise substantially, just like an increase in real wealth, it will increase your current consumption.

6. **Why do households headed by a 50-year-old tend to save a larger fraction of their incomes than those headed by either a 30-year-old or a 70-year-old?**

   A 50-year-old is in his peak earning years and is also trying to save for retirement, both of which increase saving. A 70-year-old is in retirement and drawing down previous savings. A 30-year-old has a relatively low income and is often faced with the expenses of raising a family.

15.2 Finding Equilibrium in the Aggregate Expenditure Model

1. If consumption purchases rise with disposable income, how would an increase in taxes affect consumption purchases?

An increase in taxes reduces disposable income, which in turn reduces consumption purchases.

2. If your marginal propensity to consume was 0.75, what would be your marginal propensity to save? If your marginal propensity to consume rose to 0.80, what would happen to your marginal propensity to save?

Since the marginal propensity to consume plus the marginal propensity to save must equal 1, if MPC = 0.75, MPS = 0.25. If MPC = 0.8, MPS = 0.2.

3. Could a student have a positive marginal propensity to save, and yet have negative savings (increased borrowing) at the same time?

Yes. A student could be increasing his saving (decreasing his dissaving) with each dollar of income earned, yet still have an income low enough (less than autonomous consumption divided by MPS) that he must borrow.

4. What would happen to the slope of the consumption function if the marginal propensity to save fell?

Since the slope of the consumption function equals MPC, a fall in MPS implies an increase in MPC and a steeper consumption function.

5. Why would an increase in disposable income increase induced consumption but not autonomous consumption?

Autonomous consumption is defined as consumption spending that does not depend on income, while induced consumption spending is induced by increases in disposable income.

6. What tends to happen to inventories if aggregate expenditures exceed output? What tends to happen to output?

If aggregate expenditures exceed output, inventories will fall, which will give producers incentives to increase output.

7. What tends to happen to inventories if output exceeds aggregate expenditures? What tends to happen to output?

If output exceeds aggregate expenditures, inventories will rise, giving producers incentives to decrease output.

15.3 Adding Investment, Government Purchases, and Net Exports

1. When all the nonconsumption components of aggregate expenditures are autonomous, why does the aggregate expenditures line have the same slope as the consumption function?

The slope of the aggregate expenditures line equals the change in aggregate expenditures divided by the change in income, but where only consumption depends on income, the change in aggregate expenditures equals the change in consumption, and the aggregate expenditures line has the same slope as the consumption function.

2. If net exports are negative, what happens to the aggregate expenditures line, other things equal? What will happen to equilibrium income?

Autonomous expenditures equal the sum of autonomous consumption plus investment plus government purchases plus net exports. If net exports are negative, autonomous expenditures are lower and the aggregate expenditure line shifts down, resulting in lower equilibrium income.

3. As the economy turns toward a recession, what happens to unplanned inventory investment? Why? What happens to planned investment? Why?

As the economy turns toward a recession, unplanned inventory investment is positive because sales are less than producers' planned. Planned inventory falls because it is very sensitive to perceptions of future changes in business conditions.

4. How does unplanned inventory investment signal which way real GDP will tend to change in the economy?

Unplanned inventory increases signal that demand was weaker than expected, which will tend to result in a decrease in real output and income. Unplanned inventory decreases signal that demand was stronger than expected, which will tend to result in an increase in real output and income.

15.4 Shifts in Aggregate Expenditure and the Multiplier

1. If autonomous expenditure rises and the marginal propensity to consume rises, what would happen to equilibrium income?

Either of these changes moves the *AE* intersection with the 45-degree line to the right, increasing equilibrium income.

2. **If autonomous expenditure rises and the marginal propensity to consume falls, what would happen to equilibrium income?**

Since the first change moved the *AE* intersection with the 45-degree line to the right, the second moved it left. Since the two changes would change equilibrium income in opposite directions, we do not know the net effect without more information.

3. **If the marginal propensity to consume was 0.75, what would happen to equilibrium income if government purchases increased by $500 billion and investment fell by $500 billion at the same time? What if government purchases increased by $500 billion and investment fell by $400 billion at the same time?**

If government purchases increased by $500 billion and investment fell by $500 billion at the same time, there would be no change in autonomous expenditures and therefore no change in equilibrium income. If government purchases increased by $500 billion and investment fell by $400 billion at the same time, autonomous expenditures would increase by $100 billion. It would increase equilibrium income by $100 billion times one over one minus 0.75, or $400 billion.

4. **Why does a larger marginal propensity to consume lead to a larger multiplier?**

A larger marginal propensity to consume makes the denominator of the multiplier smaller, which makes the multiplier larger.

5. **If autonomous consumption was $300 billion, investment was $200 billion, government purchases were $400 billion, and net exports were a negative $100 billion, what would autonomous consumption be? What would equilibrium income be?**

Autonomous expenditures are the autonomous components of consumption, investment, and government purchases plus net exports. Here that would be $300 billion plus $200 billion plus $400 billion minus $100 billion, or $800 billion. Equilibrium income would be $800 billion times one over one minus MPC. We cannot calculate that number without knowing MPC.

6. **What would happen to equilibrium income if, other things equal, imports increased by $100 billion and the marginal propensity to consume was 0.9?**

Net exports would decrease by $100 billion, which would decrease autonomous expenditures by $100 billion. Income would fall by $100 billion times one over one minus 0.9, or $1 trillion.

15.5 From Aggregate Expenditures to Aggregate Demand

1. **In the aggregate expenditure model, does a lower price level lead to an increase in the real quantity of goods and services demanded or on increase in demand?**

A lower price level increases the real quantity of goods and services demanded. However, because it was caused by a changing price level rather than a change in autonomous expenditures, it does not cause a change in aggregate demand.

2. **If autonomous expenditures increased by $20 billion, what is the change in aggregate demand at a given price level if the marginal propensity to consume is 0.75?**

AD would increase by the increase in autonomous expenditures times one over one minus MPC, or $20 billion × 4 = $80 billion.

3. **If autonomous expenditures decreased by $50 billion, what is the change in aggregate demand at a given price level if the marginal propensity to consume is 0.8?**

AD would decrease by the decrease in autonomous expenditures times one over one minus MPC, or $50 billion × 5 = $250 billion.

4. **Along a vertical, long-run aggregate supply curve, what effect will a $10 billion increase in government expenditures have on real output?**

A change in aggregate expenditures, increasing aggregate demand, will have no effect on real output along a vertical, long-run aggregate supply curve, regardless of MPC.

5. **If the short-run aggregate supply curve is upward sloping, why will the change in real output due to an increase in autonomous expenditures in the short run be less than that indicated by the change in aggregate demand?**

If the short-run aggregate supply curve is upward sloping, real output will increase less than the change in aggregate demand.

6. **If wages are sticky downward, why will a decrease in autonomous expenditures reduce real output much like the Keynesian expenditure model indicates?**

A decrease in autonomous expenditures will reduce *AD* by the amount indicated by the multiplier formula. If wages are sticky downward, the short-run aggregate supply curve will be nearly horizontal over the relevant range, and the fall in real output would be nearly as great as the fall in *AD*.

Problems

1. Which of the following are likely to cause a reduction in consumption?
   a. an increase in interest rates
   b. an increase in the value of stock market portfolios
   c. a decrease in disposable income
   d. an increase in income taxes
   e. deflation

2. Identify the most volatile component of aggregate expenditure. Identify its largest component.

3. Which of the following will cause the aggregate expenditure schedule to increase?
   a. an increase in consumer optimism
   b. an increase in the purchase of imports
   c. an increase in the sale of exports
   d. pessimism by business owners about the outlook of the economy
   e. an increase in government spending due to the outbreak of war

4. What would happen to autonomous consumption if household debt fell and the interest rate rose over the same time period?

5. What would happen to autonomous consumption if real wealth increased and expectations of the future became more optimistic?

6. Consumption equals $32,000 when disposable income equals $40,000. Consumption increases to $38,000 when disposable income increases to $50,000. What is the marginal propensity to consume? The marginal propensity to save?

7. If the marginal propensity to save increases, what happens to the consumption function?

8. If MPC was equal to 0.5, would doubling your income double your consumption spending?

9. Why can't an economy with an MPC greater than 1 reach a stable equilibrium in the aggregate expenditure model?

10. Why are unplanned inventory changes the key to predicting future changes in real GDP in the aggregate expenditure model?

11. Why would an increase in planned investment increase real GDP, but an unplanned increase in inventory investment decrease real GDP, in the aggregate expenditure model?

12. If the economy is a net importer, what will that do to the aggregate expenditure function and equilibrium level of real GDP?

13. Why are planned and unplanned investment unlikely to both increase over the same period of time?

14. Why do the aggregate expenditure function and the aggregate demand curve both shift upward at the same time?

15. Evaluate the following statement: The Keynesian assumption of wage and price rigidity best corresponds to the steepest portion of the aggregate supply curve where factories are operating below capacity.

16. Visit the Economy at a Glance page at the Bureau of Economic Analysis, http://www.bea.gov/newsreleases/glance .htm. Locate information about recent changes in inventory levels as well as the ratio of inventory to sales. Can you detect a trend upward or downward in inventory levels? What does the trend bode for national output according to the aggregate expenditure model?

© SIMON McCOMB/STONE/GETTY IMAGES, INC.

Macroeconomic Policy

part **6**

Fiscal Policy

AP PHOTO/CARLOS OSORIO

During the financial crisis that began in 2008, an unprecedented amount of assistance was given to banks, auto manufacturers, homeowners, and government housing agencies. Funds came from the Treasury, the Federal Reserve and the Federal Deposit Insurance Corporation. The American Recovery Act of 2009 added over $860 billion to the budget deficit. Roughly $290 billion was for tax cuts, and the rest was for government spending to increase investment and consumer spending in the hopes of creating new jobs. Proponents argued that assistance in a crisis is pulling the correct policy lever, as a briefer recession helps everyone—taxpayers, workers, and firms. But not everyone agrees. Others argue that billions were wasted on poorly managed but politically connected firms. These debates will continue. In this chapter, we talk about the role of government, particularly government purchases, taxes, and transfer payments, during recessions and booms.

The financial crisis has also led to increases in the deficit and the national debt. What are the implications of a growing debt on economic growth? on future generations? These are all fiscal policy issues.

In earlier chapters, we discussed how an economy can face a recessionary gap when aggregate demand is deficient or an inflationary gap when there is excessive aggregate demand. In this chapter, we will see how the government can employ fiscal policy—the use of government purchases, transfers, and/or taxes—to combat recessions or curb inflationary pressures. We will also see that a number of problems are associated with successfully enacting and applying fiscal policy to stabilize an economy. Finally, we will examine the automatic stabilizers and the national debt.

Fiscal Policy   16.1

📂 What is fiscal policy?

📂 How does expansionary fiscal policy affect the government's budget?

📂 How does contractionary fiscal policy affect the government's budget?

Fiscal Policy

Fiscal policy is the use of government purchases, taxes, and transfer payments to alter RGDP and the price level. Government spending takes two forms: government purchases of goods and services like national defense and education, and transfer payments like Social Security, Medicare, and Medicaid. So government expenditures (spending) are the sum of government purchases and government transfer payments. The government takes in the bulk of its tax revenues from three taxes: personal income taxes, corporate income taxes, and payroll taxes (like Social Security and Medicare).

Sometimes the government uses fiscal policy to stimulate the economy during a contraction (or recession) or to try to curb an expansion in order to bring inflation under control. In the early 1980s, large tax cuts helped the U.S. economy out of a recession. In the 1990s, Japan used large government spending programs to try to spend itself out of a recessionary slump. In 2001, a large tax cut was implemented to combat an economic slowdown and to promote long-term economic growth in the United States. And the fiscal stimulus package that the Obama administration enacted in 2009 to combat the recession was the largest fiscal stimulus since World War II. But that was small compared to the $2.5 trillion spent on the financial system. When should the government use such policies and how well do they work are just a couple of the questions we will address in this chapter.

fiscal policy
use of government purchases, taxes, and transfer payments to alter equilibrium output and prices

Why is government spending not the same as government purchases?

The Government and Total Spending

In a previous chapter, we learned that aggregate demand is equal to consumer spending, investment spending, government purchases, and net exports: $AD = C + I + G + (X - M)$. The government directly controls government purchases, but it can also indirectly affect aggregate demand through taxes and transfer programs. For example, an increase in taxes and/or a reduction in transfer payments can reduce disposable income and decrease consumer spending. Similarly, a decrease in taxes and/or an increase in transfer payment can increase disposable income and lead to an increase in consumer spending. The government can also influence investment spending through business taxes. For example, a tax cut for firms may increase investment spending and shift the aggregate demand curve to the right. Thus, the government can change aggregate demand in a number of ways.

global watch Japan's Fiscal Policy Experiment

Prior to the 1990s, Japan experienced several decades of rapid economic growth with only a mild recession in 1974. However, the 1990s were a different story—the exuberant bubble burst, as the stock market made a major correction and land values plunged. Consequently, consumption and investment spending—two major components of aggregate demand—fell.

In the decade of the 1990s, Japan grew at an unusually slow rate—1.2 percent per year—almost 3 percentage points below the average growth rate of the previous decade. In order to combat the recession, the Japanese launched a fiscal policy stimulus package of unprecedented tax cuts and spending increases. Government expenditures rose from slightly over 30 percent of GDP to almost 40 percent of GDP. The Japanese government spent well over a trillion dollars during the decade to heal their ailing economy. Because of the tax cuts,

government tax revenues fell from 34 percent to 31 percent of GDP. And the continued fiscal efforts, financed with lower taxes and higher government spending, led to a growing debt problem. (The debt-to-GDP ratio almost doubled in the decade of the 1990s—from 0.58 in 1991 to 1.1 in 2000.)

The results of the fiscal policy are mixed. The fiscal policy clearly did not bring about a full recovery. However, some economists argue that without the spending and tax cuts, the Japanese would have suffered a depression rather than a sustained period of slow economic growth. Other economists argue that the wasteful nature of government spending was the reason that fiscal policy was not more successful. The Japanese built bridges, railroad lines, tunnels, and highways to sparsely populated areas. It is safe to say that none of these projects would have been undertaken by the private sector. Thus, a better-designed fiscal policy might have been more effective.

⊘ SECTION QUIZ

1. Traditionally, government has used _____ to influence _____.
   a. taxing and spending; the demand side of the economy
   b. spending; the supply side of the economy
   c. supply management; the demand side of the economy
   d. demand management; the supply side of the economy
2. Contractionary fiscal policy consists of
   a. increased government spending and increased taxes.
   b. decreased government spending and decreased taxes.
   c. decreased government spending and increased taxes.
   d. increased government spending and decreased taxes.

(continued)

3. If the government wanted to move the economy out of a current recession, which of the following might be an appropriate policy action?

    a. decrease taxes

    b. increase government purchases of goods and services

    c. increase transfer payments

    d. any of the above

4. If government policy makers were worried about the inflationary potential of the economy, which of the following would be a correct fiscal policy change?

    a. increase taxes

    b. reduce transfer payments

    c. reduce government purchases

    d. all of the above

---

1. If, as part of its fiscal policy, the federal government increases its purchases of goods and services, is that an expansionary or contractionary tactic?

2. If the federal government decreases its purchases of goods and services, does the budget deficit increase or decrease?

3. If the federal government increases taxes and/or decreases transfer payments, is that an expansionary or contractionary fiscal policy?

4. If the federal government increases taxes or decreases transfer payments, does the budget deficit increase or decrease?

5. If the federal government increases government purchases and lowers taxes at the same time, does the budget deficit increase or decrease?

Answers: 1. a 2. c 3. d 4. d

Fiscal Policy and the *AD/AS* Model
16.2

📁 How can government stimulus of aggregate demand reduce unemployment?

📁 How can government reduction of aggregate demand reduce inflation?

Fiscal Policy and the AD/AS Model

The primary tools of fiscal policy, government purchases, taxes, and transfer payments, can be presented in the context of the aggregate supply and demand model. In Exhibit 1, we have used the *AD/AS* model to show how the government can use fiscal policy as either an expansionary or contractionary tool to help close a recessionary or an inflationary gap.

Expansionary Fiscal Policy to Close a Recessionary Gap

If the government decides to purchase more, cut taxes, and/or increase transfer payments, other things constant, total purchases will rise. That is, increased government purchases, tax cuts, or transfer payment increases can increase consumption, investment, and government purchases, shifting the aggregate demand curve to the right. The effect of this

How would you close a recessionary gap with fiscal policy?

increase in aggregate demand depends on the position of the macroeconomic equilibrium before the government stimulus. For example, in Exhibit 1, the initial equilibrium is at E_1, a recession scenario, with real output below potential RGDP. Starting at this point and moving along the short-run aggregate supply curve, an increase in government purchases, a tax cut, and/or an increase in transfer payments would increase the size of the budget deficit and lead to an increase in aggregate demand, ideally from AD_1 to AD_2. The result of such a change would be an increase in the price level, from PL_1 to PL_2, and an increase in RGDP, from $RGDP_1$ to $RGDP_{NR}$. If the policy change is of the right magnitude and timed appropriately, the expansionary fiscal policy might stimulate the economy, pull it out of the contraction and/or recession, and result in full employment at $RGDP_{NR}$. The recessionary gap is then closed.

Contractionary Fiscal Policy to Close an Inflationary Gap

Suppose that the price level is at PL_1 and that short-run equilibrium is at E_1, as shown in Exhibit 2. Say that the government decides to reduce its purchases, increase taxes, or reduce transfer payments. A government purchase change may directly affect aggregate demand.

A tax increase on consumers or a decrease in transfer payments will reduce households' disposable incomes, reducing purchases of consumption goods and services, and higher business taxes will reduce investment purchases. The reductions in consumption, investment, and/or government purchases will shift the aggregate demand curve leftward, ideally from AD_1 to AD_2. This lowers the price level from PL_1 to PL_2 and brings RGDP back to the full-employment level at $RGDP_{NR}$, resulting in a new short- and long-run equilibrium at E_2, and the inflationary gap is closed.

Exhibit 3 summarizes the preceding discussion of the tools available to the government for enacting fiscal policy.

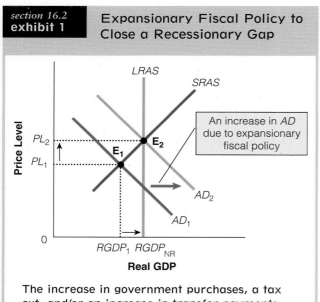

section 16.2 exhibit 1 Expansionary Fiscal Policy to Close a Recessionary Gap

The increase in government purchases, a tax cut, and/or an increase in transfer payments leads to a rightward shift in aggregate demand. This shift results in a change in equilibrium from E_1 to E_2, reflecting a higher price level and a higher RGDP. Thus, the expansionary fiscal policy can close the recessionary gap and move the economy from $RGDP_1$ to $RGDP_{NR}$. Because this result is on the *LRAS* curve, it is a long-run, sustainable equilibrium.

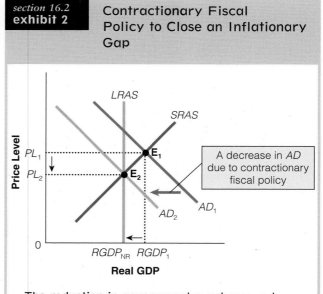

section 16.2 exhibit 2 Contractionary Fiscal Policy to Close an Inflationary Gap

The reduction in government purchases, a tax increase, or transfer payment decrease leads to a leftward shift in aggregate demand and a change in the short-run equilibrium from E_1 to E_2, reflecting a lower price level and a return to full-employment RGDP ($RGDP_{NR}$). The final long-run effect is a new lower price level and real output that has returned to $RGDP_{NR}$, and the inflationary gap is closed.

© Cengage Learning 2013

section 16.2
exhibit 3   Summary of Fiscal Policy Tools

Macroeconomic Problem	Fiscal Policy Prescription	Fiscal Policy Tools
Unemployment (Slow or negative RGDP growth rate—below $RGDP_{NR}$)	Expansionary fiscal policy to increase aggregate demand	Cut taxes Increase government purchases Increase government transfer payments
Inflation (Rapid RGDP growth rate—beyond $RGDP_{NR}$)	Contractionary fiscal policy to decrease aggregate demand	Raise taxes Decrease government purchases Decrease government transfer payments

© Cengage Learning 2013

global watch Global Tax: Revenues and Government Spending as a Percentage of GDP

In the table below, we see tax burdens for several major countries. Notice that the United States is in the middle of the pack. In fact, the U.S. tax burden is low compared to many European countries. Also, notice that some of the developing countries have lower tax burdens, like Chile, Mexico, and India. This is consistent with the history of the United States. That is, as the population of a country grows wealthier, the government often takes a larger share of income in taxes.

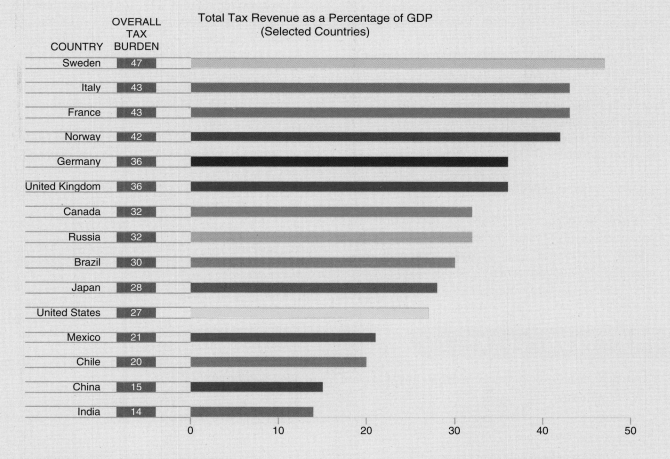

Total Tax Revenue as a Percentage of GDP (Selected Countries)

COUNTRY	OVERALL TAX BURDEN
Sweden	47
Italy	43
France	43
Norway	42
Germany	36
United Kingdom	36
Canada	32
Russia	32
Brazil	30
Japan	28
United States	27
Mexico	21
Chile	20
China	15
India	14

SOURCE: OECD (Data are for most recent date available).

POLICY application   The New Deal and Expansionary Fiscal Policy?

Roosevelt's sweep into office allowed him to push through Congress a massive amount of legislation in the first 100 days of his administration. Roosevelt did not enter the presidency with the idea that government deficit spending was a necessary stimulus to economic recovery. In fact, it was only later in his administration that he appears to have believed deficit spending would help the economy in its gravely depressed state.

Despite all of the fanfare about the first 100 days of Roosevelt's campaign for programs against the Depression, it is not really clear that they had much effect on aggregate demand. After all, besides considering what programs were instituted, we also have to look at how they were paid for and at what other programs were dropped.

In Roosevelt's campaign, he criticized Hoover for large budget deficits that had been marked up after the Crash of 1929. In fact, Hoover's administration had the largest federal deficit in the history of the United States prior to Roosevelt's election. Once elected, Roosevelt told Congress that he did not want the country to be "wrecked on the rocks of loose fiscal policy." Deficits during the Depression years were indeed small. In fact, in 1937 the total government budget, including federal, state, and local levels, had a surplus of $0.3 billion. During this time, taxes were repeatedly raised.

Fiscal policies, then, were in fact extremely weak, and even perverse. At the same time that the federal government was increasing expenditures, local and state governments were decreasing them.

If we measure the total of state, federal, and local fiscal policies, we find that they were truly expansive only in 1931 and 1936 as compared to what the government was doing prior to the Depression. These two years were expansive only because of large veterans' payments, passed by Congress in both years—by the way, over the vigorous opposition of both Hoover and Roosevelt. In both 1933 and 1937, and, to a lesser degree, in 1938, fiscal policy was quite a bit less expansionary than in 1939.

Continued tepid use of increased government spending and a slow increase in private investment led to a slow improvement, and finally by 1939 output exceeded 1929 in real terms. Because of productivity advances and a growth in the labor force, however, the return to 1929 output levels did not mean an end to unemployment. The 1939 unemployment rate of 17.2 percent was much lower than the 1933 rate, but still well above a typical unemployment rate of 5 percent.

Preparations for war in 1941 led to a 77 percent increase in government spending over the previous year. This $11 billion increase in government purchases of goods and services, followed by still greater increases in subsequent years as the United States entered World War II, led to aggregate demand increases of a magnitude to wipe out unemployment and end the Depression, which was by far the worst in U.S. history.

⑦ SECTION QUIZ

1. An increase in taxes combined with a decrease in government purchases would

   a. increase *AD*.

   b. decrease *AD*.

   c. leave *AD* unchanged.

   d. have an indeterminate effect on *AD*.

(*continued*)

2. If the economy was in a recessionary gap, in order to return to $RGDP_{NR}$, the government could

   a. decrease taxes and increase government purchases.

   b. increase taxes and increase government purchases.

   c. decrease taxes and decrease government purchases.

   d. decrease taxes and increase government purchases.

3. If the government wanted to offset the effect of a boom in consumer and investor confidence on *AD,* it might

   a. decrease government purchases.

   b. decrease taxes.

   c. increase taxes.

   d. do either (a) or (c).

4. *AD* will shift to the right, other things being equal, when

   a. the government budget deficit increases because government purchases rose.

   b. the government budget deficit increases because taxes fell.

   c. the government budget deficit increases because transfer payments rose.

   d. any of the above circumstances exist.

---

1. If the economy is in recession, what sort of fiscal policy changes would tend to bring it out of recession?

2. If the economy is at a short-run equilibrium at greater than full employment, what sort of fiscal policy changes would tend to bring the economy back to a full-employment equilibrium?

3. What effects would an expansionary fiscal policy have on the price level and real GDP, starting from a full-employment equilibrium?

4. What effects would a contractionary fiscal policy have on the price level and real GDP, starting from a full-employment equilibrium?

Answers: 1. b 2. a 3. d 4. d

The Multiplier Effect | 16.3

📁 What is the multiplier effect?

📁 How does the marginal propensity to consume affect the multiplier effect?

📁 How does investment interact with the multiplier effect?

Government Purchases, Taxes, and Aggregate Demand

Recall from our earlier discussion that any one of the major spending components of aggregate demand (*C, I, G,* or *X − M*) can initiate changes in aggregate demand, thereby producing a new short-run equilibrium. If policy makers are unhappy with the present short-run equilibrium GDP, perhaps they consider unemployment too high because of a current aggregate demand shortfall. If government were to increase its purchases of jet fighters, highways, and schools, this increased spending would lead to an increase in aggregate demand. That is, they can deliberately manipulate the level of government purchases to obtain a new short-run equilibrium value. But how much new additional government purchasing is necessary?

The Multiplier Effect

Usually, when an increase in purchases of goods or services occurs, the ultimate increase in total purchases tends to be greater than the initial increase, which is known as the **multiplier effect**. But how does this effect work? Suppose the government increases its defense budget by $10 billion to buy aircraft carriers. When the government purchases the aircraft carriers, not only does it add to the total demand for goods and services directly, but it also provides $10 billion in added income to the companies that actually construct the aircraft carriers. These companies will then hire more workers and buy more capital equipment and other inputs to produce the new output. The owners of these inputs therefore receive more income because of the increase in government purchases. What will they do with this additional income? Although behavior will vary somewhat among individuals, collectively they will probably spend a substantial part of the additional income on additional consumption purchases, pay some additional taxes incurred because of the income, and save a bit of it as well. The **marginal propensity to consume (MPC)** is the fraction of additional disposable (after-tax) income that a household consumes rather than saves. That is, MPC is equal to the *change* in consumption spending (ΔC) divided by the *change* in disposable income (ΔDY).

$$MPC = \Delta C / \Delta DY$$

For example, suppose you won a lottery prize of $1,000. You might decide to spend $750 of your winnings today and save $250. In this example, your marginal propensity to consume is 0.75 (or 75 percent), because out of the extra $1,000, you decided to spend 75 percent of it (0.75 × $1,000 = $750). The term *marginal propensity to consume* has two parts: (1) *marginal* refers to the fact that you received an *extra* amount of disposable income— an addition to your income, not your total income; and (2) *propensity to consume* refers to how much you tend to spend on consumer goods and services out of your additional income.

The flip side of the marginal propensity to consume is the **marginal propensity to save (MPS)**, which is the proportion of an addition to your income that you would save, or not spend on goods and services today. That is, MPS is equal to the change in savings (ΔS) divided by the change in disposable income (ΔDY).

$$MPS = \Delta S / \Delta DY$$

In the lottery example, your marginal propensity to save is 0.25, or 25 percent, because you decided to save 25 percent of your additional disposable income (0.25 × $1,000 = $250). Because your additional disposable income must be either consumed or saved, the marginal propensity to consume plus the marginal propensity to save must add up to 1, or 100 percent.

The Multiplier Effect at Work

Suppose that out of every dollar in *added* disposable income generated by increased investment purchases, individuals collectively spend two-thirds, or 67 cents, on consumption purchases. In other words, the MPC is 2/3. The initial $10 billion increase in government purchases causes both a $10 billion increase in aggregate demand and an income increase of $10 billion to suppliers of the inputs used to produce aircraft carriers; the owners of those inputs, in turn, will spend an additional $6.67 billion (2/3 of $10 billion) on additional consumption purchases. A chain reaction has been started. The added $6.67 billion in consumption purchases by those deriving income from the initial investment brings a

multiplier effect
a chain reaction of additional income and purchases that results in total purchases that are greater than the initial increase in purchases

marginal propensity to consume (MPC)
the additional consumption resulting from an additional dollar of disposable income

What is the marginal propensity to consume?

marginal propensity to save (MPS)
the change in savings divided by the change in disposable income

Why do the marginal propensity to consume and the marginal propensity to save add up to 1?

---

section 16.3
exhibit 1   The Multiplier Process

Change in government purchases	$10.00 billion—direct effect on *AD*
First change in consumption purchases	6.67 billion (2/3 of 10)
Second change in consumption purchases	4.44 billion (2/3 of 6.67)
Third change in consumption purchases	2.96 billion (2/3 of 4.44)
Fourth change in consumption purchases	1.98 billion (2/3 of 2.96)
Fifth change in consumption purchases	1.32 billion (2/3 of 1.98)

The sum of the indirect effect on *AD*, through induced additional consumption purchases, is equal to $20 billion

$30 billion = Total change in aggregate demand

$6.67 billion increase in aggregate demand and in new income to suppliers of the inputs that produced the goods and services. These persons, in turn, will spend some two-thirds of their additional $6.67 billion in income, or $4.44 billion, on consumption purchases. This $4.44 billion becomes aggregate demand and income to still another group of people, who will then proceed to spend two-thirds of that amount, or $2.96 billion, on consumption purchases.

The chain reaction continues, with each new round of purchases providing income to a new group of people who in turn increase their purchases. As successive changes in consumption purchases occur, the feedback becomes smaller and smaller. The added income generated and the number of resulting consumer purchases get smaller because some of the increase in income goes to savings and tax payments that do not immediately flow into greater investment or government spending. As indicated in Exhibit 1, the fifth change in consumption is indeed much smaller than the first change in consumption.

Why does each additional round of the multiplier process get smaller and smaller?

What is the total impact of the initial increase in government purchases on additional consumption and income? We can find the answer by using the multiplier formula, calculated as follows:

$$\text{Multiplier} = 1/(1 - \text{MPC})$$

In this case,

$$\text{Multiplier} = 1/(1 - 2/3) = 1/(1/3) = 3$$

An initial increase in government purchases of $10 billion will increase total purchases by $30 billion ($10 billion × 3), as the initial $10 billion in government purchases also generates an additional $20 billion in consumption.

Changes in the MPC Affect the Multiplier Process

Why does a larger marginal propensity to consume lead to a larger multiplier effect?

Note that the larger the marginal propensity to consume, the larger the multiplier effect, because relatively more additional consumption purchases out of any given income increase generates relatively larger secondary and tertiary income effects in successive rounds of the process. For example, if the MPC is 3/4, the multiplier is 4:

$$\text{Multiplier} = 1/(1 - 3/4) = 1/(1/4) = 4$$

If the MPC is only 1/2, however, the multiplier is 2:

$$\text{Multiplier} = 1/(1 - 1/2) = 1/(1/2) = 2$$

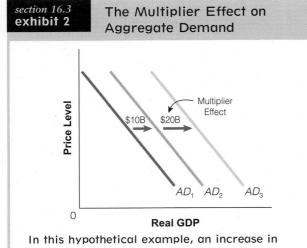

section 16.3
exhibit 2

The Multiplier Effect on Aggregate Demand

In this hypothetical example, an increase in government purchases of $10 billion for new aircraft carriers will shift the aggregate demand curve to the right by more than the $10 billion initial purchase, other things being equal. It will shift aggregate demand by a total of $30 billion, to AD_3. (The shifts are shown larger than they would really be for visual ease; $30 billion is a small shift in a $15,000 billion economy.)

The Multiplier and the Aggregate Demand Curve

As we discussed earlier, when the federal Department of Defense decides to buy additional aircraft carriers, it affects aggregate demand. It increases the incomes of owners of inputs used to make the aircraft carriers, including profits that go to the owners of the firms involved. That is the initial effect. The secondary effect—the greater income that results—will lead to increased consumer purchases. In addition, the higher profits for the firms involved in carrier construction may lead them to increase their investment purchases. So the initial effect of the government's purchases will tend to have a multiplied effect on the economy. In Exhibit 2, we can see that the initial impact of a $10 billion additional purchase by the government directly shifts the aggregate demand curve from AD_1 to AD_2. The multiplier effect then causes the aggregate demand to shift out $20 billion further, to AD_3. If MPC is 2/3, the total effect on aggregate demand of a $10 billion increase in government purchases is therefore $30 billion.

Tax Cuts and the Multiplier

If the government wants to use fiscal stimulus to move the economy to the natural rate, increased government purchases is only one alternative. The government can also stimulate business and consumer spending through tax cuts. Both Japan (1999) and the United States (2001 and 2003) have recently employed tax cuts to stimulate their economies.

How much of an *AD* shift do we get from a change in taxes? As in the case of government purchases, it depends on the marginal propensity to consume. However, the tax multiplier is smaller than the government purchases multiplier because government purchases have a direct impact on aggregate demand, while a tax cut has only an indirect impact on aggregate demand. Why? Because consumers will save some of their income from the tax cut. So if the MPC is 3/4, then when their disposable income rises by $1,000, households will increase their consumption by $750 while saving $250 of the added income.

To compare the multiplier effect of a tax cut with an increase in government purchases, suppose there were a $10 billion tax cut and that the MPC is 2/3. The initial increase in consumption spending from the tax cut would be 2/3 × $10 billion (*MPC* × tax cut) = $6.67 billion. Because in this case people would save one-third of their tax cut income, the effect on aggregate demand of the change in taxes would be smaller than that of a change of equal size in government purchases. The cumulative change in spending (the increase in *AD*) due to the $10 billion tax cut is found by plugging the initial effect of the changed consumption spending into our earlier formula: $1/(1 − MPC)$ × $6.67 billion, which is 3 × $6.67 = $20 billion. So the initial tax cut of $10 billion leads to a stimulus of $20 billion in consumer spending. Although this amount is less than the $30 billion from government purchases, it is easy to see why tax cuts and government purchases are both attractive policy prescriptions for a slow economy.

Why is the tax multiplier smaller than the government purchases multiplier?

Taxes and Investment Spending

Taxes can also stimulate investment spending. For example, if a cut in corporate-profit taxes leads to expectations of greater after-tax profits, it could fuel additional investment spending. That is, tax cuts designed for consumers and investors can stimulate both the *C* and *I* components of aggregate demand. A number of administrations have used this strategy to stimulate aggregate spending and shift the aggregate demand curve to the right: Kennedy (1963), Reagan (1981), and Bush (2001 and 2003).

A Reduction in Government Purchases and Tax Increases

Reductions in government purchases and tax increases are magnified by the multiplier effect, too. Suppose the government made cutbacks in the space program. Not only would it decrease government purchases directly, but aerospace workers would be laid off and unemployed workers would cut back on their consumption spending; this initial cutback would have a multiplying effect through the economy, leading to an even greater reduction in aggregate demand. Similarly, tax hikes would leave consumers with less disposable income, so they would cut back on their consumption, which would lower aggregate demand and set off the multiplier process, leading to an even larger cumulative effect on aggregate demand.

Does the multiplier apply to both increases and decreases in aggregate demand?

Time Lags, Saving, and Imports Reduce the Size of the Multiplier

The multiplier process is not instantaneous. If you get an additional $100 in income today, you may spend two-thirds of that on consumption purchases eventually, but you may wait six months or even longer to do it. Such time lags mean that the ultimate increase in

---

use what you've learned   The Broken Window Fallacy

Whenever a government program is justified not on its merits but by the jobs it will create, remember the broken window: Some teenagers toss a brick through a bakery window. A crowd gathers and laments, "What a shame." But before you know it, someone suggests a silver lining to the situation: Now the baker will have to spend money to have the window repaired. This will add to the income of the repairman, who will spend his additional income, which will add to another seller's income, and so on. You know the drill. The chain of spending will multiply and generate higher income and employment. If the broken window is large enough, it might produce an economic boom! . . .

Most voters fall for the broken window fallacy, but not students of economic principles. They will say, "Hey, wait a minute!" If the baker hadn't spent his money on window repair, he would have spent it on the new suit he was saving to buy. Then the tailor would have the new income to spend, and so on. The broken window didn't create net new spending; it just diverted spending from somewhere else. The broken window does not create new activity, just

different activity. People see the activity that takes place. They don't see the activity that *would* have taken place.

The broken window fallacy is perpetrated in many forms. Whenever job creation or retention is the primary objective, I call it the job-counting fallacy. Students of economics principles understand the nonintuitive reality that real progress comes from job destruction. It once took 90 percent of our population to grow our food. Now it takes 3 percent. Pardon me, but are we worse off because of the job losses in agriculture? The would-have-been farmers are now college profs and computer gurus or singing the country blues on Sixth Street.

If you want jobs for jobs' sake, trade in bulldozers for shovels. If that doesn't create enough jobs, replace shovels with spoons. But there will always be more work to do than people to work. So instead of counting jobs, we should make every job count.

purchases resulting from an initial increase in purchases may not be achieved for a year or more. The extent of the multiplier effect visible within a short time will be less than the total effect indicated by the multiplier formula. In addition, saving and money spent on import goods (which are not part of aggregate demand for domestically produced goods and services) will reduce the size of the multiplier, because each of them reduces the fraction of a given increase in income that will go to additional purchases of domestically produced consumption goods.

It is also important to note that the multiplier effect is not restricted to changes in government purchases and taxes. The multiplier effect can apply to changes that alter spending in any of the components of aggregate demand: consumption, investment, government purchases, or net exports.

Some have argued that the multiplier effect of a new sports stadium, for example, will lead to additional local spending that will be three or four times the amount of the initial investment. However, this outcome is unlikely. It is important to remember that money spent on the stadium (taxpayer dollars) could also have been spent on food, clothing, entertainment, recreation, and many other goods and services. So the expenditures on the stadium come at the expense of other consumer expenditures. In addition, the multiplier is most effective when it brings idle resources into production. If all resources are fully employed, the expansion in demand and the multiplier effect will lead to a higher price level, not increases in employment and RGDP.

The 2008–2009 Recession

The 2008–2009 recession is the worst recession since the Great Depression. It has lead to the largest peacetime fiscal expansion in history. Many countries around the world have been increasing the size of their budget deficits by cutting taxes and increasing government spending. There is debate among economists on the effectiveness of fiscal policy to stimulate the economy, and much of that debate depends on the size of the multiplier. A multiplier of 1 means that an increase in government purchases of $1 billion would increase aggregate demand and lead to an increase in $1 billion of RGDP. The economy could now have new highways, bridges, fighter jets and aircraft carriers without sacrificing other components of aggregate demand like private consumption and investment. How is this possible? The answer is that these are idle resources that are now being put to use. If the multiplier is greater than 1 it is even more magical; RGDP rises by more than than the increase in government purchases.

The Obama economists believe the multiplier for government purchases is close to 1.5 (a $1 billion increase in government purchases will increase a country's GDP by $1.5 billion) and the multiplier for taxes is closer to 1. Other economists believe that the multiplier for government purchases is much smaller, closer to 0.5. So there is debate on the size of the government purchase multiplier. And it appears that despite a $787 billion injection, the fiscal stimulus had far less impact than many policy makers anticipated.

Why is the multiplier effect on real output smaller when resources are fully employed?

However, economists do agree that the multiplier is very small—close to zero—when the economy is at or near full employment and that the effectiveness of fiscal policy depends on the type of action that is taken. For example, the short-run effect of government spending on infrastructure like highways and bridges tends to be greater than, say, that of a tax cut where individuals will save a large portion of their tax windfall. Tax cuts for poorer people may be more effective than those for richer, because the poor tend to spend a larger proportion of their additional (marginal) income. Economists also agree that tax multipliers are much higher when taxes are permanent than when they are temporary and that fiscal multipliers will be lower in heavily indebted economies than in prudent ones.

In the words of macroeconomist Robert Barro, "Do not use the cover of fiscal policy to undertake massive public works programs that do not pass muster from the perspective of cost-benefit analysis . . . it is wrong now to think that added government spending is free."

in the news   Air Force to Award $35 Billion Tanker Contract

The Air Force is poised to award one of the biggest contracts in military history—a $35 billion deal to build nearly 200 giant airborne refueling tankers. The rival companies are Chicago-based Boeing Co. and European Aeronautic Defence and Space Co.

. . . If Boeing wins, production would occur in Everett, Washington; Wichita, Kansas; and in cities in several other states. If EADS wins, the tanker would be assembled in Mobile, Alabama. The two companies say that, either way, some 50,000 jobs would be created.

ISRAEL SUN/IDF/LANDOV

In the real world, the multiplier process is important because it may help explain why small changes in consumption, investment, and government purchases can result in larger, multiplied changes in total purchases. These increased purchases, in turn, may lead to increased real output and reduced unemployment when the economy is not already fully employed. In this application, when the government purchases the refueling tankers, we are assuming that it would not have purchased other goods and services with those same dollars instead.

This assumption is important because the purchase of the refueling tankers has the potential to lead to a net increase in demand only so far as it increases total government purchases, which, if the economy is less than fully employed, will increase real output and employment. That is, the demand for the refueling tankers, other things being equal, will lead to an increase in output for Boeing or EADS (which are competing to get the defense contract to build the refueling tanker). As a result, the company that wins the contract will hire more employees, who will take their paychecks and spend some of it on clothes, restaurant meals, and other goods and services. These purchases will result in further growth in those industries, many of which are located far from the aircraft plant. In other words, a government purchase has the potential to have an impact on the economy that is greater than the magnitude of that original purchase. This is the multiplier process at work. However, if the aircraft purchases simply replace other government purchases, the multiplied expansion in defense-related industries will be offset by a multiplied contraction in industries where government purchases have fallen.

Contrast this example with government purchases of food for a school lunch program. Government purchases of school lunches rise, but private consumption falls as parents now purchase less food—perhaps by the same amount—for their children's lunches. Overall, we would expect only a small change in demand, if any, as government demand replaces private demand. In some real sense, the suppliers of apples, milk, cookies, and chips have just had the names of their customers change.

② SECTION QUIZ

1. The multiplier effect is based on the fact that _____ by one person is (are) _____ to another.

    a. income; income

    b. expenditures; expenditures

    c. expenditures; income

    d. income; expenditures

2. The expenditure multiplier is

    a. 1/MPC.

    b. 1/(1 – MPC).

    c. (1 – MPC)/1.

    d. 1/ΔMPC.

3. If the marginal propensity to consume is two-thirds, the multiplier is

    a. 30.

    b. 66.

    c. 1.5.

    d. 3.

4. The federal government buys $20 million worth of computers from Dell. If the MPC is 0.60, what will be the impact on aggregate demand, other things being equal?

    a. Aggregate demand will increase $12 million.

    b. Aggregate demand will increase $13.33 million.

    c. Aggregate demand will increase $20 million.

    d. Aggregate demand will increase $50 million.

    e. Aggregate demand will not change.

5. When taxes are increased, disposable income _____, and hence consumption _____.

    a. increases; increases

    b. increases; decreases

    c. decreases; increases

    d. decreases; decreases

    e. stays the same; stays the same

---

1. How does the multiplier effect work?

2. What is the marginal propensity to consume?

3. Why is the marginal propensity to consume always less than one?

4. Why does the multiplier effect get larger as the marginal propensity to consume gets larger?

5. If an increase in government purchases leads to a reduction in private-sector purchases, why will the effect on the economy be smaller than that indicated by the multiplier?

Answers: 1. c   2. b   3. d   4. d   5. d

Supply-Side Effects of Tax Cuts 16.4

- 📁 What is supply-side economics?
- 📁 How do supply-side policies affect long-run aggregate supply?
- 📁 What do its critics say about supply-side ideas?

What Is Supply-Side Economics?

The debate over short-run stabilization policies has been going on for some time, with no sign that it is close to being settled. When policy makers discuss methods of stabilizing the economy, the focus since the 1930s has been on managing the economy through demand-side policies. But a group of economists believes that we should be focusing on the supply side of the economy as well, especially in the long run, rather than just on the demand side. In particular, they believe that individuals will save less, work less, and provide less capital when taxes, government transfer payments (such as welfare), and regulations are too burdensome on productive activities. In other words, they believe that fiscal policy can work on the supply side of the economy as well as the demand side.

Impact of Supply-Side Policies

Supply-siders would encourage government to reduce individual and business taxes, deregulate, and increase spending on research and development. Supply-siders believe that these types of government policies could generate greater long-term economic growth by stimulating personal income, savings, and capital formation.

The Laffer Curve

High marginal income tax rates could conceivably reduce work and investment incentives and increase tax evasion to the point that government revenues are lower than they would be at some lower marginal income tax rate. Economist Arthur Laffer argued that point graphically in what has been called the Laffer curve, depicted in Exhibit 1. When marginal income tax rates are low, increasing the federal marginal tax rate will increase federal tax revenues, as shown by the movement from point B to point C in Exhibit 1. However, at higher federal marginal tax rates, disincentive effects and increased tax evasion may actually reduce federal tax revenue. Over this range of marginal income tax rates, lowering taxes may actually increase federal tax revenue. This relationship is shown by the movement from point D to point C in Exhibit 1. A high marginal income tax rate on the rich might reduce the incentive to work, save, and invest, and perhaps as important, it might produce illegal shifts in transactions to what has been termed the underground economy, meaning that people make cash and barter transactions that are difficult for any

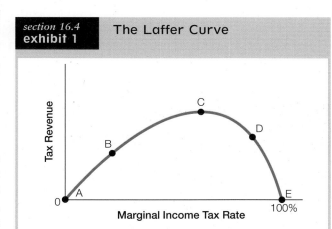

section 16.4 exhibit 1 The Laffer Curve

If the marginal income tax rate is set at 100 percent, at point E, citizens will have no incentive to work or invest and tax revenues will be zero. Tax revenues will also be zero if the tax rate is zero, at point A. If the economy has a relatively high marginal income tax rate, at point D, tax revenues could be increased by lowering the marginal income tax rate, a move toward point C. However, as marginal income tax rates are lowered beyond point C, the tax revenues fall. Moving in the other direction, from point B to point C, we see that tax revenues would increase with higher marginal income tax rates up to point C. At higher marginal income tax rates beyond point C, tax revenues would fall.

© Cengage Learning 2013

tax collector to observe. If tax evasion becomes common, the equity and revenue-raising efficiency of the tax system suffers, as does general respect for the law.

Although all economists believe that incentives matter, disagreement exists as to the shape of the Laffer curve and where the economy actually is on the Laffer curve. That is, many economists believe that tax cuts increase incentives to work and invest but current U.S. tax levels do not appear to be on the downward side of the Laffer curve. There is also no evidence that prior to the Reagan cuts of the 1980s, the average marginal tax rate was high enough that a cut in tax rates would result in larger overall tax revenues. However, it is possible that taxpayers in the high-income group were on that portion of the curve. Other studies have shown that maximum tax revenues occurred in Sweden between 70 to 80 percent marginal income tax rates. So there may actually be a point where the marginal income tax rates of a country may be so high that tax revenues will fall. Some economists believe that France might also be close to that point.

It also depends on what type of taxes. With regard to capital taxes, the United States and many developed countries may be on the left side of the Laffer curve. However, one study shows that Denmark and Sweden may be to the right of the peak on capital taxes. That is, cutting taxes might improve their budgetary situation.

Research and Development and the Supply Side of the Economy

Some economists believe that investment in research and development will have long-run benefits for the economy. In particular, greater research and development will lead to new technology and knowledge, which will permanently shift the short- and long-run aggregate supply curves to the right. The government could encourage investments in research and development by giving tax breaks or subsidies to firms. The challenge, of course, is to produce *productive* research and development.

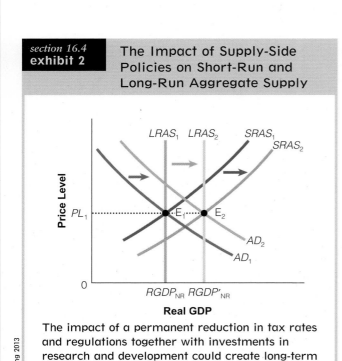

section 16.4
exhibit 2

The Impact of Supply-Side Policies on Short-Run and Long-Run Aggregate Supply

The impact of a permanent reduction in tax rates and regulations together with investments in research and development could create long-term effects on income, saving, and capital formation, shifting both the *SRAS* curve and the *LRAS* curve rightward. As income rises and is spent, the aggregate demand curve shifts to the right.

How Do Supply-Side Policies Affect Long-Run Aggregate Supply?

We see in Exhibit 2 that rather than being primarily concerned with short-run economic stabilization, supply-side policies are aimed at increasing both the short-run and long-run aggregate supply curves. If these policies are successful and maintained, output and employment will increase in the long run, as reflected in the shift from $RGDP_{NR}$ to $RGDP'_{NR}$. Both short- and long-run aggregate supply will increase over time, as the effects of deregulation and major structural changes in plant and equipment work their way through the economy. It takes workers some time to fully respond to improved work incentives.

Critics of Supply-Side Economics

Of course, those who believe in supply-side economics have their critics. These critics are skeptical about the magnitude of the impact of lower taxes on work effort and the impact of deregulation on productivity. Critics claim that the tax cuts of the 1980s led to moderate real output growth but only through a reduction in real tax revenues, inflation, and large budget deficits.

Although real economic growth followed the tax cuts, supply-side critics say that it came as a result of a large budget deficit. The critics raise several questions: What will happen to the distribution of income if most supply-side policies focus on benefits to those with capital? Will people save and invest much more if capital gains taxes are reduced (capital gains are increases in the value of an asset)? It may be more likely that saving and investment is driven by changes in income and expectations of profitability. How much more work effort will we see if marginal tax rates are lowered? The increase in the quantity of labor supplied following a tax cut is likely to be limited since most workers are already working 40 hour weeks and do not have opportunities to work more hours. Will the new production that occurs from deregulation be enough to offset the benefits thought by many to come from regulation?

The Supply-Side and Demand-Side Effects of a Tax Cut

A tax cut can lead to greater incentives to work and save—an increase in aggregate supply (short-run and long-run)—and to demand-side stimulus from the increased disposable income (income after taxes) and an increase in aggregate demand. But how much will the tax rate affect aggregate demand and aggregate supply? We do not know for sure, but let's look at two possible outcomes of the supply-side effects of a tax cut. We will focus on the aggregate demand curve and the *SRAS* curve. Suppose the tax cut leads to a large increase in *AD* but only a small increase in *SRAS*. What happens to the price level and RGDP? The more traditional view of a fiscal policy tax cut is shown in Exhibit 3(a). We can see that RGDP increases from $RGDP_1$ to $RGDP_2$ and price level increases from PL_1 to PL_2. The good news is that the price level rises less than it would if there were no supply-side effect to the tax cut. Without the supply-side effect from the tax cut, the price level would rise to PL_3. But what if the supply-side effect were much larger, as shown in Exhibit 3(b)? It could completely offset the higher price-level effect of an expansionary fiscal policy, as RGDP rises from $RGDP_1$ to $RGDP_2$ and the price level stays constant at PL_1.

Why would a tax rate reduction increase both aggregate demand and aggregate supply?

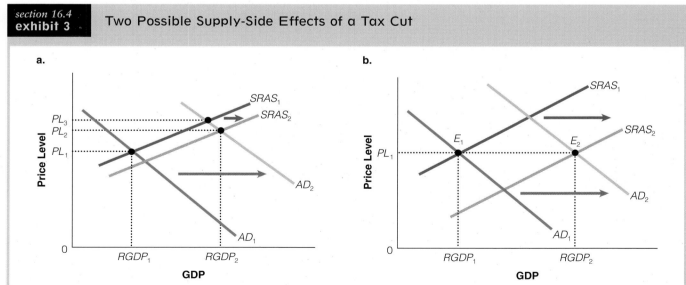

© Cengage Learning 2013

section 16.4 **exhibit 3** Two Possible Supply-Side Effects of a Tax Cut

a.

b.

If the supply-side tax cut has a small effect on the *SRAS* but a large effect on *AD*, then RGDP increases from $RGDP_1$ to $RGDP_2$, while the price level rises from PL to PL_2, as shown in (a). However, if the supply-side tax cut has a large effect on *SRAS* and a large effect on *AD*, then RGDP increases from $RGDP_1$ to $RGDP_2$, and the price level is constant at PL_1, as shown in (b).

Fiscal policy was used infrequently in the United States and Europe from the 1980s to the late 1990s because of concerns over large budget deficits. However, the budget surplus that emerged in the latter half of the 1990s opened the gate for increased government spending and the Bush tax cut in 2001. Most economists agree that taxes alter incentives and distort market outcomes, as we learned in Chapter 7. Taxes clearly change people's behavior; and the tax cuts that lead to the strongest incentives to work, save, and invest will lead to the greatest economic growth and will be the least inflationary.

ⓔSECTION QUIZ

1. Lower marginal tax rates stimulate people to work, save, and invest, resulting in more output and a larger tax base. This statement most closely reflects which of the following views?

    a. the Keynesian

    b. the multiplier view

    c. the aggregate demand theory

    d. the supply-side view

2. Other things being constant, an increase in marginal tax rates will

    a. decrease the supply of labor and reduce its productive efficiency.

    b. decrease the supply of capital and decrease its productive efficiency.

    c. encourage individuals to buy goods that are tax deductible instead of those that are more desired but nondeductible.

    d. do all of the above.

3. According to the Laffer curve,

    a. decreasing tax rates on income will always increase tax revenues.

    b. decreasing tax rates on income will always decrease tax revenues.

    c. decreasing tax rates are more likely to increase tax revenues the higher tax rates are to start with.

    d. decreasing tax rates are more likely to increase tax revenues the lower tax rates are to start with.

---

1. Is supply-side economics more concerned with short-run economic stabilization or long-run economic growth?

2. Why could you say that supply-side economics is really more about after-tax wages and after-tax returns on investment than it is about tax rates?

3. Why do government regulations have the same sort of effects on businesses as taxes?

4. Why are the full effects of supply-side policies not immediately apparent?

5. If taxes increase, what would you expect to happen to employment in the underground economy? Why?

Answers: 1. d 2. d 3. c

16.5

Possible Obstacles to Effective Fiscal Policy

📋 How does the crowding-out effect limit the economic impact of increased government purchases or reduced taxes?

📋 How do time lags in policy implementation affect policy effectiveness?

The Crowding-Out Effect

Some economists believe that fiscal policy is not as potent as we described earlier because of the crowding-out effect. The crowding-out effect occurs when household consumption and investment spending decrease as a result of financing a budget deficit. There are direct effects. For example, if the government spent more on school lunch programs, individuals might buy fewer groceries.

There are also indirect effects. If the government spends more on defense and social programs without raising taxes for those programs, the deficit will rise.

Let's see how more spending on government purchases can lead to less investment spending. The multiplier effect of an increase in government purchases implies that the increase in aggregate demand will tend to be greater than the initial fiscal stimulus, other things being equal. However, because all other things will not tend to stay equal in this case, the multiplier effect may not hold true. For example, an increase in government purchases stimulates aggregate demand. As the new spending takes place, income and real GDP will rise which will cause households and firms to increase their demand for money to accommodate increased buying and selling. The increase in the demand for money will cause the interest rate to rise. As a result of the higher interest rate, consumers may decide against buying a car, a home, or other interest-sensitive goods, and businesses may cancel or scale back plans to expand or buy new capital equipment. In short, the higher interest rate will choke off some private spending on goods and services, and as a result, the impact of the increase in government purchases may be smaller than first assumed. Economists call this the **crowding-out effect**.

In Exhibit 1, suppose government purchases initially increased by $10 billion. This change by itself would shift aggregate demand to the right by $10 billion times the multiplier, from AD_1 to AD_2. However, when the government increases its purchases of goods and services, it leads to an increase in income. The increase in income leads to an increase in the demand for money and a higher interest rate. The higher interest rate crowds out investment spending, causing the aggregate demand curve to shift left, from AD_2 to AD_3. Because both these processes are taking place at the same time, the net effect is an increase in aggregate demand from AD_1 to AD_3 rather than to AD_2.

The multiplier and crowding-out effect can also impact the size of the shift in aggregate demand from a tax change. Recall that when tax cuts stimulate consumer spending, earnings and profits rise, which further stimulates consumer spending—the multiplier effect. But the higher income leads to an increase in the demand for money, which tends to lead to higher interest rates. The higher interest rates make borrowing more costly and reduce investment spending—the crowding-out effect. Also, remember, if households view tax cuts as permanent, they are more likely to increase spending by a larger amount than if they viewed the tax as temporary.

When the government borrows to pay the deficit, can it drive up the interest rates and crowd out private consumption and investment?

crowding-out effect
theory that government borrowing drives up the interest rate, lowering consumption by households and investment spending by firms

section 16.5 **exhibit 1**	**The Crowding-Out Effect**

Government borrowing to finance a deficit leads to a higher interest rate and lower levels of private investment spending. The lower levels of private spending can crowd out the fiscal policy effect, shifting aggregate demand to the left from AD_2 to AD_3. The net effect of the fiscal policy is a small increase in aggregate demand, AD_1 to AD_3, not the larger increase from AD_1 to AD_2.

Time Lags in Fiscal Policy Implementation

How will the lag time of a fiscal policy impact its effectiveness?

It is important to recognize that in a democratic country, fiscal policy is implemented through the political process, and that process takes time. Often, the lag between the time that a fiscal response is desired and the time an appropriate policy is implemented and its effects felt is considerable. Sometimes a fiscal policy designed to deal with a contracting economy may actually take effect during a period of economic expansion, or vice versa, resulting in a stabilization policy that actually destabilizes the economy.

The Recognition Lag

Government tax or spending changes require both congressional and presidential approval. Suppose the economy is beginning a downturn. It may take two or three months before enough data are gathered to indicate the actual presence of a downturn. This time span is called the *recognition lag*. Sometimes a future downturn can be forecast through econometric models or by looking at the index of leading indicators, but usually decision makers are hesitant to plan policy on the basis of forecasts that are not always accurate.

The Implementation Lag

At some point, however, policy makers may decide that some policy change is necessary. At this point, experts are consulted, and congressional committees hold hearings and listen to testimony on possible policy approaches. During the consultation phase, many decisions have to be made. If, for example, a tax cut is recommended, what form should the cut take, and how large should it be? Across-the-board income tax reductions? Reductions in corporate taxes? More generous exemptions and deductions from the income tax (e.g., for child care, casualty losses, education of children)? In other words, who should get the benefits of lower taxes? Likewise, if the decision is made to increase government expenditures, which programs should be expanded or initiated, and by how much? Because these questions have profound political consequences, reaching decisions is seldom easy and usually involves substantial compromise and a great deal of time.

Finally, once the House and Senate have completed their separate deliberations and have arrived at a final version of the fiscal policy bill, it is presented to Congress for approval. After congressional approval is secured, the bill then goes to the president for approval or veto. These steps are all part of what is called the *implementation lag*.

During the period 1990–1991, the actual output of the economy was less than the potential output of the economy—a recessionary gap. Because automatic stabilizers resulted in lower taxes and larger transfer payments, consumption did not fall as far as it might have.

However, before President Clinton began his term in 1993, he believed that more was needed, so he put together a stimulus package of additional government spending and tax cuts. But by the time the bill reached the floor of Congress, the recession was over, illustrating how difficult it is to time fiscal stimulus. When the economy went into recession in March of 2001, it was not until a year later that the stimulus package was signed into law. Another example is when President John F. Kennedy thought the economy was operating below its potential in 1962; Congress finally passed a tax cut in 1964.

The Impact Lag

Would the impact lag generally be greater for government public works project than a tax cut?

Even after legislation is signed into law, it takes time to bring about the actual fiscal stimulus desired. If the legislation provides for a reduction in withholding taxes, for example, it might take a few months before the changes show up in workers' paychecks. With respect to changes in government purchases, the delay is usually much longer. If the government increases spending for public works projects such as sewer systems, new highways, or urban renewal, it takes time to draw up plans and get permissions, to advertise for bids from contractors, to get contracts, and then to begin work. Further delays might occur because of government regulations. For example, an environmental impact statement must be completed before most public works projects can begin, a process that often takes many months or even years, called the *impact lag*.

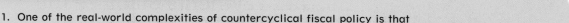

⑦ SECTION QUIZ

1. One of the real-world complexities of countercyclical fiscal policy is that
   a. fiscal policy is based on forecasts, which are not foolproof.
   b. a lag occurs between a change in fiscal policy and its effect.
   c. how much of the multiplier effect will take place in a given amount of time is uncertain.
   d. All of the above are correct.

2. According to the crowding-out effect, if the federal government borrows to finance deficit spending,
   a. the demand for money will decrease, driving interest rates down.
   b. the demand for money will increase, driving interest rates up.
   c. the supply of money will increase, driving interest rates up.
   d. the supply of money will decrease, driving interest rates down.

3. When the crowding-out effect of an increase in government purchases is included in the analysis,
   a. *AD* shifts left.
   b. *AD* doesn't change.
   c. *AD* shifts right, but by more than the simple multiplier analysis would imply.
   d. *AD* shifts right, but by less than the simple multiplier analysis would imply.

4. Which of the following statements is true?
   a. The crowding-out effect will tend to reduce the magnitude of the effects of increases in government purchases.
   b. The crowding-out effect implies that expansionary fiscal policy will tend to reduce private purchases of interest-sensitive goods.
   c. The crowding-out effect can occur as a result of direct effects (e.g., building a library may result in fewer books being purchased on Amazon).
   d. The crowding-out effect can occur as a result of financing a deficit that drives up real interest rates and crowds out private consumption and investment spending.
   e. All of the above statements are true.

---

1. Why does a larger government budget deficit increase the magnitude of the crowding-out effect?
2. Why does fiscal policy have a smaller effect on aggregate demand the greater the crowding-out effect is?
3. How do time lags affect the effectiveness of fiscal policy?

Answers: 1. d 2. b 3. d 4. e

Automatic Stabilizers

16.6

▭ What are automatic stabilizers?   ▭ Which automatic stabilizers are the most important?

Automatic Stabilizers

Some changes in government transfer payments and taxes take place automatically as business cycle conditions change, without deliberations in Congress or the executive branch of the government. Changes in government transfer payments or tax collections that automatically tend to counter business cycle fluctuations are called **automatic stabilizers**.

automatic stabilizers
changes in government transfer payments or tax collections that automatically help counter business cycle fluctuations

Automatic stabilizers work without legislative action. The stabilizers serve as shock absorbers for the economy. But the key is that they doit quickly.

How Do the Tax System and Transfer Payments Stabilize the Economy?

The most important automatic stabilizer is the tax system. Personal income taxes vary directly in amount with income and, in fact, rise or fall by greater percentages than income itself. Big increases and big decreases in GDP are both lessened by automatic changes in income tax receipts. Because incomes, earnings, and profits all fall during a recession, the government collects less in taxes. When you work less, you are paid less and therefore pay less in taxes. It's like an automatic tax cut that acts to reduce the severity of a recession. This is also true for payroll taxes, which depend on a worker's earnings, and corporate income taxes, which depend on a firm's profits. When earnings and profits fall during a recession, so do government revenues. So, like the personal income tax, the corporate income tax and payroll taxes are automatic stabilizers, too. This reduced tax burden partially offsets the magnitude of the recession. Beyond this factor, the unemployment compensation program is another source of automatic stabilization. During recessions, unemployment is usually high and unemployment compensation payments increase, providing income that will be consumed by recipients. During boom periods, such payments will fall as the number of unemployed decreases. The system of public assistance (such as food stamps, Temporary Assistance for Needy Families, and Medicaid) payments tends to be another important automatic stabilizer because the number of low-income persons eligible for some form of assistance grows during recessions (stimulating aggregate demand) and declines during booms (reducing aggregate demand). Perhaps the Great Depression would not have been so "great" if automatic stabilizers had been in place. Many had to dig into their savings and cut back on their spending, which made matters worse.

Automatic stabilizers are not strong enough to completely offset a serious recession. However, they certainly reduce the severity of a recession, without the problems associated with lags that were discussed in the last section.

Despite the shortcomings of traditional fiscal policy, it provides policy makers with another option in the event of a severe downturn. The use of fiscal policy can reassure investors and consumers that the government realizes it has the potential to make up for insufficient demand, especially if the economy is far from its potential output.

What are the advantages of automatic stabilizers?

What are the disadvantages of automatic stabilizers in a severe recession?

ⓘ SECTION QUIZ

1. Automatic stabilizers

    a. reduce the problems caused by lags, using fiscal policy as a stabilization tool.

    b. are changes in fiscal policy that act to stimulate *AD* automatically when the economy goes into recession.

    c. are changes in fiscal policy that act to restrain *AD* automatically when the economy is growing too fast.

    d. All of the above are correct.

2. During a recession, government transfer payments automatically _____ and tax revenue automatically _____.

    a. fall; falls

    b. increase; falls

    c. increase; increases

    d. fall; increases

(continued)

The National Debt   16.7

- What are budget deficits and budget surpluses?
- How is the national debt financed?
- What has happened to the federal budget balance?
- What impact does a budget deficit have on the interest rate?
- What impact does a budget surplus have on the interest rate?

Fiscal Stimulus Affects the Budget

As discussed earlier in the chapter, when government spending exceeds tax revenues, a budget deficit results. When tax revenues are greater than government spending, a budget surplus exists.

Budget Deficit:

Government Spending > Tax Revenues

Budget Surplus:

Tax Revenues > Government Spending

How Government Finances the Debt

For many years, the U.S. government ran budget deficits and built up a large federal debt. The budget deficit occurs when government expenditure exceed tax revenues in a given year. The federal, or public, debt is the total amount the federal government owes all its creditors. But how will the government pay for all of those budget deficits that have turned into debt? After all, it has to have some means of paying out the funds necessary to support government expenditures that are in excess of the funds derived from tax payments. One thing the government can do is simply print money—dollar bills. This approach was used to finance much of the Civil War budget deficit, both in the North and in the Confederate states. However, printing money to finance activities is highly inflationary and also undermines confidence in the government. Typically, the budget deficit is financed by issuing debt. The federal government in effect borrows an amount necessary to cover the deficit by issuing bonds, or IOUs, payable with interest typically at some maturity date. More specifically, the U.S. Treasury borrows by selling Treasury bills (T-bills), notes, and bonds to government agencies, banks, households, and foreigners. We also need to distinguish between the gross debt and the public debt. The gross debt includes U.S. Treasury securities purchased by U.S. federal agencies. Because the government owes this debt to itself, economists generally focus on public debt—debt held by the public excluding federal government interagency borrowing. It is important to remember that projected liabilities of programs such as Social Security and Medicare are not included in the current national debt. Adding these and other projected liabilities could more than triple the size of the public debt.

What is the difference between the gross debt and the public debt?

The total of the values of all bonds outstanding constitutes the federal debt. That is, it the amount owed by the federal government to owners of government securities. This figure does not include debt incurred by state and local government. Exhibit 1 shows the federal budget as a percentage of GDP since 1912. Notice the difference between tax revenues and government expenditures in 1945, during World War II, which is when the budget deficit was the highest. Exhibit 2 shows the projected budget until the year 2015.

Why Run a Budget Deficit?

From 1960 through 1997, the federal budget was in deficit every year except one—in 1969, the government ran a small budget surplus. Budget deficits can be important because they provide the federal government with the flexibility to respond appropriately to changing economic circumstances. For example, the government may run deficits during special emergencies such as military involvements, earthquakes, fires, or floods. The government may also use a budget deficit to avert an economic downturn.

Historically, the largest budget deficits and a growing government debt occur during war years, when defense spending escalates and taxes typically do not rise as rapidly as spending. The federal government will also typically run budget deficits during recessions, as taxes are cut and government spending increases. However, in the 1980s, deficits and debt soared in a relatively peaceful and prosperous time. In 1980, President Reagan ran a platform of lowering taxes and reducing the size of government. Although the tax cuts occurred, the reduction in the growth of government spending did not. The result was huge peacetime budget deficits and a growing national debt that continued through the early 1990s, as shown in Exhibit 1.

However, when President Clinton took office in 1993, he set a goal to reduce the budget deficit. This goal was a high priority for both Democrats and Republicans. And after nearly a decade of uninterrupted economic growth, the deficit eventually turned into a budget surplus. In 2001 the budget surplus slipped into a deficit for three primary reasons: (1) the 2001 tax cut that President Bush promised in his presidential campaign; (2) the war on terrorism and wars in Iraq and Afghanistan; and (3) the 2001 recession that led to less tax revenue and

section 16.7
exhibit 1   Federal Budget (Percentage of GDP)

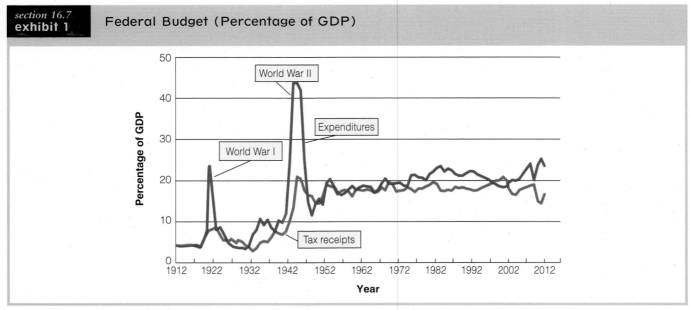

SOURCE: Economic Report of the President, 2011.
NOTE: Projections for 2011 and 2012.

section 16.7 **exhibit 2**	Public Debt Trends	
Fiscal Year	**Public Debt (billions of dollars)**	**Public Debt as a Percentage of GDP**
1929	$ 16.9	18.0%
1940	43.0	45.0
1945	260.2	120.0
1950	256.8	94.0
1955	274.4	69.0
1960	290.5	56.0
1965	322.3	47.0
1970	380.9	38.0
1975	541.9	35.0
1980	909.1	33.0
1985	1,817.5	44.0
1990	3,206.6	56.0
1995	4,921.0	67.2
2000	5,629.0	57.9
2005	7,905.3	64.6
2010	13,786.6	94.3

© Cengage Learning 2013

greater government spending. However, in looking at the future projections in Exhibit 2, it appears the United States will face large deficits for the next decade.

The Burden of Public Debt

The "burden" of the debt is a topic that has long interested economists, particularly whether the burden falls on present or future generations. Exhibit 2 shows the burden as a percentage of GDP from 1929 to 2010. Arguments can be made that the generation of taxpayers living at the time that the debt is issued shoulders the true cost of the debt, because the debt permits the government to take command of resources that might be available for other, private uses. In a sense, the resources it takes to purchase government bonds might take away from private activities, such as private investment financed by private debt. No economist can deny, however, that the issuance of debt does involve some intergenerational transfer of incomes. Long after federal debt is issued, a new generation of taxpayers is making interest payments to people of the generation that bought the bonds issued to finance that debt. But what if foreigners buy the government securities, sometimes called external national debt? This actually increases the burden of the debt on future generations of Americans, because future debt payments will go to foreigners. Almost 30 percent of the debt was held by foreigners in 2010. The positive side is that foreign investment supplements domestic saving and keeps interest rates lower than they would otherwise be.

Who bears the burden of the public debt?

However, even when foreigners hold part of the debt, if public debt is created intelligently the "burden" of the debt should be less than the benefits derived from the resources acquired as a result, particularly when the debt allows for an expansion in real economic activity or for the development of vital infrastructure for the future. The opportunity cost of expanded public activity may be small in terms of private activity that must be forgone to finance the public activity if unemployed resources are put to work. The real issue of importance is whether the government's activities have benefits that are greater than their costs; whether it is done through raising taxes, printing money, or running deficits, it is, for the most part, a "financing issue."

POLICY application   Would a Balanced Budget Amendment Work?

What are the arguments for and against balancing the budget? If we had a balanced budget, how could we allow the government to run deficits during emergencies?

From 1960 to 1998, the federal budget was in deficit every year except one, when the government ran a small balanced surplus in 1969. In 1998, the federal government ran a surplus and continued to run surpluses for the next three years. However, a series of events—the recession of 2001, the terrorist attacks, financing the wars in Iraq and Afghanistan, and a financial crisis—brought deficits back in the picture.

Some individuals believe that we must control the deficits through responsible fiscal restraint—a belief that has prompted a drive to add a balanced budget amendment to the U.S. Constitution.

But the possibility that the spending activities of the federal government may be constitutionally restricted is terrifying to some. Opponents' arguments can be summarized as follows:

First, at best, a balanced budget amendment would be ineffective because it is impossible to guarantee that revenues and expenditures will always match up on an annual basis. Second, at worst, a balanced budget amendment would reduce the fiscal flexibility of the federal government, thereby making it more difficult to respond appropriately to changing economic circumstances. Furthermore, if the public really wants the government to balance its budget, our elected representatives already have the power to respond to this desire.

It is certainly true that no amendment to the Constitution can ensure that the budget will ever be perfectly balanced. No one can exactly predict either revenues or expenditures over a specified interval. And in some circumstances, budget flexibility can be justified. Finally, it is true that Congress has the control over taxing and spending needed to eliminate the chronic deficits if it chooses to do so. Given all these factors, why should we clutter up the Constitution with a balanced budget amendment?

Proponents of a balanced budget amendment argue that, in the absence of fiscal restraints, excessive government spending will occur because the private advantages that each of us realizes from spending on our government programs are paid for almost entirely by other taxpayers. Of course, each of us suffers from having to pay for the programs of others, and most of us would be willing to reduce our special interest demands if others would do the same. But we all recognize that as long as we continue to pay for the programs of others, we enjoy no advantage from reducing our individual demands on the government treasury. In this uncontrolled setting, we are in a spending free-for-all, with penalties for the fiscally responsible and rewards for the fiscally irresponsible.

Of course, a balanced budget amendment could be written that would allow the government to run deficits in time of special emergencies such as military involvement, earthquakes, financial crises, fires, or floods. In addition, the voters might adopt a plan that would allow for a two-thirds vote to increase the deficit or that would opt for a running average balanced budget instead of balancing the budget every year. Any of these proposals could work toward controlling runaway federal spending to some degree. A balanced budget would mean greater national saving, investment and economic growth. A smaller debt would also lead to less of a burden on future generations of taxpayers. Inheriting this debt will lower future standards of living, other things equal. However, what if the deficit is reduced by cutting back on spending in education? With less education, future generations could be less productive with lower incomes. If the deficit became so large that financing the debt (sometimes called monetizing the debt) became problematic than there might be a temptation to turn to inflation to finance the debt. In addition, parents and grandparents could offset some of this problem to the extent that they save more now and bequeath larger inheritances to their children.

The most important issue of all might be at what *level* the budget should be balanced. Many would prefer deficits in a small budget to a much larger, but balanced, budget. However, the real issue, as always, is: Are we getting government goods and services with benefits that are greater than costs?

in the news Obstacle to Deficit Cutting: A Nation on Entitlements

Efforts to tame America's ballooning budget deficit could soon confront a daunting reality: Nearly half of all Americans live in a household in which someone receives government benefits, more than at any time in history.

At the same time, the fraction of American households not paying federal income taxes has also grown—to an estimated 45 percent in 2010, from 39 percent five years ago, according to the Tax Policy Center, a nonpartisan research organization. . . .

A little more than half don't earn enough to be taxed; the rest take so many credits and deductions they don't owe anything. Most still get hit with Medicare and Social Security payroll taxes, but 13 percent of all U.S. households pay neither federal income nor payroll taxes.

"We have a very large share of the American population that is getting checks from the government," says Keith Hennessey, an economic adviser to President George W. Bush and now a fellow at the conservative Hoover Institution, "and an increasingly smaller portion of the population that's paying for it."

The dimensions of the budget hole were underscored Monday, when the Treasury reported that the government ran a $1.26 trillion deficit for the first 11 months of the fiscal year, on pace to be the second-biggest on record.

Yet even as Americans express concern over the deficit in opinion polls, many oppose benefit cuts, particularly with the economy on an uneven footing. A Wall Street Journal/NBC News poll conducted late last month found 61 percent of voters were "enthusiastic" or "comfortable" with congressional candidates who support cutting federal spending in general. But 56 percent expressed the same enthusiasm for candidates who voted to extend unemployment benefits.

As recently as the early 1980s, about 30 percent of Americans lived in households in which an individual was receiving Social Security, subsidized housing, jobless benefits or other government-provided benefits. By the third quarter of 2008, 44 percent were, according to the most recent Census Bureau data.

That number has undoubtedly gone up, as the recession has hammered incomes. Some 41.3 million people were on food stamps as of June 2010, for instance, up 45 percent from June 2008. With unemployment high and federal jobless benefits now available for up to 99 weeks, 9.7 million unemployed workers were receiving checks in late August 2010, more than twice as many as the 4.2 million in August 2008.

Still more Americans—19 million by 2019, according to the Congressional Budget Office—will get federal aid to buy health insurance when legislation passed this year is implemented. . . .

. . . Government data don't show how many of the households receiving government benefits also escape federal taxes. But there is certainly some overlap between the two groups, since many benefits are aimed at those earning too little to pay income taxes and at people who don't have jobs, and who thus don't pay payroll taxes.

Cutting spending on these "entitlements" is widely seen as an inevitable ingredient in any credible deficit-reduction program. Yet despite occasional bouts of belt-tightening in Washington and bursts of discussion about restraining big government, the trend toward more Americans receiving government benefits of one sort or another has continued for more than 70 years—and shows no sign of abating.

An aging population is adding to the ranks of Americans receiving government benefits, and will continue to do so as more of the large baby-boom generation, those born between 1946 and 1964, become eligible. Today, an estimated 47.4 million people are enrolled in Medicare, up 38 percent from 1990. By 2030, the number is projected to be 80.4 million.

The difficulty of restraining benefits when so much of the population depends on them is now

(continued)

in the news   Obstacle to Deficit Cutting: A Nation on Entitlements (Cont.)

on view across Europe, where efforts to rein in deficits are forcing governments to cut popular entitlements. European countries have traditionally provided far more generous welfare benefits than the United States has, including monthly allowances for children regardless of income, free college tuition and universal health care. Public retirement programs are also bigger, since the combination of aging populations and low birth rates means fewer workers are paying into the system.

In recent months, political leaders in Europe have struggled to convince voters that change is necessary. German Chancellor Angela Merkel has exempted pensions from her government's planned budget cuts, reflecting the growing power of the retiree vote. French President Nicolas Sarkozy is facing mass protests, including a national strike week, as he tries to raise France's minimum retirement age from 60 to 62. Greece's government had to face down demonstrations this year when it slashed pension benefits, as it was forced to do to get bailout money from other European countries and the International Monetary Fund.

Still, Europe does offer examples that change is possible. Germany slashed benefits for the long-term unemployed in 2004, a step that analysts credit with prompting more Germans to get jobs as well as improving the country's budget balance. Cuts to entitlements are politically possible, says Daniel Gros, director of the Center for European Policy Studies, a nonpartisan think tank in Brussels, "but societies need some time to get used to the idea."

The U.S. government first offered large-scale assistance during Franklin Delano Roosevelt's New Deal. The Social Security Act, passed in 1935, created the popular retirement program as well as unemployment compensation, the early stages of what became known as "welfare" and assistance to the blind and elderly. In the 1940s, the G.I. Bill offered unemployment benefits, education assistance and loans to veterans. That same decade, Washington began offering free or reduced-price lunches to children from low-income families and, a decade later, monthly benefits to the disabled.

Lyndon Johnson's Great Society programs brought food stamps plus Medicare and Medicaid. In the 1970s, Supplemental Security Income was created on top of routine Social Security benefits for the poorest of the elderly and disabled, and so-called Section 8 vouchers began subsidizing rental housing. The earned-income tax credit was launched in 1975 to offer extra cash to lowwage workers, and grew in the 1990s to become one of the government's principle antipoverty programs.

Benefits for children were expanded in 1997 with the State Children's Health Insurance Program during the Clinton administration—and were expanded again in 2009. Shortly after President Barack Obama took office, Congress passed the American Recovery and Reinvestment Act, the stimulus bill, which among other things extended unemployment compensation and offered incentives for states to cover more workers.

All this is expensive. Payments to individuals—a budget category that includes all federal benefit programs plus retirement benefits for federal workers—will cost $2.4 trillion this year, up 79 percent, adjusted for inflation, from a decade earlier when the economy was stronger. That represents 64.3 percent of all federal outlays, the highest percentage in the 70 years the government has been measuring it. The figure was 46.7 percent in 1990 and 26.2 percent in 1960.

When the economy recovers, some—but not all—current recipients of federal aid are likely to lose their benefits, which some say is reason enough to keep them going for now.

. . . Cutting federal benefits while the economy is still weak would be a mistake, some analysts say, because it could hinder recovery by giving consumers less money to spend.

SOURCE: "Obstacle to Deficit Cutting: A Nation on Entitlements," by Sara Murray, WSJ, 09/14/2010. Reprinted with permission of WSJ, Copyright © 2010, Dow Jones & Company, Inc. All Rights Reserved Worldwide.

⊘ SECTION QUIZ

1. How does the government finance budget deficits?

   a. The Federal Reserve creates new money.

   b. It issues debt to government agencies, private institutions, and private investors.

   c. It is primarily financed by foreign investors.

   d. It does nothing to finance budget deficits.

2. When government debt is financed internally, future generations will

   a. inherit a lower tax liability.

   b. inherit neither higher taxes nor interest payment liability.

   c. inherit higher taxes.

   d. do none of the above.

3. Higher budget deficits would tend to

   a. raise interest rates.

   b. reduce investment.

   c. reduce the growth rate of the capital stock.

   d. do all of the above.

---

1. What will happen to the interest rate when a budget deficit occurs?

2. What will happen to the interest rate when a budget surplus occurs?

3. What are the intergenerational effects of a national debt?

4. What must be true for Americans to be better off as a result of an increase in the national debt?

Answers: 1. b   2. c   3. d

Interactive Summary

Fill in the blanks:

1. _____ is the use of government spending and/or taxes to alter real GDP and price levels.

2. When government spending (for purchases of goods and services and transfer payments) exceeds tax revenues, the result is a budget _____.

3. When the government wishes to stimulate the economy by increasing aggregate demand, it will _____ government purchases of goods and services, _____ taxes, or use some combination of these approaches.

4. Expansionary fiscal policy is associated with _____ government budget deficits.

5. If the government wishes to dampen a boom in the economy, it will _____ its purchases of goods and services, _____ taxes, or use some combination of these approaches.

6. By changing tax rates, the government can alter the amount of _____ income of households and thereby bring about changes in _____ purchases.

7. Increased budget _____ will stimulate the economy when it is operating at less than full capacity.

8. The result of an expansionary fiscal policy in the short run would be a(n) _____ in the price level and a(n) _____ in RGDP.

9. If the government wants to use fiscal policy to help "cool off" the economy when it has overheated and inflation has become a serious problem, it will tend to _____ government purchases and/or _____ taxes.

10. A tax _____ on consumers will reduce households' disposable incomes and thus their purchases of _____ goods and services, while higher business taxes will reduce _____ purchases.

11. Contractionary fiscal policy will result in a(n) _____ price level and _____ employment in the short run.

12. The _____ effect explains why, when an initial increase in purchases of goods or services occurs, the ultimate increase in total purchases will tend to be greater than the initial increase.

13. When the government purchases additional goods and services, not only does it add to the total demand for goods and services directly, but the purchases also add to people's _____.

14. When people's incomes rise because of increased government purchases of goods and services, collectively people will spend a substantial part of the additional income on additional _____ purchases.

15. The additional consumption purchases made as a portion of one's additional income is measured by the _____.

16. With each additional round of the multiplier process, the added income generated and the resulting consumer purchases get _____ because some of each round's increase in income goes to _____ and _____ payments.

17. _____ is equal to 1/(1 – MPC).

18. The larger the marginal propensity to consume, the _____ the multiplier effect.

19. If the marginal propensity to consume were smaller, a given increase in government purchases would have a(n) _____ effect on consumption purchases.

20. The extent of the multiplier effect visible within a short time period will be _____ than the total effect indicated by the multiplier formula.

21. The multiplier effect triggered by an increase in spending arises because of the additional _____ spending that it leads to.

22. If your MPC were equal to 0.7, your MPS would equal _____.

23. Savings and money spent on imported goods will each _____ the size of the multiplier.

24. The multiplier effect of an increase in government purchases implies that the increase in aggregate demand will tend to be _____ than the initial fiscal stimulus, other things being equal.

25. Supply-side economists believe that individuals will save _____, work _____,

and provide _____ capital when taxes, government transfer payments (such as welfare), and regulations are too burdensome on productive activities.

26. The _____ curve shows that high tax rates could conceivably reduce work incentives to the point that government revenues are lower at high marginal tax rates than they would be at somewhat lower rates.

27. If the demand-side stimulus from reduced tax rates is _____ than the supply-side effects, the result will be a higher price level and a greater level of real output.

28. Changes in government transfer payments or tax collections that automatically tend to counter business cycle fluctuations are called _____.

29. The most important automatic stabilizer is the _____ system.

30. Big increases and big decreases in GDP are both _____ by automatic changes in income tax receipts.

31. Because incomes, earnings, and profits all fall during a recession, the government collects _____ in taxes. This reduced tax burden partially _____ any contractionary fall in aggregate demand.

32. When the government borrows money to finance a deficit, it _____ the overall demand for money in the money market, driving interest rates _____.

33. The _____ effect refers to the theory that when the government borrows money to finance a deficit, it drives interest rates up, choking off some private spending on goods and services.

34. The monetary authorities could _____ the money supply to offset the _____ interest rates due to the crowding-out effect of expansionary fiscal policy.

35. Expansionary fiscal policy will tend to _____ the demand for dollars relative to other currencies.

36. Expansionary fiscal policy will tend to cause net exports to _____.

37. The larger the crowding-out effect, the _____ the actual effect of a given change in fiscal policy.

38. Because of the _____ in implementing fiscal policy, a fiscal policy designed to deal with a contracting economy may actually take effect during a period of economic expansion.

39. Timed correctly, contractionary fiscal policy could correct a(n) _____; timed incorrectly, it could cause a(n) _____.

40. If the federal government is running a(n) _____, the federal debt would be getting smaller.

41. Historically, the largest budget deficits have tended to be in _____ years.

42. Deficit reduction is a(n) _____ fiscal policy in the short run.

43. _____ a federal budget deficit could be an appropriate fiscal policy if the economy were in a recession.

44. If unemployed resources are put to work by government spending, the opportunity cost of expanded public activity would be _____ than otherwise.

45. Starting at a full-employment equilibrium, the only long-term effect of an increase in aggregate demand will be an increase in the _____ level.

46. Starting at a full-employment equilibrium, once the economy has returned to its long-run equilibrium after an increase in government purchases, employment will be _____ full employment.

Answers: 1. Fiscal policy 2. deficit 3. increase; increase 4. increased 5. reduce; increase 6. disposable; consumption 7. deficits 8. increase; increase 9. reduce; increase 10. increase; consumption; investment 11. lower; lower 12. multiplier 13. incomes 14. consumption 15. marginal propensity to consume 16. smaller; savings; tax 17. The expenditure multiplier 18. larger 19. smaller 20. less 21. consumption 22. 0.3 23. reduce 24. greater 25. less; less; less 26. Laffer 27. greater 28. automatic stabilizers 29. tax 30. lessened 31. less; offsets 32. increases 33. crowding-out 34. increase; higher 35. increases up 36. fall 37. smaller 38. time lags 39. inflationary boom; recession 40. surplus 41. war 42. contractionary 43. Increasing 44. lower 45. price 46. equal to

Key Terms and Concepts

fiscal policy 445
multiplier effect 452
marginal propensity to
consume (MPC) 452

marginal propensity to
save (MPS) 452

crowding-out effect 463
automatic stabilizers 465

Section Quiz Answers

16.1 Fiscal Policy

1. **If, as part of its fiscal policy, the federal government increases its purchases of goods and services, is that an expansionary or contractionary tactic?**
   An increase in government purchases of goods and services would be an expansionary tactic, increasing aggregate demand, other things equal.

2. **If the federal government decreases its purchases of goods and services, does the budget deficit increase or decrease?**
   If the federal government decreased its purchases of goods and services, for a given level of tax revenue, the budget deficit (the difference between government spending and government revenues) would decrease.

3. **If the federal government increases taxes and/or decreases transfer payments, is that an expansionary or contractionary fiscal policy?**
   Either an increase in taxes or a decrease in transfer payment would be a contractionary tactic, decreasing aggregate demand by decreasing people's disposable incomes and therefore reducing the demand for consumption goods.

4. **If the federal government increases taxes or decreases transfer payments, does the budget deficit increase or decrease?**
   If the federal government increased taxes or decreased transfer payments, for a given level of government purchases, a budget deficit (the difference between government spending and government revenues) would decrease.

5. **If the federal government increases government purchases and lowers taxes at the same time, does the budget deficit increase or decrease?**

Increased government purchases would increase a budget deficit, other things equal. Lowered taxes would also increase a budget deficit, other things equal. Therefore, both changes together would increase a budget deficit.

16.2 Fiscal Policy and the *AD/AS* Model

1. **If the economy is in recession, what sort of fiscal policy changes would tend to bring it out of recession?**

If the economy is in recession, aggregate demand intersects short-run aggregate supply to the left of the long-run aggregate supply curve. Expansionary fiscal policy—increased government purchases, decreased taxes, and/or increased transfer payments—addresses a recession by shifting aggregate demand to the right.

2. **If the economy is at a short-run equilibrium at greater than full employment, what sort of fiscal policy changes would tend to bring the economy back to a full-employment equilibrium?**

If the economy is at a short-run equilibrium at greater than full employment, aggregate demand intersects short-run aggregate supply to the right of the long-run aggregate supply curve. Contractionary fiscal policy—decreased government purchases, increased taxes, and/or decreased transfer payments—addresses a short-run equilibrium at greater than full employment by shifting aggregate demand to the left.

3. **What effects would an expansionary fiscal policy have on the price level and real GDP, starting from a full-employment equilibrium?**

Starting from a full-employment equilibrium, an expansionary fiscal policy would increase aggregate demand, increasing the price level and real GDP in the short run. However, in the long run, real GDP will return to its full-employment long-run equilibrium level as input prices adjust (the short-run aggregate supply curve shifts up or left), and only the price level will end up higher.

4. **What effects would a contractionary fiscal policy have on the price level and real GDP, starting from a full-employment equilibrium?**

Starting from a full-employment equilibrium, a contractionary fiscal policy would decrease aggregate demand, decreasing the price level and real GDP in the short run. However, in the long run, real GDP will return to its full-employment long-run equilibrium level as input prices adjust (the short-run aggregate supply curve shifts down or right), and the price level will end up lower.

16.3 The Multiplier Effect

1. **How does the multiplier effect work?**

The multiplier effect occurs because the increased purchases during each "round" of the multiplier process generate increased incomes for the owners of the resources used to produce the goods purchased, which leads them to increase consumption purchases in the next "round" of the process. The result is a final increase in total purchases, including the induced consumption purchases, that is greater than the initial increase in purchases.

2. **What is the marginal propensity to consume?**

The marginal propensity to consume is the proportion of an additional dollar of income that would be spent on additional consumption purchases.

3. **Why is the marginal propensity to consume always less than one?**

This is true because all expenditures ultimately have to be financed out of income, so each dollar of added income cannot lead to more than a dollar of added purchases. In addition, taxes and savings also have to be financed out of income.

4. **Why does the multiplier effect get larger as the marginal propensity to consume gets larger?**

The larger the marginal propensity to consume, the larger the fraction of increased income in each "round" of the multiplier process that will go to additional consumption purchases. Since each round of the multiplier process will therefore be larger the greater the marginal propensity to consume, the multiplier will also be larger.

5. **If an increase in government purchases leads to a reduction in private-sector purchases, why will the effect on the economy be smaller than that indicated by the multiplier?**

At the same time that the increased government purchases are leading to a multiple expansion of income and purchases for one set of citizens, the "crowded-out" private-sector purchases are causing a multiple contraction of income and purchases for other citizens. The net effect on the economy will therefore be smaller than the increase in government purchases times the multiplier.

16.4 Supply-Side Effects of Tax Cuts

1. Is supply-side economics more concerned with short-run economic stabilization or long-run economic growth?

Supply-side economics is more concerned with long-run economic growth than short-run economic stabilization. It is focused primarily on adopting policies that will increase the long-run aggregate supply curve (society's production possibilities curve) over time, by increasing incentives to work, save, and invest.

2. Why could you say that supply-side economics is really more about after-tax wages and after-tax returns on investment than it is about tax rates?

Changes in after-tax wages and after-tax returns on investment are the incentives that change people's behavior, not changes in the tax rates themselves.

3. Why do government regulations have the same sort of effects on businesses as taxes?

To the extent that government regulations impose added costs on businesses, the effects of these added costs are the same—a decrease (leftward or upward shift) in supply—as if a tax of that amount were imposed on the business.

4. Why are the full effects of supply-side policies not immediately apparent?

It often takes a substantial period of time before improved productivity incentives have their complete effects. For instance, an increase in the after-tax return on investment will increase investment, but it will take many years before the capital stock has completed its adjustment. The same is true for human capital investments in education, research and development, and so forth—if a student or researcher learns more today, the full effect won't be observed immediately.

5. If taxes increase, what would you expect to happen to employment in the underground economy? Why?

The primary benefit of employment in the underground economy is the savings due to not having to pay taxes (or bear some of the costs of regulations imposed on legitimate employment). The cost includes the risk of being caught, the difficulty of dealing on a cash-only or barter basis, and so on. As tax rates increase, the benefits of working in the underground economy increase relative to the costs, and employment in the underground economy will tend to increase, other things being equal.

16.5 Possible Obstacles to Effective Fiscal Policy

1. Why does a larger government budget deficit increase the magnitude of the crowding-out effect?

A larger government budget deficit increases the demand for loanable funds, thereby increasing the magnitude of the increase in interest rates and crowding out more private-sector investment as a result.

2. Why does fiscal policy have a smaller effect on aggregate demand the greater the crowding-out effect is?

The greater the crowding-out effect, the smaller the net effect (the increase in government purchases minus the private-sector purchases crowded out) fiscal policy has on aggregate demand. For example, if each dollar of added government purchases crowds out 50 cents worth of private-sector purchases, fiscal policy will have only half the effect on aggregate demand that it would if there were no crowding-out effect.

3. How do time lags affect the effectiveness of fiscal policy?

The time lag between when a policy change is desirable and when it is adopted and implemented (for data gathering, decision making, etc.), as well as the time lag between when a policy is implemented and when it has its effects, makes it difficult for fiscal policy to have the desired effect at the desired time, particularly given the difficulty in forecasting the future course of the economy.

16.6 Automatic Stabilizers

1. How does the tax system act as an automatic stabilizer?

Some taxes, such as progressive income taxes and corporate profits taxes, automatically increase as the economy grows, and this increase in taxes restrains disposable income and the growth of aggregate demand below what it would have been otherwise. Similarly, they automatically decrease in recessions, and this decrease in taxes increases disposable income and acts as a partial offset to the fall in aggregate demand. The result is reduced business cycle instability.

2. Are automatic stabilizers affected by a time lag? Why or why not?

Since automatic stabilizers respond to business cycle changes without the need for legislative or executive action, there is no appreciable lag between when business cycle conditions justify a change in them and when they do change. However, there is still a lag between when those stabilizers change and when their full effects are felt.

3. Why are transfer payments such as unemployment compensation effective automatic stabilizers?

Some transfer payment programs, such as unemployment compensation, act as automatic stabilizers because when business cycle conditions worsen, people can start receiving increased transfer payments as soon as they become eligible (lose their jobs, in the case of unemployment compensation). The same is true of some other welfare-type programs, such as food stamps.

16.7 The National Debt

1. What will happen to the interest rate when a budget deficit occurs?

When the government borrows to finance a budget deficit, it causes the interest rate to rise, other things equal.

2. What will happen to the interest rate when a budget surplus occurs?

When there is a budget surplus, it adds to national saving and lowers the interest rate, other things equal.

3. What are the intergenerational effects of a national debt?

Arguments can be made that the generation of the taxpayers living at the time that the debt is issued shoulders the true cost of the debt, because the debt permits the government to take command of resources that would be available for other, private uses. However, the issuance of debt does involve some intergenerational transfer of incomes. Long after federal debt is issued, a new generation of taxpayers is making interest payments to persons of the generation that bought the bonds issued to finance that debt. If public debt is created intelligently, however, the "burden" of the debt should be less than the benefits derived from the resources acquired as a result; this is particularly true when the debt allows for an expansion in real economic activity or for the development of vital infrastructure for the future.

4. What must be true for Americans to be better off as a result of an increase in the national debt?

For Americans to be better off as a result of an increase in the federal debt, the value of the investments and other spending financed by the debt must be greater than the cost of financing it.

Problems

1. Why are federal government actions that increase deficits considered expansionary fiscal policy and those that decrease deficits considered contractionary fiscal policy?

2. Are increases in both government purchases and net taxes at the same time expansionary or contractionary? Would both changes together increase or decrease the federal government deficit?

3. Answer the following questions.
   a. If the current budget shows a surplus, what would an increase in government purchases do to it?
   b. What would that increase in government purchases do to aggregate demand?
   c. When would an increase in government purchases be an appropriate countercyclical fiscal policy?

4. Answer the following questions.
   a. If the current budget shows a deficit, what would an increase in taxes do to it?
   b. What would that increase in taxes do to aggregate demand?
   c. When would an increase in taxes be an appropriate contractionary fiscal policy?

5. Use the accompanying diagram to answer the following questions.

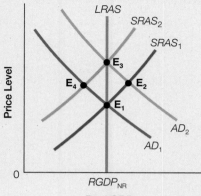

a. At what short-run equilibrium point might expansionary fiscal policy make sense to help stabilize the economy?
b. What would be the result of appropriate fiscal policy in that case?
c. What would be the long-run result if no fiscal policy action were taken in that case?
d. At what short-run equilibrium point might contractionary fiscal policy make sense to help stabilize the economy?
e. What would be the result of appropriate fiscal policy in that case?
f. What would be the long-run result if no fiscal policy action were taken in that case?

6. What is a recessionary gap? What would be the appropriate fiscal policy to combat or offset one? What is an inflationary gap? What would be the appropriate fiscal policy to combat or offset one?

7. What would the multiplier be if the marginal propensity to consume was
   a. 1/3?
   b. 1/2?
   c. 3/4?

8. If government purchases increased by $20 billion, other things being equal, what would be the resulting change in aggregate demand, and how much of that change would be a change in consumption, if the MPC were
   a. 1/3?
   b. 1/2?
   c. 2/3?
   d. 3/4?
   e. 4/5?

9. Could the multiplier be written as 1 divided by the marginal propensity to save (MPS)?

10. Why does it take a larger reduction in taxes to create the same increase in AD as a given increase in government purchases?

11. Explain why an equal dollar increase in both government purchases and net taxes would increase aggregate demand.

12. Use the accompanying diagram to answer the following questions.

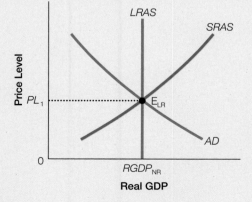

a. Starting from the initial equilibrium in the diagram, illustrate the case of a supply-side fiscal policy that left the price level unchanged.

b. Compared to your answer in (a), when would a supply-side fiscal policy result in an increase in the price level?

13. Why can a decrease in tax rates increase *AS* as well as *AD*, whereas an increase in government purchases will increase *AD* but not *AS*?

14. How do automatic stabilizers affect budget deficits and surpluses? How would automatic stabilizers be affected by an annually balanced budget rule?

15. Why do automatic stabilizers minimize the lag problem with fiscal policy?

16. Answer the following questions:
    a. Describe the crowding-out effect of an increase in government purchases.
    b. Why does the magnitude of the crowding-out effect depend on how responsive interest rates are to increased government borrowing and how responsive investment is to changes in interest rates?
    c. How would the size of the crowding-out effect affect the size of the change in aggregate demand that would result from a given increase in government purchases?

Monetary Institutions

Money is very important to the economy. Recall the circular flow model in which households trade money for the goods and services they buy in product markets, and firms exchange money for inputs they buy to produce the goods and services they sell in factor markets. In this chapter, we will discuss the different forms of money, the different functions of money, and how banks create money. We will learn how the Federal Reserve works to keep banks safe. At the end of the chapter, we will examine some periods of bank failure in the twentieth century.

17.1

What Is Money?

📁 What is money?

📁 Is using money better than barter?

📁 How does money lower the costs of making transactions?

📁 How does money serve as a store of value?

money
anything generally accepted in exchange for goods or services

What is a medium of exchange? Why is it important?

Money is anything that is generally accepted in exchange for goods and services. In colonial times, commodities such as tobacco and wampum (Native American trinkets, such as shells) were sometimes used as money. At some times and in some places, even cigarettes and whiskey have been used as money. Using commodities as money has several disadvantages, however, the most important of which is that many commodities deteriorate easily after a few trades. Precious metal coins have been used for money for millennia, partly because of their durability.

The Functions of Money

Money has four important functions in the economy: it acts as a medium of exchange, a unit of account, a store of value, and a means of deferred payment. Let's examine the four important functions of money and see how they are different than other assets in the economy like stocks, bonds, art, real estate, and a comic book collection.

medium of exchange
the primary function of money, which is to facilitate transactions and lower transaction costs

The primary function of money is to serve as a **medium of exchange**, to facilitate transactions, and to lower transaction costs. That is, sellers will accept it as payment in a transaction. However, money is not the only medium of exchange; rather, it is the only medium that is generally accepted for most transactions. How would people trade with one another in the absence of money? They would barter for goods and services that they desire.

barter
direct exchange of goods and services without the use of money

The Barter System Is Inefficient

Under a barter system, individuals pay for goods or services by offering other goods and services in exchange. Suppose you are a farmer who needs some salt. You go to the merchant selling salt and offer her 30 pounds of wheat for 2 pounds of salt. The wheat that you use to buy the salt is not money, because the salt merchant may not want wheat and therefore may not accept it as payment. This issue is one of the major disadvantages of barter: The buyer may not have appropriate items of value to the seller. The salt merchant may reluctantly take the wheat that she does not want, later bartering it away to another customer for something that she does want. In any case, barter is inefficient because several trades may be necessary to receive the desired goods. That is, the problem with barter is that it requires a double coincidence of wants both traders must be willing to trade their products with each other. Money solves the problem of double coincidence of wants because people will accept money for the items they sell.

Moreover, barter is extremely expensive over long distances. What would it cost me, living in California, to send wheat to Maine in return for an item in the L.L. Bean catalog? It is much cheaper to mail a check. Finally, barter is time consuming because of difficulties in determining the value of the product that is being offered for barter. For example, the person selling the salt may wish to inspect the wheat first to

Why is barter so inefficient?

Tobacco was once used as money in colonial America—in particular, in Virginia and Maryland. Tobacco was used rather than other commodities because it was resistant to spoilage. In the seventeenth century, colonists used wampum (polished shells) as lawful money. The ancient Chinese used chisels for money, while other societies have used fish and cattle and, of course, gold coins as money.

in the news Mackerel Economics in Prison Leads to Appreciation for Oily Fillets

When Larry Levine helped prepare divorce papers for a client a few years ago, he got paid in mackerel. Once the case ended, he says, "I had a stack of macks."

Mr. Levine and his client were prisoners in California's Lompoc Federal Correctional Complex. Like other federal inmates around the country, they found a can of mackerel—the "mack" in prison lingo—was the standard currency.

"It's the coin of the realm," says Mark Bailey, who paid Mr. Levine in fish. Mr. Bailey was serving a two-year tax-fraud sentence in connection with a chain of strip clubs he owned. Mr. Levine was serving a nine-year term for drug dealing. Mr. Levine says he used his macks to get his beard trimmed, his clothes pressed and his shoes shined by other prisoners. "A haircut is two macks," he says, as an expected tip for inmates who work in the prison barber shop.

There's been a mackerel economy in federal prisons since about 2004, former inmates and some prison consultants say. That's when federal prisons prohibited smoking and, by default, the cigarette pack, which was the earlier gold standard.

Prisoners need a proxy for the dollar because they're not allowed to possess cash. Money they get from prison jobs (which pay a maximum of 40 cents an hour, according to the Federal Bureau of Prisons) or family members goes into commissary accounts that let them buy things such as food and toiletries. After the smokes disappeared, inmates turned to other items on the commissary menu to use as currency.

Books of stamps were one easy alternative. "It was like half a book for a piece of fruit," says Tony Serra, a well-known San Francisco criminal-defense attorney who last year finished nine months in Lompoc on tax charges. Elsewhere in the West, prisoners use PowerBars or cans of tuna, says Ed Bales, a consultant who advises people who are headed to prison. But in much of the federal prison system, he says, mackerel has become the currency of choice.

Mackerel supplier Global Source Marketing Inc. says demand from prisons has grown since 2004. In recent years, demand has switched from cans—which wardens don't like because inmates can turn them into makeshift knives—to plastic-and-foil pouches of mackerel fillets, says Jon Linder, a vice president at supplier Power Commissary Inc., in Bohemia, New York.

Mackerel is hot in prisons in the United States, but not so much anywhere else, says Mark Muntz, president of Global Source, which imports fillets of the oily, dark-fleshed fish from Asian canneries. Mr. Muntz says he's tried marketing mackerel to discount retailers. "We've even tried 99-cent stores," he says. "It never has done very well at all, regardless of the retailer, but it's very popular in the prisons."

Mr. Muntz says he sold more than $1 million of mackerel for federal prison commissaries last year. It accounted for about half his commissary sales, he says, outstripping the canned tuna, crab, chicken, and oysters he offers.

Unlike those more expensive delicacies, former prisoners say, the mack is a good stand-in for the greenback because each can (or pouch) costs about $1 and few—other than weight-lifters craving protein—want to eat it.

So inmates stash macks in lockers provided by the prison and use them to buy goods, including illicit ones such as stolen food and home-brewed "prison hooch," as well as services, such as shoe-shines and cell cleaning.

The Bureau of Prisons views any bartering among prisoners as fishy. "We are aware that inmates attempt to trade amongst themselves items that are purchased from the commissary," says bureau spokeswoman Felicia Ponce in an email. She says guards respond by limiting the amount of goods prisoners can stockpile. Those who are caught bartering can end up in the "Special Housing Unit"—an isolation area also known as the "hole"—and could lose credit they get for good behavior.

(continued)

in the news Mackerel Economics in Prison Leads to Appreciation for Oily Fillets (Cont.)

For that reason—and since communications between inmates and nonprisoners are monitored by prison officials—current inmates can't discuss mackerel transactions without risking discipline, say several lawyers and consultants who represent incarcerated clients.

. . . "I paid gambling debts" with mackerel, he says. "One time I bought cigarettes for a friend who was in the hole."

Mr. Roberts and other ex-inmates say some prisoners make specially prepared food with items from the prison kitchen and sell it for mackerel.

"I knew a guy who would buy ingredients and use the microwaves to cook meals. Then people used mack to buy it from him," says Jonson Miller, an adjunct history professor at Drexel University in Philadelphia who spent two months in federal prison after being arrested at a protest on federal property.

Mr. Miller was released in 2003, when prisoners were getting ready for cigarettes to be phased out, and says inmates then were already moving to mackerel.

. . . There are other threats to the mackerel economy, says Mr. Linder, of Power Commissary. "There are shortages world-wide, in terms of the catch," he says. Combined with the weak dollar, that's led to a surging mack. Now, he says, a pouch of mackerel sells for more than $1 in most commissaries.

Another problem with mackerel is that once a prisoner's sentence is up, there's little to do with it. The fish can't be redeemed for cash and has little value on the outside. As a result, says Mr. Levine, prisoners approaching their release must either barter or give away their stockpiles.

That's what Mr. Levine did when he got out of prison last year. Since then, he's set up a consulting business offering advice to inmates and soon-to-be prisoners. He consults on various matters, such as how to request facility transfers and how to file grievances against wardens.

It's similar to the work he provided fellow inmates when he was in prison. But now, he says, "I get paid in American dollars."

ECS

economic content standards

Most people would like to have more money. Students, however, often fail to understand that the real value of money is determined by the goods and services money can buy. Doubling the amount of money in an economy would not, by itself, make people better off, because there would still be the same amount of goods and services produced and consumed, only at higher prices.

make sure that it is pure and not contaminated with dirt or insects. Barter, in short, is expensive and inefficient, and it generally prevails only where limited trade is carried out over short distances, which generally means in relatively primitive economies. The more complex the economy (e.g., the higher the real GDP per capita), the greater the economic interactions between people, and consequently, the greater the need for one or more universally accepted assets serving as money. Only in a Robinson Crusoe economy, where people live in isolated settlements and are generally self-sufficient, is the use of money unnecessary.

Money as a Unit of Account

Besides serving as a medium of exchange, money is also a unit of account. With a barter system, one does not know precisely what 30 pounds of wheat are worth relative to 2 pounds of salt. With money, a common "yardstick" exists, so people can precisely compare the values of diverse goods and services. Thus, if wheat costs 50 cents a pound and salt costs $1 a pound, we can say that a pound of salt is valued precisely two times as much as a pound of wheat ($1/$0.50 = 2). By providing a universally understood unit of account, money serves to lower the information costs involved in making transactions. Without money, a person might not know what a good price for salt is, because so many different commodities can be bartered for it. With money, only one price for salt is necessary, and that price is readily available as information to the potential consumer. We use money as a unit of account when we measure and record economic value.

Money as a Store of Value

Money also serves as a store of value. It can provide a means of saving or "storing" things of value in an efficient manner. A farmer in a barter society who wants to save for retirement might accumulate enormous inventories of wheat, which he would then gradually trade away for other goods in his old age. This approach is a terribly inefficient way to save. The farmer would have to construct storage buildings to hold all his wheat, and the interest payments he would earn on the wheat would actually be negative, because it is quite likely that rats would eat part of it or it would otherwise deteriorate. Most important, physical goods of value would be tied up in unproductive use for many years. With money, the farmer saves pieces of paper that can be used to purchase goods and services in his old age. It is both cheaper and safer to store paper rather than wheat.

Money as a Means of Deferred Payment

Finally, money is a **means of deferred payment**. Money makes it much easier to borrow and to repay loans. With barter, lending is cumbersome and subject to an added problem. What if a wheat farmer borrows some wheat and agrees to pay it back in wheat next year, but the value of wheat soars because of a poor crop resulting from drought? The debt will be paid back in wheat that is far more valuable than that borrowed, creating a problem for the borrower. Of course, fluctuations in the value of money can also occur; indeed, inflation has been a major problem in our recent past and continues to be a problem in many countries. But the value of money fluctuates far less than the value of many individual commodities, so lending in money imposes fewer risks on buyers and sellers than lending in commodities.

ECS

economic content standards
Money is important to an economy. Because it replaces barter, it makes exchange less costly. As a result, people are more likely to specialize in what they have a comparative advantage in and use the money earned to buy what they want to consume. This increases production and consumption in a nation.

How does the existence of money make borrowing and lending easier?

means of deferred payment
the attribute of money that makes it easier to borrow and to repay loans

---

② SECTION QUIZ

1. Money's principal role is to serve as

   a. a standard for credit transactions.

   b. a medium of exchange.

   c. a standard for making bank loans.

   d. a standard for the real bills doctrine.

2. Barter is inefficient compared to using money for trading because

   a. it is more expensive over long distances.

   b. potential buyers may not have appropriate items of value to sellers with which to barter.

   c. it is more time consuming, since it is more difficult to evaluate the products that are being offered for barter than to evaluate money.

   d. of all of the above.

   e. of none of the above.

3. Currency is a poor store of value when

   a. the unemployment rate is high.

   b. banks are failing at an abnormally high rate.

   c. the rate of inflation is very high.

   d. gold can be purchased at bargain prices.

   e. All of the above are correct.

(*continued*)

4. Money makes it easier to borrow and repay loans. This function of money is referred to as

a. a store of value.

b. a means of deferred payment.

c. a unit of account.

d. a standard of value.

e. none of the above.

5. Money is

a. whatever is generally accepted in exchange for goods and services.

b. an object to be consumed.

c. a highly illiquid asset.

d. widely used in a barter economy.

6. Without money to serve as a medium of exchange,

a. gains from trade would be severely limited.

b. our standard of living would probably be reduced.

c. the transaction costs of exchange would increase.

d. All of the above are true.

1. Why does the advantage of monetary exchange over barter increase as an economy becomes more complex?

2. How can uncertain and rapid rates of inflation erode money's ability to perform its functions efficiently?

3. In a world of barter, would useful financial statements such as balance sheets be possible? Would stock markets be possible? Would it be possible to build cars?

4. Why do virtually all societies create something to function as money?

Answers: 1. b 2. d 3. c 4. b 5. a 6. d

17.2 Measuring Money

☞ What is currency?
☞ What is liquidity?

☞ What is included in the money supply?
☞ What backs our money?

Currency

currency
coins and/or paper created to facilitate the trade of goods and services and the payment of debts

Currency consists of coins and/or paper that some institution or government has created to be used in the trading of goods and services and the payment of debts. Currency in the form of metal coins is still used as money throughout the world today. But metal currency has a disadvantage: It is bulky. Also, certain types of metals traditionally used in coins, such as gold and silver, are not available in sufficient quantities to meet our demands for a monetary instrument. For these reasons, metal coins have for centuries been supplemented by paper currency, often in the form of bank notes. In the United States, the Federal Reserve System (the Fed) issues Federal Reserve notes in various denominations, and this paper currency, along with coins, provides the basis for most transactions of relatively modest size in the

United States today. Note that currency in circulation refers to the paper money and coins that are not held by banks or the government.

Currency as Legal Tender

In the United States and most other nations of the world, metallic coins and paper currency are the only forms of **legal tender**. In other words, coins and paper money have been officially declared to be money—to be acceptable for the settlement of debts incurred in financial transactions. In effect, the government says, "We declare these instruments to be money, and citizens are expected to accept them as a medium of exchange." Legal tender is **fiat money**—a means of exchange that has been established not by custom and tradition or because of the value of the metal in a coin but by government fiat, or declaration.

What makes this paper and metal valuable? Paper and metal are valuable if they are acceptable to people who want to sell goods and services. Sellers must be confident that the money they accept is also acceptable where they want to buy goods and services. Imagine if money in California were not accepted as money in Texas or New York. It would certainly make it more difficult to carry out transactions.

Demand Deposits and Other Checkable Deposits

Most of the money that we use for day-to-day transactions, however, is not official legal tender. Rather, it is a monetary instrument that has become "generally accepted" in exchange over the years and has now, by custom and tradition, become money. What is this instrument? It is balances in checking accounts in banks, more formally called **demand deposits**.

Demand deposits are defined as balances in bank accounts that depositors can access on demand by simply writing checks. That is, demand deposits are convertible to currency on demand. Some other forms of accounts in financial institutions also have virtually all the attributes of demand deposits. For example, other checkable deposits earn interest but have some restrictions, such as higher monthly fees or minimum balance requirements. These interest-earning checking accounts effectively permit the depositors to write "orders" similar to checks and assign the rights to the deposit to other persons, just as we write checks to other parties. Practically speaking, funds in these accounts are the equivalent of demand deposits and have become an important component in the supply of money. Both of these types of accounts are forms of **transaction deposits** because they can be easily converted into currency or used to buy goods and services directly. **Traveler's checks**, like currency and demand deposits, are also easily converted into currency or used directly as a means of payment.

legal tender
coins and paper officially declared to be acceptable for the settlement of financial debts

fiat money
a means of exchange established by government declaration

demand deposits
balances in bank accounts that depositors can access on demand

transaction deposits
deposits that can be easily converted to currency or used to buy goods and services directly

traveler's checks
transaction instruments easily convertible into currency

The Popularity of Demand Deposits and Other Checkable Deposits

Demand deposits and other checkable deposits have replaced paper and metallic currency as the major component of money used for larger transactions in the United States and in most other relatively well-developed nations for several reasons, including the ease and safety of transactions, lower transaction costs, and transaction records.

What is legal tender? What is fiat money?

Ease and Safety of Transactions

Paying for goods and services with checks is easier (meaning cheaper) and less risky than paying with paper money. Paper money is readily transferable: If someone takes a $20 bill from you, it is gone, and the thief can use it to buy goods with no difficulty. If, however, someone steals a check that you have written to the telephone company to pay a monthly bill, that person will probably have great difficulty using it to buy goods and services because he has to be able to identify himself as a representative of the telephone company. If someone steals your checkbook, the thief can use your checks as money only if he can successfully forge your signature and provide some identification. Hence, transacting business by check is much less risky than using legal tender; an element of insurance or safety exists in the use of transaction deposits instead of currency.

Lower Transaction Costs

Suppose you decide that you want to buy a sweater that costs $81.28 from the current Urban Outfitters mail-order catalog. It is much cheaper, easier, and safer for you to send a check for $81.28 rather than four $20 bills, a $1 bill, a quarter, and three pennies. Transaction deposits are popular precisely because they lower transaction costs compared with the use of metal or paper currency. In small transactions, the gains in safety and convenience of checks are outweighed by the time and cost required to write and process them; in these cases, transaction costs are lower with paper and metallic currency. Therefore, it is unlikely that the use of paper or metallic currency will disappear entirely.

Credit and Debit Cards

Are credit cards money? Are debit cards money?

A credit card is "generally acceptable in exchange for goods and services." At the same time, however, a credit card payment is actually a guaranteed loan available on demand to the cardholder, which merely defers the cardholder's payment for a transaction using a demand deposit. After all, the word "credit" means that you are receiving money today with a promise to pay it back in the future—it really is a short-term loan. Ultimately, an item purchased with a credit card must be paid for with a check; monthly payments on credit card accounts are required to continue using the card. A credit card, then, is not money but rather a convenient tool for carrying out transactions that minimizes the physical transfer of checks or currency. In this sense, it is a substitute for the use of money in exchange and allows the cardholder to use any given amount of money in future exchanges.

A debit card is just a card that lets you access your money via your checking account, but the card is not money. They are called debit cards because they reduce or debit your bank account directly when you use them. People often prefer to use debit cards to writing a check because no checkbook is required. It is just a convenient way to access your checking account. It may be safer than a credit card too because debit cards require a personal identification number (PIN). However, there is no grace period, and the transaction immediately reduces the amount of money in your bank account. Consequently, consumers have less leverage if disputing a purchase; with a check, you can stop payment, and with a credit card you have a grace period between purchase and payment.

Savings Accounts

Economists are not completely in agreement on what constitutes money for all purposes. They agree, nearly universally, that coins, paper currency, demand and other checkable deposits, and traveler's checks are certainly forms of money, because all are accepted as direct means of payment for goods and services. Some economists, however, argue that for some purposes *money* should be more broadly defined to include **nontransaction deposits**. Nontransaction deposits are fund accounts against which the depositor *cannot* directly write checks hence the name. If these funds cannot be used directly as a means of payment but must first be converted into money, why do people hold such accounts? People use these accounts primarily because they generally pay higher interest rates than transaction deposits.

nontransaction deposits
funds that cannot be used for payment directly but must be converted into currency for general use

Two primary types of nontransaction deposits exist: savings accounts and time deposits (sometimes referred to as certificates of deposit, or CDs). Most purists would argue that nontransaction deposits are **near money** assets but not money itself. Why? Savings accounts and time deposits cannot be used directly to purchase a good or service. They are not a direct medium of exchange. For example, you cannot go into a supermarket, pick out groceries, and give the clerk the passbook to your savings account. You must convert funds from your savings account into currency or demand deposits before you can buy goods and services. Thus, strictly speaking, nontransaction deposits do not satisfy the formal definition of money. At the same time, however, savings accounts are assets that can be quickly converted into money at the face value of the account. In the jargon of finance, savings accounts are highly liquid assets. True, under federal law commercial banks legally can require depositors to request withdrawal of funds in writing and then defer making payment for several weeks. But in practice no bank prohibits immediate withdrawal, although early withdrawal from some time deposits, especially certificates of deposit, may require the depositor to forgo some interest income as a penalty.

near money
nontransaction deposits that are not money but can be quickly converted into money

Money Market Mutual Funds

Money market mutual funds are interest-earning accounts provided by brokers who pool funds into investments such as Treasury bills. These funds are invested in short-term securities, and depositors are allowed to write checks against their accounts subject to certain limitations. This type of fund experienced tremendous growth over the last 20 years. Money market mutual funds are highly liquid assets. They are considered to be near money because they are relatively easy to convert into money for the purchases of goods and services.

money market mutual funds
interest-earning accounts provided by brokers that pool funds into such investments as Treasury bills

Stocks and Bonds

Virtually everyone agrees that many other forms of financial assets, such as stocks and bonds, are not money. Suppose you buy 1,000 shares of common stock in Microsoft at $30 per share, for a total of $30,000. The stock is traded daily on the New York Stock Exchange and elsewhere; you can readily sell the stock and get paid in legal tender or a demand deposit. Why, then, is this stock not considered money? First, it will take a few days for you to receive payment for the sale of stock; you cannot turn the asset into cash as quickly as you can a savings deposit in a financial institution. Second, and more importantly, the value of the stock fluctuates over time, and as the owner of the asset, you have no guarantee that you will be able to obtain its original nominal value at any time. Thus, stocks and bonds are not generally considered to be money.

Why are stocks and bonds not money?

Liquidity

Money is an asset that we generally use to buy goods or services. In fact, it is so easy to convert money into goods and services that we say it is the most liquid of assets. When we speak of **liquidity**, we are referring to the ease with which one asset can be converted into another asset or goods and services. For example, to convert a stock into goods and services would prove to be somewhat more difficult—contacting your broker or going online, determining at what price to sell your stock, paying the commission for the service, and waiting for the completion of the transaction. Clearly, stocks are not as liquid an asset as money. But other assets are even less liquid—for example, converting your painting collection or your baseball cards or Barbie dolls into other goods and services.

liquidity
the ease with which one asset can be converted into another asset or into goods and services

The Money Supply

Because a good case can be made either for including or for excluding savings accounts, certificates of deposit (CDs), and money market mutual funds from an operational definition of the money supply depending on its intended purpose, we will compromise and do both. Economists call the narrow definition of money—currency, checkable deposits, and traveler's checks—M1. There is a little mystery involved with M1. Currency is the coins and paper bills that are in the hands of the public. It is the most widely used medium of exchange. Currency is typically a larger fraction of M1 than checkable deposits yet checks are used more often to make payments. How is that possible? First, there is nearly $3,000 per person (adults and children) of currency in circulation in the United States. How many people do you know who carry that kind of cash in their wallet? Some of that cash is in cash registers. Businesses and individuals also like to hold cash for precautionary reasons. Still others like to hold cash because they can hide illegal activities (drugs, pornography, tax evasion, and so on). However, the bulk of U.S. currency is in foreign countries—perhaps as much as 60 percent. These countries may have a currency that does not holds its value as well as the dollar; it's safer for some foreigners to hold part of their wealth in U.S. dollars than in their own country's currency.

The broader definition of money, encompassing M1 plus savings deposits, time deposits (except for some large-denomination certificates of deposit), and noninstitutional money market mutual fund shares, is called M2. The distinction between M1 and M2 is becoming smaller, as banks now allow depositors to shift funds from saving accounts to checking accounts with ATM cards or online.

The difference between M1 and M2 is striking, as evidenced by the different sizes of the total supply of money depending on which definition is used. As Exhibit 1 shows, M2 is more than four times the magnitude of M1. In other words, people strongly prefer to keep the bulk of their liquid assets in the form of savings accounts of various kinds.

How Was Money "Backed"?

Until fairly recently, coins in most nations were largely made from precious metals, usually gold or silver. These metals had a considerable intrinsic worth: If the coins were melted down, the metal would be valuable for use in jewelry, industrial applications, dentistry, and so forth. Until 1933, the United States was on an internal **gold standard**, meaning that the dollar was defined as equivalent in value to a certain amount of gold, and paper currency or demand deposits could be freely converted to gold coin. The United States abandoned the gold standard, however, eventually phasing out gold currency. Some silver coins and paper money convertible into silver remained, but by the end of the 1960s, even this tie between the monetary system and precious metals was gone. This was due in part because the price of silver soared so high that the metal in coins had an intrinsic worth greater than its face value, leading people to hoard coins or even melt them down. When two forms of money are available, people prefer to spend the form of money that is less valuable. This tendency is a manifestation of Gresham's law: "Cheap money drives out dear money."

What backing does today's money have?

What Really Backs Our Money Now?

Consequently, today no meaningful precious metal "backing" gives our money value. Why, then, do people accept dollar bills in exchange for goods? After all, a dollar bill is a piece of generally wrinkled paper about 6 inches by 2.5 inches in size, with virtually no inherent utility or worth. Do we accept these bills because it states on the front of the bills, "This note is legal tender for all debts, public and private"? Perhaps, but we accept some forms of currency and money in the form of demand deposits without that statement.

section 17.2 exhibit 1	Two Definitions of the Money Supply: M1 and M2

Currency = $977.0 billion
M1: Currency + Checkable deposits + Traveler's checks = $2,006.1 billion
M2: M1 + Savings deposits + Small-denomination time deposits + Noninstitutional money market mutual fund
shares + Money market deposit accounts = $9,313.7 billion

SOURCE: Federal Reserve, September 2011.

The true backing behind money in the United States is faith that people will take it in exchange for goods and services. People accept with great eagerness these small pieces of green paper with pictures of long-deceased people with funny-looking hair simply because we believe that they will be exchangeable for goods and services with an intrinsic value. If you were to drop two pieces of paper of equal size on the floor in front of 100 students, one a blank piece of paper and the other a $100 bill, and then leave the room, most of the group would probably start scrambling for the $100 bill, while the blank piece of paper would be ignored. Such is our faith in the green paper's practical value that some will even fight over it. As long as people have confidence in something's convertibility into goods and services, "money" will exist and no further backing is necessary.

Because governments represent the collective will of the people, they are the institutional force that traditionally defines money in the legal sense. People are willing to accept pieces of paper as money only because of their faith in the government. When people lose faith in the exchangeability of pieces of paper that the government decrees as money, even legal tender loses its status as meaningful money. Something is money only if people will generally accept it. Governments play a key role in defining money, but much of its value is actually created by private businesses in the pursuit of profit. A majority of U.S. money, whether M1 or M2, is in the form of deposits at privately owned financial institutions.

use what you've learned   Pawn Shops and Liquidity

Q What do pawn shops sell?

A The typical response is that they sell used goods. In fact, they sell few used goods. However, they do sell something that is even more important to their clientele. They sell liquidity. When individuals hock their wares at pawn shops they are usually desperate—and are willing to pledge their watches, rings, or whatever as collateral. The pawn shop will allow you to buy your pawned item back in some specified time period for a higher price (that is, an interest charge). In this sense, pawn shops are like banks and will lend you money for a specified period of time if you are willing to pay the interest. But even if individuals don't buy their pawned item back, this behavior of selling and taking a lower price than could be obtained through the classifieds in order to get the money now, demonstrates that buyers are willing to pay for liquidity.

© RANDY FARIS/CORBIS

People who hold money, then, must have faith not only in their government but also in banks and other financial institutions. If you accept a check drawn on a regional bank, you believe that bank or, for that matter, any bank will be willing to convert that check into legal tender (currency), enabling you to buy goods or services that you want to have. Thus, you have faith in the bank as well. In short, our money is money because of the confidence we have in private financial institutions and our government.

⑦ SECTION QUIZ

1. The money supply that includes only currency, checkable deposits, and traveler's checks is known as
   a. M1.
   b. M2.
   c. M3.
   d. L.

2. Credit cards
   a. are included in the M1 definition of the money supply.
   b. are included in the M2 definition of the money supply.
   c. are included in the M3 definition of the money supply.
   d. are included only in the broadest definition of the money supply.
   e. are not included in the definition of the money supply.

3. The distinction between M1 and M2 is based on
   a. liquidity—the ease with which an asset can be converted into cash.
   b. storability—the ease with which an asset can be stored.
   c. divisibility—the ease with which an asset can be used to make specific payments.
   d. portability—the ease with which an asset can be moved to make a payment on the spot.
   e. all of the above.

4. An increase in demand deposits combined with an equal decrease in currency in circulation would
   a. have no direct effect on M1 or M2.
   b. increase both M1 and M2.
   c. increase M1 and decrease M2.
   d. decrease M1 and increase M2.

5. Liquidity is defined as
   a. the cash value of fiat money.
   b. the value of fiat money when used to buy a good or service.
   c. the speed at which money is spent.
   d. the ease with which money can be divided to make payments.
   e. the ease with which an asset can be converted into cash.

---

1. If everyone in an economy accepted poker chips as payment in exchange for goods and services, would poker chips be money?
2. If you were buying a pack of gum, would using currency or a demand deposit have lower transaction costs? What if you were buying a house?
3. What is the main advantage of transaction deposits for tax purposes? What is their main disadvantage for tax purposes?
4. Are credit cards money?
5. What are M1 and M2?
6. How have interest-earning checking accounts and overdraft protection led to the relative decline in demand deposits?

Answers: 1. a   2. e   3. a   4. a   5. e

How Banks Create Money   **17.3**

📁 How is money created?

📁 What is a reserve requirement?

📁 How do reserve requirements affect how much money can be created?

Financial Institutions

The biggest players in the banking industry are **commercial banks**. Commercial banks are financial institutions organized to handle the everyday financial transactions of businesses and households through demand deposit accounts and savings accounts and by making short-term commercial and consumer loans. These banks account for more than two-thirds of all the deposits in the banking industry; they maintain almost all the demand deposits and close to half the savings accounts.

Nearly 1,000 commercial banks operate in the United States. This number is in marked contrast to most other nations, where the leading banks operate throughout the country and where a large proportion of total bank assets are held in a handful of banks. Until recently, federal law restricted banks from operating in more than one state. This law has now changed, and the structure of banking as we know it will inevitably change with the emergence of interstate banking, mergers, and "hostile" takeovers.

Aside from commercial banks, the banking system includes two other important financial institutions: **savings and loan associations** and **credit unions**. Savings and loan associations provide many of the same services as commercial banks, including checkable deposits, a variety of time deposits, and money market deposit accounts. The almost 2,000 members of savings and loan associations have typically invested most of their savings deposits in home mortgages. Credit unions are cooperatives made up of depositors with some common affiliation, such as the same employer or union.

commercial banks
financial institutions organized to handle everyday financial transactions of businesses and households through demand deposit accounts and savings accounts and by making short-term commercial and consumer loans

Are banks the only important financial institutions?

savings and loan associations
financial institutions organized as cooperative associations that hold demand deposits and savings of members in the form of dividend-bearing shares and make loans, especially home mortgage loans

credit unions
financial cooperatives made up of depositors with a common affiliation

The Functions of Financial Institutions

Financial institutions offer a large number of financial functions. For example, they often will pay an individual's monthly bills by automatic withdrawals, administer estates, and rent safe-deposit boxes, among other things. Most important, though, they are depositories for savings and liquid assets that are used by individuals and firms for transaction purposes. They can create money by making loans. In making loans, financial institutions act as intermediaries (the middle persons) between savers, who supply funds, and borrowers seeking funds to invest.

How Do Banks Create Money?

As we have already learned, most money, narrowly defined, is in the form of transaction deposits assets that can be directly used to buy goods and services. But how did the balance in, say, a checking account get there in the first place? Perhaps it was through a loan made by a commercial bank. When a bank lends to a person, it does not typically give the borrower cash (paper and metallic currency). Rather, it gives the borrower the funds by issuing a check or by adding funds to an existing checking account. If you go into a bank and borrow $1,000, the bank probably will add $1,000 to your checking account at the bank, creating a new checkable deposit money.

How does a bank loan create money?

How Do Banks Make Profits?

Banks make loans and create checkable deposits to make profits. How do they make their profits? By collecting higher interest payments on the loans they make than they pay their depositors for those funds. If you borrow $1,000 from Bank One, the interest payment you make, less the expenses the bank incurs in making the loan, including their costs of acquiring the funds, represents profit to the bank.

Reserve Requirements

reserve requirements
holdings of assets at the bank or at the Federal Reserve Bank as mandated by the Fed

Because the way to make more profit is to make more loans, banks want to make a large volume of loans. Stockholders of banks want the largest profits possible; so what keeps banks from making nearly infinite quantities of loans? Primarily, government regulatory authorities limit the loan issuance of banks by imposing **reserve requirements**. Banks are required to keep on hand a quantity of cash or reserve accounts with the Federal Reserve equal to a prescribed proportion of their checkable deposits.

Fractional Reserve System

Why is our banking system called a fractional reserve system?

fractional reserve system
a system that requires banks to hold reserves equal to some fraction of their checkable deposits

Even in the absence of regulations restricting the creation of checkable deposits, a prudent bank would put some limit on their loan (and therefore deposit) volume. Why? For people to accept checkable deposits as money, the checks written must be generally accepted in exchange for goods and services. People will accept checks only if they know that they are quickly convertible at par (face value) into legal tender. For this reason, banks must have adequate cash reserves on hand (including reserves at the Fed that can be almost immediately converted to currency, if necessary) to meet the needs of customers who wish to convert their checkable deposits into currency or spend them on goods or services.

Our banking system is sometimes called a **fractional reserve system**, because banks, by law as well as by choice, find it necessary to keep cash on hand and reserves at the Federal Reserve equal to some fraction of their checkable deposits. If a bank were to create $100 in demand deposits for every $1 in cash reserves that it had, the bank might well find itself in difficulty before too long. Why? Consider a bank with $10,000,000 in demand and time deposits and $100,000 in cash reserves. Suppose a couple of large companies with big accounts decide to withdraw $120,000 in cash on the same day. The bank would be unable to convert into legal tender all the funds requested. The word would then spread that the bank's checks are not convertible into lawful money, possibly causing a "run on the bank." The bank would have to quickly convert some of its other assets into currency, or it would be unable to meet its obligations to convert its deposits into currency, and it would have to close.

Therefore, even in the absence of reserve regulations, few banks would risk maintaining fewer reserves on hand than they thought prudent for their amount of deposits (particularly demand deposits). Reserve requirements exist primarily to control the amount of demand and time deposits and thus the size of the money supply; they do not exist simply to prevent bank failures.

In the past, banks did not want to keep any more of their funds in reserves than required because those cash assets earned no interest. However, that changed in October 2008, when the Fed began paying interest *on reserves held* with the

In the movie *It's a Wonderful Life*, there is a scene showing a run on a savings and loan that demonstrates the power of the fractional reserve banking system—"You're thinking of this place all wrong; as if I had the money in a safe. Your money is not here. Your money is in Joe's house and in the Kennedy's house and hundreds of others."

© BETTMANN/CORBIS

Fed. Paying interest on reserves encourages banks to hold additional reserves. However, the interest rate paid on reserves is currently very low, so it has not changed banks' incentives much. The change also provides the Fed with another tool to influence the money supply. We will discuss this in the next chapter. To protect themselves but also earn interest income, banks usually keep some of their assets in highly liquid investments, such as U.S. government bonds. These types of highly liquid, interest-paying assets are often called secondary reserves.

secondary reserves
highly liquid, interest-paying assets held by the bank

A Balance Sheet

Earlier in this chapter, we learned that money is created when banks make loans. We will now look more closely at the process of bank lending and its impact on the stock of money. In doing so, we will examine the structure and behavior of our hypothetical bank, Bank One. To get a good picture of the size of the bank, what it owns, and what it owes, we look at its balance sheet, which is like a financial "photograph" of the bank at a single moment. Exhibit 1 presents a balance sheet for Bank One.

balance sheet
a financial record that indicates the balance between a bank's assets and its liabilities plus capital

Assets

The assets of a bank are the items of value that the bank owns (e.g., cash, reserves at the Federal Reserve, bonds, and its buildings), including contractual obligations of individuals and firms to pay funds to the bank (loans). The largest asset category for most banks is loans. Banks maintain most of their assets in the form of loans because interest payments on loans are the primary means by which they earn revenue. Some assets are kept in the form of noninterest-bearing cash and reserve accounts at the Federal Reserve to meet legal reserve requirements (and to meet the cash demands of customers). Typically, relatively little of a bank's reserves, or cash assets, is physically kept in the form of paper currency in the bank's vault or at tellers' windows. Most banks keep the majority of their reserves as reserve accounts at the Federal Reserve. As previously indicated, banks usually also keep some assets in the form of bonds that are quickly convertible into cash if necessary (secondary reserves).

Liabilities

All banks have substantial liabilities, which are financial obligations that the bank has to other people. The predominant liability of virtually all banks is deposits. If you have money in a demand deposit account, you have the right to demand cash for that deposit at any time. Basically, the bank owes you the amount in your checking account. Time deposits similarly constitute a liability of banks.

Capital Stock

For a bank to be healthy and solvent, its assets, or what it owns, must exceed its liabilities, or what it owes others. In other words, if the bank were liquidated and all the assets converted

Why are checking account deposits a liability for a bank?

section 17.3 exhibit 1	Balance Sheet, Bank One			
Assets			**Liabilities and Capital**	
Cash (reserves)		$ 2,000,000	Transaction deposits (checking deposits)	$ 5,000,000
Loans		6,100,000	Savings and time deposits	4,000,000
Bonds (U.S. government and municipal)		1,500,000	Total Liabilities	$ 9,000,000
Bank building, equipment, fixtures		400,000	Capital	1,000,000
Total Assets		**$10,000,000**	**Total Liabilities and Capital**	**$10,000,000**

© Cengage Learning 2013

into cash and all the obligations to others (liabilities) paid off, some cash would still be left to distribute to the owners of the bank, that is, its stockholders. This difference between a bank's assets and its liabilities constitutes the bank's capital. Note that this definition of capital differs from the earlier definition, which described capital as goods used to further production of other goods (machines, structures, tools, etc.). In this case, the capital stock is the equity owned by shareholders both in and out of the community. As you can see in Exhibit 1, capital is included on the right side of the balance sheet, so that both sides (assets and liabilities plus capital) are equal in amount. Any time the aggregate amount of bank assets changes, the aggregate amount of liabilities and capital must also change by the same amount, by definition.

How is a bank's capital different from the definition of capital generally used by economists?

The Required Reserve Ratio

required reserve ratio the percentage of deposits that a bank must hold at the Federal Reserve Bank or in bank vaults

excess reserves reserve levels held above that required by the Fed

Suppose for simplicity that Bank One faces a reserve requirement of 10 percent on all deposits. This percentage is often called the **required reserve ratio**. But what does a required reserve ratio of 10 percent mean? It means that the bank *must* keep cash on hand or at the Federal Reserve Bank equal to one-tenth (10 percent) of its deposits. For example, if the required reserve ratio is 10 percent, banks are required to hold $100,000 in required reserves for every $1 million in deposits. The remaining 90 percent of cash is called excess reserves.

Reserves in the form of cash earn no revenue for the bank; no profit is made from holding cash. If bank reserves are held as accounts with the Fed, a very low interest is now paid, but that does not change banks' incentives very much from holding cash in their vaults. When banks have excess reserves, they typically invest the excess reserves in interest-earning assets—sometimes bonds but usually loans.

Loaning Excess Reserves

Let's see what happens when someone deposits $100,000 at Bank One. We will continue to assume that the required reserve ratio is 10 percent. That is, the bank is required to hold $10,000 in required reserves for this new deposit of $100,000. The remaining 90 percent, or $90,000, becomes excess reserves, most of which will likely become available for loans for individuals and businesses.

However, the story doesn't end here. Let's say that the bank loans all its new excess reserves of $90,000 to an individual who is remodeling her home. At the time the bank makes the loan, its money supply increases by $90,000. Specifically, no one has less money—the original depositor still has $100,000, and the bank adds $90,000 to the borrower's checking account (demand deposit). A new demand deposit, or checking account, of $90,000 has been created. *Because demand deposits are money, the issuers of the new loan have created money.*

Furthermore, borrowers are not likely to keep borrowed money in their checking accounts for long, because they usually take out loans to make purchases. If a loan is used for remodeling, the borrower pays the construction company; the owner of the construction company, in turn, will likely deposit the money into his account at another bank to add even more funds for additional money expansion. This whole process is summarized in Exhibit 2.

Now suppose that Bank One faces a reserve requirement of 20 percent. The bank must keep cash on hand or at the Federal Reserve Bank equal to one-fifth (20%) of its deposits. If the bank's deposits (demand and time) sum to $9,000,000, required reserves are calculated as follows:

$$\text{Deposits} \times \text{Reserve ratio} = \$9,000,000 \times 0.20$$
$$= \$1,800,000$$

section 17.3 exhibit 2   Fractional Reserve Banking System

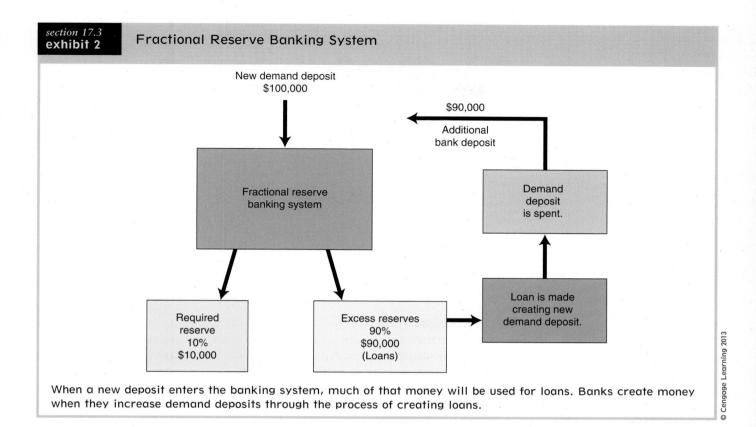

When a new deposit enters the banking system, much of that money will be used for loans. Banks create money when they increase demand deposits through the process of creating loans.

The bank, then, is required to maintain $1,800,000 in cash. Bank One, however, actually has $2 million in cash, meaning that it has excess reserves, or $200,000. (Excess reserves = Actual reserves − Required reserves, or $2,000,000 − $1,800,000.)

$$\text{Excess reserves} = \text{Actual reserves} - \text{Required reserves}$$

$$= \$2,000,000 - \$1,800,000$$

$$= \$200,000$$

Suppose Bank One decided to make loans with its $200,000 in excess reserves. For simplicity's sake, let us suppose it makes one loan of $200,000 to a manufacturer for an addition to its chocolate factory. What will be the bank's balance sheet after it makes the loan? As Exhibit 3 indicates, both assets and liabilities rise by $200,000. The bank simply gives the borrower a checking account with $200,000 in it, a new deposit liability of the bank. In return, the borrower gives the bank an IOU agreeing to pay back the $200,000 plus interest at some future date. Thus, loans rise by $200,000 over the level on the initial balance sheet.

section 17.3 exhibit 3   Balance Sheet for Bank One after Loan

Assets		Liabilities and Capital	
Cash (reserves)	$ 2,000,000	Demand deposits	$ 5,200,000
Loans	6,300,000	Time deposits	4,000,000
Bonds (U.S. government and municipal)	1,500,000	Total Liabilities	$ 9,200,000
Bank building, equipment, fixtures	400,000	Capital	1,000,000
Total Assets	**$10,200,000**	**Total Liabilities and Capital**	**$10,200,000**

section 17.3 exhibit 4	Balance Sheet for Bank One after Loan Funds Are Spent			
Assets			**Liabilities and Capital**	
Cash (reserves)		$ 1,800,000	Demand deposits	$ 5,000,000
Loans		6,300,000	Time deposits	4,000,000
Bonds (U.S. government and municipal)		1,500,000	Total Liabilities	$ 9,000,000
Bank building, equipment, fixtures		400,000	Capital	1,000,000
Total Assets		**$10,000,000**	**Total Liabilities and Capital**	**$10,000,000**

Note that in making the loan, Bank One did not have to reduce its cash reserves. It did not give the borrower cash; it simply created new money by giving the borrower $200,000 in a checking account. Therefore, even after making a loan equal to its initial excess reserves of $200,000, the bank still has some excess reserves. The bank's deposits rose to $9,200,000; 20 percent of that is $1,840,000. Yet the bank has $2,000,000 in actual reserves. Excess reserves are still $160,000 ($2,000,000 − $1,840,000 = $160,000).

If it still has some excess reserves, should the bank make still more loans? No. Why? Because when the chocolate manufacturer borrowed $200,000, it did so in order to expand the factory. Few people borrow money and simply let the money sit in a checking account while they pay interest on the loan. It is reasonable to assume that the chocolate maker will shortly take all or part of the $200,000 out of the checking account, probably in the form of a check to a construction company for $200,000. What will the construction company do with the check? Put it in its bank. With many different banks in the United States, it is likely that the construction company has its checking account in another bank. Suppose its account is in Bank Two. Bank Two credits the account of the construction company with $200,000 in demand deposits, then takes the check and uses the facilities of the Federal Reserve System or a bank clearinghouse to present the check to Bank One for payment. Bank One will then have to pay Bank Two $200,000 in cash.

Therefore, Bank One will eventually (depending on how long it takes the chocolate manufacturer to spend the $200,000 it borrowed) face losing cash reserves equal to the loan. After Bank Two presents the check that was written by the chocolate manufacturer to Bank One for payment, Bank One's balance sheet changes again, as indicated in Exhibit 4.

As the chocolate maker spends the $200,000, demand deposits fall by that amount, so that the bank's liabilities also decline by $200,000. The bank transfers $200,000 in cash to Bank Two. Incidentally, rarely is cash actually physically moved, given the expense and risk. Typically, the local Federal Reserve Bank simply reduces the reserves of Bank One at the Fed by $200,000 and increases Bank Two's by $200,000.

When the smoke clears, the chocolate manufacturer has its factory addition, and Bank One has an interest-paying IOU equal to $200,000. Bank One's cash reserves have fallen, however, to an amount ($1,800,000) exactly equal to its required reserves. Had the bank initially loaned out more than its $200,000 in excess reserves, the bank would have found its reserves below the required level as soon as the borrower spent the loan, assuming that the receiver of the funds had his or her bank account in another bank. Therefore, one important rule of thumb in banking is that a single bank in a banking system of many banks can safely make loans only equal to the amount of its excess reserves.

Does the creation of additional money create additional wealth?

Is More Money More Wealth?

When banks create more money by putting their excess reserves to work, they make the economy more liquid by providing more of a medium of exchange. Clearly, more money is in the economy after the loan, but is the borrower any wealthier? The answer is no. Even though borrowers have more money to buy goods and services, they are not any richer, because the new liability, the loan, has to be repaid.

In short, banks create money when they increase demand deposits through the process of creating loans. However, the process does not stop here. In the next section, we will see how the process of loans and deposits has a multiplying effect throughout the banking industry.

? SECTION QUIZ

1. Under fractional reserve banking, when a bank lends to a customer,

    a. bank credit decreases.

    b. reserves drain away from the system.

    c. the bank is protected from a run.

    d. borrowers receive a newly created demand deposit; that is, money is created.

    e. bank profitability is decreased.

2. Required reserves of a bank are a specific percentage of their

    a. loans.

    b. cash on hand.

    c. total assets.

    d. deposits.

3. Which of the following will lead to an increase in the money supply?

    a. You pay back a $10,000 loan that you owe to your bank.

    b. Your bank gives you a $10,000 loan by adding $10,000 to your checking account.

    c. You pay $10,000 in cash for a new motorcycle.

    d. You bury $10,000 in cash in your backyard.

4. Which of the following statements is true?

    a. Unlike in other nations, few separate commercial banks operate in the United States.

    b. Financial institutions can create money by making loans.

    c. If you go into a bank and borrow $1,000, the bank probably will simply add $1,000 to your checking account at the bank, but the process will not create new money in the banking system.

    d. Excess reserves equals actual reserves plus required reserves.

---

1. What is happening to the number of banks now that interstate banking is allowed?

2. In what way is it true that "banks make money by making money"?

3. How do legal reserve deposit regulations lower bank profits?

4. Is a demand deposit an asset or a liability?

5. If the Bonnie and Clyde National Bank's only deposits were demand deposits of $20 million and it faced a 10 percent reserve requirement, how much money would it be required to hold in reserves?

6. Suppose you found $10,000 while digging in your backyard, and you deposited it in the bank. How would your new demand deposit account create a situation of excess reserves at your bank?

Answers: 1. d 2. d 3. b 4. b

The Money Multiplier

▱ How does the process of multiple expansions of the money supply work?

▱ What is the money multiplier?

The Multiple Expansion Effect

How do new loans create excess reserves in other banks?

We just learned that banks can create money (demand deposits) by making loans and that the monetary expansion of an individual bank is limited to its excess reserves. However, this point ignores the further effects of a new loan and the accompanying expansion in the money supply. New loans create new money directly, but they also create excess reserves in other banks, which leads to still further increases in both loans and the money supply. With this multiple expansion effect, a given volume of bank reserves creates a multiplied amount of money.

New Loans and Multiple Expansions

To see how the process of multiple expansion works, consider what happens when Bank One receives a new cash deposit of $100,000. For convenience, say the bank is only required to keep new cash reserves equal to one-tenth (10 percent) of new deposits. Thus, Bank One is only required to hold $10,000 of the $100,000 deposit for required reserves. The bank therefore has $90,000 in excess reserves as a consequence of the new cash deposit.

Bank One will probably put its newly acquired excess reserves to work in some fashion earning income in the form of interest. Most likely, it will make one or more new loans totaling $90,000.

When the borrowers from Bank One get their loans, the borrowed money will almost certainly be spent on something new—machinery, a new house, a new car, or greater store inventories. The new money will lead to new spending.

The $90,000 spent by people borrowing from Bank One will likely end up in bank accounts in still other banks, such as Bank Two in Exhibit 1. Bank Two now has a new deposit of $90,000 with which to make more loans and create still more money. So Bank Two's T-account now looks like this:

Bank Two

Assets		Liabilities	
Reserves	$ 9,000	Checking	
Loans	81,000	deposits	$90,000

After the deposits, Bank Two has liabilities of $90,000. Thus, Bank Two creates $81,000 of money. Now if the money deposited in Bank Two is made available for a loan and is then deposited in Bank Three, the T-account for Bank Three will be:

Bank Three

Assets		Liabilities	
Reserves	$ 8,100	Checking	
Loans	72,900	deposits	$81,000

This process continues with Bank Three, Bank Four, Bank Five, and others. The initial cash deposit made by Bank One thus has a chain-reaction effect that ultimately involves many banks and a total monetary impact that is far greater than would be suggested by the size of the original deposit of $100,000. That is, every new loan gives rise to excess reserves, which lead to still further lending and deposit creation. Of course, each round of lending is smaller than the preceding one, because some (we are assuming 10 percent) of the new money created must be kept as required reserves.

The Money Multiplier

The **money multiplier** measures the potential amount of money that the banking system generates with each dollar of reserves. The following formula can be used to measure the total maximum potential impact on the supply of money:

$$\text{Potential money creation} = \text{Initial deposit} \times \text{Money multiplier}$$

To find the size of the money multiplier, we simply divide 1 by the reserve requirement ($1/R$). The larger the reserve requirement, the smaller the money multiplier. Thus, a reserve requirement of 25 percent, or one-fourth, means a money multiplier of 4. Likewise, a reserve requirement of 10 percent, or one-tenth, means a money multiplier of 10.

What happens to the money multiplier when the reserve requirement is raised?

In the example given in Exhibit 1, where Bank One (facing a 10 percent reserve requirement) receives a new $100,000 cash deposit, the initial deposit equals $100,000. Potential money creation, then, equals $100,000 (initial deposit) multiplied by 10 (the money multiplier), or $1,000,000. Using the money multiplier, we can calculate that the total potential impact of the initial $100,000 deposit is some $1,000,000 in money being created. In other words, the final monetary impact is 10 times as great as the initial deposit. Most of this increase, $900,000, has been created by the increase in demand deposits generated when banks make loans; the remaining $100,000 is from the initial deposit.

Why Is It Only "Potential" Money Creation?

Note that the expression "potential money creation" was used in describing the impact of creating loans and deposits out of excess reserves. Why "potential"? Some banks could choose not to lend all their excess reserves. Some banks might be extremely conservative and keep some extra newly acquired cash assets in that form. When they do, the chain reaction effect is reduced by the amount of excess reserves not loaned out.

What happens to money creation if borrowers don't spend all their newly acquired bank deposits?

Moreover, some borrowers may not spend all their newly acquired bank deposits, or they may wait a considerable period before doing so. Others may put their borrowed funds into time deposits rather than checkable deposits, which would reduce the M1 expansion process but not the M2 money expansion process. Still others may choose to keep some of their loans as currency in their pockets. Such leakages and time lags in the bank money expansion process usually mean that the actual monetary impact of an initial deposit created out of excess reserves within a short time is less than that indicated by the money multiplier. Still, the multiplier principle does work, and a multiple expansion of deposits will generally occur in a banking system that is characterized by fractional reserve requirements.

Leverage and the Financial Crisis of 2008

The financial crisis of 2008, like many previous financial crises, was blamed in part on "excessive leverage." Borrowing to finance investments is frequently cited as a major contributor to financial crises. When a financial institution (or an individual) only invests its own money, it can, in the very worst case, only lose its own money. But when it borrows in order to invest more, it can potentially earn more from its investment, but it can also lose more than its initial investment. For example, suppose you purchased a home for $500,000 and put down 20 percent ($100,000) at closing. You now have $100,000 of equity in the house. If the value of the house appreciates in the next year by 10 percent to $550,000,

section 17.4 exhibit 1   The Multiple Expansion Process

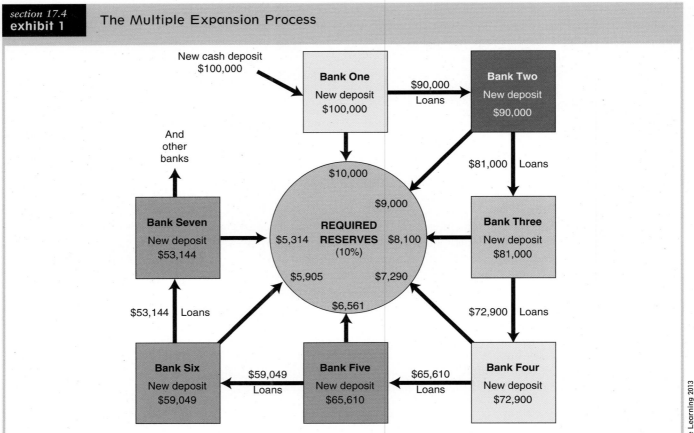

A $100,000 new cash deposit at Bank One has the potential to create $1,000,000 in a chain reaction that involves many banks. The process repeats itself, as the money lent by one bank becomes a new deposit in another bank.

© Cengage Learning 2013

you now have $150,000 in equity, a 50 percent increase. However, if the value of the home falls 10 percent in the next year to $450,000, you now have lost 50 percent of your equity. If it fell to $400,000, you would lose all your equity. Imagine if you only had to put 5 percent down. Then even a small reduction in the value of the home could leave you upside down, that is with negative equity. Thus, the larger the fraction of an investment financed by borrowing, the greater the degree of leveraging, and the greater potential for profit if the investment is favorable and loss if the investment falls in value. During the financial crisis, many new subprime borrowers, with 5 percent or less down, soon found themselves with negative equity—upside down on their loans—and either went through foreclosure or walked away from their homes. Whether it is a bank or a homeowner, leveraging magnifies both the potential returns and the risks from investment.

Financial institutions are often highly leveraged—$10 of assets may be financed with $1 of equity and $9 of debt, a leverage ratio of nine to one. Investment banks before the financial crisis had leverage ratios that were much greater than this. If bank assets fell 15 percent, it could easily lose all of its equity if it was "highly" leveraged. The assets would no longer be large enough to cover their liabilities (what the bank owes to others), and the bank could go bankrupt. For some large financial institutions, losses magnified by the ill-effects of leveraging had a ripple effect; that is, as one firm failed to pay other firms, it spread financial troubles throughout the industry. When Bear Stearns went under, their leverage was reported to have been close to 35 to 1, while holding complex portfolios that included a significant amount of "toxic" assets. This soon spelt disaster, as $1 of equity was supporting $35 of borrowing. Other financial institutions were also highly leveraged. Lehman Brothers, for example, in its last annual financial statement, showed accounting leverage of roughly 30 to 1 ($691 billion in assets divided by $22 billion in stockholders' equity).

It easy to see how the whole financial system can be impacted by highly leveraged financial institutions. A bank has to meet a capital requirement, say 5 percent of capital to back every $1 of loans or assets, so if a bank has $100 billion in loans outstanding it must have $5 billion in capital. If the value of its assets falls, then the bank must either raise additional capital or cut back its loans. If a number of banks find themselves in the same situation, then there is less lending in financial markets, leading to less consumption and investment and, ultimately, lower real GDP and employment.

In the years leading up to the financial crisis, the power of leveraging was working in favor of the financial institutions, who made huge profits. However, both the decline in the stock market and the fall in housing prices, magnified by leverage, caused many financial institutions to falter in 2007–2008. Because banks borrow from other banks, it can cause problems for the whole financial system. In the words of former Treasury secretary, Paul O'Neill, "If you have 10 bottles of water and one is poisoned, but you do not know which, no one drinks the water." That is, banks were frightened *to loan to* other banks. The collapse of the housing bubble that was built on wide-scale leveraging almost took down the whole financial structure.

Many banks were in desperate need of capital because of the losses that were backed by mortgages that went bad. Because the shortage of capital meant less lending, the Treasury department and the Fed put billions dollars into the banking system to increase the amount of bank capital and get lending back to normal levels, which began to occur in late 2009.

⊚ SECTION QUIZ

1. If a banking transaction created new excess reserves in the banking system, the result would tend to be

   a. an increase in the amount of loans made by banks and an increase in the supply of money.

   b. an increase in the amount of loans made by banks and a decrease in the supply of money.

   c. a decrease in the amount of loans made by banks and an increase in the supply of money.

   d. a decrease in the amount of loans made by banks and a decrease in the supply of money.

2. A reserve requirement of 20 percent means a money multiplier of

   a. 1.25.

   b. 2.

   c. 5.

   d. 20.

3. If the required reserve ratio were increased, then

   a. the money supply would tend to decrease, but the outstanding loans of banks would tend to increase.

   b. both the money supply and the outstanding loans of banks would tend to decrease.

   c. the money supply would tend to increase, but the outstanding loans of banks would tend to decrease.

   d. both the money supply and the outstanding loans of banks would tend to increase.

4. Which of the following statements is true?

   a. When someone invests only their own money, they cannot lose more than that amount.

   b. When someone borrows money to invest, they can lose more than their initial investment.

   c. The greater the extent of leverage in an investment, the greater the potential for both profit and loss.

   d. When home prices decline, borrowers with low down payments may end up with negative equity.

   e. All of the above are true.

(*continued*)

5. Which of the following is true?

   a. Financial institutions are often highly leveraged.

   b. Highly leveraged financial institutions could be at risk of bankruptcy if the value of their investments fell substantially.

   c. When one financial firm goes bankrupt, it can increase the risk that other financial firms could also go bankrupt.

   d. When banks cannot meet their capital requirements, the value of loans is often contracted in order to do so.

   e. All of the above are true.

1. Why do the supply of money and the volume of bank loans both increase or decrease at the same time?

2. Why would each bank involved in the process of multiple expansions of the money supply lend out a larger fraction of any new deposit it receives the lower the reserve requirement?

3. If a particular bank with a reserve requirement of 10 percent has $30,000 in new cash deposits, how much money could it create through making new loans?

4. Why do banks choosing to hold excess reserves or borrowers choosing to hold some of their loans in the form of currency reduce the actual impact of the money multiplier below that indicated by the multiplier formula?

5. How did excessive leverage play a role in the financial crisis?

Answers: 1. a 2. c 3. b 4. e 5. e

17.5 | The Collapse of America's Banking System, 1920–1933

▢ What caused the collapse of the banking system between 1920 and 1933?

▢ How are bank failures avoided today?

Perhaps the most famous utterance from Franklin D. Roosevelt, the president of the United States from 1933 to 1945, was made on the day he assumed office, when he declared, "The only thing we have to fear is fear itself." These 10 words succinctly summarize the problems that led the world's leading economic power to a near total collapse in its system of commercial banking and, with that, to an abrupt and unprecedented decline in the money supply. The decline in the money supply, in turn, contributed to an economic downturn that had dire consequences for many, especially for the one-fourth of the labor force unemployed at the time of Roosevelt's first inaugural address.

What Happened to the Banking Industry?

In 1920, 30,000 banks were operating in the United States; by 1933, the number declined to about 15,000. What happened? In some cases, bank failure reflected imprudent management or even criminal activity on the part of bank officers (stealing from the bank). More often, though, banks in rural areas closed as a consequence of having large sums of assets tied up in loans to farmers who, because of low farm prices, were not in a position to pay off the loans when they came due. Rumors spread that a bank was in trouble, and those rumors, even if false, became self-fulfilling prophecies. Bank "runs" developed, and even conservatively managed banks with cash equal to 15 percent or 20 percent of their deposit liabilities found themselves with insufficient cash reserves to meet the withdrawal requests of panicky depositors.

The bank failures of the 1920s, while numerous, were generally scattered around small towns in the country. In general, confidence in banks actually increased during that decade; and by the fall of 1929, there were $11 in bank deposits for every $1 in currency in circulation.

The first year following the stock market crash of 1929 saw little dramatic change in the banking system, but in late 1930, a bank with the unfortunately awesome-sounding name of the Bank of the United States failed—the largest bank failure in the country up to that time. This failure had a ripple effect. More runs on banks occurred as depositors became jittery. Banks, fearing runs, stopped lending their excess reserves, thereby aggravating a fall in the money supply and reducing business investment.

As depositors converted their deposits to currency, bank reserves fell, as did the ability of banks to support deposits. The situation improved a bit in 1932, when a newly created government agency, the Reconstruction Finance Corporation (RFC), made loans to distressed banks. By early 1933, however, the decline in depositor confidence had reached the point that the entire banking system was in jeopardy. On March 4, newly inaugurated President Roosevelt declared a national bank holiday, closing every bank in the country for nearly two weeks. Then, only the "good" banks were allowed to reopen, an action that increased confidence. By this time the deposit-currency ratio had fallen from 11 to 1 (in 1929) to 4 to 1. Passage of federal deposit insurance in mid-1933 greatly strengthened depositor confidence and led to money reentering the banks. The recovery process began.

Why were there so many bank failures during the Great Depression?

What Caused the Collapse?

The collapse occurred for several reasons. First, the nation had thousands of relatively small banks. Customers believed that depositor withdrawals could force a bank to close, and the mere fear of bank runs made them a reality. Canada, with relatively few banks, most of them large with many branches, had no bank runs. Second, governmental attempts to stem the growing distress were weak and too late. Financial aid to banks was nonexistent; the Federal Reserve System and other governmental efforts began only in 1932—well into the decline. Third, deposit insurance, which would have bolstered customer confidence, did not exist. The financial consequences of bank failures were correctly perceived by the public to be dire. Fourth, growing depositor fear was enhanced by the fact that the economy was in a continuous downward spiral, eroding the basis for any optimism that bank loans would be safely repaid.

Can the fear of a bank run lead to a bank run?

Bank Failures Today

The combination of the Federal Deposit Insurance Corporation (FDIC) and the government's greater willingness to assist distressed banks has reduced the number of bank failures in recent times. Now, when a bank runs into financial difficulty, the FDIC may assist another bank in taking over the assets and liabilities of the troubled bank so that no depositor loses a cent. We do not see depositors run on banks because the FDIC will make good on deposits. Today, if a depository institution fails, its deposits are guaranteed up to $250,000 per depositor per bank. Over 90 percent of banks now hold FDIC insurance. Other insurance programs handle the rest. There are costs and benefits of insuring deposits. On the cost side is that bankers whose deposits are insured may take greater risks—which is called moral hazard. On the benefit side deposit insurance means that changes in the money supply due to a loss of deposits from failed banks are no longer a big problem. Better bank stability means a greater stability in the money supply, which means, as will be more explicitly demonstrated in the next chapter, a greater level of economic stability. There are also other mechanisms in place that can prevent bank runs: capital requirements, reserve requirements and the ability of banks to borrow at the Fed's discount window (more on this in the next chapter). Depositors

What are the benefits and costs of the Federal Deposit Insurance Corporation (FDIC)?

do not have to monitor the risky behavior of their banks as a result of being insured. That is, if a bank makes a risky loan and it goes well, they make a profit; if it goes poorly, they are protected by federal deposit insurance. So to keep banks from behaving recklessly, they are required to maintain more assets. Now, if risky loans go bad, banks can draw on their other assets. The excess of bank assets over deposits and other liabilities is called their bank capital. A bank's capital is typically required to be at least 7 percent of the value of their assets.

However, in the 1980s, a savings and loan crisis occurred, one of the worst financial crises since the Great Depression. The inflation of the 1970s had created a problem for many savings and loans. They had made a large number of long-term (30 years) real estate loans in the early 1970s, when the inflation rate was relatively low, at about 5 percent. Then, during most of the rest of that decade, inflation rates rose rapidly and nominal interest rates soared. The savings and loans were in a squeeze—they had to pay high interest rates to attract depositors but were earning low interest rates on their real estate loans from the early 1970s. This disastrous combination for the savings and loans caused many of them to go belly up.

Unfortunately, interest rates were not the only problem. The government eased regulations to make it easier for savings and loans to compete for deposits with other financial institutions in the national market. Deregulation, coupled with deposit insurance, put savings and loans in a gambling mood. Many savings and loans poured money into high-risk real estate projects and other risky ventures. Depositors had little incentive to monitor their banks because they knew they would be protected up to $100,000 on their accounts by the government. Eventually, more than a thousand thrift institutions went bankrupt. Depositors were saved, but taxpayers were not. Taxpayers ended up paying the bill for much of the savings and loan—debacle the bailout for the financial losses has been estimated to be more than $150 billion. The Thrift Bailout Bill of 1989 provided funds for the bailout and new, stricter provisions for banks.

Financial crisis are a little like earthquakes. We know that they will happen, but we don't know exactly when and the magnitude. For example, not many economists forecasted the financial crisis of 2008.

② SECTION QUIZ

1. Which of the following is true of the Great Depression?

    a. It involved a near-collapse of America's commercial banking system.

    b. Problems with the commercial banking system caused an abrupt and unprecedented decline in the money supply.

    c. Even rumors of a bank being in financial trouble could cause a run on that bank.

    d. Banks, fearing runs, chose to increase their excess reserves as a precaution.

    e. All of the above are true.

2. Which of the following statements is true?

    a. The banking system collapse in the Great Depression was at least partly caused by a fear of bank runs.

    b. Government attempts to deal with the Great Depression's banking distress were too weak to prevent it.

    c. Bank distress in the Great Depression was not reduced by federal deposit insurance.

    d. In the Great Depression, the Federal Reserve System did not adopt efforts to ease banking distress until 1932.

    e. All of the above are true.

1. How did the combination of increased holding of excess reserves by banks and currency by the public lead to bank failures in the 1930s?

2. What are the four reasons cited in the text for the collapse of the U.S. banking system in this period?

3. What is the FDIC, and how did its establishment increase bank stability and reassure depositors?

Answers: 1. e   2. e

Interactive Summary

Fill in the blanks:

1. The most important disadvantage of using commodities as money is that they _____ easily after a few trades.

2. _____ consists of coins and/or paper that some institution or government has created to be used in the trading of goods and services and the payment of debts.

3. Legal tender is _____ money.

4. Assets in checking accounts in banks are more formally called _____ deposits.

5. Demand deposits are deposits in banks that can be _____ on demand by simply writing a check.

6. _____ deposits are assets that can be easily converted into currency or used to buy goods and services directly.

7. _____ deposits and _____ deposits have replaced paper and metallic currency as the primary source of money used for transactions in the United States.

8. Transaction deposits are a popular monetary instrument precisely because they lower _____ costs compared with the use of metal or paper currency.

9. Credit card payments are actually guaranteed _____, which merely defer customer payment.

10. Credit cards are not money; they are _____ for the use of money in exchange.

11. _____ deposits are fund accounts against which the depositor cannot directly write checks.

12. Two primary types of nontransaction deposits exist: _____ accounts and _____ deposits.

13. Assets that can be quickly converted into money are considered highly _____ assets.

14. Money market mutual funds are considered _____ money because they are relatively easy to convert into money for the purchase of goods and services.

15. _____ includes M1, plus saving accounts, time deposits (except for some large-denomination certificates of deposit), and money market mutual funds.

16. _____ law states that "cheap money drives out dear money."

17. Something is money only if people will generally _____ it.

18. Our money is money because of confidence that we have in _____ institutions as well as in our _____.

19. The primary function of money is to serve as a(n) _____.

20. The more complex the economy, the _____ the need for one or more universally accepted assets serving as money.

21. Money is both a(n) _____ of value and a(n) _____ of value.

22. With money, a common _____ exists, so that the values of diverse goods and services can be precisely compared.

23. The value of money fluctuates far _____ than the value of many individual commodities.

24. The biggest players in the banking industry are _____.

25. Aside from commercial banks, the banking system includes two other important financial institutions: _____ and _____.

26. Most important, financial institutions are _____ for savings and liquid assets that are used by individuals and firms for transaction purposes.

27. In making loans, financial institutions act as intermediaries between _____, who supply funds, and _____ seeking funds to invest.

28. If you go into a bank and borrow $1,000, the bank probably will simply _____ to your checking account at the bank.

29. Banks make their profit by collecting _____ interest payments on the loans they make than they pay their depositors for those funds.

30. _____ require banks to keep on hand a quantity of cash or reserve accounts with the Federal Reserve equal to a prescribed proportion of their checkable deposits.

31. Our banking system is sometimes called a(n) _____ system because banks find it necessary to keep cash on hand and reserves at the Federal Reserve equal to some fraction of their checkable deposits.

32. Money is created when banks _____.

33. The largest asset item for most banks is _____.

34. Most banks keep a majority of their reserves as _____.

35. Checking account deposits and time deposits constitute _____ of banks.

36. Any time the aggregate amount of bank _____ changes, the aggregate amount of liabilities and capital must also change by the same amount, by definition.

37. Required reserves equal _____ times _____.

38. Whenever excess reserves appear, banks will convert the _____ reserves into other _____ assets.

39. The monetary expansion of an individual bank is limited to its _____ reserves.

40. Potential money creation from a cash deposit equals that initial deposit times _____.

41. The actual monetary impact of an initial deposit created out of excess reserves within a short time period is _____ indicated by the money multiplier.

42. When a person pays a loan back to a bank, demand deposits _____ and the money supply _____.

Answers: 1. deteriorate 2. Currency 3. fiat 4. demand 5. withdrawn 6. Transaction 7. Demand; other checkable 8. transaction 9. loans 10. substitutes 11. Nontransaction 12. savings; time 13. liquid 14. near 15. M2 16. Gresham's 17. accept 18. private financial; government 19. medium of exchange 20. greater 21. standard; store 22. yardstick 23. less 24. commercial banks 25. savings and loan associations; credit unions 26. depositories 27. savers; borrowers 28. add $1,000 29. higher 30. Reserve requirements 31. fractional reserve 32. make loans 33. loans 34. reserve accounts at the Federal Reserve 35. liabilities 36. assets 37. deposits; the required reserve ratio 38. non-interest-earning; interest-earning 39. excess 40. the money multiplier 41. less than that 42. decline; declines

Key Terms and Concepts

money 482
medium of exchange 482
barter 482
means of deferred payment 485
currency 486
legal tender 487
fiat money 487
demand deposits 487
transaction deposits 487
traveler's checks 487

nontransaction deposits 488
near money 489
money market mutual funds 489
liquidity 489
M1 490
M2 490
gold standard 490
Gresham's law 490
commercial banks 493
savings and loan associations 493

credit unions 493
reserve requirements 494
fractional reserve system 494
secondary reserves 495
balance sheet 495
required reserve ratio 496
excess reserves 496
money multiplier 501

Section Quiz Answers

17.1 What Is Money?

1. Why does the advantage of monetary exchange over barter increase as an economy becomes more complex?

As the economy becomes more complex, the number of exchanges between people in the economy grows very rapidly. This means that the transaction cost advantages of using money over barter for those exchanges also grows very rapidly as the economy becomes more complex.

2. How can uncertain and rapid rates of inflation erode money's ability to perform its functions efficiently?

Uncertain and rapid rates of inflation erode money's ability to perform its functions efficiently because money lowers transaction costs most effectively when its value is stable and therefore more predictable. Uncertain and rapid rates of inflation reduce the stability and predictability of the value of money, reducing its usefulness as a universally understood store of value. It therefore reduces money's ability to reduce transaction costs.

3. In a world of barter, would useful financial statements such as balance sheets be possible? Would stock markets be possible? Would it be possible to build cars?

In a world of barter, there is no common standard of value to allow comparisons of all the "apples and oranges" that must be summarized in financial statements, making such statements virtually impossible. Without money to act as a common standard of value, stock and other financial markets, as well as very complex (many transactions) production processes, would also be virtually impossible.

4. Why do virtually all societies create something to function as money?

Having some good function as money lowers transaction costs, allowing increasing specialization and exchange to create increasing wealth for a society. That increase in wealth made possible by using money is why virtually all societies create something to function as money.

17.2 Measuring Money

1. If everyone in an economy accepted poker chips as payment in exchange for goods and services, would poker chips be money?

Since money is anything that is generally accepted in exchange for goods or services (a medium of exchange), if everyone in an economy accepted poker chips as payment in exchange for goods and services, poker chips would be money.

2. If you were buying a pack of gum, would using currency or a demand deposit have lower transaction costs? What if you were buying a house?

If you were buying a pack of gum, or making any other such small purchase, using currency would generally have lower transaction costs than a demand deposit (checking account). However, if you were buying a house, or any other very large purchase, using a demand deposit would generally have lower transaction costs than paying with currency (it would be cheaper, easier, and safer, and it would generate a more reliable financial record).

3. What is the main advantage of transaction deposits for tax purposes? What is their main disadvantage for tax purposes?

The main advantage of transaction deposits for tax purposes is that they provide more reliable financial records for complying with record-keeping requirements for tax purposes. The financial records that transaction deposits generate, on the other hand, are their main disadvantage for those who wish to hide their financial activities from tax authorities.

4. Are credit cards money?

Credit cards are not money. They are actually guaranteed loans available on demand to users, which can be activated by consumers. Credit cards are convenient substitutes for making transactions directly with money; that is, they are substitutes for the use of money in exchange.

5. What are M1 and M2?

M1 is a narrow definition of money that focuses on money's use as a means of payment (for transaction purposes). M1 includes currency in circulation, checkable deposits, and traveler's checks. M2 is a broader definition of money, which focuses on money's use as a highly liquid store of purchasing power or savings. M2 equals M1 plus other "near moneys," including savings accounts, small-denomination time deposits, and money market mutual funds.

6. How have interest-earning checking accounts and overdraft protection led to the relative decline in demand deposits?

Interest-earning checking accounts provide the same ability to make transactions as non interest-earning demand deposit accounts but are more attractive to many consumers because they earn interest. Overdraft protection means that consumers do not have to keep as much money in demand deposit accounts "just in case" in order to protect against overdrawing their accounts.

17.3 How Banks Create Money

1. What is happening to the number of banks now that interstate banking is allowed?

Laws against interstate banking prevented the formation of large, interstate banking organizations, resulting in a large number of American banks. However, now that interstate banking is allowed, mergers are resulting in fewer, larger, interstate banks.

2. In what way is it true that "banks make money by making money"?

Banks make money (profits) by loaning out their deposits at a higher interest rate than they pay their depositors. However, it is the extension of new loans in search of profits that creates new demand deposits, thereby increasing the stock of money.

3. How do legal reserve deposit regulations lower bank profits?

Unlike other bank assets, legal reserves do not earn interest. Therefore, requiring a larger portion of bank assets to be held in such non-interest-earning accounts than prudent banking practice would dictate reduces bank earnings and profits.

4. Is a demand deposit an asset or a liability?

A demand deposit is an asset for its owner but a liability for the bank at which the account is kept.

5. If the Bonnie and Clyde National Bank's only deposits were demand deposits of $20 million, and it faced a 10 percent reserve requirement, how much money would it be required to hold in reserves?

The Bonnie and Clyde National Bank would have to hold 10 percent of its $20 million in demand deposits, or $2 million, as reserves.

6. Suppose you found $10,000 while digging in your backyard and you deposited it in the bank. How would your new demand deposit account create a situation of excess reserves at your bank?

A new $10,000 deposit adds that amount both to your demand deposit account and to the reserves of your bank. But only a fraction of the added reserves are required by the addition to your demand deposit account. The rest are excess reserves, which the bank will look to convert to interest-earning loans or other assets.

17.4 The Money Multiplier

1. Why do the supply of money and the volume of bank loans both increase or decrease at the same time?

The supply of money and the volume of bank loans both increase or decrease at the same time because issuing new bank loans adds to the money supply, while calling in existing bank loans reduces the money supply.

2. Why would each bank involved in the process of multiple expansions of the money supply lend out a larger fraction of any new deposit it receives the lower the reserve requirement?

Each bank involved in the process of multiple expansions of the money supply can lend up to the amount of its excess reserves. But the excess reserves created by each dollar deposited in a bank equals 1 minus the required reserve ratio. The lower this reserve requirement, the greater the excess reserves created by each new deposit, and therefore the greater the fraction of any new deposit that will be loaned out in this process.

3. If a particular bank with a reserve requirement of 10 percent has $30,000 in new cash deposits, how much money could it create through making new loans?

A bank can loan up to the amount of its excess reserves. If it faces a reserve requirement of 10 percent, a new $30,000 cash deposit would add $3,000 (10 percent of $30,000) to its required reserves but $30,000 to its total reserves. This deposit would therefore create $27,000 in excess reserves that the bank could lend out, and that $27,000 in increased loans would increase the money stock by an equal amount.

4. Why do banks choosing to hold excess reserves or borrowers choosing to hold some of their loans in the form of currency reduce the actual impact of the money multiplier below that indicated by the multiplier formula?

If banks choose to hold excess reserves, each bank involved in the process of creating additional money will lend out less, and therefore create less new money, than if it loaned out all its excess reserves. The result will be a smaller money supply than that indicated by the multiplier formula because the formula assumes that banks lend out all their excess reserves. If borrowers hold some of their loans as currency, this will reduce the amount of vault cash, which counts as a reserve, at banks. This then will reduce the amount that can be loaned at each stage of the money-supply creation process and will therefore reduce the actual money multiplier below the level indicated by the multiplier formula.

5. How did excessive leverage play a role in the financial crisis?

Financial institution leveraging can increase risk and lead to bankruptcy. In addition, losses borne by one financial institution can have a ripple effect, increasing losses by others. The collapse of the housing market, built on wide-scale leveraging, almost took down the whole financial structure.

17.5 The Collapse of America's Banking System, 1920–1933

1. How did the combination of increased holding of excess reserves by banks and currency by the public lead to bank failures in the 1930s?

The desire by the public for increased currency holdings, caused largely by the fear of bank failures, also forced banks to sharply increase excess reserves and reduce lending, together resulting in a sharp fall in the money stock. Despite substantial excess reserves, however, bank runs led to the failure of even many conservatively run banks.

2. What are the four reasons cited in the text for the collapse of the U.S. banking system in this period?

The cited reasons include (1) the large number of small banks, which were more at risk from bank runs; (2) governmental attempts to stem the distress in the banking industry that were both weak and too late; (3) the absence of deposit insurance, which would have bolstered consumer confidence; and (4) fear that the economy was in a continuous downward cycle, so that there was little basis for optimism that bank loans would be safely repaid.

3. What is the FDIC, and how did its establishment increase bank stability and reassure depositors?

The Federal Deposit Insurance Corporation insures bank deposits. This guarantee of deposits eliminated the risk to depositors if their bank failed, thus eliminating the bank runs that resulted from the fear of bank insolvency. Without having to face the risk of bank runs, banks became more stable.

Problems

1. Explain the difficulties that an economics professor might face in purchasing a new car under a barter system.

2. Why do people who live in countries experiencing rapid inflation often prefer to hold U.S. dollars rather than their own country's currency? Explain.

3. An alternative version of Gresham's law is that "Bad money drives out good money." Why is it true that, in choosing between different currencies to transact in, good money drives out bad money?

4. Which one of each of the following pairs of assets is most liquid?
   a. Microsoft stock or a traveler's check
   b. a 30-year bond or a six-month Treasury bill
   c. a certificate of deposit or a demand deposit
   d. a savings account or 10 acres of real estate

5. Indicate whether each of the following belongs on the asset or liability side of a bank's balance sheet.
   a. loans
   b. holdings of government securities
   c. demand deposits
   d. vault cash
   e. deposits at the Fed
   f. bank buildings
   g. certificates of deposit

6. Why do you think asking whether money is an asset or a liability is a trick question in economics?

7. Why have ATMs and online banking made savings accounts more liquid than they used to be?

8. Why would the increasing liquidity of savings accounts make some monetary economists track the size of M1 plus savings account balances (called MZM) over time?

9. What would each of the following changes do to M1 and M2?

Change	M1	M2
An increase in currency in circulation	_____	_____
A decrease in demand deposits	_____	_____
An increase in savings deposits	_____	_____
An increase in credit card balances	_____	_____
A conversion of savings account balances into checking account balances	_____	_____
A conversion of savings account balances into time account balances	_____	_____
A conversion of checking account balances into money market mutual funds	_____	_____

10. Given that the Fed currently imposes reserve requirements on checking deposits, but not on savings deposits, why would banks prefer to hold deposits as savings accounts rather than checking accounts, other things equal?

11. Since the Fed has begun paying interest on bank reserves at the Fed, do banks still want to avoid holding excess reserves?

12. What would the money multiplier be if the required reserve ratio were

5 percent?   _____
10 percent?   _____
20 percent?   _____
25 percent?   _____
50 percent?   _____

13. Assume there was a new $100,000 deposit into a checking account at a bank.
    a. What would be the resulting excess reserves created by that deposit if banks faced a reserve requirement of

    10 percent?   _____
    20 percent?   _____
    25 percent?   _____
    50 percent?   _____

    b. How many additional dollars could that bank lend out as a result of that deposit if banks faced a reserve requirement of

    10 percent?   _____
    20 percent?   _____
    25 percent?   _____
    50 percent?   _____

    c. How many additional dollars of money could the banking system as a whole create in response to such a new deposit if banks faced a reserve requirement of

    10 percent?   _____
    20 percent?   _____
    25 percent?   _____
    50 percent?   _____

14. If the required reserve ratio is 10 percent, calculate the potential change in demand deposits under the following circumstances:
    a. You take $5,000 from under your mattress and deposit it in your bank.
    b. You withdraw $50 from the bank and leave it in your wallet for emergencies.
    c. You write a check for $2,500 drawn on your bank (Wells Fargo) to an auto mechanic who deposits the funds in his bank (Bank of America).

15. Calculate the magnitude of the money multiplier if banks were to hold 100 percent of deposits in reserve. Would banks be able to create money in such a case? Explain.

16. Answer the following questions.
    a. If a bank had reserves of $30,000 and demand deposits of $200,000 (and no other deposits), how much could it lend out if it faced a required reserve ratio of

       10 percent?   _____
       15 percent?   _____
       20 percent?   _____

    b. If the bank then received a new $40,000 deposit in a customer's demand deposit account, how much could it now lend out if it faced a required reserve ratio of

       10 percent?   _____
       15 percent?   _____
       20 percent?   _____

chapter eighteen

The Federal Reserve System and Monetary Policy

What do we know about the amount of money in the economy and its impact on other important macro-economic variables such as the price level, employment and real GDP? In the previous chapter, we demonstrated how banks create money. In this chapter, we see how the Federal Reserve can use its power over the money supply to impact interest rates in the short run via the aggregate demand and supply model and how money impacts the price level in the long run through the equation of exchange. We will also see that macroeconomic policy, whether it is fiscal or monetary

policy, is very difficult to implement. Is it easy to nudge the economy back on track? The latest recession suggests it's not so easy.

The chairperson of the Federal Reserve System is one of the most important policy makers in the country. The importance of the Federal Reserve System and monetary policy cannot be overestimated. In this chapter, we will see how deliberate changes in the money supply can affect aggregate demand and lead to short-run changes in the output of goods and services as well as the price level. That is, monetary policy can be an effective tool for helping to achieve and maintain price stability, full employment, and economic growth. We will also see that monetary-policy tools, just like fiscal-policy tools, have problems of implementation.

18.1   The Federal Reserve System

📂 What are the functions of a central bank?

📂 Who controls the Federal Reserve System?

📂 How is the Fed tied to Congress and the executive branch?

The Functions of a Central Bank

What does a central bank do? Why is it important?

In most countries of the world, the job of manipulating the supply of money belongs to the "central bank." A central bank performs many functions. First, the central bank is a "banker's bank." It is the bank where commercial banks maintain their own cash deposits—their reserves. Second, the central bank performs a number of service functions for commercial banks, such as transferring funds and checks between various commercial banks in the banking system. Third, the central bank typically serves as the primary bank for the central government, handling, for example, its payroll accounts. Fourth, the central bank buys and sells foreign currencies and generally assists in the completion of financial transactions with other countries. Fifth, it serves as the "lender of last resort," helping banking institutions in financial distress. Sixth, the central bank is concerned with the stability of the banking system and the money supply, which, as we have already seen, results from the loan decisions of banks. The central bank can and does impose regulations on private commercial banks; it thereby regulates the size of the money supply and influences the level of economic activity. The central bank also implements monetary policy, which, along with fiscal policy, forms the basis of efforts to direct the economy to perform in accordance with macroeconomic goals.

Commercial banks keep reserves with the central bank. Roughly 4,000 U.S. banks are members of the Federal Reserve System. While this is less than half the number of total banks, the member banks hold roughly 75 percent of U.S. bank deposits. Furthermore, all banks must meet the Fed's requirements, whether they are members or not.

Location of the Federal Reserve System

In most countries, the central bank is a single bank; for example, the central bank of Great Britain, the Bank of England, is a single institution located in London. In the United States, however, the central bank is 12 institutions, closely tied together and collectively called the Federal Reserve System. The Federal Reserve System, or Fed, as it is nicknamed, comprises separate banks in Boston, New York, Philadelphia, Richmond, Atlanta, Dallas, Cleveland, Chicago, St. Louis, Minneapolis–St. Paul, Kansas City, and San Francisco. As Exhibit 1

© Cengage Learning 2013

section 18.1
exhibit 1   Boundaries of Federal Reserve Districts and Their Branch Territories

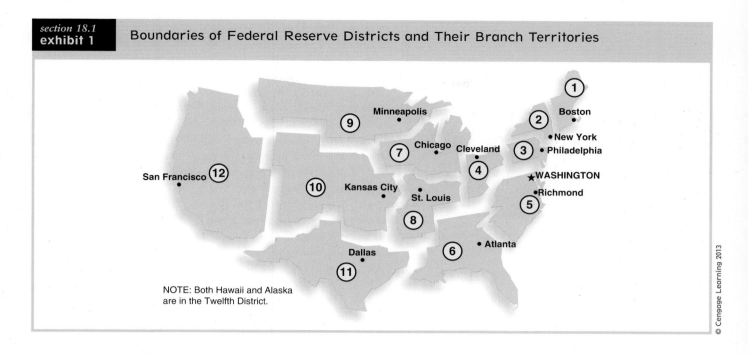

NOTE: Both Hawaii and Alaska
are in the Twelfth District.

shows, these banks and their branches are spread all over the country, but they are most heavily concentrated in the eastern states.

Each of the 12 banks has branches in key cities in its district. For example, the Federal Reserve Bank of Cleveland serves the fourth Federal Reserve district and has branches in Pittsburgh, Cincinnati, and Columbus. Each Federal Reserve Bank has its own board of directors and, to a limited extent, can set its own policies. Effectively, however, the 12 banks act in unison on major policy issues, with control of major policy decisions resting with the Board of Governors and the Federal Open Market Committee, headquartered in Washington, D.C. The chairman of the Federal Reserve Board of Governors (currently Ben Bernanke) is generally regarded as one of the most important and powerful economic policy makers in the country.

The Fed's Relationship to the Federal Government

The Federal Reserve System was created in 1913 because the U.S. banking system had so little stability and no central direction. Technically, the Fed is privately owned by the banks that "belong" to it. Banks are not required to belong to the Fed; however, since the passage of new legislation in 1980, virtually no difference exists between the requirements for member and nonmember banks.

The private ownership of the Fed is essentially meaningless, because the Federal Reserve Board of Governors, which controls major policy decisions, is appointed by the president of the United States, not by the stockholders. The owners of the Fed have relatively little control over its operations and receive only small fixed dividends on their modest financial stake in the system. Again, the feature of private ownership but public control was a compromise made to appease commercial banks opposed to direct public (government) regulation.

The Fed's Ties to the Executive Branch

An important aspect of the Fed's operation is that, historically, it has enjoyed a considerable amount of independence from both the executive and legislative branches of government. In fact, central banks with greater degrees of independence appear to have a lower annual

The chair of the Fed is truly the chief executive officer of the system. The Fed chair is required by law to testify to Congress twice a year. In addition to the chair, all seven members are appointed by the president and confirmed by the Senate to sit on the Board of Governors. Governors are appointed for 14-year terms, staggered every two years, in an attempt to insulate them from political pressure.

inflation rate. True, the president appoints the seven members of the Board of Governors, subject to Senate approval, but the term of appointment is 14 years. No member of the Federal Reserve Board will face reappointment from the president who initially made the appointment, because presidential tenure is limited to two four-year terms. Moreover, the terms of board members are staggered, so a new appointment is made only every two years. Hence, it is unlikely that a single president would appoint a majority of the members of the board; even were it possible, members have little fear of losing their jobs as a result of presidential wrath. The chair of the Federal Reserve Board is a member of the Board of Governors and serves a four-year term. The chair is truly the chief executive officer of the system and effectively runs it, with considerable help from the presidents of the 12 regional banks.

Fed Operations

Many of the key policy decisions of the Federal Reserve are actually made by its Federal Open Market Committee (FOMC), which consists of the seven members of the Board of Governors, the president of the New York Federal Reserve Bank, and four other presidents of Federal Reserve Banks, who serve on the committee on a rotating basis. The FOMC makes most of the key decisions influencing the direction and size of changes in the money supply; their regular, closed meetings are accordingly considered important by the business community, news media, and government.

ⓘ SECTION QUIZ

1. The most important role of the Federal Reserve System is

   a. raising or lowering taxes.

   b. regulating the supply of money.

   c. increasing or reducing government spending.

   d. none of the above.

2. Which of the following is not a function of the Federal Reserve System?

   a. being a lender of last resort

   b. being concerned with the stability of the banking system

   c. serving as a major bank for the central government

   d. setting currency exchange rates

3. The Fed is institutionally independent. A major advantage of this is that

   a. monetary policy is subject to regular ratification by congressional votes.

   b. monetary policy is not subject to control by politicians.

   c. monetary policy cannot be changed once it has been determined.

   d. monetary policy will always be coordinated with fiscal policy.

   e. monetary policy will always offset fiscal policy.

(continued)

How Does the Federal Reserve Change the Money Supply?

18.2

📂 What are the three major tools of the Fed?   📂 What other powers does the Fed have?

📂 What is the purpose of the Fed's tools?   📂 How are bank failures avoided today?

As noted previously, the Federal Reserve Board of Governors and the FOMC are the prime decision makers for U.S. monetary policy. They decide whether to expand the money supply and, it is hoped, the real level of economic activity, or to contract the money supply, hoping to cool inflationary pressures. How does the Fed control the money supply, particularly when it is the privately owned commercial banks that actually create and destroy money by making loans, as we discussed earlier?

The Fed has three major methods by which to control the supply of money: It can engage in open market operations, change reserve requirements, or change its discount rate. Of these three, by far the most important is open market operations.

Open Market Operations

Open market operations involve the purchase and sale of U.S. government bonds by the Federal Reserve System. The FOMC decides at its regular meetings to buy or sell government bonds. Open market operations are the most important method the Fed uses to influence the money supply for several reasons. First, it is a device that can be implemented quickly and cheaply—the Fed merely calls an agent who buys or sells bonds. Second, it can be done quietly, without a lot of political debate or a public announcement. Third, it is a rather powerful tool, as any given purchase or sale of bonds has an ultimate impact several times the amount of the initial transaction. Fourth, the Fed can use this tool to change the money supply by a small or large amount on any given day.

The trading desk at the Federal Reserve Bank in New York is responsible for buying and selling the government bonds. When the Fed wants to increase the money supply, the FOMC tells the trading desk at the Federal Reserve Bank in New York to buy U.S. government bonds from the public in the nation's bond market. The seller of the bonds will likely deposit their new funds in the bank, increasing excess reserves. The new reserves would lead to new loans and checking account deposits, putting the money multiplier in motion and ultimately increasing the money supply.

If the Fed wanted to decrease the money supply, the FOMC would tell the trading desk to sell government bonds to the public in the nation's bond market. The buyers of the

open market operations purchase and sale of U.S. government bonds by the Federal Reserve System

What is the most important tool of the Federal Reserve?

government bonds would pay with checks drawn from their bank. The reserves at their bank will fall. The decrease in reserves leads to fewer loans and checkable account deposits, setting the money multiplier in motion in reverse, leading to a reduction in the money supply.

In short, if the Fed believes the economy needs to be stimulated, it will buy government bonds. If the Fed wishes to slow the economy down, it will sell government bonds.

The Reserve Requirement

Even though open market operations are the most important and widely utilized tool for achieving monetary objectives that the Fed has at its disposal, open market operations are not the Fed's potentially most powerful tool. The Fed possesses the power to change the reserve requirements of member banks by altering the reserve ratio. It can have an immediate and significant impact on the ability of member banks to create money. Suppose the banking system as a whole has $500 billion in deposits and $60 billion in reserves, with a reserve ratio of 12 percent. Because $60 billion is 12 percent of $500 billion, the system has no excess reserves. Suppose now that the Fed lowers reserve requirements by changing the reserve ratio to 10 percent. Banks then are required to keep only $50 billion in reserves ($500 billion × 0.10), but they still have $60 billion. Thus, the lowering of the reserve requirement gives banks $10 billion in excess reserves. The banking system as a whole can expand deposits and the money supply by a multiple of this amount, in this case 10 (10% equals 1/10; the banking multiplier is the reciprocal of this, or 10). The lowering of the reserve requirement in this case, then, would permit an expansion in deposits of $100 billion, which represents a 20 percent increase in the stock of money, from $500 to $600 billion.

When Does the Fed Use This Tool?

Relatively small reserve requirement changes can thus have a big impact on the potential supply of money. This tool is so potent, in fact, that it is seldom used. In other words, the power of the reserve requirement is not only its advantage but also its disadvantage, because a small reduction in the reserve requirement can make a huge change in the number of dollars that are in excess reserves in banks all over the country. Such huge changes in required reserves and excess reserves have the potential to disrupt the economy.

Frequent changes in the reserve requirement would make it difficult for banks to plan. For example, a banker might worry that if she makes loans now and then the Fed raises the reserve requirement, she would not have enough reserves to meet the new reserve requirements. If she does not make loans and the Fed leaves the reserve requirement alone, she loses the opportunity to earn income on those loans.

Carpenters don't use sledgehammers to hammer small nails or tacks; the tool is too big and powerful to use effectively. For the same reason, the Fed changes reserve requirements rather infrequently, and when it does make changes, it is by small amounts. For example, between 1970 and 1980, the Fed changed the reserve requirement only twice, and less than 1 percent on each occasion. Furthermore, changes in the reserve requirement, because they are so powerful, are a sign that monetary policy has swung strongly in a new direction.

Why doesn't the Fed change the reserve requirement often?

Fed Now Pays Interest on Reserves

In October of 2008, the Fed began to pay interest on reserves held with the Fed—both required reserves and excess reserves. This provides the Fed with a new tool. If the Fed raised the interest rate it paid on reserves, we would expect banks to hold more in excess reserves, decreasing the size of the money multiplier and reducing the money supply. If the Fed wanted to increase the money supply, it could decrease the interest rate it pays on reserves, lowering holdings of excess reserves and increasing the money multiplier.

The Discount Rate

Banks having trouble meeting their reserve requirement can borrow funds directly from the Fed at its discount window. The interest rate the Fed charges on these borrowed reserves is called the **discount rate**. The Fed can control the money supply by altering the discount rate. If the Fed raises the discount rate, it discourages banks from borrowing reserves from the Fed. This reduces the quantity of reserves in the banking system, which leads to a reduction in the money supply. That is, if the Fed wants to contract the money supply, it will raise the discount rate, making it more costly for banks to borrow reserves.

If the Fed is promoting an expansion of money and credit, it will lower the discount rate, making it cheaper for banks to borrow reserves. Thus, a lower discount rate will encourage banks to borrow from the Fed, increasing the quantity of reserves and the money supply.

The discount rate sometimes changes fairly frequently, often several times a year. Sometimes the rate will be moved several times in the same direction within a single year, which has a substantial cumulative effect.

discount rate
interest rate that the Fed charges commercial banks for the loans it extends to them

The Significance of the Discount Rate

The discount rate is a relatively unimportant tool, mainly because member banks do not rely heavily on the Fed for borrowed funds and often the Fed would not lend them all they want to borrow. It is something most of them believe should be reserved for real emergencies. In October of 1987, when the stock market crashed, Fed Chair Alan Greenspan used discount lending to help financial institutions that were in trouble. Many Wall Street brokerage firms needed temporary funds to finance the high volume of stock trades. The Fed was there to help. Also, in the financial crisis of 2008, the collapse of the housing market coupled with mortgage defaults meant that many financial institutions were in trouble. The Fed provided loans to many of these financial institutions that were in trouble.

When banks have short-term needs for cash to meet reserve requirements, they are more likely to take a short-term (often overnight) loan from another bank in the **federal funds market**. For that reason, many people pay a lot of attention to the interest rate on federal funds.

In recent years, the Federal Reserve has increased its focus on the federal funds rate as the primary indicator of its stance on monetary policy. The Fed announces a federal funds rate target at each FOMC meeting. This rate is watched closely, because it affects all the interest rates throughout the economy—auto loans, mortgages, and so on.

Normally the discount rate is set 1.0 percentage point above the federal funds rate target. Setting the discount rate above the fund rate is designed to keep banks from turning to this source. Thus, most of discount lending is small.

The Fed could use the discount rate by altering the discount rate relative to the federal funds rate. However, the discount rate's main significance is that changes in the rate are commonly viewed as a signal of the Fed's intentions with respect to monetary policy. Discount rate changes are widely publicized, unlike open market operations, which are carried out in private and announced several weeks later in the minutes of the FOMC.

However, in response to the financial crisis, there was considerable amount of lending through the discount window beginning in the fall of 2008. The Fed reduced the spread between the discount rate and the federal funds rate; by the spring of 2008, the discount rate was only 0.25 percentage point above the federal funds rate, when it had usually been a full percentage point higher.

Why do banks typically not borrow at the discount window?

federal funds market
market in which banks provide short-term loans to other banks that need cash to meet reserve requirements

ECS

economic content standards

The major monetary policy tool that the Fed uses is open market purchases or sales of government securities. Other policy tools used by the Fed include increasing or decreasing the discount rate charged on loans it makes to commercial banks and raising or lowering reserve requirements for commercial banks.

How the Fed Reduces the Money Supply

The Fed can do three things to reduce the money supply or reduce the rate of growth in the money supply: (1) sell bonds, (2) raise reserve requirements, or (3) raise the discount rate. Of course, the Fed could also opt to use some combination of these three tools in its approach.

These moves tend to decrease aggregate demand, reducing nominal GDP—ideally, through a decrease in P rather than Q. These actions are the monetary policy equivalent of a fiscal policy of raising taxes, lowering transfer payments, and/or reducing government purchases.

How the Fed Increases the Money Supply

If the Fed is concerned about underutilizing resources (e.g., unemployment), it can engage in precisely the opposite policies: (1) buy bonds, (2) lower reserve requirements, or (3) lower the discount rate. The Fed can also use some combination of these three approaches.

These moves tend to increase aggregate demand, increasing nominal GDP—ideally, through an increase in Q (in the context of the equation of exchange) rather than P. Equivalent expansionary fiscal policy actions include reducing taxes, increasing transfer payments, and/or increasing government purchases.

Difficulties in Controlling the Money Supply

Why is it so hard to control the money supply?

In a fractional reserve banking system, the Fed cannot precisely control the money supply because of two problems: people and banks.

The Fed cannot precisely control the amount of money that people want to hold as currency in circulation versus as deposits in their financial institutions. The more cash people put in the bank, the more excess reserves the bank has for lending purposes and the more money created. Alternatively, if people are concerned about the health of the financial system and choose to take money out of the bank in order to hold more currency, it would reduce banks' excess reserves, reducing lending and the money supply. Either change can alter the money supply without any action from the Fed.

Banks can also choose to not lend out all of their excess reserves. When banks keep more excess reserves, the Fed has less control over the money supply because banks rather than Fed policy dictates how much will be lent out. If banks make money by making loans, why would they keep excess reserves? Banks may choose to become more cautious because of the current economic climate; to avoid risk they may choose to hold on to more excess reserves. Consequently, the banking system would create less money with a given level of reserves than it normally would and the money supply would fall.

This may not be a huge problem because the Fed keeps massive amounts of data on the behavior of banks and their depositors. As a result, changes in currency circulation or excess reserve holdings by banks can be remedied with offsetting policies the Fed can control.

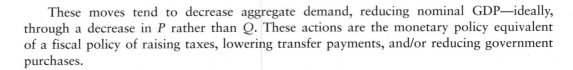

policy watch   QE2 to the Rescue?

In the fall of 2010, the Federal Reserve announced a plan to resume monetary easing by purchasing $600 billion in long-term Treasuries. The plan, which expired in June of 2011, was quantitative easing, number 2 (QE2). It was called number 2 because the Fed had already used asset purchases earlier, during the financial crisis. Japan used a similar policy in the 1990s, when its interest rates were also near zero.

Despite potential risks, the Federal Reserve's plans to buy $600 billion in U.S. Treasury bonds by June of next year will expand the money supply and should stimulate the economy, according to National Center for Policy Analysis Distinguished Fellow Bob McTeer, former president of the Federal Reserve Bank of Dallas and member of the Federal Open Market Committee (FOMC).

(*continued*)

POLICY watch QE2 to the Rescue? (Cont.)

According to McTeer, "Banks aren't exactly hoarding cash, but they're not lending enough either, that's because holding extra cash reserves has been prudent during these turbulent times. By providing more reserves through the purchase of Treasuries, however, there will be fewer benefits to holding additional cash and it will increasingly be in bankers' interest to put their excess reserves to work through loans and investments."

McTeer acknowledged that the magnitude of quantitative easing—$600 billion by June 2011—is "large but all of it may not be needed." "The fear, of course, is inflation," McTeer warned. However, "some measures of inflation are below one percent and there is a great deal of slack in the economy; capacity utilization is low and unemployment is high. So the Fed believes that under these conditions it can stimulate growth in the money supply without a high risk of inflation."

A number of economists are also concerned that quantitative easing could depreciate the value of the dollar in foreign exchange markets. McTeer states, "More dollars created might depress it in foreign exchange markets but, if the monetary surge works, a healthier U.S. economy might strengthen it. In any case, flexible exchange rates are intended to reconcile whatever domestic policies are appropriate for domestic conditions with the rest of the world. Internal policies may have external circumstances, but charges that the intent is to spur the domestic economy through currency depreciation are way off base."

The QE2 program has increased bank reserves, but banks have added to their excess reserves rather than creating large amounts of money through lending and investing. There has been no multiple expansion of the money supply, as would be the case if the banking system kept very few excess reserves.

Monetary Easing versus Blockage

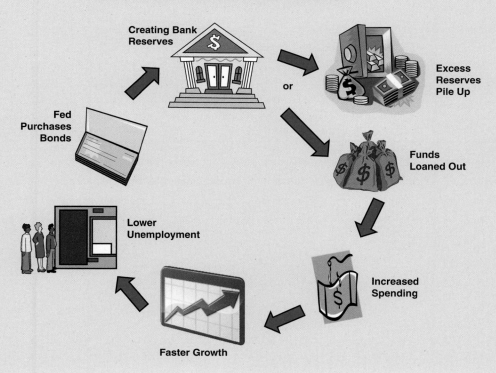

② SECTION QUIZ

1. In order to increase the rate of growth of the money supply, the Fed can

   a. raise the discount rate.

   b. raise the reserve requirement.

   c. buy U.S. governemnt bonds on the open market.

   d. sell U.S. government bonds on the open market.

2. If the Fed wishes to decrease the money supply, it

   a. buys stocks.

   b. sells stocks.

   c. can buy government bonds from the public in the nation's bond market.

   d. can sell government bonds to the public in the nation's bond market.

3. If the Fed sells U.S. government bonds to the public in the the nation's bond market,

   a. the banking system has more reserves, and the money supply tends to grow.

   b. the banking system has fewer reserves, and the money supply tends to grow.

   c. the banking system has more reserves, and the money supply tends to fall.

   d. the banking system has fewer reserves, and the money supply tends to fall.

4. If the Fed lowers the discount rate, what will be the effect on the money supply?

   a. The money supply will tend to increase.

   b. The money supply will tend to decrease.

   c. The money supply will not change nor influence an expansion or contraction process.

   d. Not enough data are given to answer.

5. Reducing reserve requirements, other things being equal, would tend to

   a. increase the dollar volume of loans made by the banking system.

   b. increase the money supply.

   c. increase aggregate demand.

   d. do all of the above.

   e. do (a) and (b), but not (c).

---

1. What three main tactics could the Fed use in pursuing a contractionary monetary policy?

2. What three main tactics could the Fed use in pursuing an expansionary monetary policy?

3. Would the money supply rise or fall if the Fed made an open market purchase of government bonds, *ceteris paribus?*

4. If the Fed raised the discount rate from 1 to 2 percent, what effect would this have on the money supply?

Answers: 1. c   2. d   3. d   4. a   5. d

Money, Interest Rates, and Aggregate Demand

- What causes the demand for money to change?

- How do changes in income change the money market equilibrium?

- How does the Fed's buying and selling bonds affect RGDP in the short run?

- What is the relationship between bond prices and the interest rate?

- Why does the Fed target the interest rate rather than the money supply?

- How are the real and nominal interest rates connected in the short run?

The Money Market

The Federal Reserve's policies with respect to the money supply have a direct effect on short-run nominal interest rates and, accordingly, on the components of aggregate demand. The **money market** is the market where money demand and money supply determine the equilibrium *nominal* interest rate. When the Fed acts to change the money supply by changing one of its policy variables, it alters the money market equilibrium.

Money has several functions, but why would people hold money instead of other financial assets? That is, what is responsible for the demand for money? Transaction purposes, precautionary reasons, and asset purposes are at least some of the determinants of the demand for money.

money market
market in which money demand and money supply determine the equilibrium interest rate

How does the Federal Reserve impact short-run nominal interest rates?

Transactions Demand for Money

First, the primary reason that money is demanded is for transaction purposes—to facilitate exchange. Workers are generally paid by the week or month. However, most people want to hold on to money so they can buy goods and services on a continual basis, not just on payday. They want to keep money for everyday predictable expenses. For example, nobody would want to buy pizza with stocks and bonds. How costly would it be to convert less liquid assets like stocks or bonds into goods and services? Those costs would include the loss of interest and possible withdrawal penalties. In addition, the higher a person's income, the more transactions that person is likely to make (because consumption is income related); the greater will be GDP; and the greater will be the demand for money from transaction purposes, other things being equal.

Precautionary Demand for Money

Second, people like to have money on hand for precautionary reasons—so called "mattress money." If unexpected medical or other expenses require an unusual outlay of cash, people want to be prepared. The extent to which an individual holds cash for precautionary reasons depends partly on that person's income and partly on the opportunity cost of holding money, which is determined by market rates of interest. The higher the market interest rates, the higher the opportunity cost of holding money; and so people will hold less of their financial wealth as money.

Why do people hold money?

Asset Demand for Money

Third, money has a trait—liquidity—that makes it a desirable asset. Other things being equal, people prefer assets that are more liquid to those that are less liquid. That is, people want to be able to easily convert some of their money into goods and services. For this reason, most people wish to have some of their portfolio in the form of money. At higher interest rates on other assets, the amount of money desired for this purpose will be smaller, because the opportunity cost of holding money will have risen.

The Demand for Money and the Nominal Interest Rate

The quantity of money demanded varies inversely with the nominal interest rate. When interest rates are higher, the opportunity cost—in terms of the interest income on alternative assets—of holding monetary assets is higher, and persons will want to hold less money. At the same time, the demand for money, particularly for transaction purposes, is highly dependent on income levels, because the transaction volume varies directly with income. Finally, the demand for money depends on the price level. If the price level increases, buyers will need more money to purchase their goods and services. If the price level falls, buyers will need less money to purchase their goods and services.

The demand curve for money is presented in Exhibit 1. At lower interest rates, the quantity of money demanded is greater, illustrated by a movement from A to B. That is, the lower the interest rate the lower the opportunity cost of holding money. An increase in income will lead to an increase in the demand for money, depicted by a rightward shift in the money demand (MD) curve, a movement from A to C.

How would an increase in income impact your demand for money?

Why Is the Supply of Money Relatively Inelastic?

The supply of money is largely governed by the regulatory policies of the central bank. Whether interest rates are 4 percent or 14 percent, banks seeking to maximize profits will increase lending as long as they have reserves above their desired level. Even a 4 percent return on loans provides more profit than maintaining those assets in non-interest-bearing cash or reserve accounts at the Fed, which currently earn very low interest rate from the Fed. Given this fact, the money supply is effectively almost perfectly inelastic with respect to interest rates over their plausible range. Therefore, we draw the money supply (MS) curve as vertical, other things being equal, in Exhibit 2, with changes in Federal Reserve policies acting to shift the money supply curve.

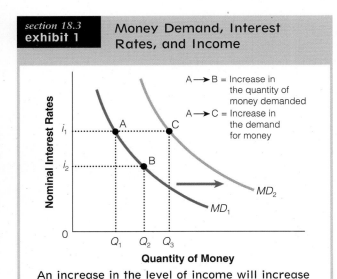

section 18.3 exhibit 1 — Money Demand, Interest Rates, and Income

An increase in the level of income will increase the amount of money that people want to hold for transaction purposes for any given interest rate; the demand for money therefore shifts to the right, from MD_1 to MD_2. The money demand curve is downward sloping, because at the lower nominal interest rate, the opportunity cost of holding money is lower.

The Money Market

Equilibrium in the money market is found by combining the money demand and money supply curves in Exhibit 2. Money market equilibrium occurs at that *nominal* interest rate where the quantity of money demanded equals the quantity of money supplied. Initially, the money market is in equilibrium at i^* in Exhibit 2.

Money Market Equilibrium

In Exhibit 2, we see that equilibrium occurs at point E, where the quantity of money demanded by the public is equal to the quantity of the money supplied by the banking system, given the policies adopted by the Fed. At i_2, below the equilibrium interest rate, the quantity of money that people want to hold is greater than the quantity that is available from the banking system—there is a shortage at i_2. Consequently, people will try to increase their holdings of money by reducing their holdings of bonds or other interest-bearing assets. Because many people are trying to rid themselves of bonds, bond sellers realize they must increase interest on bonds to attract buyers. Thus, the interest rate rises to the equilibrium level, i^*.

At i_1, the interest rate is above the equilibrium level, the quantity of money people want to hold is less than the quantity that is available from the banking system; there is a surplus of money at i_1. Those that are holding the surplus of money (cash and checkable deposits) will try to exchange money for other assets such as bonds. As the demand for bonds rises, bond sellers can pay less interest but still attract enough buyers. As the interest rate falls, people become more willing to hold money, until the interest rate reaches equilibrium at i^*, where people are content holding the money the banking system has supplied.

The Money Market and the Aggregate Demand Curve

Recall the interest rate effect that moved us along the aggregate demand curve when the price level changed. We now look at that relationship in more detail. Specifically, when the price level rises from PL_1 to PL_2 in Exhibit 3, people demand more money and the money demand curve shifts from MD_1 to MD_2. That is, at the new higher price level, PL_2, many goods and services will have higher prices, so people will want to hold more money, MD_2 rather than MD_1.

How does an increase in the demand for money affect the money market? The increase in the demand for money, coupled with a fixed money supply (controlled by the Fed), will cause the interest rate to increase from i_1 to i_2. At the higher interest rate, the cost of borrowing and the return to saving are higher. In short, fewer households will be borrowing for houses and cars, and fewer firms will be investing in new factories and equipment. Thus, the quantity at RGDP demanded falls from $RGDP_1$ to $RGDP_2$.

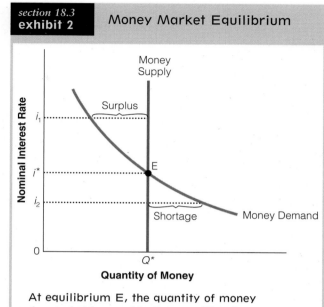

section 18.3
exhibit 2   **Money Market Equilibrium**

At equilibrium E, the quantity of money demanded is equal to the quantity of money supplied by the banking system. The equilibrium interest rate is i^* and the equilibrium quantity of money is Q^*. At i_1, there is a surplus. At i_2 there is a shortage.

© Cengage Learning 2013

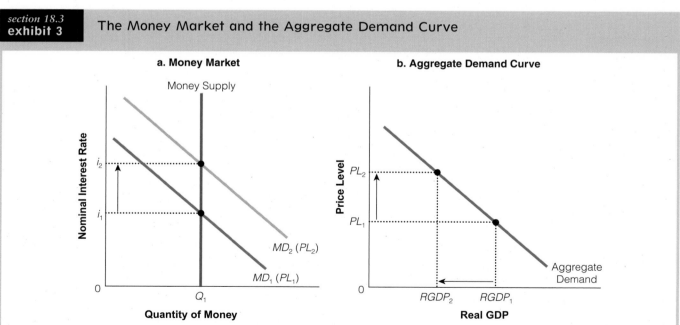

section 18.3
exhibit 3   **The Money Market and the Aggregate Demand Curve**

When the price level increases from PL_1 to PL_2, people desire to hold more money—an increase in the demand for money from MD_1 to MD_2. The increase in the demand for money causes the interest rate to rise from i_1 to i_2. The increase in interest leads to a reduction in RGDP demanded from $RGDP_1$ to $RGDP_2$.

© Cengage Learning 2013

How does a change in the price level affect the demand for money?

Of course, the reverse is true as well. A lower price level leads to a decrease in the demand for money because, on average, goods and services have lower price tags. The reduction in the demand for money causes a reduction in the interest rate, which encourages consumption and investment that reduces RGDP demanded. Hence, this leads to the downward-sloping aggregate demand curve—a higher price level leads to reduction in RGDP demanded.

How Do Income Changes Affect the Equilibrium Position?

Rising national income increases the demand for money, shifting the money demand curve to the right from MD_1 to MD_2, and leading to a new higher equilibrium interest rate.

How Would an Increase in the Money Supply Affect Equilibrium Interest Rates and Aggregate Demand?

A Federal Reserve policy change that increased the money supply would be depicted by a shift in the money supply curve to the right. As a result of this shift, the equilibrium quantity of money demanded increases as equilibrium interest rates fall. The immediate impact of expansionary monetary policy is to decrease the interest rate. Because the money demand curve has not changed, the interest rate falls to the new equilibrium at E_2. The interest rate falls to induce people to hold the additional money supplied by the banking system, MS_2. The lower interest rate, or the fall in the cost of borrowing money, then leads to an increase in aggregate demand for goods and services at the current price level. The lower interest rate will increase home sales, car sales, business investments, and so on. That is, an increase in the money supply will lead to lower interest rates and an increase in aggregate demand, as seen in Exhibit 4. Thus, when the Fed changes policy to increase the money supply, the interest rate falls. This increases RGDP demanded at each and every price level. If the Fed

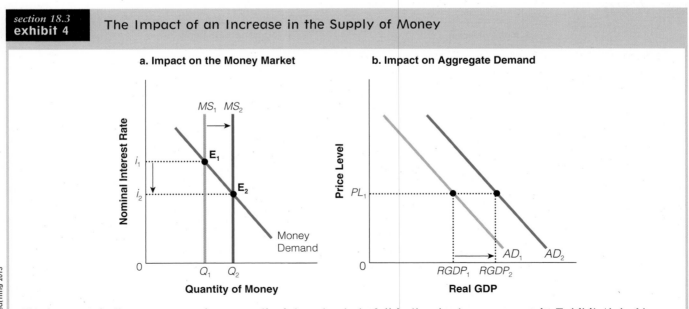

section 18.3 exhibit 4   The Impact of an Increase in the Supply of Money

The increase in the money supply causes the interest rate to fall in the short run, as seen in Exhibit 4(a). At lower interest rates, households and businesses invest more and buy more goods and services, shifting the aggregate demand curve to the right, as shown in Exhibit 4(b).

changes policy to reduce the money supply, the interest rate would rise, which would lower RGDP demanded at each and every price level.

Does the Fed Target the Money Supply or Interest Rates?

Some economists believe that the Fed should try to control the money supply. Other economists believe that the Fed should try to control interest rates. Unfortunately, the Fed cannot do both—it must pick one or the other.

The economy is initially at point A in Exhibit 5, where the interest rate is i_1 and the quantity of money is at Q_1. Now, suppose the demand for money were to increase because of an increase in national income, an increase in the price level, or because people desire to hold more money. As a result, the demand curve for money shifts to the right, from MD_1 to MD_2. If the Fed decides it does not want the money supply to increase, it can pursue a policy of no monetary growth, which leads to an increase in the interest rate to i_2 at point C. The Fed could also try to keep the interest rate stable at i_1, but it can only do so by increasing the growth in the money supply through expansionary monetary policy. The Fed cannot simultaneously pursue policies of no monetary growth and monetary expansion; it must choose—a higher interest rate, a greater money supply, or some combination of both. The Fed cannot completely control both the growth in the money supply and the interest rate. If it attempts to keep the interest rate steady in the face of increased money demand, it must increase the growth in the money supply. If it tries to keep the growth of the money supply in check in the face of increased money demand, the interest rate will rise.

In short, monetary policy can be applied in terms of the money supply or the interest rate (the federal funds rate). When FOMC sets a federal funds rate target, the Fed's bond traders are told to do whatever is necessary to get the equilibrium interest rate to the target level. To lower the federal funds rate, Fed bond traders buy government bonds. This increases the money supply and lowers the interest rate. If FOMC raises the target for the federal funds rate, its bond traders sell government bonds. This decreases the money supply and raises the interest rate.

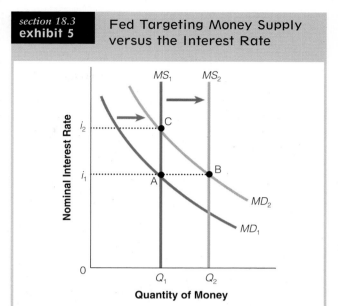

section 18.3 exhibit 5 — Fed Targeting Money Supply versus the Interest Rate

When the demand curve for money shifts outward, the Fed must settle for either a higher interest rate, a greater money supply, or some combination of both. The Fed cannot completely control both the growth in the money supply and the interest rate. If it attempts to keep the interest rate steady, it must increase the growth in the money supply. If it tries to keep the growth of the money supply in check, the interest rate will rise.

Why can't the Fed target the growth in the money supply and the interest rate at the same time?

The Problem

The problem with targeting the money supply is that the demand for money fluctuates considerably in the short run. Focusing on the growth in the money supply when the demand for money is changing unpredictably leads to large fluctuations in interest rates, as occurred in the U.S. economy during the late 1970s and early 1980s. These erratic changes in interest rates could seriously disrupt the investment climate.

Keeping interest rates in check also creates problems. For example, when the economy grows, the demand for money also grows, so the Fed has to increase the money supply to keep interest rates from rising. If the economy is in a recession, the demand for money falls, and the Fed has to contract the money supply to keep interest rates from falling. This approach leads to the wrong policy prescription—expanding the money supply during a boom eventually leads to inflation, and contracting the money supply during a recession makes the recession even worse.

Which Interest Rate Does the Fed Target?

The Fed targets the federal funds rate. Remember the federal funds rate is the interest rate that banks charge each other for short-term loans. A bank that may be short of reserves might borrow from another bank that has excess reserves. The Fed has been targeting the federal funds rate since about 1965. At the close of the meetings of the FOMC, the Fed usually announces whether the federal funds rate target will be increased, decreased, or left alone as shown in Exhibit 6.

Monetary policy decisions may be enacted either through the money supply or through the interest rate. That is, if the Fed wants to pursue a contractionary monetary policy (a reduction in aggregate demand), this policy can take the form of a reduction in the money supply or a higher interest rate. If the Fed wants to pursue an expansionary monetary policy (an increase in aggregate demand), this policy can take the form of an increase in the money supply or a lower interest rate. So why is the interest rate used? First, many economists believe that the primary effects of monetary policy are felt through the interest rate. Second, the money supply is difficult to measure accurately. Third, as we mentioned earlier, changes in the demand for money may complicate money supply targets. Last, people are more familiar with changes in the interest rate than with changes in the money supply.

Does the Fed Influence the Real Interest Rate in the Short Run?

Most economists believe that in the short run the Fed can control the nominal interest rate and the real interest rate. Recall that the real interest rate is equal to the nominal interest rate minus the expected inflation rate. Therefore, a change in the nominal interest rate tends to change the real interest rate by the same amount, because the expected inflation rate is slow to change in the short run. That is, if the expected inflation rate does not change, the

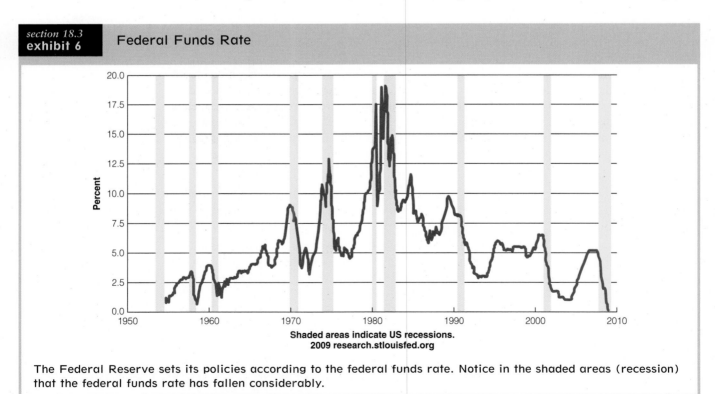

section 18.3
exhibit 6   Federal Funds Rate

Shaded areas indicate US recessions.
2009 research.stlouisfed.org

The Federal Reserve sets its policies according to the federal funds rate. Notice in the shaded areas (recession) that the federal funds rate has fallen considerably.

SOURCE: Board of Governors of the Federal Reserve System.

relationship between the nominal and real interest rates is a direct relationship: A 1 percent reduction in the nominal interest rate will generally lead to a 1 percent reduction in the real interest rate in the short run. However, for the long run—several years after the inflation rate has adjusted—the equilibrium real interest rate will be given by the intersection of the demand and supply of loanable funds curves.

Exhibit 7 summarizes the preceding discussion of the tools available to the Fed for enacting monetary policy.

section 18.3 **exhibit 7**	Summary of Fed Tools for Monetary Policy	
Macroeconomic Problem	**Monetary Policy Prescription**	**Fed Policy Tools**
Unemployment (Slow or negative RGDP growth rate—below $RGDP_{NR}$)	Expansionary monetary policy to increase aggregate demand	Buy bonds Lower discount rate Lower reserve requirement
Inflation (Rapid RGDP growth rate—beyond $RGDP_{NR}$)	Contractionary monetary policy to decrease aggregate demand	Sell bonds Raise discount rate Raise reserve requirement

© Cengage Learning 2013

POLICY application   The Fed's Exit Strategy

The depth and breadth of the global recession has required a highly accommodative monetary policy. Since the onset of the financial crisis nearly two years ago, the Federal Reserve has reduced the interest-rate target for overnight lending between banks (the federal-funds rate) nearly to zero. We have also greatly expanded the size of the Fed's balance sheet through purchases of longer-term securities and through targeted lending programs aimed at restarting the flow of credit.

These actions have softened the economic impact of the financial crisis. They have also improved the functioning of key credit markets, including the markets for interbank lending, commercial paper, consumer and small-business credit, and residential mortgages.

My colleagues and I believe that accommodative policies will likely be warranted for an extended period. At some point, however, as economic recovery takes hold, we will need to tighten monetary policy to prevent the emergence of an inflation problem down the road. The Federal Open Market Committee, which is responsible for setting U.S. monetary policy, has devoted considerable time to issues relating to an exit strategy. We are confident we have the necessary tools to withdraw policy accommodation, when that becomes appropriate, in a smooth and timely manner.

The exit strategy is closely tied to the management of the Federal Reserve balance sheet. When the Fed makes loans or acquires securities, the funds enter the banking system and ultimately appear in the reserve accounts held at the Fed by banks and other depository institutions. These reserve balances now total about $800 billion, much more than normal. And given the current economic conditions, banks have generally held their reserves as balances at the Fed.

But as the economy recovers, banks should find more opportunities to lend out their reserves. That would produce faster growth in broad money (for example, M1 or M2) and easier credit conditions, which could ultimately result in inflationary pressures—unless we adopt countervailing policy measures. When the time comes to tighten monetary policy, we must either eliminate these large reserve balances or, if they remain, neutralize any potential undesired effects on the economy.

To some extent, reserves held by banks at the Fed will contract automatically, as improving financial conditions lead to reduced use of our short-term lending facilities, and ultimately to their wind down. Indeed, short-term credit extended by the Fed to financial institutions and other market

(*continued*)

policy
application
The Fed's Exit Strategy (Cont.)

participants has already fallen to less than $600 billion as of mid-July from about $1.5 trillion at the end of 2008. In addition, reserves could be reduced by about $100 billion to $200 billion each year over the next few years as securities held by the Fed mature or are prepaid. However, reserves likely would remain quite high for several years unless additional policies are undertaken.

Even if our balance sheet stays large for a while, we have two broad means of tightening monetary policy at the appropriate time: paying interest on reserve balances and taking various actions that reduce the stock of reserves. We could use either of these approaches alone; however, to ensure effectiveness, we likely would use both in combination.

Congress granted us authority last fall to pay interest on balances held by banks at the Fed. Currently, we pay banks an interest rate of 0.25 percent. When the time comes to tighten policy, we can raise the rate paid on reserve balances as we increase our target for the federal funds rate.

Banks generally will not lend funds in the money market at an interest rate lower than the rate they can earn risk-free at the Federal Reserve. Moreover, they should compete to borrow any funds that are offered in private markets at rates below the interest rate on reserve balances because, by so doing, they can earn a spread without risk.

Thus the interest rate that the Fed pays should tend to put a floor under short-term market rates, including our policy target, the federal-funds rate. Raising the rate paid on reserve balances also discourages excessive growth in money or credit, because banks will not want to lend out their reserves at rates below what they can earn at the Fed.

Considerable international experience suggests that paying interest on reserves effectively manages short-term market rates. For example, the European Central Bank allows banks to place excess reserves in an interest-paying deposit facility. Even as that central bank's liquidityoperations substantially increased its balance sheet, the overnight interbank rate remained at or above its

deposit rate. In addition, the Bank of Japan and the Bank of Canada have also used their ability to pay interest on reserves to maintain a floor under short-term market rates.

Despite this logic and experience, the federal-funds rate has dipped somewhat below the rate paid by the Fed, especially in October and November 2008, when the Fed first began to pay interest on reserves. This pattern partly reflected temporary factors, such as banks' inexperience with the new system.

However, this pattern appears also to have resulted from the fact that some large lenders in the federal-funds market, notably government-sponsored enterprises such as Fannie Mae and Freddie Mac, are ineligible to receive interest on balances held at the Fed, and thus they have an incentive to lend in that market at rates below what the Fed pays banks.

Under more normal financial conditions, the willingness of banks to engage in the simple arbitrage noted above will tend to limit the gap between the federal-funds rate and the rate the Fed pays on reserves. If that gap persists, the problem can be addressed by supplementing payment of interest on reserves with steps to reduce reserves and drain excess liquidity from markets—the second means of tightening monetary policy. Here are four options for doing this.

First, the Federal Reserve could drain bank reserves and reduce the excess liquidity at other institutions by arranging large-scale reverse repurchase agreements with financial market participants, including banks, government-sponsored enterprises and other institutions. Reverse repurchase agreements involve the sale by the Fed of securities from its portfolio with an agreement to buy the securities back at a slightly higher price at a later date.

Second, the Treasury could sell bills and deposit the proceeds with the Federal Reserve. When purchasers pay for the securities, the Treasury's account at the Federal Reserve rises and reserve balances decline.

The Treasury has been conducting such operations since last fall under its Supplementary Financing

(continued)

POLICY application   The Fed's Exit Strategy (Cont.)

Program. Although the Treasury's operations are helpful, to protect the independence of monetary policy, we must take care to ensure that we can achieve our policy objectives without reliance on the Treasury.

Third, using the authority Congress gave us to pay interest on banks' balances at the Fed, we can offer term deposits to banks—analogous to the certificates of deposit that banks offer their customers. Bank funds held in term deposits at the Fed would not be available for the federal funds market.

Fourth, if necessary, the Fed could reduce reserves by selling a portion of its holdings of long-term securities into the open market.

Each of these policies would help to raise short-term interest rates and limit the growth of broad measures of money and credit, thereby tightening monetary policy.

Overall, the Federal Reserve has many effective tools to tighten monetary policy when the economic outlook requires us to do so. As my colleagues and I have stated, however, economic conditions are not likely to warrant tighter monetary policy for an extended period. We will calibrate the timing and pace of any future tightening, together with the mix of tools to best foster our dual objectives of maximum employment and price stability.

consider this:

The Fed was there to rescue many banks during the financial crisis of 2007–2008. It infused the banking system with newly created reserves.

SOURCE: Ben Bernanke, "The Fed's Exit Strategy," *The Wall Street Journal*, July 21, 2010. Reprinted from The Wall Street Journal © 2010 Dow Jones & Company. All rights reserved.

⑦ SECTION QUIZ

1. The money demand curve shows
   a. the various amounts of money that individuals will hold at different price levels.
   b. the various amounts of money that individuals will spend at different levels of GDP.
   c. the various amounts of money that individuals will hold at different interest rates.
   d. the quantity of bonds that the Fed will buy at different price levels.

2. What will happen to the demand for money if real GDP rises?
   a. It will decrease.
   b. It will be unchanged.
   c. It will increase.
   d. It depends on what happens to interest rates.

3. Contractionary monetary policy will tend to have what effect?
   a. Increase the money supply and lower interest rates.
   b. Increase the money supply and increase interest rates.
   c. Decrease the money supply and lower interest rates.
   d. Decrease the money supply and increase interest rates.

4. When money demand increases, the Fed can choose between
   a. increasing interest rates or increasing the supply of money.
   b. increasing interest rates or decreasing the supply of money.
   c. decreasing interest rates or increasing the supply of money.
   d. decreasing interest rates or decreasing the supply of money.

(*continued*)

⑦ SECTION QUIZ (Cont.)

5. If a reduction in the money supply were desired in order to slow inflation, the Federal Reserve might

   a. decrease reserve requirements.

   b. buy U.S. government bonds on the open market.

   c. raise the discount rate.

   d. do either (b) or (c).

---

1. What are the determinants of the demand for money?

2. If the earnings available on other financial assets rose, would you want to hold more or less money? Why?

3. For the economy as a whole, why would individuals want to hold more money as GDP rises?

4. Why might people who expect a major market "correction" (a fall in the value of stock holdings) wish to increase their holdings of money?

5. How is the money market equilibrium established?

6. Who controls the supply of money in the money market?

7. How does an increase in income or a decrease in the interest rate affect the demand for money?

8. What Federal Reserve policies would shift the money supply curve to the left?

9. Will an increase in the money supply increase or decrease the short-run equilibrium real interest rate, other things being equal?

10. Will an increase in national income increase or decrease the short-run equilibrium real interest rate, other things being equal?

11. What is the relationship between interest rates and aggregate demand in monetary policy?

Answers: 1. c 2. c 3. d 4. a 5. c

18.4 Expansionary and Contractionary Monetary Policy

📁 What is expansionary monetary policy?

📁 What is contractionary monetary policy?

📁 How does monetary policy work in the open economy?

📁 How does monetary policy impact real GDP and the price level?

Expansionary Monetary Policy in a Recessionary Gap

What can the Fed do to close a recessionary gap?

If the Fed engages in expansionary monetary policy to combat a recessionary gap, the increase in the money supply will lower the interest rate. The lower interest rate reduces the cost of borrowing and the return to saving. Therefore, firms invest in new plant and equipment, while households increase their investment in housing at the lower interest rate. In short, when the Fed increases the money supply, interest rates fall and the quantity demanded of goods and services increases at each and every price level. The aggregate demand curve shifts from AD_1 to AD_2, as seen in Exhibit 1. The result is greater RGDP growth at a higher price level at E_2. In this case, the Fed has eliminated the recession, and RGDP is equal to the potential level of output at $RGDP_{NR}$. During the recession of 2001, the Fed aggressively lowered the federal funds rate to stimulate aggregate demand when it was faced with a recessionary gap.

For example, in the first half of 2001, the Fed slashed interest rates to their lowest levels since August 1994. Between January 2001 and August 2001, the Fed cut the federal funds rate target by 3 percentage points, clearly demonstrating that it was concerned that the economy was dangerously close to falling into a recession. Then came the events of September 11 and the corporate scandals. By the end of the year, the federal funds rate, which began at 6.5 percent, was at 1.75 percent, the lowest rate since 1961. With the slow recovery, the Fed pushed the rate down further, to 1.25 percent in November 2002. The Fed's actions were aimed at increasing consumer confidence, restoring stock market wealth, and stimulating investment. That is, the Fed's move was designed to increase aggregate demand in an effort to increase output and employment to long-run equilibrium at E_2.

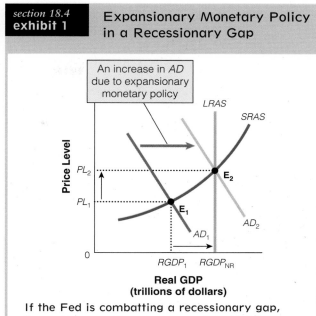

section 18.4
exhibit 1   Expansionary Monetary Policy in a Recessionary Gap

If the Fed is combatting a recessionary gap, it can increase the money supply, which leads to a change in aggregate demand from AD_1 to AD_2. The result is greater RGDP of a higher price level. The expansionary monetary policy has moved the economy to the natural rate (where RGDP = potential GDP).

© Cengage Learning 2013

Contractionary Monetary Policy in an Inflationary Gap

The Fed may engage in contractionary monetary policy if the economy faces an inflationary gap. Suppose the economy is at initial short-run equilibrium, E_1, in Exhibit 2. In order to combat inflation, suppose the Fed engages in an open market sale of bonds. This would lead

to a decrease in the money supply, causing the interest rate to rise. The higher interest rate means that borrowing is more expensive and the return to saving is higher. Consequently, firms find it more costly to invest in plant and equipment and households find it more costly to finance new homes. In short, when the Fed increases the money supply it lowers the interest rate and increases the quantity of goods and services demanded at every price level. That is, the aggregate demand curve shifts leftward from AD_1 to AD_2 in Exhibit 2. The result is a lower RGDP and a lower price level, at E_2. The economy is now at $RGDP_{NR}$ where RGDP equals the potential level of output.

Monetary Policy in the Open Economy

For simplicity, we have assumed that the global economy does not affect domestic monetary policy. This assumption is incorrect. Suppose the Fed decides to pursue an expansionary policy by buying bonds on the open market. As we have seen, when the Fed buys bonds on the open market, the

section 18.4
exhibit 2   Contractionary Monetary Policy in an Inflationary Gap

A decrease in AD due to contractionary monetary policy

If the Fed is combating an inflationary gap at E_1, it can decrease the money supply, which would lead to a change from AD_1 to AD_2. The result is a lower RGDP and a lower price level at E_2, and the economy moves to the natural rate (where RGDP = potential GDP).

© Cengage Learning 2013

in the **news** The U.S. Economy in the Wake of September 11

The devastating events of September 11 further set back an already fragile economy. Heightened uncertainty and badly shaken confidence caused a widespread pullback from economic activity and from risk taking in financial markets, where equity prices fell sharply for several weeks and credit risk spreads widened appreciably. The most pressing concern of the Federal Reserve in the first few days following the attacks was to help shore up the infrastructure of financial markets and to provide massive quantities of liquidity to limit potential disruptions to the functioning of those markets. The economic fallout of the events of September 11 led the Federal Open Market Committee (FOMC) to cut the target federal funds rate after a conference call early the following week and again at each meeting through the end of the year.

Displaying the same swift response to economic developments that appears to have characterized much business behavior in the current cyclical episode, firms moved quickly to reduce payrolls and cut production after mid-September. Although these adjustments occurred across a broad swath of the economy, manufacturing and industries related to travel, hospitality, and entertainment bore the brunt of the downturn. Measures of consumer confidence fell sharply in the first few weeks after the attacks, but the deterioration was not especially large by cyclical standards, and improvement in some of these indexes was evident in October. Similarly, equity prices started to rebound in late September, and risk spreads began to narrow somewhat by early November, when it became apparent that the economic effects of the attacks were proving less severe than many had feared.

Consumer spending remained surprisingly solid over the final three months of the year in the face of enormous economic uncertainty, widespread job losses, and further deterioration of household balance sheets from the sharp drop in equity prices immediately following September 11. Several factors were at work in support of household spending during this period. Low and declining interest rates provided a lift to outlays for durable goods and to activity in housing markets. Nowhere was the boost from low interest rates more apparent than in the sales of new motor vehicles, which soared in response to the financing incentives offered by manufacturers. Low mortgage interest rates not only sustained high levels of new home construction but also allowed households to refinance mortgages and extract equity from homes to pay down other debts or to increase spending. Fiscal policy provided additional support to consumer spending. The cuts in taxes enacted [in 2001], including the rebates paid out over the summer, cushioned the loss of income from the deterioration in labor markets. And the purchasing power of household income was further enhanced by the sharp drop in energy prices during the autumn. With businesses having positioned themselves to absorb a falloff of demand, the surprising strength in household spending late in the year resulted in a dramatic liquidation of inventories. In the end, real gross domestic product posted a much better performance than had been anticipated in the immediate aftermath of the attacks.

SOURCE: Federal Reserve Board of Governors, "Monetary Policy and the Economic Outlook," *88th Annual Report,* 2001, pp. 3–5.

immediate effect is that the money supply increases and interest rates fall. With lower domestic interest rates, some domestic investors will invest funds in foreign markets, exchanging dollars for foreign currency, which leads to a depreciation of the dollar (a decrease in the value of the dollar). The depreciation of the dollar makes the U.S. market more attractive to foreign buyers and foreign markets relatively less attractive to domestic buyers. That is, this shift means an increase in net exports—fewer imports and greater exports—and an increase in RGDP in the short run.

Similarly, the Fed may pursue a contractionary monetary policy by selling bonds on the open market. When the Fed sells bonds on the open market, the immediate effect is it reduces

use what you've learned   Money and the *AD/AS* Model

QDuring the Great Depression in the United States, the price level fell, the money wage rate fell, real GDP fell, and unemployment reached 25 percent. Investment fell, and as banks failed, the money supply fell dramatically. Can you show the effect of these changes from a vibrant 1929 economy to a battered 1932 economy using the *AD/AS* model?

AThe 1929 economy was at PL_{1929} and $RGDP_{NR}$ in Exhibit 3. The lack of consumer confidence coupled with the large reduction in the money supply, wealth lost in the stock market crash, and falling investment sent the aggregate demand curve reeling. As a result, the aggregate demand curve fell from AD_{1929} to AD_{1932}, real GDP fell to $RGDP_{1932}$, and the price level fell to PL_{1932}.

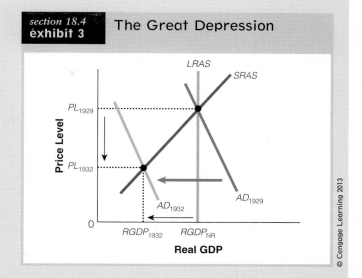

**section 18.4
exhibit 3**   The Great Depression

© Cengage Learning 2013

the money supply and causes interest rates to rise; foreign investors will convert their currencies to dollars to take advantage of the relatively higher interest rates. These purchases will lead to an appreciation of the dollar (an increase in the value of a currency), which will make U.S. goods and services relatively more expensive—foreigners will import less and domestic consumers will buy more exports. The result is a decrease in net exports and a reduction in RGDP in the short run.

⑦ SECTION QUIZ

1. Which of the following Federal Reserve actions would most likely help counteract an oncoming recession?

   a. an increase in reserve requirements and an increase in the discount rate

   b. the sale of government bonds and an increase in the discount rate

   c. the sale of foreign currencies and an increase in reserve requirements

   d. the purchase of government bonds and a reduction in the discount rate

2. In a recession, appropriate monetary policy would tend to be for the Fed to _____ bonds to _____ AD.

   a. buy; increase

   b. buy; decrease

   c. sell; increase

   d. sell; decrease

(*continued*)

② SECTION QUIZ (Cont.)

3. To offset an inflationary boom, appropriate Fed policy could be to _____ reserve requirements to _____ *AD.*

   a. increase; increase

   b. increase; decrease

   c. decrease; increase

   d. decrease; decrease

4. Which one of the following would be the most appropriate stabilization policy if the economy is operating beyond its long-run potential capacity?

   a. the Fed sells government bonds to the public in the nation's bond market

   b. an increase in government purchases, holding taxes constant

   c. a reduction in reserve requirements

   d. a reduction in taxes, holding government purchases constant

1. How will an expansionary monetary policy affect RGDP and the price level at less than full employment?

2. How will a contractionary monetary policy affect RGDP and the price level at a point beyond full employment?

Answers: 1. d 2. a 3. b 4. a

18.5

Money and Inflation—The Long Run

📂 What is the equation of exchange?

📂 What is the velocity of money?

📂 What is the quantity theory of money and prices?

For many centuries, scholars have known that there is a positive relationship between the money supply, the price level, the growth in the money supply, and the inflation rate. In the 1500s, there was a huge influx of gold and silver that flowed into Europe following the Spanish conquest in the New World. The influx of precious metals almost tripled the money supply of Europe. Too many coins were chasing what goods were available and prices rose steadily in the sixteenth century.

The Inflation Rate and the Growth in the Money Supply

Can inflation last a long time without increases in the money supply?

One of the major reasons that the control of the money supply is so important is that, in the long run, the amount of money in circulation and the overall price level are closely linked. It is virtually impossible for a country to have sustained inflation without a rapid growth in the money supply. The inflation rate tends to be greater in periods of rapid monetary expansion than in periods of slower growth in the money supply. In Exhibit 1, we see that international data supports the relationship between higher money growth and a higher inflation rate.

The Equation of Exchange

In the early twentieth century, Yale economist Irving Fisher formalized the relationship between money and the price level with the equation of exchange. The equation of exchange (or quantity equation) can be written as:

$$M \times V = P \times Q$$

where M is the money supply, however defined (usually M_1 or M_2), V is the velocity of money, P is the price level, and Q is real output (RGDP).

The **velocity of money** refers to its "turnover" rate, or the intensity with which money is used. Specifically, V represents the average number of times that each dollar is used in purchasing final goods or services in a one-year period. For example, a $20 bill may travel from you to the delicatessen owner, who passes it on to a doctor for the co-payment on medical services, who passes it on to a car dealership as part of a down payment for a new car. The faster money circulates, the higher the velocity. Velocity is defined as the nominal or current dollar value of output divided by the money supply, or:

$$V = RGDP/M$$

Suppose we have a simple economy that only produces frozen yogurt. The economy produces 200 quarts of frozen yogurt per year. The frozen yogurt sells for $5 a quart and the quantity of money in the economy is $100. Plugging the numbers into our equation, we get:

$$
\begin{aligned}
V &= RGDP/M \\
&= P \times Q/M \\
&= (\$5 \times 200)/\$100 = 10
\end{aligned}
$$

What is the velocity of money?

velocity of money
a measure of how frequently money is turned over

ECS
economic content standards

In the long run, inflation results from increases in a nation's money supply that exceed increases in its output of goods and services.

---

section 18.5
exhibit 1   Money Supply Growth and Inflation Rates in Selected Countries, 1980–2002

We often see a strong positive correlation between a country's average annual inflation rate and its annual growth in money supply.

SOURCE: *International Financial Statistics*, International Monetary Fund, Washington, D.C., 2008, Volume LXI, pp. 51–53 and 79–81.

That is, the people in the economy spend $1,000 per year on frozen yogurt. If there is only $100 of money in the economy, each dollar must change hands on average 10 times per year. Thus, the velocity is 10.

The Quantity Theory of Money and Prices

quantity theory of money and prices
a theory of the connection between the money supply and the price level when the velocity of money is constant

If we make certain assumptions about the variables in the equation of exchange we can clearly see the relationship between the money supply and the price level. This relationship is called the **quantity theory of money and prices**. If velocity (V) and real GDP (Q) both remain constant, then a 10 percent increase in the money supply will lead to a 10 percent increase in the price level—that is, the money supply and the price level change by the same proportion. We can then extend this equation to link the growth rates of these four variables. Using the *growth version of the quantity equation*, we can transform $M \times V = P \times Q$ into:

$$\text{Growth rate of the money supply} + \text{Growth rate of velocity} =$$
$$\text{Growth rate of the price level (inflation rate)} +$$
$$\text{Growth rate of real output}$$

This makes it easier to see the effects of the money supply on the inflation rate. Suppose money growth is 5 percent per year, the growth of real output is 3 percent per year, and velocity has not changed at all—its growth rate is 0 percent. What is the inflation rate? The growth rate of M (5 percent) + the growth rate of V (0 percent) = the growth rate of prices __?__ + the growth rate of Q (3 percent). In this situation, the growth rate of prices (the inflation rate) is equal to 2 percent. We can also extend the analysis to predict the inflation rate when real GDP and velocity also vary. For example, if velocity grew at 1 percent annually rather than zero in our example, the inflation rate would be 3 percent rather than 2 percent.

If velocity remains constant, then the growth rate of velocity (the percentage change from one year to the next) will be zero. Then we can simplify our equation once more:

$$\text{Inflation rate} = \text{Growth rate of the money supply} - \text{Growth rate of real GDP}$$

If this is the case, there are three possible scenarios:

1. If money supply grows at a faster rate than real GDP, then there will be inflation.
2. If money supply grows at a slower rate than real GDP, then there will be deflation.
3. If money supply grows at the same rate as real GDP, the price level will be stable.

Economists once expected they could treat the velocity of money as a given, because the determinants of velocity they focused on would change only very slowly. We now know that velocity is not constant, but often moves in a fairly predictable pattern. Historically, the velocity of money has been quite stable over a long period of time, particularly when using the M_2 definition of money. Thus, the connection between money supply and the price level is still fairly predictable, especially during periods of high inflation.

If an increase in the money supply leads to inflation in the long run, why do countries allow the growth rate of their money supply to increase so rapidly? There are several possible reasons. For example, during wars or political instability, countries may spend more than they can raise through borrowing from the public or taxation, so they create more money to pay their bills. The more money they create, the larger amount of inflation they will experience.

What is hyperinflation? What causes it? How can you get rid of it?

Hyperinflation

The relationship between the growth rate of the money supply and the inflation rate is particularly strong when there is very rapid inflation, called hyperinflation. One of the most famous cases of hyperinflation was in Germany in the 1920s—inflation rose to roughly 300 percent *per month* for over a year. The German government had incurred large amounts of debt as a result of World War I and could not raise enough money to pay its expenses, so it printed huge amounts of money. The inflation rate became so rapid that store owners would change their prices in the middle of the day, firms had to pay workers several times a week, and many resorted to barter. Recently, Zimbabwe, Brazil, Argentina, and Russia have all experienced hyperinflation. The cause of hyperinflation is simply excessive money growth.

② SECTION QUIZ

1. In the long run, a sustained increase in growth of the money supply relative to the growth rate of potential real output will most likely
   a. cause the nominal interest rate to fall.
   b. cause the real interest rate to fall.
   c. reduce the natural rate of unemployment.
   d. increase real output growth.
   e. do none of the above.

2. The equation of exchange can be written as
   a. $M \times P = V \times Q$.
   b. $M \times V = P \times Q$.
   c. $M \times Q = P \times V$.
   d. $Q \times M = P \times V$.

3. The P in the equation of exchange represents the
   a. profit earned in the economy.
   b. average level of prices of final goods and services in the economy.
   c. marginal level of prices.
   d. marginal propensity to spend.

4. If nominal GDP is $3,200 billion and M1 is $800 billion, then velocity is
   a. 0.5.
   b. 2.
   c. 4.
   d. 8.
   e. 400.

5. According to the simple quantity theory of money, a change in the money supply of 6.5 percent would, holding velocity constant, lead to
   a. a 6.5 percent change in real GDP.
   b. a 6.5 percent change in nominal GDP.
   c. a 6.5 percent change in velocity.
   d. a 6.5 percent change in aggregate supply.

6. If M increases and V increases,
   a. nominal GDP increases.
   b. nominal GDP decreases.
   c. nominal GDP stays the same.
   d. the effect on nominal GDP is indeterminate.

(*continued*)

18.6

Problems in Implementing Monetary and Fiscal Policy

📁 What problems exist in implementing monetary policy?

📁 What problems exist in coordinating monetary and fiscal policies?

Problems in Conducting Monetary Policy

The lag implementation problem inherent in adopting fiscal policy changes is less acute for monetary policy, largely because the decisions are not slowed by the same budgetary process. That is, the implementation lag is longer for fiscal policy. The FOMC of the Federal Reserve, for example, can act quickly (in emergencies almost instantly, by conference call) and even secretly to buy or sell government bonds, the key day-to-day operating tool of monetary policy. However, the length and variability of the lag before its effects on output and employment are felt are still significant, and the time before the full price-level effects are felt is even longer and more variable. According to the Federal Reserve Bank of San Francisco, the major effects of a change in policy on growth in the overall production of goods and services usually are felt within three months to two years; the effects on inflation tend to involve even longer lags, one to three years or more.

How Do Commercial Banks Implement the Fed's Monetary Policies?

One limitation of monetary policy is that it ultimately must be carried out through the commercial banking system. The central bank (the Federal Reserve System in the United States) can change the environment in which banks act, but the banks themselves must take the steps necessary to increase or decrease the money supply. Usually, when the Fed is trying to constrain monetary expansion, it has no difficulty in getting banks to make appropriate responses. Banks must meet their reserve requirements; if the Fed raises bank reserve requirements, sells bonds, and/or raises the discount rate, banks must obtain the necessary cash or reserve deposits at the Fed to meet their reserve requirements. In response, banks will call in loans that are due for collection, sell secondary reserves, and so on in order to obtain the necessary reserves. In the process of collecting loans, the banks decrease the money supply.

When the Federal Reserve wants to induce monetary expansion, however, it can provide banks with excess reserves (e.g., by lowering reserve requirements or buying government bonds), but it cannot force the banks to make loans, thereby creating new money. Ordinarily, of course, banks want to convert their excess reserves to interest-earning income by making loans. But in a deep recession or depression, banks might be hesitant to make enough loans to put all those reserves to work, fearing that they will not be repaid. Their pessimism might lead them to perceive that the risks of making loans to many normally creditworthy borrowers outweigh any potential interest earnings (particularly at the low real interest rates that are characteristic of depressed times). Some have argued that banks maintaining excess reserves rather than loaning them out was, in fact, one of the monetary policy problems that arose during the Great Depression.

Banks That Are Not Part of the Federal Reserve System and Policy Implementation

A second problem with monetary policy relates to the fact that the Fed can control deposit expansion at member banks, but it has no control over global and nonbank institutions that also issue credit (loan money) but are not subject to reserve requirement limitations;

great economic thinkers   Milton Friedman (1912–2006)

© BROOKS KRAFT/CORBIS

Milton Friedman was born in New York City in 1912. He was an undergraduate at Rutgers and a graduate student at Columbia University. Prior to his death in November 2006, he was a senior research fellow at the Hoover Institute at Stanford University. He was also Paul Snowden Russell Distinguished Service Professor Emeritus of Economics at the University of Chicago, where he taught from 1946 to 1976, and was a member of the research staff of the National Bureau of Economic Research from 1937 to 1981.

He is probably best known as the leader of the Chicago School of Monetary Economics, which stressed the importance of the quantity of money as an instrument of government policy and as a determinant of business cycles and inflation.

During the 1950s and 1960s, researching the relationship between the money supply and the economy was considered a waste of time. But in the 1970s Friedman convinced many of his colleagues, even his most ardent critics, that money matters in the economy. Friedman knew that money mattered, but he also knew that it is not easy to successfully manipulate monetary policy to stabilize the economy when the lags between implementation and impact can be long and unpredictable. Friedman thought that continued aggregate demand stimulation would not increase output, but would cause inflation. He believed that most recessions were caused by monetary misuse. Friedman also developed the permanent income hypothesis: People's spending decisions depend on expectations of future income not just current income.

In addition to his work on monetary economics, Friedman wrote extensively on public policy, always with a primary emphasis on the preservation and extension of individual freedom. In fact, many of Friedman's economic ideas have been tested: flexible exchange rates, educational vouchers, an all-volunteer army, and the privatization and deregulation of many industries.

examples are pension funds and insurance companies. Therefore, while the Fed may be able to predict the impact of its monetary policies on loans issued by member banks, global and nonbanking institutions can alter the impact of monetary policies adopted by the Fed. Hence, the real question is how precisely the Fed can control the short-run real interest rates and the money supply through its monetary policy instruments.

Fiscal and Monetary Coordination Problems

Another problem that may arise out of existing institutional policy making arrangements is the coordination of fiscal and monetary policy. Congress and the president make fiscal policy decisions, while monetary policy making is in the hands of the Federal Reserve System. A macroeconomic problem arises if the federal government's fiscal decision makers differ with the Fed's monetary decision makers on policy objectives or targets. For example, the Fed may be more concerned about keeping inflation low, while fiscal policy makers may be more concerned about keeping unemployment low.

Alleviating Coordination Problems

In recognition of potential macroeconomic policy coordination problems, the chairman of the Federal Reserve Board has participated for several years in meetings with top economic advisers of the president. An attempt is made in these meetings to reach a consensus on the appropriate policy responses, both monetary and fiscal. Still, they sometimes disagree, and the Fed occasionally works to partly offset or even neutralize the effects of fiscal policies that it views as inappropriate. Some people believe that monetary policy should be more directly controlled by the president and Congress, so that all macroeconomic policy will be determined more directly by the political process. Also, it is argued that such a move would enhance coordination considerably. Others, however, argue that it is dangerous to turn over control of the nation's money supply to politicians, rather than allowing decisions to be made by technically competent administrators who are more focused on price stability and more insulated from political pressures applied by the public and special interest groups.

Timing Is Critical

The timing of fiscal policy and monetary policy is crucial. Because of the significant lags before the fiscal and monetary policy has its impact, the increase in aggregate demand may occur at the wrong time. For example, imagine that we are initially at AD_1 in Exhibit 1. The economy is currently suffering from low levels of output and high rates of unemployment. In response, policy makers decide to increase government purchases and implement a tax cut, or alternatively they could have increased the money supply. But from the time when the policy makers recognize the problem to the time when the policies have a chance to work themselves through the economy, business and consumer confidence both increase, shifting the aggregate demand curve rightward from AD_1 to AD_2—increasing RGDP and employment. When the fiscal policy takes hold, the policies will have the undesired effect of causing inflation, with little permanent effect on output and employment. This effect may be seen in Exhibit 1, as the aggregate demand curve shifts from AD_2 to AD_3. At E_3, input owners will require higher input prices, shifting the $SRAS$ leftward from $SRAS_1$ to $SRAS_2$ and to the new long-run equilibrium at E_4.

Imperfect Information

In addition, the problem of imperfect information enters the picture. For example, in order to know how much to stimulate the economy, policy makers must know the size of the multiplier and by how much RGDP should increase. But some economists disagree on the natural rate of real output ($RGDP_{NR}$), and it may be diffi-cult to know where RGDP is at any given moment in time; government estimates are approximations and are often cor-rected at a later period. The government must also know the exact *MPC*. If the estimate is too low, the multiplier will be less than expected, and the stimulus will be too small. If the estimate of *MPC* is too high, the multiplier will be more than expected, and the stimulus will be too large.

Overall Problems with Monetary and Fiscal Policy

Much of macroeconomic policy in this country is driven by the idea that the federal government can counteract eco-nomic fluctuations: stimulating the economy (with increased government spending, tax cuts, and easy money) when it is weak and restraining it when it is overheating. However, policy makers must adopt the right policies in the right amounts at the right time for such "stabilization" to do more good than harm; and to do this, government policy makers need far more accurate and timely information than experts can give them.

First, economists must know not only which way the economy is heading but also how rapidly it is changing. Even the most current data on key variables such as employ-ment, growth, productivity, and so on, reflect conditions in the past, not the present. The unvarnished truth is that in our incredibly complicated world, no one knows exactly what the economy will do, no matter how sophisticated the econometric models used; our models are only approximations. It has often been said, and not completely in jest, that the purpose of economic forecasting is to make astrology look respectable.

But let's assume that economists can outperform astrologers at forecasting. Indeed, let's be completely unrealistic and assume that economists can provide completely accurate eco-nomic forecasts of what will happen if macroeconomic policies are unchanged. Even then, they cannot be certain of how best to promote stable economic growth.

If economists knew, for example, that the economy was going to dip into another recession in six months, they would then need to know exactly how much each possible policy would spur activity to keep the economy stable. But such precision is unattainable, given the complexity of economic forecasting. Furthermore, despite assurances to the contrary, economists aren't always certain what effect a policy will have on the economy. Will an increase in government purchases quicken economic growth? It is widely assumed so but how much? Moreover, increasing government purchases increases the budget deficit, which could send a frightening signal to the bond markets. The result might be to drive up interest rates and choke off economic activity. Thus, even when policy makers know in which direction to nudge the economy, they cannot be sure which policy levers to pull, or how hard to pull them, in order to fine-tune the economy to stable economic growth.

But let's further assume that policy makers know when the economy will need a boost and which policy will provide the

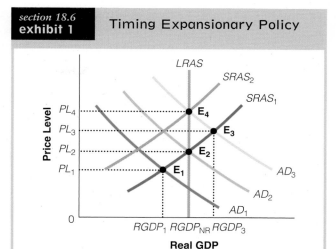

section 18.6 exhibit 1   **Timing Expansionary Policy**

Initially, the macroeconomy is at equilibrium at point E_1. With high unemployment (at $RGDP_1$), the government decides to increase government purchases and cut taxes to stimulate the economy, or the Fed could have increased the money supply. Aggregate demand shifts from AD_1 to AD_2 over time, perhaps 12 to 16 months. In the meantime, if consumer confidence increases, the aggregate demand curve might shift to AD_3, leading to much higher prices (PL_4) in the long run, rather than at the target level, point E_2, at price level PL_2.

© Cengage Learning 2013

Is it difficult to fine tune an economy?

Some economists believe that fine-tuning the economy is like driving a car with an unpredictable steering lag on a winding road, or driving while looking only through the rearview mirror.

© BRAND X PICTURES/GETTY IMAGES

right boost. A third crucial consideration is how long it will take a policy before it has its effect on the economy. The trouble is that, even when increased government purchases or an expansionary monetary policy does give the economy a boost, no one knows precisely how long it will take to do so. The boost may come quickly or it may come many months (even years) in the future, when it may add inflationary pressures to an economy already overheating rather than help the economy to recover from a recession.

Macroeconomic policy making is rather like driving down a twisting road in a car with an unpredictable lag and degree of response in the steering mechanism. If you turn the wheel to the right, the car will eventually veer to the right, but you don't know exactly when or how much. In short, severe practical difficulties are inherent in trying to fine-tune the economy. Even the best forecasting models and methods are far from perfect. Economists are not exactly sure where the economy is or where or how fast it is going, making it difficult to prescribe an effective policy. Even if we do know where the economy is headed, we cannot be sure how large a policy's effect will be or when it will take effect.

? SECTION QUIZ

1. Compared to fiscal policy, which of the following is an advantage of using monetary policy to attain macroeconomic goals?
   a. It takes a long time for fiscal policy to have an effect on the economy, but the effects of monetary policy are immediate.
   b. The effects of monetary policy are certain and predictable, while the effects of fiscal policy are not.
   c. The implementation of monetary policy is not slowed down by the same budgetary process as fiscal policy.
   d. The economists who help conduct monetary policy are smarter than those who help with fiscal policy.

2. An important limitation of monetary policy is that
   a. it is conducted by people in Congress who are under pressure to get reelected every two years.
   b. when the Fed tries to buy bonds, it is often unable to find a seller.
   c. when the Fed tries to sell bonds, it is often unable to find a buyer.
   d. it must be conducted through the commercial banking system, and the Fed cannot always make banks do what it wants them to do.

3. Which of the following statement is true?
   a. The FOMC of the Federal Reserve is unable to act quickly in emergencies.
   b. When the Fed is trying to constrain monetary expansion, it can be difficult to get banks to respond appropriately.
   c. Economic advisers, using sophisticated econometric models, can forecast what the economy will do in the future with reasonable accuracy.
   d. For government policy makers to be sure of doing more good than harm, they need far more accurate and timely information than experts can give them.

4. Which of the following statements is true?
   a. The Fed can change the environment in which banks act, but the banks themselves must take the steps necessary to increase or decrease the supply of money.
   b. Banks maintaining excess reserves hinder attempts by the Fed to induce monetary expansion.
   c. The Fed may be able to predict the impact of its monetary policies on loans by member banks, but the actions of global and nonbanking institutions can serve to offset, at least in part, the impact of monetary policies adopted by the Fed on the money and loanable funds markets.
   d. Given the difficulties of timing stabilization policy, an expansionary monetary policy intended to reduce the severity of a recession may instead add inflationary pressures to an economy that is already overheating.
   e. All of the above are true.

(continued)

⑦ S E C T I O N   Q U I Z (Cont.)

1. Why is the lag time for adopting policy changes shorter for monetary policy than for fiscal policy?

2. Why would a banking system that wanted to keep some excess reserves rather than lending out all of them hinder the Fed's ability to increase the money supply?

3. How can the activities of global and nonbank institutions weaken the Fed's influence on the money market?

4. If fiscal policy was expansionary, but the Fed wanted to counteract the fiscal policy effect on aggregate demand, what could it do?

5. What are the arguments for and against having monetary policy more directly controlled by the political process?

6. How is fine-tuning the economy like driving a car with an unpredictable steering lag on a winding road?

Answers: 1. c   2. d   3. d   4. e

Interactive Summary

Fill in the blanks:

1. In most countries, the job of manipulating the supply of money belongs to the _____.

2. Effective control of major monetary policy decisions rests with the _____ and the _____ of the Federal Reserve System.

3. The Federal Reserve was created in 1913 because the U.S. banking system had little _____ and no _____ direction.

4. The _____ consists of the seven members of the Board of Governors, the president of the New York Federal Reserve Bank, and four other presidents of Federal Reserve banks, who serve on the committee on a rotating basis.

5. Perhaps the most important function of the Federal Reserve is its ability to regulate the _____.

6. The Fed has three major methods that it can use to control the supply of money: It can engage in _____ operations, change _____ requirements, or change its _____ rate.

7. _____ are by far the most important device used by the Fed to influence the money supply.

8. Open market operations involve the purchase or sale of _____ by _____.

9. When the Fed buys government bonds in an open market operation, it _____ the money supply.

10. The most a bank can lend out at a given time is equal to its _____.

11. If the reserve requirement is 10 percent, a total of up to _____ in new money is potentially created by the purchase of $100,000 of government bonds by the Fed.

12. When the Fed sells a bond, the reserves of the bank where the bond buyer keeps his bank account will _____.

13. If the Fed _____ reserve requirements, other things being equal, it will create excess reserves in the banking system.

14. An increase in the required reserve ratio would result in a(n) _____ in the money supply.

15. Small reserve requirement changes have a(n) _____ impact on the potential supply of money.

16. Banks having trouble meeting their reserve requirement can borrow reserves directly from the Fed at an interest rate called the _____ rate.

17. If the Fed raises the discount rate, it makes it _____ costly for banks to borrow funds from it to meet their reserve requirements, which will result in _____ new loans being made and _____ money created.

18. If the Fed wants to expand the money supply, it will _____ the discount rate.

19. When banks have short-term needs for cash to meet reserve requirements, they are more likely to take a short-term (often overnight) loan from other banks in the _____ market than to borrow reserves directly from the Fed.

20. The current extent of discount lending is _____.

21. In recent years, the Federal Reserve has _____ its focus on the federal funds rate as the primary indicator of its stance on monetary policy.

22. The Fed can do three things if it wants to reduce the money supply: _____ government bonds, _____ reserve requirements, or _____ the discount rate.

23. An increase in the money supply would tend to _____ nominal GDP.

24. People have three basic motives for holding money instead of other assets: for _____ purposes, _____ reasons, and _____ purposes.

25. The quantity of money demanded varies _____ with the rate of interest.

26. If the price level falls, buyers will need _____ money to purchase their goods and services.

27. We draw the money supply curve as _____, other things being equal, with changes in _____ policies acting to shift the money supply curve.

28. Money market equilibrium occurs at that _____ interest rate where the quantity of money demanded equals the quantity of money supplied.

29. Rising national income will shift the demand for money to the _____, leading to a new _____ equilibrium nominal interest rate.

30. An increase in the money supply will lead to _____ interest rates and a(n) _____ in aggregate demand.

31. When the Fed sells bonds, it _____ the price of bonds, _____ interest rates, and _____ aggregate demand in the short run.

32. If the demand for money increases but the Fed doesn't allow the money supply to increase, interest rates will _____, and aggregate demand will _____.

33. When the economy grows, the Fed would have to _____ the money supply to keep interest rates from rising.

34. The _____ is the interest rate the Fed targets.

35. A contractionary policy can be thought of as a(n) _____ in the money supply or a(n) _____ in the interest rate.

36. The real interest rate is equal to _____ minus _____.

37. Countercyclical monetary policy would _____ the supply of money to combat a potential inflationary boom.

38. The Fed selling bonds will lead to a(n) _____ in the money supply, a(n) _____ in interest rates, a(n) _____ of the dollar, a(n) _____ in net exports, and a(n) _____ in RGDP in the short run.

39. The quantity equation of money can be presented as: _____ = _____.

40. _____ represents the average number of times that a dollar is used in purchasing final goods or services in a one-year period.

41. If M increases and V remains constant, then P must _____, Q must _____, or P and Q must each _____.

42. Expanding the money supply, other things being equal, will have a similar impact on aggregate demand as _____ government spending or _____ taxes.

43. Some economists, often called _____, believe that monetary policy is the most powerful determinant of macroeconomic results.

44. Velocity is _____ stable when measured using the M1 definition and over shorter periods of time.

45. An increase in the interest rates will cause people to hold _____ money, which, in turn, means that the velocity of money _____.

46. Higher rates of anticipated inflation would tend to _____ velocity.

47. The inflation rate tends to rise _____ in periods of rapid monetary expansion.

48. The lag problem inherent in adopting fiscal policy changes is much _____ acute for monetary policy.

49. According to the Federal Reserve Bank of San Francisco, the major effects of a change in policy on growth in the overall production of goods and services usually are felt within _____ months to _____ years, and the effects on inflation tend to involve even longer lags, perhaps _____ to _____ years or more.

50. In the process of calling in loans to obtain necessary banking reserves, banks _____ the supply of money.

51. Ordinarily, banks want to convert excess reserves into interest-earning _____, but in a deep recession or a depression, banks might be hesitant to make enough loans to put all those reserves to work.

52. The Fed can control deposit expansion at _____ banks, but it has no control over global and nonbank institutions that also _____.

53. Decision making with respect to fiscal policy is made by _____ and _____, while monetary-policy decision making is in the hands of _____.

54. Some people believe that monetary policy should be more directly controlled by the president and Congress, so that all macroeconomic policy will be determined _____ directly by the political process, which will _____ policy coordination.

55. Policy makers must adopt the _____ policies in the _____ amounts at the _____ time for such "stabilization" to do more good than harm.

56. When increased government purchases or expansionary monetary policy does give the economy a boost, _____ knows precisely how long it will take to do so.

Answers: 1. central bank 2. Board of Governors; Federal Open Market Committee 3. stability; central 4. Federal Open Market Committee 5. money supply 6. open market; reserve; discount 7. Open market operations 8. government securities; the Federal Reserve System 9. increases 10. excess reserves 11. $1,000,000 12. fall 13. lowers 14. decrease 15. big 16. discount 17. more; fewer; less 18. lower 19. federal funds 20. small 21. increased 22. sell; raise; raise 23. raise 24. transaction; precautionary; asset 25. inversely 26. less 27. vertical; Federal Reserve 28. nominal 29. right; holder 30. lower; increase 31. lowers; raises; reduces 32. rise; fall 33. increase 34. federal funds rate 35. decrease; increase 36. the nominal interest rate; the expected inflation rate 37. reduce 38. decrease; increase; appreciation; decrease; decrease 39. M × V; P × Q 40. Velocity 41. rise; rise 42. increasing; reducing 43. monetarists 44. less 45. less; increases 46. increase 47. more 48. less 49. three; two; one; three 50. reduce 51. loans 52. member; issue credit 53. Congress; the president; the Federal Reserve System 54. more; improve 55. right; right; right; right 56. no one

Key Terms and Concepts

open market operations 519
discount rate 521
federal funds market 521

money market 525
velocity of money 539

quantity theory of money
  and prices 540

Section Quiz Answers

18.1 The Federal Reserve System

1. What are the six primary functions of a central bank?

A central bank (1) is a "banker's bank," where commercial banks maintain their own deposits; (2) provides services, such as transferring funds and checks, for commercial banks; (3) serves as the primary bank for the federal government; (4) buys and sells foreign currencies and assists in transactions with other countries; (5) serves as a "lender of last resort" for banking institutions in financial distress; and (6) regulates the size of the money supply.

2. What is the FOMC, and what does it do?

The Federal Open Market Committee is a committee of the Federal Reserve System, made up of the seven members of the Board of Governors, the president of the New York Federal Reserve Bank and four other presidents of Federal Reserve banks. It makes most of the key decisions influencing the direction and size of changes in the money stock.

3. How is the Fed tied to the executive branch? How is it insulated from executive branch pressure to influence monetary policy?

The president selects the seven members of the Board of Governors, subject to Senate approval, one every two years, for 14-year terms. He also selects the chair of the Board of Governors for a four-year term. However, since the president can only select one member every two years, he cannot appoint a majority of the Board of Governors during his term in office. Also, the president cannot use reappointment of his nominees or threats of firing members to pressure the Fed on monetary policy.

18.2 How Does the Federal Reserve Change the Money Supply?

1. What three main tactics could the Fed use in pursuing a contractionary monetary policy?

The Fed could conduct an open market sale of government securities (bonds), mandate an increase in reserve requirements, and/or mandate an increase in the discount rate if it wanted to pursue a contractionary monetary policy.

2. What three main tactics could the Fed use in pursuing an expansionary monetary policy?

The Fed could conduct an open market purchase of government securities (bonds), mandate a decrease in reserve requirements, and/or mandate a decrease in the discount rate if it wanted to pursue an expansionary monetary policy.

3. Would the money supply rise or fall if the Fed made an open market purchase of government bonds, *ceteris paribus*?

An open market purchase of government bonds by the Fed would increase banking reserves, thereby increasing the money stock, *ceteris paribus*.

4. If the Fed raised the discount rate from 1 to 2 percent, what effect would this have on the money supply?

Raising the discount rate makes it more costly for banks to borrow reserves directly from the Fed. To the extent that banks borrow fewer reserves directly from the Fed, this reduces total banking reserves, thereby decreasing the money stock, *ceteris paribus*.

18.3 Money, Interest Rates, and Aggregate Demand

1. What are the determinants of the demand for money?

There are three motives for the demand for money: transaction purposes (to facilitate exchange), precautionary purposes (just in case), and asset purposes (to keep some assets in the liquid form of money). The demand for money increases (shifts to the right) if either real incomes or the price level is higher, because that will increase the nominal amount of transactions. A decrease in the interest rate will

decrease the opportunity cost of holding money, increasing the quantity of money people wish to hold (moving down along the demand for money curve), but not increasing the demand for money (shifting the demand for money curve).

2. If the earnings available on other financial assets rose, would you want to hold more or less money? Why?

Since holding wealth in the form of other financial assets is the alternative to holding it in the form of money, nonmoney financial assets are substitutes for holding money. When the earnings (interest) available on alternative financial assets rise, the opportunity cost of holding money instead also rises; so you would want to hold less money, other things being equal.

3. For the economy as a whole, why would individuals want to hold more money as GDP rises?

Individuals conduct a larger volume of transactions as GDP rises. Therefore, they would want to hold more money as GDP rises in order to keep the costs of those increasing transactions down.

4. Why might people who expect a major market "correction" (a fall in the value of stock holdings) wish to increase their holdings of money?

When the value of alternative financial assets is expected to fall, holding money, which will not similarly fall in value, becomes more attractive. Therefore, in the case of an expected fall in the value of stocks, bonds, or other financial assets, people would want to increase their holdings of money as a precaution.

5. How is the money market equilibrium established?

In the money market, money demand and money supply determine the equilibrium nominal interest rate.

6. Who controls the supply of money in the money market?

The banking system, through the loan expansion process, directly determines the supply of money in the money market. However, the Fed, through the policy variables it controls (primarily open market operations, reserve requirements, and the discount rate), indirectly controls the supply of money by controlling the level of reserves and the money multiplier.

7. How does an increase in income or a decrease in the interest rate affect the demand for money?

An increase in income increases (shifts right) the demand for money, as people want to hold down the transactions costs on the increasing volume of transactions taking place. A decrease in interest rates, on the other hand, increases the quantity of money demanded (moving down along the money demand curve) but does not change the demand for money.

8. What Federal Reserve policies would shift the money supply curve to the left?

An open market sale of government securities (bonds), an increase in reserve requirements, and/or an increase in the discount rate would shift the money supply curve to the left.

9. Will an increase in the money supply increase or decrease the short-run equilibrium real interest rate, other things being equal?

An increase in the money supply would decrease the short-run equilibrium real interest rate, other things being equal, as the rightward shift of the money supply curve pushes the money market equilibrium down along the money demand curve.

10. Will an increase in national income increase or decrease the short-run equilibrium real interest rate, other things being equal?

An increase in national income will shift the money demand curve to the right, which would increase the short-run equilibrium real interest rate, other things being equal.

11. What is the relationship between interest rates and aggregate demand in monetary policy?

Lower interest rates will tend to stimulate aggregate demand for goods and services, other things being equal.

18.4 Expansionary and Contractionary Monetary Policy

1. How will an expansionary monetary policy affect RGDP and the price level at less than full employment?

An expansionary monetary policy shifts aggregate demand to the right. Starting from less than full employment, the result will be an increase in the price level, an increase in real output, and a decrease in unemployment as the economy moves up along the short-run aggregate supply curve. This increased output will be sustainable if it does not exceed the natural level of real output.

2. How will a contractionary monetary policy affect RGDP and the price level at a point beyond full employment?

A contractionary monetary policy, starting from a point beyond full employment, will reduce aggregate demand and will move the economy from the short-

run equilibrium position beyond full employment toward the new long-run equilibrium position at full employment, preventing an inflationary boom. There is, then, a reduction in both RGDP and the price level.

18.5 Money and Inflation— The Long Run

1. If M1 is $10 billion and velocity is 4, what is the product of the price level and real output (nominal GDP)? If the price level is 2, what does the dollar value of output (nominal GDP) equal?

If the money supply is $10 billion and velocity is 4 (so that $M \times V = \$40$ billion), the product of the price level and real output ($P \times Q$, or nominal output), must also be $40 billion. If the price level is 2, real output would equal the $40 billion nominal output divided by the price level of 2, or $20 billion.

2. If nominal GDP is $200 billion and the money supply is $50 billion, what must velocity be?

Since $M \times V = P \times Q$, $V = P \times Q/M$. $V = \$200$ billion/$50 billion, or 4, in this case.

3. If the money supply increases and velocity does not change, what will happen to nominal GDP?

If M increases and V does not change, $M \times V$ must increase. Since $M \times V = P \times Q$, and $P \times Q$ equals nominal GDP, nominal GDP must also increase as a result.

4. If velocity is unstable, does stabilizing the money supply help stabilize the economy? Why or why not?

If V is unstable, stabilizing M does not stabilize $M \times V$. Since $M \times V$ will not be stabilized, $P \times Q$, or nominal GDP, will not be stabilized either.

18.6 Problems in Implementing Monetary and Fiscal Policy

1. Why is the lag time for adopting policy changes shorter for monetary policy than for fiscal policy?

The lag time for adopting monetary policy changes is shorter than for fiscal policy changes because decisions regarding monetary policy are not slowed by the budgetary process that fiscal tax and expenditure policy changes must go through.

2. Why would a banking system that wanted to keep some excess reserves rather than lending out all of them hinder the Fed's ability to increase the money supply?

A desire on the part of the banking system to keep some excess reserves would reduce the money supply, other things being equal. Such a change would thus at least partly offset the effects of the Fed's expansionary policy changes, which would hinder the Fed's ability to successfully use expansionary monetary policy to increase the money supply.

3. How can the activities of global and nonbank institutions weaken the Fed's influence on the money market?

The Fed has no control over global and nonbank institutions, which issue credit (loan money) like U.S. commercial banks but are not subject to reserve requirement limitations. The Fed cannot control their behavior and the resulting effects on economic activity through its policy variables, as it can with U.S. commercial banks.

4. If fiscal policy was expansionary, but the Fed wanted to counteract the fiscal policy effect on aggregate demand, what could it do?

Expansionary fiscal policy would increase aggregate demand. To counteract that fiscal policy effect on aggregate demand, the Fed would want to adopt contractionary monetary policy (through an open market sale of government securities, an increase in reserve requirements, and/or an increase in the discount rate), which would tend to reduce aggregate demand, other things being equal.

5. What are the arguments for and against having monetary policy more directly controlled by the political process?

The argument for having monetary policy more directly controlled by the political process is basically that since fiscal policy is already determined by the political process, and since monetary policy (which is not determined by the same political process) can offset or even neutralize the macroeconomic effects of fiscal policy, it would be better for all macroeconomic policy to be directly controlled by the political process. The argument against having monetary policy more directly controlled by the political process is that it would be dangerous to turn over control of the nation's money supply to politicians rather than having monetary policy decisions be made by technically competent administrators who are focused more on price stability and are more insulated from political pressures coming from the public and special interest groups.

6. How is fine-tuning the economy like driving a car with an unpredictable steering lag on a winding road?

Fine-tuning the economy is like driving a car with an unpredictable steering lag on a winding road because to steer the economy successfully requires that policy makers have an accurate map of both which way and how rapidly the economy is headed, they need to know exactly how much each possible policy would affect the economy, so that they "turn the policy wheels" just the right amount, and know how long it will take each possible policy to "turn" the economy.

Problems

1. Why is the private ownership of the Federal Reserve System essentially meaningless?

2. How is central bank independence related to average inflation rates across countries? How is the Fed insulated from executive branch pressures?

3. Why does the fact that the Fed finances its operations out of interest earned on its portfolio, with the excess returned to the U.S. Treasury, make it more independent of congressional pressure?

4. How does an open market purchase by the Fed increase bank reserves? How does it increase the money supply?

5. Why would the Fed seldom do an open market purchase of government securities at the same time that it raises the discount rate or the required reserve ratio?

6. Why is a reduction in the required reserve ratio such a powerful monetary policy tool? Why is it so seldom used?

7. Why would a reduction in the required reserve ratio not be a powerful tool when banks choose to hold substantial quantities of excess reserves?

8. In which direction would the money supply change if
   a. the Fed raised the reserve requirement?
   b. the Fed conducted an open market sale of government bonds?
   c. the Fed raised the discount rate?
   d. the Fed conducted an open market sale of government bonds and raised the discount rate?
   e. the Fed conducted an open market purchase of government bonds and raised reserve requirements?

9. Why would the transactions motive and the precautionary motive for holding money both tend to vary directly with the price level? Why would the quantity of money people desire to hold for both motives tend to vary inversely with interest rates?

10. In the move from a below-equilibrium interest rate to the equilibrium interest rate, what happens in the bond market and the loan market? In the move from an above-equilibrium interest rate to the equilibrium interest rate, what happens in the bond market and the loan market?

11. How does a higher price level affect the money market? How does it affect aggregate demand?

12. Why can't the Fed target both the money supply and the interest rate at the same time?

13. Answer the following questions.
    a. What is the equation of exchange?
    b. In the equation of exchange, if V doubled, what would happen to nominal GDP as a result?
    c. In the equation of exchange, if V doubled and Q remained unchanged, what would happen to the price level as a result?
    d. In the equation of exchange, if M doubled and V remained unchanged, what would happen to nominal GDP as a result?
    e. In the equation of exchange, if M doubled and V fell by half, what would happen to nominal GDP as a result?

14. Why have ATMs and online banking made savings accounts more liquid than they used to be?

15. Given that the Fed currently imposes reserve requirements on checking deposits, but not on savings deposits, why would banks prefer to hold deposits as savings accounts rather than checking accounts, other things being equal?

Issues in Macroeconomic Theory and Policy

We begin this chapter by asking whether policy makers face a trade-off between inflation and unemployment. If a trade-off is inevitable, does it exist in the short run and the long run? If the economy is faced with a recessionary or an inflationary gap, how quickly will it recover to its long-run equilibrium position? And what is the best way to stabilize the economy? Should policy makers use expansionary and contractionary monetary and fiscal policies? Or should policy makers allow the economy to self-correct?

Macroeconomists do not completely agree on this question, a topic we will discuss throughout this chapter.

After 10 years of unprecedented economic growth, the economy started to slip into a recession in early 2001, although it was one of the mildest recessions on record. This recession was set off by a serious drop in investment spending. The technology sector led to higher productivity during the 1990s, but the bursting of the dot-com bubble resulted in a considerable loss in stock market wealth. The slowdown in the tech sector started to affect other segments of the economy. This situation, coupled with the 9/11 terrorist attacks, created a negative shock that rippled through the economy, especially in the travel sector. Hotels and airlines were hit particularly hard. The corporate accounting scandals of Enron and WorldCom also influenced investment attitudes. Uncertainty and fading optimism reduced both investment and consumption spending and reduced aggregate demand. To combat the recession, the government stimulated aggregate demand with increases in government expenditures for security and defense, the tax cut of 2001, and aggressive reductions in the federal funds rate by the Federal Reserve. The Fed started to cut its federal funds rate by 0.5 percentage point (it usually only changes the rate by 0.25 percent at a given meeting) in January of 2001. In the week following the attacks on the World Trade Center (September 2001), it temporarily set the federal funds rate as low as 1.25 percent. By November 2001, the recession was officially over, but the federal funds rate had fallen from 6.5 percent to 2 percent—4.5 percent lower than the previous year. The Fed looked like it had done its job.

However, the Fed may have set the federal funds rate too low for too long. This Fed policy may have been at least partially responsible for causing a housing bubble that was reminiscent of the stock market bubble of the 1990s. The 2007–2008 period also witnessed risky lending that was similar to the lending practices that occurred during the saving and loans crisis of the 1980s. There were also bank runs as a crisis of confidence in our financial institutions ensued, not unlike the Great Depression (but certainly smaller in scope).

Was lowering the federal funds rate the best way to stabilize an economy?

The Phillips Curve   19.1

☞ What is the Phillips curve?

☞ How does the Phillips curve relate to the aggregate supply and demand model?

Unemployment and Inflation

Despite legislation committing the federal government to the goal of full employment and the development of macroeconomic theory arguing that full employment can be achieved by manipulating aggregate demand, periods of high unemployment still occur.

We usually think of inflation as an evil—higher prices mean lower real incomes for people on fixed incomes, while those with the power to raise the prices charged for goods or services they provide may actually benefit. Nevertheless, some economists believe that inflation could actually help eliminate unemployment. For example, if output prices rise but money wages do not go up as quickly or as much, real wages fall. At the lower real wage, unemployment is less because the lower wage makes it profitable to hire more, now cheaper, employees than before. The result is real wages that are closer to the full-employment equilibrium wage that clears the labor market. Hence, with increased inflation, one might expect lower unemployment in the short run.

Why is there a possible short-run relationship between the inflation rate and the unemployment rate?

The Phillips Curve

In fact, an inverse relationship between the rate of unemployment and the changing level of prices has been observed in many periods and places in history. Credit for identifying this relationship generally goes to British economist A. H. Phillips, who in the late 1950s published a paper setting forth what has since been called the *Phillips curve*. Phillips and many others since suggested that at higher rates of inflation, the rate of unemployment is lower, while during periods of relatively stable or falling prices, unemployment is substantial. In short, the cost of lower unemployment appears to be greater inflation, and the cost of greater price stability appears to be higher unemployment.

Exhibit 1 shows the actual inflation-unemployment relationship for the United States for the 1960s. The points in this graph represent the combination of the inflation rate and the rate of unemployment in each of the 10 years of the decade. The curved line—the Phillips curve—is the smooth line that best "fits" the data points.

The Slope of the Phillips Curve

In examining Exhibit 1, it is evident that the slope of the Phillips curve is not the same throughout its length. The curve is steeper at higher rates of inflation and lower levels of unemployment. This relationship suggests that once the economy has relatively low unemployment rates, further reductions in the unemployment rate can occur only if the economy can accept larger increases in the inflation rate. Once the unemployment rate is low, it takes larger and larger doses of inflation to eliminate a given quantity of unemployment. Presumably, at lower unemployment rates, an increased part of the economy is already operating at or near full capacity. Further fiscal or monetary stimulus primarily triggers inflationary pressures in sectors already at capacity, while eliminating decreasing amounts of unemployment in those sectors where some excess capacity and unemployment still exist.

What does the steepness of the Phillips curve measure?

| section 19.1 **exhibit 1** | The Phillips Curve Relationship, United States, 1960s |

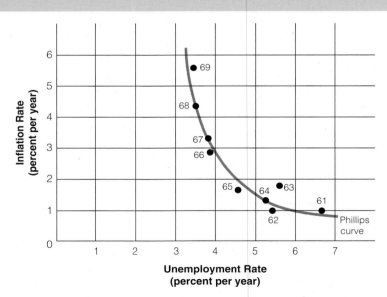

The Phillips curve illustrates an inverse relationship between the rate of unemployment and the rate of inflation. The slope of the Phillips curve becomes more steep as the unemployment rate drops, indicating that at low unemployment rates, further decreases in unemployment can occur only if the economy can accept much larger increases in inflation rates.

The Phillips Curve and the *AD/AS* Curves

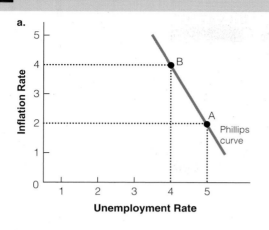

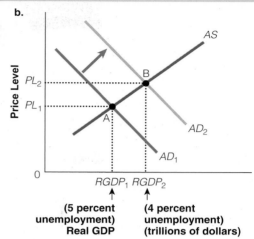

As shown in (b), if the aggregate supply curve is positively sloped, an increase in aggregate demand will cause higher prices and higher output (lower unemployment); a decrease in aggregate demand will cause lower prices and lower output (higher unemployment). This same trade-off is illustrated in the Phillips curve in (a), in the shift from point A to point B.

© Cengage Learning 2013

The Phillips Curve and Aggregate Supply and Demand

In Exhibit 2, we see the relationship between aggregate supply and demand analysis and the Phillips curve. Suppose the economy moved from a 2 percent annual inflation rate to a 4 percent inflation rate, and the unemployment rate simultaneously fell from 5 percent to 4 percent. In the Phillips curve, we see this shift as a move up the curve from point A to point B in Exhibit 2(a). We can see a similar relationship in the *AD/AS* model in Exhibit 2(b). Imagine that an increase in aggregate demand occurs. Consequently, the price level increases from PL_1 to PL_2 (the inflation rate rises) and output increases from $RGDP_1$ to $RGDP_2$ (the unemployment rate falls). To increase output, firms employ more workers, so employment increases and unemployment falls—the movement from point A to point B in Exhibit 2(b).

How is moving up the Phillips curve like moving up along the short-run aggregate supply curve?

② SECTION QUIZ

1. Society faces a

   a. long-run trade-off between price inflation and unemployment.

   b. short-run trade-off between inflation and unemployment.

   c. short-run trade-off between the actual unemployment rate and the natural rate of unemployment.

   d. long-run trade-off between inflation and real output.

   e. Both (b) and (d) are correct.

2. If policy makers expand aggregate demand, they can lower unemployment _____, but only by _____.

   a. temporarily; decreasing inflation

   b. temporarily; increasing inflation

   c. permanently; decreasing inflation

   d. permanently; increasing inflation

(*continued*)

3. If the Phillips curve is steeper at higher rates of inflation, it suggests that

   a. once the economy has relatively low unemployment rates, further reductions in the unemployment rate can occur only by accepting larger increases in the inflation rate.

   b. once the economy has relatively low unemployment rates, further reductions in the unemployment rate can occur only by reducing the rate of inflation.

   c. only reducing the rate of inflation can reduce the high unemployment rate.

   d. When the economy is experiencing low inflation rates, the unemployment rate can be reduced only by accepting lower rates of inflation.

4. Which of the following is consistent with a movement along a short-run Phillips curve?

   a. a decrease in the inflation rate with no change in unemployment

   b. a decrease in unemployment with no change in the inflation rate

   c. a decrease in inflation with an increase in unemployment

   d. a decrease in unemployment and a decrease in inflation

1. How does the rate of inflation affect real wage rates if nominal wages rise less or more slowly than output prices?

2. How does the change in real wage rates (relative to output prices) as inflation increases affect the unemployment rate?

3. What is the argument for why the Phillips curve is relatively steeper at lower rates of unemployment and higher rates of inflation?

4. For a given upward-sloping short-run aggregate supply curve, how does an increase in aggregate demand correspond to a movement up and to the left along a Phillips curve?

Answers: 1. b 2. b 3. a 4. c

19.2

The Phillips Curve over Time

▭ How reliable is the Phillips curve?

▭ Is the Phillips curve stable over time?

▭ What is the difference between the long-run and short-run Phillips curves?

The Phillips Curve—The 1960s

It became widely accepted in the 1960s that to pursue the appropriate economic policies, policy makers merely had to decide on the combination of unemployment and inflation they wanted from the Phillips curve. To be sure, a reduction in the rate of unemployment came at a cost (more inflation), as did a reduction in the amount of inflation (more unemployment). Nonetheless, policy makers believed they could influence economic activity so that some goals could be met, though with a trade-off in terms of other macroeconomic goals. The empirical evidence on prices and unemployment seemed to fit the Phillips curve approach so beautifully at first that it is not surprising that it was embraced so rapidly and completely. Economists such as Milton Friedman and Edmund Phelps, who questioned the long-term validity of the Phillips curve, were largely ignored in the 1960s. These economists believed there might be a short-term trade-off between unemployment and inflation but not a permanent trade-off. That is, a trade-off happens in the short run but not in the long run. According to Friedman, the short-run trade-off comes from *unanticipated* inflation.

The Short-Run Phillips Curve versus the Long-Run Phillips Curve

The **natural rate hypothesis** states that the economy will self-correct to the natural rate of unemployment. Let us examine the reasoning behind the natural rate hypothesis. Suppose the economy is at point A in Exhibit 1(a). At that point, the inflation rate is 3 percent and the unemployment rate is at the natural rate, 5 percent. Now suppose the growth rate of the money supply increases. The increase in the growth rate of the money supply stimulates aggregate demand. In the short run, the increase in aggregate demand increases output and decreases unemployment. As the economy moves up along the short-run Phillips curve, from point A to point B, the actual inflation rate increases from 3 percent to 6 percent, and the unemployment rate falls below the natural rate to 3 percent.

natural rate hypothesis
states that the economy will self-correct to the natural rate of employment

Because the increase in inflation was unanticipated, real wages fall. Firms are now receiving higher prices relative to their input costs, so they expand output. Consequently, unemployment rates fall, seen in Exhibit 1(a) as a movement along the short-run Phillips curve from A to B. Eventually, workers (and other input owners) realize that their real wages have fallen because of the increase in the inflation rate that was not initially anticipated—in short, they were fooled in the short run. Workers now vigorously negotiate for higher wages. These demands increase costs to producers, and as a result, they reduce output and unemployment rises—causing a rightward shift in the short-run Phillips curve in Exhibit 1(a).

In short, the higher-than-expected inflation rate shifts the short-run Phillips curve to the right. If the 6 percent inflation rate continues, the adjustment of expectations will move the economy from point B to point C, where the expected and actual inflation rates are equal at the natural level of output and the natural rate of unemployment.

In the long run, the economy moves from A to C as inflation increases from 3 percent to 6 percent. This graph reveals that no trade-off occurs between the inflation rate and the unemployment rate in the long run. The policy implication is that the use of fiscal or monetary policy to alter real output from the natural level of real output or unemployment from the natural rate of unemployment is ineffective in the long run.

What causes the short-run Phillips curve to shift?

section 19.2
exhibit 1   The Short-Run and Long-Run Phillips Curve

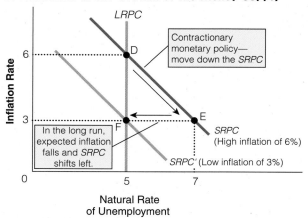

a. An Increase in the Growth of the Money Supply

b. Reduction in the Growth of the Money Supply

The economy initially moves along the short-run Phillips curve (*SRPC*) as actual inflation deviates from expected inflation. When expected inflation rates then adapt to actual inflation rates, the *SRPC* shifts to intersect the long-run Phillips curve (*LRPC*) at the new inflation rate—point C in (a) and point F in (b). If the actual inflation rate remains at the new level, then output returns to the natural level of real output, and unemployment returns to the natural rate of unemployment at that inflation rate on the *LRPC*.

Alternatively, suppose the rate of growth in the money supply decreases as a result of the Federal Reserve System's inflationary concerns. The decrease in the rate of growth in the money supply reduces aggregate demand. In the short run, the decrease in aggregate demand moves the economy down along the short-run Phillips curve from point D to point E, where the actual inflation rate has decreased from 6 percent to 3 percent and the unemployment rate has risen above the natural rate to 7 percent. The decrease in aggregate demand leads to lower production and a higher unemployment rate.

Initially, the reduction in the inflation rate is unanticipated, and real wages rise; firms are now receiving lower prices relative to their input costs, so they reduce their output. This leads to a higher unemployment rate, as seen in the movement from point D to point E in Exhibit 1(b). If this new inflation rate remains steady at 3 percent, the actual and expected inflation rates will eventually become the same. The growth in wages will slow, lowering the cost of production, increasing output, and lowering the unemployment rate as the short-run Phillips curve shifts leftward in Exhibit 1(b).

If the 3 percent inflation rate continues, the adjustment of expectations will move the economy from point E to point F in Exhibit 1(b), where the expected and actual inflation rates are equal at the natural level of output and the natural rate of unemployment. In this scenario, a lower inflation rate comes at the expense of higher unemployment in the short run, until people adapt their expectations to the new lower inflation rate in the long run. These expectations are called **adaptive expectations**—individuals believe that the best indicator of the future is recent information on inflation and unemployment. That is, individuals will see what has happened to help predict what will happen.

In Exhibit 2 (a), we see that the negative relationship between the inflation rate and the unemployment rate broke down in the early 1970s. Notice that the inflation rate was in the 5 to 6 percent range in the early 1970s, and consumers and firms expected it to remain high. However, the unemployment rate rose back to the rates of the early 1960s. The movement from point A to point B in Exhibit 2(a) resembles the movement along the short-run Phillips curve, and the movement from point B to point C resembles the curve shifting back toward the natural rate of unemployment.

In Exhibit 2(b), we see inflation and unemployment data for the period 1979 to 1985. The late 1970s and early 1980s was a period of very high inflation, and the chair of the Federal Reserve, Paul Volker, decided to reduce the growth rate of the money supply to slow

adaptive expectations
an individual's belief that the best indicator of the future is recent information on inflation and unemployment

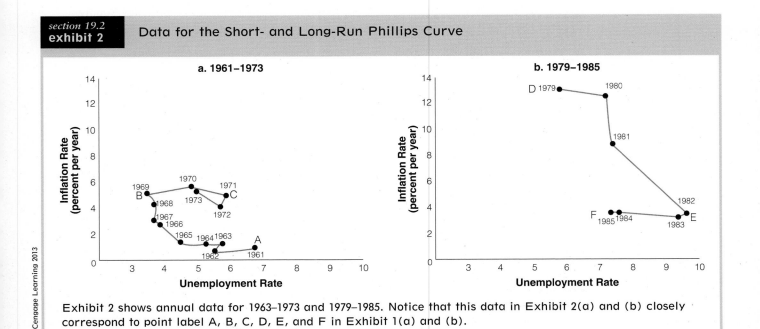

section 19.2
exhibit 2   **Data for the Short- and Long-Run Phillips Curve**

a. 1961–1973

b. 1979–1985

Exhibit 2 shows annual data for 1963–1973 and 1979–1985. Notice that this data in Exhibit 2(a) and (b) closely correspond to point label A, B, C, D, E, and F in Exhibit 1(a) and (b).

the rate of inflation. The contractionary monetary policy moved the economy down along the short-run Phillips curve from point D to point E. When workers and firms lowered their inflationary expectations, the short-run Phillips curve shifted inward from point E to point F.

Supply Shocks

Earlier in this chapter, we assumed that the inverse relationship in the short-run Phillips curve was created by changes in aggregate demand. We have also seen that a change in the expected inflation rate can cause a shift in the short-run Phillips curve. However, recently economists have focused on a different source for shifts in the short-run Phillips curve—supply shocks.

Many economists believe that the higher energy prices in the early and late 1970s created a negative supply shock. Higher oil prices had important implications for the macroeconomy because they meant higher production costs for many goods and services. Higher production costs caused a leftward shift in the $SRAS$ curve from $SRAS_1$ to $SRAS_2$, as seen in Exhibit 3(a). As a result, the price level increased from PL_1 to PL_2 and $RGDP$ fell from $RGDP_1$ to $RGDP_2$ in Exhibit 3(a). The negative supply shock led to a higher price level and less output—stagflation. A stagnant economy means fewer jobs and a higher unemployment rate. A higher price level leads to a higher inflation rate (the percentage change in the price level from the previous year) and a higher rate of unemployment. The short-run Phillips curve shifts to the right from $SRPC_1$ to $SRPC_2$, in Exhibit 3(b). Point B indicates a higher rate of inflation and a higher rate of unemployment than at point A.

A positive supply shock (large technological improvements, bountiful harvest, or lower energy prices) lowers the inflation rate and lowers the rate of unemployment. Specifically, a favorable supply shock lowers the costs of production and causes a rightward shift in the $SRAS$ curve from $SRAS_1$ to $SRAS_2$, as seen in Exhibit 4(a). As a result, the price level falls

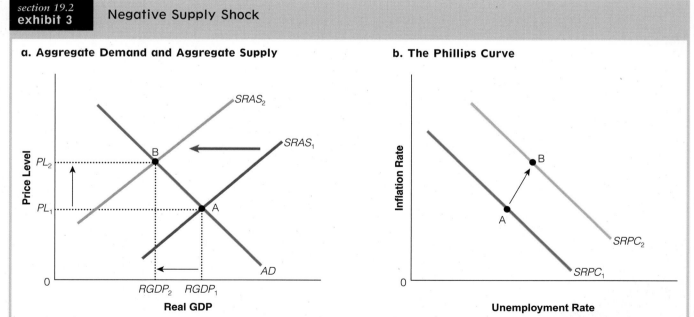

section 19.2 exhibit 3   **Negative Supply Shock**

a. Aggregate Demand and Aggregate Supply

b. The Phillips Curve

The higher energy prices in the early and late 1970s created a negative supply shock. In (a), the higher production costs causes a leftward shift in the $SRAS$ curve from $SRAS_1$ to $SRAS_2$, an increase in the price level from PL_1 to PL_2, and a decrease in RGDP from $RGDP_1$ to $RGDP_2$. With a higher price level comes a higher inflation rate, and with less output comes a higher rate of unemployment. The short-run Phillips curve shifts to the right from $SRPC_1$ to $SRPC_2$ in (b). At point B, both the inflation rate and the unemployment rate are higher than at point A.

© Cengage Learning 2013

section 19.2
exhibit 4 Positive Supply Shock

a. Aggregate Demand and Aggregate Supply

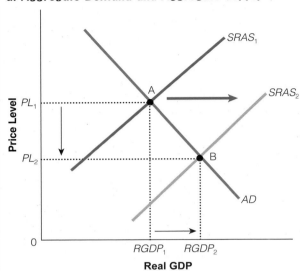

b. The Phillips Curve

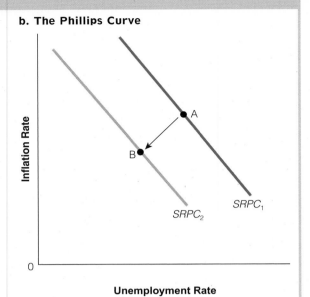

In (a), lower costs of production caused by the positive supply shock cause a rightward shift in the *SRAS* curve from *SRAS*$_1$ to *SRAS*$_2$, the price level falls from *PL*$_1$ to *PL*$_2$, and RGDP rises from *RGDP*$_1$ to *RGDP*$_2$. The positive supply-side shock leads to a lower price level and greater output. With a lower price level comes a lower inflation rate and a lower rate of unemployment. The short-run Phillips curve shifts to the left, from *SRPC*$_1$ to *SRPC*$_2$ in (b). At point B, both the inflation rate and the unemployment rate are lower than at point A.

How does a negative supply shock impact the short-run Phillips curve?

How does a positive shock impact the short-run Phillips curve?

from *PL*$_1$ to *PL*$_2$, and *RGDP* rises from *RGDP*$_1$ to *RGDP*$_2$ in Exhibit 4(a). The positive supply-side shock leads to a lower price level and greater output. A growing economy means more jobs and a lower unemployment rate. With a lower price level, a lower inflation rate and a lower rate of unemployment occur; the short-run Phillips curve shifts to the left, from *SRPC*$_1$ to *SRPC*$_2$ in Exhibit 4(b). That is, at point B, both the rate of inflation and the rate of unemployment are lower than at point A. For example, in the late 1990s, a number of economists believed we witnessed a positive supply shock because of rapidly changing new technology, favorable exchange rates, and lower oil prices, all of which led to lower production costs. These factors caused the aggregate supply curve to shift to the right—a higher level of *RGDP* and a lower price level—and the Phillips curve shifted to the left to a lower inflation rate and a lower unemployment rate.

It is important to note that the impact a positive or negative shock depends on expectations. If people expect the change to be permanent, the Phillips curve will stay in the new position until something else changes. As we are finding out, expectations can have widespread implications in the macroeconomy. However, if the shock is expected to be temporary, the Phillips curve will soon shift back to its original position. For example, people viewed the negative supply shocks of the 1970s as permanent and the Phillips curve shifted to the right—a new position with a higher rate of inflation and a higher rate of unemployment.

Why did the United States not experience a substantial negative supply shock in 2005 when oil prices jumped to more than $70 a barrel? The answer is based on several possible reasons. One, although the nominal price of oil reached $70, oil prices would have had to reach $90 before hitting record high levels in terms of inflation adjusted prices. Two, industry has become less oil dependent: Machinery is more energy efficient, and the higher number of service-oriented jobs requires less energy. Three, households are more fuel efficient: cars typically get better gas mileage, and appliances are much more energy efficient than in the 1970s. The amount of oil used to produce a unit of output has fallen an estimated 35 percent since the OPEC oil shocks of the 1970s. Lastly, through the leadership of the last two Federal Reserve chairs, Volcker and Greenspan, the Fed established increased credibility as an inflation fighter by being careful to make sure that temporary spikes in oil prices do not lead to sustained inflation.

in the news   The Lure of Inflation's Siren Song

Inflation is a tempting seductress, especially in an economy overburdened by debt and unemployment.

Why not, the thinking goes, keep the stimulus taps open longer than necessary to ensure a vigorous recovery by allowing inflation to overshoot targets for a year or two? Think of it as another dose of adrenaline helping unemployment fall faster and helping to erode budget deficits.

The problem: Once unleashed, inflation can't be easily contained, and sometimes the measures needed to do so can choke off growth.

So far, the Federal Reserve believes substantial slack in the economy makes inflation a distant prospect. Even if prices do rise, it has strong faith it can control them.

But there is a growing drumbeat of support for higher inflation. Olivier Blanchard, IMF chief economist, recently suggested central banks consider raising inflation targets so they have more room to cut interest rates when crises hit. Some others argue employers and politicians are unwilling to address structural problems in the economy, leaving inflation as a more practical alternative.

"Inflation can achieve what no congress can, fast reductions in fiscal deficits," Christian Broda, head of international research at Barclays Capital, wrote in a research note on Monday.

Mr. Broda estimated that letting inflation run at 5 percent for two years, compared with the Fed's 1.5 percent to 2 percent target for core inflation, would reduce the unemployment rate by three percentage points.

Of course, that is beguiling with consumers and the country as a whole struggling. And given tame inflation in the face of huge stimulus in recent years, the idea of runaway prices seems a distant threat, as the Fed said Tuesday.

But the risk that the central bank gets softer on inflation lies in its dual mandate to achieve both price stability and maximum employment. A desire to attack unemployment could lead to calls for letting inflation run up quietly, even if the target rate remains unchanged. After all, if the economy really is recovering, zero interest rates could quickly become distortive.

Remember also that Fed Chairman Ben Bernanke's life study has been the Great Depression and how to avoid a repeat. Interestingly, that is at odds with the European Central Bank, whose view is heavily influenced by the hyperinflation of Germany's Weimar Republic.

Congress, which has attacked the Fed's independence, could also be an issue. It may push for inflation as an alternative to spending cuts or tax increases.

While attractive in the short-term, inflation would quickly be reflected in the cost of debt, hammering the value of fixed-income securities and pushing up the cost of borrowing. It could also hit the dollar and push commodity prices even higher. The experience of the 1970s shows how painful it can be to rein in inflation once unleashed.

So investors should be alert for any signs that the Fed is taking price stability for granted, or is willing to let inflation run above target. Heavy borrowers need to work through their problems to create a sustainable rebound.

Inflation would be a false fix.

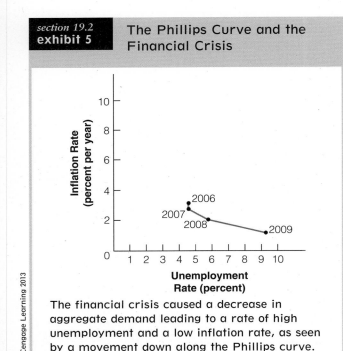

© Cengage Learning 2013

**section 19.2
exhibit 5**

The Phillips Curve and the
Financial Crisis

The financial crisis caused a decrease in
aggregate demand leading to a rate of high
unemployment and a low inflation rate, as seen
by a movement down along the Phillips curve.

In sum, if people expect economic fluctuations to be permanent and caused primarily by supply-side shifts, then the result is likely to be a positive relationship between the inflation rate and the unemployment rate—a shifting Phillips curve. Higher rates of inflation will be coupled with higher rates of unemployment, and lower rates of inflation will be coupled with lower rates of unemployment.

The Phillips Curve and Financial Crisis of 2008

As we stated earlier, the financial crisis of 2008 led to massive declines in wealth from plummeting asset values in the stock market and housing market. The decrease in aggregate demand caused the inflation rate to fall and the unemployment rate in rise, as seen in the Phillips curve in Exhibit 5. In other words, there has been a downward movement along the Phillips curve. Policy makers are hoping that with the use of fiscal and monetary policy they can increase aggregate demand and move the economy up along the Phillips curve and trade a little more inflation for less unemployment.

⑦ SECTION QUIZ

1. At the natural rate of unemployment, the long-run Phillips curve is
   a. horizontal.
   b. upward sloping.
   c. downward sloping.
   d. vertical.

2. Most economists today believe that the Phillips curve is
   a. downward sloping in the short run but vertical in the long run.
   b. vertical in the short run but downward sloping in the long run.
   c. upward sloping in the short run but vertical in the long run.
   d. vertical in the short run but upward sloping in the long run.

3. The short-run Phillips curve trade-off implies
   a. that if the curve shifts over time, society must accept decreases in unemployment for decreases in inflation.
   b. that if the curve is stable, society must accept increases in inflation for increases in unemployment.
   c. that if the curve shifts over time, society must accept increases in inflation for decreases in unemployment.
   d. that if the curve is stable, society must accept increases in unemployment for decreases in inflation.

4. Which of the following would shift the Phillips curve to the left?
   a. a negative supply shock
   b. an increase in inflationary expectations
   c. a positive supply shock
   d. all of the above

5. The short-run Phillips curve could shift to the right as a result of either _____ or _____.
   a. rising oil prices; increasing inflation expectations
   b. rising wages; falling prices
   c. declining oil prices; falling inflation expectations
   d. falling wages; rising prices
   e. none of the above

(continued)

6. As the economy moves up and to the right along a short-run aggregate supply curve, it
   a. moves up and to the right along the short-run Phillips curve.
   b. moves up and to the left along the short-run Phillips curve.
   c. moves down and to the right along the short-run Phillips curve.
   d. moves down and to the left along the short-run Phillips curve.

7. If the actual unemployment rate exceeds the natural rate of unemployment, there will be a tendency toward
   a. increased inflation and a leftward shift of the short-run Phillips curve.
   b. decreased inflation and a rightward shift of the short-run Phillips curve.
   c. increased inflation and a rightward shift of the short-run Phillips curve.
   d. decreased inflation and a leftward shift of the short-run Phillips curve.

1. Is the Phillips curve stable over time?

2. Why would you expect no relationship between inflation and unemployment in the long run?

3. Why is the economy being on the long-run Phillips curve equivalent to its being on the long-run aggregate supply curve?

4. Why would inflation have to accelerate over time to keep unemployment below its natural rate (and real output above its natural level) for a sustained period?

5. What does the long-run Phillips curve say about the relationship between macroeconomic policy stimulus and unemployment in the long run?

Answers: 1. d   2. a   3. b   4. c   5. c   6. c   7. d

Rational Expectations   19.3

🗀 What is rational expectations theory?

🗀 What do critics say about rational expectations theory?

Can Human Behavior Counteract Government Policy?

Is it possible that people can anticipate the plans of policy makers and alter their behavior quickly to neutralize the intended impact of government action? For example, if workers see that the government is allowing the money supply to expand rapidly, they may quickly demand higher money wages to offset the anticipated inflation. In the extreme form, if people could instantly recognize and respond to government policy changes, it might be impossible to alter real output or unemployment levels through policy actions, because government policy makers could no longer surprise households and firms. An increasing number of economists believe that there is at least some truth to this point of view. At a minimum, most economists accept the notion that real output and the unemployment rate cannot be altered with the ease that was earlier believed; some believe that the unemployment rate can seldom be influenced by fiscal and monetary policies.

What if people anticipate and react to government policy changes?

theory of rational expectations belief that workers and consumers incorporate the likely consequences of government policy changes into their expectations by quickly adjusting wages and prices

Rational Expectations Theory

The relatively new extension of economic theory that leads to this rather pessimistic conclusion regarding macroeconomic policy's ability to achieve our economic goals is called the **theory of rational expectations**. The notion that expectations or anticipations of future events are relevant to economic theory is not new; for decades, economists have incorporated expectations into models analyzing many forms of economic behavior. Only in the recent past, however, has a theory evolved that tries to incorporate expectations as a central factor in the analysis of the entire economy.

The interest in rational expectations has grown rapidly in the last decade. Acknowledged pioneers in the development of the theory include Professor Robert Lucas of the University of Chicago Professor Thomas Sargent of New York University and Christopher Sims of Princeton University. In 1995, Professor Lucas won the Nobel Prize for his work in rational expectations. In 2011, Sargent and Sims won the Nobel Prize for their contributions to rational expectations. Their combined work made us rethink the way we look at policy actions.

Rational expectations economists believe that wages and prices are flexible and that households and firms incorporate the likely consequences of government policy changes quickly into their expectations. In addition, rational expectations economists believe that the economy is inherently stable after macroeconomic shocks and that tinkering with fiscal and monetary policy cannot have the desired effect unless households and firms are caught "off guard" (and catching them off guard gets harder the more you try to do it).

Rational Expectations and the Consequences of Government Macroeconomic Policies

Why do rational expectation economists believe that fiscal and monetary policy will not have the desired effect?

Rational expectations theory, then, suggests that government economic policies designed to alter aggregate demand to meet macroeconomic goals are of limited effectiveness. When policy targets become public, it is argued, people will alter their own behavior from what it would otherwise have been to maximize their own utility, and in so doing, they largely negate the intended impact of policy changes. If government policy seems tilted toward permitting more inflation to try to reduce unemployment, people start spending their money faster than before, become more adamant in their demands for wages and other input prices, and so on. In the process of quickly altering their behavior to reflect the likely consequences of policy changes, they make it more difficult (costly) for government authorities to meet their macroeconomic objectives. Rather than fooling people into changing real wages, and therefore unemployment, with inflation "surprises," changes in inflation are quickly reflected into expectations with little or no effect on unemployment or real output even in the short run. As a consequence, policies intended to reduce unemployment through stimulating aggregate demand will often fail to have the intended effect. Fiscal and monetary policy, according to this view, will work only if the people are caught off guard or are fooled by policies and thus do not modify their behavior in a way that reduces policy effectiveness.

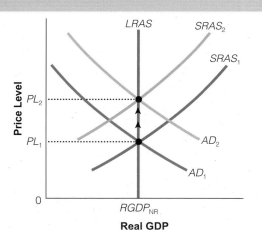

section 19.3 exhibit 1   **Rational Expectations and the AD/AS Model**

Expansionary monetary policy (or fiscal policy) will not affect RGDP if wages and prices are completely flexible, as in the rational expectations model. This means that the SRAS curve will shift leftward from $SRAS_1$ to $SRAS_2$ at the same time as the AD curve. Therefore, an expansionary policy, an increase in aggregate demand from AD_1 to AD_2, will lead to a higher price level but no change in RGDP or unemployment.

Anticipation of an Expansionary Monetary Policy

Consider the case in which an increase in aggregate demand is a result of an expansionary monetary policy. This increase is reflected in Exhibit 1 in the shift from AD_1 to AD_2. Because of the predictable inflationary consequences of that expansionary policy, prices immediately adjust to a new level at PL_2. Consumers, producers, workers, and lenders who *anticipated* the effects of the expansionary policy simply build the higher inflation rates into their product prices, wages, and interest rates. That is, households and firms realize that expansionary monetary policy can cause inflation if the economy is working close to capacity. Consequently, in an effort to protect themselves from the higher anticipated inflation, workers ask for higher wages, suppliers increase input prices, and producers raise their product prices. Because wages, prices, and interest rates are assumed to be flexible, the adjustments take place immediately. This increase in input costs for wages, interest, and raw materials causes the aggregate supply curve to shift up or leftward, shown as the movement from $SRAS_1$ to $SRAS_2$ in Exhibit 1. So the desired policy effect of greater real output and reduced unemployment from a shift in the aggregate demand curve is offset by an upward or leftward shift in the aggregate supply curve caused by an increase in input costs.

Unanticipated Expansionary Policy

How does unanticipated expansionary policy differ from anticipated expansionary policy?

Again, consider the case of an increase in aggregate demand that results from an expansionary monetary policy. However, this time it is *unanticipated*. The increase in the money supply is reflected in Exhibit 2 in the shift from AD_1 to AD_2. This unanticipated change in monetary policy stimulates output and employment in the short run, as the equilibrium moves from point A to point B. At the new short-run equilibrium, the output is at $RGDP_2$, and the price level is at PL_2. This output is beyond $RGDP_{NR}$, so it is not sustainable in the long run. Because it is unanticipated, workers and other input owners are expecting the price level to remain at PL_1, rather than PL_2. However, when input owners eventually realize that the actual price level has changed, they will require higher input prices, shifting the $SRAS$ from $SRAS_1$ to $SRAS_2$. At point C, we see that output has returned to $RGDP_{NR}$ but at a higher price level, PL_3.

Therefore, when the expansionary policy is unanticipated, it leads to a short-run expansion in output and employment. But in the long run, the only impact of the change in monetary policy is a higher price level—inflation. In short, when the change is correctly anticipated, expansionary monetary (or fiscal) policy does not result in a change in real output. However, if the expansionary monetary (fiscal) policy is unanticipated, the result is a short-run increase in RGDP and employment, but in the long run, it just means a higher price level.

In fact, the only way that monetary or fiscal policy can change output in the rational expectations model is with a surprise—an unanticipated change. For example, on April 18, 2001, between regularly scheduled meetings of the Federal Open Market Committee, the Fed surprised financial markets with an aggressive half-point cut in the interest rate. The Fed was trying to boost consumer confidence and impact falling stock market wealth. The surprise reduction in the interest rate sent the stock market soaring as the Dow posted one of its largest single-day point gains, and the NASDAQ had its fourth largest percentage gain. Former Fed Chairman Greenspan hoped that this move would shift the *AD* curve rightward, leading to higher levels of output.

section 19.3
exhibit 2

An Expansionary Policy That Is Unanticipated

An unanticipated change in monetary policy stimulates output and employment in the short run, as the equilibrium moves from point A to point B. At the new shortrun equilibrium, the output is at *RGDP*₂ and the price level is at *PL*₂. Because the expansionary policy is unanticipated, workers and other input owners are expecting the price level to remain at *PL*₁, rather than *PL*₂. When input owners eventually realize that the actual price level has changed, they will require higher input prices, shifting the *SRAS* curve from *SRAS*₁ to *SRAS*₂. At point C, we see that output has returned to *RGDP*ₙᵣ but at a higher price level, *PL*₃. If the expansionary policy is unanticipated, it leads to a short-run expansion in output and employment. In the long run, however, the impact of the change in the expansionary policy is a higher price level.

Critics of Rational Expectations Theory

What do the critics say about rational expectations theory?

Of course, rational expectations theory does have its critics. Critics want to know whether households and firms are completely informed about the impact that, say, an increase in money supply will have on the economy. In general, all citizens will not be completely informed, but key players such as corporations, financial institutions, and labor organizations may well be informed about the impact of these policy changes. But other problems arise. For example, are wages and other input prices really that flexible? That is, even if decision makers could anticipate the eventual effect of policy changes on prices, those prices may still be slow to adapt (e.g., what if you had just signed a three-year labor or supply contract when the new policy was implemented?).

Most economists reject the extreme rational expectations model of complete wage and price flexibility. In fact, most economists still believe a short-run trade-off between inflation and unemployment results because some input prices are slow to adjust to changes in the price level. However, in the long run, the expected inflation rate adjusts to changes in the actual inflation rate at the natural rate of unemployment, $RGDP_{NR}$.

⑦ SECTION QUIZ

1. According to rational expectations, if workers and firms forecast inflation accurately,
   a. the real wage will not decline as the price level rises.
   b. workers will not lose from inflation, and firms will not gain.
   c. the aggregate supply curve will be vertical.
   d. all of the above are correct.

2. If expectations are rational,
   a. a predictable change in inflation can make the expected inflation rate deviate from the actual inflation rate.
   b. unemployment can exceed the full-employment rate even in the long run.
   c. the inflation rate cannot be reduced without a sustained period of high unemployment, because the short-run Phillips curve is downward sloping.
   d. an increase in aggregate demand due to government policy will not necessarily increase real output.

3. According to the rational expectations view, the government can change real output
   a. with appropriate, well-publicized fiscal and monetary policies.
   b. with appropriate, well-publicized fiscal and monetary policies in the short run, but not in the long run.
   c. only by making unexpected changes in aggregate demand.
   d. without ever affecting the price level.

4. If expectations are rational, can fiscal and monetary policy control real output?
   a. Yes, provided policies are announced in advance.
   b. Yes, both policies are effective in altering real output in the desired way.
   c. No, because policy makers can't accurately predict how people's expectations will be affected by the policies policy makers adopt.
   d. No, only fiscal policy can alter unemployment in the short run.
   e. No, only monetary policy can alter unemployment in the short run.

5. If an increase in the growth rate of *AD* leads to an increase in real GDP in the short run,
   a. the increase in *AD* could have been correctly anticipated.
   b. the increase in *AD* could have been greater than anticipated.
   c. the increase in *AD* could have been less than anticipated.
   d. the increase in *AD* could have been any of the above.

(*continued*)

⓺ SECTION QUIZ (Cont.)

6. With rational expectations, a policy that would increase *AD* would lead to

   a. higher inflation and lower unemployment in the short run if people underestimated the effect of the policy on inflation.

   b. higher inflation and higher unemployment in the short run if people underestimated the effect of the policy on inflation.

   c. higher inflation and no change in unemployment in the short run, if people's expectations were correct.

   d. higher inflation and an indeterminate effect on unemployment in the short run, if people's expectations were correct.

   e. both (a) and (c).

7. If the rational expectations theory is accurate, equilibrium real GDP will change in the short run

   a. whenever the aggregate demand curve shifts.

   b. only if discretionary fiscal policy is used.

   c. only if there is a shift in aggregate demand that could not have been predicted from the information available to the public.

   d. only if discretionary monetary policy is used.

   e. None of the above is correct.

8. Which of the following statements is true?

   a. A correctly anticipated increase in *AD* from expansionary monetary or fiscal policy will not change real output, employment, or unemployment in the short run.

   b. In the rational expectations model, when people expect a larger increase in *AD* than actually results from a policy change, it leads to a lower price level and a higher level of RGDP in the short run.

   c. If some input prices are slow to adjust to changes in the price level, the rational expectations model of complete wage and price flexibility will be correct.

   d. In the long run and the short run, the expected inflation rate equals the actual inflation rate.

---

1. What is rational expectations theory?

2. Why could an unexpected change in inflation change real wages and unemployment, while an expected change in inflation could not?

3. Why can the results of rational expectations be described as generating the long-run results of a policy change in the short run?

4. In a world of rational expectations, why is it harder to reduce unemployment below its natural rate but potentially easier to reduce inflation rates?

5. Even if individuals could quickly anticipate the consequences of government policy changes, how could long-term contracts (e.g., three-year labor agreements and 30-year fixed rate mortgages) and the costs of changing price lists and catalogs result in unemployment still being affected by those policy changes?

6. Why do expected rainstorms have different effects on people than unexpected rainstorms?

Answers: 1. d 2. d 3. c 4. c 5. b 6. d 7. c 8. a

19.4

Controversies in Macroeconomic Policy

- 📁 Are fiscal and monetary policies effective?
- 📁 Should monetary policy use a rule or discretion?
- 📁 Should central banks target inflation?
- 📁 Could indexing reduce the costs of inflation?

What are the different views of the effectiveness of discretionary fiscal and monetary policy?

Are Fiscal and Monetary Policies Effective?

Economies tend to fluctuate. Consumer or business pessimism leads to a reduction in aggregate demand. As aggregate demand falls, so does output and employment. The rising unemployment and the fall in income cause additional damage to the economy. The economy is now operating to the left of the *LRAS* (or inside its production possibilities curve); resources are not being used efficiently when actual output is less than potential output. Many economists believe that in the short run, policy makers have the ability to alter aggregate demand. If the aggregate demand is insufficient, policy makers can stimulate aggregate demand by increasing government spending, cutting taxes, and increasing the growth rate of the money supply. If aggregate demand is excessive, policy makers can reduce aggregate demand by decreasing government spending, increasing taxes, and reducing the growth rate of the money supply.

These macroeconomists are called *activists,* and they believe that in the short run, discretionary monetary and fiscal policy can stimulate the economy that is in a recessionary gap or dampen the economy that is in an inflationary boom with aggregate demand management. However, other economists believe that aggregate demand stimulus cannot *keep* the rate of unemployment below the natural rate. Most economists accept the basic notion of the natural rate hypothesis that suggests the unemployment rate will be close to the natural rate in the long run. Other economists, *rational expectations theorists,* believe that government economic policies designed to alter aggregate demand are not all that effective because households and firms form expectations to economic policy causing prices and wages to adjust quickly, leaving the output roughly the same but at a higher price level. To these economists, monetary and fiscal policy will only work if it comes as a surprise to the public.

However, most economists do not accept the notion that households and firms have rational expectations and that wages and prices adjust quickly because of wage and other input contracts. Even if households and firms formed rational expectations, if prices and wages adjusted slowly, expansionary monetary policy could lead to a lower unemployment level.

Most macroeconomists believe both that monetary and fiscal policy can shift the aggregate demand and that the intervention can be counterproductive. Recall our discussion in the previous chapter about the lags associated with both fiscal and monetary policies. The long and uncertain lags may lead to policies that are counterproductive. In other words, the policies aimed at closing a recessionary gap may cause an inflationary gap if the stimulus occurs at the wrong time. Or policies aimed at closing an inflationary gap may overshoot the goal and cause a recessionary gap. The problem is that we do not operate with a crystal ball. For policy makers, timing and the exact size of the stimulus are essential for effective stabilization policies.

Other economists believe that the potency of expansionary fiscal policy will be diminished by the crowding-out effect. That is, expansionary fiscal policy increases the real interest rate when it borrows money to finance its deficit, which crowds out private investment. It is also possible that the economy is stimulated with fiscal or monetary policy in the short run for political gains that will only be inflationary in the long run. Recall that expansionary monetary policy lowers the real interest rate and stimulates private investment.

Other questions the policy makers will have to answer are: What are the output effects of the fiscal or monetary policy? What is the marginal propensity to consume (MPC) of the tax cut? How much will the central bank have to change the real interest rate to get the desired change in residential and commercial spending?

For most economists, monetary policy is the preferred tool for stabilization because the inside lags (the time from when a policy is needed to the time it is implemented) are much shorter. Recall that the federal open market committee (FOMC) meets eight times a year. Fiscal policy requires Congress to convene and debate the tax cuts or expenditure increases. However, fiscal policy may be used in special circumstances when monetary policy alone cannot do the job. Automatic stabilizers (e.g., taxes that impact disposable income and unemployment compensation) are an important part of fiscal policy and have a much smaller lag because they are implemented automatically.

Policy Difficulties with Supply Shocks

Recall that a negative supply shock, like those the United States experienced in the 1970s and 2007–2008, leads to an increase in the price level and a reduction in real aggregate output ($RGDP$), as seen in Exhibit 1.

After a negative demand shock (not shown but a leftward shift in the AD curve from say point A), policy makers can employ expansionary fiscal and/or monetary policy which can help shift the economy back to its original position. However, this is not the case with a negative supply shock. For example, suppose policy makers choose to use expansionary fiscal and/or monetary policy as a response to the recession caused by the supply shock; this increase in aggregate demand causes an increase in aggregate output ($RGDP$) but leads to even greater inflation, as seen in Exhibit 2(a). Or if policy makers choose to use contractionary fiscal and/or monetary policy to control inflation, this decrease in aggregate demand leads to a lower price level but causes an even lower level of aggregate output with higher rates of unemployment, as seen in Exhibit 2(b). In short, stagflation caused by a supply shock makes economic policy making very difficult.

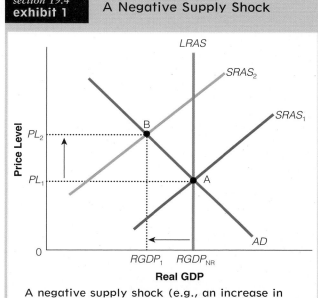

section 19.4 exhibit 1   **A Negative Supply Shock**

A negative supply shock (e.g., an increase in global oil prices) cause production costs to rise and lowers the amount producers are willing to supply at any given aggregate price level. The result is a lower aggregate output at $RGDP_1$ and a higher price level at PL_2.

© Cengage Learning 2013

What Should the Central Bank Do?

Most economists believe that monetary policy should take the lead in stabilization policy and that the central bank should be independent and insulated from political pressure to avoid political business cycles. Political business cycles may occur if central banks ally themselves with an incumbent party and pursue expansionary monetary policy prior to an election. Even though the short-run impact may be increased output, employment, and a victory for the incumbent party in the election, the long-run impact will be inflation. So, faced with these potential problems, how should the central bank set its monetary policy?

How do negative supply shocks make policy more difficult?

Some macroeconomists believe that the central bank should adopt rules, such as a constant growth rate in the money supply. According to the rule advocates, if the money supply were only allowed to increase by say 3 to 5 percent per year (enough to accommodate new economic growth), the result would be less uncertainty and greater economic stability. In other words, if the fixed rule is followed and the real economic growth rate is 3 percent per year and the monetary growth rate is 3 percent per year, the average rate of inflation is zero. This situation seldom occurs, but the point here is that it would add credibility to the Federal Reserve as being tough on inflation. It would make it clear that what the Fed says it's going to do is consistent with what it actually does.

section 19.4
exhibit 2   Policy Response to a Supply Shock

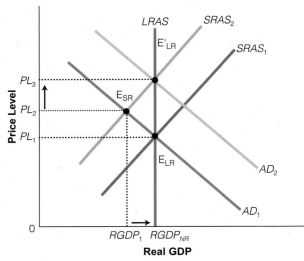

a. Expansionary Monetary and/or Fiscal Policy

If policy makers increase aggregate demand at E_{SR}, aggregate output increase to $RGDP_{NR}$, and employment increases, but the price level rises to PL_3. The increase in AD helps aggregate output but causes even more inflation.

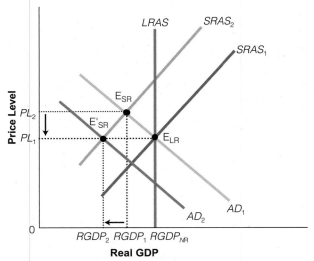

b. Contractionary Monetary and/or Fiscal Policy

If policy makers decrease aggregate demand at E_{SR} aggregate output falls further to $RGDP_2$, but the price level returns to PL_1. The decrease in AD curbs inflation but causes a reduction in aggregate output and a rise in unemployment.

In 1985, Bolivia had an inflation rate approaching 12,000 percent per year, and the government decided to put the brakes on the money supply. The result, hyperinflation was over in a month, no output was lost, and credibility was restored. The public must believe the government's anti-inflation policy, or it will not work.

Inflation Targeting

Some macroeconomists believe that we can do better than targeting the growth rate of monetary aggregates. These economists believe we should target the inflation rate. Targeting the inflation rate would require the central bank to attempt to stay in a certain band of inflation for a specified period of time—say 2 to 3 percent. The key to targeting is that it enhances credibility and could help to "anchor" inflationary expectations and lead to greater price stability. After all, successful monetary policy hinges critically on the ability to manage expectations. Several countries have inflation targets in place: the Bank of England is at 2 percent; the Bank of Canada is at 2 percent; Brazil is at 4.5 percent; and Chile is at the range between 2 percent and 4 percent. Empirical studies show a tendency for inflation rates to fall in countries that use inflation targeting.

Critics of inflation targeting will argue that central banks need flexibility. Good leaders, like Volker and Greenspan, proved that they can handle the job without set rules or targets. In other words, the United States has kept inflation low without rules or targeting, so those opposed to targets say, "If it ain't broke, don't fix it." Others argue that it may cause banks to focus too much attention on inflation at the expense of other goals such as output and employment. For example, a recessionary gap will normally cause the central bank to lower the interest rate to stimulate spending, output, and employment rather than just focus on inflation. Some might ask: If the Fed is going to put a target band on inflation, why not put one on unemployment and long-term interest rates too?

Targeting Inflation at Zero

So, if central banks are targeting low inflation rates of 2 percent, why not target inflation rates at 0 percent? After all, we have seen the costs to inflation: shoe leather costs, menu costs, changes in tax liabilities, changes in the distribution of income—and it leads to a distortion of the price system. However, these costs are probably small if inflation rates are low and expected to stay low. The other problem associated with a zero inflation rate is that it would be difficult to precisely hit the target all the time, and it could lead to deflation (the average price level of goods and services are falling) as it did in Japan in the 1990s. Also, some macroeconomists worry that if the inflation rate is targeted at zero, the interest rate may fall to zero in a recession and render expansionary macroeconomic policy powerless. Other problems are unanticipated shocks and unanticipated financial crises. Monetary authorities need the flexibility to respond to these shocks by temporarily going outside the target range. In recent times, the Federal Reserve was there to respond to the stock market crash of October 19, 1987—when stock prices fell by more than 20 percent in a single day (the biggest ever one-day decline)—and to the shock created by the terrorist attacks on September 11, 2001, when the Federal Reserve made massive discount loans to banks to avoid a financial crisis.

Should central banks try to target inflation rates at 0 percent?

Critics of targeting a zero inflation rate believe that achieving zero inflation is almost impossible and the costs are too high. The costs of disinflation (lowering the rate of inflation) can be high. Reducing the inflation rate can reduce output substantially. Disinflation is not painless.

The Taylor Rule

A variant of monetary rules and inflation targeting is the Taylor rule. It is a hybrid—part rule, part discretion. Taylor's formula uses a rule to decide when to use discretionary decisions. According to John Taylor, "The federal funds rate is increased or decreased according to what is happening to both real GDP and inflation. In particular, if real GDP rises 1 percent above potential GDP the federal funds rate should be raised, relative to the current inflation rate, by 0.5 percent. And if inflation rises by 1 percent above its target of 2 percent, then the federal funds rate should be raised by 0.5 percent relative to the inflation rate. When real GDP is equal to potential GDP and inflation is equal to its target of 2 percent, then the federal funds rate should remain at about 4 percent, which would imply a real interest rate of 2 percent on average. The policy rule was purposely chosen to be simple. Clearly, the equal weights on inflation and the GDP gap are an approximation reflecting the finding that neither variable should be given a negligible weight." If the central bank used this rule, market participants could easily predict central bank behavior, creating greater stability and certainty.

What is the Taylor rule?

Asset Price Inflation

Some economists believe that the Fed should be concerned about asset pricing—especially housing and stock market prices. The period 1999–2004 saw inflation at a low rate of about 2.5 percent per year, yet housing prices were rising 25 percent and higher in some markets. In some countries, Australia and Great Britain, the central banks are paying closer attention to the growth in asset prices even when consumer price inflation is low. Others believe that the central bank should not concern itself with the value that consumers place on stocks and housing. If the bubble bursts, the Fed can lower interest rates to bolster the economy.

Of course, as we found out during the financial crisis of 2007–2008, there are several questions that must be answered. One of the most important is: Can you identify housing or stock bubbles when they are appearing? The extent of monetary policy intervention may depend on the bubble. In the recession of 2007–2008, the housing bubble spread throughout the economy quickly and violently, before interest rate policy could be used to offset the damaging effects.

Indexing and Reducing the Costs of Inflation

Another approach to some of the problems posed by inflation is **indexing**. As you recall, inflation poses substantial equity and distributional problems only when it is unanticipated or unexpected. One means of protecting parties against unanticipated price increases is

indexing
use of payment contracts that automatically adjust for changes in inflation

to write contracts that automatically change the prices of goods or services whenever the overall price level changes, effectively rewriting agreements in terms of dollars of constant purchasing power. Wages, loans, and mortgage payments—everything possible—would be changed every month or so by an amount equal to the percentage change in some broad-based price index. Thus, if prices rose by 1.2 percent this month and your last month's wage was $1,000, your wage this month would be $1,012 ($1,000 × 1.012). By making as many contracts as possible payable in dollars of constant purchasing power, those involved could protect themselves against unanticipated changes in inflation.

Why Isn't Indexing More Extensively Used?

Indexing seems to eliminate most of the wealth transfers associated with unexpected inflation. Why then is it not more commonly used? One main argument against indexing is that it can worsen inflation. As prices go up, wages and certain other contractual obligations (e.g., rents) also automatically increase. This immediate and comprehensive reaction to price increases leads to greater inflationary pressures. One price increase leads to a second, which in turn leads to a third, and so on.

Other Problems Associated with Indexing

We might ask, so what? If prices rise rapidly, but wages, rents, and so forth move up with prices, real wages and rents remain constant. However, if inflation gets bad enough, it could become almost impossible administratively to maintain the indexing scheme. The index, to be effective, might have to be changed every few days, but the information to make such frequent changes is not currently available. To get the necessary information quickly, then, might be quite expensive, involving a small army of price-checking bureaucrats and a massive electronic communications system. Other inefficiencies occur as well. During the German hyperinflation of the early 1920s, prices at one point rose so rapidly that workers demanded to be paid twice a day, at noon and at the end of the workday. During their lunch hour, workers would rush money to their wives, who would then run out and buy real goods before prices increased further.

Other big problems include the fact that indexing reduces the ability for relative price changes to allocate resources where they are more valuable. Not everything can be indexed, so indexing would cause wealth redistribution. In addition, costs would necessarily be incurred as a result of renegotiating cost-of-living (COLA) clauses.

Excessive inflation, then, leads to great inefficiency, as well as to a loss of confidence in the issuer of money—namely, the government. Furthermore, inflation influences world trade patterns. Limited indexing, in fact, has already been adopted, as some wage and pension payments are changed with changes in the cost-of-living index. Whether on balance those escalator clauses are "good" or "bad" is a debatable topic—a normative judgment that we will leave to the reader to make.

---

② SECTION QUIZ

1. Under the Taylor rule, the federal funds rate would be increased by half a point when

   a. real GDP exceeds target real GDP by 1 percentage point.

   b. target GDP exceeds real GDP by 1 percentage point.

   c. inflation exceeds the inflation target by 1 percentage point.

   d. either (a) or (c) occurs.

(continued)

2. The primary purpose of indexing is to

   a. lower the inflation rate.

   b. reduce the social costs of inflation.

   c. help the government maintain wage and price controls.

   d. All of the above are primary purposes of indexing.

3. Indexing is a method of fighting inflation by

   a. tying monetary payments to changes in price indexes.

   b. lowering the level of the consumer price index.

   c. keeping prices from rising above government set ceilings.

   d. all of the above.

4. Indexing

   a. is a process of adjusting payment contracts to automatically adjust for changes in the price level.

   b. can reduce the impact of inflation on the distribution of income.

   c. may intensify the inflationary effects of expansionary monetary policy by increasing inflationary pressures.

   d. is characterized by all of the above.

5. Which of the following statements is true?

   a. Activist economists believe that discretionary macroeconomic policy can make the economy less unstable.

   b. One of the advantages of monetary policy rules is to increase the Federal Reserve System's credibility in its fight against inflation.

   c. If monetary authorities respond to political pressures during a recession, the result could be a decrease in interest rates and a decrease in unemployment in the short run, but higher inflation in the long run.

   d. Some economists oppose widespread indexing on the grounds that it could worsen inflation.

   e. All of the above are true.

6. Which of the following statements is true?

   a. Most economists think that unemployment will remain close to the natural rate of unemployment in the short run.

   b. For many economists, monetary policy's shorter outside lag is an advantage in using monetary policy for stabilization efforts.

   c. Monetary policy rules have the advantage of giving the Fed discretion to deal with sudden shocks and crises.

   d. As a practical matter, indexing can only be used with wage contracts.

   e. All of the above are true.

---

1. What impact do lags have on discretionary fiscal and monetary policy?

2. What is a political business cycle? What are the possibilities for conflict of interest to arise?

3. How does credibility impact inflation?

4. What are the arguments for and against inflation targeting?

5. What are the problems associated with targeting a zero rate on inflation?

6. If each possible good were indexed to changes in the general price level, would it be easy for relative price changes to signal changing relative scarcities? Why or why not?

Answers: 1. d 2. b 3. a 4. d 5. e 6. e

Interactive Summary

Fill in the blanks:

1. The recession in early 2001 was set off by a serious drop in _____.

2. The Phillips curve describes a short-run trade-off between _____ and _____.

3. If output prices rise but money wages do not go up as quickly, real wages will _____, tending to _____ unemployment.

4. The Phillips curve suggests that at lower rates of inflation, the rate of unemployment will be _____.

5. The Phillips curve is _____ at higher rates of inflation and lower rates of unemployment.

6. An increase in aggregate demand would cause the economy to move _____ along a Phillips curve, causing the inflation rate to _____ and the rate of unemployment to _____.

7. When moving up along a Phillips curve, employment rates tend to _____.

8. Economists who questioned the long-term validity of the Phillips curve were largely _____ in the 1960s.

9. According to Milton Friedman, a trade-off occurs between inflation and unemployment in the _____ run but not in the _____ run; the trade-off comes from _____ inflation.

10. The data from the 1970s indicated that the Phillips curve _____ remain in place.

11. In the long run when the expected inflation rate falls, the short-run Phillips curve shifts _____.

12. The _____ hypothesis states that the economy will self-correct to the natural rate of unemployment.

13. An increase in the growth rate of the money supply _____ aggregate demand, _____ output, _____ inflation, and _____ unemployment.

14. An unanticipated increase in inflation will _____ real wages, resulting in a _____ unemployment rate.

15. In the long run, when expected inflation rises, workers adjust to the higher rate of inflation by shifting the short-run Phillips curve _____.

16. When actual inflation equals expected inflation, real output equals its _____ level and unemployment equals the _____.

17. In the long run, when inflation increases, there is _____ in unemployment.

18. A decrease in inflation will _____ real wages at first, _____ real output and _____ unemployment.

19. If inflation is steady, actual inflation _____ expected inflation.

20. When people adapt their inflationary expectations after actual inflation changes, it is called _____ expectations.

21. Higher production costs due to adverse supply shocks shift the short-run Phillips curve _____.

22. A negative supply shock _____ cause inflation to increase and unemployment to increase at the same time.

23. A positive supply shock can result in both unemployment and inflation _____ at the same time.

24. If people expect supply shocks to be permanent, the result would be inflation and unemployment both _____ for adverse supply shocks and both _____ for favorable supply shocks.

25. An increase in oil prices is considered a(n) _____ supply shock.

26. If people could _____ to policy changes, it might not be possible to increase real output or employment through policy actions.

27. The theory of rational expectations leads to a(n) _____ conclusion about macroeconomic policy's ability to achieve our economic goals.

28. Rational expectations economists believe that wages and prices are _____ and workers _____ incorporate the likely consequences of government policy changes into their expectations.

29. Rational expectations economists think the economy tends to be inherently _____ and that government policy has the desired effects only when consumers and workers are caught _____.

30. According to rational expectations, when policy targets become public, people will alter their behavior to largely _____ the intended effects.

31. If changes in the inflation rate are quickly reflected in expectations, unemployment or real output from macroeconomic policy would experience _____ effect.

32. An increase in aggregate demand that is correctly anticipated and responded to will _____ the price level, _____ real output and _____ the unemployment rate.

33. When expansionary macroeconomic policy is unanticipated, the short-run aggregate supply curve _____ in the short run, but when it is correctly anticipated, the short-run aggregate supply curve _____.

34. Whether a macroeconomic policy change is anticipated or unanticipated, it will not change real output or unemployment in the _____ run.

35. In the short run, an increase in aggregate demand will _____ the price level, whether it is anticipated or not, but it will increase real output only if it is _____.

36. If people expect a larger increase in aggregate demand than the actual increase in aggregate demand that occurs, the price level would _____ and real output would _____ in the short run.

37. If input prices adjust _____, the rational expectations view that changes in government policy would have no effect on real output in the short run would be incorrect.

38. If aggregate demand is insufficient, policy makers can stimulate aggregate demand by _____ government spending, _____ taxes, or _____ the growth rate of the money supply.

39. Activist macroeconomists believe that in the short run, discretionary macroeconomic policy can _____ economic fluctuations.

40. Most economists accept the notion that unemployment will be close to the natural rate of unemployment in the _____ run.

41. The rational expectations school, the form that assumes instant adjustment, believes that government _____ impact real output in the short run.

42. With _____ expectations, but not _____ expectations, inflation could potentially be lowered by macroeconomic policy without causing a recession.

43. If the timing or the magnitude of a macroeconomic policy change is not what is intended, it could make the economy _____ stable.

44. Monetary policy is often the preferred stabilization tool due to its _____ inside lags.

45. Monetary policy rules and inflation targeting are intended to add _____ to the Federal Reserve's determination to hold inflation down.

46. Inflation targeting is intended to help _____ inflation expectations and lead to _____ price stability.

47. Shoe leather costs and menu costs are probably small if inflation is _____ and expected to _____.

48. One worry about inflation targeting is that it would reduce monetary authorities' _____ to respond to _____ shocks and crises.

49. To reduce the inflation rate by one percentage point may require reducing real output by _____ 1 percent.

50. The Taylor approach uses a(n) _____ to decide when to use _____ actions.

51. The Taylor rule suggests changes in the _____ rate when real output or inflation rates deviate from their targets.

52. Under a Taylor rule, when real GDP falls below potential GDP, the federal funds rate should _____, and when inflation falls above the target the federal funds rate should _____.

53. Under a Taylor rule, for each one percentage point deviation from potential GDP or from the target inflation rate, the federal funds rate should change by _____ point.

54. _____ is a way of protecting parties against unanticipated changes in inflation by using contracts that automatically adjust to changes in purchasing power.

55. One main argument against indexing is that it can _____ inflation, by making one price increase lead to others.

56. If _____ becomes rapid, it could be almost impossible to administer an indexing scheme.

57. Another problem with indexing is that it reduces the ability for _____ changes to efficiently allocate resources.

Answers: 1. investment 2. inflation; unemployment 3. falls; reduce 4. higher 5. steeper 6. up; rise; fall 7. rise 8. ignored 9. short; long; unanticipated 10. did not 11. leftward 12. natural rate 13. increases; increasing; increasing; decreasing 14. decrease; lower 15. rightward 16. natural; natural rate of unemployment 17. no change 18. increase; lowering; raising 19. equals 20. adaptive 21. rightward 22. can 23. falling 24. increasing; decreasing 25. negative 26. instantly recognize and respond 27. pessimistic 28. flexible; quickly 29. stable; off-guard 30. negate 31. little or no 32. increase; leave unchanged; leave unchanged 33. does not change; shifts upward 34. long 35. long 36. increase; unanticipated 37. slowly 38. increasing; decreasing; increasing 39. reduce 40. long 41. cannot 42. rational; adaptive 43. less 44. shorter 45. credibility 46. anchor; lower 47. low; stay low 48. flexibility; unanticipated 49. more than 50. rule; discretionary 51. federal funds 52. fall; rise 53. 0.5 54. Indexing 55. worsen 56. inflation 57. relative price

Key Terms and Concepts

natural rate hypothesis 559
adaptive expectations 560

theory of rational expectations 565

indexing 573

Section Quiz Answers

19.1 The Phillips Curve

1. How does the rate of inflation affect real wage rates if nominal wages rise less or more slowly than output prices?

When nominal wages rise less or more slowly than output prices, real (adjusted for inflation) wages fall.

2. How does the change in real wage rates (relative to output prices) as inflation increases affect the unemployment rate?

The fall in real wage rates (relative to output prices) as inflation increases reduces the unemployment rate, because the lower real wage rates make it profitable to hire more, now relatively cheaper, employees than before.

3. What is the argument for why the Phillips curve is relatively steeper at lower rates of unemployment and higher rates of inflation?

The argument is that once capacity utilization is high and unemployment is low, an increased part of the economy is already operating at or near full capacity, and further fiscal or monetary policy stimulus primarily triggers inflationary pressures in sectors already at capacity, while eliminating decreasing amounts of unemployment in those fewer sectors where excess capacity and high unemployment still exist.

4. For a given upward-sloping, short-run aggregate supply curve, how does an increase in aggregate demand correspond to a movement up and to the left along a Phillips curve?

For a given upward-sloping, short-run aggregate supply curve, an increase in aggregate demand moves the economy up along the short-run aggregate supply curve to an increased price level and increased RGDP. The increase in the price level is an increase in inflation and the increase in RGDP is accompanied by a decrease in unemployment, so the same effect is shown by a move up (higher inflation) and to the left (lower unemployment) along a Phillips curve.

19.2 The Phillips Curve over Time

1. Is the Phillips curve stable over time?

No. While the short-run Phillips curve was once considered to be stable, economists now recognize that it is unstable and does not represent a permanent relationship between unemployment and inflation rates.

2. Why would you expect no relationship between inflation and unemployment in the long run?

This is the natural rate hypothesis. You would expect there to be no relationship between inflation and unemployment in the long run because the long run represents what happens once people have completely adjusted to changed conditions. Therefore, in the long run, actual and expected rates of inflation are the same, and changes in rates of inflation do not change people's "real" behavior (reflected in unemployment and real GDP) because those changes are not unexpected.

3. Why is the economy being on the long-run Phillips curve equivalent to its being on the long-run aggregate supply curve?

Unemployment equals its natural rate along the long-run Phillips curve. Real GDP is equal to its natural level along the long-run aggregate supply curve. But the natural level of real GDP is the output level consistent with unemployment equal to its natural rate, so points on both curves illustrate the same results.

4. Why would inflation have to accelerate over time to keep unemployment below its natural rate (and real output above its natural level) for a sustained period of time?

Inflation would have to accelerate over time to keep unemployment below its natural rate (and real output above its natural level) for a sustained period of time because over time, people would adapt to any given level of inflation. Therefore, at a given rate of inflation, unemployment would return to its natural rate over time. To keep people "fooled" into unemployment below its natural rate requires more inflation than people expected, and to maintain this requires accelerating inflation over time.

5. What does the long-run Phillips curve say about the relationship between macroeconomic policy stimulus and unemployment in the long run?

The vertical long-run Phillips curve indicates that there is no relationship between macroeconomic policy stimulus and unemployment in the long run, once people have had time to completely adapt to it. Unemployment will equal its natural rate in the long run, and macroeconomic policy will therefore only change the inflation rate in the long run.

19.3 Rational Expectations

1. What is the rational expectations theory?

The rational expectations theory incorporates expectations as a central factor in the analysis of the entire economy. It is essentially the idea that people will rationally anticipate the predictable future consequences of present decisions, and change their behavior today to reflect those future consequences. For example, this would mean that people can anticipate the inflationary long-run consequences of macroeconomic policies adopted today, and that anticipation leads them to change their current behavior in a way that can quickly neutralize the intended impact of a government action.

2. Why could an unexpected change in inflation change real wages and unemployment, while an expected change in inflation could not?

An unexpected change in inflation could change real wages and unemployment precisely because it was unexpected, and people were "fooled" into changing their behavior (in the short run). An expected change in inflation would not change real wages and unemployment because no one is fooled, so people don't change their real behavior as a result.

3. Why can the results of rational expectations be described as generating the long-run results of a policy change in the short run?

The long run refers to the situation once people have had time to completely adjust their behavior to current circumstances. But under rational expectations, the long-run consequences will be anticipated and responded to today, so that people have completely adjusted their behavior to new policies in the short run. Therefore, the results of rational expectations can be described as generating the long-run results of a policy change in the short run.

4. In a world of rational expectations, why is it harder to reduce unemployment below its natural rate but potentially easier to reduce inflation rates?

Reducing unemployment below its natural rate requires that inflation be greater than expected.

But under rational expectations, people are not fooled by inflationary policies (unless they are surprised), so this is very hard to do. It is potentially easier to reduce inflation rates under rational expectations, though, because people will be more quickly convinced that inflation will fall when credible government policies are put in place, and it will not take an extended period of high unemployment before they adapt to the lower inflation rate that results.

5. Even if individuals could quickly anticipate the consequences of government policy changes, how could long-term contracts (e.g., three-year labor agreements and 30-year fixed rate mortgages) and the costs of changing price lists and catalogs result in unemployment still being affected by those policy changes?

Even if individuals could quickly anticipate the consequences of government policy changes, long-term contracts can't be instantly adjusted, so the real prices and wages subject to such contracts will be at least temporarily changed by inflation "surprises," at least until such contracts can be rewritten. Similarly, price lists and catalogs will not be changed instantly when new policies are adopted, because of the cost of doing so, and those prices will not instantly adapt to new inflationary expectations. Since these prices will be "wrong" for a period after new policies are adopted, real wages and prices, and therefore unemployment, can still be affected for a period of time by policy changes.

6. Why do expected rainstorms have different effects on people than unexpected rainstorms?

Expected rainstorms don't catch you by surprise, so you prepare for them in a way that minimizes their effects (umbrellas, jackets, etc.). Unexpected rainstorms catch you by surprise, and have much greater effects, because they haven't been prepared for.

19.4 Controversies in Macroeconomic Policy

1. What impact do lags have on discretionary fiscal and monetary policy?

For stabilization policy to be effective policy must be appropriate in direction, magnitude, and timing, so lag problems can cause policy to be ineffective or even worsen problems. This means that policies aimed at closing a recessionary gap may cause an inflationary gap, or that policies aimed at closing an inflationary gap may cause a recessionary gap, if the policies have their effects at the wrong time. Further, this leads many economists to believe that monetary authorities should take the lead in stabilization policy, because of the much shorter inside lags for monetary policy. Shorter lags are also an advantage for automatic stabilizers over discretionary fiscal policy.

2. What is a political business cycle? What are the possibilities for conflict of interest to arise?
Political business cycles can occur when economic policies are timed for political effect, as when a central bank pursues expansionary monetary policy prior to an election. The conflict of interest arises because while the short-run impact may be electoral success because of the increased output and employment, the long-run effect will be inflation and the costs entailed in dealing with it or overcoming it.

3. How does credibility impact inflation?
Credibility is particularly important to make it clear that government authorities, such as the Federal Reserve, will actually do what they say they will do (e.g., when they say they will be tough on inflation, they actually will be). This dramatically reduces the risk that such government policy will fool you in substantial ways, so that you need not worry so much about protecting yourself against policy-induced mistakes, and social coordination is improved as a result.

4. What are the arguments for and against inflation targeting?
The argument for inflation targeting is that rules are important in creating policy credibility and that inflation targeting works more effectively than other rules, such as targeting the growth of monetary aggregates. Targeting inflation is said to enhance credibility and to help "anchor" inflationary expectations and lead to greater price stability. Critics argue that inflation targeting removes the flexibility that central banks need to respond to changing situations and may focus too much attention on inflation and not enough on employment and output.

5. What are the problems associated with targeting a zero rate on inflation?
While there are costs of low rates of inflation (e.g., shoe leather and menu costs), those costs are small when inflation is low and expected to remain low. A zero inflation rate, however, would be difficult to precisely hit, and could even lead to deflation, which also causes economic problems. Some economists also worry that targeting zero inflation could sometimes result in a zero interest rate, which would render expansionary monetary policy powerless to stimulate the economy. Further, when there are unanticipated shocks and crises, it would eliminate the flexibility that central banks need to respond.

6. If each possible good were indexed to changes in the general price level, would it be easy for relative price changes to signal changing relative scarcities? Why or why not?
When all prices tend to change together (e.g., when one price goes up, the price level goes up, and so other indexed prices also go up as a result), it is harder for relative prices to change to reflect changing relative scarcity.

Problems

1. Use the following diagrams and
   a. show in both diagrams what would happen if government purchases increase in the short run.
   b. show in both diagrams what would happen if the growth rate of the money supply was reduced in the short run.
   c. show in both diagrams what would happen if people came to expect a higher rate of inflation.
   d. show in both diagram what would happen if a favorable supply shock occurred.

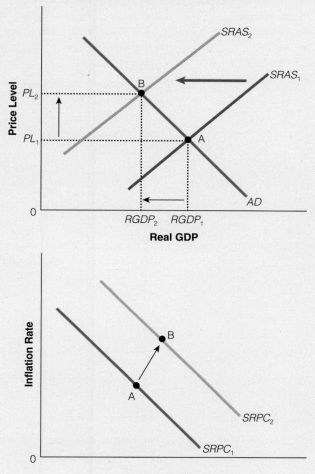

2. Use the diagram to answer the following questions.
   a. At which point might expansionary government policy help stabilize the economy?
   b. At which point might contractionary government policy help stabilize the economy?

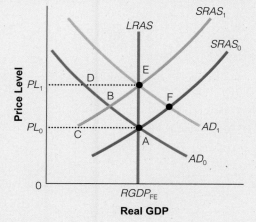

3. Use the diagram from problem 2 and indicate
   a. which movement would correspond to an unanticipated expansionary government policy in the short run.
   b. which movement would correspond to an unanticipated contractionary government policy in the short run.
   c. which movement would correspond to a completely anticipated expansionary government policy, under rational expectations.
   d. which movement would correspond to a completely anticipated contractionary government policy in the short run.
   e. what would happen if an expansionary government policy occurred, but its inflationary effects were smaller than they were expected to be.

4. Abraham Lincoln once said "You can fool all of the people some of the time, and some of the people all of the time, but you cannot fool all of the people all of the time." How can a central bank that conducts monetary policy "fool people" and thereby affect the level of unemployment in the economy? What happens if people begin to anticipate future monetary policy correctly based on past experience?

5. Predict the impact an unexpected decrease in the money supply would have on the following variables in the short run and in the long run.
   a. the inflation rate
   b. the unemployment rate
   c. real output
   d. real wages

6. Predict whether unemployment will increase or decrease as a result of each of the following monetary policies. If it is unanticipated? What if it is anticipated?
   a. a reduction in the discount rate from 6 percent to 5.5 percent
   b. an open market sale by the Federal Reserve Bank
   c. an increase in the required reserve ratio from 10 percent to 12 percent

7. If money wages are rising faster than output prices,
   a. what is happening to real wages?
   b. what would happen to unemployment as a result?
   c. what would happen to SRAS as a result?

8. Answer the following questions.
   a. Why does an upward shift in the Phillips curve correspond to an upward shift in the short-run aggregate supply curve?
   b. Why does a movement up and to the left along a Phillips curve correspond to a movement up and to the right along a short-run aggregate supply curve?

9. Why is the credibility of the monetary authorities so crucial to quickly overcoming expected inflation?

10. Suppose the following data represent points along a short-run Phillips curve. Are the data consistent with what you would expect? Why or why not?

	Inflation Rate	Unemployment Rate
A	0%	5%
B	1	4.5
C	2	3.75
D	3	2.75
E	4	1.5

11. How are the long-run Phillips curve and the long-run aggregate supply curve related?

12. How would each of the following likely affect long-run and/or short-run aggregate supply and employment in the macro economy?
   a. an increase in the productivity of the labor force due to increased education
   b. the coldest year in a century leads to frequent ice and snow storms
   c. major advances in computer and Internet technologies

13. Why do economists who believe people form rational expectations have little faith that announced changes in monetary policy will have substantial effects on real output?

14. Does stagflation contradict the theory of the Phillips curve?

© SIMON McCOMB/STONE/GETTY IMAGES, INC.

part

The Global Economy

International Trade

Why do countries trade? Hong Kong has no oil—how is it going to get it? What is comparative advantage? Bananas could be grown in the most tropical parts of the United States or in expensive greenhouses, but wouldn't it be easier to import bananas from Honduras? Stop for a moment and imagine a world without international trade. Chocolate is derived from cocoa beans that are imported from South America and Africa. There are imported cars from Germany and Japan, shoes and sweaters from Italy, shirts from India, and watches and clocks from Switzerland. Consumers love trade because it provides them with more choices. It is good for producers, too; the speed of transportation and communication has opened up world markets. In addition,

lower costs are sometimes the result of economies of scale. Free trade gives firms access to large world markets. It also fosters more competition, which helps to keep prices down.

Economics is largely about exchange. But up to this point we have focused on trade between individuals within the domestic economy. In this chapter, we extend our coverage to international trade. In this chapter, we will study the theoretical reasons for the importance of trade. We will also look at the arguments for and against trade protection.

The Growth in World Trade   20.1

- What has happened to the volume of international trade over time?
- Who trades with the United States?
- What does the United States export? Import?

Importance of International Trade

In a typical year, about 15 percent of the world's output is traded in international markets. Of course, the importance of the international sector varies enormously from place to place across the world. Some nations are virtually closed economies (no interaction with other economies), with foreign trade equaling only a small proportion (perhaps 5 percent) of total output, while in other countries, trade is much more important. In the last three decades, the sum of U.S. imports and exports has increased from 11 percent of GDP to roughly 30 percent. In addition, incoming and outgoing investments (capital flows) have risen from less than 1 percent to roughly 3 percent of GDP. In Germany, roughly 30 percent of all output produced is exported, while Ireland and Belgium each export more than 70 percent of GDP.

U.S. exports include capital goods, automobiles, industrial supplies, raw materials, consumer goods, and agricultural products. U.S. imports include crude oil and refined petroleum products, machinery, automobiles, consumer goods, industrial raw materials, food, and beverages.

Is the trade between the United States and other countries becoming more important over time?

Trading Partners

In the early history of the United States, international trade largely took place with Europe and with Great Britain in particular. Now the United States trades with a number of countries, the most important of which are Canada, China, Japan, Mexico, Germany, and the United Kingdom as seen in Exhibit 1.

section 20.1 **exhibit 1**	Major U.S. Trading Partners				
Top Trading Partners—Exports of Goods in 2010			Top Trading Partners—Imports of Goods in 2010		
Rank	Country	Percent of Total	Rank	Country	Percent of Total
1	Canada	19.4%	1	China	19.5%
2	Mexico	12.8	2	Canada	14.2
3	China	7.2	3	Mexico	11.8
4	Japan	4.7	4	Japan	6.3
			5	Germany	4.3

SOURCE: CIA, *The World Factbook* 2011.

20.2

Comparative Advantage and Gains from Trade

📁 Does voluntary trade lead to an improvement in economic welfare?

📁 What is the principle of comparative advantage?

📁 What benefits are derived from specialization?

Economic Growth and Trade

Can trade raise output and income levels?

Using simple logic, we conclude that the very existence of trade suggests that trade is economically beneficial. Our conclusion is true if we assume that people are utility maximizers and are rational, are intelligent, and engage in trade on a voluntary basis. Because almost all trade is voluntary, it would seem that trade occurs because the participants feel that they are better off because of the trade. Both participants in an exchange of goods and services anticipate an improvement in their economic welfare. Sometimes, of course, anticipations are not realized (because the world is uncertain), but the motive behind trade remains an expectation of some enhancement in utility or satisfaction by both parties.

Granted, "trade must be good because people do it" is a rather simplistic explanation. The classical economist David Ricardo is usually given most of the credit for developing the economic theory that more precisely explains how trade can be mutually beneficial to both parties, raising output and income levels in the entire trading area.

The Principle of Comparative Advantage

Ricardo's theory of international trade centers on the concept of comparative advantage. Persons, regions, or countries can gain by specializing in the production of the good in which they have a comparative advantage. That is, if they can produce a good or service at a lower opportunity cost than others, we say that they have a **comparative advantage** in the production of that good or service. In other words, a country or a region should specialize in producing and selling those items that it can produce at a lower opportunity cost than other regions or countries.

Comparative advantage analysis does not mean that nations or areas that export goods will necessarily be able to produce those goods or services more cheaply than other nations in an absolute sense. What is important is *comparative* advantage, not *absolute* advantage. For example, the United States may be able to produce more cotton cloth per worker than India can, but this capability does not mean that the United States should necessarily sell cotton cloth to India. For a highly productive nation to produce goods in which it is only marginally more productive than other nations, the nation must take resources from the production of other goods in which its productive abilities are markedly superior. As a result, the opportunity costs in India of making cotton cloth may be less than in the United States. With that, both can gain from trade, despite potential absolute advantages for every good in the United States.

comparative advantage
occurs when a person or country can produce a good or service at a lower opportunity cost than others

What is the difference between absolute advantage and comparative advantage?

Comparative Advantage, Specialization, and the Production Possibilities Curves

Wendy and Calvin live on opposite ends of a small town. Wendy can produce either food or cloth. On a daily basis, she can produce 10 pounds of food, five yards of cloth, or any linear combination between the two goods along her production possibilities curve in Exhibit 1 (to simplify the calculations we have drawn linear production possibilities curves). If Wendy spends the whole day producing food, she can produce 10 pounds. If she spends the whole day producing cloth, she can produce five yards. Recall that the production possibilities curve represents the maximum possible combinations of food and cloth she can produce, given her fixed set of resources and technology. The negatively sloped production possibilities curve means that when she produces one good, with her fixed resources, she gives up the opportunity to produce another good.

What is Wendy's opportunity cost of producing cloth? It is what Wendy gives up in food production for each unit of cloth production, which is two pounds of food per yard of cloth. Therefore, her opportunity cost of producing a yard

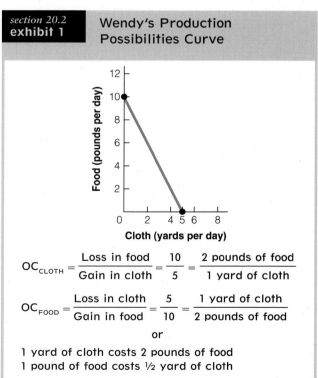

© Cengage Learning 2013

of cloth is two pounds of food. What is the opportunity cost of Wendy producing food? It is what she gives up in cloth production for each unit increase in food production, or one yard of cloth per two pounds of food. That is, for each pound of food Wendy produces, she gives up producing ½ yard of cloth.

Calvin, who lives on the other side of town, can also produce food or cloth. On a daily basis, he could produce three pounds of food, four yards of cloth, or any linear combination between the two along his production possibilities curve in Exhibit 2. When he spends the

great economic thinkers   David Ricardo (1772–1823)

HULTON ARCHIVES/GETTY IMAGES

David Ricardo was born in London to a wealthy, Jewish immigrant stockbroker, the third of 17 children. His father trained him in the stock brokerage business, which he entered at age 14. At 21, he married a young Quaker woman, leaving the Jewish faith to become a Unitarian. This upset his father, who disowned David. The young Ricardo joined a bank and entered the stock market on his own. He was very successful in this enterprise, making millions of pounds and quickly surpassing the wealth accumulated by his father, with whom he later reconciled. Ricardo retired from the stock exchange business at age 43 and died of an ear infection at 51, leaving behind a large fortune.

Ricardo could accredit much of his success in the stock market to his brilliant ability to predict human nature and public reaction. As a member of the House of Commons, he was also an undaunted advocate of government reform, religious and political freedom, and free trade. A man of firm convictions, he often lobbied for class-leveling policies that conflicted with his personal interests as a landowner and a man of wealth.

In his late 20s, while vacationing in Bath, England, Ricardo picked up a copy of Adam Smith's The *Wealth of Nations* and became interested in economics. It was a few years later that Ricardo, who had no formal education past age 14, improved upon Smith's principle of absolute advantage. Ricardo's ideas, though difficult for many of his fellow politicians to understand, were ingenious.

Smith argued that two countries should engage in trade if one was better at producing one good than the other—absolute advantage. For example, if one country is better at producing hats and the other at producing shoes, the two countries can produce more total output by producing those goods that they can produce best. However, Ricardo demonstrated that even if one country was absolutely more productive than another in making all goods and services, it would still be mutually beneficial for the two countries to engage in trade, as each had a comparative advantage in one of the goods.

Ricardo argued this point at a time in British history when the wealthy landowners, who had a clutch on parliament, had a virtual monopoly on grain in England in the form of the Corn Laws, passed in 1815. These acts prevented the importation of grain from France, although, as Ricardo argued, France could afford to feed the British for less than it would cost them to feed themselves. Despite Ricardo's argument and the fact that English laborers were spending one-fourth of their income on bread, the Corn Laws persisted until 1846. Ricardo did, however, leave behind a remarkable concept that convinced future economists that free trade is almost always in the best interest of an economy as a whole.

day producing cloth, he can produce four yards. When he spends the day producing food, he can produce three pounds. To produce cloth, Calvin must decrease his production of food. What is Calvin's opportunity cost of producing cloth? It is what he gives up in producing food for each unit of cloth production, which is three pounds of food per four pounds of cloth. Therefore, his opportunity cost of producing cloth is ¾ pound of food. What is Calvin's opportunity cost of producing food? It is what he gives up in cloth production for each unit of food production which is four yards of cloth per three pounds of food. Therefore, the opportunity cost of producing a pound of food is 4/3 yards of cloth per day.

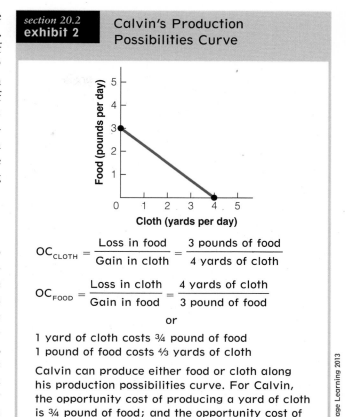

section 20.2
exhibit 2   **Calvin's Production
Possibilities Curve**

$$OC_{CLOTH} = \frac{\text{Loss in food}}{\text{Gain in cloth}} = \frac{3 \text{ pounds of food}}{4 \text{ yards of cloth}}$$

$$OC_{FOOD} = \frac{\text{Loss in cloth}}{\text{Gain in food}} = \frac{4 \text{ yards of cloth}}{3 \text{ pound of food}}$$

or

1 yard of cloth costs ¾ pound of food
1 pound of food costs ⅓ yards of cloth

Calvin can produce either food or cloth along his production possibilities curve. For Calvin, the opportunity cost of producing a yard of cloth is ¾ pound of food; and the opportunity cost of producing a pound of food is ⅓ yards of cloth.

Absolute and Comparative Advantage

Now let's compare Wendy's production possibilities curve to Calvin's production possibilities curve to see who has an absolute advantage in producing cloth and who has an absolute advantage in producing food. An absolute advantage occurs when one producer can do a task using fewer inputs than the other producer. In Exhibit 3, we see that Wendy is more productive than Calvin at producing food. Along the vertical axis, we can see that if Wendy uses all of her resources to produce food, she can produce 10 pounds of food per day. If Calvin devotes all of his resources to producing food, he can only produce 3 pounds of food per day. We say that Wendy has an absolute advantage over Calvin in the production of food.

Along the horizontal axis in Exhibit 3, we can see that Wendy is also more productive than Calvin at producing cloth. If Wendy devotes all of her resources to producing cloth, she can produce five yards of cloth per day. If Calvin devotes all of his resources to producing cloth, he can only produce four yards of cloth per day. We say that Wendy also has an absolute advantage over Calvin in the production of cloth. She has an absolute advantage in producing both food and cloth. Therefore, should Wendy produce both food and cloth and Calvin produce nothing? No!

Recall from Chapter 2 that a comparative advantage exists when one person can produce a good at a lower opportunity cost than another person. So who has the comparative advantage (lowest opportunity cost) in producing food? In this case, Wendy's opportunity cost of producing food is less than Calvin's. Wendy's opportunity cost of producing a pound of food is ½ yard of cloth, whereas Calvin's opportunity cost of producing one pound of food is ⅓ yards of cloth. Therefore, Wendy is the more efficient producer of food—she gives up less in cloth when she produces food, compared to Calvin. Remember, comparative advantage is always a relative concept.

Who has the comparative advantage in producing cloth? That is, who can produce cloth at the lowest opportunity cost? That would be Calvin, because he gives up only ¾ pound of food to produce one yard of cloth. If Wendy were to produce a yard of cloth, she would have to give up two pounds of food. The lowest opportunity cost producer of cloth is Calvin. In other words, to produce one more yard of cloth, Calvin gives up fewer pounds of food than Wendy. Therefore, Calvin is the more efficient producer of cloth—he gives up less in food when he produces cloth, compared to Wendy. Calvin has a comparative advantage in producing cloth.

If Wendy has an absolute advantage in producing both food and clothes, why doesn't she just produce both?

Gains from Specialization and Exchange

Suppose Wendy and Calvin meet and decide to specialize in those activities in which they have a comparative advantage. Wendy would specialize in the production of food and Calvin would specialize in the production of cloth. By specializing, Wendy can produce ten pounds

section 20.2
exhibit 3   Absolute and Comparative
Advantage

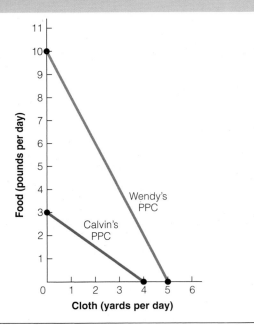

	Cloth (yds./day)	Food (lbs./day)	OC of Cloth	OC of Food
Wendy	5	10	2 lbs. of food	½ yd. of cloth
Calvin	4	3	¾ lb. of food	⅓ yds. of cloth

In this case, Wendy has an absolute advantage producing food and cloth. If she devotes all her resources to producing cloth she can produce ten yards per day, while Calvin could only produce five yards. In addition, if Wendy devotes all her resources to producing food she could produce ten pounds of food and Calvin could only produce three pounds of food.

Wendy has a comparative advantage in producing food. Wendy's opportunity cost of producing a pound of food is 1/2 yard of cloth; Calvin's opportunity cost of producing a pound of food is 4/3 yards of cloth. Calvin has a comparative advantage in producing cloth. Wendy's opportunity cost of producing a yard of cloth is 2 pounds of food. If Calvin were to produce a yard of cloth, he would only give up 3/4 of a pound of food.

Why does there have to be trade to capture the gains from comparative advantage and specialization?

© Cengage Learning 2013

of food per day (point B′ in Exhibit 4) and Calvin can produce four yards of cloth per day (point B in Exhibit 4). However, *to achieve any of the gains from comparative advantage and specialization, there must be trade.*

After specializing in the good in which they have a comparative advantage, suppose Wendy and Calvin agree to trade at the exchange "price" of one pound of food for one yard of cloth. If Wendy trades three pounds of cloth for three pounds of food, she can obtain a position along the new production possibilities curve that is beyond her original production possibilities curve, point C in Exhibit 4. Wendy can now have seven pounds of food and three yards of cloth—a combination she could not have obtained without specialization and trade.

Calvin also benefits from specialization and trade. In the trade, he receives three pounds of food for three yards of cloth and now can enjoy three pounds of food and one yard of cloth a combination, at point C, he could not have obtained without specialization and trade. In sum, the exchange has allowed both Wendy and Calvin to produce and consume a combination of the two goods beyond what would have been attainable if it were not for specialization and exchange.

Individuals and Nations Gain from Specialization and Trade

Just as Calvin and Wendy benefit from specialization and trade, so do the people of different nations. Because of specialization, according to comparative advantage, both nations can be better off, even if one nation has an absolute advantage in both goods over the other. Furthermore, the greater the difference in opportunity cost between the two trading partners, the greater the benefits from specialization and exchange.

Note that when we say nations trade with nations, we really mean that the people of a nation trade with people of other nations. When China trades clothes to the United States for Boeing 787 jetliners, they both benefit from the exchange, because they are able to obtain them at a lower cost than if they produced those goods themselves. Free trade does not guarantee that each individual will be better off or that everyone will receive the same benefits, but it does mean that collectively, the population of each nation will benefit from the trade. Indeed, unskilled workers in high wage countries may temporarily lose jobs. Recall that when NAFTA was passed, its critics argued that low-skilled workers would lose jobs because of U.S. trade with Mexico. However, that does not appear to have happened to any large extent. Instead, consumers have been enjoying lower priced goods because of the trade.

Regional Comparative Advantage

Using a production possibilities curve, we saw how Wendy and Calvin could benefit from specialization and trade. The principle of comparative advantage can be applied to regional markets as well. In fact, trade has evolved in large part because different geographic areas

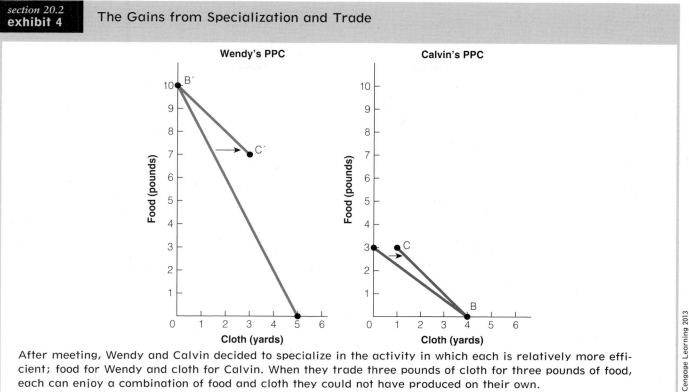

section 20.2
exhibit 4

The Gains from Specialization and Trade

Wendy's PPC

Calvin's PPC

After meeting, Wendy and Calvin decided to specialize in the activity in which each is relatively more efficient; food for Wendy and cloth for Calvin. When they trade three pounds of cloth for three pounds of food, each can enjoy a combination of food and cloth they could not have produced on their own.

© Cengage Learning 2013

---

have different resources and therefore different production possibilities. The impact of trade between two areas with differing resources is shown in Exhibit 5. To keep the analysis simple, suppose two trading areas can produce only two commodities, grain and computers. A "trading area" may be a locality, a region, or even a nation, but for our example suppose we think in terms of two hypothetical regions, Grainsville and Techland.

Grainsville and Techland have various potential combinations of grain and computers that they can produce. For each region, the cost of producing more grain is the output of computers that must be forgone, and vice versa. We see in Exhibit 5 that Techland can produce more grain (40 bushels) and more computers (100 units) than Grainsville can (30 bushels and 30 units, respectively), perhaps reflecting superior resources (more or better labor, more land, and so on). These numbers mean that Techland has an absolute advantage in both products.

Suppose that, before specialization, Techland chooses to produce 75 computers and 10 bushels of grain per day. Similarly, suppose Grainsville decides to produce 12 computers and 18 bushels of grain. Collectively, then, the two areas are producing 87 computers (75 + 12) and 28 bushels of grain (10 + 18) per day before specialization.

Now, suppose the two nations specialize. Techland decides to specialize in computers and devotes all its resources to making that product. As a result, computer output in

section 20.2
exhibit 5

Production Possibilities, Techland and Grainsville

Region	Grain (bushels per day)	Computers (units per day)
Techland	0	100
	10	75
	20	50
	30	25
	40	0
Grainsville	0	30
	6	24
	12	18
	18	12
	24	6
	30	0
Before Specialization		
Techland	10	75
Grainsville	18	12
Total	28	87
After Specialization		
Techland	0	100
Grainsville	30	0
Total	30	100

© Cengage Learning 2013

Techland rises to 100 units per day, some of which is sold to Grainsville. Grainsville, in turn, devotes all its resources to grain, producing 30 bushels of grain per day and selling some of it to Techland. Together, the two areas are producing more of both grain and computers than before—100 instead of 87 computers and 30 instead of 28 bushels of grain. Both areas could, as a result, have more of both products than before they began specializing and trading.

How can this happen? In Techland, the opportunity cost of producing grain is high—25 computers must be forgone to get 10 more bushels of grain. The cost of one bushel of grain, then, is 2.5 computers (25 divided by 10). In Grainsville, by contrast, the opportunity cost of producing six more units of grain is six units of computers that must be forgone; so the cost of one unit of grain is one unit of computers. In Techland, a unit of grain costs 2.5 computers, while in Grainsville the same amount of grain costs only one computer. Grain is more costly in Techland in terms of the computers forgone than in Grainsville, so Grainsville has the comparative advantage in the production of grain, even though Techland has an absolute advantage in grain.

With respect to computers, an increase in output by 25 units, say from 25 to 50 units, costs 10 bushels of grain forgone in Techland. The cost of one more computer is 0.4 bushel of grain (10 divided by 25). In Grainsville, an increase in computer output of six units, say from 12 to 18, is accompanied by a decrease in grain production by 6 bushels, as resources are converted from grain to computer manufacturing. The cost of one computer is 1 bushel of grain. Computers are more costly (in terms of opportunity cost) in Grainsville and cheaper in Techland, so Techland should specialize in the production of computers.

Thus, by specializing in products in which it has a comparative advantage, an area has the potential of having more goods and services, assuming it trades the additional output for other desirable goods and services that others can produce at a lower opportunity cost. In the scenario presented here, the people in Techland would specialize in computers, and the people in Grainsville would specialize in farming (grain). We can see from this example that specialization increases both the division of labor and the interdependence among groups of people.

⊘ SECTION QUIZ

1. Comparative advantage
   a. means that nations or areas that export goods will necessarily be able to produce those goods or services more cheaply than other nations in an absolute sense.
   b. means a country, or a region, should specialize in producing and selling those items that it can produce at a lower opportunity cost than other regions or countries.
   c. Both (a) and (b) are true.
   d. Neither (a) nor (b) is true.

2. If a nation does not have an absolute advantage in producing anything, it
   a. can have no comparative advantage either.
   b. will have a comparative advantage in the activity in which its disadvantage is the least.
   c. will benefit if it refuses to trade.
   d. will export raw materials and import finished products.

3. Which of the following statements is true?
   a. If two nations with different opportunity costs of production specialize, total output of both products may be higher as a result.
   b. By specializing in products in which it has a comparative advantage, an area can have more goods and services if it trades the added output for other goods and services that others can produce at a lower opportunity cost.
   c. By specialization according to comparative advantage and trade, two parties can each achieve consumption possibilities that would be impossible for them without trade.
   d. All of the statements are correct.

(continued)

⑦ SECTION QUIZ (Cont.)

4. Assume that the opportunity cost of producing a pair of pants in the United States is 2 pounds of rice, while in China it is 5 pounds of rice. As a result,

   a. the United States has a comparative advantage over China in the production of pants.

   b. China has a comparative advantage over the United States in the production of rice.

   c. mutual gains from trade can be realized by both countries if the United States exports rice to China in exchange for shoes.

   d. mutual gains from trade can be realized by both countries if the United States exports pants to China in exchange for rice.

   e. all of the above except (c) are true.

5. In Samoa the opportunity cost of producing one coconut is four pineapples, while in Guam the opportunity cost of producing one coconut is five pineapples. In this situation,

   a. if trade occurs, both countries will be able to consume beyond the frontiers of their original production possibilities.

   b. Guam will be better off if it exports coconuts and imports pineapples.

   c. both Samoa and Guam will be better off if Samoa produces both coconuts and pineapples.

   d. mutually beneficial trade cannot occur.

---

1. Why do people voluntarily choose to specialize and trade?

2. How could a country have an absolute advantage in producing one good or service without also having a comparative advantage in its production?

3. Why do you think the introduction of the railroad reduced self-sufficiency in the United States?

4. If you can wash the dishes in two-thirds the time it takes your younger sister to wash them, do you have a comparative advantage in washing the dishes with respect to her?

Answers: 1. a   2. b   3. d   4. e   5. a

Supply and Demand in International Trade

20.3

📁 What is consumer surplus?

📁 What is producer surplus?

📁 Who benefits and who loses when a country becomes an exporter?

📁 Who benefits and who loses when a country becomes an importer?

The Importance of Trade: Producer and Consumer Surplus

Recall from Chapter 7 that the difference between the most a consumer would be willing to pay for a quantity of a good and what a consumer actually has to pay is called **consumer surplus**. The difference between the lowest price for which a supplier would be willing to supply a quantity of a good or service and the revenues a supplier actually receives

> **consumer surplus**
> the difference between the price a consumer is willing and able to pay for an additional unit of a good and the price the consumer actually pays; for the whole market, it is the sum of all the individual consumer surpluses—the area below the market demand curve and above the market price

section 20.3 exhibit 1   Consumer and Producer Surplus

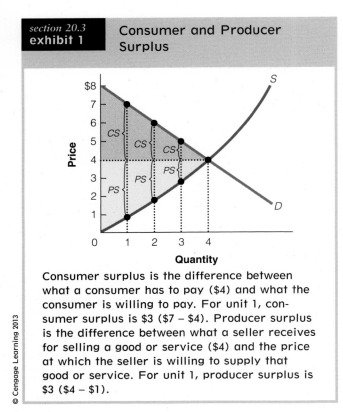

Consumer surplus is the difference between what a consumer has to pay ($4) and what the consumer is willing to pay. For unit 1, consumer surplus is $3 ($7 − $4). Producer surplus is the difference between what a seller receives for selling a good or service ($4) and the price at which the seller is willing to supply that good or service. For unit 1, producer surplus is $3 ($4 − $1).

producer surplus
the difference between what a producer is paid for a good and the cost of producing that unit of the good; for the market, it is the sum of all the individual sellers' producer surpluses— the area above the market supply curve and below the market price

for selling it is called **producer surplus**. With the tools of consumer and producer surplus, we can better analyze the impact of trade. Who gains? Who loses? What happens to net welfare?

The demand curve represents the maximum prices that consumers are willing and able to pay for different quantities of a good or service; the supply curve represents the minimum prices suppliers require to be willing to supply different quantities of that good or service. For example, in Exhibit 1, the consumer is willing to pay up to $7 for the first unit of output and the producer would demand at least $1 for producing that unit. However, the equilibrium price is $4, as indicated by the intersection of the supply and demand curves. It is clear that the two would gain from getting together and trading that unit, because the consumer would receive $3 of consumer surplus ($7 − $4), and the producer would receive $3 of producer surplus ($4 − $1). Both would also benefit from trading the second and third units of output—in fact, from every unit up to the equilibrium output. Once the equilibrium output is reached at the equilibrium price, all the mutually beneficial opportunities from trade between suppliers and demanders will have taken place; the sum of consumer surplus and producer surplus is maximized.

It is important to recognize that the total gain to the economy from trade is the sum of the consumer and the producer surpluses. That is, consumers benefit from additional amounts of consumer surplus, and producers benefit from additional amounts of producer surplus.

Free Trade and Exports—Domestic Producers Gain More Than Domestic Consumers Lose

Using the concepts of consumer and producer surplus, we can graphically show the net benefits of free trade. Imagine an economy with no trade, where the equilibrium price, P_{BT}, and equilibrium quantity, Q_{BT}, of wheat are determined exclusively in the domestic economy, as shown in Exhibit 2. Suppose that this imaginary economy decides to engage in free trade. You can see that the world price (established in the world market for wheat), P_{AT}, is higher than the domestic price before trade, P_{BT}. In other words, the domestic economy has a comparative advantage in wheat, because it can produce wheat at a lower relative price than the rest of the world. So this wheat-producing country sells some wheat to the domestic market and some wheat to the world market, all at the going world price.

The price after trade (P_{AT}) is higher than the price before trade (P_{BT}). Because the world market is huge, the demand from the rest of the world at the world price (P_{AT}) is assumed to be perfectly elastic. That is, domestic wheat farmers can sell all the wheat they want at the world price. If you were a wheat farmer in Nebraska, would you rather sell all your bushels of wheat at the higher world price or the lower domestic price? As a wheat farmer, you would surely prefer the higher world price. But this preference is not good news for domestic cereal and bread consumers, who now have to pay more for products made with wheat because P_{AT} is greater than P_{BT}.

Graphically, we can see how free trade and exports affect both domestic consumers and domestic producers. At the higher world price, P_{AT}, domestic wheat producers are receiving larger amounts of producer surplus. Before trade, they received a surplus equal to area e + f; after trade, they received surplus b + c + d + e + f, for a net gain of area b + c + d. However, part of the domestic producers' gain comes at domestic consumers' expense. Specifically,

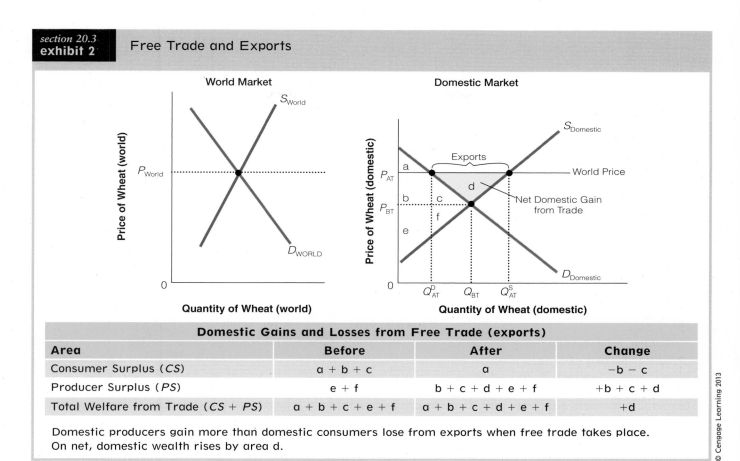

section 20.3
exhibit 2   Free Trade and Exports

Domestic Gains and Losses from Free Trade (exports)

Area	Before	After	Change
Consumer Surplus (*CS*)	a + b + c	a	−b − c
Producer Surplus (*PS*)	e + f	b + c + d + e + f	+b + c + d
Total Welfare from Trade (*CS* + *PS*)	a + b + c + e + f	a + b + c + d + e + f	+d

Domestic producers gain more than domestic consumers lose from exports when free trade takes place. On net, domestic wealth rises by area d.

consumers had a consumer surplus equal to area a + b + c before the trade (at P_{BT}), but they now have only area a (at P_{AT})—a loss of area b + c.

Area b reflects a redistribution of income, because producers are gaining exactly what consumers are losing. Is that good or bad? We can't say objectively whether consumers or producers are more deserving. However, the net benefits from allowing free trade and exports are clearly visible in area d. Without free trade, no one gets area d. That is, on net, members of the domestic society gain when domestic wheat producers are able to sell their wheat at the higher world price. Although domestic wheat consumers lose from the free trade, those negative effects are more than offset by the positive gains captured by producers. Area d is the net increase in domestic wealth (the welfare gain) from free trade and exports.

Are there winners and losers with free trade and exports?

Free Trade and Imports—Domestic Consumers Gain More Than Domestic Producers Lose

Now suppose that our economy does not produce shirts as well as other countries of the world. In other words, other countries have a comparative advantage in producing shirts, and the domestic price for shirts is above the world price. This scenario is illustrated in Exhibit 3. At the new, lower world price, the domestic producer will supply quantity Q^{S}_{AT}. However, at the lower world price, the domestic producers will not produce the entire amount demanded by domestic consumers, Q^{D}_{AT}. At the world price, reflecting the world supply and demand for shirts, the difference between what is domestically supplied and what is domestically demanded is supplied by imports.

---

section 20.3
exhibit 3   Free Trade and Imports

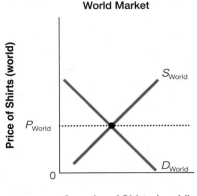

World Market

Price of Shirts (world)

P_{World}

S_{World}

D_{World}

0

Quantity of Shirts (world)

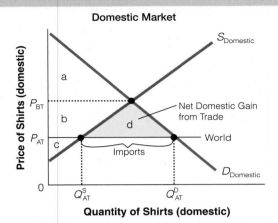

Domestic Market

Price of Shirts (domestic)

$S_{Domestic}$

a

P_{BT}

b

Net Domestic Gain
from Trade

d

P_{AT}

c

World

Imports

$D_{Domestic}$

0   Q^S_{AT} Q^D_{AT}

Quantity of Shirts (domestic)

Domestic Gains and Losses from Free Trade (imports)			
Area	**Before Trade**	**After Trade**	**Change**
Consumer Surplus (*CS*)	a	a + b + d	b + d
Producer Surplus (*PS*)	b + c	c	−b
Total Welfare from Trade (*CS* + *PS*)	a + b + c	a + b + c + d	+d

Domestic consumers gain more than domestic producers lose from imports when free trade is allowed. On net, domestic wealth rises by area d.

At the world price (established in the world market for shirts), we assume that the world supply to the domestic market curve is perfectly elastic—that the producers of the world can supply all that domestic consumers are willing to buy at the going price. At the world price, Q^S_{AT} is supplied by domestic producers, and the difference between Q^D_{AT} and Q^S_{AT} is imported from other countries.

Who wins and who loses from free trade and imports? Domestic consumers benefit from paying a lower price for shirts. In Exhibit 3, before trade, consumers only received area a in consumer surplus. After trade, the price fell and quantity purchased increased, causing the area of consumer surplus to increase from area a to area a + b + d, a gain of b + d. Domestic producers lose because they are now selling their shirts at the lower world price, P_{AT}. The producer surplus before trade was b + c. After trade, the producer surplus falls to area c, reducing producer surplus by area b. Area b, then, represents a redistribution from producers to consumers, but area d is the net increase in domestic wealth (the welfare gain) from free trade and imports.

Are there winners and losers with free trade and imports?

---

in the news   What to Expect When You're Free Trading

. . . All economists know that when American jobs are outsourced, Americans as a group are net winners. What we lose through lower wages is more than offset by what we gain through lower prices. In other words, the winners can more than afford to compensate the losers. Does that mean they ought

to? Does it create a moral mandate for the taxpayer-subsidized retraining programs . . .?

Um, no. Even if you've just lost your job, there's something fundamentally churlish about blaming the very phenomenon that's elevated you above

(*continued*)

in the **news** **What to Expect When You're Free Trading (Cont.)**

the subsistence level since the day you were born. If the world owes you compensation for enduring the downside of trade, what do you owe the world for enjoying the upside?

I doubt there's a human being on earth who hasn't benefited from the opportunity to trade freely with his neighbors. Imagine what your life would be like if you had to grow your own food, make your own clothes and rely on your grandmother's home remedies for health care. Access to a trained physician might reduce the demand for grandma's home remedies, but—especially at her age—she's still got plenty of reason to be thankful for having a doctor.

Some people suggest, however, that it makes sense to isolate the moral effects of a single new trading opportunity or free trade agreement. Surely we have fellow citizens who are hurt by those agreements, at least in the limited sense that they'd be better off in a world where trade flourishes, except in this one instance. What do we owe those fellow citizens?

One way to think about that is to ask what your moral instincts tell you in analogous situations. Suppose, after years of buying shampoo at your local pharmacy, you discover you can order the same shampoo for less money on the Web. Do you have an obligation to compensate your pharmacist? If you move to a cheaper apartment, should you compensate your landlord? When you eat at McDonald's, should you compensate the owners

of the diner next door? Public policy should not be designed to advance moral instincts that we all reject every day of our lives.

In what morally relevant way, then, might displaced workers differ from displaced pharmacists or displaced landlords? You might argue that pharmacists and landlords have always faced cutthroat competition and therefore knew what they were getting into, while decades of tariffs and quotas have led manufacturing workers to expect a modicum of protection. That expectation led them to develop certain skills, and now it's unfair to pull the rug out from under them. Once again, that argument does not mesh with our everyday instincts. For many decades, schoolyard bullying has been a profitable occupation. All across America, bullies have built up skills so they can take advantage of that opportunity. If we toughen the rules to make bullying unprofitable, must we compensate the bullies?

Bullying and protectionism have a lot in common. They both use force (either directly or through the power of the law) to enrich someone else at your involuntary expense. If you're forced to pay $20 an hour to an American for goods you could have bought from a Mexican for $5 an hour, you're being extorted. When a free trade agreement allows you to buy from the Mexican after all, rejoice in your liberation. . . .

⑦ SECTION QUIZ

1. Which of the following statements is true?

   a. The difference between what a consumer is willing and able to pay and what a consumer actually has to pay is called consumer surplus.

   b. The difference between what a supplier is willing and able to supply and the price a supplier actually receives for selling a good or service is called producer surplus.

   c. Both (a) and (b) are true statements.

   d. None of the above is true.

(*continued*)

SECTION QUIZ (Cont.)

2. Compared to the no-trade situation, when a country imports a good,

   a. domestic consumers gain, domestic producers lose, and the gains outweigh the losses.

   b. domestic consumers lose, domestic producers gain, and the gains outweigh the losses.

   c. domestic consumers gain, domestic producers lose, and the losses outweigh the gains.

   d. domestic consumers gain and domestic producers lose by an equal amount.

3. Compared to the no-trade situation, when a country exports a good:

   a. domestic consumers gain, domestic producers lose, and the gains outweigh the losses.

   b. domestic consumers lose, domestic producers gain, and the gains outweigh the losses.

   c. domestic consumers gain, domestic producers lose, and the losses outweigh the gains.

   d. domestic consumers gain and domestic producers lose by an equal amount.

---

1. How does voluntary trade generate both consumer and producer surplus?

2. If the world price of a good is greater than the domestic price prior to trade, why does it imply that the domestic economy has a comparative advantage in producing that good?

3. If the world price of a good is less than the domestic price prior to trade, why does it imply that the domestic economy has a comparative disadvantage in producing that good?

4. When a country has a comparative advantage in the production of a good, why do domestic producers gain more than domestic consumers lose from free international trade?

5. When a country has a comparative disadvantage in a good, why do domestic consumers gain more than domestic producers lose from free international trade?

6. Why do U.S. exporters, such as farmers, favor free trade more than U.S. producers of domestic products who face competition from foreign imports, such as the automobile industry?

Answers: 1. c 2. a 3. b

20.4

Tariffs, Import Quotas, and Subsidies

📁 What is a tariff?
📁 What are the effects of a tariff?

📁 What are the effects of an import quota?
📁 What is the economic impact of subsidies?

Tariffs

tariff
a tax on imports

What is a tariff?

A tariff is a tax on imported goods. Tariffs are usually relatively small revenue producers that retard the expansion of trade. They bring about higher prices and revenues for domestic producers, and lower sales and revenues for foreign producers. Moreover, tariffs lead to higher prices for domestic consumers. In fact, the gains to producers are more than offset by the losses to consumers. With the aid of a graph we will see how the gains and losses from tariffs work.

The Domestic Economic Impact of Tariffs

The domestic economic impact of tariffs is presented in Exhibit 1, which illustrates the supply and demand curves for domestic consumers and producers of shoes. In a typical international supply and demand illustration, the intersection of the world supply and

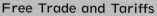

section 20.4
exhibit 1   **Free Trade and Tariffs**

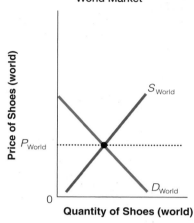

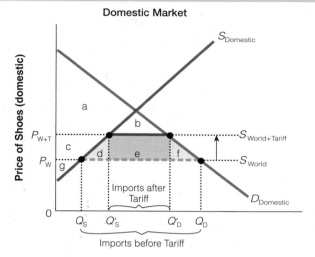

Gains and Losses from Tariffs			
Area	**Before Tariffs**	**After Tariffs**	**Change**
Consumer Surplus (*CS*)	a + b + c + d + e + f	a + b	−c − d − e − f
Producer Surplus (*PS*)	g	c + g	+c
Government Revenues (Tariff)	0	e	+e
Total Welfare from Tariff (*CS* + *PS* + Tariff Revenues)	a + b + c + d + e + f + g	a + b + c + e + g	−d − f

In the case of a tariff, we see that consumers lose more than producers and government gain. On net, the deadweight loss associated with the new tariff is represented by area d + f.

© Cengage Learning 2013

demand curves would determine the domestic market price. However, with import tariffs, the domestic price of shoes is greater than the world price, as in Exhibit 1. We consider the world supply curve (S_W) for domestic consumers to be perfectly elastic; that is, we can buy all we want at the world price (P_W). At the world price, domestic producers are only willing to provide quantity Q_S, but domestic consumers are willing to buy quantity Q_D—more than domestic producers are willing to supply. Imports make up the difference.

As you can see in Exhibit 1, the imposition of the tariff shifts the perfectly elastic supply curve from foreigners to domestic consumers upward from S_{World} to $S_{World+Tariff}$, but it does not alter the domestic supply or demand curve. At the resulting higher domestic price (P_{W+T}), domestic suppliers are willing to supply more, Q'_S, but domestic consumers are willing to buy less, Q'_D. At the new equilibrium, the domestic price (P_{W+T}) is higher and the quantity of shoes demanded (Q'_D) is lower. But at the new price, the domestic quantity demanded is lower and the quantity supplied domestically is higher, reducing the quantity of imported shoes. Overall, then, tariffs lead to (1) a smaller total quantity sold, (2) a higher price for shoes for domestic consumers, (3) greater sales of shoes at higher prices for domestic producers, and (4) lower sales of foreign shoes.

Although domestic producers do gain more sales and higher earnings, consumers lose much more. The increase in price from the tariff results in a loss in consumer surplus, as shown in Exhibit 1. After the tariff, shoe prices rise to P_{W+T}, and consequently, consumer surplus falls by area c + d + e + f, representing the welfare loss to consumers from the tariff. Area c in Exhibit 1 shows the gain to domestic producers as a result of the tariff. That is, at the higher price, domestic producers are willing to supply more shoes, representing a welfare

Do domestic producers like tariffs?

gain to producers resulting from the tariff. As a result of the tariff revenues, government gains area e. This is the import tariff—the revenue government collects from foreign countries on imports. However, we see from Exhibit 1 that consumers lose more than producers and government gain from the tariff. That is, on net, the deadweight loss associated with the tariff is represented by area d + f.

Arguments for Tariffs

Despite the preceding arguments against trade restrictions, they continue to be levied. Some rationale for their existence is necessary. Three common arguments for the use of trade restrictions deserve our critical examination.

Temporary Trade Restrictions Help Infant Industries Grow

A country might argue that a protective tariff will allow a new industry to more quickly reach a scale of operation at which economies of scale and production efficiencies can be realized. That is, temporarily shielding the young industry from competition from foreign firms will allow the infant industry a chance to grow. With early protection, these firms will eventually be able to compete effectively in the global market. It is presumed that without this protection, the industry could never get on its feet. At first hearing, the argument sounds valid, but it involves many problems. How do you identify "infant industries" that genuinely have potential economies of scale and will quickly become efficient with protection? We do not know the long-run average total cost curves of industries, a necessary piece of information. Moreover, if firms and governments are truly convinced of the advantages of allowing an industry to reach a large scale, would it not be wise to make massive loans to the industry, allowing it to begin large-scale production all at once rather than slowly and at the expense of consumers? In other words, the goal of allowing the industry to reach its efficient size can be reached without protection. Finally, the history of infant industry tariffs suggests that the tariffs often linger long after the industry is mature and no longer in need of protection.

Tariffs Can Reduce Domestic Unemployment

Exhibit 1 shows how tariffs increase output by domestic producers, thus leading to increased employment and reduced unemployment in industries where tariffs have been imposed. Yet the overall employment effects of a tariff imposition are not likely to be positive; the argument is incorrect. Why? First, the imposition of a tariff by the United States on, say, foreign steel is going to be noticed in the countries adversely affected by the tariff. If a new tariff on steel lowers Japanese steel sales to the United States, the Japanese will likely retaliate by imposing tariffs on U.S. exports to Japan, say, on machinery exports. The retaliatory tariff will lower U.S. sales of machinery and thus employment in the U.S. machinery industries. As a result, the gain in employment in the steel industry will be offset by a loss of employment elsewhere.

Even if other countries did not retaliate, U.S. employment would likely suffer outside the industry gaining tariff protection. The way that other countries pay for U.S. goods is by getting dollars from sales to the United States—imports to us. If new tariffs lead to restrictions on imports, fewer dollars will be flowing overseas in payment for imports, which means that foreigners will have fewer dollars available to buy our exports. Other things being equal, this situation will tend to reduce our exports, thus creating unemployment in the export industries.

Tariffs Are Necessary for Reasons of National Security

Sometimes it is argued that tariffs are a means of preventing a nation from becoming too dependent on foreign suppliers of goods vital to national security. That is, by making foreign goods more expensive, we can protect domestic suppliers. For example, if oil is vital to operating planes and tanks, losing foreign supplies of oil during wartime could cripple a nation's defenses.

What are the arguments for having tariffs?

The national security argument is usually not valid. If a nation's own resources are depletable, tariff-imposed reliance on domestic supplies will hasten depletion of domestic reserves, making the country even *more* dependent on imports in the future. If we impose a high tariff on foreign oil to protect domestic producers, we will increase domestic output of oil in the short run. In the process, however, we will deplete the stockpile of available reserves. Thus, the defense argument is of questionable validity. From a defense standpoint, it makes more sense to use foreign oil in peacetime and perhaps stockpile "insurance" supplies so that larger domestic supplies would be available during wars.

Are Tariffs Necessary to Protect against Dumping?

Dumping occurs when a foreign country sells its products at prices below their costs or below the prices for which they are sold on the domestic market. For example, the Japanese government has been accused for years of subsidizing Japanese steel producers as they attempt to gain a greater share of the world steel market and greater market power. That is, the short-term losses from selling below cost may be offset by the long-term economic profits from employing this strategy. Some have argued that tariffs are needed to protect domestic producers against low-cost dumpers because they will raise the cost to foreign producers and offset their cost advantage.

The United States has antidumping laws; if a foreign country is found guilty of dumping, the United States can impose antidumping tariffs on that country's products, thereby raising the price of the foreign goods that are being dumped. In practice, however, it is often difficult to prove dumping; foreign countries may simply have lower steel production costs. So what may seem like dumping may in fact be comparative advantage.

Import Quotas

Like tariffs, **import quotas** directly restrict imports, leading to reductions in trade and thus preventing nations from fully realizing their comparative advantage. The case for quotas is probably even weaker than the case for tariffs. Unlike what occurs with a tariff, the U.S. government does not collect any revenue as a result of the import quota. Despite the higher prices, the loss in consumer surplus, and the loss in government revenue, quotas come about because people often view them as being less protectionist than tariffs—the traditional, most-maligned form of protection.

import quota
a legal limit on the imported quantity of a good that is produced abroad and can be sold in domestic markets

Besides the rather blunt means of curtailing imports by using tariffs and quotas, nations have devised still other, more subtle means of restricting international trade. For example, nations sometimes impose product standards, ostensibly to protect consumers against inferior merchandise. Effectively, however, those standards may be simply a means of restricting foreign competition. For example, France might keep certain kinds of wine out of the country on the grounds that they are made with allegedly inferior grapes or have an inappropriate alcoholic content. Likewise, the United States might prohibit automobile imports that do not meet certain standards in terms of pollutants, safety, and gasoline mileage. Even if these standards are not intended to restrict foreign competition, the regulations may nonetheless have that impact, restricting consumer choice in the process.

The Domestic Economic Impact of an Import Quota

The domestic economic impact of an import quota on sugar is presented in Exhibit 2. The introduction of an import quota increases the price from the world price, P_W (established in the world market for autos) to P_{W+Q}. The quota causes the price to rise above the world price. The domestic quantity demanded falls and the domestic quantity supplied rises. Consequently, the number of imports is much smaller than it would be without the import

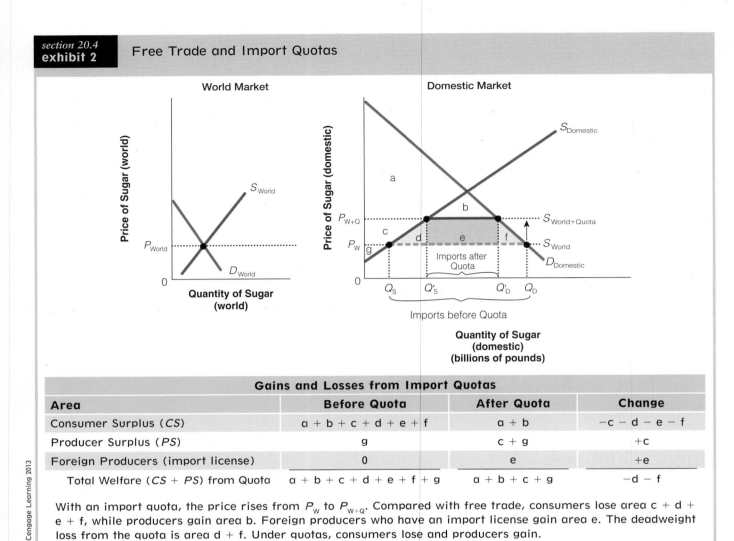

section 20.4
exhibit 2   Free Trade and Import Quotas

World Market

Domestic Market

Gains and Losses from Import Quotas

Area	Before Quota	After Quota	Change
Consumer Surplus (*CS*)	a + b + c + d + e + f	a + b	−c − d − e − f
Producer Surplus (*PS*)	g	c + g	+c
Foreign Producers (import license)	0	e	+e
Total Welfare (*CS* + *PS*) from Quota	a + b + c + d + e + f + g	a + b + c + g	−d − f

With an import quota, the price rises from P_W to P_{W+Q}. Compared with free trade, consumers lose area c + d + e + f, while producers gain area b. Foreign producers who have an import license gain area e. The deadweight loss from the quota is area d + f. Under quotas, consumers lose and producers gain.

What are import quotas?

quota. Compared with free trade, domestic producers are better off, but domestic consumers are worse off. Specifically, the import quota results in a gain in producer surplus of area c and a loss in consumer surplus of area c + d + e + f. However, unlike the tariff case, where the government gains area e in revenues, the government does not gain any revenues with a quota. So the difference between a tariff and a quota is that the tariff brings in revenue to the government while the quota benefits the foreign producer who is lucky enough to receive an import license. They are lucky because they can sell their allotted amount of output at the higher domestic price rather than the lower world price. In the United States, import licenses are given to foreign producers of clothes and, to a lesser extent, sugar. However, if the government charges a fee for the import license, then it is very similar to the tariff—especially if the fee is the difference between the domestic and world price. In this case, the import quota and the tariff would be identical. In reality, countries very seldom sell their import licenses, so the gains accrue to the firms that receive the licenses. Consequently, the deadweight loss is even greater with quotas than with tariffs.

If tariffs and import quotas hurt importing countries, why do they exist? The reason they exist is that producers can make large profits or "rents" from tariffs and import quotas. Economists call these efforts to gain profits from government protection **rent seeking**. Because this money, time, and effort spent on lobbying could have been spent producing something else, the deadweight loss from tariffs and quotas will likely understate the true deadweight loss to society.

rent seeking
efforts by producers to gain profits from government protections such as tariffs and import quotas

The Economic Impact of Subsidies

Working in the opposite direction, governments sometimes try to encourage exports by subsidizing producers. With a subsidy, revenue is given to producers for each exported unit of output, which stimulates exports. Although not a barrier to trade like tariffs and quotas, subsidies can distort trade patterns and lead to inefficiencies. How do these distortions happen? With subsidies, producers will export goods not because their costs are lower than those of a foreign competitor but because their costs have been artificially reduced by government action, transferring income from taxpayers to the exporter. The subsidy does not reduce the amounts of actual labor, raw material, and capital costs of production—society has the same opportunity costs as before. The nation's taxpayers end up subsidizing the output of producers who, relative to producers in other countries, are inefficient. The nation, then, is exporting products in which it does not have a comparative advantage. Gains from trade in terms of world output are eliminated or reduced by such subsidies. Thus, subsidies, usually defended as a means of increasing exports and improving a nation's international financial position, are usually of dubious worth to the world economy and even to the economy doing the subsidizing.

According to the World Bank and the International Monetary Fund (IMF), world trade has benefited enormously from greater openness in trade since 1950. Tariffs on goods have fallen from a worldwide average of 26 percent to less than 9 percent today. On average, trade has grown more than twice as fast as world output.

Buy American. The Job You Save May Be Your Own. A common myth is that it's better for Americans to spend their money at home than abroad. The best way to expose the fallacy in this argument is to take it to its logical extreme. If it's better for me to spend my money here than abroad, then it's even better to buy in Texas than in New York, better yet to buy in Dallas than in Houston . . . in my own neighborhood . . . within my own family . . . to consume only what I can produce. Alone and poor.

In a comprehensive study, Professor Matthew Slaughter of Dartmouth found that when U.S. firms hired lower-cost labor at foreign subsidiaries overseas, their parent companies hired even more people in the United States to support expanded operations. For every job "outsourced" to India and other foreign countries, nearly two new jobs were generated here in the United States. And the new U.S. jobs were higher-skilled—filled by scientists, engineers, marketing professionals, and others hired to meet the new demand.

ⓘ SECTION QUIZ

1. The infant-industry argument for protectionism claims that an industry must be protected in the early stages of its development so that

   a. firms will be protected from subsidized foreign competition.

   b. domestic producers can attain the economies of scale to allow them to compete in world markets.

   c. adequate supplies of crucial resources will be available if needed for national defense.

   d. None of the above reflect the infant-industry argument.

(*continued*)

⌨ SECTION QUIZ (Cont.)

2. After the United States introduces a tariff in the market for steel, the price of steel in the United States will

   a. decrease.

   b. increase.

   c. remain the same.

   d. change in an indeterminate manner.

3. Introducing a tariff on vitamin E would

   a. reduce imports of vitamin E.

   b. increase U.S. consumption of domestically produced vitamin E.

   c. decrease total U.S. consumption of vitamin E.

   d. do all of the above.

   e. do none of the above.

4. Import quotas and tariffs

   a. reduce the quantity of imports.

   b. raise the domestic price of the good.

   c. decrease the welfare of domestic consumers.

   d. increase the welfare of domestic producers.

   e. lead to deadweight loss.

   f. do all of the above.

5. Which of the following is (are) true?

   a. An import quota raises the domestic price, while a tariff does not.

   b. A tariff reduces the quantity of imports, while an import quota does not.

   c. A tariff raises revenue for the government.

   d. An import quota benefits the foreign producer who is lucky enough to receive an import license.

   e. Both (c) and (d) are true.

---

1. Why do tariffs increase domestic producer surplus but decrease domestic consumer surplus?

2. How do import tariffs increase employment in "protected" industries but at the expense of a likely decrease in employment overall?

3. Why is the national security argument for tariffs questionable?

4. Why is the domestic argument for import quotas weaker than the case for tariffs?

5. Why does subsidizing exports by industries without a comparative advantage tend to harm the domestic economy, on net?

Answers: 1. b 2. b 3. d 4. f 5. e

Interactive Summary

Fill in the blanks:

1. In a typical year, about _____ percent of the world's output is traded in international markets.

2. In the global economy, one country's exports are another country's _____.

3. _____ trade implies that both participants in an exchange of goods and services anticipate an improvement in their economic welfare.

4. The theory that explains how trade can be beneficial to both parties centers on the concept of _____.

5. A person, a region, or a country has a comparative advantage over another person, region, or country in producing a particular good or service if it produces a good or service at a lower _____ than others do.

6. What is important for mutually beneficial specialization and trade is _____ advantage, not _____ advantage.

7. Trade has evolved in large part because different geographic areas have _____ resources and therefore _____ production possibilities.

8. If Techland can produce more of both grain and computers than Grainsville, Techland has a(n) _____ advantage in both products.

9. The difference between the most a consumer would be willing to pay for a quantity of a good and what a consumer actually has to pay is called _____ surplus.

10. We can better analyze the impact of trade with the tools of _____ and _____ surplus.

11. Once the equilibrium output is reached at the equilibrium price, the sum of _____ and _____ is maximized.

12. When the domestic economy has a comparative advantage in a good because it can produce it at a lower relative price than the rest of the world can, international trade _____ the domestic market price to the world price, benefiting domestic _____ but harming domestic _____.

13. When the domestic economy has a comparative advantage in a good, allowing international trade redistributes income from domestic _____ to domestic _____, but _____ surplus increases more than _____ surplus decreases.

14. When a country does not produce a good relatively as well as other countries do, international trade will _____ the domestic price to the world price, with the difference between what is domestically supplied and what is domestically demanded supplied by _____.

15. When a country does not produce a good relatively as well as other countries do, international trade redistributes income from domestic _____ to domestic _____ and causes a net _____ in domestic wealth.

16. A(n) _____ is a tax on imported goods.

17. Tariffs bring about _____ prices and revenues to domestic producers, _____ sales and revenues to foreign producers, and _____ prices to domestic consumers.

18. With import tariffs, the domestic price of goods is _____ than the world price.

19. If import tariffs are imposed, at the new price the domestic quantity demanded is _____, and the quantity supplied domestically is _____, _____ the quantity of imported goods.

20. Import tariffs benefit domestic _____ and _____ but harm domestic _____.

21. One argument for tariffs is that tariff protection is necessary _____ to allow a new industry to more quickly reach a scale of operation at which economies of scale and production efficiencies can be realized.

22. Tariffs lead to _____ output and employment and reduced unemployment in domestic industries where tariffs are imposed.

23. If new tariffs lead to restrictions on imports, _____ dollars will be flowing overseas in payment for imports, which means that foreigners will have _____ dollars available to buy U.S. exports.

24. If a nation's own resources are depletable, tariff-imposed reliance on domestic supplies will _____ depletion of domestic reserves.

25. An import _____ gives producers from another country a maximum number of units of the good in question that can be imported within any given time span.

26. Tariffs and import quotas are rather suspect and exist because of producers' lobbying efforts to gain profits from government protection, which is called _____.

27. Dumping occurs when a foreign country sells its products at prices _____ their costs or _____ the prices they are sold at in the domestic market.

28. If a foreign country is found guilty of dumping, the United States can impose _____ tariffs.

29. Governments sometimes try to encourage exports by _____ producers.

30. With subsidies, a nation's taxpayers end up subsidizing the output of producers who, relative to producers in other countries, are _____.

31. Gains from trade in terms of world output are _____ by export subsidies.

Key Terms and Concepts

comparative advantage 589
consumer surplus 595

producer surplus 596
tariff 600

import quota 603
rent seeking 604

Section Quiz Answers

20.1 The Growth in World Trade

1. **Why is it important to understand the effects of international trade?**

   All countries are importantly affected by international trade, although the magnitude of the international trade sector varies substantially by country. International connections mean that any of a large number of disturbances that originate elsewhere may have important consequences for the domestic economy.

2. **Why would U.S. producers and consumers be more concerned about Canadian trade restrictions than Swedish trade restrictions?**

   The United States and Canada are the two largest trading partners in the world. This means that the effects of trade restrictions imposed by Canada would have a far larger effect on the United States than similar restrictions imposed by Sweden. (For certain items, however, the magnitude of our trade with Sweden is greater than it is with Canada, so for these items Swedish restrictions would be of more concern.)

20.2 Comparative Advantage and Gains from Trade

1. **Why do people voluntarily choose to specialize and trade?**

   Voluntary specialization and trade among self-interested parties only takes place because all the parties involved expect that their benefits from this specialization (according to comparative advantage) and exchange will exceed their costs.

2. **How could a country have an absolute advantage in producing one good or service without also having a comparative advantage in its production?**

   If one country was absolutely more productive at everything than another country but wasn't equally more productive at everything, there would still be some things in which it had a comparative disadvantage. For instance, if country A was three times as productive in making X and two times as productive in making Y as country B, it would have a comparative advantage in making X (it gives up less Y for each X produced) and a comparative disadvantage in making Y (it gives up more X for each Y produced), relative to country B.

3. **Why do you think the introduction of the railroad reduced self-sufficiency in the United States?**

   Prior to the introduction of the railroad, the high cost of transportation overwhelmed the gains from specializing according to comparative advantage in much of the United States (production cost differences were smaller than the costs of transportation). The railroads reduced transportation costs enough that specialization and exchange became beneficial for more goods and services, and self-sufficiency due to high transportation costs declined.

4. **If you can wash the dishes in two-thirds the time it takes your younger sister to wash them, do you have a comparative advantage in washing the dishes with respect to her?**

   We can't know the answer to this question without more information. It is not the time taken to wash the dishes that matters in determining comparative advantage but the opportunity cost of the time in terms of forgone value elsewhere. If your younger sister is less than two-thirds as good at other chores than you, she is relatively better at washing the dishes and so would have a comparative advantage in washing the dishes. If she is more than two-thirds as good at other chores, she is relatively better at these chores and so would have a comparative disadvantage in washing the dishes.

20.3 Supply and Demand in International Trade

1. How does voluntary trade generate both consumer and producer surplus?

Voluntary trade generates consumer surplus because a rational consumer would not purchase if he did not value the benefits of purchase at greater than its cost, and consumer surplus is the difference between that value and the cost he is forced to pay. Voluntary trade generates producer surplus because a rational producer would not sell additional units unless the price he received was greater than his marginal cost, and producer surplus is the difference between the revenues received and the costs producers must bear to produce the goods that generate those revenues.

2. If the world price of a good is greater than the domestic price prior to trade, why does it imply that the domestic economy has a comparative advantage in producing that good?

If the world price of a good is greater than the domestic price prior to trade, this implies that the domestic marginal opportunity cost of production is less than the world marginal opportunity cost of production. But this means that the domestic economy has a comparative advantage in that good.

3. If the world price of a good is less than the domestic price prior to trade, why does it imply that the domestic economy has a comparative disadvantage in producing that good?

If the world price of a good is less than the domestic price prior to trade, this implies that the domestic marginal opportunity cost of production is greater than the world marginal opportunity cost of production. But this means that the domestic economy has a comparative disadvantage in that good.

4. When a country has a comparative advantage in the production of a good, why do domestic producers gain more than domestic consumers lose from free international trade?

When a country has a comparative advantage in producing a good, the marginal benefit from exporting is the world price, which is greater than the forgone value domestically (along the domestic demand curve) for those units of domestic consumption "crowded out" and greater than the marginal cost of

the expanded output. Therefore, there are net domestic gains to international trade (the gains to domestic producers exceed the losses to domestic consumers).

5. When a country has a comparative disadvantage in a good, why do domestic consumers gain more than domestic producers lose from free international trade?

When a country has a comparative disadvantage in producing a good, the marginal cost of importing is the world price, which is less than the additional value (along the domestic demand curve) for those units of expanded domestic consumption and less than the marginal cost of the domestic production "crowded out." Therefore, there are net domestic gains to international trade (the gains to domestic consumers exceed the losses to domestic producers).

6. Why do U.S. exporters, such as farmers, favor free trade more than U.S. producers of domestic products who face competition from foreign imports, such as the automobile industry?

Exporters favor free trade over restrictions on what they sell in other countries because it increases the demand and therefore the price for their products, which raises their profits. Those who must compete with importers want those imports restricted rather than freely traded because it increases the demand and therefore the price for their domestically produced products, which raises their profits.

20.4 Tariffs, Import Quotas, and Subsidies

1. Why do tariffs increase domestic producer surplus but decrease domestic consumer surplus?

Tariffs raise the price of imported goods to domestic consumers, resulting in higher prices received by domestic producers as well. Thus, the higher price reduces domestic consumer surplus but increases domestic producer surplus.

2. How do import tariffs increase employment in "protected" industries but at the expense of a likely decrease in employment overall?

Import tariffs increase employment in "protected" industries because the barriers to lower-price imports increase the demand faced by domestic producers, increasing their demand for workers. However, imports are the means by which foreigners get the dollars to buy our exports, so restricted imports will mean restricted exports (even more so if other countries retaliate with import restrictions of their own). In addition, by raising the prices domestic consumers pay for the protected products (remember that domestic consumers lose more than domestic producers gain from protectionism), consumers are made poorer in real terms, which will reduce demand for goods, and therefore the labor to make them, throughout the economy.

3. Why is the national security argument for tariffs questionable?

The national security argument for tariffs is questionable because tariffs increase current reliance on domestic supplies, which depletes the future stockpile of available reserves. With fewer domestic reserves, the country will be even more dependent on foreign supplies in the future. Buying foreign supplies and stockpiling them makes more sense as a way of reducing reliance on foreign supplies in wartime.

4. Why is the domestic argument for import quotas weaker than the case for tariffs?

Tariffs at least use the price system as the basis of trade. Tariff revenues end up in a country's treasury, where they can be used to produce benefits for the country's citizens or to reduce the domestic tax burden. Import quotas, however, transfer most of those benefits to foreign producers as the higher prices they receive.

5. Why does subsidizing exports by industries without a comparative advantage tend to harm the domestic economy, on net?

Subsidizing industries in which a country has a comparative disadvantage (higher costs) must, by definition, require shifting resources from where it has a comparative advantage (lower costs) to where it has a comparative disadvantage. The value of the output produced from those resources (indirectly in the case of specialization and exchange) is lower as a result.

Problems

1. Bud and Larry have been shipwrecked on a deserted island. Their economic activity consists of either gathering berries or fishing. We know that Bud can catch four fish in one hour or harvest two buckets of berries. In the same time Larry can catch two fish or harvest two buckets of berries.

   a. Fill in the following table assuming that they *each* spend four hours a day fishing and four hours a day harvesting berries.

	Fish per Day	Buckets of Berries per Day
Bud	_____	_____
Larry	_____	_____
Total	_____	_____

   b. If Bud and Larry don't trade with each other, who is better off? Why?

   c. Assume that Larry and Bud operate on straight-line production possibilities curves. Fill in the following table:

	Opportunity Cost of a Bucket of Berries	Opportunity Cost of a Fish
Bud	_____	_____
Larry	_____	_____

   d. If they traded, who has the comparative advantage in fish? In berries?

   e. If Larry and Bud specialize in and trade the good in which they have a comparative advantage, how much of each good will be produced in an eight-hour day? What are the gains from trade?

2. The following table represents the production possibilities in two countries:

Country A		Country B	
Good X	Good Y	Good X	Good Y
0	32	0	24
4	24	4	18
8	16	8	12
12	8	12	6
16	0	16	0

   Which country has a comparative advantage at producing Good X? How can you tell?

   Which country has a comparative advantage at producing Good Y?

3. Suppose the United States can produce cars at an opportunity cost of two computers for each car it produces. Suppose Mexico can produce cars at an opportunity cost of eight computers for each car it produces. Indicate how both countries can gain from free trade.

4. Evaluate the following statement: "Small, developing economies must first become self-sufficient before benefiting from international trade."

5. Evaluate the following statement: "The United States has an absolute advantage in growing wheat. Therefore, it must have a comparative advantage in growing wheat."

6. NAFTA (North American Free Trade Agreement) is an agreement among the United States, Canada, and Mexico to reduce trade barriers and promote the free flow of goods and services across borders. Many U.S. labor groups were opposed to NAFTA.

   Can you explain why? Can you predict how NAFTA might alter the goods and services produced in the participating countries?

7. If country A is the lowest opportunity cost producer of X and country B is the lowest opportunity cost producer of Y, what happens to their absolute and comparative advantages if country A suddenly becomes three times more productive at producing both X and Y than it was before?

8. Assume that Freeland could produce 8 units of X and no Y, 16 units of Y and no X, or any linear combination in between, and Braveburg could produce 32 units of X and no Y, 48 units of Y and no X, or any linear combination in between.
   a. What is the opportunity cost of producing X in Freeland? In Braveburg?
   b. If Freeland and Braveburg specialize according to comparative advantage, which directions will goods flow in trade?
   c. If trade occurs, what will the terms of trade between X and Y be?
   d. How large would transactions costs, transportation costs, or tariffs have to be to eliminate trade between Freeland and Braveburg?

9. To protect its domestic apple industry, Botswana has for many years prevented international trade in apples. The following graph represents the Botswana domestic market for apples. P_{BT} is the current price, and P_{AT} is the world price.

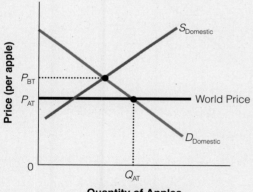

   a. If the government allows world trade in apples, what will happen to the price of apples in Botswana? Why?
   b. Indicate the amount of apples domestic producers produce after there is trade in apples as Q_{DT}. How many apples are imported?
   c. Trade in imports causes producer surplus to be reduced by the amount b. Show b on the graph.
   d. The gains from trade equal the amount increased consumer surplus exceeds the loss in producer surplus. Show this gain, g, on the graph.
   e. Explain why consumers in Botswana would still be better off if they were required to compensate producers for their lost producer surplus.

10. Use the accompanying graphs to illustrate the effects of imposing a tariff on imports on the domestic price, the domestic quantity purchased, the domestic quantity produced, the level of imports, consumer surplus, producer surplus, the tariff revenue generated, and the total welfare effect from the tariff.

World Market

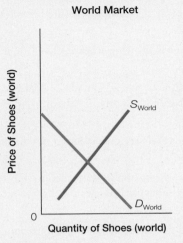

Domestic Market

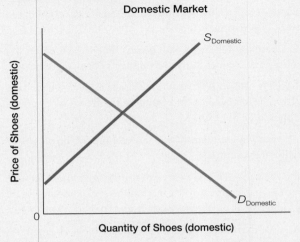

11. Using the accompanying graphs, illustrate the effects of opening up the domestic market to international trade on the domestic price, the domestic quantity purchased, the domestic quantity produced, imports or exports, consumer surplus, producer surplus, and the total welfare gain from trade.

World Market

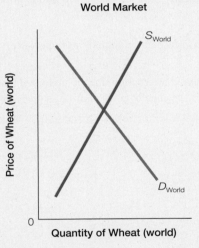

Domestic Market

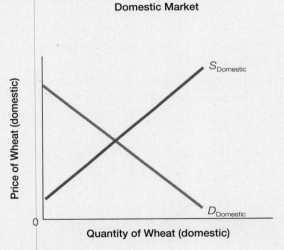

12. Explain why imposing a tariff causes a net welfare loss to the domestic economy.

13. If imposing tariffs and quotas harms consumers, why don't consumers vigorously oppose the implementation of these protectionist policies?

14. Why does rent seeking imply that the traditional measure of deadweight loss from tariffs and quotas will likely understate the true deadweight loss to society?

15. Would you be in favor of freer trade or against it in the following circumstances?
    a. The move to freer trade is in another country, and you are an exporter to that country.
    b. The move to freer trade is in your country, and you compete with imports from other countries.
    c. The move to freer trade is in your country, and you import parts for products you sell domestically.

16. Go through your local newspaper and locate four news items regarding the global economy. Identify the significance of each of these news items to the U.S. economy and whether they are likely to affect international trade.

International Finance

When people travel to foreign countries, they pay for their goods and services in foreign currencies. For example, if we were in Italy and were buying Italian shoes, we would have to pay in euros—and we might want to know how much that will cost us in U.S. currency. In this chapter, we will learn how nations pay each other in world trade and how we measure how much buying and selling is going on. We will also learn about exchange rates.

COUNTRY	CURRENCY	WE SELL
UNITED STATES ÉTAS-UNIS		1.1998
EUROPEAN UNION UNION EUROPÉENNE		1.4996
ENGLAND ANGLETERRE		2.1998
JAPAN JAPON		0.0109
SWITZERLAND SUISSE		0.9895
AUSTRALIA AUSTRALIE		0.9596
DENMARK DANEMARK		.2084

21.1   The Balance of Payments

📁 What is the balance of payments?   📁 What is the balance of trade?

📁 What are the three main components of the
    balance of payments?

Balance of Payments

balance of payments
the record of international transactions in which a nation has engaged over a year

The record of all of the international financial transactions of a nation over a year is called the balance of payments. The **balance of payments** is a statement that records all the exchanges requiring an outflow of funds to foreign nations or an inflow of funds from other nations. Just as an examination of gross domestic product accounts gives us some idea of the economic health and vitality of a nation, the balance of payments provides information about a nation's world trade position. The balance of payments is divided into three main sections: the current account, the capital account, and an "error term" called the statistical discrepancy. These are highlighted in Exhibit 1. Let's look at each of these components, beginning with the current account, which is made up of imports and exports of goods and services.

The Current Account

Export Goods and the Current Account

current account
a record of a country's imports and exports of goods and services, net investment income, and net transfers

A **current account** is a record of a country's imports and exports of goods and services, net investment income, and net transfers. Any time a foreign buyer purchases a good from a U.S. producer, the foreign buyer must pay the U.S. producer for the good. Usually, the foreign buyer must pay for the good in U.S. dollars, because the producer wants to pay his workers' wages and other input costs with dollars. Making this payment requires the foreign buyer to exchange units of her currency at a foreign exchange dealer for U.S. dollars. Because the United States gains claims for foreign goods by obtaining foreign currency in exchange for the dollars needed to buy exports, all exports of U.S. goods abroad are considered a credit,

---

section 21.1
exhibit 1   **U.S. Balance of Payments, 2011 (billions of dollars)**

Type of Transaction

Current Account			Capital Account		
1. Exports of goods	$ 1,289		10. U.S.-owned assets abroad	$ −1,005	
2. Imports of goods	−1,934		11. Foreign-owned assets in the United States	1,246	
3. Balance of trade (lines 1 + 2)		−646	12. Capital account balance (lines 10 + 11)		241
4. Service exports	549		13. Statistical discrepancy	230	
5. Service imports	−403		14. Net Balance (lines 9 − 12 + 13)		$0
6. Balance on goods and services (lines 3 + 4 + 5)		−500			
7. Unilateral transfers (net)	−136				
8. Investment income (net)	165				
9. Current account balance (lines 6 + 7 + 8)		−471			

SOURCE: Bureau of Economic Analysis, Table 1.

or plus (+), item in the U.S. balance of payments. Those foreign currencies are later exchangeable for goods and services made in the country that purchased the U.S. exports.

Import Goods and the Current Account

When a U.S. consumer buys an imported good, however, the reverse is true: The U.S. importer must pay the foreign producer, usually in that nation's currency. Typically, the U.S. buyer will go to a foreign exchange dealer and exchange dollars for units of that foreign currency. Imports are thus a debit (−) item in the balance of payments, because the dollars sold to buy the foreign currency add to foreign claims for foreign goods, which are later exchangeable for U.S. goods and services. U.S. imports, then, provide the means by which foreigners can buy U.S. exports.

Nations import and export services like tourism.

Services and the Current Account

Even though imports and exports of goods are the largest components of the balance of payments, they are not the only ones. Nations import and export services as well. A particularly important service is tourism. When U.S. tourists go abroad, they are buying foreign-produced services in addition to those purchased by citizens there. Those services include the use of hotels, sightseeing tours, restaurants, and so forth. In the current account, these services are included in imports. On the other hand, foreign tourism in the United States provides us with foreign currencies and claims against foreigners, so they are included in exports. Airline and shipping services also affect the balance of payments. When someone from Italy flies American Airlines, that person is making a payment to a U.S. company. Because the flow of international financial claims is the same, this payment is treated just like a U.S. export in the balance of payments. If an American flies on Alitalia, however, Italians acquire claims against the United States, and so it is included as a debit (import) item in the U.S. balance-of-payments accounts.

Net Transfer Payments and Net Investment Income

Other items that affect the current account are private and government grants and gifts to and from other countries. When the United States gives foreign aid to another country, a debit occurs in the U.S. balance of payments because the aid gives foreigners added claims against the United States in the form of dollars. Private gifts, such as individuals sending money to relatives or friends in foreign countries, show up in the current account as debit items as well. Because the United States usually sends more humanitarian and military aid to foreigners than it receives, net transfers are usually in deficit.

If your Australian cousin flies here from Sydney on American Airlines, how does that impact the balance of payments?

Net investment income is also included in the current account (line 8)—U.S. investors hold foreign assets and foreign investors hold U.S. assets. Payments received by U.S. residents are added to the current account and payments made by U.S. residents are subtracted from the current account. In 2011, a net flow of $241 billion came into the United States.

The Current Account Balance

The balance on the current account is the net amount of credits or debits after adding up all transactions of goods (merchandise imports and exports), services, and transfer payments (e.g., foreign aid and gifts). If the sum of credits exceeds the sum of debits, the nation is said to run a balance-of-payments surplus on the current account. If debits exceed credits, however, the nation is running a balance-of-payments deficit on the current account.

The Balance of Trade and the Balance of the Current Account

balance of trade
the net surplus or deficit resulting from the level of exportation and importation of merchandise

What is the difference between the balance of trade and the balance on current account?

The balance of payments of the United States for 2011 is presented in Exhibit 1. Notice that exports and imports of goods and services are by far the largest credits and debits. Notice also that U.S. exports of goods were $646 billion less than imports of goods. The import/export goods relationship is often called the **balance of trade**. The United States, therefore, experienced a balance-of-trade deficit that year of $646 billion. However, some of the $646 billion trade deficit is offset by credits from a $146 billion surplus in services. This difference leads to a $500 billion deficit in the balance of goods and services. When $136 billion of net unilateral transfers (gifts and grants between the United States and foreigners) and $165 billion of investment income (net) from the United States are added (the foreigners gave more to the United States than the United States gave to the foreigners), the total deficit on the current account is $471 billion. Exhibit 2 shows the balance on the current account since 1975.

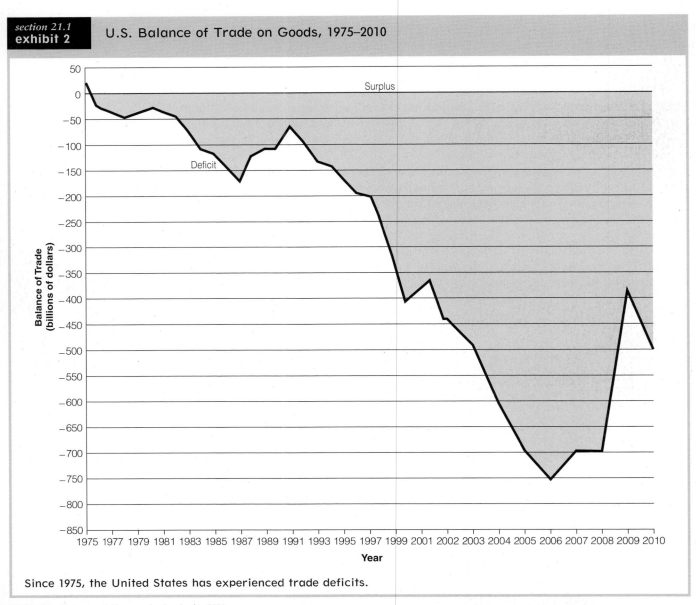

section 21.1
exhibit 2   U.S. Balance of Trade on Goods, 1975–2010

Since 1975, the United States has experienced trade deficits.

SOURCE: Bureau of Economic Analysis, 2011.

The Capital Account

How was this deficit on the current account financed? Remember that U.S. credits give us the financial means to buy foreign goods and that our credits were $545 billion less than our debits from imports and net unilateral transfers to foreign countries. This deficit on the current account balance is settled by movements of financial, or capital, assets. These transactions are recorded in the *capital account,* so that a current account deficit is financed by a capital account surplus. In short, the **capital account** records the foreign purchases or assets in the United States (a monetary inflow) and U.S. purchases of assets abroad (a monetary outflow).

capital account records the foreign purchases or assets in the domestic economy (a monetary inflow) and domestic purchases of assets abroad (a monetary outflow)

What Does the Capital Account Record?

Capital account transactions include such items as international bank loans, purchases of corporate securities, government bond purchases, and direct investments in foreign subsidiary companies. In 2011, the United States purchased foreign assets of $1,005 billion, which was a further debit because it provided foreigners with U.S. dollars. On the other hand, foreign investments in U.S. bonds, stocks, and other items totaled more than $1,246 billion. In addition, the United States and other governments buy and sell dollars. On net in 2011, foreign-owned assets in the United States made about $241 billion more than did U.S. assets abroad. On balance, then, a surplus (positive credit) in the capital account from capital movements amounted to $241 billion, offsetting the $471 billion deficit on current account.

The Statistical Discrepancy

In the final analysis, it is true that the balance-of-payments account (current account minus capital account) must balance so that credits and debits are equal. Why? Due to the reciprocal aspect of trade, every credit eventually creates a debit of equal magnitude. These errors are sometimes large and are entered into the balance of payments as the *statistical discrepancy.* Including the errors and omissions recorded as the statistical discrepancy, the balance of payments does balance. That is, the number of U.S. dollars demanded equals the number of U.S. dollars supplied when the balance of payments is zero.

Balance of Payments: A Useful Analogy

In concept, the international balance of payments is similar to the personal financial transactions of an individual. Each individual has a personal "balance of payments," reflecting that person's trading with other economic units: other individuals, corporations, and governments. People earn income or credits by "exporting" their labor service to other economic units or by receiving investment income (a return on capital services). Against that, they "import" goods from other economic units; we call these imports consumption. This debit item is sometimes augmented by payments made to outsiders (e.g., banks) on loans and so forth. Fund transfers, such as gifts to children or charities, are other debit items (or credit items for recipients of the assistance).

As individuals, if our spending on consumption exceeds our income from exporting our labor and capital services, we have a "deficit" that must be financed by borrowing or selling assets. If we "export" more than we "import," however, we can make new investments and/or increase our "reserves" (savings and investment holdings). Like nations, an individual who runs a deficit in daily transactions must make up for it through accommodating transactions (e.g., borrowing or reducing personal savings or investment holdings) to bring about an ultimate balance of credits and debits in his or her personal account.

⊘ SECTION QUIZ

1. Which of the following would be recorded as a credit in the U.S. balance-of-payments accounts?

   a. the purchase of a German business by a U.S. investor

   b. the import of Honda trucks by a U.S. automobile distributor

   c. European travel expenditures of an American college student

   d. the purchase of a U.S. Treasury bond by a French investment company

2. What is the difference between the balance of merchandise trade and the balance of payments?

   a. Only the value of goods imported and exported is included in the balance of merchandise trade, while the balance of payments includes the value of all payments to and from foreigners.

   b. The value of goods imported and exported is included in the balance of merchandise trade, while the balance of payments includes only capital account transactions.

   c. The value of all goods, services, and unilateral transfers is included in the balance of merchandise trade, while the balance of payments includes both current account and capital account transactions.

   d. Balance of merchandise trade and balance of payments both describe the same international exchange transactions.

3. If consumers in Europe and Asia develop strong preferences for U.S. goods, the U.S. current account will

   a. not be affected, because purchases of U.S. goods by foreigners are recorded in the capital account.

   b. not be affected, because purchases of U.S. goods based on mere preferences are recorded under statistical discrepancy.

   c. move toward surplus, because purchases of U.S. goods are recorded as credits on our current account.

   d. move toward deficit, because purchases of U.S. goods by foreigners are counted as debits in our current account.

4. Which of the following will enter as a credit in the U.S. balance-of-payments capital account?

   a. the purchase of a Japanese automobile by a U.S. consumer

   b. the sale of Japanese electronics to an American

   c. the sale of an American baseball team to a Japanese industrialist

   d. the purchase of a Japanese electronic plant by an American industrialist

5. If the value of a nation's merchandise exports exceeds merchandise imports, then the nation is running a

   a. balance-of-payments deficit.

   b. balance-of-payments surplus.

   c. merchandise trade deficit.

   d. merchandise trade surplus.

---

1. What is the balance of payments?

2. Why must British purchasers of U.S. goods and services first exchange pounds for dollars?

3. How is it that our imports provide foreigners with the means to buy U.S. exports?

4. What would have to be true for the United States to have a balance-of-trade deficit and a balance-of-payments surplus?

5. What would have to be true for the United States to have a balance-of-trade surplus and a current account deficit?

6. With no errors or omissions in the recorded balance-of-payments accounts, what should the statistical discrepancy equal?

7. A Nigerian family visiting Chicago enjoys a Chicago Cubs baseball game at Wrigley Field. How would this expense be recorded in the balance-of-payments accounts? Why?

Answers: 1. d 2. a 3. c 4. c 5. d

Exchange Rates   21.2

What are exchange rates?

How are exchange rates determined?

How do exchange rates affect the demand for foreign goods?

The Need for Foreign Currencies

When a U.S. consumer buys goods from a seller in another country—who naturally wants to be paid in her own domestic currency—the U.S. consumer must first exchange U.S. dollars for the seller's currency in order to pay for those goods. American importers must, therefore, constantly buy yen, euros, pesos, and other currencies in order to finance their purchases. Similarly, someone in another country buying U.S. goods must sell his domestic currency to obtain U.S. dollars to pay for those goods.

If I am buying something from a person in a foreign country, do I need to exchange my dollars for their foreign currency?

The Exchange Rate

The price of a unit of one foreign currency in terms of another is called the **exchange rate**. If a U.S. importer has agreed to pay euros (the currency of the European Union) to buy a cuckoo clock made in the Black Forest in Germany, she would then have to exchange U.S. dollars for euros. If it takes $1 to buy 1 euro, then the exchange rate is $1 per euro. From the German perspective, the exchange rate is 1 euro per U.S. dollar.

exchange rate
the price of one unit of a country's currency in terms of another country's currency

Changes in Exchange Rates Affect the Domestic Demand for Foreign Goods

Prices of goods in their currencies combine with exchange rates to determine the domestic price of foreign goods. Suppose the cuckoo clock sells for 100 euros in Germany. What is the price to U.S. consumers? Let's assume that tariffs and other transaction costs are zero. If the exchange rate is $1 = 1 euro, then the equivalent U.S. dollar price of the cuckoo clock is 100 euros times $1 per euro, or $100. If the exchange rate were to change to $2 = 1 euro, fewer clocks would be demanded in the United States, because the effective U.S. dollar price of the clocks would rise to $200 (100 euros × $2 per euro). The higher relative value of a

Why do they say a strong dollar is a mixed blessing?

use what you've learned   Exchange Rates

Q Why is a strong dollar (i.e., exchange rate for foreign currencies is low) a mixed blessing?

A A strong dollar will lower the price of imports and make trips to foreign countries less expensive. Lower prices on foreign goods also help keep inflation in check and make investments in foreign financial markets (foreign stocks and bonds) relatively cheaper. However, it makes U.S. exports more expensive. Consequently, foreigners will buy fewer U.S. goods and services. The net effect is a fall in exports and a rise in imports—net exports fall. Note that some Americans are helped (vacationers going to foreign countries and those preferring foreign goods), while others are harmed (producers of U.S. exports, operators of hotels dependent on foreign visitors in the United States). A stronger dollar also makes it more difficult for foreign investors to invest in the United States.

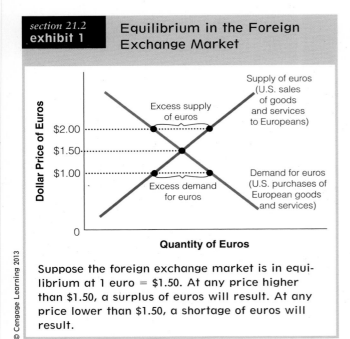

section 21.2 exhibit 1

Equilibrium in the Foreign Exchange Market

Suppose the foreign exchange market is in equilibrium at 1 euro = $1.50. At any price higher than $1.50, a surplus of euros will result. At any price lower than $1.50, a shortage of euros will result.

On January 1, 1999, the euro became the currency in 11 countries: Belgium, Germany, Spain, France, Ireland, Italy, Luxembourg, the Netherlands, Austria, Portugal, and Finland. If the euro becomes relatively less expensive in terms of dollars (it now costs less to buy a euro), what will happen to the U.S. demand for European goods? If the price of the euro falls relative to the dollar, European products become relatively less expensive to U.S. consumers, who will tend to buy more European goods.

derived demand
the demand for an input derived from consumers' demand for the good or service produced with that input

euro compared to the dollar (or, equivalently, the lower relative value of a dollar compared to the euro) would lead to a reduction in U.S. demand for German-made clocks.

The Demand for a Foreign Currency

The demand for foreign currencies is known as a **derived demand**, because the demand for a foreign currency derives directly from the demand for foreign goods and services or for foreign investment. The more that goods from a foreign country are demanded, the more of that country's currency is needed to pay for those goods. This increased demand for the currency will push up the exchange value of that currency relative to other currencies.

The Supply of a Foreign Currency

Similarly, the supply of foreign currency is provided by foreigners who want to buy the exports of a particular nation. For example, the more that foreigners demand U.S. products, the more of their currencies they will supply in exchange for U.S. dollars, which they use to buy our products.

Determining Exchange Rates

We know that the demand for foreign currencies is derived from the demand for foreign goods, but how does that affect the exchange rate? Just as in the product market, the answer lies with the forces of supply and demand. In this case, it is the supply of and demand for a foreign currency that determine the equilibrium price (exchange rate) of that currency.

The Demand Curve for a Foreign Currency

As Exhibit 1 shows, the demand curve for a foreign currency—the euro, for example—is downward sloping, just as it is in product markets. In this case, however, the demand curve has a negative slope because as the price of the euro falls relative to the dollar, European products become relatively more inexpensive to U.S. consumers, who therefore buy more European goods. To do so, the quantity of euros demanded by U.S. consumers will increase to buy more European goods as the price of the euro falls. For this reason, the demand for foreign currencies is considered to be a derived demand.

The Supply Curve for Foreign Currency

The supply curve for a foreign currency is upward sloping, just as it is in product markets. In this case, as the price, or value, of the euro increases relative to the dollar, U.S. products will become relatively less expensive to European buyers, who will thus increase the quantity of dollars they demand. Europeans will, therefore, increase the quantity of euros supplied to the United States by buying more U.S. products.

Hence, the supply curve is upward sloping.

Equilibrium in the Foreign Exchange Market

Equilibrium is reached where the demand and supply curves for a given currency intersect. In Exhibit 1, the equilibrium price of a euro is $1.50. As in the product market, if the dollar price of euros is higher than the equilibrium price, an excess quantity of euros will be supplied at that price; that is, a surplus of euros will exist. Competition among euro sellers will push the price of euros down toward equilibrium. Likewise, if the dollar price of euros is lower than the equilibrium price, an excess quantity of euros will be demanded at that price; that is, a shortage of euros will occur. Competition among euro buyers will push the price of euros up toward equilibrium.

⑦ SECTION QUIZ

1. If the price in dollars of Mexican pesos changes from $0.10 per peso to $0.14 per peso, the peso has
   a. appreciated.
   b. depreciated.
   c. devalued.
   d. stayed at the same exchange rate.

2. If the exchange rate between the dollar and the euro changes from $1 = 1 euro to $2 = 1 euro, then
   a. European goods will become less expensive for Americans, and imports of European goods to the United States will rise.
   b. European goods will become less expensive for Americans, and imports of European goods to the United States will fall.
   c. European goods will become more expensive for Americans, and imports of European goods to the United States will rise.
   d. European goods will become more expensive for Americans, and imports of European goods to the United States will fall.

3. If the dollar appreciates relative to other currencies, which of the following is true?
   a. It takes more of the other currency to buy a dollar.
   b. It takes less of the other currency to buy a dollar.
   c. No change occurs in the currency needed to buy a dollar.
   d. Not enough information is available to make a determination.

4. Suppose that the dollar rises from 100 to 125 yen. As a result,
   a. exports to Japan will likely increase.
   b. Japanese tourists will be more likely to visit the United States.
   c. U.S. businesses will be less likely to use Japanese shipping lines to transport their products.
   d. U.S. consumers will be more likely to buy Japanese-made automobiles.

5. A depreciation in the U.S. dollar would
   a. discourage foreigners from making investments in the United States.
   b. discourage foreign consumers from buying U.S. goods.
   c. reduce the number of dollars it would take to buy a Swiss franc.
   d. encourage foreigners to buy more U.S. goods.

---

1. What is an exchange rate?
2. When a U.S. dollar buys relatively more British pounds, why does the cost of imports from England fall in the United States?
3. When a U.S. dollar buys relatively fewer yen, why does the cost of U.S. exports fall in Japan?

(*continued*)

4. How does an increase in domestic demand for foreign goods and services increase the demand for those foreign currencies?

5. As euros get cheaper relative to U.S. dollars, why does the quantity of euros demanded by Americans increase? Why doesn't the demand for euros increase as a result?

6. Who brings exchange rates down when they are above their equilibrium value? Who brings exchange rates up when they are below their equilibrium value?

Answers: 1. a   2. d   3. a   4. d   5. d

21.3

Equilibrium Changes in the Foreign Exchange Market

📂 What factors cause the demand curve for a currency to shift?

📂 What factors cause the supply curve for a currency to shift?

Determinants in the Foreign Exchange Market

What can cause a change in the demand for a currency?

The equilibrium exchange rate of a currency changes many times daily. Sometimes, these changes can be quite significant. Any force that shifts either the demand for or supply of a currency will shift the equilibrium in the foreign exchange market, leading to a new exchange rate. Among such factors are changes in consumer tastes for goods, income levels, relative real interest rates, and relative inflation rates, as well as speculation.

Increased Tastes for Foreign Goods

Because the demand for foreign currencies is derived from the demand for foreign goods, any change in the U.S. demand for foreign goods will shift the demand schedule for foreign currency in the same direction. For example, if a cuckoo clock revolution sweeps through the United States, German producers will have reason to celebrate, knowing that many U.S. buyers will turn to Germany for their cuckoo clocks. However, because Germans will only accept payment in the form of euros, U.S. consumers and retailers must convert their dollars into euros before they can purchase their clocks. The increased taste for European goods in the United States will, therefore, lead to an increased demand for euros. As shown in Exhibit 1, this increased demand for euros shifts the demand curve to the right, resulting in a new, higher equilibrium dollar price of euros.

Relative Income Increases or Reductions in U.S. Tariffs

Any change in the average income of U.S. consumers will also change the equilibrium exchange rate, *ceteris paribus*. If on the whole incomes were to increase in the United States, Americans would buy more goods, including imported goods, hence more European goods

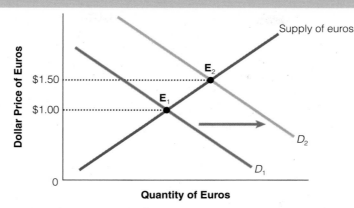

section 21.3
exhibit 1 | Impact on the Foreign Exchange Market of a U.S. Increase in Taste, Income Increase, or Tariff Decrease

An increase in the taste for European goods, an increase in U.S. incomes, or a decrease in U.S. tariffs can cause an increase in the demand for euros, shifting the demand for euros to the right from D_1 to D_2 and leading to a higher equilibrium exchange rate.

would be bought. This increased demand for European goods would lead to an increased demand for euros, resulting in a higher exchange rate for the euro. A decrease in U.S. tariffs on European goods would tend to have the same effect as an increase in incomes, by making European goods more affordable. Exhibit 1 shows that it would again lead to an increased demand for European goods and a higher short-run equilibrium exchange rate for the euro.

What can cause a change in the supply of a currency?

European Incomes Increase, Reductions in European Tariffs, or Changes in European Tastes

If European incomes rose, European tariffs on U.S. goods fell, or European tastes for American goods increased, the supply of euros in the euro foreign exchange market would increase. Any of these changes would cause Europeans to demand more U.S. goods and therefore more U.S. dollars to purchase those goods. To obtain these added dollars, Europeans would have to exchange more of their euros, increasing the supply of euros on the euro foreign exchange market. As Exhibit 2 demonstrates, the result would be a rightward shift in the euro supply curve, leading to a new equilibrium at a lower exchange rate for the euro.

How Do Changes in Relative Real Interest Rates Affect Exchange Rates?

If interest rates in the United States were to increase relative to, say, European interest rates, other things being equal, the rate of return on U.S. investments would increase relative to that on European investments. European investors would then increase their demand for U.S. investments and therefore offer euros for sale in order to buy dollars to buy U.S. investments, shifting the supply curve for euros to the right, from S_1 to S_2 in Exhibit 3.

What impact will an increase in travel to Paris by U.S. consumers have on the dollar price of euros? For a consumer to buy souvenirs at the Eiffel Tower, she will need to exchange dollars for euros. It will increase the demand for euros and result in a new, higher dollar price of euros.

section 21.3
exhibit 2   Impact on the Foreign Exchange Market of a European Increase in Taste, Income Increase, or Tariff Decrease

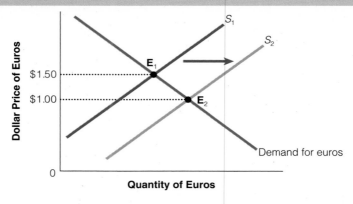

If European incomes increase, European tariffs on U.S. goods fall, or European tastes for American goods increase, the supply of euros increases. The increase in demand for dollars causes an increase in the supply of euros, shifting it to the right, from S_1 to S_2.

In this scenario, U.S. investors would also shift their investments away from Europe by decreasing their demand for euros relative to their demand for dollars, from D_1 to D_2 in Exhibit 3. A subsequent, lower equilibrium price ($1.50) would result for the euro as a result of the increase in U.S. interest rates. That is, the euro would depreciate, because euros could now buy fewer units of dollars than before. In short, the higher U.S. interest rates would attract more investment to the United States, leading to a relative appreciation of the dollar and a relative depreciation of the euro.

Changes in the Relative Inflation Rate

If Europe experienced an inflation rate greater than that experienced in the United States, other things being equal, what would happen to the exchange rate? In this case, European products would become more expensive to U.S. consumers. Americans would then decrease the quantity of European goods demanded and thus decrease their demand for euros. The result would be a leftward shift of the demand curve for euros.

On the other side of the Atlantic, U.S. goods would become relatively cheaper to Europeans, leading Europeans to increase the quantity of U.S. goods demanded and thus to demand more U.S. dollars. This increased demand for dollars would translate into an increased supply of euros, shifting the supply curve for euros outward. Exhibit 4 shows the shifts of the supply and demand curves and the new lower equilibrium price for the euro resulting from the higher European rate.

Expectations and Speculation

What impact do speculation and expectations have on the value of a currency?

Every trading day, roughly a trillion dollars in currency trades hands in the foreign exchange markets. Suppose currency traders believe that in the future, the United States will experience more rapid inflation than will Japan. If currency speculators believe that the value of the dollar will soon be falling because of the anticipated rise in the U.S. inflation rate, those who are holding dollars will convert them to yen. This move will lead to an increase in the demand for yen—the yen appreciates and the dollar depreciates relative to the yen, *ceteris paribus*. In short, if speculators believe that the price of a country's currency is going to rise, they will buy more of that currency, pushing up the price and causing the country's currency to appreciate.

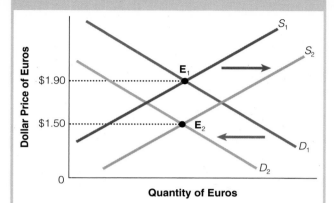

section 21.3
exhibit 3

Impact on the Foreign Exchange Market from an Increase in the U.S. Interest Rate

When U.S. interest rates increase, European investors increase their supply of euros to buy dollars—the supply curve of euros increases from S_1 to S_2. In addition, U.S. investors shift their investments away from Europe, decreasing their demand for euros and shifting the demand curve from D_1 to D_2. This shift leads to a depreciation of the euro; that is, euros can now buy fewer units of dollars.

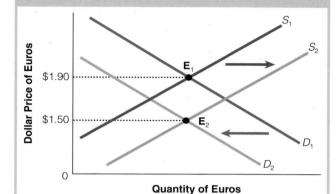

section 21.3
exhibit 4

Impact on the Foreign Exchange Market from an Increase in the European Inflation Rate

If Europe experiences a higher inflation rate than does the United States, European products become more expensive to U.S. consumers. As a result, those consumers demand fewer euros, shifting the demand for euros to the left, from D_1 to D_2. At the same time, U.S. goods become relatively cheaper to Europeans, who then buy more dollars by supplying euros, shifting the euro supply curve to the right, from S_1 to S_2. The result: a new, lower equilibrium price for the euro.

use what you've learned   Determinants of Exchange Rates

Q How will each of the following events affect the foreign exchange market?
a. American travel to Europe increases.
b. Japanese investors purchase U.S. stock.
c. U.S. real interest rates abruptly increase relative to world interest rates.
d. Other countries become less politically and economically stable relative to the United States.

A a. The demand for euros increases (demand shifts right in the euro market), the dollar will depreciate, and the euro will appreciate, *ceteris paribus.*

b. The demand for dollars increases (demand shifts right in the dollar market), the dollar will appreciate, and the yen will depreciate, *ceteris paribus.* Alternatively, you could think of it as an increase in supply in the yen market.

c. International investors will increase their demand for dollars in the dollar market to take advantage of the higher interest rates. The dollar will appreciate relative to other foreign currencies, *ceteris paribus.*

d. More foreign investors will want to buy U.S. assets, resulting in an increase in demand for dollars.

ⓘ SECTION QUIZ

1. Which of the following is most likely to favor the appreciation of the American dollar?

   a. a German professor on vacation in Iowa

   b. an American professor on extended vacation in Paris

   c. an American farmer who relies on exports

   d. Disney World

2. If the dollar appreciates relative to other currencies, which of the following is true?

   a. It takes more of the other currency to buy a dollar.

   b. It takes less of the other currency to buy a dollar.

   c. No change occurs in the currency needed to buy a dollar.

   d. Not enough information is available to make a determination.

3. If the United States experiences a sharp increase in exports, what will happen to demand for the U.S. dollar?

   a. It will decrease.

   b. It will increase.

   c. It will be unchanged.

   d. It will change at the same rate as the supply of dollars will change.

   e. There is not enough information to make a determination.

4. If fewer British tourists visit the Grand Canyon, what is the effect in the exchange market?

   a. It will increase the supply of British pounds.

   b. It will decrease the supply of British pounds.

   c. It will increase the demand for British pounds.

   d. It will decrease the demand for British pounds.

5. Suppose that the dollar rises from 100 to 125 yen. As a result,

   a. exports to Japan will likely increase.

   b. Japanese tourists will be more likely to visit the United States.

   c. U.S. businesses will be less likely to use Japanese shipping lines to transport their products.

   d. U.S. consumers will be more likely to buy Japanese-made automobiles.

6. Other things being constant, which of the following will most likely cause the dollar to appreciate on the exchange rate market?

   a. higher domestic interest rates

   b. higher interest rates abroad

   c. expansionary domestic monetary policy

   d. reduced inflation abroad

7. A depreciation in the U.S. dollar would

   a. discourage foreigners from making investments in the United States.

   b. discourage foreign consumers from buying U.S. goods.

   c. reduce the number of dollars it would take to buy a Swiss franc.

   d. encourage foreigners to buy more U.S. goods.

8. In foreign exchange markets, the effect of an increase in the demand for dollars on the value of the dollar is the same as that of

   a. an increase in the supply of foreign currencies.

   b. a decrease in the supply of foreign currencies.

   c. a decrease in the demand for dollars.

   d. none of the above.

(*continued*)

⊙ SECTION QUIZ (Cont.)

1. Why will the exchange rates of foreign currencies relative to U.S. dollars decline when U.S. domestic tastes change, reducing the demand for foreign-produced goods?

2. Why does the demand for foreign currencies shift in the same direction as domestic income? What happens to the exchange value of those foreign currencies in terms of U.S. dollars?

3. How would increased U.S. tariffs on imported European goods affect the exchange value of euros in terms of dollars?

4. Why do changes in U.S. tastes, income levels, or tariffs change the demand for euros, while similar changes in Europe change the supply of euros?

5. What would happen to the exchange value of euros in terms of U.S. dollars if incomes rose in both Europe and the United States?

6. Why does an increase in interest rates in Germany relative to U.S. interest rates increase the demand for euros but decrease their supply?

7. What would an increase in U.S. inflation relative to Europe do to the supply and demand for euros and to the equilibrium exchange value (price) of euros in terms of U.S. dollars?

Answers: 1. b   2. a   3. b   4. d   5. d   6. a   7. d   8. a

---

Flexible Exchange Rates   21.4

📂 How are exchange rates determined today?

📂 How are exchange rate changes different under a flexible-rate system than in a fixed system?

📂 What major problems exist in a fixed-rate system?

📂 What are the major arguments against flexible rates?

The Flexible Exchange Rate System

Since 1973, the world has essentially operated on a system of flexible exchange rates. Flexible exchange rates mean that currency prices are allowed to fluctuate with changes in supply and demand, without governments stepping in to prevent those changes. Before that, governments operated under what was called the *Bretton Woods fixed exchange rate system,* in which they would maintain a stable exchange rate by buying or selling currencies or reserves to bring demand and supply for their currencies together at the fixed exchange rate. The present system evolved out of the Bretton Woods fixed-rate system and occurred by accident, not design. Governments were unable to agree on an alternative fixed-rate approach when the Bretton Woods system collapsed, so nations simply let market forces determine currency values.

Are Exchange Rates Managed at All?

To be sure, some governments are sensitive to sharp changes in the exchange value of their currencies. These governments will intervene from time to time to prop up their currency's exchange rate if it is considered too low or falling too rapidly, or will actively depress its exchange rate if it is considered to be too high or rising too rapidly. Such was the case when the U.S. dollar declined in value in the late 1970s, but the U.S. government intervention appeared to have little if any effect in preventing the dollar's decline. However, present-day fluctuations in

What are fixed exchange rates?

What do economists mean when they say there is a dirty float system?

dirty float system
a description of the exchange rate system that means that fluctuations in currency values are partly determined by government intervention

exchange rates are not determined solely by market forces. Economists sometimes say that the current exchange rate system is a **dirty float system**, meaning that fluctuations in currency values are partly determined by market forces and partly influenced by government intervention. Over the years, however, such governmental support attempts have been insufficient to dramatically alter exchange rates for long, and currency exchange rates have changed dramatically.

When Exchange Rates Change

When exchange rates change, they affect not only the currency market but the product markets as well. For example, if U.S. consumers were to receive fewer and fewer British pounds and Japanese yen per U.S. dollar, the effect would be an increasing price for foreign imports, *ceteris paribus*. It would now take a greater number of dollars to buy a given number of yen or pounds, which U.S. consumers use to purchase those foreign products. It would, however, lower the cost of U.S. exports to foreigners. If, however, the dollar increased in value relative to other currencies, then the relative price of foreign goods would decrease, *ceteris paribus*. But foreigners would find that U.S. goods were more expensive in terms of their own currency prices, and, as a result, would import fewer U.S. products.

The Advantages of Flexible Rates

As mentioned earlier, the present system of flexible exchange rates was not planned. Indeed, most central bankers thought that a system where rates were not fixed would lead to chaos. What in fact has happened? Since the advent of flexible exchange rates, world trade has not only continued but expanded. Over a one-year period, the world economy adjusted to the shock of a fourfold increase in the price of its most important internationally traded commodity, oil. Although the OPEC oil cartel's price increase certainly had adverse economic effects, it did so without paralyzing the economy of any one nation.

The most important advantage of the flexible-rate system is that the recurrent crises that led to speculative rampages and major currency revaluations under the fixed Bretton Woods system have significantly diminished. Under the fixed-rate system, price changes in currencies came infrequently, but when they came, they were of a large magnitude: 20 percent or 30 percent changes overnight were fairly common. Today, price changes occur daily or even hourly, but each change is much smaller in magnitude, with major changes in exchange rates typically occurring only over periods of months or years.

What are the advantages of flexible exchange rates?

The exchange rate is the rate at which one country's currency can be traded for another country's currency. Under a flexible-rate system, the government allows the forces of supply and demand to determine the exchange rate. Changes in exchange rates occur daily or even hourly.

Fixed Exchange Rates Can Result in Currency Shortages

Perhaps the most significant problem with the fixed-rate system is that it can result in currency shortages, just as domestic price and wage controls lead to shortages. Suppose we had a fixed-rate system with the price of one euro set at $1.00, as shown in Exhibit 1. In this example, the original quantity of euros demanded and supplied is indicated by curves D_1 and S, so $1.00 is the equilibrium price. That is, at a price of $1.00, the quantity of euros demanded (by U.S. importers of European products and others wanting euros) equals the quantity supplied (by European importers of U.S. products and others).

Suppose that some event happens to increase U.S. demand for Dutch goods. For this example, let us assume that Royal Dutch Shell discovers new oil reserves in the North Sea and thus has a new product to export. As U.S. consumers begin to demand Royal Dutch Shell oil, the demand for euros increases. That is, at any given dollar price of euros, U.S. consumers want more euros, shifting the demand curve to the right, to D_2. Under a fixed exchange rate system, the dollar price of euros must remain at $1, where the quantity of euros demanded (Q_2) now exceeds the quantity supplied, Q_1. The result is a shortage of euros—a shortage that must be corrected in some way. As a solution to the shortage, the United States may borrow euros from the Netherlands, or perhaps ship the Netherlands some of its reserves of gold. The ability to continually make up the shortage (deficit) in this manner, however, is limited, particularly if the deficit persists for a substantial time.

Flexible Rates Solve the Currency Shortage Problem

Under flexible exchange rates, a change in the supply or demand for euros does not pose a problem. Because rates are allowed to change, the rising U.S. demand for European goods (and thus for euros) would lead to a new equilibrium price for euros, say at $1.50. At this higher price, European goods are more costly to U.S. consumers. Some of the increase in demand for European imports, then, is offset by a decrease in quantity demanded resulting from higher import prices. Similarly, the change in the exchange rate will make U.S. goods cheaper to Europeans, thus increasing U.S. exports and, with that, the quantity of euros supplied. For example, a $40 software program that cost Europeans 40

section 21.4 exhibit 1 How Flexible Exchange Rates Work

An increase in demand for euros shifts the demand curve to the right, from D_1 to D_2. Under a fixed-rate system, this increase in demand results in a shortage of euros at the equilibrium price of $1, because the quantity demanded at this price, Q_2, is greater than the quantity supplied, Q_1. If the exchange rate is flexible, however, no shortage develops. Instead, the increase in demand forces the exchange rate higher, to $1.50. At this higher exchange rate, the quantity of euros demanded doesn't increase as much, and the quantity of euros supplied increases as a result of the now relatively lower cost of imports from the United States.

© Cengage Learning 2013

euros when the exchange rate was $1 per euro costs less than 27 euros when the exchange rate increases to $1.50 per euro ($40 divided by $1.50).

Flexible Rates Affect Macroeconomic Policies

With flexible exchange rates, the imbalance between debits and credits arising from shifts in currency demand and/or supply is accommodated by changes in currency prices, rather than through the special financial borrowings or reserve movements necessary with fixed rates. In a pure flexible exchange rate system, deficits and surpluses in the balance of payments tend to disappear automatically. The market mechanism itself is able to address world trade imbalances, dispensing with the need for bureaucrats attempting to achieve some administratively determined price. Moreover, the need to use restrictive monetary and/or fiscal policy to end such an imbalance while maintaining a fixed exchange rate is alleviated. Nations are thus able to feel less constraint in carrying out internal macroeconomic policies under flexible exchange rates. For these reasons, many economists welcomed the collapse of the Bretton Woods system and the failure to arrive at a new system of fixed or quasi-fixed exchange rates.

The Disadvantages of Flexible Rates

Despite the fact that world trade has grown and dealing with balance-of-payments problems has become less difficult, flexible exchange rates have not been universally endorsed by everyone. Several disadvantages of this system have been cited.

What are the disadvantages of flexible exchange rates?

Flexible Rates and World Trade

Traditionally, the major objection to flexible rates was that they introduce considerable uncertainty into international trade. For example, if you order some perfume from France with a commitment to pay 1,000 euros in three months, you are not certain what the dollar price of euros, and therefore of the perfume, will be three months from now, because the exchange rate is constantly fluctuating. Because people prefer certainty to uncertainty and are generally risk averse, this uncertainty raises the costs of international transactions. As a result, flexible exchange rates can reduce the volume of trade, thus reducing the potential gains from international specialization.

Proponents of flexible rates have three answers to this argument. First, the empirical evidence shows that international trade has, in fact, grown in volume faster since the introduction of flexible rates. The exchange rate risk of trade has not had any major adverse effect. Second, it is possible to, in effect, buy insurance against the proposed adverse effect of currency fluctuations. Rather than buying currencies for immediate use in what is called the "spot" market for foreign currencies, one can contract today to buy foreign currencies in the future at a set exchange rate in the "forward" or "futures" market. By using this market, a perfume importer can buy euros now for delivery to her in three months; in doing so, she can be certain of the dollar price she is paying for the perfume. Since floating exchange rates began, booming futures markets in foreign currencies have opened in Chicago, New York, and in foreign financial centers. The third argument is that the alleged certainty of currency prices under the old Bretton Woods system was fictitious, because the possibility existed that nations might, at their whim, drastically revalue their currencies to deal with their own fundamental balance-of-payments problems. Proponents of flexible rates, then, argue that flexible rates are therefore no less disruptive to trade than fixed rates.

Flexible Rates and Inflation

A second, more valid criticism of flexible exchange rates is that they can contribute to inflationary pressures. Under fixed rates, domestic monetary and fiscal authorities have an incentive to constrain their domestic prices, because lower domestic prices increase the attractiveness of exported goods. This discipline is not present to the same extent with flexible rates. The consequence of a sharp monetary or fiscal expansion under flexible rates would be a decline in the value of one's currency relative to those of other countries. Yet even that may not seem to be as serious a political consequence as the Bretton Woods solution of an abrupt devaluation of the currency in the face of a severe balance-of-payments problem.

Advocates of flexible rates would argue that inflation need not occur under flexible rates. Flexible rates do not cause inflation; rather, it is caused by the expansionary macroeconomic policies of governments and central banks. Actually, flexible rates give government decision makers greater freedom of action than fixed rates; whether they act responsibly is determined not by exchange rates but by domestic policies.

global watch   The Trilemma of International Finance

As the world economy struggles to recover from its various ailments, the international financial order is coming under increased scrutiny. Currencies and exchange rates, in particular, are getting a hard look.

Various pundits and politicians, including President Obama himself, have complained that the Chinese renminbi is undervalued and impeding a global recovery. The problems in Greece have caused many people to wonder whether the euro is a failed experiment and whether Europe's nations would have been better off maintaining their own currencies.

(*continued*)

global watch   The Trilemma of International Finance (Cont.)

In thinking about these issues, the place to start is what economists call the fundamental trilemma of international finance. Yes, trilemma really is a word. It has been a term of art for logicians since the 17th century, according to the Oxford English Dictionary, and it describes a situation in which someone faces a choice among three options, each of which comes with some inevitable problems.

What is the trilemma in international finance? It stems from the fact that, in most nations, economic policy makers would like to achieve these three goals:

- *Make the country's economy open to international flows of capital.* Capital mobility lets a nation's citizens diversify their holdings by investing abroad. It also encourages foreign investors to bring their resources and expertise into the country.

- *Use monetary policy as a tool to help stabilize the economy.* The central bank can then increase the money supply and reduce interest rates when the economy is depressed, and reduce money growth and raise interest rates when it is over-heated.

- *Maintain stability in the currency exchange rate.* A volatile exchange rate, at times driven by speculation, can be a source of broader economic volatility. Moreover, a stable rate makes it easier for households and businesses to engage in the world economy and plan for the future.

But here's the rub: You can't get all three. If you pick two of these goals, the inexorable logic of economics forces you to forgo the third.

In the United States, we have picked the first two. Any American can easily invest abroad, simply by sending cash to an international mutual fund, and foreigners are free to buy stocks and bonds on domestic exchanges. Moreover, the Federal Reserve sets monetary policy to try to maintain full employment and price stability. But a result of this decision is volatility in the value of the dollar in foreign exchange markets.

By contrast, China has chosen a different response to the trilemma. Its central bank conducts monetary policy and maintains tight control over the exchange value of its currency. But to accomplish these two goals, it has to restrict the international flow of capital, including the ability of Chinese citizens to move their wealth abroad. Without such restrictions, money would flow into and out of the country, forcing the domestic interest rate to match those set by foreign central banks.

Most of Europe's nations have chosen the third way. By using the euro to replace the French franc, the German mark, the Italian lira, the Greek drachma and other currencies, these countries have eliminated all exchange-rate movements within their zone. In addition, capital is free to move among nations. Yet the cost of making these choices has been to give up the possibility of national monetary policy.

The European Central Bank sets interest rates for Europe as a whole. But if the situation in one country—Greece, for example—differs from that in the rest of Europe, that country no longer has its own monetary policy to address national problems.

Is there a best way to deal with this trilemma? Perhaps not surprisingly, many American economists argue for the American system of floating exchange rates determined by market forces. This preference underlies much of the criticism of China's financial policy. It also led to skepticism when Europe started down the path toward a common currency in the early 1990s. Today, those euro skeptics feel vindicated by the problems in Greece.

But economists should be cautious when recommending exchange-rate policy, because it is far from obvious what is best. In fact, Americans' embrace of floating exchange rates is relatively recent. From World War II to the early 1970s, the

(continued)

global watch The Trilemma of International Finance (Cont.)

United States participated in the Bretton Woods system, which fixed exchange rates among the major currencies. Moreover, in 1998, as much of Asia was engulfed in a financial crisis, Robert E. Rubin, then the Treasury secretary, praised China's exchange-rate policy as an "island of stability" in a turbulent world.

Even the euro experiment is based in part on an American model. Anyone taking a trip across the United States doesn't need to change money with every crossing of a state border. A common currency among the 50 states has served Americans well. Europeans were aspiring for similar benefits.

To be sure, Europe is different from the United States, which has a large central government that can redistribute resources among regions as needed. More important, our common language and heritage allow labor to move freely among regions in a way that will always be harder in Europe. The United States of Europe may have been too much to hope for.

Without doubt, the world financial system presents policy makers with difficult tradeoffs. Americans shouldn't be too harsh when other nations facing the trilemma reach conclusions different from ours. In this area of economic policy, as well as many others, there is room for reasonable nations to disagree.

ⓠ SECTION QUIZ

1. If a dollar is cheaper in terms of a foreign currency than the equilibrium exchange rate, a _____ exists at the current exchange rate that will put _____ pressure on the exchange value of a dollar.

   a. surplus of dollars; downward

   b. surplus of dollars; upward

   c. shortage of dollars; downward

   d. shortage of dollars; upward

2. Which of the following statements is true?

   a. The world has always been on a flexible exchange rate system.

   b. Governments do not intervene in international currency markets under a flexible exchange rate system.

   c. Currently, exchange rates do not change very frequently.

   d. Changing exchange rates can change both a country's exports and its imports.

3. Which of the following statements is true?

   a. World trade has expanded under flexible exchange rates.

   b. An increased exchange value of the U.S. dollar would tend to reduce American net exports.

   c. Under fixed exchange rates, rates change less frequently but by larger amounts than under flexible exchange rates.

   d. Currency shortages can arise under fixed exchange rates, but not under flexible exchange rates.

   e. All of the above are true.

(continued)

② SECTION QUIZ (Cont.)

4. Which of the following statements is true?

   a. Exchange rates never changed under fixed exchange rate systems.

   b. Changing from fixed to flexible exchange rates does not impact a country's domestic macroeconomic policies.

   c. It is not possible to insure against adverse currency fluctuations.

   d. Flexible exchange rates can contribute to inflationary pressures.

1. What are the arguments for and against flexible exchange rates?

2. When the U.S. dollar starts to exchange for fewer Japanese yen, other things equal, what happens to U.S. and Japanese imports and exports as a result?

3. Why is the system of flexible exchange rates sometimes called a dirty float system?

4. Were exchange rates under the Bretton Woods system really stable? How could you argue that exchange rates were more uncertain under the fixed-rate system than with floating exchange rates?

5. What is the uncertainty argument against flexible exchange rates? What evidence do proponents of flexible exchange rates cite in response?

6. Do flexible exchange rates cause higher rates of inflation? Why or why not?

Answers: 1. d 2. d 3. e 4. d

Interactive Summary

Fill in the blanks:

1. A current account is a record of a country's current _____ and _____ of goods and services.

2. Because the United States gains claims over foreign buyers by obtaining foreign currency in exchange for the dollars needed to buy U.S. exports, all exports of U.S. goods abroad are considered a(n) _____ or _____ item in the U.S. balance of payments.

3. Nations import and export _____, such as tourism, as well as _____ (goods).

4. The merchandise import/export relationship is often called the balance of _____.

5. Foreigners buying U.S. goods must _____ their currencies to obtain _____ in order to pay for exported goods.

6. The price of a unit of one foreign currency in terms of another is called the _____.

7. A change in the euro-dollar exchange rate from $1 per euro to $2 per euro would _____ the

U.S. price of German goods, thereby _____ the number of German goods that would be demanded in the United States.

8. The demand for foreign currencies is a derived demand because it derives directly from the demand for foreign _____ or for foreign _____.

9. The more foreigners demand U.S. products, the _____ of their currencies they will supply in exchange for U.S. dollars.

10. The supply of and demand for a foreign currency determine the equilibrium _____ of that currency.

11. The quantity of euros demanded by U.S. consumers will increase to buy more European goods as the price of the euro _____.

12. As the price, or value, of the euro increases relative to the dollar, American products become relatively _____ expensive to European buyers, which will _____ the quantity of dollars they will demand.

13. The supply curve of a foreign currency is _____ sloping.

14. If the dollar price of euros is higher than the equilibrium price, an excess quantity of euros will be _____ at that price, and competition among euro _____ will push the price of euros _____ toward equilibrium.

15. An increased demand for euros will result in a(n) _____ equilibrium price (exchange value) for euros, while a decreased demand for euros will result in a(n) _____ equilibrium price (exchange value) for euros.

16. Changes in a currency's exchange rate can be caused by changes in _____ for goods, changes in _____, changes in relative _____ rates, changes in relative _____ rates, and _____.

17. An increase in tastes for European goods in the United States would _____ the demand for euros, thereby _____ the equilibrium price (exchange value) of euros.

18. A decrease in incomes in the United States would _____ the amount of European

imports purchased by Americans, which would _____ the demand for euros, resulting in a(n) _____ exchange rate for euros.

19. If European incomes _____, European tariffs on U.S. goods _____, or European tastes for U.S. goods _____, Europeans would demand more U.S. goods, leading them to increase their supply of euros to obtain the added dollars necessary to make those purchases.

20. If interest rates in the United States were to increase relative to European interest rates, other things being equal, the rate of return on U.S. investments would _____ relative to that on European investments, thereby _____ Europeans' demand for U.S. investments.

21. If Europe experienced a higher inflation rate than the United States, European products would become _____ expensive to U.S. consumers, thereby _____ the quantity of European goods demanded by Americans, and thus _____ the demand for euros.

Answers: 1. imports; exports 2. credit; plus 3. services; merchandise 4. trade 5. sell; U.S. dollars 6. exchange rate 7. increase; reducing 8. goods and services; capital 9. more 10. exchange rate 11. falls 12. less; increase 13. upward 14. supplied; sellers; down 15. higher; lower 16. tastes; income; real interest; inflation; speculation 17. increase; increasing 18. decrease; decrease; lower 19. rose; increased; increased 20. increase; increasing 21. more; decreasing; decreasing

Key Terms and Concepts

balance of payments 614
current account 614
balance of trade 616

capital account 617
exchange rate 619

derived demand 620
dirty float system 628

Section Quiz Answers

21.1 The Balance of Payments

1. What is the balance of payments?
The balance of payments is the record of all the international financial transactions of a nation—both those involving inflows of funds and those involving outflows of funds—over a year.

2. Why must British purchasers of U.S. goods and services first exchange pounds for dollars?
Since U.S. goods and services are priced in dollars, a British consumer who wants to buy U.S. goods must first buy dollars in exchange for British pounds before he can buy the U.S. goods and services with dollars.

3. How is it that our imports provide foreigners with the means to buy U.S. exports?
The domestic currency Americans supply in exchange for the foreign currencies to buy imports also supplies the dollars with which foreigners can buy American exports.

4. What would have to be true for the United States to have a balance-of-trade deficit and a balance-of-payments surplus?
A balance-of-trade deficit means that we imported more merchandise (goods) than we exported. A balance-of-payments surplus means that the sum of our goods and services exports exceeded the sum of

our goods and services imports, plus funds transfers from the United States. For both to be true would require a larger surplus of services (including net investment income) and/or net fund transfer inflows than our trade deficit in merchandise (goods).

5. What would have to be true for the United States to have a balance-of-trade surplus and a current account deficit?
A balance-of-trade surplus means that we exported more merchandise (goods) than we imported. A current account deficit means that our exports of goods and services (including net investment income) were less than the sum of our imports of goods and services, plus net fund transfers. For both to happen would require that the sum of our deficit in services plus net transfers must be greater than our surplus in merchandise (goods) trading.

6. With no errors or omissions in the recorded balance-of-payments accounts, what should the statistical discrepancy equal?
If there were no errors or omissions in the recorded balance-of-payments accounts, the statistical discrepancy should equal zero, since when properly recorded, credits and debits must be equal because every credit creates a debit of equal value.

7. A Nigerian family visiting Chicago enjoys a Chicago Cubs baseball game at Wrigley Field. How would this expense be recorded in the balance-of-payments accounts? Why?
This would be counted as an export of services, because it would provide Americans with foreign currency (a claim against Nigeria) in exchange for those services.

21.2 Exchange Rates

1. What is an exchange rate?
An exchange rate is the price in one country's currency of one unit of another country's currency.

2. When a U.S. dollar buys relatively more British pounds, why does the cost of imports from England fall in the United States?
When a U.S. dollar buys relatively more British pounds, the cost of imports from England falls in the United States because it takes fewer U.S. dollars to buy a given number of British pounds in order to pay English producers. In other words, the price in U.S. dollars of English goods and services has fallen.

3. When a U.S. dollar buys relatively fewer yen, why does the cost of U.S. exports fall in Japan?
When a U.S. dollar buys relatively fewer yen, the cost of U.S. exports falls in Japan because it takes fewer yen to buy a given number of U.S. dollars in order to pay American producers. In other words, the price in yen of U.S. goods and services has fallen.

4. How does an increase in domestic demand for foreign goods and services increase the demand for those foreign currencies?
An increase in domestic demand for foreign goods and services increases the demand for those foreign currencies because the demand for foreign currencies is derived from the demand for foreign goods and services and foreign capital. The more foreign goods and services are demanded, the more of that foreign currency that will be needed to pay for those goods and services.

5. As euros get cheaper relative to U.S. dollars, why does the quantity of euros demanded by Americans increase? Why doesn't the demand for euros increase as a result?
As euros get cheaper relative to U.S. dollars, European products become relatively more inexpensive to Americans, who therefore buy more European goods and services. To do so, the quantity of euros demanded by U.S. consumers will rise to buy them, as the price (exchange rate) for euros falls. The demand (as opposed to quantity demanded) of euros doesn't increase because this represents a movement along the demand curve for euros caused by a change in exchange rates, rather than a change in demand for euros caused by some other factor.

6. Who brings exchange rates down when they are above their equilibrium value? Who brings exchange rates up when they are below their equilibrium value?
When exchange rates are greater than their equilibrium value, there will be a surplus of the currency, and frustrated sellers of that currency will bring its price (exchange rate) down. When exchange rates are less than their equilibrium value, there will be a shortage of the currency, and frustrated buyers of that currency will bring its price (exchange rate) up.

21.3 Equilibrium Changes in the Foreign Exchange Market

1. Why will the exchange rates of foreign currencies relative to U.S. dollars decline when U.S. domestic tastes change, reducing the demand for foreign-produced goods?
When U.S. domestic tastes change, reducing the demand for foreign-produced goods, the reduced demand for foreign-produced goods will also reduce the demand for the foreign currencies to buy

them. This reduced demand for those foreign currencies will reduce their exchange rates relative to U.S. dollars.

2. Why does the demand for foreign currencies shift in the same direction as domestic income? What happens to the exchange value of those foreign currencies in terms of U.S. dollars?

An increase in domestic income increases the demand for goods and services, including imported goods and services. This increases the demand for foreign currencies with which to buy those additional imports, which increases their exchange rates (the exchange value of those currencies) relative to U.S. dollars.

3. How would increased U.S. tariffs on imported European goods affect the exchange value of euros in terms of dollars?

Increased U.S. tariffs on imported European goods would make them less affordable in the United States. This would lead to a reduced demand for European goods in the United States, and therefore a reduced demand for euros. And this would reduce the exchange value of euros in terms of dollars.

4. Why do changes in U.S. tastes, income levels, or tariffs change the demand for euros, while similar changes in Europe change the supply of euros?

Changes in U.S. tastes, income levels, or tariffs change the demand for euros because they change the American demand for European goods and services, thereby changing the demand for euros with which to buy them. Similar changes in Europe change the supply of euros because they change the European demand for U.S. goods and services, thus changing their demand for dollars with which to buy those goods and services. This requires them to change their supply of euros in order to get those dollars.

5. What would happen to the exchange value of euros in terms of U.S. dollars if incomes rose in both Europe and the United States?

These changes would increase both the demand (higher incomes in the United States) and supply (higher incomes in Europe) of euros. The effect on the exchange value of euros would be determined by whether the supply or demand for euros shifted more (rising if demand shifted relatively more and falling if supply shifted relatively more).

6. Why does an increase in interest rates in Germany relative to U.S. interest rates increase the demand for euros but decrease their supply?

An increase in interest rates in Germany relative to U.S. interest rates increases the rates of return on German investments relative to U.S. investments. U.S. investors therefore increase their demand for German investments, increasing the demand for euros with which to make these investments. This would also reduce the demand by German investors for U.S. investments, decreasing the supply of euros with which to buy the dollars to make the investments.

7. What would an increase in U.S. inflation relative to Europe do to the supply and demand for euros and to the equilibrium exchange value (price) of euros in terms of U.S. dollars?

An increase in U.S. inflation relative to Europe would make U.S. products relatively more expensive to European customers, decreasing the amount of U.S. goods and services demanded by European customers and thus decreasing the supply of euros with which to buy the dollars necessary for those purchases. It would also make European products relatively cheaper to U.S. customers, increasing the amount of European goods and services demanded by Americans and thus increasing the demand for euros needed for those purchases. The decreased supply of and increased demand for euros results in an increasing exchange value of euros in terms of U.S. dollars.

21.4 Flexible Exchange Rates

1. What are the arguments for and against flexible exchange rates?

The arguments for flexible exchange rates include: the large expansion of world trade under flexible exchange rates; the fact that they allowed the economy to adjust to a quadrupling in the price of the world's most important internationally traded commodity—oil; and especially that it diminished the recurring crises that caused speculative rampages and currency revaluations, allowing the market mechanism to address currency shortages and world trade imbalances. The arguments against flexible exchange rates are that it increases exchange rate uncertainty in international trade, and can contribute to inflationary pressures, due to the lack of the fixed-rate system's incentives to constrain domestic policies, which would erode net exports.

2. When the U.S. dollar starts to exchange for fewer Japanese yen, other things equal, what happens to U.S. and Japanese imports and exports as a result?

When the U.S. dollar starts to exchange for fewer Japanese yen, other things equal, the U.S. cost of Japanese imports rises, decreasing the value of Japanese exports to the United States. It also decreases the cost to the Japanese of buying U.S. goods, increasing the value of U.S. exports to Japan.

3. Why is the system of flexible exchange rates sometimes called a dirty float system?

The system of flexible exchange rates is sometimes called a dirty float system because governments do intervene at times in foreign currency markets to alter their currencies' exchange rates, so that exchange rates are partly determined by market forces and partly by government intervention.

4. Were exchange rates under the Bretton Woods system really stable? How could you argue that exchange rates were more uncertain under the fixed-rate system than with floating exchange rates?

Exchange rates under the Bretton Woods system were not really stable. While exchange rate changes were infrequent, they were large, with large effects. It could be argued that the cost of the uncertainty about the less frequent but larger exchange rate changes that resulted was actually greater as a result than for the more frequent but smaller exchange rate changes under the fixed-rate system.

5. What is the uncertainty argument against flexible exchange rates? What evidence do proponents of flexible exchange rates cite in response?

The uncertainty argument against flexible exchange rates is that flexible exchange rates add another source of uncertainty to world trade, which would increase the cost of international transactions, reducing the magnitude of international trade. Proponents of flexible exchange rates cite the faster growth of international trade since the introduction of flexible exchange rates, the fact that markets exist on which to hedge exchange rate risks (through forward, or futures, markets), and that the alleged exchange rate certainty was fictitious, since large changes could take place at a nations' whim, in response.

6. Do flexible exchange rates cause higher rates of inflation? Why or why not?

Flexible exchange rates do not cause higher rates of inflation. However, they do reduce the incentives to constrain domestic inflation for fear of reducing net exports under the fixed exchange rate system. Inflation, though, is ultimately caused by expansionary macroeconomic policies adopted by governments and their central banks.

Problems

1. Indicate whether each of the following represents a credit or debit on the U.S. current account.
   a. An American imports a BMW from Germany.
   b. A Japanese company purchases software from an American company.
   c. The United States gives $100 million in financial aid to Israel.
   d. A U.S. company in Florida sells oranges to Great Britain.

2. Indicate whether each of the following represents a credit or debit on the U.S. capital account.
   a. A French bank purchases $100,000 worth of U.S. Treasury notes.
   b. The central bank in the United States purchases 1 million euros in the currency market.
   c. A U.S. resident buys stock on the Japanese stock market.
   d. A Japanese company purchases a movie studio in California.

3. How are each of the following events likely to affect the U.S. trade balance?
   a. The European price level increases relative to the U.S. price level.
   b. The dollar appreciates in value relative to the currencies of its trading partners.
   c. The U.S. government offers subsidies to firms that export goods.
   d. The U.S. government imposes tariffs on imported goods.
   e. Europe experiences a severe recession.

4. How are each of the following events likely to affect the value of the dollar relative to the euro?
   a. Interest rates in the European Union increase relative to the United States.
   b. The European Union price level rises relative to the U.S. price level.
   c. The European central bank intervenes by selling dollars on currency markets.
   d. The price level in the United States falls relative to the price level in Europe.

5. If the demand for a domestic currency decreases in a country using a fixed exchange rate system, what must the central bank do to keep the currency value steady?

6. What happens to the supply curve for dollars in the currency market under the following conditions?
   a. Americans wish to buy more Japanese consumer electronics.
   b. The United States wishes to prop up the value of the yen.

7. Evaluate the following statement: "The balance of payments equals −$200 million and the statistical discrepancy equals zero."

8. Assume that a product sells for $100 in the United States.
   a. If the exchange rate between British pounds and U.S. dollars is $2 per pound, what would the price of the product be in the United Kingdom?
   b. If the exchange rate between Mexican pesos and U.S. dollars is 125 pesos per dollar, what would the price of the product be in Mexico?
   c. In which direction would the price of the $100 U.S. product change in a foreign country if Americans' tastes for foreign products increased?
   d. In which direction would the price of the $100 U.S. product change in a foreign country if incomes in the foreign country fell?
   e. In which direction would the price of the $100 U.S. product change in a foreign country if interest rates in the United States fell relative to interest rates in other countries?

9. How would each of the following affect the supply of euros, the demand for euros, and the dollar price of euros?

Change	Supply of Euros	Demand for Euros	Dollar Price of Euros
Reduced U.S. tastes for European goods			
Increased incomes in the United States			
Increased U.S. interest rates			
Decreased inflation in Europe			
Reduced U.S. tariffs on imports			
Increased European tastes for U.S. goods			

10. How are each of the following classified, as debits or credits, in the U.S. balance-of-payments accounts?

	Credit	Debit
a. Americans buy autos from Japan.		
b. American tourists travel to Japan.		
c. Japanese consumers buy rice grown in the United States.		
d. The United States gives foreign aid to Rwanda.		
e. General Motors, a U.S. company, earns profits in France.		
f. Royal Dutch Shell earns profits from its U.S. operations.		
g. General Motors builds a new plant in Vietnam.		
h. Japanese investors purchase U.S. government bonds.		

11. What will happen to the supply of dollars, the demand for dollars, and the equilibrium exchange rate of the dollar in each of the following cases?

	Supply of Dollars	Demand for Dollars	Equilibrium Exchange Rates
a. Americans buy more European goods.			
b. Europeans invest in U.S. stock market.			
c. European tourists flock to the United States.			
d. Europeans buy U.S. government bonds.			
e. American tourists flock to Europe.			

ability-to-pay principle belief that those with the greatest ability to pay taxes should pay more than those with less ability to pay

adaptive expectations an individual's belief that the best indicator of the future is recent information on inflation and unemployment

adverse selection a situation where an informed party benefits in an exchange by taking advantage of knowing more than the other party

aggregate the total amount—such as the *aggregate level of output*

aggregate demand (AD) the total demand for all the final goods and services in the economy

aggregate demand curve graph that shows the inverse relationship between the price level and RGDP demanded

aggregate supply (AS) curve the total quantity of final goods and services suppliers are willing and able to supply at a given price level

asymmetric information occurs when the available information is initially distributed in favor of one party relative to another in an exchange

automatic stabilizers changes in government transfer payments or tax collections that automatically help counter business cycle fluctuations

autonomous determinants of consumption expenditures expenditures not dependent on the level of current disposable income that can result from factors such as real wealth, the interest rate, household debt, expectations, and tastes and preferences

bads items that we do not desire or want, where less is preferred to more, like terrorism, smog, or poison oak

balance of payments the record of international transactions in which a nation has engaged over a year

balance of trade the net surplus or deficit resulting from the level of exportation and importation of merchandise

balance sheet a financial record that indicates the balance between a bank's assets and its liabilities plus capital

bar graph visual display showing the comparison of quantities

barter direct exchange of goods and services without the use of money

bonds an obligation issued by the corporation that promises the holder to receive fixed annual interest payments and payment of the principal upon maturity

boom period of prolonged economic expansion

business cycles short-term fluctuations in the economy relative to the long-term trend in output

capital the equipment and structures used to produce goods and services

capital account records the foreign purchases or assets in the domestic economy (a monetary inflow) and domestic purchases of assets abroad (a monetary outflow)

capital intensive production that uses a large amount of capital

causation when one event brings about another event

ceteris paribus holding all other things constant

change in quantity demanded a change in a good's own price leads to a change in quantity demanded, a move along a given demand curve

Coase theorem states that where property rights are defined in a clear-cut fashion, externalities are internalized

command economy economy in which the government uses central planning to coordinate most economic activities

commercial banks financial institutions organized to handle everyday financial transactions of businesses and households through demand deposit accounts and savings accounts and by making short-term commercial and consumer loans

common resource a rival good that is nonexcludable

common stock residual claimants of corporate resources who receive a proportion of profits based upon the ratio of shares held

comparative advantage occurs when a person or country can produce a good or service at a lower opportunity cost than others

competitive market a market where the many buyers and sellers have little market power—each buyer's or seller's effect on market price is negligible

complements an increase (decrease) in the price of one good shifts the demand curve for another good to the left (right)

consumer price index (CPI) a measure of the cost of a market basket that represents the consumption of a typical household

consumer sovereignty consumers vote with their dollars in a market economy; this accounts for what is produced

consumer surplus the difference between the price a consumer is willing and able to pay for an additional unit of a good and the price the consumer actually pays; for the whole market, it is the sum of all the individual consumer surpluses

consumption purchases of final goods and services

contraction when the economy is slowing down—measured from the peak to the trough

correlation when two events occur together

cost-push inflation a price-level increase due to a negative supply shock or increases in input prices

credit unions financial cooperatives made up of depositors with a common affiliation

cross-price elasticity of demand the measure of the impact that a price change of one good will have on the demand of another good

crowding-out effect theory that government borrowing drives up the interest rate, lowering consumption by households and investment spending by firms

currency coins and/or paper created to facilitate the trade of goods and services and the payment of debts

current account a record of a country's imports and exports of goods and services, net investment income, and net transfers

cyclical unemployment unemployment due to short-term cyclical fluctuations in the economy

deadweight loss net loss of total surplus that results from an action that alters a market equilibrium

deflation a decrease in the overall price level, which increases the purchasing power of money

demand deposits balances in bank accounts that depositors can access on demand

demand-pull inflation a price-level increase due to an increase in aggregate demand

depreciation annual allowance set aside to replace worn-out capital

depression severe recession or contraction in output

derived demand the demand for an input derived from consumers' demand for the good or service produced with that input

diminishing marginal utility a good's ability to provide less satisfaction with each successive unit consumed; the concept that states that as an individual consumes more and more of a good, each successive unit generates less and less utility (or satisfaction)

dirty float system a description of the exchange rate system that means that fluctuations in currency values are partly determined by government intervention

discount rate interest rate that the Fed charges commercial banks for the loans it extends to them

discouraged worker an individual who has left the labor force because he or she could not find a job

disposable personal income the personal income available after personal taxes

dividend the annual per share payment to shareholders based upon realized profits

double counting adding the value of a good or service twice by mistakenly counting the intermediate goods and services in GDP

durable goods longer-lived consumer goods, such as automobiles

economic goods scarce goods created from scarce resources— goods that are desirable but limited in supply

economic growth an upward trend in the real per capita output of goods and services

the economic problem scarcity forces us to choose, and choices are costly because we must give up other opportunities that we value

economics the study of choices we make among our many wants and desires given our limited resources

efficiency when an economy gets the most out of its scarce resources

efficiency wage model theory stating that higher wages lead to greater productivity

elastic when the quantity demanded is greater than the percentage change in price ($E_D > 1$)

empirical analysis the use of data to test a hypothesis

Employment Act of 1946 a commitment by the federal government to hold itself accountable for short-run economic fluctuations

entrepreneurship the process of combining labor, land, and capital to produce goods and services

equilibrium price the price at the intersection of the market supply and demand curves; at this price, the quantity demanded equals the quantity supplied

equilibrium quantity the quantity at the intersection of the market supply and demand curves; at the equilibrium quantity, the quantity demanded equals the quantity supplied

excess reserves reserve levels held above that required by the Fed

exchange rate the price of one unit of a country's currency in terms of another country's currency

excise tax a sales tax on individual products such as alcohol, tobacco, and gasoline

expansion when output (real GDP) is rising significantly—the period between the trough of a recession and the next peak

expenditure approach calculation of GDP by adding the expenditures by market participants on final goods and services over a given period

expenditure multiplier the multiplier that only considers the impact of consumption changes on aggregate expenditures

externality a benefit or cost from consumption or production that spills over onto those who are not consuming or producing the good

factor (or input) markets markets where households sell the use of their inputs (capital, land, labor, and entrepreneurship) to firms

factor payments wages (salaries), rent, interest payments, and profits paid to the owners of productive resources

fallacy of composition the incorrect view that what is true for the individual is always true for the group

federal funds market market in which banks provide short-term loans to other banks that need cash to meet reserve requirements

fiat money a means of exchange established by government declaration

fiscal policy use of government purchases, taxes, and transfer payments to alter equilibrium output and prices

fixed investment all new spending on capital goods by producers

flat tax a tax that charges all income earners the same percentage of their income

fractional reserve system a system that requires banks to hold reserves equal to some fraction of their checkable deposits

free rider deriving benefits from something not paid for

frictional unemployment the unemployment that results from workers searching for suitable jobs and firms looking for suitable workers

GDP deflator a price index that helps measure the average price level of all final consumer goods and services produced

gold standard defining the dollar as equivalent to a set value of a quantity of gold, allowing direct convertibility from currency to gold

goods items we value or desire

Gresham's Law the principle that "cheap money drives out dear money"; given an alternative, people prefer to spend less valuable money

gross domestic product (GDP) the measure of economic performance based on the value of all final goods and services produced within a country during a given period

gross national product (GNP) the difference between net income of foreigners and GDP

human capital the productive knowledge and skill people receive from education, on-the-job training, health, and other factors that increase productivity

hyperinflation extremely high rates of inflation for sustained periods of time

hypothesis a testable proposition

import quota a legal limit on the imported quantity of a good that is produced abroad and can be sold in domestic markets

income elasticity of demand the percentage change in demand divided by the percentage change in consumer's income

increasing opportunity cost the opportunity cost of producing additional units of a good rises as society produces more of that good

indexing use of payment contracts that automatically adjust for changes in inflation

indirect business taxes taxes, such as sales tax, levied on goods and services sold

individual demand curve a graphical representation that shows the inverse relationship between price and quantity demanded

individual demand schedule a schedule that shows the relationship between price and quantity demanded

individual supply curve a graphical representation that shows the positive relationship between the price and quantity supplied

inelastic when the quantity demanded is less than the percentage change in price ($E_D < 1$)

inferior good if income increases, the demand for a good decreases; if income decreases, the demand for a good increases

inflation a rise in the overall price level, which decreases the purchasing power of money

inflationary gap the output gap that occurs when the actual output is greater than the potential output

innovation applications of new knowledge that create new products or improve existing products

intangible goods goods that we cannot reach out and touch, such as friendship and knowledge

inventory investment purchases that add to the stocks of goods kept by the firm to meet consumer demand

investment the creation of capital goods to augment future production

job leaver a person who quits his or her job

job loser an individual who has been temporarily laid off or fired

labor the physical and human effort used in the production of goods and services

labor force the number of people aged 16 and over who are available for employment

labor force participation rate the percentage of the working age population in the labor force

labor intensive production that uses a large amount of labor

labor productivity output per unit of worker

land the natural resources used in the production of goods and services

law of demand the quantity of a good or service demanded varies inversely (negatively) with its price, *ceteris paribus*

law of supply the higher (lower) the price of the good, the greater (smaller) the quantity supplied

leading economic indicators factors that economists at the Commerce Department have found typically change before changes in economic activity

legal tender coins and paper officially declared to be acceptable for the settlement of financial debts

liquidity the ease with which one asset can be converted into another asset or into goods and services

logrolling exchanging votes to get support for legislation

long-run aggregate supply (*LRAS*) curve the graphical relationship between RGDP and the price level when output prices and input prices can fully adjust to economic changes

M1 the narrowest definition of money; includes currency, checkable deposits, and traveler's checks

M2 a broader definition of money that includes M1 plus savings deposits, time deposits, and noninstitutional money market mutual fund shares

macroeconomics the study of the whole economy, including the topics of inflation, unemployment, and economic growth

marginal cost (MC) the change in total costs resulting from a one-unit change in output

marginal propensity to consume (MPC) the additional consumption resulting from an additional dollar of disposable income

marginal propensity to save (MPS) the additional saving that results from an additional dollar of income

marginal thinking focusing on the additional, or marginal, choices; marginal choices involve the effects of adding or subtracting, from the current situation, the small (or large) incremental changes to a plan of action

market the process of buyers and sellers exchanging goods and services

market demand curve the horizontal summation of individual demand curves

market economy an economy that allocates goods and services through the private decisions of consumers, input suppliers, and firms

market equilibrium the point at which the market supply and market demand curves intersect

market failure when the economy fails to allocate resources efficiently on its own

market supply curve a graphical representation of the amount of goods and services that suppliers are willing and able to supply at various prices

means of deferred payment the attribute of money that makes it easier to borrow and to repay loans

median voter model a model that predicts candidates will choose a position in the middle of the distribution

medium of exchange the primary function of money, which is to facilitate transactions and lower transaction costs

menu costs the costs imposed on a firm from changing listed prices

microeconomics the study of household and firm behavior and how they interact in the marketplace

minimum wage rate an hourly wage floor set above the equilibrium wage

mixed economy an economy where government and the private

sector determine the allocation of resources

money anything generally accepted in exchange for goods or services

money market market in which money demand and money supply determine the equilibrium interest rate

money market mutual funds interest-earning accounts provided by brokers that pool funds into such investments as Treasury bills

money multiplier measures the potential amount of money that the banking system generates with each dollar of reserves

moral hazard taking additional risks because you are insured

multiplier effect a chain reaction of additional income and purchases that results in total purchases that are greater than the initial increase in purchases

national income (NI) a measure of income earned by owners of the factors of production

national income accounting a uniform means of measuring economic performance

natural rate hypothesis states that the economy will self-correct to the natural rate of employment

natural rate of unemployment the median, or "typical," unemployment rate, equal to the sum of frictional and structural unemployment when they are at a maximum

near money nontransaction deposits that are not money but can be quickly converted into money

negative externality occurs when costs spill over to an outside party who is not involved in producing or consuming the good

negative incentive an incentive that either increases costs or reduces benefits, resulting in a decrease in the activity or behavior

negative relationship when two variables change in opposite directions

net benefit the difference between the expected marginal benefits and the expected marginal costs

net exports the difference between the value of exports and the value of imports

net national product (NNP) GNP minus depreciation

new entrant an individual who has not held a job before but is now seeking employment

nominal interest rate the reported interest rate that is not adjusted for inflation

nondurable goods tangible items consumed in a short period of time, such as food

nontransaction deposits funds that cannot be used for payment directly but must be converted into currency for general use

normal good if income increases, the demand for a good increases; if income decreases, the demand for a good decreases

normative statement a subjective, contestable statement that attempts to describe what should be done

open economy a type of model that includes international trade effects

open market operations purchase and sale of government securities by the Federal Reserve System

opportunity cost the value of the best forgone alternative that was not chosen

peak the point in time when expansion comes to an end, that is, when output is at the highest point in the cycle

personal income (PI) the amount of income received by households before personal taxes

pie chart visual display showing the relative size of various quantities that add up to 100 percent

positive externality occurs when benefits spill over to an outside party who is not involved in producing or consuming the good

positive incentive an incentive that either reduces costs or increases benefits, resulting in an increase in an activity or behavior

positive relationship when two variables change in the same direction

positive statement an objective, testable statement that describes what happens and why it happens

potential output the amount of real output the economy would produce if its labor and other resources were fully employed, that is, at the natural rate of unemployment

preferred stock a stock that pays fixed, regular dividend payments despite the profits of the corporation

present value the value in today's dollars of home future benefit

price ceiling a legally established maximum price

price controls government-mandated minimum or maximum prices

price-earnings ratio (PE) a measure of stock value that is determined by dividing the price of the stock by the amount of annual corporate earnings per share

price elasticity of demand the measure of the responsiveness of quantity demanded to a change in price

price elasticity of supply the measure of the sensitivity of the quantity supplied to changes in price of a good

price floor a legally established minimum price

price index a measure of the trend in prices paid for a certain bundle of goods and services over a given period

price level the average level of prices in the economy

private good a good with rivalrous consumption and excludability

producer goods capital goods that increase future production capabilities

producer price index a measure of the cost of goods and services bought by firms

producer surplus the difference between what a producer is paid for a good and the cost of producing that unit of the good; for the market, it is the sum of all the individual sellers' producer surpluses—the area above the market supply curve and below the market price

product markets markets where households are buyers and firms are sellers of goods and services

production possibilities curve the potential total output combinations of any two goods for an economy

productivity output per worker

progressive tax tax designed so that those with higher incomes pay a greater proportion of their income in taxes

public good a good that is nonrivalrous in consumption and nonexcludable

quantity theory of money and prices a theory of the connection between the money supply and the price level when the velocity of money is constant

rational behavior people do the best they can, based on their values and information, under current and anticipated future circumstances

rational decision making people do the best they can, based on their values and information, under current and anticipated future circumstances.

rational ignorance lack of incentive to be informed

real gross domestic product per capita real output of goods and services per person

real gross domestic product (RGDP) the total value of all final goods and services produced in a given period, such as a year or a quarter, adjusted for inflation

real interest rate the nominal interest rate minus the inflation rate; also called the inflation-adjusted interest rate

recession a period of significant decline in output and employment

recessionary gap the output gap that occurs when the actual output is less than the potential output

reentrant an individual who worked before and is now reentering the labor force

regressive tax as a person's income rises, the amount his or her tax as a proportion of income falls

relative price the price of a specific good compared to the price of other goods

rent seeking efforts by producers to gain profits from government

protections such as tariffs and import quotas

required reserve ratio the percentage of deposits that a bank must hold at the Federal Reserve Bank or in bank vaults

research and development (R&D) activities undertaken to create new products and processes that will lead to technological progress

reserve requirements holdings of assets at the bank or at the Federal Reserve Bank as mandated by the Fed

resources inputs used to produce goods and services

retained earnings the practice of using corporate profits for capital investment rather than dividend payouts

rule of rational choice individuals will pursue an activity if the expected marginal benefits are greater than the expected marginal costs

savings and loan associations financial institutions organized as cooperative associations that hold demand deposits and savings of members in the form of dividend-bearing shares and make loans, especially home mortgage loans

scarcity exists when human wants (material and nonmaterial) exceed available resources

secondary reserves highly liquid, interest-paying assets held by the bank

securities stocks and bonds

services intangible items of value provided to consumers, such as education

shifts in the demand curve a change in one of the variables, other than the price of the good itself, that affects the willingness of consumers to buy

shoe-leather cost the cost incurred when individuals reduce their money holdings because of inflation

shortage a situation where quantity demanded exceeds quantity supplied

short-run aggregate supply (SRAS) curve the graphical relationship between RGDP and the price level when output prices can change but input prices are unable to adjust

simple circular flow model an illustration of the continuous flow of goods, services, inputs, and payments between firms and households

slope the ratio of rise (change in the Y variable) over run (change in the x variable)

special interest groups groups with an intense interest in particular voting issues that may be different from that of the general public

specializing concentrating in the production of one, or a few, goods

stagflation a situation in which lower growth and higher prices occur together

stockholders entities that hold shares of stock in a corporation

structural unemployment the unemployment that results from workers not having the skills to obtain long-term employment

substitutes an increase (decrease) in the price of one good causes the demand curve for another good to shift to the right (left)

supply shocks unexpected temporary events that can either increase or decrease aggregate supply

surplus a situation where quantity supplied exceeds quantity demanded

tangible goods items we value or desire that we can reach out and touch

tariff a tax on imports

theory statement or proposition used to explain and predict behavior in the real world

theory of rational expectations belief that workers and consumers incorporate the likely consequences of government policy changes into their expectations by quickly adjusting wages and prices

time-series graph visual tool to show changes in a variable's value over time

total revenue (TR) the amount sellers receive for a good or service, calculated as the product price times the quantity sold

total welfare gains the sum of consumer and producer surpluses

transaction deposits deposits that can be easily converted to currency or used to buy goods and services directly

transferable pollution rights a right given to a firm to discharge a specified amount of pollution; its transferable nature creates incentive to lower pollution levels

traveler's checks transaction instruments easily convertible into currency

trough the point in time when output stops declining, that is, when business activity is at its lowest point in the cycle

underemployment a situation in which a worker's skill level is higher than necessary for a job

unemployment rate the percentage of the population aged 16 and older

who are willing and able to work but are unable to obtain a job

unintended consequences the secondary effects of an action that may occur after the initial effects

unit elastic demand demand with a price elasticity of 1; the percentage change in quantity demanded is equal to the percentage change in price

unplanned inventory investment collection of inventory that results when people do not buy the products firms are producing

variable something that is measured by a number, such as your height

velocity of money a measure of how frequently money is turned over

vertical equity different treatment based on level of income and the ability to pay principle

wage and price inflexibility the tendency for prices and wages to only adjust slowly downward to changes in the economy

welfare effects the gains and losses associated with government intervention in markets

winner's curse a situation that arises in certain auctions where the winner is worse off than the loser because of an overly optimistic value placed on the good

X-axis the horizontal axis on a graph

Y-axis the vertical axis on a graph

Index